Argentina

From Insolvency to Growth

The World Bank
Washington, D.C.

World Bank Country Studies are among the many reports originally prepared for internal use as part of the continuing analysis by the Bank of the economic and related conditions of its developing member countries and of its dialogues with the governments. Some of the reports are published in this series with the least possible delay for the use of governments and the academic, business and financial, and development communities. The typescript of this paper therefore has not been prepared in accordance with the procedures appropriate to formal printed texts, and the World Bank accepts no responsibility for errors.

The World Bank does not guarantee the accuracy of the data included in this publication and accepts no responsibility whatsoever for any consequence of their use. Any maps that accompany the text have been prepared solely for the convenience of readers; the designations and presentation of material in them do not imply the expression of any opinion whatsoever on the part of the World Bank, its affiliates, or its Board or member countries concerning the legal status of any country, territory, city, or area or of the authorities thereof or concerning the delimitation of its boundaries or its national affiliation.

The material in this publication is copyrighted. Requests for permission to reproduce portions of it should be sent to the Office of the Publisher at the address shown in the copyright notice above. The World Bank encourages dissemination of its work and will normally give permission promptly and, when the reproduction is for noncommercial purposes, without asking a fee. Permission to copy portions for classroom use is granted through the Copyright Clearance Center, 27 Congress Street, Salem, Massachusetts 01970, U.S.A.

The complete backlist of publications from the World Bank is shown in the annual *Index of Publications*, which contains an alphabetical title list (with full ordering information) and indexes of subjects, authors, and countries and regions. The latest edition is available free of charge from the Distribution Unit, Office of the Publisher, The World Bank, 1818 H Street, N.W., Washington, D.C. 20433, U.S.A., or from Publications, The World Bank, 66, avenue d'Iéna, 75116 Paris, France.

ISSN: 0253-2123

Library of Congress Cataloging-in-Publication Data

Argentina : from insolvency to growth.
      p.   cm. — (World Bank country study, ISSN 0253-2123)
   ISBN 0-8213-2463-2
   1. Argentina—Economic conditions—1983– 2. Argentina—Economic
policy.   I. International Bank for Reconstruction and Development.
II. Series.
HC175.A8615   1993
338.982—dc20   93-4348
                                           CIP

COUNTRY DATA - ARGENTINA

MONEY, CREDIT AND PRICES	1980	1985	1988	1989	1990	1991	1992 g/
			(Million Pesos; end of period)				
Money and Quasi Money	0.0008	0.8	24	298	5,593	12,726	20,570
Domestic Bank Credit to Public Sector	0.0002	0.7	28	1,442	15,853	17,437	17,378
Domestic Bank Credit to Private Sector	0.0008	1.0	18	367	4,772	14,243	19,013
Money and Quasi Money as % of GDP	22.3	14.2	29.2	11.7	10.9	10.3	13.4
Wholesale Price Index (1985=100)	0.0673	133	3,156	173,153	1,555,570	2,439,141	2,604,846
Annual percentage changes in:							
General Wholesale Price Index	57	364	432	5,386	798	57	7
Bank Credit to Public Sector	70	377	527	5,009	999	10	0
Bank Credit to Private Sector	109	372	285	1,914	1,199	199	33

BALANCE OF PAYMENTS	1980	1985	1990	1991	1992 g/
		(US$ Million)			
Exports of Goods, NFS	10,765	10,242	14,953	14,755	15,062
Imports of Goods, NFS	14,024	5,891	7,057	11,779	18,756
Resource Balance	(3,259)	4,351	7,896	2,976	(3,694)
Interest Payments (net)	(947)	(4,879)	(5,724)	(4,930)	(3,846)
Other Factor Payments (net) a/	(584)	(425)	(479)	(868)	(411)
Net Current Transfers	23	0	71	0	(32)
Balance on Current Account	(4,767)	(953)	1,764	(2,822)	(7,983)
Direct Investment	788	919	1,668	2,481	4,676
Total M&LT Loans (net)	3,400	2,786	(969)	1,288	(272)
Disbursements	5,809	7,564	-	-	-
Amortization	2,409	4,778	-	-	-
Other Capital (net) b/	-2217	-881	345	1,757	7,571
Changes in Net Reserves (- = increase)	2,796	(1,871)	(2,808)	(2,704)	(3,992)
Gross Reserves (end year) c/	6,743	4,801	6,010	9,093	12,496

MERCHANDISE EXPORTS (Average 1988-1991)

	US$ Mln.	% of Total
Agricultural goods d/	2,631	27.6
Manuf. goods of agric. orig. e/	4,354	45.7
Manuf. of industrial origin f/	2,551	26.8
Total Merchandise Exports	9,536	100.0

EXTERNAL DEBT (as of Dec.31, 1992) g/

	US$ Mln.
Total Debt Outstanding & Disbursed (DOD)	72,062
IBRD	2,579
IDB and Other Multilateral	3,697
IMF	2,474
Bilaterals	14,482
Bonds	8,683
Commercial Banks h/	40,147

DEBT SERVICE RATIO, 1992 i/	42.3%
Interest service ratio (% of exports G&NFS)	17.7%

IBRD/IDA LENDING. DECEMBER 31, 1992 (Mln. US$)

	IBRD	IDA
Outstanding & Disbursed	2,579	-
Undisbursed	-	-
Outstanding incl. Undisbursed	-	-

RATE OF EXCHANGE j/

1980	1992
US$ 1.00 = A$ 0.000000018	US$ 1.00 = A$ 0.9906
A$ 1.00 = US$ 55,555,555	A$ 1.00 = US$ 1.0095

a/ Direct investment income plus other factor service income.
b/ Includes short-term capital, net IMF resources, changes in arrears,
   and valuation adjustments.
c/ Includes valuation and other adjustments.
d/ BCRA categories I, II, and III: livestock and other animal products; agricultural
   products; fats and oils.
e/ BCRA categories IV, VIII, and XI: i.e. manufactured food, beverages and tobacco;
   leather, furs and related products; textiles and clothing.
f/ All other manufactured goods categories.
g/ Preliminary estimate.
h/ Includes financial markets, private non-guaranteed, short term and public sector financing debt
i/ Amortization and interest payments on medium- and long-term (MLT) debt as a percentage
   of exports of G&NFS. Excludes arrears; includes rescheduling of debt.
j/ Period average in pesos.

CURRENCY EQUIVALENTS
Currency Unit - Peso

EXCHANGE RATE
A$1.00 = US$1.00

FISCAL YEAR
January 1 - December 31

ABBREVIATIONS

AFJP	Pension Funds	Administradoras de Fondos de Jubilación y Pensiones
AGP	Port Authority	Administración General de Puertos
AyEE	Water and Electric Company	Agua y Energía Eléctrica
ANA	National Customs Administration	Administración Nacional de Aduanas
ANSSAL	National Administration of Health Insurance	Administración Nacional de Seguros de Salud
ATN	Discretionary Treasury Grants	Aportes del Tesoro Nacional
BANADE	National Development Bank	Banco Nacional de Desarrollo
BCRA	Central Bank	Banco Central
BHN	National Housing Bank	Banco Hipotecario Nacional
BIC	Investment and Growth Bonds	Bonos de Inversion y Crecimiento
BICE	Bank of Investment and External Trade	Banco de Inversiones y Comercio Externo
BOCE	Economic Consolidation Bond	Bonos de Consolidación Económica
BOCON	Consolidation Bonds	Bonos de Consolidación
BONEX	External Treasury Bonds	Bonos Externos del Tesoro
CNEA	Atomic Energy Commission	Comisión Nacional de Energía Atómomica
CONAE	National Commission for Space Activities	Comisión Nacional de Actividades Espaciales
CONFER	National Committee of Radio Telecommunications	Comité National de Radio y Telecomunicaciones
CONFESA	Federal Health Council	Consejo Federal de Salud
CONICET	National Council on Science and Technology	Consejo Nacional de Ciencia y Tecnología
CRM	Monetary Regulation Account	Cuenta de Regulación Monetaria
DGI	General Tax Board	Dirección General de Impositiva
DNCFP	Federal Commission of Provinces	Dirección Nacional de Consejo Federal de Provincias
DGFM	General Directorate for Military Factories	Dirección General de Fábricaciones Militares
DNC	National Highway Board	Dirección Nacional de Carreteras
DNRP	Provincial Tax Boards	Dirección Nacional de Recaudación Provincial
DVP	Provincial Highways Departments	Dirección de Vialidad Provincial
ENADEP	National Sports Agency	Ente Nacional de Deportes
ENATUR	National Tourism Agency	Ente Nacional de Turismo
ENTel	National Telephone Company	Empresa Nacional de Telecomunicaciones
FIEL	Foundation for Latin America Economic Research	Fundación de Investigaciones Económicas Latinoamericanas
FONAVI	National Housing Fund	Fondo Nacional de Vivienda
GdE	National Gas Company	Gas del Estado
GPP	Gross Provincial Product	Producto Bruto Provincial
IAF	Institute for Financial Aid to Retired Military Personnel	Instituto para Ayuda Financiera al Personal Militar Retirado
INAP	National Institute of Public Administration	Instituto Nacional de Administración Pública
INDER	Reinsurance Institute	Institutos de Reaseguros
INOS	National Institute of Social Insurance	Instituto Nacional de Seguro Social
INSSJP	Institute of Health Insurance for Retirees and Pensioners	Instituto de Seguro de Salud para Jubilados y Pensionados
IPV	Provincial Housing Institutes	Instituto Provincial de Vivienda
MERCOSUR	Southern Common Market	Mercado Común del Sur
MHSA	Ministry of Health and Social Action	Ministerio de Salud y Acción Social
NFPS	Non-Financial Public Sector	Sector Público No-Financiero
NPS	National Pension System	Sistema Nacional de Pensiones
NPV	Present Net Value	Valor Actual Neto
OSN	National Sanitation Company	Obras Sanitarias de la Nación
PAMI	Program of Integral Medical Care	Programa Integral de Cuidados Médicos
PAN	National Food Program	Programa Nacional de Alimentación
PAYG	Pay-As-You-Go	Sistema de Reparto
QRs	Quantitative Restrictions	Restrictiones Cuantitativas
SEGBA	Electricity Company of the Province	Servicios Eléctricos del Gran Buenos Aires
SICE	Secretary of Commerce and Industry	Secretaría de Industria y Comercio Exterior
SIDE	National Intelligence System	Sistema de Inteligencia del Estado
SIPRI	Stockholm International Peace Research Institute	Instituto Internacional Stockholmo de Paz e Investigación
SOFI	French Customs Administration	Administración Francesa de Aduanas
SVOA	Secretary of Housing	Secretaría de Vivienda
VAT	Value-Added Tax	Impuesto al Valor Agregado
YPF	State Oil Company	Yacimientos Petrolíferos Fiscales

Preface

This report is based on missions which visited Argentina in November 1991, March 1992 and October 1992. The main mission comprised the following members:

Richard Newfarmer (Mission Leader, Macro, Public Finance)
Daniel Artana (Industrial Promotion, Subsidies, and Provincial
    Finance)
Nicole Ball (Military Expenditures)
Egbert Gerken (Social Security)
Shahrzad Gohari (Education and Health)
Daniel Hewitt (Military Expenditures)
Felipe Larrain (Public Investment)
Roberto Manrique (Presidency and Military Expenditures)
Jacques Morisset (Revenues, Public Enterprises, Central Bank,
    Macroconsistency)
Philip Musgrove (Education and Health)
Victor Thuronyi (Direct Taxes)
Jaime Vasquez-Caro (Tax Policy and Administration)
Mario Vicens (Monetary Policy and Macroconsistency)
Matthew Vogel (Budget Analysis, Statistical Annexes, and
    Projections)

The mission also benefitted from contributions from Raul Auzmendi (Transport), James Hanson (External Debt), Antonio Martin del Campo (Budget Processes), Nelson de Franco (Power), Oscar Libonatti (Fiscal Accounts), John Stoddart (Hydrocarbons), and David Vetter (Provinces). Alejandro Izquierdo helped prepare the Statistical Annexes and graphs. James Hanson provided valuable comments. Diane Bievenour and Mila Divino provided secretarial support.

The mission also produced a companion report on provincial public finance, *Argentina: Towards a New Federalism* (June 1992), World Bank.

Contents

PART III - EXPENDITURES

EXECUTIVE SUMMARY

A. Overview

Three Years of Progress

1.　　　　The Menem Administration assumed office in July 1989 after a decade of crisis in public finances that had culminated in hyperinflation. The new team inherited weak public institutions accustomed to deficit spending and reliance on the inflation tax. Claims on the state's resources were far greater than its capacity to mobilize resources--meaning the Argentine state was insolvent. Dependence on the inflation tax had caused the macroeconomy to become progressively more unstable by shrinking the monetary base to levels that made it impossible to control inflation with even small fiscal gaps.

2.　　　　In response to the crisis, the Menem Administration enacted a series of structural reforms in its first 42 months that progressively recast the foundations of public finance. The Government undertook difficult-to-reverse reforms in the legal framework, institutions, and policies. These involved restructuring the state through reforms in *revenue mobilization* to increase the quantity and quality of federal revenues and *expenditure reforms* that have redrawn the boundaries of the national government and private sector. Expenditure reforms included an *administrative reform* to reduce the size and scope of government and improve control over expenditures, a *new federalism* that made revenue-sharing with the provinces transparent and decentralized selected expenditures, and an extensive program of *privatizations and asset sales* to end irreversibly subsidies through public entities and facilitate new private investment. Finally, the Government has also attempted to delink the nonfinancial public sector from the source of inflationary finance through *reforms of the Central Bank.*

3.　　　　The results have been impressive: revenues increased, expenditures declined, and the noninterest balance moved into sustainable surplus for the first time in decades. Aggregate expenditures have not fallen more as a share of GDP because increases associated with automatic transfers to the provinces and social security offset expenditure reductions elsewhere. The transfers have helped to alleviate (at least initially) latent structural deficits in social security and the provinces as well. Progress in controlling inflation was not smooth--in part because institutional weaknesses took time to redress, and because small errors of macroeconomic management superimposed on small and skittish financial markets quickly were amplified into runs on the currency. Nonetheless, the underlying fundamentals in public finance improved steadily, as the combined deficit of the public sector fell from 10.5 percent of GDP in 1989 to a projected slight surplus in 1992. The macroeconomy has become more stable and the economy is now in its third year of strong expansion.

The Challenges Ahead

4.　　　　Maintaining balance in public finances is an essential prerequisite for continued price stability and economic expansion. This idea is now broadly accepted among Government officials at all levels and the public at large. Nonetheless, weaknesses in the structural underpinnings of public finance remain in social security, provincial finances, health insurance, and defense expenditures--and these pose medium-term threats to fiscal balance. Maintaining the intensity of the reform effort--with their implied sacrifices--in an environment of price stability, growth, and fading memories of hyperinflation is the challenge now facing the Government. Moreover, if economic growth should slow, then tax growth will decline and demands for wage increases, new subsidies, and public spending may intensify.

5. Aware of this, the Government has shown its resolve to implement and/or consolidate the ambitious set of reforms already underway. The Government intends to consolidate the *administrative reform* by implementing the recently passed Law of Public Financial Management, by improving control over the wage bill, by seeking passage of the Law of Public Procurement, and by completing the bureaucratic restructuring. *Social security reform*, the linchpin of several other reforms, is intended to provide an adequate and reliable pension to beneficiaries and, by capitalizing the system, create a huge pool of savings available for investment, albeit at transitional cost to the Government. Social security reform also is linked to the reform of *direct taxes*, since income tax collection is central to funding of social security from general revenues. Also as part of the social security financing, the Government has proposed changes in *federal-provincial fiscal relations*, designed to improve the balance between revenue and expenditure responsibilities; it is also encouraging provinces to undertake their own adjustment programs. In other areas, the Government has formulated a reform of the *health insurance* program that would provide universal health coverage, reduce inefficiencies in the health system, and eventually reduce wage taxes, while offering the promise of improved health status and worker productivity. Finally, the Government has also begun a reform of the *defense complex*, including the privatization of military-run public enterprises, restructuring personnel and revising the use of military facilities. These reforms constitute the basis of future improvements in public finance and will help eradicate the structural deficit and improve the quality of revenue mobilization and expenditures. The Government merits full external support in these efforts.

6. If these reforms are consummated, the public sector accounts are projected to be in approximate balance over the medium term. The remaining small financing gaps toward the end of the decade should be financeable in a world of price stability, low interest rates, steady four percent growth, and continued confidence in economic management.

7. However, public finances have little cushion in the event that favorable economic and policy assumptions do not materialize. First, slower-than-projected growth of output or unexpected increases in inflation may reduce public sector revenues below projected levels; while the revenue problem is no longer structural, the Government still has minimal scope for offsetting adverse events through revenue increases. Second, the process of adjustment has given rise to new uncertainties that may place unanticipated claims on public resources. The Government needs to increase spending on social services and investment in the near term to improve service delivery. The downsizing of the state has reduced the demand for investment in public goods and services but only partially; the deterioration from a decade of neglect requires new and more efficient spending. Third, the proposed new social security regime entails

unknown but substantial transition costs. While the near-term costs are to be offset by general revenues, changes in the design of the reform as it makes its way through Congress may increase these costs. Fourth, levels of public sector indebtedness are still high, and fiscal accounts are vulnerable to unanticipated interest rate surges. Finally, the Government is consolidating past arrears to social security recipients, suppliers, and others with claims on the state through issue of as much as US$15-20 billion in new debt (the consolidation bond, BOCON); the service of this debt is capitalized for the first six years, but payments on the order of US$3 billion will be required in the last years of this decade. Although some of this new debt will be canceled with future asset sales, cash payments on the BOCON will come due at exactly the time when payments to commercial banks under the recent debt reduction agreement peak at about US$3 billion. These uncertainties mean that Argentina must not slow the pace of medium-term reforms, and the Government should therefore strive to exceed its current fiscal objectives.

8.   With federal revenues approaching historic highs of more than 24 percent of GDP, the main outstanding issues are to improve the neutrality of the tax policy framework and its progressivity. As discussed below, reducing payroll taxes (perhaps as part of the health insurance reform) and broadening the base of the income tax would serve both ends well while at the same time contributing to revenue increases. Tax administration, much improved in recent years, also holds the promise of some revenue increases, mainly through vigilant administration of recent controls on costly subsidies to promoted industries. New revenues from these sources could in the future be used to eliminate remaining small taxes and ease rates on main taxes. Finally, provincial tax policy and administration are potential sources of additional revenues and efficiency.

9.   On the expenditure side, the stop-go austerity programs of the 1980s and the post-1989 adjustment program--notably the administrative reform and the privatization program--brought down federal public expenditures to levels that are a tolerable burden on the economy. Public expenditures, equal to 22 percent of GDP at the federal level and 40 percent for all public expenditures, are below the average for the industrial countries, and comparable to middle-income countries.

10.   The main problems with expenditures are: (i) to buttress mechanisms that prevent surges in expenditure in the future; (ii) to increase the productivity of all public expenditures; and (iii) to reduce the excessive current expenditures of the provinces. Expenditure surges arise from spending compression, inadequate control of the wage bill and other expenditures, and precarious financing for spending authorities receiving transfers. The administrative reform, by reducing employment in the Federal Government by over 50 percent and increasing wages, has relieved wage compression; the privatization program has had a similar effect. Also, the Government has taken important strides to improve Budget Office's control over cash management, budgeting, and programming. The new Law of Financial Administration, passed in September 1992, will establish the legal basis for fiscal control, including expenditure authorization and *ex post* auditing. Also, regularizing financial relations with the provinces and public enterprises have reduced pressures for discretionary allocations. Nonetheless, important actions remain: full implementation of the control and *ex post* auditing systems in Financial Administration Law, improved control of the wage bill, and gaining fiscal control over the health insurance system.

11.   Sustaining the recovery in the private sector requires a more efficient delivery of publicly supplied goods and services, and a sound macroeconomic and regulatory framework. At the national level, expenditure compression in the 1980s reduced the already-low productivity of public expenditures. While recent employment reductions and privatizations have relieved the compression, only better management and resource allocation across programs can realize potential productivity gains.

12.   At the provincial level, spending is nearly twice the noninterest expenditure of the national administration. Current expenditures are excessive and investment is low.[1] Most provinces, long accustomed to a share of the inflation tax, are only now beginning the adjustment that the Federal Government started three years ago. While provinces are being asked to supply an increasing share of public service, they have received windfall gains in co-participated revenues, and this could reduce the incentive to adjust. For that reason, the Government has last year obtained proportional payment for administration of taxes, an increased share of co-participated taxes for social security, transferred responsibility for secondary education and health to the provinces, and required repayment of rediscounts. Adjustment in the provinces--through reforms of tax systems, administration, and employment practices--is the only way that provinces can begin to provide educational, health and other services more efficiently. Moreover, from a macroeconomic point of view, a slowdown in growth and revenue collection would generate considerable demands to increase transfers unless provincial administrations make headway in implementing their own reforms. The next section elaborates on these themes by summarizing the specific recommendations of this report.

B. Policy Options to Consolidate Fiscal Stability

13.   Several new policies and reforms, summarized below, could increase the fiscal surplus by an estimated 1.2-1.4 percent of GDP, and provide the cushion necessary to offset contingencies in the medium-term fiscal program. Moreover, the reforms would provide considerable improvement in the quality of public revenue mobilization and productivity of expenditures. This report suggests specific policy initiatives in tax policy and administration, current expenditures, and public investment as well as spending in the social security system, public enterprises and provinces.

Tax Policy

14.   The tax policy framework over the last two years has produced dramatic improvements in tax collection at the same time that it has evolved into a more efficient system. The Government has markedly increased its reliance on VAT and reduced the coverage of inefficient taxes, especially those on exports. The system now relies on four modern taxes: the general and uniform VAT, the income/assets tax, import tariffs, and excise taxes on selected final products (notably fuel, cigarettes, and alcoholic beverages). The abolition of the remaining inefficient taxes will be possible as revenues from efficient taxes become compatible with the current public expenditures. The main

---

1   Provincial public finances are treated in summary form in this report based on a detailed review in a separate report. See World Bank, *Argentina: Towards a New Federalism*, June 1992.

outstanding issues are neutrality with respect to use of capital and labor and the progressivity of the system.

15.   The Government is poised to address these issues in the context of its social security and pension funds reforms. One proposal would be to reduce the wage taxes by making some portion of the employers' contribution deductible against the VAT, and thus increase social security funding from the VAT and income taxes. This would generate an important incentive for employers to declare social security contributions and help reduce evasion. The burden of the income tax on the middle and lower-middle class would be reduced by raising the minimum monthly taxable income. This proposal would be a salutary step toward reducing the bias against employment, but is only a partial solution. Although the increase in the minimum taxable income will in principle improve the progressivity because of the reduction of taxation on low-income workers, it would effectively narrow the base for the income tax by excluding many mid- and upper-income taxpayers as well. While the annual average income per family is estimated at about US$19,000, the minimum taxable income is above US$20,000. Also, the loss of the wage taxes may require the Government to increase the VAT rate.

16.   A more direct way of addressing both the factor bias and progressivity is to explore ways of reducing the wage taxes and increasing taxes on income from capital. Assuming that the social security system is financeable through the elimination of evasion at a 26 percent contribution rate, the Government should consider linking a reform of the health insurance system with a reduction in both the family funds and the health insurance quotas. Contributions to health and family funds account for nearly 24 percent of gross salaries, much higher than nonpension wage taxes in all OECD countries. Health reform--discussed at length in Chapter 5--and more efficient use of the family funds might permit reductions of the payroll taxes by half.

17.   At the same time, the Government could increase the taxation of income from capital directly through modifications to the corporate and personal income tax. For the *corporate income tax*, the deduction of interest payments from the corporate income tax should be retained, provided that interest income is taxed at the individual level. At the same time the Government should review the expensing of investment to ensure that the depreciation deduction is consistent with economic rates of depreciation.

18.   For the *personal income tax*, the Government should reintroduce taxation on income from capital, which is now virtually exempt. First, the Government should disallow the interest deduction; this would allow taxation of the interest earnings. Second, the Government should also institute taxation of at least the real portion of capital gains. Finally, the Government should not raise the already generous minimum threshold on income subject to taxation, but, as tax administration improves, lower it. In addition, the Government should eliminate miscellaneous deductions and review the possibility of taxation of fringe benefits. The effect of these measures would be to broaden the base rather than to narrow it.

19.   Reducing the payroll tax through reduction of health funds contributions, which are fully deductible from the base of the personal income tax, will automatically increase the base of the personal income tax. Lower contributions can lead to an

increase in after-tax wages since a reduction in labor cost leads to an increase in labor demand, which in turn affects positively real wages (and can also reduce unemployment). The positive impact on real wages will be reinforced if a decline in the price level occurs. The price of capital would be positively influenced since labor costs directly affect the production cost of investment goods. Finally, simultaneous reductions in the wage tax, coupled with other reforms in service delivery, will also improve the equity of the tax system.

20.   The August 1992 agreement with provinces helps redress the earmarked imbalance between the social security system and other demands on Treasury resources fixed in the coparticipation regime. The package assigns 15 percent of total coparticipated tax revenues to the social security system, but does not create maximum incentives for provincial governments to adjust. Tax revenues allocated to provinces are projected to increase by nearly US$3.8 billion between 1992 and 1993. The agreement left in place about US$1.5 billion in transfers other than co-participation, including FONAVI, which are less effective in achieving their stated objectives. Transfers to the provinces other than coparticipation should be considered as an instrument of structural adjustment and in that sense should be linked to improvements in the fiscal performance of the provinces.

Tax Administration

21.   Reforms in tax administration have been a major cause of revenue improvements to date, and have allowed the Government to gain strong control of revenue streams. Nonetheless, programs to improve control of industrial promotion, internal administration, the tax court, and the customs administration merit priority attention because of their high revenue potential.

22.   Of these, perhaps the highest tax yield could come from the Government's efforts to control industrial promotion. The program, implemented in November 1992, involves exchanging self-declared benefits for an audited tax credit applicable against future taxes, cancellation of benefits not yet activated, and careful auditing of existing beneficiaries. The DGI should devote the necessary resources to audit firms that did not pay taxes during the suspension of benefits in the year following the Emergency Law; the effort to control provincial firms has achieved only 50 percent of its targeted rate of audit thus far, but could yield revenues of more than US$300 million. In looking to the future, the Government should make permanent the suspension of new industrial promotion benefits, the suspension of which is scheduled to expire in September 1993.

23.   The entire reform program of the industrial promotion system will produce large fiscal savings. Estimates of DGI staff suggest that the tax credit substitution program will reduce the fiscal cost of the industrial promotion from US$2.7 billion to US$1.4 billion in 1993.

Current Expenditures: The Wage Bill

24.   The Government has undertaken an unprecedented administrative reform to downsize and reorganize the Federal Government. Officials reorganized the main ministries and selected decentralized agencies. Employment in the national

administration will have fallen from roughly 670,000 in 1990 to under 285,000 by end 1992; of this reduction, 105,000 employees have left the Government and the remainder have been transferred to the provincial governments. Employment reductions in the public enterprise sector have been no less dramatic: employment has fallen from 295,000 to almost 50,000. Of this 245,000 reduction, about one-third has been through retrenchment, and the rest via privatization.

25.   To complete the reduction program, the Government should: (i) complete the restructuring process for those remaining governmental organizations that have yet to be restructured, including CONICET, CNEA, civilian personnel in the Armed Forces, the national universities, the National Sugar Board, and health insurance funds (*obras sociales*), which in total would reduce employment by an additional 27,000 positions; (ii) continue to work with the budget office to disaggregate reductions by jurisdiction to ensure proper accounting and budgeting in the future; (iii) realize a special study on reductions, including the preparation of names and identification numbers for the purpose of ensuring that those who leave and receive indemnification will not reenter public service.

26.   To complete the reform of the wage payment system and pay scale, the Government must: (i) establish its own computerized registry of civil service and centralize the payment function directly or through the Ministries' accounts in line with the new law of Public Finances, possibly absorbing the staff of the Office of Civil Service into the Ministry of Economy--where it was located before the Military Government of 1976; (ii) implement a computerized check payment system through the banking system to control the wage bill, a measure that might save as much as US$200 million in administrative costs plus additional savings through reduction in wages to nonexistent workers. If the new system is well designed, it will ensure greater accountability and establish firm control over the wage bill. These actions may help reduce further the resources devoted solely to "administration"--amounting to a savings of nearly US$400 million spent through the various ministries.

Health and Social Welfare

27.   The Government is now beginning to formulate an effective strategy for the social sectors. The Federal Government is a relatively small actor in health compared to the provinces and the quasi-public health insurance funds. Federal outlays for health, housing, and welfare absorb US$800 million of the US$8 billion in noninterest, non-transferrable expenditures--10 percent of the national administration's actual spending. An additional US$1.5 billion are spent as direct transfers from the federal budget--US$1 billion is transferred to the provinces through the FONAVI housing program and US$200 million to subsidize the health insurance funds operated by the unions (*obras sociales*).

28.   **Health.** Most public health expenditures--whose resources flow from the wage tax as well as budgetary allocation--go through the health funds, which represent US$5.6 billion (estimated on the basis of 1986 data, the latest available) compared to federal expenditures of US$745 million by the Federal Government and perhaps US$2.0-3.5 billion by the provincial governments. Improvement in the efficiency of expenditure in this sector must, therefore, focus on improving the accountability and efficiency of

the health funds and provinces. A major reform of the social insurance funds could provide both a source of savings in 1993 as well as major improvements in productivity of health care expenditures.

29.   The Government has prepared a major reform of the health insurance funds and made its main principles law through a Presidential decree in January 1993. The new program would: (i) allow contributors to choose their own providers; (ii) allow free entry after a transition phase; (iii) require providers to offer a minimum package of health care at a specified price; and (iv) universal coverage with subsidies for indigent individuals (as distinct from current institutional subsidies). This would be combined with close monitoring of both the insurance system and the medical package, including limitations on administrative expenditures. The new system would in effect finance universal coverage by reducing the acknowledged very high costs of administration and waste in the current system. The new program remains to be defined through regulations and institutions but should be created along the lines of the original draft law.

30.   A stronger insurance system, such as that contemplated in the recently prepared draft law on obras sociales, would also relieve the federal bureaucracy of major expenditures through the budget for financing the deficits of the insurance funds-- through the ANSSAL (US$217 million in 1992). Remaining expenditures could be focused on core national objectives: vaccinations, preventive medicine, prevention of drug abuse, sanitation regulation, and targeted programs of maternal and child health care. Selected programs, such as the Ministry of Education's Student Health Program (US$48 million) and the Congressional Medical Plan (US$15 million), might be less necessary in the context of a national health insurance program.

31.   **Other Welfare.** The MHSA has welfare programs other than housing (discussed under investment) that collectively amount to US$140 million. These programs should be reviewed for possible reductions in light of the Government decision to decentralize expenditure responsibility to the provinces. In addition, other jurisdictions, especially the Ministry of Labor, spend US$240 million on several programs that merit review for effectiveness.

Education

32.   The Argentine educational system, once among the best in Latin America, has become a shadow of its former preeminence. Entrenching privileges for teachers and granting free admission and education for students beginning in the 1970s interacted with cycles of austerity in the 1980s to produce fiscally eroded public institutions. Under budget pressure, the primary schools were decentralized to the provinces beginning in the early 1970s, where many of the same forces continued at play. The secondary and vocational schools were transferred in 1992 by agreement, with implicit funding from the increase in the co-participated revenues. Quality, salaries, and teaching conditions now vary widely among provinces.

33.   After transferring secondary education to the provinces, the Government now spends about US$1.3 billion on education at the federal level, about half of which (US$720 million) is transferred to the federal universities. The largest potential

efficiency gains in federal spending are therefore to be found at the university level. This spending has not been sufficient to prevent the decline of the quality of public university education in Argentina. Because competing private universities can fulfill much of the demand and because low public tuition tends to be a regressive subsidy-- most graduates are from above-average-income families and go on to earn better-than- average salaries--the Government should consider a program of phased divestiture of the university system. This would allow resources to be concentrated on subsidies designated for low-income student scholarships at universities and enrichment programs for primary and secondary education administered at the provincial level.

34. As an interim policy, the Government should consider the establishment of a combination of user fees (i.e., tuition) and targeted subsidies (i.e., loans and scholarships for low-income, meritorious students) to enhance financing. Adopting a needs-based, targeted student loan program would ensure that low-income students would have access to university education. If the system's 700,000 students were charged a modest tuition of US$100 per term plus US$20 per month (private universities charge US$250-600 for tuition plus US$300-800 month), the Government would mobilize nearly US$300 million in additional funds. Adopting a needs-based, targeted student loan program would ensure that low-income students would have access to university education.

35. At the same time, the shift of secondary education to the provinces should facilitate the downsizing or even closure of the Ministry of Education. Selected programs, such as Budget and Education Policy (US$45 million), Teacher Education and Training Programs (US$83 million), the Cultural Budget (US$16 million), Technical Education Council (US$17 million), and Scientific Research (US$42 million), should be reviewed for their effectiveness.

36. In the future, it will be necessary to increase educational spending to pay for the equalization of teacher salaries for secondary education, increase overall pay linked to other productivity measures, improve school materials that are woefully out of date, and rehabilitate deteriorating plant and equipment. These demands will fall on the provinces. This cost could be at least partially offset by reducing the number of teachers, consistent with reasonable class sizes. At present student-teacher ratios are quite low (about 11) and highly variable across provinces (6-15). Also, paid leaves are excessive and poorly monitored. A structural reform could substantially offset costs of higher wages.

Defense

37. Military expenditures absorb the second largest share of the non-interest federal budget, and the largest share of discretionary Treasury expenditures, 32 percent. Military outlays excluding pensions have fallen from over 6.0 percent of GDP in 1980-81 to less than 2 percent at present, now among the lowest proportions of GDP in the hemisphere. The Government has recognized that Argentina's security environment has improved significantly since 1983. Resolution of long-standing conflicts with Chile, Brazil, and Great Britain, coupled with a reduction in the perceived threat of external support for domestic subversion following disintegration of the Soviet Union, has led

the Government to take the opportunity to reconsider levels of military spending, and at the same time redirect military spending to more effectively fulfill its function.

38.   The Government has identified several imbalances that currently hamper military efficiency to achieve this objective. First, with personnel costs absorbing over 70 percent of the defense budget, the military's operational capacity has been severely curtailed.   Second, as the size of the force has decreased since the mid 1980s, the traditional rank pyramid for the Army, Navy and Air Force has become distorted, with the ratio of officers to enlisted personnel rising substantially.   Third, the military pension system is in urgent need of rationalization to remain solvent, to bring it into line with the civilian pension system, and ensure mobility between the defense and civilian systems. Fourth, the facilities operated by the armed forces need to be consolidated and relocated to areas from which they can most effectively defend Argentine territory. On the other hand, wages do not appear to be a problem--military pay is significantly higher than civilian pay, and on a par with other countries when compared to mean incomes at similar grades and length of service.

39.   The reform strategy the Government has begun to implement the rationalization of the entire military sector. This includes defense-industry privatization, personnel retrenchment, and facilities consolidation.   Thirty defense-related public enterprises are currently being privatized. This exercise will eliminate their substantial losses and allow the Government to retire their associated debt, possibly even producing some revenue. Present plans to reduce civilian Ministry of Defense personnel by 40 percent will restore the ratio of civilian to military personnel that existed prior to 1985 and lead to an estimated annual savings of US$80 million.

40.   The Government is also considering retrenchment of military personnel. A decrease in the level of military employees would enable the Ministry of Defense to further lower personnel costs and facilitate the restoration of a more pyramid-shaped personnel structure. Additionally, by using some of the funds to increase operations and maintenance, and possibly making some strategic capital purchases, the Government feels it could achieve the same level of security at a lower annual cost. One way to achieve this is, for example, to implement a program that restored the personnel pyramid existing in 1984; this would entail a 25 percent personnel reduction and would save an estimated US$155 million annually.   An important principle for military restructuring is that revenues from asset sales should be used to support the reform process--for the program of restructuring of the defense establishment, severance payments and adjustment assistance, reform for the military pension system, or investments in relocation and enhanced mobility of forces in line with the Government's new strategy--instead of consumed in support of normal current expenditures. Otherwise, when the revenue stream from asset sales ends, the Government will have the same spending levels and no way to support them. In other words, proceeds from asset sales should be used to reduce liabilities or for selected strategic investment consistent with the new defense strategy.

Presidency

41.   The Presidency has evolved into a major spending entity in the Federal Government, responsible for 14 percent of spending in the national administration. The

Argentine Constitution mandates the existence of no more than 8 Ministries in the National Administration, a limit recently reenforced with the administrative reform in 1991/92. However, governments have used the Presidency jurisdiction as the sphere of Government where secretariats with Ministerial rank could be established. The four largest units--the Communication Secretariat (responsible for the Public Broadcasting Company), the National Tourism Agency, CONICET (the research institute program), and the nuclear power agency (CNEA) are responsible for 80 percent of staff and expenditures in the Presidency.

42.   A close examination of these agencies suggests unnecessarily high employment levels in the central administration and decentralized agencies in light of the new role of the state. The Presidency has been relatively untouched by the administrative reform, and overall employment levels are virtually the same as before the reform began. Since this is a jurisdiction that most needs reform, the Government should apply the same principles of downsizing to the Presidency that were applied throughout the rest of the public sector. Specifically, for the largest executing units, the Government might consider: (i) eliminating the Communications Secretariat and establishing a Directorate of Communications under the new General Subsecretariat of the Presidency; eventually, the National Service of Radio Telecommunications could be privatized, removing 950 positions from public sector accounts; (ii) rationalizing the National Tourism Agency and establishing a new National Directorate also under the jurisdiction of the Ministry of Economy, thereby eliminating 500 positions; and (iii) privatizing CONICET and the Miguel Lillo Foundation, resulting in the abolition of 5,589 positions from the public sector budget, since research and development activities could be undertaken in public and private universities.

43.   Finally, the nuclear power company (CNEA) should be restructured into business and research units for privatization and transferred out of Presidency. Two possible business units (power production and heavy water) could be established under the Secretariat of Electric Energy in the Ministry of Economy until privatization is completed. Privatization would lead to an eventual public sector savings of US$850 million. The rationalization of the Presidency jurisdiction could result in net savings of US$570 million.

Public Enterprises

44.   Public enterprises accounted for 25 percent of total public spending in Argentina as late as 1990, but the privatization program has already shrunk this to 17 percent. The Government's program of privatization of public enterprises has produced enormous benefits. Among them are capital revenues to support the transition to a sustainable public finance position, relief from investment demand in the sector, an end to pricing distortions, and macroeconomic shocks associated with political pricing. Assuming that the privatization program is completed as scheduled, resources for the Government are at estimated between US$4-5 billion in 1992, somewhat higher than official projections, which do not take into account the privatization of Encotel, Puertos A.G., OSN, and Gas del Estado. The program, if maintained on schedule, will also facilitate reductions in transfers from the federal budget.

45.   Capital revenues from asset sales are to be used in the program to cancel liabilities. It is essential that the Government maintain this policy and avoid using asset sales to finance current expenditures. Because of the debt consolidation (discussed below), the indebtedness of the Government will increase in 1993 despite the debt reduction agreement with commercial creditors. Therefore, any one-time extraordinary revenues through asset sales should be used to reduce debt.

46.   Budget transfers amount to US$2 billion annually and should be phased down in accordance with the privatization and enterprise restructuring schedule. In 1993, transfers should be scaled down to less than US$800 million--virtually all to the remaining segments of the railways and Yacyreta--and to less than US$400 million in 1994, nearly all to Yacyreta. Special effort should be devoted to reductions in railway transfers, since they are economically inefficient and costly.

47.   A prerequisite for economic success in privatization is the enactment of a clear regulatory framework, especially for pricing, in those sectors not subject to the discipline of price competition from competing sellers. In particular, output prices must be fixed according to their international production costs and not only according to the evolution of the benefits of the formerly public firm. Finally, the new Law of Procurement, submitted to Congress in January 1993, would establish the basis for a long-term, non-discriminatory regime for the entire public sector.

Provincial Finance

48.   Provinces account for about one-third of public spending in Argentina. Though preliminary estimates suggest the provinces collectively will be in fiscal balance in 1991, in the past they have been major sources of deficit in the consolidated public sector accounts. The Government has undertaken major efforts to improve the federal fiscal structure, and reduce the incentives to spend without regard to revenues. Several problems exist that can prevent the new federalism from realizing its full potential. First, imbalances between current and capital spending within provincial finances are becoming evident; provincial *real* current expenditures jumped by 41 percent between 1982 and 1990, while capital expenditures dropped by 25 percent. Second, the large rise in coparticipated taxes and the large federal-provincial transfers have reduced the fiscal urgency to reform as new revenues absolve provinces of the political cost of raising taxes; for example, in 1992, the provinces will be able to spend an estimated US$500 million more than in 1991, over and above the cost of transferred secondary education and health. A third problem is the inefficiency of provincial and municipal tax systems, characterized by distortionary taxes, poor tax administration, and poor use of the revenue potential of local tax bases. Finally, provincial governments financed more than 60 percent of their deficits in 1990 with loans through the provincial banks, and reforms initiated do not go far enough to ensure that the provincial banks will not again become a source of deficit finance and macroeconomic instability during the next economic downturn.

49.   **Federal Framework.** To maintain the incentive to adjust in the context of the present primary distribution in the Revenue Sharing Law, one option is to improve the distribution of the *marginal* increases that result from improved federal tax administration or new revenue measures at the federal level. This would require seeking

an accord to reduce the marginal transfers from future improvements and/or seeking to transfer additional expenditures to the provinces with projected "windfall" gains from marginal increases from future federal revenues. This is the strategy the Government has followed to date. Another option is to recast the US$2.2 billion of noncoparticipated transfers in the budget. The largest of these include the FONAVI housing program (US$900 million), special aid to Buenos Aires and Tierra del Fuego (two programs totalling US$300 million), the Tobacco Fund (US$100 million), and the National Highway Fund (US$100 million). With the agreement of the provinces, some or all of these resources might be consolidated into a program of block grants to be disbursed in proportion to current savings performance of provinces and/or to reimburse the cost of agreed reforms, such as severance payments to redundant workers or provincial social security reforms. This fund could be supplemented with: (i) incremental improvements in aggregate coparticipated resources; and (ii) loan proceeds from international financial institutions. A fund of US$2.0-3.0 billion could provide a powerful incentive to adjust current expenditures and revenues and provide a continuing source of much needed investment at the provincial level. The fund would be administered by a project execution unit established in the budget office; the unit would calculate the net present value, and would disburse against projects meeting the test of a positive net present value.

50.   **Revenues.** The Government should also work with the provinces to: (i) transfer to the provinces the tax administration system now in operation at the DGI, including the computerized control of the largest taxpayers, cross-checks with DGI regional offices and accounts, and improved collections of sales and land taxes; and (ii) revamp the tax policy framework to eliminate inefficient taxes.

51.   **Expenditures.** Provinces will be the main agents providing public services in the future. Their efficiency in doing so will have a profound effect on the long-term growth rate of Argentina. The most pressing need is a comprehensive administrative reform to reduce public employment similar to that designed at the national level to reduce employment and raise average salaries as well as a review of the allocation of human and fiscal resources to service delivery.

Social Security

52.   Social security spending, after accounting for 12-14 percent of spending of the nonfinancial public sector during most of the 1980s, is projected to increase to 21 percent by 1992. This represents increases in the pensions themselves, as well as payment of a larger share of accrued pensions in lieu of accumulating arrears. The August 1992 agreement with the provinces ended the accumulation of arrears by increasing paid pensions with the use of co-participated resources. The new system would create an integrated pension system for workers, comprised of a public new minimum pension for all workers, a transitional pension for retired workers and those about to retire, and a capitalized, privately-managed system. The move to a capitalized system can, if properly managed and financed, restore credibility to the social security system.

53.   The most important issue is that the Government create sufficient fiscal "space" to finance the decade-long transition to a fully capitalized system. This entails

planning for an increased deficit in the social security system (before general revenues) to about US$5-7 billion annually in 1994-97. In 1993, general revenues more than covered the system's deficit because that share of the wage tax going to the capitalized system would not take effect (and therefore be lost to the public system) until 1994, the date of implementation. As of that time, however, general revenues of US$5-7 billion are needed in 1994 and beyond, if the deficit is not to be increased. This suggests that at least the 15 percent of coparticipated revenues temporarily allocated to social security in 1993 be continued.

54.   Moreover, the annual system deficit could turn out to be US$1-$2 billion higher than the Government's present projections, depending on several possible adverse developments during the passage of the law and the transition-phase implementation: unfinanced pension increases, slow progress in controlling evasion (and therefore a slower decline of the dependency ratio), and overly generous treatment of workers during the transition with insufficient years of contribution, who might otherwise have to delay retirement until age 70. Since the financing is so dependent on general revenues, changes to the reform package that increase benefits could easily destabilize public finances.

55.   **Policies to Reinforce the Reform.**   To address the risks mentioned above, the Government should: (i) protect the new system against demands that it raise benefits for pre-reform pensioners beyond levels mandated by the old laws; (ii) resist demands for raising the compensatory pension above levels established in the December modification of the draft law; (iii) lower the average level of pension insurance from about 70 percent of the average wage to 55-65 percent--levels common in Western Europe; (iv) resist pressure for weakening the rules for the transition to higher minimum years of contribution and age at retirement; instead, allow workers not qualifying under the rules to retire at age 65 or later with actuarially fair deductions from their pensions; (v) strengthen the audit program for disability pensions; (vi) further strengthen social security collections through systematic cross-checks with the DGI; (vii) extend mandatory affiliation to all economically active, including provincial and municipal public employees; at a minimum require provincial and municipal schemes to adopt the same criteria as to minimum years of contribution and age at retirement.

56.   **Pension Fund Investments.**   The Government must design investment rules for the pension funds that will ensure the security of these resources, as the pension funds (as opposed to the pension system) will accumulate a large surplus in their first two decades of growth. These funds will produce investible resources of about US$3 billion annually in this decade. An important step is taken in the present draft law, which prohibits any minimum investment requirements in particular instruments (notably Government paper); requiring the funds to invest in financing the deficit of the rest of government would have reduced confidence in the performance of the funds.

57.   Confidence in the private pension fund scheme also depends on a coherent set of rules, and on the credible policing of the rules by a professional supervisory body free of conflicts of interest and political intervention. The draft law, however, lacks rules on the composition of the superintendency, and a recent agreement between the Government and the unions would staff the superintendency with representatives from the state, the unions, employers, and the affiliates rather than a professional management

and staff which is accountable to the Executive or Congress. This arrangement might undermine confidence that all AFJPs will be held to the strict standards of the law including application of the ultimate sanction, i.e., revocation of the AFJP license and transfer of the pension fund to other AFJPs. A weak superintendency risks that the state guarantee for a minimum fund performance will be called. Therefore, the Government should establish a professional superintendency for AFJPs.

Public Investment

58.   After nearly two decades of decline, public investment in Argentina is at historic lows. Though public investment averaged about 10 percent of GDP in the 1970s, it now has fallen to under 5 percent. The privatization program has reduced the demand for public investment and opened many sectors to private investment--notably, telecommunications, hydrocarbons, and transportation. Under private stewardship, these sectors may become dynamic, even leading sectors in Argentina. These facts, however, do not mitigate the need for new investment in those sectors remaining in the public domain--including highways, energy (for the near term), and social infrastructure.

59.   Although the Government of Argentina has made progress in the planning of public investment, with the appearance of public investment plans for both 1991 and 1992, the process of capital budgeting can be greatly improved, thereby increasing the efficiency of public investment. A serious shortcoming in the public investment process is the absence of a consistent mechanism of project evaluation that can guide investment decisions of the authorities. Out of more than 20 investment projects of over US$5 million identified, economic evaluations exist for only a handful. The government is now strengthening its technical group to establish the capacity to conduct proficient economic evaluations, including the calculation of relevant social prices to be used in all these evaluations.

60.   Several principles should guide this process. *First*, all investments should undergo an economic evaluation. *Second*, no project with a negative net present value at social prices should be carried out; having a positive net present value at social prices is a necessary, but not sufficient condition to go ahead with an investment project. In Argentina, where the public sector faces significant financial constraints, it may be impossible to finance all projects with a positive net present value. Thus, *third*, a project ranking is needed. Resources would then be allocated from the highest ranked project down, until resources are fully and efficiently allocated. Recent improvements in investment planning now establish the basis for a multi-year program that would establish out-year priorities for budgetary funding.

61.   **Power.** The annual investment budgets for 1992 of Atucha II and Pichi Picun Leufu were US$395 million and US$146 million, respectively. Taken together, the two absorb over 20 percent of the total investment budget of the national government (including central administration, special accounts, decentralized agencies and public enterprises), which was US$2.6 billion for 1992. Both of these projects have negative net present values at any discount rate over 12 percent. In the case of Pichi Picun Leufu, the Government contributions are very small and given the favorable conditions of financing, it should be completed. The completion of Atucha II should be postponed if financing cannot be obtained; as long as counterpart funds are scarce, any financing

scheme for its completion should include the minimum Government contribution during the 1993-94.

62.   **Housing.** The FONAVI housing program also appears uneconomical. Although no benefit-cost evaluation is available, there is good reason to believe that its NPV would be negative at reasonable discount rates. The program absorbed over US$900 million of resources in the budget for 1992 and has some serious flaws. An attractive and feasible option may be to phase out the program over the next two to three years. These funds have a high component of government saving, mainly because the FONAVI program does not attract any outside financing.

63.   Possible savings from these measures would amount to some US$1.4 billion, and could be used for investments in road maintenance, acceleration of Yacyreta and Piedra de Aguila hydropower projects, and increased investments in worthwhile provincial health and education projects.

Central Bank

64.   Since the conversion of short-term domestic debt into 10-year BONEX bonds in January 1990, the Government has moved vigorously to shut off the sources of finance to the nonfinancial and financial public sector through the monetary program. The trade financing facilities were closed and the function transferred to the new trade bank, Bank of International Trade (BICE). Second, financing the social security system through the OPP account has been ended. Third, debt service on the public debt held by the Central Bank is now charged to the Treasury. Fourth, rediscounts to the industrial bank (BANADE) and the Housing Bank (BHN) were gradually closed between 1987 and 1990, and net rediscount flows to the other public banks have been negative since these banks are repaying the emergency infusion of liquidity they received during the January 1991 run on the austral.

65.   These events have set the stage for improving the legal framework of the Central Bank and strengthening it as an institution. The passage of the new Central Bank Charter in September 1992 was a milestone in the creation of a modern monetary authority; the highest priority for Argentina is to implement the new Charter. The Charter provides the monetary authority with substantial independence, proscribe rediscounts--except for emergencies, and then only for limited periods against a pledge of the borrower's capital--and legally prohibits lending to the nonfinancial public sector. This is a necessary complement to the Law of Convertibility.

66.   **Administration and Management.** Management should revamp the structure of the Board of Directors to relieve them of operational line responsibilities. As it stands, Board members play both roles of supervising the President and carrying out his mandate. This dilutes responsibility and compromises the advice a Board member must give its President. The Government should use the opportunity presented by the Charter to appoint people of stature in the financial community and invest them with the responsibility of ensuring that the goals of the Charter are faithfully attained by the President and his management. Management must also devote special attention to tasks that have a high cost if not handled properly and immediately, most notably the reconciliation of the balances with external creditor banks.

67.   **Accounting**. Many changes carried out in recent years have significantly improved the Central Bank's accounting system. In particular, the recalculation of the end-1989 balance sheet and the elimination of forced investments and of the Monetary Regulation Account helped to simplify the accounting system. Nevertheless, the present system is still severely deficient. Reconstitution of the accounting system must move in parallel with the reorganization process. The reconstitution of the accounting system must also be carried out with a view to ensuring that it generate the appropriate statistics for the Central Bank's new responsibilities in a timely way. The Central Bank's operations must be defined precisely along with the specific ways and means by which data will be entered into the accounting system. Specific personnel would then be responsible for recording designated transactions. The fundamental question is whether the present system can be salvaged or if the system should be entirely replaced. Along these lines, it is noteworthy that an external audit of Central Bank accounts will be required by the new Charter.

68.   **Liquidation Function**. The Government in September 1992 modified the Financial Entities Law to require that all future liquidation of bankrupt financial institutions be handled directly by the court system. This leaves on the on-going liquidations with the Central Bank, many of the liquidations are more than a decade old, yet are still time-consuming and costly. The Central Bank should accelerate efforts to finish the process as soon as possible.

69.   **Superintendency**. Consistent with the new Charter of the Central Bank, the Government should: (i) consolidate the reform of the Superintendency of Banks by ensuring greater administrative independence and enactment of its upgraded salary and organizational structure; (ii) assign responsibility for issuing norms pertaining to banking regulation; and (iii) assign responsibility for the timely publication of financial indicators, including the balance sheets and income statement information as well as portfolio classification of banks. Also, (iv) the management relations between the Central Bank and the Superintendency should be made clearer and more predictable; (v) more enforcement power should be attributed to the Superintendency; and (vi) instruments used to evaluate commercial bank activities should be revised. Of particular concern is the need to reduce the incentives for large banks to take too many risks (too-big-to-fail policy). One possibility may be to tie bank supervision more directly to the amount of bank capital. Well-capitalized banks would be allowed to be the most diversified in financial services, since increasing the bank's own capital requirements is probably the most effective way of reducing moral hazard incentives.

C. Conclusions

70.   The Menem administration has made the most impressive progress in improving Argentina's growth prospects of any recent administration. It has done so by improving the fundamentals of public finance. These efforts have brought price stability within reach, and with it the possibility of enjoying sustained high economic growth. The next three years, however, will be as critical as the last three years. As the experience of other countries in the hemisphere has shown, only persistent, resolute and unrelenting pursuit of fiscal stability and efficient policies can realize a country's growth potential. Argentina has shown itself willing to pursue this course.

RESUMEN DE LAS PRINCIPALES RECOMENDACIONES DE POLITICA

A. Panorama General

Tres Años de Progreso

1.   La administración Menem llegó al poder en julio de 1989 después de una crisis de diez años en las finanzas públicas que culminó en la hiperinflación. El nuevo equipo heredó instituciones públicas débiles, acostumbradas a gastos deficitarios y a la recurrencia al impuesto inflacionario. Los reclamos por recursos estatales fueron mucho mayores que la capacidad estatal para movilizar recursos--en otras palabras, el Estado argentino era insolvente. La dependencia en el impuesto inflacionario tornó a la macroeconomía cada vez más inestable, reduciendo la base monetaria a niveles que hacían imposible controlar la inflación aún con pequeñas brechas fiscales.

2.   En respuesta a la crisis, la administración Menem introdujo una serie de reformas estructurales durante los primeros 42 meses de gobierno que fueron recomponiendo progresivamente los pilares de las finanzas públicas. El Gobierno llevó a cabo reformas difíciles de revertir, tanto en el marco legal como en las instituciones y políticas. Estas incluyeron la reestructuración del Estado a través de reformas en la movilización de ingresos para acrecentar la cantidad y calidad de los ingresos federales y reformas en los gastos que han redefinido los límites entre el gobierno nacional y el sector privado. Las reformas en las erogaciones incluyeron una reforma administrativa para reducir el tamaño y la ingerencia del gobierno y mejoras en el control de los gastos, un nuevo federalismo que hizo transparente la coparticipación de ingresos con las provincias y descentralizó gastos seleccionados, y un programa extensivo de privatizaciones y venta de activos que asegurara irreversiblemente el corte de subsidios via entidades públicas y facilitara nuevas inversiones privadas. Finalmente, el Gobierno también ha intentado desligar al sector público no financiero de la fuente del financiamiento inflacionario a través de reformas en el Banco Central.

3.   Los resultados han sido impresionantes: los ingresos aumentaron mientras que los gatos declinaron, y el balance primario llegó a ser superavitario por primera vez en varias décadas. El gasto agregado no cayó en mayor medida como proporción del PBI debido a incrementos en las transferencias automáticas a las provincias y a la seguridad social, que contrapesaron las reducciones en los gastos realizadas en otros sectores. Las transferencias ayudaron (al menos inicialmente) a aliviar los déficits estructurales latentes tanto en la seguridad social como en las provincias. El progreso en el control inflacionario no fue parejo--en parte porque algunas debilidades institucionales tomaron tiempo en subsanarse, y porque pequeños errores en el manejo macroeconómico, aplicados a mercados financieros pequeños y fluctuantes, prontamente se amplificaron produciendo corridas cambiarias. De todos modos, las variables fundamentales subyacentes en las finanzas públicas mejoraron constantemente, tal como lo indica la caída del déficit combinado, que pasó de 10.5 porciento del PBI en 1989, a un pequeño

superavit proyectado para 1992. La macroeconomía se ha tornado más estable y la economía se encuentra en su tercer año de fuerte expansión.

Los Próximos Desafíos

4.   El sostenimiento de una política de finanzas públicas balanceadas constituye un prerrequisito esencial para la continuidad de la estabilidad de precios y la expansión económica. Esta idea es ampliamente aceptada por los miembros del Gobierno a todo nivel así como también por el público en general. Aún así, subsisten todavía debilidades en los cimientos estructurales de las finanzas públicas, especialemente en las áreas de seguridad social, finanzas provinciales, salud y gastos de defensa--éstas atentan contra el balance fiscal en el mediano plazo. El Gobierno debe enfrentarse con el desafío que implica mantener la intensidad en el esfuerzo de las reformas--con los sacrificios que ello presupone--en un ambiente de estabilidad de precios, crecimiento, y recuerdos hiperinflacionarios en desaparición. Más aún, si el crecimiento económico declina, el crecimiento en la recaudacion tributaria bajará y las demandas de incrementos salariales, nuevos subsidios y gasto público pueden intensificarse.

5.   Conciente de esto, el Gobierno ha demostrado su resolución para implementar y/o consolidar el ambicioso grupo de medidas en marcha. El Gobierno se ha propuesto consolidar la reforma administrativa mediante la implementación de la recientemente aprobada Ley de Administración Financiera y Control de Gestión del Sector Público, mejoras en el control de la masa salarial, buscando la sanción de la ley de Compre Nacional, y completando la reestructuración burocrática. La reforma de la Seguridad Social, el eje de varias otras reformas, tiene como propósito proveer una adecuada y confiable pensión a sus beneficiarios, y mediante la capitalización del sistema, crear una amplia masa de ahorros disponible para inversiones, aunque a un costo inicial para el Gobierno. La reforma del sistema previsional también está ligada a la reforma de los impuestos directos, dado que la recaudación del impuesto a las ganancias es crucial para el financiamiento de la seguridad social a partir de los ingresos generales. Además, como parte del financiamiento de la seguridad social, el Gobierno ha propuesto cambios en las relaciones fiscales nación-provincias, diseñados para mejorar el balance entre las responsabilidades de ingresos y gastos; también ha alentado a las provincias para que realicen sus propios programas de ajuste. En otras áreas, el Gobierno ha formulado una reforma del programa de salud que proveería asistencia de tipo universal, reduciría las ineficiencias en el sistema de salud, y eventualmente reduciría las cargas laborales, prometiendo mejoras en el estado del sistema en general y en la productividad laboral. Finalmente, el Gobierno ha comenzado la reforma del complejo de defensa, incluyendo la privatización de las empresas militares, reestructuración de personal y una revisión del uso de las instalaciones militares. Dichas reformas constituyen la base de futuras mejoras en las finanzas públicas y permitirán la erradicación de déficits estructurales, mejorando al mismo tiempo la calidad de la movilización de ingresos y de gastos. El Gobierno merece total apoyo externo en estos esfuerzos.

6.   Si estas reformas se llevan a cabo, las cuentas proyectadas del sector público podrían estar aproximadamente equilibradas en el mediano plazo. Las pequeñas brechas de financiamiento hacia el fin de la década deberían ser financiables en un mundo de estabilidad de

precios, bajas tasas de interés, crecimento sostenido del 4 porciento, y una continua confianza en el equipo económico.

7.   De todos modos, las finanzas públicas tienen un escaso colchón si no se materializan los favorables supuestos económicos y de política mencionados. Primero, tasas de crecimiento del Producto más bajas que las proyectadas o incrementos inesperados en la tasa de inflación pueden reducir los ingresos proyectados del sector público; aunque el problema de ingresos ya no es estructural, el Gobierno tiene poco margen para compensar eventos adversos con aumnentos en la recaudación. Segundo, el proceso de ajuste ha dado lugar a nuevas incertidumbres que pueden implicar reclamos no anticipados sobre los recursos públicos. El Gobierno necesita incrementar el gasto en servicios sociales e inversión en el corto plazo para mejorar la prestación de servicios. El achicamiento del estado ha reducido la demanda de inversión en bienes y servicios públicos, pero sólo parcialmente; los deterioros, producto de una década de negligencia, requieren nuevos y más eficientes gastos. Tercero, el nuevo régimen de seguridad social propuesto implica costos de transición no conocidos pero de sustancial magnitud. Mientras que los costos de corto plazo podrían ser compensados con ingresos generales, cambios en la legislación que se produzcan cuando esta reforma circule por el Congreso bien podrían incrementar dichos costos. Cuarto, los niveles de deuda pública son aún altos, por lo que las cuentas fiscales son vulnerables a incrementos no anticipados en las tasas de interés. Finalmente, el Gobierno está consolidando los atrasos con jubilados, proveedores y otros, con acreencias sobre el estado, mediante la emisión de entre US$ 15.000 y US$ 20.000 millones de nueva deuda (el bono de consolidación, BOCON); el servicio de esta deuda se capitalizará durante los primeros seis años, pero se requerirán pagos de alrededor de US$ 3.000 millones durante los últimos años de la década. Aunque parte de esta deuda se cancelará con la venta de activos, los pagos en efectivo del BOCON vencerán exactamente cuando los pagos a los bancos comerciales, producto del reciente acuerdo de reducción de deuda, lleguen a un pico de alrededor de US$ 3.000 millones. Estas incertidumbres significan que Argentina no debe aminorar el paso de sus reformas de mediano plazo, y el Gobierno debería esforzarse en sobrepasar sus objetivos fiscales.

8.   Con un pico histórico en los ingresos federales de más del 24 porciento del PBI, los asuntos más importantes por atender son las mejoras en la neutralidad del marco impositivo y su progresividad. Como se discutirá posteriormente, la reducción de las cargas laborales (quizás como parte de la reforma del sistema de salud) y el aumento de la base del impuesto a las ganancias serviría para ambos propósitos, contribuyendo al mismo tiempo en la expansión de la recaudación. La administración impositiva, muy mejorada en los años recientes, también promete algunos aumentos en los ingresos, principalmente a través de una atenta administración sobre recientes controles efectuados a las industrias promocionadas. Los nuevos ingresos provenientes de estas fuentes podrían ser utilizados en el futuro para eliminar impuestos de escasa relevancia y disminuir las tasas de los impuestos más importantes. Finalmente, tanto la política como la administración impositiva provincial son fuentes potenciales de ingresos adicionales y eficiencia.

9.   Por el lado de las erogaciones, los programas de austeridad del tipo "stop-go" de los años ochenta y el programa de ajuste posterior a 1989--básicamente la reforma administrativa y el programa de privatizaciones--redujeron el gasto público federal a niveles que constituyen una carga tolerable para la economía. El gasto público, igual al 22 porciento del PBI a nivel federal y al 40 porciento para el gasto público total, se encuentra por debajo del promedio de los países industrializados, y a niveles comparables con los de los países de medianos ingresos.

10.   Los principales problemas referidos a los gastos son: (i) afianzar mecanismos que prevengan futuros aumentos en el gasto; (ii) incrementar la productividad de todas las erogaciones públicas; y (iii) reducir los excesivos gastos corrientes de las provincias. Los incrementos en el gasto surgen de la compresión en las erogaciones, el control inadecuado de la masa salarial y otros gastos, y el financiamiento precario de las autoridades de gasto que reciben transferencias. La reforma administrativa, al reducir el empleo federal por encima del 50 porciento e incrementar salarios, ha aliviado la compresión salarial; el programa de privatizaciones ha provocado efectos similares. Además, el Gobierno ha dado pasos importantes en cuanto al control de la Oficina de Presupuesto sobre la administración de fondos en efectivo, presupuestación y programación. La nueva Ley de Administración Financiera, promulgada en septiembre de 1992, establecerá las bases legales para el control fiscal, incluyendo la autorización de gastos y la auditoría ex post. También, la regularización de las relaciones financieras con las provincias y las empresas públicas ha reducido las presiones de asignaciones discrecionales. De todos modos, aún quedan por tomar medidas importantes: la total implementación de los sistemas de control y auditoría ex post de la Ley de Administración Financiera, mejoras en el control de la masa salarial y el control fiscal sobre el sistema de salud.

11.   El sostenimiento de la recuperación del sector privado requiere una eficiente provisión de bienes y servicios públicos, junto con un sólido marco regulatorio y macroeconómico. A nivel nacional, la compresión en las erogaciones durante los años ochenta redujo aún más los ya bajos niveles de productividad del gasto público. Si bien las recientes reducciones de empleo y privatizaciones han aliviado dicha compresión, sólo una mejor administración y asignación de recursos entre programas permitirán obtener potenciales ganancias de productividad.

12.   A nivel provincial, el gasto es aproximadamente el doble de las erogaciones netas de intereses de la administración nacional. Los gastos corrientes son excesivos y la inversión es baja [1]. La mayoría de las provincias, acostumbradas durante largo tiempo a financiarse con el impuesto inflacionario, están comenzando el ajuste que el Gobierno Federal empezó tres años atrás. Si bien se ha solicitado a las provincias que se encarguen de la provisión de una mayor cantidad de servicios públicos, éstas han recibido ganancias inesperadas a través de los ingresos coparticipados, lo cual puede reducir el incentivo a ajustarse. Por esta razón, el Gobierno ha obtenido el año pasado un pago proporcional de los gastos por administración impositiva, una

---

[1] Las finanzas públicas provinciales han sido tratadas resumidamente en este informe a partir de una revisión detallada, descripta en un informe por separado. Ver Banco Mundial Argentina: Hacia un Nuevo Federalismo 1992.

mayor proporción de los impuestos coparticipados para la seguridad social, ha transferido la educación secundaria y el sistema de salud a las provincias, y ha requerido el pago de redescuentos. El ajuste en las provincias--a través de reformas en los sistemas tributarios, de administración, y políticas de empleo--es el único camino para que éstas puedan proveer servicios educativos, de salud y de otra índole con mayor eficiencia. Más aún, desde un punto de vista macroeconómico, una detención en el ritmo de crecimiento y en la recaudación podrían generar considerables demandas para incrementar transferencias, salvo que las administraciones provinciales avancen en la implementación de sus propias reformas. La sección siguiente analiza estos temas resumiendo las recomendaciones específicas de este informe.

B. Opciones de Política para Consolidar la Estabilidad Fiscal

13.	Varias nuevas políticas y reformas, resumidas en los párrafos siguientes, podrían incrementar estimativamente el superávit fiscal en 1,2-1,4 porciento del PBI, proveyendo el colchón necesario para compensar las contingencias que pudieran ocurrir durante el programa fiscal de mediano plazo. Más aún, las reformas permitirían obtener mejoras considerables en la calidad de la movilización de ingresos públicos y en la productividad de los gastos. Este informe sugiere iniciativas específicas de política en temas tales como la administración y política tributaria, erogaciones corrientes e inversión pública, el gasto del sistema de seguridad social, las empresas públicas y las provincias.

Política Tributaria

14.	El marco de la política tributaria en los últimos dos años ha producido notables mejoras en la recaudación y al mismo tiempo se ha transformado en un sistema más eficiente. El Gobierno ha incrementado marcadamente su dependencia en el IVA y ha reducido la participación de impuestos ineficientes, especialmente los de exportación. El sistema se basa actualmente en cuatro impuestos modernos: el IVA general y uniforme, el impuesto a las ganancias/activos, impuestos a la importación e impuestos al consumo de algunos bienes finales (especialmente combustibles, cigarrillos y bebidas alcohólicas). La abolición de impuestos ineficientes será posible en la medida que los ingresos provenientes de impuestos eficientes sean compatibles con las actuales erogaciones públicas. Los asuntos más relevantes son la neutralidad con respecto al uso del capital y el trabajo, y la progresividad del sistema.

15.	El Gobierno se dispone a atender estos asuntos en el contexto de la reforma de la seguridad social y de las obras sociales. Una propuesta consistiría en reducir las cargas laborales permitiendo la deducción de una parte de las contribuciones patronales sobre los pagos de impuesto al valor agregado, e incrementar el financiamiento de la seguridad social a través del IVA y el impuesto a las ganancias. Esto generaría un incentivo importante para que los empleadores declaren sus contribuciones a la seguridad social, lo cual contribuiría en la reducción de la evasión. La carga del impuesto a las ganacias que recae sobre la clase media y media-baja sería reducida mediante el aumento del ingreso mensual mínimo imponible. Esta propuesta sería un paso saludable hacia la reducción del sesgo contra el empleo, pero es sólo una solución parcial. Aunque el aumento en el ingreso mínimo imponible mejoraría, en principio, la progresividad al reducir las cargas correspondientes a los trabajadores de bajos ingresos, al mismo tiempo estrecharía efectivamente la base del impuesto a las ganancias, al excluir a varios contribuyentes de ingresos medios y altos. Mientras que el ingreso promedio anual por familia se estima en alrededor de US$ 19.000, el ingreso mínimo imponible es superior a los US$ 20.000. Además, la caída en la recaudación de los impuestos laborales puede requerir que el Gobierno aumente la tasa del IVA.

16.   Un modo más directo de atender tanto el sesgo en los factores como la progresividad consiste en explorar caminos que reduzcan los impuestos laborales e incrementen las cargas sobre los ingresos de capital. Asumiendo que el sistema de seguridad social sea financiable a través de la eliminación de la evasión a una tasa contributiva del 26 %, el Gobierno debería considerar vincular la reforma del sistema de salud con una reducción en las asignaciones familiares y las cuotas del seguro de salud. Las contribuciones a los fondos de familia y salud representan aproximadamente el 24 porciento de los salarios brutos, una proporción mucho más alta que los impuestos laborales no previsionales de todos los países de la OECD. La reforma del sistema de salud--discutida ampliamente en el Capítulo 5--junto con una utilización más eficiente de las asignaciones familiares podrían permitir una reducción de los impuestos sobre la nómina salarial de un 50 porciento.

17.   Al mismo tiempo, el Gobierno podría incrementar las cargas sobre el capital directamente mediante modificaciones en los impuestos sobre los ingresos de las corporaciones e ingresos personales. Con respecto al impuesto a los ingresos de las corporaciones, se debería conservar la deducción de pagos de intereses, si es que tributan los ingresos por intereses a nivel personal. Al mismo tiempo, el Gobierno debería revisar los gastos de inversión, asegurándose que las deducciones por depreciaciones sean consistentes con tasas económicas de depreciación.

18.   En lo que concierne al impuesto personal a las ganancias, el Gobierno debería reintroducir las cargas sobre los ingresos de capital, virtualmente exentos en la actualidad. Primero, el Gobierno debería prohibir la deducción de intereses; esto permitiría cobrar impuestos sobre las ganancias de intereses. Segundo, el Gobierno debería institucionalizar gravámenes sobre al menos la porción real de las ganancias de capital. Finalmente, el Gobierno no debería aumentar el ya generoso límite mínimo de ingreso imponible; en vez, a medida que mejore la administración impositiva, debería bajarlo. Además, el Gobierno debería eliminar otras reducciones existentes y rever la posibilidad de fijar cargas sobre beneficios adicionales. El efecto de dichas medidas contribuiría en la expansión de la base del impuesto a las ganancias, en vez de contraerla.

19.   La reducción de los impuestos sobre la nómina salarial a través de la reducción de las contribuciones a los fondos de salud, que son totalmente deducibles de la base del impuesto a los ingresos personales, provocaría automáticamente un incremento de dicha base. Menores contribuciones podrían llevar a un incremento en los salarios después de impuestos, dado que las reducciones sobre los costos laborales tienden a expandir la demanda de trabajo que a su vez impacta positivamente sobre los salarios reales (pudiendo incluso reducir el desempleo). Dicho impacto sobre los salarios reales sería reforzado si se produce una caída en el nivel de precios.

El precio del capital se vería influenciado positivamente, dado que los costos laborales afectan directamente al costo de producción de los bienes de inversión. Finalmente, las simultáneas reducciones que se efectúen sobre los impuestos laborales, junto con otras reformas en la prestación de servicios, mejorarían también la equidad del sistema impositivo.

20.   El entendimiento de agosto de 1992 con las provincias ayuda a remediar los desequilibrios entre el sistema de seguridad social y otras demandas sobre recursos del Tesoro fijados en el régimen de coparticipación. Dicho paquete asigna el 15 porciento de los ingresos provenientes del IVA al sistema de seguridad social, pero no genera incentivos máximos para que los gobiernos provinciales se ajusten. La proyección de ingresos tributarios asignados a las provincias indica un aumento de los mismos de alrededor de US$ 3.800 millones entre 1992 y 1993. El entendimiento dejó en pie otras transferencias (no coparticipadas) cercanas a US$ 1.500 millones, incluyendo el FONAVI, que son menos efectivas en términos de los objetivos fijados. Aquellas transferencias no coparticipadas deberían ser consideradas como un instrumento de ajuste estructural y en ese sentido, deberían estar ligadas a mejoras en el desempeño fiscal de las provincias.

Administración Impositiva

21.   Las reformas en la administración impositiva han sido una de las principales causas de las mejoras en la recaudación a la fecha, y han permitido al Gobierno obtener el control sobre los flujos de ingresos. Aún así, dado el alto potencial de ingresos, programas para mejorar el control de la promoción industrial, la administración interna, la corte impositiva y la administración de aduanas merecen especial atención.

22.   Entre éstos, quizás el más alto rendimiento fiscal podría provenir de los esfuerzos que el Gobierno realice en materia de control de la promoción industrial. El programa, implementado en noviembre de 1992, implica cambiar los beneficios de auditoría propia por un crédito fiscal auditado deducible de futuros impuestos, la cancelación de los beneficios aún no activados, y una cuidadosa auditoría de los beneficiarios existentes. La DGI debería asignar los recursos necesarios para auditar a aquellas empresas que no pagaron impuestos durante la suspensión de los beneficios en el año siguiente a la Ley de Emergencia; el esfuerzo de control sobre las firmas provinciales ha logrado hasta ahora solamente el 50 porciento de la tasa de auditoría fijada como meta, aunque podría obtener recursos de más de US$ 300 millones por esta vía. Mirando hacia el futuro, el Gobierno debería hacer permanente la suspensión de nuevos beneficios de promoción industrial, que expiraría en septiembre de 1993.

23.   El programa completo de reforma de la promoción industrial producirá grandes ahorros fiscales. Estimaciones del personal de la DGI sugieren que el programa de sustitución de créditos fiscales reducirá el costo fiscal de la promoción industrial de US$ 2.700 millones a US$ 1.400 millones en 1993.

Erogaciones Corrientes: la Masa Salarial

24.   El Gobierno ha realizado una reforma administrativa sin precedentes para reorganizar y reducir el tamaño del Gobierno Federal. Los principales ministerios y organismos descentralizados seleccionados fueron reorganizados. El empleo en la administración nacional habrá caído de aproximadamente 670.000 en 1990 a menos de 285.000 agentes hacia fines de 1992; de esta reducción, 105.000 empleados han dejado el Gobierno y el resto ha sido transferido a las provincias. La reducción de empleo en las empresas públicas no ha sido menos dramática: el nivel de empleo ha pasado de 295.000 a casi 50.000. De esta reducción de 245.000 empleados, alrededor de la tercera parte se debe a despidos, y el resto a privatizaciones.

25.   Para completar el programa de reducciones, el Gobierno debería: (i) completar el proceso de reestructuración en aquellas organizaciones gubernamentales que aún no han sido reestructuradas, incluyendo el CONICET, la CNEA, el personal civil de las Fuerzas Armadas, las universidades nacionales, la Dirección Nacional del Azúcar, y las obras sociales, que en total reduciría el nivel de empleo en 27.000 empleados; (ii) continuar trabajando con la oficina de presupuesto para desagregar las reducciones por jurisdicción para asegurar una contabilización y presupuestación apropiadas en 1993; (iii) realizar un estudio especial sobre reducciones, incluyendo la preparación de nombres y números de identificación, con el propósito de asegurar que aquéllos que se retiren y reciban indemnizaciones no reingresen al servicio público.

26.   Para completar la reforma del sistema de pago de salarios y el escalafón de pagos, el Gobierno debe (i) establecer su propio registro computarizado del personal y centralizar la función de pago directamente o a través de las cuentas ministeriales de acuerdo con la nueva ley de Finanzas Públicas, trasladando posiblemente a los miembros de la Oficina de Personal al Ministerio de Economía--donde se encontraba con anterioridad al gobierno militar de 1976; (ii) implementar un sistema computarizado de pagos por medio de cheques a través del sistema bancario para controlar la masa salarial, medida que ahorraría alrededor de US$ 200 millones en costos administrativos y ahorros adicionales a través de reducciones en los salarios pagados a trabajadores inexistentes. Si el nuevo sistema es diseñado apropiadamente, asegurará una mejor contabilización y un firme control sobre la masa salarial. Estas acciones podrían contribuir en la reducción de recursos dedicados solamente a "administración"--llegando a un ahorro cercano a los US$ 400 millones actualmente gastado a través de los diversos ministerios.

Salud y Bienestar Social

27.   El Gobierno está comenzando a formular una estrategia efectiva para los sectores sociales. El Gobierno Federal es un actor relativamente pequeño comparado con las provincias y los fondos de salud cuasi-públicos. Los gastos Federales en salud, vivienda y bienestar absorben US$ 800 millones de los US$ 8.000 millones de gastos (excluidos intereses y transferencias)--10 porciento de las actuales erogaciones de la administración nacional. Una suma adicional de US$ 1.500 millones provenientes del presupuesto federal se transfiere a las provincias--US$ 1.000 millones son transferidos a las provincias a través del programa de vivienda FONAVI, y US$ 200 millones se transfieren a los fondos de salud controlados por las obras sociales.

28.   **Salud.** La mayor parte del gasto en salud--cuyos recursos provienen de impuestos al trabajo y asignaciones presupuestarias--se realiza a través de los fondos de salud, que gastan estimativamente US$ 5.600 millones (estimados en base a datos de 1986, los últimos disponibles) mientras que los gastos del gobierno federal son de US$ 745 millones, y quizas de US$ 2.000-3.500 millones en los gobiernos provinciales. Las mejoras en la eficiencia del gasto en este sector deberán centrarse entonces en mejoras en la contabilidad y eficiencia de los fondos de salud y de las provincias. Una reforma importante de estos fondos de cobertura social podría ser una fuente de ahorro en 1993 y de mejoras de envergadura en la productividad de los gastos en salud.

29.   El Gobierno ha preparado una importante reforma de los fondos de salud, convirtiendo sus principios fundamentales en ley a través del decreto Presidencial de enero de 1993. El nuevo programa debería: (i) permitir a los contribuyentes elegir sus propios proveedores; (ii) permitir la libre entrada después de una fase de transición; (iii) requerir a los proveedores que ofrezcan un paquete mínimo de salud a un precio especificado; y (iv) cobertura universal con subsidios a individuos indigentes (distintos de los subsidios institucionales corrientes). Esto sería combinado con un estricto monitoreo tanto del sistema de cobertura como del paquete médico, incluyendo limitaciones en los gastos administrativos. El nuevo sistema financiaría en efecto una cobertura universal reduciendo los altísimos costos de administración existentes y malgastos del sistema vigente.

30.   Un sistema de cobertura más sólido, contemplado en el recientemente preparado proyecto de ley de obras sociales, también aliviaría a la burocracia federal de grandes gastos realizados a través del presupuesto para el financiamiento de déficits de los fondos de salud--a través del ANSSAL (US$ 217 millones en 1992). Los gastos restantes podrían dedicarse a objetivos nacionales básicos: vacunación, medicina preventiva, prevención en el abuso de drogas, regulación sanitaria, y programas de salud para madres y niños. Puede ser que algunos programas, como el Programa de Salud Estudiantil del Ministerio de Educación (US$ 48 millones) y el Plan Médico del Congreso (US$ 15 millones) sean menos necesarios en el contexto de un programa nacional de salud.

31.   **Otras Areas de Bienestar.** El Ministerio de Salud y Acción Social cuenta con otros programas además del de vivienda (analizado en el capítulo de inversión) que en conjunto suman US$ 140 millones. Estos programas deberían ser revisados con el propósito de efectuar reducciones, teniendo en cuenta la decisión del Gobierno de descentralizar la responsabilidad sobre los gastos a las provincias. Además, otras jurisdicciones, especialmente el Ministerio de Trabajo, gastan US$ 240 millones en varios programas que merecen ser revisados en términos de efectividad.

Educación

32.   El sistema educativo argentino, alguna vez entre los mejores de América Latina, se ha transformado en una sombra de lo que fuera en épocas anteriores. El otorgamiento de excesivos privilegios a los educadores junto con la libre admisión de alumnos que comenzaron

en la década del 70, interactuaron con ciclos de austeridad en la década del 80, dando como resultado instituciones públicas fiscalmente erosionadas. Bajo presión presupuestaria, las escuelas primarias fueron transferidas a las provincias en los primeros años de la década del 70, donde se siguieron repitiendo este tipo de vaivenes. Los colegios secundarios y vocacionales fueron transferidos en 1992 por convenio, con financiamiento implícito a partir del incremento de los ingresos coparticipados. Tanto la calidad y condiciones educativas, así como los salarios docentes ahora varían ampliamente entre las distintas provincias.

33.   Después de haber transferido la educación secundaria a las provincias, el Gobierno gasta actualmente US$ 1.300 millones en educación a nivel federal, de lo cual aproximadamente la mitad--US$ 720 millones--es transferida a las universidades federales. Las mayores ganancias potenciales en eficiencia se encuentran entonces a nivel universitario. Estas erogaciones no han sido suficientes para frenar el deterioro en la calidad de la enseñanza universitaria pública en Argentina. Dado que las universidades privadas pueden satisfacer gran parte de la demanda y dado que la los bajos aranceles educativos en la enseñanza pública tienden a ser un subsidio regresivo--la mayoría de los graduados provienen de familias de ingresos por encima del promedio, luego ganan salarios mejores que el promedio--el Gobierno debería considerar un programa en fases de traspaso del sistema universitario al sector privado. Esto le permitiría concentrar sus recursos en subsidios específicos como becas universitarias por bajos ingresos y programas de enriquecimiento para la educación primaria y secundaria administrada a nivel provincial.

34.   Interinamente, el Gobierno debería considerar la ejecución de una política que combine el cobro de aranceles educativos y subsidios selectivos (como préstamos y becas por bajos ingresos o por mérito estudiantil) para mejorar el financiamiento. La adopción de un programa selectivo basado en las necesidades del estudiantado aseguraría que aquellos con bajos ingresos tengan acceso a una educación universitaria. Si se cobrara a los 700.000 alumnos del sistema una modesta suma de US$ 100 por período lectivo más US$ 20 por mes (las instituciones privadas cobran US$ 250-600 de matrícula más US$ 300-800 por mes), el Gobierno movilizaría un fondo adicional de alrededor de US$ 300 millones.

35.   Al mismo tiempo, el traspaso de la educación secundaria a las provincias debería facilitar el achicamiento o aún el cierre del Ministerio de Educación. Programas como el de Política Educativa y Presupuestaria (US$ 45 millones), el de Educación y Entrenamiento Docente (US$ 83 millones), el Presupuesto Cultural (US$ 16 millones), el Consejo de Educación Técnica (US$ 17 millones), y el de Investigación Científica (US$ 42 millones), deberían ser revisados en términos de su efectividad.

36.   En el futuro será necesario incrementar el gasto educativo para pagar la equiparación salarial de los docentes de los colegios secundarios, aumentar el pago total asociado a otras medidas de productividad, mejorar los materiales educativos que se encuentren calamitosamente desactualizados, y rehabilitar la planta y equipo en estado deteriorado. Estas demandas recaerán sobre las provincias. Este costo podría ser disminuido parcialmente con la reducción del número de docentes, de manera consistente con tamaños de clase razonables. En la actualidad las

relaciones estudiantes-maestro son bastante bajas (alrededor de 11) y altamente variables entre provincias (6-15). Además, las licencias con goce de sueldo son excesivas y poco controladas. Una reforma estructural podría compensar sustancialmente los costos de mayores salarios.

Defensa

37.   Los gastos militares son los segundos en volumen dentro del presupuesto federal primario, y la mayor parte de los gastos discrecionales del Tesoro (32 porciento). Los gastos militares excluyendo pensiones han caído de cifras superiores al 6% del PBI en 1980-81 a menos del 2% en la actualidad, siendo ésta una de las menores proporciones del PBI en el hemisferio. El Gobierno ha reconocido que el entorno de la seguridad en la Argentina ha mejorado notablemente desde la restauración de la democracia en 1983. La resolución de conflictos de larga data con Chile, Brasil y Gran Bretaña, junto con la reducción de las amenazas de apoyo externo a la subversión doméstica como consecuencia de la desintegración de la Unión Soviética, han dado la oportunidad al Gobierno de reconsiderar el nivel de los gastos militares, y al mismo tiempo reorientar el gasto militar para cumplir más efectivamente con su función.

38.   El Gobierno ha identificado varios desequilibrios que actualmente obstaculizan la eficiencia militar para cumplir con este objetivo. Primero, los costos de personal absorben más del 70 porciento del presupuesto de defensa, con lo cual la capacidad operativa militar ha sido severamente restringida. Segundo, dado que el tamaño de la fuerza se ha reducido desde mediados de la década del 80, la pirámide tradicional de rangos para el Ejército, la Marina y la Aviación se ha distorsionado, provocando sustanciales subas en la relación oficiales/personal alistado. Tercero, el sistema militar de pensiones necesita urgentemente una racionalización para mantener su solvencia, para alinearlo con el sistema civil de pensiones y para asegurar la movilidad entre ambos sistemas. Cuarto, las instalaciones operadas por las fuerzas armadas necesitan ser consolidadas y reubicadas en áreas en las que puedan defender el terreno argentino de una manera más efectiva. Por otra parte, los salarios no parecen ser un problema--los pagos a militares son significativamente mayores que los pagos a civiles, y son similares a los de otros países cuando se los compara por salarios medios para grados similares y antigüedad de servicio.

39.   La estrategia de reforma que el Gobierno ha comenzado a implementar incluye la racionalización de todo el sector militar. Esto incluye la privatización de las industrias de defensa, la reducción de personal y la consolidación de las instalaciones. En estos momentos treinta empresas del área de defensa se encuentran en proceso de privatización. Esta tarea eliminará sus sustanciales pérdidas y permitirá al Gobierno cancelar su deuda asociada, obteniendo quizás algún beneficio. Los planes actuales para reducir el personal civil del Ministerio de Defensa en un 40 porciento permitirán volver a la relación personal civil/personal militar existente con anterioridad a 1985, y generar ahorros anuales estimados en US$ 80 millones.

40.   El Gobierno también está considerando la reducción del personal militar. Un decremento en el nivel del personal militar permitiría al Ministerio de Defensa reducir los costos

de personal y contribuiría a la restauración de una estructura de personal de forma más piramidal. Adicionalmente, utilizando algunos de los fondos para mejorar las operaciones y el mantenimiento y, posiblemente, efectuando algunas compras estratégicas de capital, se podría obtener el mismo nivel de seguridad a un costo anual menor. Por ejemplo, un programa que restaurara la pirámide de personal a los niveles existentes en 1984 mediante una reducción de personal del 25 porciento, ahorraría estimativamente unos US$ 155 millones por año. Un principio importante es que los ingresos provenientes de la venta de activos deberían ser utilizados para respaldar el proceso de reforma--para el programa de reestructuración de la institución militar, el pago de indemnizaciones y la asistencia para el ajuste, la reforma del sistema de pensiones militares, o inversiones en la reubicación y mayor movilidad de las fuerzas de acuerdo con la nueva estrategia del Gobierno--en vez de ser consumidos para hacer frente a los gastos corrientes. De otro modo, cuando el flujo de ingresos por venta de activos cese, el Gobierno tendrá los mismos niveles de gasto y no contará con medios para financiarlos. Dicho de otra manera, cuanto proviene de la venta de activos debería utilizarse en la reducción de obligaciones o en inversiones consistentes con la nueva estrategia de defensa.

Presidencia

41.   La presidencia se ha transformado en una de las entidades de mayor gasto en el Gobierno Federal, siendo responsable por el 14 porciento del gasto de la administración nacional. La Constitución Argentina establece la existencia de no mas de 8 Ministerios en la Administración Nacional, límite que fuera recientemente reimplantado con la reforma administrativa de 1991-92. De todos modos, los gobiernos han utilizado la jurisdicción presidencial como la esfera de gobierno donde podían establecerse secretarías con rango ministerial. Las cuatro unidades más grandes--la Secretaría de Comunicaciones, a cargo de la compañía pública de radiodifusión, el Ente Nacional de Turismo, el CONICET (instituto de investigación), y la Comisión Nacional de Energía Atómica (CNEA) representan el 80 porciento del personal y de los gastos en la Presidencia.

42.   Un examen cuidadoso de estas agencias sugiere que existen niveles innecesariamente altos de empleo en la administración central y las agencias descentralizadas a la luz del nuevo rol del estado. La Presidencia prácticamene no ha sido afectada por la reforma administrativa, y el nivel total de empleo es virtualmente el mismo que el existente con anterioridad a la reforma. Dado que esta es una jurisdicción que realmente necesita ser reformada, el Gobierno debería aplicar los mismos principios de achicamiento que fueron empleados en el resto del sector público sobre la Presidencia. Específicamente, para las unidades ejecutivas más grandes, el Gobierno podría considerar: (i) la eliminación de la Secretaría de Comunicaciones, y el establecimiento de una Dirección de Comunicaciones dependiente de la nueva Subsecretaría General de la Presidencia; eventualmente, el Servicio Nacional de Radiotelecomunicaciones podría ser privatizado, quitando 950 puestos de las cuentas del sector público; (ii) la racionalización del Ente Nacional de Turismo y el establecimiento de una nueva Dirección Nacional también bajo jurisdicción del Ministerio de Economía, eliminando así 500 puestos; (iii) la privatización del CONICET y la Fundación Miguel Lillo, reduciendo 5.589 puestos del

presupuesto del sector público, dado que las actividades de investigación y desarrollo podrían llevarse a cabo en universidades públicas y privadas.

43. Finalmente, la compañía de energía nuclear (CNEA) debería ser reestructurada, transformándola en unidades comerciales y de investigación que serían luego transferidas fuera del ámbito de la Presidencia. Dos posibles unidades comerciales (productoras de energía y agua pesada, respectivamente) podrían pasar a manos de la Secretaría de Energía Eléctrica del Ministerio de Economía hasta que se proceda a su privatización. Dicha privatización permitiría al sector público obtener un ahorro eventual de US$ 850 millones. La racionalización de la jurisdicción presidencial podría resultar en ahorros netos de US$ 570 millones.

Empresas Públicas

44. Las empresas públicas absorbieron un cuarto del total del gasto público de Argentina en 1990, pero el programa de privatizaciones ha reducido esta cifra al 17 porciento. Dicho programa encarado por el Gobierno ha producido enormes beneficios: ingresos de capital para apoyar la transición hacia una posición sostenible de las finanzas públicas, alivio en la demanda de inversión en el sector, y el fin de las distorsiones de precios y shocks macroeconómicos asociados con el establecimiento de precios políticos, entre otros. Suponiendo que el programa de privatizaciones fuera completado según lo programado, los recursos para el Gobierno serían del orden de los US$ 4.000-5.000 millones 1992, algo mayores que las proyecciones oficiales, que no tienen en cuenta la privatización de Encotel, AGP, OSN y Gas del Estado. Si el programa se ajusta al cronograma previsto, permitirá efectuar reducciones en las transferencias del presupuesto federal.

45. Los ingresos de capital producto de la venta de activos deben ser utilizados dentro del actual programa para cancelar obligaciones. Es esencial que el Gobierno mantenga esta política, evitando el uso de los fondos provenientes de la venta de activos para el financiamiento de erogaciones corrientes. Dada la consolidación de la deuda (analizada posteriormente), el endeudamiento del Gobierno se incrementará en 1993 a pesar del acuerdo de reducción de deuda con los bancos comerciales. Por lo tanto, todo ingreso extraordinario proveniente de la venta de activos debería ser utilizado en la reducción de deuda.

46. Las transferencias presupuestarias suman US$ 2.000 millones por año, y deberían caer progresivamente de acuerdo con el cronograma de privatizaciones y reestructuración de empresas. En 1993, éstas deberían descender a menos de US$ 800 millones--virtualmente destinadas en su totalidad a los segmentos prevalecientes de los ferrocarriles y a Yacyretá--y a menos de US$ 400 millones en 1994, casi en su totalidad para Yaciretá. Se deberían realizar especiales esfuerzos para reducir las transferencias a los ferrocarriles dado que son económicamente ineficientes y costosos.

47. Un prerrequisito para que las privatizaciones arriben a buen puerto es la instrumentación de un marco regulatorio, especialmente para la fijación de precios en aquellos sectores que no estén sujetos a la competencia de precios. En particular, se deben fijar precios

de producción de acuerdo con los costos internacionales de producción y no sólo según la evolución de los beneficios de las ex-empresas públicas. Finalmente, la nueva Ley de Compre Nacional, enviada al Congreso en enero de 1993, establecería las bases de un régimen no discriminatorio de largo plazo para todo el sector público.

Finanzas Provinciales

48.   Las provincias participan en un tercio del total del gasto público en Argentina. Aunque estimaciones preliminares sugieren que en conjunto las provincias estarán en una situación balanceada en 1991, en el pasado han sido una de las fuentes principales de déficit en las cuentas consolidadas del sector público. El Gobierno ha dedicado grandes esfuerzos en mejorar la estructura fiscal federal, y en reducir los incentivos a gastar sin tener en cuenta el volumen de ingresos. Existen varios problemas que pueden frenar al nuevo federalismo en la implementación de todo su potencial. Primero, los desajustes entre los gastos corrientes y de capital en las finanzas provinciales son evidentes; los gatos corrientes provinciales en términos reales subieron un 41 porciento entre 1982 y 1990, mientras que los gastos de capital cayeron en un 25 porciento. Segundo, el importante incremento en los impuestos coparticipables y las grandes transferencias federales a las provincias han reducido la urgencia de reformas fiscales, puesto que los nuevos ingresos absuelven a las provincias del costo político de recolectar impuestos; por ejemplo, en 1992, las provincias podrán gastar US$ 500 millones más que en 1991, muy por encima del costo que implica la transferencia de los colegios secundarios y los servicios de salud. Un tercer problema es la ineficiencia de los sistemas impositivos provinciales y municipales, caracterizados por distorsiones impositivas, una pobre administración impositiva, y un uso pobre de los ingresos potenciales de las bases imponibles existentes. Finalmente, los gobiernos provinciales financiaron más del 60 porciento de sus déficits en 1990 con créditos de los bancos provinciales, y las reformas iniciadas no tienen el alcance necesario como para asegurar que esto no sucederá otra vez durante próximas caídas en el nivel de actividad.

49.   **Estructura Federal.** Para mantener el incentivo a realizar ajustes en el contexto de la actual distribución primaria según la Ley de Coparticipación, una opción posible es mejorar la distribución de los incrementos marginales que resulten de una mejor administración impositiva federal o de nuevas medidas recaudatorias a nivel federal. Esto requeriría la búsqueda de un acuerdo para reducir las transferencias marginales de futuras mejoras y/o la transferencia de gastos adicionales a las provincias con ganancias extraordinarias provenientes de los futuros aumentos marginales de los ingresos federales. Esta es la estrategia que el Gobierno ha seguido a la fecha. Otra opción es redistribuir los US$ 2.200 millones de transferencias no coparticipadas canalizados a través del presupuesto. Las mayores transferencias se realizan a través del programa de vivienda FONAVI (US$ 900 millones), las ayudas especiales a Buenos Aires y Tierra del Fuego (dos programas que suman US$ 300 millones), el Fondo del Tabaco (US$ 100 millones), y el Fondo Nacional de Autopistas (US$ 100 millones). Con el acuerdo de las provincias, parte o la totalidad de estos recursos puede consolidarse en un programa de subvenciones, desembolsadas proporcionalmente al desempeño de las provincias en la obtención de ahorros corrientes y/o reembolsos equivalentes al costo de las reformas acordadas, como las

indemnizaciones a trabajadores redundantes o reformas en los programas de seguridad social. Este fondo podría ser suplementado con (i) mejoras incrementales en los recursos coparticipados, y (ii) créditos de las instituciones financieras internacionales. Un fondo de US$ 2.000-3.000 millones podría provocar fuertes incentivos para ajustar gastos e ingresos corrientes y convertirse en una continua fuente de inversión muy necesitada a nivel provincial. El fondo sería administrado por una unidad de ejecución de proyectos establecida en la oficina de presupuesto; dicha unidad calcularía el valor actual neto, y desembolsaría fondos para aquellos proyectos que cuenten con valores actuales netos positivos.

50.   **Ingresos.** El Gobierno debería trabajar también con las provincias para (i) transferir los sistemas de administración impositiva (actualmente operativos en la DGI) a las provincias, incluyendo el control computarizado de los mayores contribuyentes, controles cruzados con las oficinas y cuentas regionales de la DGI, y mejoras en la recaudación de impuestos a las ventas y a la tierra; y (ii) renovar la estructura impositiva para eliminar impuestos ineficientes.

51.   **Gastos.** Las provincias serán los principales agentes proveedores de servicios públicos en el futuro, y su eficiencia en este campo tendrá profundos efectos en la tasa de crecimiento de largo plazo de Argentina. Es indispensable la instrumentación de una amplia reforma administrativa, similar a la reforma encarada a nivel nacional, para reducir el nivel de empleo e incrementar los salarios medios, y revisar la asignación de recursos humanos y fiscales dedicados a la prestación de servicios.

Seguridad Social

52.   Se proyecta que el gasto en Seguridad Social, estimado alrededor del 12-14 porciento del gasto del sector público no financiero durante los años 80, subirá al 21 porciento en 1992. Esto reflejada los aumentos en las jubilaciones, además del pago de pensiones adeudadas para no acumular retrasos. El acuerdo de agosto de 1992 con las provincias, terminó con la acumulación de atrasos, pues se incrementaron los pagos jubilatorios con el uso de recursos coparticipados. El nuevo sistema crearía un sistema de pensión integrada para los trabajadores, un sistema de transición para jubilados y trabajadores por jubilarse, y un sistema capitalizado manejado por el sector privado. El cambio a un sistema capitalizado puede restaurar la credibilidad del sistema de seguridad social si es adecuadamente administrado y financiado.

53.   El punto más importante es que el Gobierno debe crear suficiente "espacio" fiscal como para financiar la transición a lo largo de la década hacia un sistema totalmente capitalizado. Esto significa realizar planes para hacer frente a un déficit en la seguridad social (antes de ingresos generales) de alrededor de US$ 5.000-7.000 millones en 1993-97. En 1993, los ingresos generales sobraron para cubrir el déficit del sistema, porque la proporción de las contribuciones laborales que iría al sector capitalizado recién se haría efectiva a partir de 1994, la fecha de implementación. De todos modos, a partir de esta fecha se necesitarán entre US$ 5.000 y US$ 7.000 millones anuales, si no se incrementa el déficit. Esto sugiere que la asignación a la seguridad social de por lo menos el 15 porciento de los ingresos coparticipados debe continuar.

54.   Aún más, el déficit anual del sistema puede llegar a ser entre US$ 1.000 y US$ 2.000 millones superior a las proyecciones presentadas por el Gobierno, dependiendo de varios cambios posiblemente adversos durante el tratamiento legislativo del proyecto de ley y la fase de transición en la implementación: incrementos no financiados en las pensiones, escasos progresos en el control de la evasión (con menores caídas en la relación de dependencia) y un trato extremadamente generoso con los trabajadores con insuficientes años de contribución durante la transición, que de otro modo deberían retrasar su jubilación hasta el cumplimiento de 70 años. Dedo que el financiamiento depende tanto de los ingresos generales, cambios en el paquete de reforma que incrementen los beneficios podrían fácilmente desestabilizar las finanzas públicas.

55.   **Políticas para Reforzar la Reforma.** Para atender los mencionados riesgos, el Gobierno debería: (i) proteger al nuevo sistema contra las demandas para que se suban los beneficios de pensionados del sistema anterior a la reforma, por encima de los niveles correspondientes a la antigua legislación; (ii) resistir las demandas de aumentos de las pensiones compensatorias por encima de los niveles acordados en las modificaciones efectuadas en diciembre sobre el proyecto de ley; (iii) disminuir el nivel de las pensiones de alrededor del 70 porciento del salario medio a 55-60 porciento--niveles nomales en Europa occidental; (iv) resistir la presión para debilitar las reglas durante la transición, referidas a mayores niveles del mínimo de años de contribución y la edad de jubilación; al contrario, permitir que se realicen deducciones actuariales razonables sobre las pensiones de aquellos trabajadores que no cumplan con las reglas de retiro a la edad de 65 años; (v) reforzar el programa de auditoría sobre las pensiones para discapacitados; (vi) reforzar aún más la recaudación del sistema de seguridad social a través de controles por cruzamiento sitemáticos con la DGI; (vii) extender la afiliación obligatoria a toda la población económicamente activa, incluyendo a los empleados municipales y provinciales; como mínimo, requerir a los sistemas provinciales y municipales que adopten los mismos criterios con respecto al mínimo de años de contribución y la edad de retiro.

56.   **Inversiones de los Fondos de Pensión.** El Gobierno debe diseñar reglas de inversión para los fondos de pensión que garanticen la seguridad de estos recursos, dado que los fondos de pensión (contrariamente al sistema de pensiones) acumularán un amplio superávit durante las dos primeras décadas de crecimiento. Estos fondos producirán recursos de inversión equivalentes a US$ 3.000 millones anuales en esta década. Se ha dado un paso importante en el actual proyecto de ley, al prohibir requerimientos mínimos de inversión en determinado tipo de instrumentos (especialmente papeles del Gobierno); haber requerido a los fondos que invirtieran en el financiamiento del déficit del resto del Gobierno hubiera reducido la confianza en el desempeño de los fondos.

57.   La confianza en el esquema de pensión privado también depende de un grupo coherente de normas, y de un poder de policía creíble ejercido por un cuerpo de supervisión profesional, libre de conflictos de interés e intervención política. De todos modos, el proyecto de ley carece de reglas sobre la composición de la superintendencia, y un reciente acuerdo entre el Gobierno y los sindicatos incluiría dentro de la superintendencia a representantes del estado, los sindicatos y los afiliados, en vez de contar con un gerenciamiento profesional y personal que

responda al Poder Ejecutivo o al Congreso. Este acuerdo puede disminuir la confianza sobre el control que recae sobre las AFJPs siguiendo el estricto cumplimiento de la ley, incluyendo la aplicación de sanciones máximas, como la revocación de licencias de las AFJPs y la transferencia de los fondos de pensión a otras AFJPs. Una superintendencia débil pone en riesgo que surja la necesidad de que el estado deba garantizar un beneficio mínimo de los fondos. Por lo tanto, el Gobierno debería establecer una superintendencia profesional para las AFJPs.

Inversión Pública

58.   Después de casi dos décadas declinantes, la inversión pública argentina se encuentra en un mínimo histórico. Aunque la inversión pública promediaba alrededor del 10 porciento del PBI en la década del 70, actualmente ésta es inferior al 5 porciento. El programa de privatizaciones ha reducido la demanda de inversión pública, dejando espacio para las inversiones privadas--en especial, telecomunicaciones, hidrocarburos y transporte. Bajo dirección privada, estos sectores pueden transformarse en sectores dinámicos, quizás líderes en Argentina. Aún así, estos hechos no mitigan la necesidad de nueva inversión en aquellos sectores que aún se encuentran bajo dominio público--incluyendo autopistas, energía (en el corto plazo), e infraestructura social.

59.   Aunque el Gobierno de Argentina ha realizado progresos en el planeamiento de la inversión pública reflejados en los planes de inversión pública para 1991 y 1992, el proceso de presupuestación de capital puede ser ampliamente mejorado, incrementando la eficiencia de la inversión pública. Un serio inconveniente en el proceso de inversión pública es la ausencia de un mecanismo consistente de evaluación de proyectos que guíe las decisiones de inversión de las autoridades. Sobre más de 20 proyectos de inversión de más de US$ 5 millones identificados, sólo fue posible encontrar evaluaciones económicas para unos pocos. El Gobierno está fortaleciendo ahora su grupo técnico para conducir las evaluaciones económicas con mayor capacidad, incluyendo el cálculo de los precios sociales relevantes necesarios para estas evaluaciones.

60.   Varios principios deberían guiar este proceso. Primero, todas las inversiones deberían contar con una evaluación económica. Segundo, no se debería encarar ningún proyecto cuyo valor actual neto (VAN) sea negativo a precios sociales. El hecho de contar con un valor actual neto positivo a precios sociales es una condición necesaria, pero no suficiente para encarar un proyecto de inversión. En Argentina, donde el sector público enfrenta restricciones financieras significativas, puede resultar imposible financiar todos aquellos proyectos con un valor actual neto positivo. Entonces, tercero, se necesitará un ordenamiento de proyectos. El criterio económico sería entonces el empleo de los recursos, comenzando por el proyecto mejor posicionado, continuando descendentemente hasta que los recursos se hallen plenamente asignados. Recientes avances en el planeamiento de inversiones establecen en la actualidad las bases para un programa de varios años que establezca a su vez las prioridades por año para el financiamiento presupuestario.

61.   **Energía.** Los presupuestos anuales de inversión en 1992 para Atucha II y Pichi Picún Leufú son de US$ 395 millones y US$ 146 millones, respectivamente. Ambos absorben arriba del 20 porciento del presupuesto total de inversión del gobierno nacional (incluyendo la administración central, cuentas especiales, organismos descentralizados y empresas públicas), unos US$ 2.600 millones en 1992. Ambos proyectos tienen VAN negativos a cualquier tasa de descuento superior al 12 porciento. En el caso de Pichi Picún Leufú, las contribuciones del Gobierno son pequeñas y dadas las condiciones favorables de financiamiento, la obra debería ser completada. La terminación de Atucha II debería ser pospuesta si no se puede obtener financiamiento; mientras los fondos correspondientes sean escasos, cualquier financiamiento para su terminación debería incluir mínimas contribuciones del Gobierno durante el período 1993-1994.

62.   **Vivienda.** El programa de vivienda FONAVI no parece ser económico. Aunque no hay disponible ninguna evaluación de costo-beneficio, existen buenas razones para suponer que su VAN sería negativo a tasas de descuento razonables. El programa absorbe arriba de US$ 900 millones de los recursos del presupuesto de 1992, y tiene algunos serios inconvenientes. Una opción atractiva y asequible puede ser discontinuar el programa durante los próximos dos o tres años. Estos fondos tienen un alto componente de ahorro público, básicamente porque el programa FONAVI no atrae financiamiento externo.

63.   Los ahorros posibles a partir de estas medidas podrían llegar a US$ 1.400 millones, y podrían ser empleados para inversiones en mantenimiento de rutas, la aceleración de los proyectos hidroeléctricos Yaciretá y Piedra del Aguila, así como en proyectos provinciales relevantes de salud y educación.

Banco Central

64.   Desde la conversión de deuda doméstica de corto plazo en bonos (BONEX) a 10 años en enero de 1990, el Gobierno ha actuado vigorosamente para cortar las fuentes de financiamiento del sector público no financiero y del sector público financiero a través del programa monetario. Las facilidades de financiamiento comercial fueron cerradas y la función fue transferida al nuevo banco comercial, Banco Internacional de Comercio Exterior (BICE). Segundo, el financiamiento del sistema de seguridad social a través de la cuenta de OPP ha sido cortado. Tercero, el servicio de la deuda pública con el Banco Central es cobrado al Tesoro. Cuarto, los redescuentos otorgados al banco industrial (BANADE) y al banco de vivienda (BHN) fueron gradualmente eliminados entre 1987 y 1990, y el flujo neto de redescuentos hacia los otros bancos públicos ha sido negativo, ya que estos bancos están repagando la inyección de liquidez de emergencia que recibieron durante la corrida de enero de 1991 sobre el austral.

65.   Estos eventos ahora crean el escenario necesario para mejorar la estructura legal del Banco Central y fortalecer la institución. La implementación de la Carta Orgánica del Banco Central en septiembre de 1992 fue un hito en la crecación de una autoridad monetaria moderna; la más alta prioridad para Argentina es implementar esta nueva Carta Orgánica. Dicha Carta otorga a la autoridad monetaria una gran independencia, prohíbe los redescuentos--excepto para

emergencias y por períodos limitados, contra una garantía del capital prestatario--y los préstamos al sector público no financiero. Constituye un complemento necesario para la Ley e Convertibilidad.

66.   **Administración y Gerenciamiento.** El gerencia debería modificar la estructura del Directorio para quitarle la carga de las responsabilidades operacionales. Actualmente, los miembros del Directorio tienen tanto el rol de supervisar al Presidente como el de ejecutar su mandato. Esto diluye las responsabilidades y compromete el asesoramiento que los miembros del Directorio deben dar al Presidente. El Gobierno debería utilizar la oportunidad que presenta la Carta Orgánica de nombrar personas de renombre en la comunidad financiera para otorgarles la responsabilidad de asegurar que los objetivos de dicha Carta son fehacientemente respetados por el Presidente y su gerencia. La gerencia debe prestar especial atención a aquellas tareas que poseen un alto costo si no se ejecutan adecuada y rápidamente, especialmente la reconciliación de balances con los acreedores bancarios externos.

67.   **Contabilidad.** Varios cambios realizados en los últimos años ha mejorado de manera significativa el sistema contable del Banco Central. En particular, el recálculo del balance de fines de 1989 y la eliminación de inversiones forzosas y la Cuenta de Regulación Monetaria han contribuido en la simplificación del sitema de contabilidad. De todos modos, el sistema es aún extremadamente deficiente. La reconstitución del sistema de contabilidad ebe progresar paralelamente con el proceso de reorganización. Dicha reconstitución contable debe realizarse con miras a asegurar que ésta genere las estadísticas apropiadas en el corto plazo, dadas las nuevas responsabilidades del Banco Central. Las operaciones del Banco Cntral deben ser definidas con precisión junto con las formas y medios específicos a través de los cuales se ingresarán los datos en el sistema contable. Se nombraría entones personal específico para realizar determinadas tareas. La pregunta fundamental es si el actual sistema puede ser salvado, o si el mismo debería ser reemplazado completamente. En ésta línea, es digno e mención que la nueva Carta Orgánica requerirá una auditoría externa del Banco Central.

68.   **Función de Liquidación.** El Gobierno modificó la Ley de Entidades Financieras en septiembre de 1992, requiriendo que todas las liquidaciones futuras de instituciones financieras en bancarrota sean manejadas por el Poder Judicial. Esto deja las liquidaciones en proceso entro de la jurisdicción del Banco Central; muchas de las liquidaciones llevan ya más de una década, y aún consumen mucho tiempo y son costosas. El Banco Central debería acelerar sus esfuerzos para terminar con estos procesos lo antes posible.

69.   **Superintendencia.** De manera consistente con la nueva Carta Orgánica del Banco Central, el Gobierno debería: (i) consolidar la reforma de la Superintendencia de Bancos, asegurando una mayor independencia administrativa, promulgando su mejorada estructura salarial y organizacional; (ii) asignar responsabilidades para reglamentar normas relativas a la regulación bancaria; y (iii) asignar responsabilidades sobre la publicación de indicadores financieros, incluyendo los balances e información sobre las declaraciones de ingresos, junto con la clasificación de portafolio de los bancos. Además, (iv) las relaciones gerenciales entre el Banco Central y la Superintendencia deberían ser más claras y predecibles; (v) se debería asignar

a la Superintendencia mayores poderes para asegurar el cumplimiento de la ley; y (vi) los instrumentos utilizados para evaluar las actividades comerciales de los bancos deberían ser revisados. Es de particular interés reducir los incentivos que tienen los bancos más grandes a tomar muchos riesgos (política de muy-grande-para-quebrar). Una posibilidad sería ligar la supervisión de los bancos directamente con el tamaño de su capital. Los bancos bien capitalizados tendrían permiso para ser los más diversificados en servicios financieros, dado que el incremento en los requerimientos de capital de los bancos es probablemente el modo más efectivo de reducir los incentivos de riesgos morales.

C. Conclusiones

70.   La administración Menem ha realizado el progreso más impresionante en mejorar las perspectivas de crecimiento de la Argentina, comparada con cualquiera de las recientes administraciones. Esto fue realizado mediante mejoras en los pilares de las finanzas públicas. Estos esfuerzos trajeron consigo la estabilidad de precios, y con ella, la posibilidad de disfrutar de un alto y sostenido crecimiento económico. Aún así, los próximos tres años serán tan críticos como los primeros tres. Tal como lo demuestra la experiencia de otros países del hemisferio, sólo la persecución resuelta, persistente e implacable del objetivo de estabilidad fiscal y políticas eficientes, puede hacer realidad el potencial de crecimiento de un país. Argentina ha demostrado su resolución en la persecución de este curso.

CHAPTER 1. FINANCIAL INSTABILITY AND PUBLIC FINANCES

A. Public Sector Deficits, Inflation, and Slow Growth

1.   Imbalances in public finance have been central to Argentina's prolonged economic decline. Once among the world's most prosperous economies, Argentina has experienced slow economic growth since the 1940s. During the 1970s, the country's long-term growth rate slowed, and in the 1980s the country suffered from its longest period of stagnation in the century (Figure 1.1). Savings and investment rates fell precipitously from the 1970s until 1989 (Figure 1.2). Argentines, responding to the unstable macroeconomic environment, increasingly saved and invested abroad, labor productivity fell, and poverty worsened. The value of the currency plummeted as the price level increased, and the ratio of public debt to GDP rose to nearly 100 percent.

Figure 1.1   **Figure 1.2**

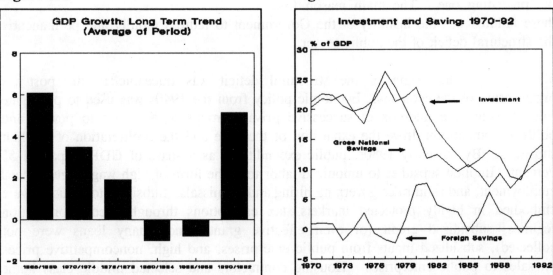

2.   Underlying this economic performance were several macroeconomic and institutional distortions that manifested themselves in chronic public sector deficits and endemic inflation (Figure 1.3). Public sector deficits in the late 1970s ranged from 5-14 percent of GDP, and in the early 1980s surpassed 15 percent of GDP. Central Bank losses, difficult to calculate in 1980-83, undoubtedly pushed the combined deficit to over 20 percent of GDP. After the return to constitutional democracy in 1983, public demands to control inflation were translated into four major stabilization programs. All of them failed to eradicate inflation, and each ended in a more virulent inflation than the preceding one. The main reason for

Figure 1.3

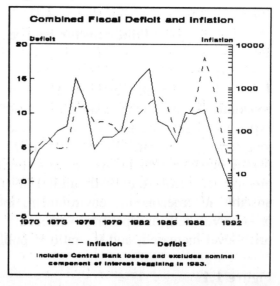

these failures was the inability of the Government to redress rapidly and permanently the structural deficit of the public sector.

3.   The origin of the structural deficit was traceable to the post-war organization of the economy. Economic policy from the 1940s was used to propagate rules favoring the interests of successive private groups with access to power, and political competition drove the expansion of the state and the proliferation of implicit subsidies. By the early 1980s, public expenditures as a share of GDP surpassed 55 percent. Implicit subsidies to unionized labor took the form of high wages, guaranteed employment, and rigid rules governing hiring and dismissals. Subsidies to industry were embodied in highly protected markets, tax exemptions through special promotion regimes, subsidized credit (or even effective grants since many loans were not collected), subsidized inputs from public enterprises, and high, noncompetitive prices on sales to public enterprises. Housing contractors and selected middle class home buyers benefitted from enormous public subsidies through earmarked taxes and effective grants through the Housing Bank (BHN). Tobacco growers benefitted from special taxes, as did the sugar growers, the merchant marine, and other small interest groups. Consumers, mainly in the urban middle classes, enjoyed below-cost tariffs from public enterprise and lax collection practices. Provincial governments could avail themselves of costless credit from the provincial banks, which the Central Bank reimbursed. The military enjoyed expanding budgets, especially in 1976-82, as well as management perquisites in state companies. By 1987-89, subsidies through the budget, tax exemptions, agricultural regulations, public enterprise tariffs, and central bank rediscounts were estimated to amount to some US$7 billion[1] roughly 8 percent of GDP.

4.   The growth of the state and concomitant rents and subsidies were financeable during the late 1970s largely because of high private savings after the 1975/76 stabilization, and then the expanding Eurodollar market with low or even negative international interest rates. This permitted the Government to run debt-financed

---

1   See Annex 1.1 "Subsidies to the Private Sector."

deficits of 7-8 percent of GDP with rates of inflation between 200-300 percent annually for the second half of the 1970s. However, the sudden rise in real international interest rates and the abrupt end to voluntary foreign commercial bank credit in the early 1980s provoked a financial collapse, and placed additional pressure on the economy. The economy was forced to divert domestic savings into foreign interest payments. After the public sector took over much of the private debt in 1980-82, the larger public interest bill only exacerbated the existing structural public deficit.

5.   The public sector had difficulty extracting more resources from the private sector, since the ever-greater share of the combined public sector borrowing requirement had to be financed through the domestic financial system and, eventually, money creation (Figure 1.4). The private sector, in an effort to avoid the inflation tax, gradually withdrew its resources from the financial system and reduced its holdings of currency; this, together with the effects of inflation on real revenue collection, made the macroeconomy progressively more unstable in the 1980s, and weakened the instruments of monetary policy (Figure 1.5). Even though the level of the deficit fell from near 20 percent of GDP in the early 1980s to an average of about 10 percent in 1987-89, the base of the inflation tax had shrunk because efforts to reduce the deficit were not fast or permanent enough to convince the private sector that its savings in domestic currency would not be taxed by inflation. Inflation became high and unpredictable, and thus became the main impediment to the recovery of private savings and investment. The decade ended with two episodes of hyperinflation in 1989.

Figure 1.4   **Figure 1.5**

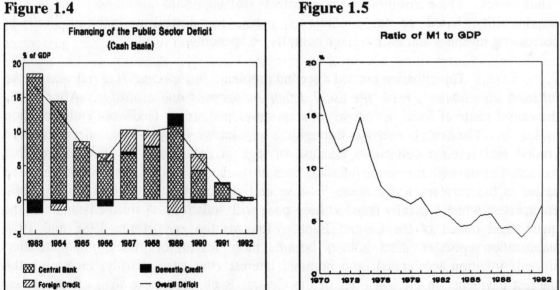

Macroeconomic Problems Confronting the Menem Administration

6.   When the Menem administration assumed office, it confronted three macroeconomic problems grounded in public finance. First, the economic team inherited *public institutions that for years had incentives favoring spending without incentives to raise revenues*. The national administration, enjoying access to Central Bank financing for its bonds and resorting to arrears, had a reduced incentive to collect taxes. Other levels of government--the decentralized agencies, public enterprises, the social security system, and provinces--were not subject to effective budget constraints and were usually able to push their deficits back onto the Treasury and ultimately the Central Bank. Many public enterprises had evolved into nonaccountable fiefdoms, and the Treasury covered deficits through direct transfers and progressive assumption of their liabilities. Public banks were able to draw on rediscounts from the Central Bank. The capacity of the social security system to collect and record properly its revenues from high wage taxes diminished and it had little incentive to reform because it relied progressively more on earmarked taxes, central bank financing, and arrears to pensioners. Provinces, relying on revenue-sharing and special grants from the Federal Government, were able to increase expenditures, especially on employment and generous social security benefits; when federal transfers proved insufficient to finance expenditures, these governments borrowed from their provincial banks, whose deficits had been historically covered by the Central Bank. The private health insurance funds, which administered a compulsory public tax that collectively amounted to 3-4 percent of GDP, had no accountability to the public at large or minimal accountability to their beneficiaries. These institutional arrangements had important corollaries: the lack of responsibility, based on the absence of public accountability, manifest itself in decreasing revenues and ever weaker controls on spending.

7.   This situation created a second problem: *institutionalizing reliance on the inflation tax ultimately made the fiscal deficit endogenous and explosive*. After 1988, the causal chain of fiscal deficits to inflation developed strong feedbacks from inflation to deficits. The first channel was through the well-known Olivera-Tanzi effect; inflation eroded real revenue collections because of lags in collections, a phenomenon that worsened at the higher average inflation rates of the late 1980s because evasion became easier as the currency lost meaning.[2] A second channel was through tariffs of public enterprises, which typically failed to keep pace with inflation. A third channel was the quasi-fiscal deficit of the Central Bank. Towards the end of the 1988 and 1989 stabilization episodes, asset holders became more fearful of losses, remonetization slowed, inflation accelerated, and nominal interest rates rose sharply, increasing the interest payments on the liabilities of the Central Bank; this more than offset interest receipts on assets, most of which were unlinked to domestic market rates. Finally, financial markets, leery of inflation surges, responded to indicators of future inflation-- notably movements in the exchange rate, increases in public enterprise prices, and fiscal deficits--with rapid portfolio shifts against the austral that from time to time reduced the money base by 50 percent in a matter of days.

---

2   In 1988, for example, Tanzi losses were estimated to be 2.1 percent of GDP. See World Bank, *Argentina: Tax Policy for Stabilization and Economic Recovery* (8067-AR).

8.　　　　In 1989 these pressures became intense: collection lags mattered more because of higher average inflations, and rapid price increases hung a cloak of opaqueness over tax returns and evasion became pervasive. Public enterprise prices became the indicator of success or failure of a program, and so were keep frozen so long that they became sources of deficit. The Central Bank's quasi-fiscal deficit assumed greater importance in the Plan Primavera and Plan Bunge Born, and financing the Central Bank's deficit became the principal source of money creation after domestic interest rates began to rise at the end of these programs. Finally, by the end of the decade, only professional market players dominated the market, heightening responsiveness of financial markets to increasingly skittish expectations of future inflation, and making the macroeconomy highly susceptible to even minor shocks.[3] These problems were especially apparent around the end of each calendar year when the public sector required substantial financing for its heavy end-of-year payments; however, demand for financial assets decreased substantially as individuals closed out their asset portfolios in preparation for vacation.

9.　　　　By the advent of the Menem administration, the history of deficits had created the third problem: *the state had become insolvent.* Claims on state resources were far greater than its capacity to mobilize resources. The high ratio of foreign public debt to GDP (approaching 100 percent in 1989) was only one manifestation of insolvency; others included the unfinanced obligation of the social security system (which was not recorded in the fiscal accounts), estimated to be US$7-10 billion and rising by US$200 million per month; excessive employment in the public sector with lifetime guarantees; and "acquired rights" granted to beneficiaries of subsidies, including promoted industries with tax credits of 10-15 years' duration. A priority for the Government, therefore, was increasing revenues, reducing flow claims on the Treasury-- wage payments and subsidies--as well as restructuring the stock of existing liabilities to foreigners, the financial system, social security recipients, and suppliers.

3　　　Rudiger Dornbusch and Juan Carlos de Pablo formalized these relationships in a model designed to show the relationship between inflation, growth, the budget deficit, and money creation under various macroeconomic and financial conditions. The model states:

$$\pi = (\alpha g - y)/(1-\beta g); \ 1 \le \beta g$$

where π is inflation, α is the velocity of money under noninflationary circumstances, g is the rate of growth, and β is the response of velocity to the rate of inflation. This equation states that (i) inflation will be less the higher the rate of growth because growth generates a demand for money; (ii) inflation will be greater the larger the budget deficit; and (iii) the rate of inflation depends on the parameters for velocity; the higher the velocity of money (say, associated with dollarization), the greater will be inflation associated with any level of deficit; similarly, the higher the responsiveness of financial markets and velocity of money to inflation, the greater will be inflation. See Chapter 4 of *Deuda Externa e inestabilidad macroeconomica en la Argentina* (Buenos Aires: Editorial Sudamericana, 1988), especially pp. 77-79 and Appendix II.

B. Main Problems in Public Finance: 1970-89

10.   The insolvency problems which the Menem administration encountered were traceable to decades of public sector imbalance. The accounts of the public sector had not been in surplus in three decades.[4] The public sector deficit averaged 14 percent of GDP in 1980-84, and fell to 8.9 percent in 1985-89 (Table 1.1). The noninterest or primary balance was in deficit by an average of 9 percent of GDP in the first half of the 1980s, improving to a deficit of 2.2 percent of GDP in the second half. These endemic deficits had their origin in an erosion of revenue capacity and an inability to contain expenditures.

Revenues

11.   The tax burden as a share of GDP, which had reached 19.5 percent of GDP in 1980, fell to 16 percent in 1989. But more important, this fall was accompanied by an increasing reliance on inefficient taxes that discouraged growth. The Argentine tax system was fairly sophisticated and efficient in the early 1970s; however, tax exemptions were granted for various purposes beginning in 1973. As time passed, inflation, combined with the lack of political resolve to enforce tax laws, progressively eroded the tax structure and administration. The tax system effectively collapsed during the 1989/90 hyperinflations.

12.   In an attempt to maintain revenues as the tax system was eroding, the Government began to rely increasingly on inefficient but easily collectable taxes--so-called tax handles. The VAT became riddled with exemptions, primarily for industrial promotion. Revenues from the VAT, which reached a peak of over 5 percent of GDP in 1981, had fallen to under 2 percent in 1989; their contribution to total revenues fell from some 23 percent in 1980-84 to under 15 percent in 1989. The income tax withered to less than one percent of GDP. The tax handles included export taxes, taxes on bank checks, and excessive energy taxes. To complicate matters, the Executive agreed to earmark selected taxes to enlist support from selected regional or special interests when negotiating tax packages through Congress, and these reduced the flexibility of the Treasury to allocate resources.

13.   The decline in revenues from efficient taxes (VAT and income taxes) reflected three factors: improper indexing, tax administration and exemptions. Income tax receipts suffered particularly from the inappropriate definition of the inflation adjustments for loss carryovers as well as tax exemptions for income from interest and dividends. Improper indexing of other taxes also lowered real receipts in inflationary times, leading to a procyclical bias in revenue shortfalls.

---

4   There are difficulties in comparing public sector figures across time, because of variations in accounting. For time series information on fiscal accounts, see FIEL *El Gasto Publico en la Argentina, 1960-1988* (Buenos Aires: Fundacion de Investigaciones Economicas Latinoamericanas, 1990).

Table 1.1: Argentina - Fiscal Accounts of the Consolidated Public Sector, 1983 - 1992
(Accrual basis, as percent of GDP)

	1983	1984	1985	1986	1987	1988	1989	1990	1991	1992e
Current Revenue a/	19.3	22.4	23.1	21.7	20.0	19.1	17.6	17.7	20.4	25.0
Tax Revenue	15.7	19.1	18.7	18.6	17.8	16.8	16.3	16.6	19.1	23.8
DGI and Customs Revenue	11.0	16.5	15.1	14.6	14.0	12.1	13.0	11.5	13.5	15.9
Social Security Revenue	4.7	2.6	3.6	4.0	3.9	4.7	3.3	5.0	5.7	7.9
Non-tax Revenue	3.6	3.3	4.4	3.1	2.2	2.3	1.3	1.1	1.3	1.2
Current Expenditures	28.0	24.4	25.2	23.5	23.4	23.1	19.9	21.6	21.8	23.7
Personnel	4.8	4.8	4.1	3.6	4.1	4.1	3.4	4.1	3.9	3.6
Goods and Services	2.9	1.9	2.2	2.0	2.1	2.0	1.6	1.4	1.3	1.6
Transfers	14.5	12.7	13.5	14.1	13.8	14.1	11.6	13.1	14.5	16.8
Provinces	7.6	5.9	6.1	6.7	6.6	7.0	6.1	5.7	7.0	8.2
Social Security	6.1	5.6	5.6	5.5	5.1	5.2	3.6	5.7	6.0	8.2
Others	0.8	1.2	1.8	1.9	2.1	1.9	2.0	1.7	1.6	0.4
Interest Payments b/	5.8	5.0	5.4	3.8	3.5	2.8	3.3	3.1	2.1	1.7
Domestic c/	0.9	0.8	0.7	0.3	0.5	0.4	0.2	0.5	0.3	0.1
External d/	4.9	4.2	4.7	3.5	3.0	2.4	3.1	2.6	1.8	1.6
Public Enterprise Non-interest Savings	-0.1	0.6	1.0	1.9	1.8	1.0	0.9	1.2	0.3	0.8
Current Revenues	11.0	10.5	13.6	12.1	11.8	12.8	12.8	8.8	6.7	6.0
Current Non-interest Expenditures	11.1	9.9	12.6	10.1	9.9	11.8	11.9	7.6	6.4	5.2
Savings	-8.8	-1.4	-1.1	0.1	-1.5	-3.0	-1.4	-2.7	-1.1	2.1
Capital Revenue	0.2	0.2	0.2	0.1	0.1	0.4	0.6	0.2	1.7	1.3
Capital Expenditures	6.8	5.1	4.5	4.4	5.3	6.0	3.9	2.6	2.3	1.7
General Government	2.9	1.6	1.5	1.6	1.7	1.5	1.0	0.8	0.7	1.2
Public Enterprises	3.9	3.6	2.9	2.8	3.6	4.5	2.8	1.9	1.6	0.5
Non-Financial Public Sector Balance	-15.4	-6.3	-5.4	-4.2	-6.7	-8.6	-4.7	-5.1	-1.7	1.7
Quasi-fiscal Balance of Central Bank e/	-1.1	-2.5	-2.8	-1.6	-3.4	-1.4	-5.8	-1.0	-0.6	-0.2
Overall Balance	-16.5	-8.8	-8.2	-5.8	-10.1	-10.0	-10.5	-6.1	-2.3	1.5
Memo:										
Primary Surplus	-9.6	-1.3	0.0	-0.4	-3.2	-5.8	-1.4	-2.0	0.4	3.4
Operational Primary Surplus f/	-9.8	-1.5	-0.2	-0.5	-3.3	-6.2	-2.0	-2.2	-1.3	2.1
Net Federal Expenditure g/	36.0	31.4	31.5	27.5	30.2	29.4	28.7	24.0	24.4	24.8
Provincial Revenue, incl. transfers	11.6	10.4	10.8	11.2	8.0	10.3	9.4	9.0	10.3	13.2
Provincial Expenditure	11.4	11.9	11.4	11.1	12.9	12.3	10.6	13.2	13.5	12.8
Health Funds Expenditures h/	4.4	4.1	4.3	4.4	4.6	4.7	3.8	3.8	4.2	4.7
Total Non-interest Expenditures	48.4	44.5	46.4	43.1	46.1	48.1	40.7	40.0	39.1	38.2
Total Expenditure, incl. quasifiscal balance of BCRA i/	55.3	52.0	54.6	48.5	53.0	52.3	49.8	44.1	41.8	40.1

a/ Includes coparticipated revenues.
b/ Interest payments of the entire Federal Government.
c/ Real component of domestic interest payments for 1983-1991; 1992 is nominal due to return to stability.
d/ Accrued interest due.
e/ Real earnings on assets less real interest costs; IMF definition, 1983-87; IBRD definition 1988-1992 (see Ch.13)
f/ Primary surplus less capital revenue.
g/ Includes non-interest current account of the public enterprises and quasi-fiscal balance (- = expenditure).
h/ 1983-1987 from FIEL "Gasto Público" report (1988); 1988-1992 based on Bank staff estimates.
i/ Gross expenditure of national government, public enterprises, provinces, health funds and quasifiscal balance of the Central Bank.

Source: Secretary of Finance; Executed Budgets, 1983-1991; Cash Basis, 1992.

14.   The capacity to administer efficient taxes eroded with inattention to management and systems development early in the decade and the sharp deterioration in public sector salaries after 1984. The General Tax Office (DGI) had an inadequate tax roll, a low rate of inspections and audits, a low level of efficiency in processing returns, and low rate of collection per audit. In 1989, an audit that cost the DGI on average US$800 produced US$35 in new revenues. The customs administration also became less reliable and effective in the 1980s.

15.   The use of tax expenditures in support of industrial activity beginning in the late 1970s was pernicious to revenues. Fiscal incentives for industrial promotion were built around Law 21608 of 1977 to promote industrial investment and supporting the creation of industries in less developed regions of the country. Additional laws expanded the incentives for investment and production in Tierra del Fuego and in four provinces.[5] Inadequate control and inspection have led to widespread abuses and tax evasion. The system engendered fiscal losses without significant employment effects. The fiscal cost of the national and regional promotion schemes as well as the scheme for Tierra del Fuego was estimated to have been as much as 1.0 percent of GDP in 1989.

Expenditures

16.   Driven by powerful interest groups with minimal accountability to the electorate, total expenditures of the nonfinancial public sector as a percent of GDP increased from a level of slightly less than 30 percent in 1966-70 to a peak of over 55 percent in 1980-83. The stop-go austerity programs of the 1980s produced temporary reversals of these trends, but no sustained reduction. Noninterest expenditures fell by five percentage points of GDP to 1986, only to surge again as mid-term elections approached in late 1987. Expenditures were compressed again in 1988-89--this time by seven percent of GDP--mainly by accumulating arrears in social security and denying resources to the provinces (which in turn accumulated arrears with workers and suppliers, and borrowed from their banks). Efforts at stabilization tended to contract those expenditures that were least objectionable politically--investment, the wage bill of the civil service, other public expenditures. The 1980s left public expenditures plagued with both process and composition problems.

17.   **Process Problems.** The inability to control expenditures was the result of: (i) a fragmented fiscal administration with perverse incentives, including proliferation of decentralized agencies, unclear financial relations with the provinces, and overearmarking of revenue streams; (ii) the complete breakdown within the budgetary process; and (iii) the institutional failure to properly control expenditures. *Fragmentation* with perverse incentives meant that most public expenditures occurred outside the direct control of the Executive (i.e., the Secretary of Finance), instead residing with the decentralized agencies, special accounts, public enterprises, provinces

---

5   The fiscal incentives for industrial promotion were awarded through six different instruments: (i) exemption from import duties and VAT purchases on capital goods; (ii) deferral of tax payments by investors up to a certain percentage of the amount invested; (iii) exemption from profit taxes; (iv) exemption from capital taxes; (v) exemption from the VAT; (vi) exemption from the stamp duty; and (vii) exemptions for suppliers of promoted firms.

and social security funds. In 1992, for example, the Secretary of Finance had direct responsibility for only 20 percent of all spending--and one-quarter of this was interest payments. At the same time, the Federal Government assumed a greater responsibility for providing resources, either through taxes or the Central Bank. As the various components of government reached the limits of their budgets, they customarily arranged for *ad hoc*, discretionary bailouts from the central government or Central Bank--financed ultimately from the inflation tax.

18.　　　　The *budget process* itself weakened under the weight of unstable macroeconomic conditions. Cycles of inflation and austerity forced the Treasury to manage short-term flows on the basis of the immediate priorities of continually changing quarterly fiscal targets rather than an agreed budget. High and variable inflation soon rendered budgets prepared in nominal terms meaningless. The budgetary process itself was plagued by several other problems, including the omission from coverage of important sources of expenditures (e.g., public enterprises); absence of budget programming and therefore of a regular programmatic review of public expenditures, oriented towards improved resource reallocation under severe resource constraints; *ex-ante* and ineffectual control of budget execution; inconsistent accounts and the absence of timely budget processing and therefore weak senior-level monitoring, and unenforceable reporting requirements; the breakdown of the public investment planning process and the absence of a link to the budget. The very institutions of public financial management were inadequate.[6]

19.　　　　In this environment, the *expenditure control* strategy of the Alfonsin Administration after 1987 was to limit the access of the decentralized public sector to the Treasury and Central Bank--attempting to force each component of government to put itself in balance. Thus, the public enterprises were to have been put in balance by requiring the surplus companies to cross-subsidize the deficit companies, in exchange for taking over the service burden on commercial bank debt; the provinces were taken out of the consolidated public sector accounts with the passage of revenue sharing legislation, and the social security system was to be made financially independent. This strategy necessarily entailed distortions--especially in the cross-subsidies in the public enterprises and in the central government absorbing a disproportionate share of the initial expenditure reductions and liabilities of the public sector. This effort ultimately failed--the decentralized components pressed claims to obtain emergency financing via the budget, provincial banks, and even issuance of quasi-money by some provinces.

6　　The institutions of fiscal control were weak. The accounting function (National Accounting Office-CGN) was not fully developed, and accounts were inconsistent because there were no accounting norms for the public sector as a whole; the internal control function--expenditure recording--in the Executive was only effective for public enterprises (General Accounting Office for Public Enterprises-SIGEP) and partially for procurement in the rest of the public sector (National Court of Accounts-TCN); and there was no external auditing because there was inadequate internal control. The control system emphasized formal decisions on an *ex-ante* basis, instead of following a modern approach, which implied *ex-post* performance control measured against an approved budget. It also did not separate the three basic functions--accounting, internal registration/control, and external auditing--that have to be independent in a modern institutional structure on control. Finally, the TCN was charged with judicial responsibilities for prosecution of public fraud cases that should be the sole responsibility of the judicial branch.

However, it did begin a process to regularize accounts and institutionalize fiscal responsibility.

20. **Composition Problems (Economic Classification).** As austerity programs began to take hold in the late 1980s, the fragmentation of spending authority forced a disproportionate compression on those elements securely in the control of the Treasury--wages, service quality, and investment of the Federal Government. This form of adjustment distorted the composition of expenditures substantially over time as seen through an analysis of expenditures by economic classification. (A functional analysis is discussed below.) The aggregate wage bill and investment fell as a share of the total to make room for a relative increase in interest payments and transfers to nonfederal components of government--namely, the provinces, public enterprises (primarily railways), and social security.

21. The *wage bill* of the national administration declined from about 4.9 percent of GDP in 1980 to about 3.4 percent in 1989, a period when overall employment in the national administration increased and GDP was contracting. This pattern of adjustment eroded the capacity of the Government to perform its core functions as well as exacerbated existing weaknesses in its budgetary capacity. During the 1980s, the Federal Government increased the number of public employees by 36 percent between 1980 and 1990 from about 495,000 to about 670,000 workers (see Annex Tables 3.1-3.7).[7] By 1990, average real wages had fallen to under 35 percent of their January 1984 levels, the peak for the decade. The salary compression ratio--the ratio of the highest to lowest salary--had fallen to less than 3:1 by February 1990 compared with historical levels of 10-12:1. Provincial public sector employment exhibited the same pattern with even greater distortion.

22. By 1990, the Government could not attract qualified managers and technicians, had limited staff capacity to perform on-going programmatic functions (let alone design and implement broad reforms), and could not adequately monitor policies for compliance and effect. More important, limited human resources were badly deployed across an overextended public sector still designed with a heavily interventionist and market-regulating legal framework. Morale was low, and the average civil servant worked only a few hours a day because of the need for part-time work elsewhere and lack of supervisory control.

23. At the same time, the capacity of the Government to supply its workers with *goods and services* necessary to perform their duties had fallen: teachers worked without adequate suppliers, hospitals were inadequately supplied and maintained, and maintenance throughout the public sector deteriorated. The balance between non-wage operating costs and wages fell to about 15 percent, down from previous levels of 35 percent in the 1970s. This ratio improved slightly in 1992 because of the general improvement in public finances and administrative reform.

---

7   In addition, employment in the public enterprises is about 300,000, in the official banks about 33,000, and employment in the provincial governments is estimated at about 1 million (excluding nonconsolidated municipalities and provincial corporations) (see Annex Table). Also, the military has enlisted personnel of 86,000, paid through the budget.

24.		Almost three-quarters of noninterest federal expenditures shown in Table 1.1 were *transfers* to the provinces, public enterprises, social security and other. Transfers to the provinces were *ad hoc* and somewhat discretionary during the mid-1980s, but the coparticipation law enacted in 1988 required the Federal Government to transfer automatically 58 percent of selected taxes to the provinces. This primary distribution formula was significantly higher than at any time in the history of the Republic, and much higher than the 34 percent prevailing in 1980-84.[8] The shift in the tax base toward more efficient taxes also shifted the base in favor of coparticipated taxes. As a result, transfers to the provinces rose from an average of 6.5 percent of GDP in 1983-85 to over 8 percent in 1992.

25.		Transfers to the public enterprises were primarily to subsidize the operating losses of several money-losing enterprises, most importantly the railways. For most of the 1980s, enterprises enjoyed considerable autonomy in planning and budgeting, and deficits would be covered by the Treasury; subsidies varied inversely with stabilization programs because most programs froze enterprise tariffs, and managers bargained over the transfers and sought federally guaranteed loans from suppliers that would later revert to the Federal Government to pay.

26.		The social security system was massively in deficit throughout the 1980s. This deficit was even larger than that shown in the fiscal accounts because the arrears were not officially recorded or acknowledged until much later (1992). Revenue collections were poorly administered and benefits were generous. Other transfers were military pensions, universities and private education, and the housing program.

27.		Public *investment* during the expenditure compression of the 1980s declined to its lowest level in history. From 5.5 percent in 1983-85, public investment as a share of GDP fell to under 4 percent in 1988. Investment in the Federal Government--roads, schools, hospitals, power--fell especially precipitously since their resources were linked more closely to tax performance. Investment spending in the public enterprises also declined sharply, but in response to their deteriorating savings performance and shrinking borrowing capacity. As a consequence, the quality and quantity of publicly provided goods and services greatly deteriorated. Since 1990, the privatization program has partially relieved the public sector of the pent-up demand for public investment.

The Quasi-Fiscal Deficit

28.		After its takeover of private debt in 1980-82, the Central Bank assumed the external liabilities of several failed banks as well the expenses of liquidation. In addition, the Central Bank provided subsidized exchange rates for external payments, which added to its losses. After 1985, the Central Bank began to finance the repayment of government bonds, to permit rediscounts to public banks that effectively financed fiscal expenditures (in the form of provincial expenditures or subsidies to housing and industry), and, of lesser importance, to finance an increasing float with the social security system. The Central Bank also absorbed losses associated with trade financing.

8		See World Bank, *Towards a New Federalism*, May 1992, Chapter 2.

All these efforts produced a hugely negative capital position; writing in 1989, the current president of the Central Bank, Mr. Roque Fernandez, estimated the recorded and unrecorded losses of the Central Bank up to 1990 to be about US$67 billion. Annual recorded losses averaged 2 percent of GDP in 1983-86 and 3.5 percent in 1987-89.

29.   Financing these quasi-fiscal expenditures required funds. The Central Bank increased demand for its liabilities through ever-higher legal reserve requirements and "forced investments" from the commercial banking system. It also sold its own bonds. These mechanisms in 1987-89 resulted in a substantial debt to the financial system that in itself was destabilizing because of the explosive interest bill. Since its asset portfolio was built on fixed interest loans (many of which were to the Housing and Industrial Banks and were thus nonperforming) and its liabilities composed mainly of forced investments bearing market interest rates, high real interest rates and/or high inflation widened the domestic quasi-fiscal deficit. Towards the end of stabilization episodes based on fixed exchange rates, real interest rates rose as financial markets began to fear devaluations, the interest bill of the Central Bank became an endogenous and destabilizing source of money creation.[9] This mechanism eventually led to the collapse of the Plan Primavera (August 1988-February 1989), the Plan Bunge Borne (July 1989-December 1989), and ended the Central Bank's capacity to carry out monetary policy.

C. Post-1989 Structural Reforms in Public Finance

30.   The incoming Menem Administration enacted a series of structural reforms over 30 months that recast the basis of public finance. The Government undertook difficult-to-reverse reforms in the legal framework, institutions, and policies. Gradually, these have begun to change Argentine culture. This process, not unlike a bankruptcy procedure, was characterized by three sets of actions. First, the Government improved *revenue mobilization* to increase the quantity and quality of federal revenues. Second, it enacted *expenditure reforms* to reduce the scope and size of government through administrative reforms that reduced public employment, undertook privatizations to ensure a permanent end to subsidies through public entities, and implemented fiscal decentralization to make revenue-sharing with the provinces transparent and bring service delivery closer to local constituencies. Finally, the Government is in the process

---

[9]   These interest rate rules and the quasi-fiscal deficit generally are analyzed in Chapter 4 of *Argentina: Reforms for Price Stability and Growth*. Washington: World Bank, 1989. See also L. Barbone and P. Beckerman, "Argentina's Quasifiscal Deficit," October 1988, and P. Beckerman, "Public Sector Debt Distress in Argentina," World Bank, WPS 902, May 1992.

of *restructuring its liabilities with domestic and foreign creditors* to adjust them to serviceable levels. Other reforms have aided the process of activating efficient private investment, notably *trade and financial sector reform.*[10]

Revenue Mobilization

31.   The Government improved revenues by broadening the VAT, extending its coverage first to all goods in February 1990, and later to services in November 1990. It also adopted an assets tax in 1990. The Government also improved the efficiency of the tax administration-- establishing a control system for the largest taxpayers in February 1991 and rebuilding the tax rolls through more than 400,000 site inspections in late 1990. The tax penalty law, adopted by Congress in 1990, provided much-needed sanctions for tax non- compliance. The tax package of February 1991 improved the *quality* of the revenue mobilization effort because it eliminated

Figure 1.6

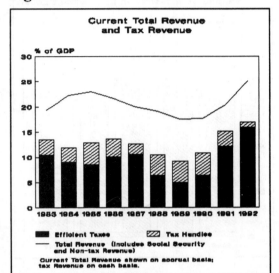

many of the so-called tax handles--easy to collect but growth-inhibiting taxes, such as export taxes, taxes on financial transactions, and several low yield taxes. These efforts cumulatively produced dramatic rises in tax collections (Figure 1.6).

---

10   The fiscal reforms had important antecedents. In retrospect, the mid-term elections of 1987 marked a turning point for public finance. By that time, demand management approaches had failed, the fiscal deficit had mushroomed, and the Plan Austral was unsalvageable. In the last two years of the Alfonsin Administration, the Government took several significant steps down the path of reform later accelerated in the Menem years. It began--slowly at first--to change incentives facing the decentralized public sector. Efforts included the revenue sharing law, which purported to eliminate discretionary transfers to the provinces and was implemented in 1988; the idea was to compel the provinces to live within budget and preempt requests for unbudgeted federal revenues (although the new law entailed a historical high in lost revenues. Second, interest rate liberalization in 1987-88, coupled with the payment of interest on mandatory reserves at the Central Bank, was designed to end the sequestration of resources from the financial system, and improve intermediation by reducing spreads; attaching a cost to reserves would supposedly discipline the Central Bank's practice of increasing reserve requirements to finance the nonfinancial public sector and its own deficit but the cost of interest on the reserves added to the fiscal deficit. Third, the Government ought to end disguised fiscal subsidies via rediscounts to official banks as a way to discipline the provinces, the industry and the housing banks. Fourth, the Government sought to discipline the decentralized components outside the Treasury--social security, public enterprises, and the provinces--by setting up clear rules circumscribing access of these agencies to the federal treasury and to Central Bank finance. Incipient efforts at opening the economy also were begun in 1987/88.

Expenditure Reduction and Restructuring

32. **Administrative Reform.** Because the wage bill dominated expenditures, the Government reduced the federal bureaucracy in 1990-92. Federal employment was cut by more than 103,000 in 1991-92, a total decline of 15 percent since 1990; in addition, 284,000 teachers and health workers were transferred to the provincial governments (Figure 1.7). Rather than simply lay off workers, this effort was based on a ministerial reorganization that focused on federal activities related to core objectives, and improvements in the civil service system through an improved salary structure and other efficiency measures. These efforts allowed the Government to increase average salaries, salary dispersion, and still reduce its wage expenditures as a share of GDP and by almost 10 percent in real terms in 1992 (Table 1.2). The Government improved its control of public expenditures in earnest beginning in February 1991; one indication was the reduction in spending jurisdictions by more than 50 percent between 1990 and 1992; the number of earmarked accounts fell from 152 in 1989 to 59 in 1992. The Government also enacted a law of Public Financial Administration in September 1992 that will revamp national fiscal accounting, improve expenditure control systems, and establish modern auditing systems for public expenditures.[11]

Figure 1.7

33. **Public Enterprises.** The new Government adopted an accelerated timetable upon taking office in July 1989 for privatization or partial divestiture of nearly all its enterprises. The program's objective was reducing the budgetary burden of the enterprises on the Treasury, making the firms more competitive, and increasing the volume and efficiency of new investment. The Government sold two television stations, ENTel (US$214 million plus US$5 billion in external debt) and Aerolineas Argentinas (US$260 million plus US$2 billion in external debt). Remaining minority government shares in the new telephone company were sold for US$1.2 billion in early 1992. The Government began a comprehensive restructuring of the petroleum industry--the first in Latin America--by auctioning off areas of YPF (realizing by end-1991 US$1.6 billion in cash). It granted road and railroad concessions to the private sector and restructured the railways, including the privatization of long distance cargo lines, and reduction of 15 percent of the railway's work force. The Government intends to privatize most of the remaining public enterprises in 1992, including shares in the petroleum industry,

---

11   The World Bank supported reforms of both revenues and expenditures of the Federal Government as well as those of the Central Bank mentioned below with a US$325 million Public Sector Reform Loan (PSRL) (cofinanced by the IDB) and a US$23 million Technical Assistance Loan in July 1991.

TABLE 1.2:   ARGENTINA - INDICATORS OF ADMINISTRATIVE REFORM: NATIONAL ADMINISTRATION

	1990	1991	1992	Total Reductions	Lay-offs a/	Transfers
National Administration Personnel	671,479	581,539	284,215	387,264	103,469	283,795
Administrative Reform Program	341,021	267,081	227,677	113,344	90,913	22,431
Central Administration	123,646	87,596	61,276	62,370	39,939	22,431
Decentralized Agencies	144,600	126,183	123,391	21,209	21,209 ...	
Other National Administration	72,775	53,302	43,010	29,765	29,765 ...	
Other Programs	330,458	314,458	56,538	273,920	12,556	261,364
Memo:						
Armed Forces (A.F.) and Conscripts	131,297	121,946	112,594	18,703	18,703	
National Administration and Armed Forces	802,776	703,485	396,809	405,967	122,172	283,795
Gross lay-offs (exc. tax agencies, Police and A.F.)					121,600	
Wages						
Wage Expenditures (1992 US$ Million) b/	3,229.49	3,555.16	3,443.05			
Wage Expenditures (% of GDP)	3.05	2.62	2.23			
Implicit Average Wage (1992 US$) c/	4,742	6,320	9,538			
Ratio of Highest to Lowest Salary d/	3.5	6.0	10.0			
Senior Government Salary (Percent of Private Sector Equivalent) e/	20.0	33.3	74.1			
Administration Structure						
Spending Jurisdictions	39	30	18			
Government Agencies	38	38	30			
Special Accounts	93	86	59			
Structure of Civil Service						
Secretaries	47	36	43			
Subsecretaries	99	29	62			
National Directorates	304	185	187			

Source: Ministry of Economy, Presidential Address to Congress (5/1/92) and Annex Table 3.1

a/ Total net lay-offs.
b/ Net of indemnizations, previsions for early retirement and changes in pay-scales; includes payroll taxes,
    overtime, 13th month salary and other benefits.
c/ Estimated considering Budgeted National Administration Personnel plus Armed Forces personnel (excluding
    conscripts; including health funds till 1992).
d/ Data from March 1990, December 1991, March 1992, for SINAPA regime.
e/ Preliminary figures; 1992 are projected.

defense industries, the nation's largest distributor of electricity Table 1.2 Indicators of Administration (SEGBA), ports and maritime transport, reinsurance, and the entire power sector. Capital revenues from privatizations have provided an important source of transitional finance to the fiscal accounts (Figure 1.8).[12]

Figure 1.8

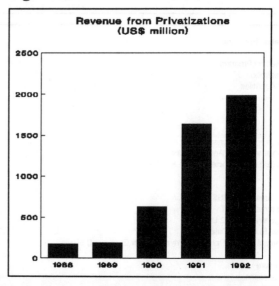

34.   **Decentralization.**   The Government also sought to restructure fiscal relationships with the provinces. Building on the coparticipation law of 1988, which fixed the share of federal revenues automatically transferred to the provinces at 58 percent, the Government sought to limit macro instability arising from deficits in the provinces. This entailed limiting the resources provincial governments could access from their provincial banks by progressively terminating Central Bank lending to provincial banks. It also meant reducing extra-coparticipation transfers through the budget. Finally, it meant transferring classes of expenditures to provincial administration in 1992, notably secondary education and hospitals.

35.   The aggregate decline in total public spending was mainly owing to the efforts at the federal level in the national administration and privatizations. Automatic transfers to the provinces and social security increased in 1991/92 and thus prevented aggregate expenditures from falling more; but these--at least initially--helped to alleviate latent structural deficits in these areas. Overall, total expenditures are 15 percentage points of GDP lower than in 1980, and 10 percent lower than in 1983, the time of return to constitutional democracy (Figure 1.9). Including the provinces and health funds, public expenditures fell from near 60 percent of GDP in the early 1980s to about 40 percent at present.

Figure 1.9

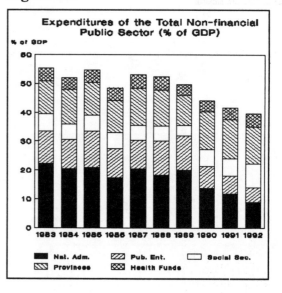

12   The World Bank supported this effort with the approval of a US$300 million Public Enterprise Reform Loan (PERAL I) and a US$23 million Technical Assistance Loan in February 1991, as well as with the PERAL II of US$ 300 million approved in December 1992.

36.   Present levels of public spending are below the average for the industrial countries, and are comparable to middle income countries.   The average level of Federal Government expenditures for industrial countries was 28.6 percent of GDP in 1985; middle-income countries averaged 27.5 percent.   Argentina's federal spending was about 25 percent of GDP in 1992. Combined federal and state (provincial) spending in six OECD countries--the US, United Kingdom, France, Germany, Sweden and Japan-- averaged 47 percent in 1985, with a range of 33 (Japan) to 65 (Sweden).[13]   In Argentina, total public sector spending was 40 percent in 1992.   Nonetheless, this conclusion must be somewhat tempered by

Figure 1.10

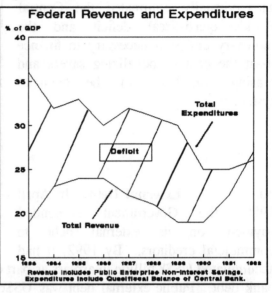

public expenditures not included in the Argentine numbers--the quasi-fiscal deficit, tax expenditures for industrial promotion, and higher-than-OECD average tariffs.

37.   Taken together, the structural measures facilitated an increase in revenues and a decrease in expenditures. On the basis of reforms enacted in 1990, revenues jumped sharply beginning in 1991. Expenditures fell sharply after 1988, especially noninterest expenditures (shown in Figure 1.10 on a net basis).

Restructuring Domestic and Foreign Debt

38.   The Government's final step in dealing with its insolvency involved restructuring its financing obligations. The Government had financed its deficit through borrowing from the financial system (US$3.5 billion) and by accumulating arrears to external creditors (US$8 billion), social security pensioners (estimated at US$12-14 billion), and others (US$4 billion). Each of these required major initiatives.

39.   **Quasi-Fiscal Deficit and Debt with the Financial System**. Although the Government ended new rediscounts to the housing and industrial banks as well as liberal rediscounts to provincial banks in 1988, the Central Bank continued money emission to finance the Treasury as well as its own deficit. In the fourth quarters of both 1988 and 1989, the rising interest bill of the Central Bank drove up the domestic interest bill and widened the deficit, such as occurred with foreign interest payments in the early 1980s (Figure 1.11). In late December 1989, faced with an exploding interest bill, rising Central Bank deficits and the renewed threat of hyperinflation, the Government took the drastic action of converting the domestic, short-term (mainly seven

---

13   See World Bank, *World Development Report*, 1988, Washington: World Bank, 1988, pp.45-46.

Figure 1.11

day), interest-bearing obligations of the Central Bank into US$3.5 billion of 10-year external Treasury bonds (BONEX). This virtually eliminated the Central Bank's quasi-fiscal deficit and the monetary emission necessary to finance it--at the cost of penalizing savers and erasing confidence in the financial system.[14]

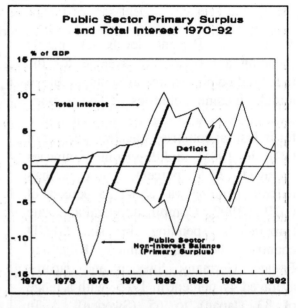

40. **External Debt.** In April 1988, the Government suspended payment on its external debt to commercial creditors. By 1992, it had accumulated US$8 billion in arrears as part of a US$33 billion medium-term commercial bank debt. Public external debt was US$61 billion (Figures 1.12). The Government reinitiated partial payments in June 1990, and established a consistent track record of paying about 25 percent of interest due. At the same time, it allowed external debt to be used in exchange for the sale of assets, which reduced the debt stock by US$7 billion. The measures, together with the progressive improvement in fiscal fundamentals in 1990/91, allowed the Government to begin negotiations with commercial banks on a debt reduction deal. In December 1992, **Figure 1.12**

the Government achieved an agreement with the banks. The agreement formalizes arrears in a 12-year uncollateralized bond at LIBOR with a 3-year grace period, after a US$700 million downpayment; it would exchange existing debt for either a collateralized *par bond* with a fixed interest rate (beginning at 4 percent and rising to 6 percent by the sixth year), or a collateralized *discount bond* at 65 percent of face value at LIBOR; new collateralized bonds would have a 12 month rolling interest guarantee. The agreement, although increasing the cash payment, will end the accumulation of arrears and provide for debt reduction

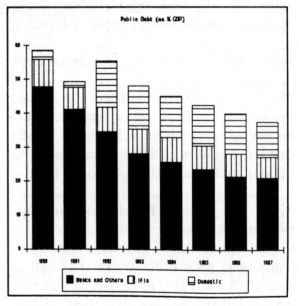

---

14   This is discussed in Chapter 12.

similar to Mexico's. Debt service payments would begin at US$1.5 billion in 1993 and rise to US$3.0 billion by the end of the decade.[15]

41.   **Arrears to Pensioners and Suppliers.**   For the last decade, the Government has paid only about half the legally mandated pension owed to social security recipients.   Arrearages were not recorded in the fiscal accounts, but are estimated to be US$7-10 billion, and accumulating at a rate of US$200 million per month. Also, the Government accumulated arrears in 1990 with suppliers through the formal suspension of payment for goods and services already provided. In addition, the health funds have arrears with their service providers that will also result in new debt. Finally, the Government, as part of its income tax reform, suspended the poorly designed loss-carry-forward deductions for the corporate income tax, with the agreement to issue some US$1.5-2.5 billion in compensatory bonds.

42.   To settle these claims, Congress authorized the Government to issue consolidation bonds (BOCONs) that will have terms of 10 or 16 years (with shorter terms for social security recipients) and a five-year grace period on principal and interest. It is estimated that the Government will have to issue US$15-20 billion. Suppliers and pensioners will have the choice between a bond denominated in local currency with a domestic interest rate and a bond denominated in US dollars at LIBOR. The service of the debt will be capitalized until 1997, but payments on the order of US$3 billion will be required in the last years of this decade.

Supporting Sectoral Reforms: Trade and Finance

43.   **Trade Regime.** After October 1988, the Government began opening the economy to import competition, a process accelerated under the Menem Administration. Quantitative restrictions (QRs) were reduced from about 50 percent of domestic production coverage to 7 percent by late 1990 (Figure 1.13); the ad valorem tariff band was narrowed from 0-115 percent to 0-24 percent, with an average rate of about 18 percent; and the production coverage of industrial export taxes was reduced to 30 percent. In February 1991, the tariff band was reduced further to 0-22 percent, the Government announced that specific duties would be converted to ad valorem tariffs, and the number of tariff rates was reduced to three (i.e., 0, 11, and 22 percent). In October 1991, the statistical tax on exports was eliminated through the decree on deregulation.

Figure 1.13

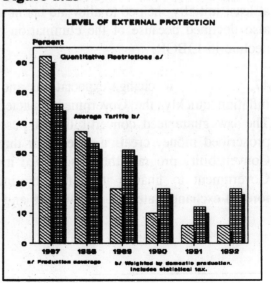

---

15   The financing implications are analyzed in Chapter 13.

44.   The deterioration in the trade balance, a consequence of massive capital inflows and fixed convertibility that deprived the Government of the exchange rate instrument, compelled the Government to use commercial policy to achieve an effective devaluation.   In October 1992, the Government announced measures to increase the competitiveness of exports in the form of partial tax rebate; on average, rebates would be raised from 8 to 13 percent.   The Government also decreased slightly the average tariff on imported goods but increased the across-the-board statistical tax from 3 percent to 10 percent.   Thus, while nominal average *ad valorem* taxes fell slightly, the average effective tariff rose from 14.8 percent to 19.8 percent.   At the same time, it lowered the maximum *ad valorem* tariff from 35 percent to 20 percent, thus narrowing tariff dispersion.

45.   **Financial System.**   The publicly-owned housing and development banks, long subject to political influence and dependent on government financial support, are undergoing major restructuring.   The National Development Bank (BANADE) and the National Housing Bank (BHN) closed their branches in March 1990 and reduced their staff by almost 75 percent.   The Government is now considering liquidating BANADE and closing BHN's remaining retail functions.   The Government also is moving to form a "second-tier" bank that will be managed and ultimately owned by the private sector for its investment needs.

Macroeconomic Results

46.   Fiscal performance has improved notably in the last two years.   The primary balance moved into surplus in 1992 for only the second time in the last two decades.   The combined deficit fell from 10.5 percent of GDP in 1989 to a projected 0.6 percent surplus in 1992. Automatic transfers to the provinces and social security increased in 1991/92, which prevented aggregate expenditures from falling more; these-- at least initially--helped to alleviate latent structural deficits there as well.   Interest costs also declined because of the elimination of the quasi-fiscal deficit and because of the decline in LIBOR.

47.   To change expectations and increase investor confidence so as to lower inflation quickly, the Government enacted the Law of Convertibility, in April 1991. The law guaranteed convertibility of pesos to dollars at US$1:A$1, and effectively proscribed money creation other than through increases in net foreign reserves.   The Convertibility program thus disciplined monetary policy and limited the powers of the Government to finance its deficit by inflation.[16]   The Law markedly reduced the foreign exchange rate risk to investors and the inflation risk to business and labor.

---

16   The Central Bank still can use reserve requirements as a instrument of monetary policy.   It also can affect government dollar-denominated bonds in its reserve backing (though these monetary aggregates are legally limited to less than 10 percent of reserves) through open-market operations to the extent of "excess" in international reserves or by varying the amount of government funds.

Figure 1.14

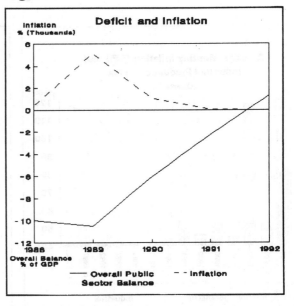

48.   As a consequence, the macroeconomic situation improved dramatically. The elimination of the deficit on the basis of sustainable policies made it possible to bring inflation down (Figure 1.14). As inflation fell, capital returned, and the increased availability of credit produced an economic recovery. The creditworthiness of the Government --as reflected in the secondary market price of private external debt--improved (Figure 1.15).

Figure 1.15

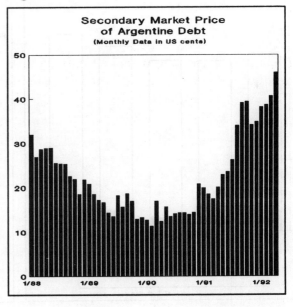

49.   Most important, the program initiated a strong and sustained economic recovery, rising incomes of the poor, and new employment creation. Because of the reforms of the public sector and consistent macroeconomic policies, the economy has grown rapidly since 1990. The economic expansion has increased real GDP by more than 15 percent (Figure 1.16). At the same time, investment rates have increased and international liquid reserves have more than tripled since 1990, and now back virtually the entire money base. Most important, indicators of poverty show substantial improvement. Unemployment has fallen to less than 6.9 percent, despite the incorporation of new workers

Figure 1.16

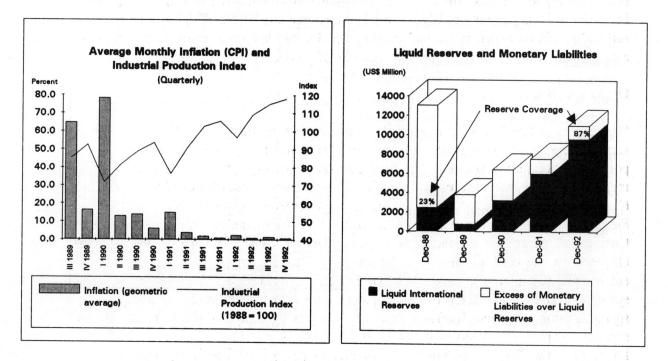

Average Monthly Inflation (CPI) and Industrial Production Index (Quarterly)

Inflation (geometric average)

Industrial Production Index (1988 = 100)

Liquid Reserves and Monetary Liabilities

(US$ Million)

Reserve Coverage

87%

23%

Liquid International Reserves

Excess of Monetary Liabilities over Liquid Reserves

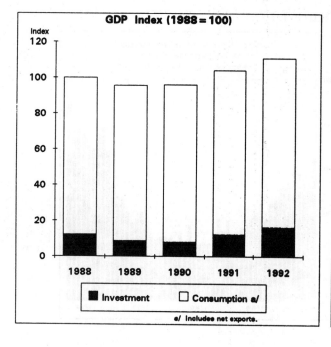

GDP Index (1988 = 100)

Investment   Consumption a/

a/ Includes net exports.

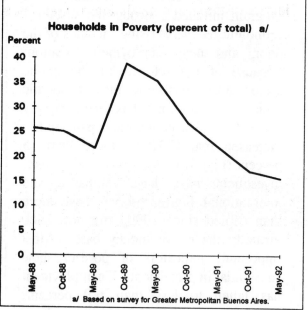

Households in Poverty (percent of total) a/

a/ Based on survey for Greater Metropolitan Buenos Aires.

into the labor market. The number of households unable to achieve an income twice thatnecessary to purchase the minimum nutritional basket has fallen from 25.7 percent in 1988 to 15.6 percent in 1992. While much remains to be done--and that is the subject of this report--it is worth underscoring that the last three years have witnessed a major turn away from the economic policies of the last 40 years.

Outline of Study

50.   The following chapter describes the organization of the Argentine public sector. The second part of the present study examines revenues with chapters on tax policy and tax administration. The third part examines expenditures, with chapters on major functional expenditures at the national level--social expenditures (Chapters 5 and 6), defense expenditures (Chapter 7), and expenditures through the Presidency (Chapter 8). The economic sectors are treated as part of the discussion on public investment in Chapter 12, except for expenditures on tax collection, treated in Chapter 4. Separate chapters are devoted to the three largest recipients of federal transfers--the public enterprises (Chapter 9), provincial governments (Chapter 10), and social security systems (Chapter 11). Each of the chapters reviews the major problems in the sector, spending programs, and discusses their effectiveness in achieving their objectives. A separate chapter is devoted to the quasi-fiscal deficit of the Central Bank and inflation financing of the Treasury (Chapter 13). A final chapter projects revenues, expenditures, and financing to the year 2000, indicates areas of uncertainty, and quantifies the fiscal impact of the recommendations in this report.

CHAPTER 2. THE ARGENTINE PUBLIC SECTOR

1.   The Argentine public sector is an aggregation of several administrative jurisdictions, woven together in a complex system of transfers, often with conceptually different fiscal accounts. To give transparency, this chapter begins with a discussion of concepts behind the different consolidations and accounting methodologies used in this report. To establish comprehensiveness, the subsequent section then disaggregates revenue mobilization and expenditures by jurisdiction for the whole public sector. Finally, the chapter concludes with an overview of expenditures by function for the national administration.

2.   Three conclusions are worth underscoring at the outset. First, the Argentine public sector can only be understood when viewed through several lenses-- level of government, economic and functional classifications, cash and accrual accounts-- hence the importance of the first section. Second, the provinces constitute the most important element of the Argentine public sector when measured by expenditures, a point emphasized in the second section. Third, the role of the Federal Government has shrunk dramatically--because of the administrative reform, decentralization, and privatization--to the point where its main functions are to raise revenues, provide for defense, and provide policy orientation for the provinces; almost half of expenditures in the national budget are transfers to the provinces, public enterprises, health funds, and other spending entities over which the Federal Government exercises only partial control.

A. Concepts and Definitions

Jurisdiction and Level of Government

3.   The Argentine public sector is comprised of the Federal Government, provinces, health funds, and the financial public sector. The Federal Government includes the national administration (synonymous with the Treasury), public enterprises, and the national social security system. The national administration comprises the central administration (Ministries), decentralized agencies, and special accounts; it has generally not been necessary to disaggregate these accounts in this report. The provincial level of government includes 22 provinces as well as the Municipality of Buenos Aires and Tierra del Fuego. Although these have their own public enterprises and social security systems, this report does not disaggregate these expenditures.[1] This report also includes the quasi-public health insurance funds (*obras sociales*) because they are funded through a federally mandated wage tax as well as transfers from the public budget. The financial public sector includes the Central Bank, 4 nationally administered banks, and 23 provincial banks.

4.   As an overview, total public expenditures amounted to about 40 percent of GDP--US$60 billion in 1992. In broad strokes, federal expenditures constitute roughly 60 percent of all public expenditures in the nonfinancial public sector (Table

---

1   See World Bank, *Towards A New Federalism*, June 1992 for a more detailed treatment of provincial public finances.

2.1). The national administration (the Treasury) comprises the central administration (Ministries), decentralized agencies, and special accounts. It has accounted for about one-third of federal expenditures and one-fifth of total expenditures. Also, within the federal administration, public enterprises have administered expenditures roughly equal to the Treasury, though with the privatization program it share of expenditures is falling. The share of the social security system, also comparable in level to the Treasury, has been rising in recent years, as the Government has increased the percentage payment of accrued obligations. Provincial spending as a share of GDP is estimated to have fallen in recent years. Even though their revenues have increased, provinces have struggled to reduce their deficits, so the gap is closing. Their collective expenditures are 50 percent larger than the Treasury's. Finally, the quasi-public health insurance funds (*obras sociales*), funded through a federally mandated wage tax as well as transfers from the public budget, are the most opaque of public expenditures; the Government does not require public reporting on these expenditures, which are estimated using data from the mid-1980s. Before analyzing flows in greater detail, it is important to clarify methods of consolidation and define key fiscal concepts.

Table 2.1: Expenditures Share by Level of the Nonfinancial Public Sector, 1990-92
(As Percent of GDP)

Level of Government	1990	1991	1992
Federal Government	26.1	23.5	22.4
National Administration-Treasury a/	11.0	9.5	8.5
Central Administration	6.8	6.4	7.2
Decentralized Agencies	2.4	1.6	0.7
Special Accounts	1.8	1.5	0.6
Public Enterprises	9.5	8.0	5.7
Social Security	5.7	6.0	8.2
Provinces and Municipalities	13.2	13.5	12.8
Health Funds	3.8	4.2	4.7
Total	43.1	41.2	39.9

a/ Net of transfers to public enterprises, social security, and provinces.

Source: Government Fiscal Accounts and Bank staff estimates.

Consolidations and Concepts

5.   This report uses different consolidations, depending on the analytical lens. The previous chapter presented the fiscal accounts according to international conventions. Only net transfers to the provinces and the health funds are included, and these components of government are assumed to be in balance. The federal public enterprises in this presentation are shown in the current account as recipients of transfers as well as having either positive or negative noninterest (operating) balances, which are included in current savings; their expenditures for investment are recorded separately in the capital account. Social security taxes are shown as revenue, and social security payments appear as transfers to the private sector.

6.　　　　This treatment of course does not show the total revenue or expenditure activity of the public sector. For that reason, the report as appropriate uses the concept of *gross federal expenditure*, which includes the total expenditure of public enterprises in federal expenditures of the nonfinancial public sector. Table 2.1 presented *total public expenditures*, including the estimated gross revenues and expenditures of the provinces, as well as revenues and expenditures of the health funds. Generally, revenues and spending by the provinces and from the health funds are not included in the totals unless otherwise specified.

7.　　　　In addition, the report includes the concept of the *combined public sector,* which is the balance of the overall public sector including the deficit of the Central Bank and implicitly the whole financial public sector. The quasi-fiscal deficit is the earnings on Central Bank assets less interest on liabilities (deducting interest income on loans to public entities that will not be paid as uncollectable losses in the years in which they accrue). This is treated in Chapter 13 in detail.

8.　　　　The concept of *primary surplus* is the balance for the nonfinancial public sector before interest payments. Because the report concentrates on the governmental accounts, this concept does not include the provinces or health funds. The *operational primary surplus* excludes any capital revenues from asset sales from the noninterest balance of the nonfinancial public sector, and is intended to convey the underlying fiscal effort during a period of high privatization receipts.

The National Budget (Treasury) and Fiscal Accounts (Savings-Investment)

9.　　　　The national budget presents the Treasury accounts, which deal solely with the national administration. Historically, only the national budget was presented to Congress for its approval; in 1988, the Government began to inform Congress of quasi-fiscal expenditures through the Central Bank at the time of budget submission, but these did not require approval. As will be seen below, Treasury expenditures are a relatively small portion of the Argentine state because not only are Treasury expenditures low relative to the rest of the state, but because more than half of these are transfers to other executing units outside the jurisdiction of the state. Revenues associated with the co-participation law are not recorded in the budget as a transfers, since these legally are the property of the state. The proposed law governing public financial administration will change Congress's role by requiring the Government to submit the consolidated public accounts to Congress and request its approval to change the overall level of indebtedness.

10.　　　　The fiscal accounts presented in the (Savings-Investment presentation)(*Esquema Ahorro-Inversion*) are more comprehensive since they show the gross expenditures of the Federal Government on a disaggregated basis as well as the main transfers among principal executing units. These fiscal accounts are the basis for macroeconomic programming. Since 1986 the accounts have not included the provinces, other than federal transfers to them. Prior to that date, provincial revenues and expenditures were also shown. However, the automatic provisions of the 1987 revenue-sharing law and the emphasis on insulating provincial accounts from the national accounts to enforce discipline was the justification for taking these out of the national accounts.

11.　　　　　Another idiosyncracy of fiscal accounts in Argentina is the treatment of interest payments. Since 1982, the domestic interest bill has been calculated on a real basis, meaning that only the real component of domestic interest payments is contained in the savings investment fiscal accounts. This was done for macroeconomic programming purposes based on the belief that the Government would be able to roll over the nominal portion of its debt; in fact, this proved impossible after 1989.[2] In 1992, with the return of price stability and the post-Plan Bonex dollarization of the domestic debt, the Treasury changed the fiscal accounts to carry the full nominal portion of the interest bill in the accounts.

Cash and Accrual Accounts

12.　　　　　Argentine accounts are maintained on different bases, and the distinction between the cash and accrual accounts is particularly important (discussed at length in Annex 2.1). Revenues and expenditures recorded on an accrual basis that produced NFPS balances that were as much as 1.5-3.0 percent of GDP more in deficit than the cash accounts (Annex Table A2.1.1). The budget and executed expenditures are presented to Congress and the public solely on an accrued basis. Since these were presented in nominal terms, budget limits usually soon lost their relevance, and during the late 1980s bore little relationship to actual spending.

13.　　　　　The reasons for the differences were related neither to accounting for foreign interest payments nor to social security. Foreign interest payments in the cash accounts were recorded on an accrual basis throughout the period, perhaps in recognition that they would have to be paid. Social security payments, the largest source of present public sector arrears, were not recorded in either set of accounts. Instead, the discrepancy between cash and accrual was attributable to the effects of high inflation on delayed actual revenue receipts and expenditures, the effects of expenditure delays associated with deferring payments (especially of the so-called 13th month (annual bonus) salary in December into January) for macroeconomic purposes, the effects of delaying payments to suppliers, and the effects of inadequate recording in both sets of accounts. In general, revenues in the accrual accounts were lower on a cash basis in 1987-89 (rising inflations and long collection lags) and higher after 1990 (falling inflation and shorter lags); expenditures, particularly in 1990, were always higher on an accrued than a cash basis.

14.　　　　　The cash accounts were used in the latter part of the decade for macroeconomic programming on the theory they best reflected the effects of net balances on monetary emission. This was accurate except insofar as the public sector was incurring debt through arrears unregistered in the accounts, and which, since known to the private sector, influenced expectations about future inflation and therefore present money demand. This was especially true in 1990, when the Government formally suspended payment to suppliers. The accrual accounts register the total changes in

---

2　　Because of weaknesses in the Treasury's office in calculating domestic interest and the foreign interest bill, in 1990 the IMF began to use the Central Bank's calculation of these payments, usually on a nominal basis. For these reasons for 1990/91, the IMF numbers may differ from the official accounts during those years. The Treasury and Central Bank began to coordinate more effectively in late 1991, so the discrepancy disappeared in the 1992 accounts.

indebtedness of the public sector in a given period; the deficit may be overstated, however, to the extent that inflation actually reduced real outlays associated with delays between the time expenditures were committed and when they were recorded. The two sets of accounts tended to converge after 1990 with reduced inflation and improved cost accounting and expenditure registration in the Treasury.

15.　　　　This report uses the accrual basis accounts, except in the Chapter 13 discussion of sources of finance, because the accrual accounts by and large present a more accurate picture of the state's total liability to the private sector over the longer periods analyzed in the report, and they are consistent with the post-1992 data on the macroeconomic program. Using the accrual accounts also facilitates an understanding of the complex transfers among the public sector, the subject of the next section.

B. Revenues and Expenditures by Level of Government

16.　　　　The total nonfinancial public sector in Argentina is shown in Table 2.2, organized according to revenue sources and expenditure uses among the various segments of Government for 1992. Revenues are shown by source along the vertical axis of the table, and use across the horizontal axis. Total federal revenues are shown on the far right of the table, and total 31 percent of GDP. This accounts for about three-quarters of all revenue mobilization effort including public enterprise revenues on a gross basis. The Treasury, comprising the central administration and special accounts, accounts for 17 percent of GDP in revenue. However, the Treasury spends only 9 percent of GDP, after netting out coparticipation transfers to the rest of the public sector (see expenditures under national administration), and only 6.4 percent after interest payments and other transfers to the private sector are subtracted. The national budget does not include revenues collected and disbursed to the provinces under the revenue sharing law (law of co-participation). These are legally deemed to be the property of the provinces. Expenditures of the National Administration are discussed in greater detail below.

17.　　　　The social security system receives funds from the VAT, direct taxes, and from its own collections drawn from the wage tax in 1992. It therefore is dependent on general revenues even as it accumulates a not insignificant flow deficit and a massive actuarial deficit. This would change with the proposed tax and social security reforms (see Chapter 11). Its expenditures, listed as "other", are solely for pensions.

18.　　　　Public enterprise sales and current expenditures in 1992 include most importantly the state oil company (YPF), the coal company (YCF), the hydroelectric power generating companies (Yacyreta, Hidronor, and Salto Grande), and the postal company (ENcotel). While most of their revenues are from sales (and hence are not shown in conventional consolidations), they collectively receive US$2 billion in transfers directly from the budget. In 1992, most of these transfers are dedicated to Yacyreta to complete the giant hydroelectric project and to the railways, the latter of which incur operating losses amounting to more than US$1 million per day. Reforms underway are designed to reduce these transfers, and they are projected to decline in 1993 (see Chapter 9).

Table 2.2a: Argentina - Public Sector Revenues, Expenditures and Flow of Funds, 1992
(As percent of GDP)

	Federal Government				Health Funds	Provinces	Total
	National Administration (Treasury)	Social Security	Public Enterprises	Total Federal Government			
Revenues	10.1	7.9	6.0	24.0	4.7	13.2	41.9
Current Revenues	8.8	7.9	6.0	22.7	4.7	13.2	40.6
Federal Government	8.8	7.9	6.0	22.7	0.1	8.2	31.0
Treasury a/	9.9	0.0		9.9	0.0	7.2	17.1
Transfers to other PS b/	-1.1		0.0	-1.1	0.1	1.0	0.0
Social Security		7.9		7.9			7.9
Public Enterprises			6.0	6.0			6.0
Health Funds c/				0.0	4.53		4.5
Provinces d/						5.0	5.0
Financial Public Sector							0.0
Capital revenues	1.3			1.3			1.3
Expenditures	8.5	8.2	5.7	22.4	4.7	12.8	39.9
Current Expenditures	7.3	8.2	5.2	20.7	4.7	11.0	36.3
Wages	3.6		1.2	4.8		6.7	11.5
Goods	1.6		4.0	5.6		1.6	7.2
Interest	1.7		0.0	1.7		0.1	1.8
Transfers to Priv. Sector e/	0.4	8.2	0.0	8.6	4.7	2.6	15.8
Capital Expenditures	1.2		0.5	1.7		1.9	3.6
Net Balance	1.6	-0.3	0.3	1.6	0.0	0.4	2.0
Memo:							
Expenditures	8.5						
Plus:Transfers to other PS	1.1						
Minus: Interest	1.7						
=Non-interest Budget	7.9						

26-Jan-93

a/ Includes non-tax revenues and tax revenues.

b/ Excludes transfers derived from tax revenues (see note a/).

c/ Estimated by taking the ratio of health taxes to social security wage tax and multiplying by social security revenue.

d/ These figures are derived from the Federalism report, April 1992. The total and the composition of provincial revenues
    and expenditures are those of 1990 (in percent of total revenues). In addition, transfers from the Central Government
     to provinces in 1992 (Education and Health) are equivalent to a 0.75 of GDP increase in the wages bill.

e/ Includes transfers to private and public universities.

Source : Ministry of Economy, 1992 Budget and Fiscal Accounts, January 1992.

Table 2.2b: Argentina - Public Sector Revenues, Expenditures and Flow of Funds, 1992
(US$ million)

	Federal Government				Health Funds	Provinces	Total
	National Administration (Treasury)	Social Security	Public Enterprises	Total Federal Government			
Revenues	15454	12087	9180	36721	7141	20197	64059
Current Revenues	13464	12087	9180	34732	7141	20197	62070
Federal Government	13464	12087	9180	34732	214	12546	47493
Treasury a/	15147	0	0	15147	0	11016	26164
Transfers to other PS b/	-1683	0	0	-1683	214	1530	61
Social Security	0	12087	0	12087	0	0	12087
Public Enterprises	0	0	9180	9180	0	0	9180
Health Funds c/	0	0	0	0	6927	0	6927
Provinces d/	0	0	0	0	0	7650	7650
Financial Public Sector	0	0	0	0	0	0	0
Capital revenues	1989	0	0	1989	0	0	1989
Expenditures	13005	12546	8721	34273	7141	19661	61075
Current Expenditures	11169	12546	7956	31672	7141	16769	55583
Wages	5508	0	1836	7344	0	10205	17550
Goods	2448	0	6120	8568	0	2433	11001
Interest	2601	0	0	2601	0	199	2800
Transfers to Priv. Sector e/	612	12546	0	13158	7141	3932	24232
Capital Expenditures	1836	0	765	2601	0	2892	5493
Net Balance	2448	-459	459	2448	0	536	2984
Memo:							
Expenditures	13005						
Plus:Transfers to other PS	1683						
Minus: Interest	2601						
=Non-interest Budget	12087						

26-Jan-93

a/ Includes non-tax revenues and tax revenues.

b/ Excludes transfers derived from tax revenues (see note a/).

c/ Estimated by taking the ratio of health taxes to social security wage tax and multiplying by social security revenue.

d/ These figures are derived from the Federalism report, April 1992. The total and the composition of provincial revenues and expenditures are those of 1990 (in percent of total revenues). In addition, transfers from the Central Government to provinces in 1992 (Education and Health) are equivalent to a 0.75 of GDP increase in the wages bill.

e/ Includes transfers to private and public universities.

Source: Ministry of Economy, 1992 Budget and Fiscal Accounts, January 1992.

19.　　　　　The health funds, which administer a tax on wages, are estimated to mobilize about 4.7 percent of GDP, and are the least transparent of public accounts. The funds receive some US$200 million in direct transfers from the budget to the Superintendency of Health Funds (ANSSAL), which is supposed to be sufficient to cover the deficit of the system, though it is believed that the funds are incurring arrears with their suppliers (see Chapter 5). Some portion of past arrears will be consolidated in the BOCON.

20.　　　　　The provinces are collectively the largest net expenditure agent in the comprehensive public sector. This in itself reveals a major issue: Provinces spend 12.8 percent of GDP but themselves raise only 4.3 percent of their total required revenues. The balance between federal and provincial net expenditures (i.e., spending less revenues) is heavily weighted in favor of the provinces. Of 15 countries recently surveyed, for example, Argentina's provincial governments had the largest net expenditure and its Federal Government the largest net surplus.[3] This creates an incentive for provinces to spend resources since they do not have to pay the political cost of raising taxes. Treasury transfers to the provinces include coparticipated revenues of 7.7 percent of GDP, which are not recorded in the Treasury accounts, and 1.2 percent which are listed in the budget for selected programs (see Chapter 10).

C. Budget Expenditures by Function: the National Administration

National Budget

21.　　　　　The national budget covers about 10 percent of GDP in noninterest expenditures, about US$15 billion. The memo item in Table 2.2 provides the statistical bridge between the comprehensive expenditure picture and the Treasury accounts in the national budget: from the 9.1 percent in GDP in total Treasury expenditures, subtract the 2 percent of GDP in interest payments and then add back the transfers to the public sector of 2.7 percent of GDP shown under revenues. The Treasury programmed noninterest expenditures of US$15 billion for 1992.

22.　　　　　A disaggregation of the national budget underscores the limited control the Federal Government has over spending. Of the US$15 billion in noninterest expenditures, only US$7.8 billion was spent directly by the national administration, and US$7.2 transferred to other executing jurisdictions (Table 2.3). In other words, the national administration actually executed only 12 percent of total public sector spending in 1992. Improving spending efficiency cannot therefore solely focus on the national administration.

23.　　　　　Of the US$7.8 billion in noninterest expenditures, 76 percent was spent in four areas: defense (32 percent), economic sectors (19 percent, primarily tax collection and highway investment), the Presidency (16 percent), and social sectors (10

3　　See Anwar Shah "Perspectives on the Design of Intergovernmental Fiscal Relations," World Bank Working Papers, July 1991, WPS 726, pp. 82-83. This survey was based on 1987 data for Argentina; the situation since then has, if anything, become more accentuated.

percent). The Legislative and Judicial Branches absorb the remainder. The composition over the last three years has remained relatively stable, though significant shifts have occurred since the early 1980s.

24.	Military spending, now about one-third of 1980-82 levels, represents an important domain for budget policy, an amount that is higher when military pensions of some US$900 million (shown as Treasury obligations) are included. Spending for the economic sectors, under the auspices of the Ministry of Economy, is mainly for revenue mobilization and highway expenditures. The Presidency constitutes a diverse set of activities, and because of its oversight of the nuclear power program, represents the most investment activity of any national jurisdiction. Social sector spending is carried out through the Ministries of Health and Social Action, Education, and Labor. The largest single program is the US$900 million FONAVI housing program, an earmarked portion of the fuel tax which is transferred directly to the provinces' local housing institutes.

25.	"Treasury obligations" are a separate jurisdiction, though they are in fact executed through ministerial jurisdictions. Three quarters of these treasury obligations are transfers to the public enterprises and military pensions. The rest--nearly US$900 million--are funds administered by the Treasury to improve salaries of selected labor Table 2.3. National Budget, 1992 groups with the administration as required during the fiscal year. These are slated for phasing down as fiscal administration improves in 1993.

26.	A given *jurisdiction* rarely covers all expenditures in its principal *function*. The Ministry of Education, for example, is responsible for only about two-thirds of expenditures on education and research at the national level (Table 2.4). The table reveals the diverse expenditures for higher education and research, evident in the proliferation of substantial expenditures for low-productivity scientific research. Similarly, the Ministry of Health and Social Action is responsible for only about three quarters of health spending.

27.	On the other hand, selected ministries have spending responsibilities across several issue areas: the Presidency and the Ministry of Health and Social Action have extremely diffuse spending authorities, with major programs in multiple areas of competence. In the case of the Presidency, these areas range from public administration to nuclear power. The Ministry of Health and Social Action spends only US$640 million of its US$1.3 billion budget on health, and the remainder is for welfare programs. Subsequent chapters of this report present the budget by jurisdiction aggregated along the broad lines in Table 2.4 because jurisdictions have spending authority.

Table 2.3: Argentina - Federal Non-interest Expenditures by Functional Group
(US$ million)   8-Feb-93

| | Total | National Administration | | | Transfers a/ | As percent of: | |
		Total	Current	Capital		Total	National Administration
Legislative and Judicial Branches b/	695	676	631	45	19	4.6	8.7
Senate and Congress	308	302	300	3	6	2.1	3.9
Judiciary	387	374	331	42	13	2.6	4.8
Presidency and Foreign Ministry	1447	1240	740	500	207	9.6	15.9
Presidency	1178	1055	584	470	123	7.8	13.6
Foreign Ministry	269	185	156	30	84	1.8	2.4
Ministries of Interior and Justice	951	684	626	58	267	6.3	8.8
Defense	2696	2470	2385	86	225	18.0	31.8
Ministry and Joint Chiefs	1004	779	767	12	224	6.7	10.0
Army	743	742	734	9	0	4.9	9.5
Navy	451	450	442	9	0	3.0	5.8
Air Force	499	498	442	57	1	3.3	6.4
Social Sectors	3310	804	704	99	2506	22.1	10.3
Education c/	1391	474	406	68	917	9.3	6.1
Health	476	223	211	13	253	3.2	2.9
Housing d/	1100	19	19	1	1081	7.3	0.3
Welfare	141	59	42	18	82	0.9	0.8
Labor	202	27	27	0	174	1.3	0.4
Economic Sectors	1844	1487	1173	314	357	12.3	19.1
Tax and Customs Administration	687	680	664	16	8	4.6	8.7
National Highway System	321	221	88	133	100	2.1	2.8
Agricultural e/	405	294	215	78	111	2.7	
Others	432	292	206	87	139	2.9	3.8
Treasury Obligations f/	4066	416	416	0	3650	27.1	5.3
Salary Enhancements	355	288	288	0	67	2.4	3.7
Public Enterprises	2100	0	0	0	2100	14.0	0.0
Military Pensions	897	0	0	0	897	6.0	0.0
Provinces g/	421	42	42	0	379	2.8	0.5
Others	294	86	86	0	208	2.0	1.1
Total	15009	7777	6675	1102	7232	100.0	100.0

a/ "Own" spending of national administration; transfers by economic classification ("incisos" 31, 32, and 61).
b/ Tribunal de Cuentas included in Senate and Congress.
c/ Includes US$724 million for universities.
d/ FONAVI Housing Fund administered by Ministry of Health and Social Action.
e/ Includes MOSP expenditures in INTA, agriculture policy, grain storage and veterinary medicine.
f/ Does not include revenue sharing under law of coparticipation; consists solely of jurisdiction 91.
g/ Includes aid to Tierra del Fuego and Buenos Aires and Provincial Education Fund.

Source: 1992 Congressionally-approved Budget (February 1992) and Contaduria General de la Nacion.

Budgetary Transfers

28.   Transfers in the Argentine budget[4] amount to US$7.2 billion, nearly half the noninterest budget. These transfers include US$2.1 billion for provincial programs other than coparticipation, US$2.1 billion for public enterprises, nearly US$221.0 billion for the universities and research institutes, and US$900 million for military pensions (Table 2.5). In addition to US$10.9 billion in automatic coparticipated tax transfers, the extra-coparticipation resources sent to the *provinces* of US$2.1 billion are transferred through 27 separate programs, ranging from the largest, FONAVI, the housing program, to the small program to help veterinary medicine. The largest expenditures are for housing (US$900 million), aid to Buenos Aires and Tierra del Fuego (US$300 million), supplemental transfers for secondary education (US$200 million), the Tobacco Fund, benefitting primarily Tucuman, and the national highway fund (US$100 million, respectively); in addition, the Government spent US$194 million to finance the provinces through the Provincial Deficit Fund.

29.   The *public enterprises* also receive about US$2.1 billion. In the 1992 budget, 30 percent went to the railways, 20 percent to Hidronor, and 15 percent to Yacyreta, as well as roughly 10 percent each for SEGBA, Agua y Energia, and YPF. Transfers also include funds for the COVIARA housing program for the Defense Ministry and the Reinsurance Institute (INDER). Although these transfers have risen since 1990, they are slated to be phased down to under US$400 million by 1994 (as discussed in Chapter 9).

30.   *Higher Education and Research* accounts for another US$900 million in transfers. About US$800 million is to support the tuition-free public universities, and another US$100 million is to support the technology institutes (CONOCIT) in the Presidency.

31.   Finally, the Treasury supports *pensions and health systems* through transfers to the respective social security systems of the military, coast guard, and police force. The *obras sociales* receive US$211 million through the national health regulatory agency (the ANSSAL).

---

4   Transfers shown under line 31-32 of the national budget which are distinct from the concept of transfers in the fiscal accounts (Savings-Investment Accounts). The latter includes coparticipated revenues not included in the budget; transfers to public enterprises, provinces (other than coparticipation), universities, and military pensions are common to both; while several less important transfers are included only in the budget.

Table 2.4: Argentina - Expenditures by Jurisdiction and Function, 1992
(US$ millions)

9-Feb-93

	Administration	Defense	Security	Health	Welfare	Education & Research a/	Economic Development	Total
Legislature and Judiciary	654	0	0	15	6	20	0	695
Senate and Congress	268	0	0	15	6	20	0	308
Judiciary	387	0	0	0	0	0	0	387
Presidency and Foreign Ministry	513	0	0	0	7	248	679	1447
Presidency b/	244	0	0	0	7	248	679	1178
Foreign Ministry	269	0	0	0	0	0	0	269
Mins. of Interior and Justice c/	320	0	571	2	58	0	0	951
Defense	6	1616	476	39	215	39	303	2696
Ministry d/	0	114	476	0	215	14	182	1000
Army	6	729	0	3	0	5	0	743
Navy	0	383	0	24	0	8	35	451
Air Force	0	388	0	12	0	13	86	499
Joint Chiefs	0	3	0	0	0	0	0	3
Social Sector Ministries	0	0	0	534	1433	1343	0	3311
Education e/	0	0	0	48	0	1343	0	1391
Health and Social Action	0	0	0	485	1232	1	0	1718
Health f/	0	0	0	485	0	1	0	486
Social Action	0	0	0	0	132	0	0	132
Housing g/	0	0	0	0	1100	0	0	1100
Labor and Social Security	0	0	0	0	202	0	0	202
Economic Sectors	712	0	0	29	0	134	969	1844
Tax and Customs Admin.	687	0	0	0	0	0	0	687
National Highway System	0	0	0	0	0	0	325	325
Others h/	24	0	0	29	0	134	644	832
Treasury Obligations	548	18	120	22	927	254	2176	4066
Salary Enhancements i/	54	18	120	22	7	2	131	355
Public Enterprises j/	55	0	0	0	0	0	2045	2100
Military Pensions	0	0	0	0	897	0	0	897
Provinces	183	0	0	0	0	0	0	183
Others k/	257	0	0	0	24	251	0	532
Total	**2752**	**1635**	**1168**	**641**	**2647**	**2039**	**4128**	**15010**

a/ Groupings based on government categories, except "Education & Research, which consists of education and "science & technology," finalidad 8.

b/ Expenditures in education & research are CONICET and CNEA's research program; those in economic development are in CNEA projects.

c/ Regular and Federal Police forces.

d/ Security expend. are the National and Coast Guards; econ. dev. programs are Fabricaciones Militares; welfare is the National and Coast Guard pensions.

e/ Expenditures are primarily transfers to universities and high schools.

f/ Expenditures for ANSSAL and general health care.

g/ Consists of three primary housing projects, FONAVI, World Bank, and Urban Development.

h/ Expenditures in various programs, principally the Tobacco Fund, FEDEI, grain storage, INTA, and veterinary medicine.

i/ Transfers form the Treasury to government agencies and ministries.

j/ Primarily consists of transfers to Railroads, Yacyretá, YPF, and other energy sector enterprises.

k/ Administrative expenditures include transfers to international organizations; education expend. is a reserve account for secondary education.

Source: 1992 Congressionally-approved Budget (February 1992) and Contaduría General de la Nación

Table 2.5: Transfers from the 1992 Budget

(US$ millions)   9-Feb-93

	Total	Provinces	Public Enterprises	Education & Research	Obras Sociales	Pensions	Others
Legislative and Judicial Branches	19	0	0	0	0	13	6
Senate and Congress a/	6	0	0	0	0	0	6
Judiciary Pensions	13	0	0	0	0	13	0
Presidency and Foreign Ministry	205	4	0	111	0	2	89
Presidency b/	121	4	0	111	0	0	6
Foreign Ministry c/	84	0	0	0	0	2	82
Ministries of Interior and Justice d/	266	194	0	0	0	55	17
Defense	225	0	0	0	5	212	7
Ministry of Defense e/	224	0	0	0	5	212	7
Army	0	0	0	0	0	0	0
Navy	0	0	0	0	0	0	0
Air Force	1	0	0	0	0	0	0
Social Sectors	2502	1229	0	838	211	174	50
Education f/	917	66	0	838	0	0	13
Health g/	269	24	0	0	211	0	35
Housing h/	1081	1081	0	0	0	0	0
Welfare	61	58	0	0	0	0	3
Labor i/	174	0	0	0	0	174	0
Economic Sectors	363	318	0	29	8	0	8
Tobacco Fund	102	102	0	0	0	0	0
National Highway Board (DNV)	100	100	0	0	0	0	0
Others	161	116	0	29	8	0	8
Treasury Obligations	3650	379	2103	0	0	897	272
Salary Enhancements j/	184	0	0	0	0	0	184
Public Enterprises	2103	0	2103	0	0	0	0
Military and Police Pensions (IAF)	897	0	0	0	0	897	0
Provinces k/	379	379	0	0	0	0	0
Private Sector Grants	4	0	0	0	0	0	4
Foreign Transfers l/	84	0	0	0	0	0	84
Total	7231	2125	2103	978	224	1352	449

a/ Includes Tribunal de Cuentas.
b/ Consists primarily of grants and scholarships to research institutes and individuals from CONICET.
c/ Aid to bordering countries.
d/ Transfer to provinces is the ATN Provincial Deficit Fund.
e/ Coast Guard and National Guard Pensions.
f/ Includes grants to universities.
g/ Includes ANSSAL.
h/ Includes FONAVI.
i/ Non-contributory pension system; includes old-age pensions, veterans of the Malvinas, and Congressional pensions.
j/ Includes Treasury programs 112, 114, and 181.
k/ Includes program for Tierra del Fuego and Buenos Aires and Provincial Education Fund.
l/ Payments for dues and services to international organizations.

Source: 1992 Congressionally-approved Budget (February 1992) and Contaduría General de la Nación.

CHAPTER 3. FEDERAL REVENUES AND TAX POLICY

1.   In general terms, a tax system should be administratively efficient, equitable, neutral on prices and on the cost of the factors of production, and flexible with respect to macroeconomic and expenditures policies. Over the last three years, the Menem Administration has increased tax collection significantly by improving the efficiency of the tax administration and by enacting some important tax policy changes such as the extension of the VAT to almost all goods and services. By broadening the base of the efficient taxes, policy changes in the last 36 months have increased revenues and made the system more efficient and economically neutral.

2.   However, there is still room to improve the present tax system with regard to the equity, neutrality, and flexibility objectives. Direct taxes are almost non-existent in Argentina and labor effectively is taxed more heavily than capital. The revenue system is also inflexible because of severe constraints associated with earmarking. The August 1992 proposal to finance the social security system with a higher share of co-participated revenues will partially address the neutrality problem.

A. Revenue Problems

Historical Performance

3.   Over the last two decades, the tax system has performed poorly. The ratio of tax receipts to GDP between 1970 and 1991 varied widely (see Table 2.7 of the Statistical Appendix). Tax collection virtually collapsed in 1975, but revenues steadily recovered in the ensuing years. Buoyed by a series of reform measures, they reached 18 percent of GDP in 1980. Tax revenues deteriorated markedly during the Alfonsin Administration, except during 1985 and 1986. Tax reform was an integral part of the *Austral Plan*, initiated in June 1985. The anti-evasion powers of DGI were increased and VAT rates were unified at 18 percent; however, on balance, the reform was unsuccessful and improvements proved to be transitory, resulting more from price stability than from improved policy and administration. The fragmentation of the tax system was not reduced, and revenues continued to erode due to fiscal incentives and evasion.   In 1989, as a result of two hyperinflations, tax revenues reached an unprecedented low level (12.7 percent of GDP). Since the beginning of the Menem Administration, tax revenues have increased significantly and are expected to be as high as 22.5 percent of GDP in 1992.

4.   Three prominent features of Argentina's tax system characterized the 1980s. First, tax revenues showed a secular tendency to fall after 1981. Second, collections became increasingly volatile (especially quarterly). During the 1980-89 period, the ratio of taxes to GDP varied between a low of 12.7 percent in 1989 and a high of 18.7 percent in 1980. The tax system also became progressively more inefficient as the share of efficient taxes in total revenues decreased. Several factors explain this volatility and deteriorating efficiency.

5.   **Unstable Macroeconomic Environment**. Changes in macroeconomic conditions have affected tax revenues in Argentina through at least two channels. First, variations in GDP have affected tax receipts through changes in the taxable base. In the 1980s, real economic growth averaged only 0.78 percent, thereby depressing significantly VAT revenues. Second, tax revenues were affected by inflationary volatility through the Olivera-Tanzi effect. During the 1980s, the estimated loss of tax revenues due to this effect was over 1 percent of GDP and about 2 percent of GDP in 1988. Overall, the performance of the tax system has been systematically stronger during periods of macroeconomic stability.

6.   **Tax Policy and Unstable Legal Framework**. The poor performance of efficient taxes compelled the Government to rely increasingly on easily attained revenues. The result was the composition of revenues progressively shifted from modern taxes to inefficient but easily collectable ones (tax handles in Figure 3.1). Modern taxes include income taxes, social security contributions, the VAT, and wealth taxes.[1] The contribution of tax handles to fiscal revenues increased significantly during the second part of the 1980s and reached 4.4 percent of GDP in 1990. Revenues from both efficient taxes and tax handles are negatively correlated over the entire period. Tax handles were usually established for a limited time by the legislature and their yield

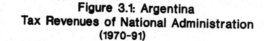

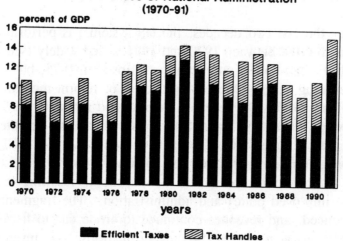

**Figure 3.1: Argentina
Tax Revenues of National Administration
(1970-91)**

---

1   Modern taxes satisfy three basic conditions: (i) generalized application on solid economic grounds; (ii) the existence of a current account in their administration--since there is a separation between the tax return and tax payments; and (iii) the delegation of important administrative duties to the tax-payer himself or to third parties economically involved with the taxpayer. Tax handles, although relatively easy to administer, are not general taxes, and typically are not economically sound. However, they share with modern taxes condition (iii), since most of the administrative work is performed by the taxpayers.

quickly diminished as taxpayers devised schemes to avoid them. Indeed, the extensive use of tax handles may have contributed to greater variability in revenues. Their diminishing returns, coupled with legislative hiatuses between approval of new handles, resulted in sudden revenue loss and equally sudden increases, complicating the task of both tax administration and policymakers. Moreover, tax handles tended to reduce the equity of the tax system. The burden of taxation tended to fall disproportionately on those of medium and low incomes because these individuals are less able to avoid paying these taxes.

7. **Tax Loopholes**. The expansion of tax expenditures and the associated opportunities for tax evasion were the most important reasons for the deterioration of the efficient taxes. For example, industrial promotion laws were developed as a result of piecemeal legislation dating as far back as the 1960s; however, these laws were substantially expanded by the end of the 1970s. At the end of 1987, virtually all investment activity was subsidized to some extent (the only exception being in the federal capital). The fiscal cost of the national and regional promotion schemes as well as the scheme for Tierra del Fuego was estimated at about 1.5 percent of GDP in 1989. Those economic actors who ended up being fully taxed were discouraged from economic activity by the relatively higher tax burden imposed on them to compensate for the revenue lost through evasion. Some of the deficiencies were attributable to the tax laws; but by far the largest inequities arose from an uneven compliance with the laws that was not effectively countered by the tax administration. Non-compliance led to serious inequities because those who got away without paying tax were treated beneficially compared with those taxpayers who, for whatever reason, ended up paying the full amount of tax due.

8. **Tax Administration Performance**. Poor performance of the tax administration during these years was central to the erosion of tax revenues and gave rise to rampant evasion. Tax administration in Argentina was chaotic and reflexive instead of intentional and remedial. Attempts to compensate for public revenue shortfalls by changing the tax laws created an unstable legal framework that resulted in an unmanageable and inequitable tax system. The constant battle with inflation induced a short-term approach to the administration of tax collection, with little attention to accuracy of compliance or implementation of remedies needed to produce an efficient tax administration in the long term. In addition to the Olivera-Tanzi effect, high and volatile inflation greatly complicated tax administration. The excessive fragmentation of the tax system, variability in legislation, and the complex, confused, and at times contradictory laws and regulations produced a legal framework difficult to enforce. Tax administration and loopholes are discussed in Chapter 4, while the remainder of this chapter focuses on the tax policy framework--its efficiency, equity, flexibility, and neutrality.

B. Tax Policy: Toward Greater Efficiency

9.   The Menem Administration, through several decrees, resolutions, and regulations,[2] has markedly strengthened the major efficient taxes. These included: the broadening of the VAT base at a uniform rate, the elimination of minor taxes, and the enactment of the gross-assets tax as a minimum income tax. While the broad thrust of tax policy has been to improve revenues and the system's efficiency, other legislation eroded the income tax (repeal of capital gains, enactment of investment expensing) and, in some cases, tax policy has been inconsistent (repeal of net wealth tax and subsequent enactment of the tax on personal goods).

Value-Added Tax

10.   The major achievement of tax reform legislation under the Menem Administration was broadening the base of the value-added tax. Tax reform legislation and improvements in tax administration resulted in a significant increase in VAT collections over the last 3 years. Under the Menem Administration, VAT receipts increased from 9.1 percent of GDP in the second quarter of 1989 to 6.6 percent of GDP in the fourth quarter of 1992 (Figure 3.2). While part of this increase is due to an improvement in macroeconomic conditions, the important effort in tax administration and tax legislation has contributed to this evolution. On average, only about 30 percent of the increase in VAT revenues is explained by the decline in inflation through the Olivera-Tanzi effect.[3]

11.   These improvements occurred in stages, beginning with Congressional passage of the general VAT reform in December 1989. In February 1990, the VAT was implemented on goods, and the rate was reduced to 13 percent. Also, the regime for small taxpayers was changed, establishing the concept of non-registered responsible persons, sales to whom were taxable at a higher rate.[4] As part of the Industrial Promotion Regime (see Chapter 3), suppliers from promoted firms continued to be exempt from the VAT. In April 1990, this exemption regime was suspended, thereby contributing to the increase in VAT revenues. In September 1990, the base of the VAT was broadened to include most services. (Previously, the VAT had been applicable only to those services specifically listed in the law; the new law contained few exemptions.) In February 1991, the general VAT rate increased from 15.6 to 16 percent; a year later it was increased to 18 percent. In the case of sales of gas, electricity, water, and other public utilities (except sales to residences), when the purchaser is registered the rate of tax is 25 percent. An 11 percent rate applies to the provision of telephone services to final consumers. Finally, in March 1992, the general VAT rate was increased from 16 to 18 percent.

---

2   The number of laws, decrees, and resolutions was 15, 36 and 3, respectively, in 1989, and 7, 53 and 33 in 1990.

3   See Annex 4.1.

4   Law 23,760 established a tax on financial services, based on value added calculated under the addition method. While this is not formally part of the VAT, it fulfills the functional role of taxing value added of the financial sector.

Fig. 3.2: VAT Revenues (1988-I-1991-IV)

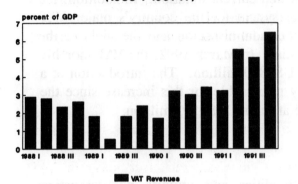

VAT Revenues

Fig. 3.3: Trade Tax Revenues (1988-I-1991-IV)

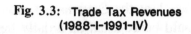

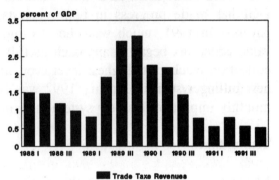

Trade Taxe Revenues

Fig. 3.4: Excise and Fuel Tax Revenues (1988-I-1991-IV)

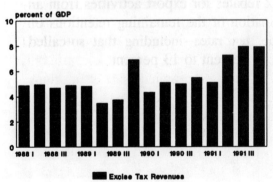

Excise Tax Revenues

Fig. 3.5: Income Tax Revenues (1988-1-1991-IV)

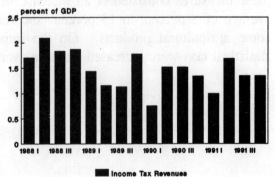

Income Tax Revenues

12.　　　　To improve the efficiency of the tax administration, all registered value-added taxpayers are now required to file monthly returns, and the administration of the tax is to become fully automated to handle the extra volume of returns. Payment can now be made through the banks. The fiscal reform package of mid-February 1990 required VAT and income-tax payments to be made within 10 days to reduce the collection lag; the Government also instituted an indexation system, under which taxes due would be adjusted on a daily basis for estimated current inflation. In addition, the DGI has made progress in improving its filing system for the country's major VAT payers. In 1991, much was done to improve tax administration and the yield of the value-added tax began to approach its full potential. In March 1992, the VAT monthly collection reached its highest level ever, about US$880 million. The introduction of a new billing system in January 1992 was largely responsible for this increase since the monthly impact of this new system is estimated at about US$100 million.

Trade Taxes

13.　　　　Argentina mostly exports commodities and imports non-competing intermediate and capital goods. The trade regime reflected an extreme overall anti-export bias. The Government made considerable progress in liberalizing trade since the change of government in July 1989. Substantial reductions in import tariff rates and in their dispersion implemented in late 1989 and early 1990 have greatly abetted the Government's medium-term goal of a tariff structure with only three to four rates, ranging from 10-20 percent. In February 1991, the tariff band was reduced further to 0-22 percent, it was announced that specific duties would be converted to *ad valorem* tariffs, and the number of tariff rates was reduced to three (0, 11, and 22 percent). In October 1991, the statistical tax on exports was eliminated and import taxes were slightly increased to offset the negative impact of these measures on fiscal revenues. The average tax rate on imports probably increased about 2 percent.[5] Finally, in November 1992, the Government modified its commercial policy. On the export side, these measures consisted of an increase in the tax rebates for export activities from an average of 8 percent to 13 percent and the elimination of the remaining retentions on some agricultural products. On the import side, tax rates--including that so-called statistical tax--were increased from an average of 17 percent to 13 percent.

5　　Although the rates of import taxes declined dramatically during the last four years, it is not clear whether the effective rate of protection declined as well. The effective rate of VAT on imported goods is much higher than on domestic goods because tax evasion is less prevalent.

Table 3.1: Trade Taxes
(in percent of GDP)

	Export Tax	Import Tax	Statistical Tax	Total
1988	0.24	1.04	0.2	1.48
1989	1.64	0.55	0.3	2.49
1990	1.35	0.31	0.42	2.08
1991	0.20	0.41	0.41	1.02
1992	0.00	0.94	0.30	1.24

Source: Government of Argentina.

14.　　　　As a result of the trade liberalization policies, export tax revenues declined over the 1985-90 period. While the ratio of export tax revenues to GDP was about 2.2 percent in 1985, it was estimated at only 0.2 percent in 1991 and almost 0 percent in 1992. Import revenues also declined during the 1988-90 years as import duties were progressively reduced, and import levels were historically low. Since the end of 1990, import tax revenues increased from 0.27 percent of GDP in the first quarter of 1991 to 1 percent in the third quarter of 1992. This increase can be explained by the boom in imports resulting from the macroeconomic policies, the recent raises in import tariffs (see above), and the improvement in customs administration (see Chapter 4).

Energy, Excise and Miscellaneous Taxes

15.　　　　Under pressure to increase revenues, the Menem Administration relied on several excises and *ad hoc* taxes in 1989 and 1990. Taxation on energy-related products has become progressively more important (see Figure 3.4) and contributed to distortions in relative prices. Rather than being linked to international prices, or to marginal cost, energy prices are set by the Government in ways that attempt to accommodate conflicting priorities of different sectors and special interest groups, as well as a variety of macroeconomic objectives.[6] The gasoline tax rate increased to 33 percent in February 1991 and the revenues collected from the fuel tax increased from 0.4 percent of GDP in the second quarter of 1989 to 2.7 percent in the third quarter of 1991. Also, a one-time tax known as the solidarity contribution and an emergency tax on the ownership of automobiles, yachts, and airplanes were established in October 1989, as well as an emergency tax on the profits of financial entities. In January 1990, the Government fixed the tax on bank debits (i.e., bank checks and similar transfers) at 3 per mil, effective as of January 1, 1990. In February 1991, the rate of the tax on debits was raised to 12 per mil, with 9 points of the tax being creditable against the taxpayer's income tax and VAT liability (half against each).[7] However, in February

---

6　　For a detailed discussion on energy taxes in Argentina, see "Argentina: Tax Policy for Stabilization and Economic Recovery," a World Bank Country Study, 1990.

7　　See Law 23,905 (published Feb. 18, 1991), art. 1. Under Law 23,549 (Tax on Bank Debits), which had been in effect through 1989, 70 percent of the tax had been creditable against the income tax.

1992, the rate was reduced to 3 per mil, with no portion being creditable against another tax.

16.   The recent improvement in VAT collection permitted the elimination of some excise taxes. Decree No. 2284/91, which dealt with deregulation of the economy, repealed the taxes on transfers of equity [8] and debt [9] instruments. It exempted the issuance of certain securities from the stamp tax. It also repealed a number of miscellaneous taxes on specific products, the proceeds of which were designated for dealing with trade regulation and promotion. The progressive elimination of inefficient taxes, such as debits and stamp taxes, is closely related to the performance of efficient taxes. If revenues of direct taxes grow satisfactorily, then inefficient taxes can be reduced further; otherwise pressure to keep the deficit low will undoubtedly lead to the retention of inefficient taxes.

Direct Taxes

17.   Further improvement in the tax system in Argentina is closely related to the future performance of direct taxes. Argentina relies on direct taxation much less than other countries. Revenues collected from income taxes declined from 1.9 percent of GDP in 1987 to 0.8 percent of GDP in 1991. In countries with a comparable per capita income level, the average income tax to GDP ratio was about 8.1 percent. In contrast, Argentina relies more than countries of similar income levels on direct taxes on wages and salaries to finance social security funds. Specific recommendations are advanced below.

18.   Part of this performance was attributable to poor administration. As an illustration, between 1975 and 1986, only about 17 percent of potential taxpayers were known to the tax administration; only 8 percent bother to file a tax return; and less than 4 percent pay income tax.[10] In addition, the tax was poorly designed with improper indexing of loss carry-forwards, numerous exceptions, and the effective exemption of virtually all capital income and most labor income.

19.   Over the last two years, the Government has implemented several measures to modify direct taxes. The tax reform legislation created a new tax on business assets and eliminated the taxes on company net worth, personal wealth, and capital gains--all of which were administratively costly and low yielding. In addition, the tax reform legislation made several changes to the personal and corporate tax laws. In February 1990, income taxes on corporations were lowered to 20 percent from 33 percent, with a minimum tax payment of 1 percent of assets; income taxes on individuals were simplified to a new 10-30 percent rate with 5 brackets, with a withholding tax for wage earners. Finally, the February 1991 package raised the assets

---

8   Impuesto Sobre las Ventas Compras, Cambio, o Permuta de Divisas.

9   Impuesto a la Transferencia de Títulos Valores.

10   See "Argentina: Tax Policy for Stabilization and Economic Recovery," a World Bank Country Study, 1990.

tax from 1 to 2 percent for one year, and widened the income tax base by suspending loss carry-overs from the 1988-89 period.

20.   In spite of all these efforts, the income tax remained clearly unsatisfactory. Under these circumstances, the Government modified the legislation on income tax in April 1992 to include the following changes: (i) an increase in the rate of the corporate income tax from 20 to 30 percent; (ii) the replacement of accumulated loss carry-overs through March 1991 by a bond exchange program; and (iii) a widening of the tax base on personal wealth to include foreign assets holdings.

21.   These measures are likely to have a positive impact on tax revenues in 1993. Official projections estimate that income tax receipts may reach 3.5 percent of GDP in 1993 in comparison to 1.8 percent of GDP in 1992. However, this figure is relatively sensitive to changes in several factors. First, it is difficult to determine foreign asset holdings by Argentine residents even though the DGI has launched an aggressive campaign over the last few months. Second, this projection does not account for provisions on the future debt service of the new bond (BOCON) that will be issued to settle the problem of loss carry-overs. The BOCON would be peso-denominated, with 16 years maturity and 6 years' grace on capital and interest, and would carry the savings deposit rate of interest. The total amount of BOCON is estimated at US$2.4 billion and provisioning could reach 0.3-0.5 percent of GDP in 1993.

C. Remaining Issues

22.   The Government has made major advances in reforming the tax system. Important outcomes have been improved revenue mobilization and greater revenue efficiency. The Government can now turn its attention to second-order issues: tax system progressivity, neutrality, and flexibility.

The Progressivity of the Tax System

23.   The decline in the share of direct taxes in total revenues has adversely affected the progressivity of the tax system with respect to income.[11] While in 1970 the income tax represented 15 percent of total revenues, its share declined to 4 percent in 1991. Although some recent empirical studies have stressed that direct taxes are not as progressive as potentially expected because higher-income individuals are better able to evade direct taxation than low- and middle-income individuals, income taxes are still a major source of progressivity of the tax system in the long run.

24.   While in some cases trade taxes and VAT systems are progressive, this is debatable for Argentina. Assuming that the share of imported goods is more important for the highest income households, these taxes may contain an element of progressivity. However, in the case of Argentina, imports are less than 6 percent of

---

11   We are mainly concerned with the vertical equity of the tax system, or how to tax individuals who differ in their level of income. The question of what tax produces horizontal equity is difficult to answer. One could potentially suggest several practical bases for taxation--income, consumption, wages, and wealth.

GDP and, above all, trade taxes have declined dramatically since 1988. Consumption is mainly composed of domestic products and, in this case, indirect taxes such as the VAT are clearly regressive with respect to income.[12] The VAT rate increased substantially over the last two years, which had a negative impact on the equity of the tax system.

25. There are several ways of making the tax system more progressive. One is to reduce the regressivity of the VAT by exempting the VAT tax base goods on which low-income individuals spend heavily. This approach has two major drawbacks--it would distort consumption choices and induce administrative inefficiency and it would reduce tax revenues if this measure is not offset by an increase in the VAT rate. A second method is to allow a credit against income taxes, presumably primarily for low-income individuals. This method would complicate tax administration. None of these options contemplate transforming the VAT into a tax like the individual income tax, which is progressive at the upper level of the income distribution. Therefore, the major recommendation of the report is to strengthen rather than reduce the personal income tax (see recommendations for details).

The Neutrality of the Tax System

26. An additional remaining weakness of the tax system is its bias against labor relative to capital. While labor is heavily taxed, taxes on capital are extremely low.

27. **Tax on Labor**. Wage taxes represent nearly 50 percent of gross salary in Argentina. Pension insurance is supported by a 26 percent tax on wages; health insurance by a 14 percent tax; and the Family Fund receives 9 percent (Table 3.2).

28. While social security contributions are not extremely high by international standards, payroll taxes linked to Health Insurance and the Family Fund are higher than in all developed countries (see Table 3.3).

---

12   See "Assessing a Value-Added Tax: Efficiency and Equity," J. Granelle, *Tax Notes*, March 1988, for an illustrative example.

Table 3.2: Wage Taxes
(in percent of gross salary)

	Employers	Employees	Total
Pension Insurance	16.0	10	26.0
Payroll Taxes	17.9	6	23.9
Health Insurance for:			
Pensioners	2.0	3	5.0
Active Workers a/	6.9	3	9.9
Family Fund	7.5	-	7.5
Housing Fund b/	-	-	
Unemployment Insurance	1.5	-	
			1.5
Total	33.9	16	49.9

a/   Includes 0.9 percent contribution for the administration
of health insurance institutions.

b/   Until late 1991, employers paid 11 percent for pension
insurance and 5 percent for the Housing Fund. Law 23966
raised the pension contribution by 5 percent and eliminated
the wage tax for the Housing Fund.

Source: Government of Argentina; Bank staff.

Table 3.3: Payroll Taxes and Social Security Payments:
An International Comparison
(in percent of gross wages)

Country	Payroll Taxes	Social Security		
		Employers	Employee	Total
Argentina	23.9	16.0	10.0	49.9
Austria	5.0	22.2	15.4	42.6
France	7.1	46.4	13.9	67.4
Germany	-	18.8	17.3	36.1
Luxembourg	0.8	19.6	12.1	32.5
Sweden	5.8	30.5	-	36.3
UK	1.4	10.5	9.0	20.9
USA	-	16.0	6.7	22.7

Source: OECD (1986) and staff estimates.

29.   However, a narrow focus on social security contributions and payroll taxes overlooks the fact that individual tax rates act together to influence private decisions so that gauging the effect of taxes on incentives means understanding their interaction. The typical argument for Argentina is that high payroll taxes are offset by low direct taxes. For employment decisions, one must distinguish between the taxes that a firm or household pays and the totality of tax payments that would apply to incremental employment for an extra job or an extra hour.

30.   The impact of the tax system on the labor cost is generally measured by the effective rate of taxation on labor use.[13] This rate is defined as the difference between gross labor cost to the employer and wages net of taxes available to the worker.

---

13   For a description see "Marginal Tax Rates on the Use of Labor and Capital in OECD Countries," by M. McKee, J. Visser and P. Saunders, *OECD Economic Studies*, Autumn 1986.

The advantage of this measure is that the impact of wage taxes is taken into account together with other direct and indirect taxes. The average effective rate of labor taxation appears much higher in Argentina than in most industrial countries (see Table 3.4).

Table 3.4: The Effective Rate of Taxation on Labor Use

Country	Rate a/
Argentina	63.5
Austria	42.4
France	51.7
Germany	41.3
Luxembourg	42.1
Sweden	62.8
UK	42.7
USA	34.8
Total Weighted Average	
OECD Europe	46.3
OECD Non-Europe	33.5
OECD	43.3

a/ The effective rate of taxation on labor (ERTL) is defined as:
$$ERTL = 1 - [1 - t_{le} - t_y + t_y t_{le}]/[(1 + t_c)(1 + t_{lr} + t_{lp})]$$
where t_{le} and t_{lr} are employees' and employers social security contribution rates, t_{lp} is the payroll tax, t_y is the personal income tax rate, and t_c is the rate of indirect taxation. This calculation used the following tax rates: $t_{le} = 0.10$; $t_y = 0.30$; $t_{lr} = 0.16$; $t_{lp} = 0.239$; and $t_c = 0.116$.

Source: OECD (1986) and Bank staff estimates.

31.   The taxation of labor is relatively high in Argentina because of payroll taxes. In addition, the high indirect tax rates also contribute to the taxation of labor. In fact, an increase in indirect taxes may affect negatively the supply of labor because households will have less incentive to consume. Real wages may be bid up, thereby reducing the incentives for firms to hire additional workers. The effective rate of taxation is certainly overestimated in the case of Argentina since tax evasion lowers the effective average income tax rate relative to the legal tax rate used in the calculation. If the income tax rate were 0, the effective taxation of labor would be equal to 42.3. In such a case, the taxation of labor would not be higher than in most industrial countries--but the progressivity of the tax system would be fully eliminated. This suggests that an increase in income taxes should be compensated by a reduction in wage taxes; otherwise the cost of labor would increase dramatically.

32.   **Tax on Capital**. The tax rate on capital use is extremely low in Argentina.[14] This can be illustrated by the following example. Since October 1990,

[14] Measuring the tax rate on capital use is in all instances extremely complex. The tax code is such that the tax rate differs according to the asset and industry composition of investment, the form of finance used for the project, and whether funds are obtained directly from households or channelled through a financial intermediary.

expensing has been allowed for investments in equipment. At the same time, interest expense continues to be deductible. Thus, in the case of a debt-financed investment, the taxpayer can deduct both the cost of the investment and the cost of the interest to finance it. In the case of leveraged investments, this treatment can result in negative tax rates. In other words, the amount of revenue would be greater if the investment were completely exempt from tax.[15]

Earmarked Funds

33.   Another issue is the flexibility of the Argentine tax system. A substantial fraction of tax revenues collected at the federal level is automatically earmarked to the provinces, special accounts and the social security system. The most important source is the law governing the revenue-sharing between the Federal Government and the provinces. This coparticipation mechanism was validated in 1988 (Law 23548) by assigning 57.7 percent of the total coparticipated tax revenues to the provinces (before the August 1992 package (discussed next page)). The distribution of the fuel tax was changed in September 1991.

34.   The distribution of tax revenues that was presented in the 1992 budget is summarized in percentage of total tax revenues in Table 3.4. According to this allocation system, Provinces were the most important recipients of tax revenues transfers, about US$12,590 million. In fact, the provinces were likely to receive more revenues from taxes collected at the federal level than the central administration itself. Special accounts were expected to receive 40 percent of the fuel tax, about US$1,235 million, which was mostly used to finance the government housing program (FONAVI). Finally, the social security system were projected to receive about US$1,440 million, resulting from the partial transfer of VAT revenues.

D. The August 1992 Agreement with Provinces

35.   On August 12, 1992, the Central Administration reached an agreement with Provinces regarding the allocation of tax revenues among national administration, provinces, and the social security system. The modification became necessary to finance the transition costs associated with the social security system. In the 1992 budget, 11 percent of total VAT revenues were allocated to the social security system (the so-called Social Security VAT) and the rest was divided between the national administration (43.7 percent) and the provinces (50.1 percent). In the new system, in addition to the existing allocation described above, 15 percent of total coparticipated tax revenues will go to the

---

15   Suppose that a taxpayer borrows A$100 to make an investment. Both the rate of interest and the rate of return on the investment are 10 percent. The investment yields A$110 one year later, at which time the cash from disposition of the investment is used to pay off the loan. Before taking taxes into account, there is a net profit of zero. However, if the taxpayer is allowed to deduct the cost of the investment, there is a deduction of A$100 in year 1, and income of A$100 in year 2 (supposing that the interest of 10 is deductible from the income of A$110). In present value terms, the taxpayer is ahead, because he has in effect received an interest-free loan of A$100 from the Government. Instead of receiving tax revenue, the government has given a subsidy to the investment. The subsidy could be compensated if someone paid tax on the interest income from granting the loan, but in Argentina interest income of individuals is generally not taxable.

social security system. Therefore, the new allocation is 29.6 percent to the National administration, 49.1 percent to the Provinces, and 21.2 percent to the Social Security system. (See Table 3.4). In principle, this regime will be valid until December 1993.

36.   The Government chose to link new changes in tax policy to the social security reform.   These changes provide additional resources to the social security system, from 6.2 percent to 21.2 percent of total tax revenues.   This additional financing is particularly important since the annual transition cost of the social security system is high (see Chapter 11).

37.   The proposed package also involves a decline in the share of tax revenues allocated to the national administration and provinces.   However, provinces will get an additional US$3.8 billion in tax revenues between 1992 and 1993 as a result of the (projected) improvement in the Central Government's tax administration.   Moreover, the package insures a monthly payment of US$725 million in coparticipated tax revenues to provinces.[16]   Therefore, in case of a fall in tax revenues, the burden of adjustment would be supported by the national administration and the social security system.   A negative implication is that provinces will have less pressure to adjust their inefficient tax administration and fiscal expenditures since they will receive more coparticipated revenues in 1993 than in 1992, even though the share of total revenues is lower under the new allocation system.

38.   The allocation system would also be improved by reducing further transfers to special accounts, reallocating them to the social security system or to the provinces. While the Government has made considerable progress in reducing the proliferation of special accounts (their number and value has declined by over half since the 1990 budget year), the government housing program, which accounts for about 70 percent of the transfers to special accounts in 1992, should be reevaluated.

E. Recommendations

39.   The tax policy framework over the last two years has produced dramatic improvements in tax collection at the same time that it has evolved into a more efficient system.   The Government has markedly increased its reliance on VAT and reduced the coverage of inefficient taxes, especially those on exports.   The system now relies on four modern taxes: the general and uniform VAT, the income/assets tax, import tariffs, and excise taxes on selected final products (notably fuel, cigarettes, and alcoholic beverages).   The abolition of the inefficient taxes will be possible as revenues from efficient taxes become compatible with the current public expenditures.   The main outstanding issues are neutrality with respect to use of capital and labor and the progressivity of the system.

---

16   The Provinces also benefit from a fund of US$43.8 million per month, and an
        additional 14 percent from income tax revenues. In order to ensure the neutrality of
        the transfers of education and health expenditure responsibilities from the Central
        Government to the Provinces, additional revenues are transferred to about US$110
        million per month.

40.　　　　The Government is poised to address these issues in the context of its social security reform. One proposal would be to reduce the wage taxes by making some portion of the employers' contribution deductible against the VAT, and thus increase social security funding from the VAT and income taxes.[17] This would generate an important incentive for employers to declare social security contributions and help reduce evasion. The burden of the income tax on the middle and lower-middle class would be reduced by raising the minimum monthly taxable income. This would be a salutary step toward reducing the bias against employment, but is only a partial solution. Although the increase in the minimum taxable income will in principle improve the progressivity because of the reduction of taxation on low-income workers, it would effectively narrow the base for the income tax by excluding many mid- and upper-income taxpayers as well. While the annual average income per family is estimated at about US$19,000, the minimum taxable income is above US$20,000.

41.　　　　A more direct way of addressing both the factor bias and progressivity is to explore ways of reducing the wage taxes and increasing taxes on income from capital. Assuming that the social security system is financeable through the elimination of evasion at a 26 percent contribution rate, the Government should consider linking a reform of the health insurance system with a reduction in both the family funds and the health insurance quotas. Contributions to health and family funds account for nearly 24 percent of gross salaries, much higher than nonpension wage taxes in all OECD countries. Health reform--discussed at length in Chapter 5--and more efficient use of the family funds might permit reductions of the payroll taxes by half.

42.　　　　At the same time, the Government could increase the taxation of income from capital directly through modifications to the corporate and personal income tax. For the *corporate income tax*, the deduction of interest payments from the corporate income tax should be retained, provided that interest income is taxed at the individual level. At the same time the Government should review the expensing of investment to ensure that the depreciation deduction is consistent with economic rates of depreciation.

43.　　　　For the *personal income tax*, the Government should reintroduce taxation on income from capital, which is now virtually exempt. First, the Government should disallow the interest deduction; this would allow taxation of the interest earnings. Second, the Government should also institute taxation of at least the real portion of capital gains. Finally, the Government should not raise the already generous minimum threshold on income subject to taxation, but, as tax administration improves, lower it. In addition, the Government should eliminate miscellaneous deductions and review the possibility of taxation of fringe benefits. The effect of these measures would be to broaden the base rather than to narrow it.

17　　In that sense, this new proposal replaces the "nonwage value-added" proposal that has been abandoned by the Government. In order to limit the loss in tax revenues, this measure may be limited to export sectors. This would present the advantage to reduce the price distortion between tradable and non-tradable goods.

Table 3.5: Argentina - Revenue Earmarking, 1992/1993: Effects of the Third Quarter 1992 Agreement

	1992				1993			
	Total	National Admin.	Social Security	Provinces	Total	National Admin.	Social Security	Provinces
				-- Percent --				
Total (weighted) a/	100.0	43.7	6.2	50.1	100.0	29.6	21.2	49.1
VAT b/	100.0	37.7	11.0	51.3	100.0	21.8	24.4	53.9
Income c/	100.0	42.3	0.0	57.7	100.0	19.3	32.0	48.7
Assets d/	100.0	38.7	0.0	61.3	100.0	36.0	15.0	49.0
Excise taxes	100.0	42.3	0.0	57.7	100.0	36.0	15.0	49.0
Cigarette	100.0	42.3	0.0	57.7	100.0	36.0	15.0	49.0
Others	100.0	42.3	0.0	57.7	100.0	36.0	15.0	49.0
Trade Taxes	100.0	100.0	0.0	0.0	100.0	100.0	0.0	0.0
Fuel e/	100.0	47.0	0.0	53.0	100.0	47.0	0.0	53.0
Personal Goods	100.0	0.0	100.0	0.0	100.0	0.0	100.0	0.0
Others, coparticipated f/	100.0	42.3	0.0	57.7	100.0	36.0	15.0	49.0
Others g/	100.0	0.0	0.0	100.0	100.0	0.0	0.0	100.0
				-- US$ millions --				
Total a/	24899	10870	1544	12485	32730	9701	6953	16075
VAT	13067	4926	1437	6703	17857	3892	4348	9617
Income	2540	1074	0	1466	6076	1173	1944	2958
Assets	719	278	0	441	539	194	81	264
Excise taxes	2293	970	0	1323	2474	890	371	1213
Cigarette	1410	597	0	814	1515	545	227	743
Others	883	373	0	509	959	345	144	470
Trade Taxes	1760	1760	0	0	2154	2154	0	0
Fuel	2647	1244	0	1403	2424	1139	0	1285
Personal Goods	107	0	107	0	101	0	101	0
Others, coparticipated	1459	617	0	842	718	258	108	352
Others	308	0	0	308	387	0	0	387

a/ Percentages reflect earmarking policies in effect during first semester of 1992; values are calculated based
   on 1993 budget.   In 1993, Provinces are guaranteed a minimum of US$725 million from coparticipated tax revenues.
   Weigthed total represents share of total tax revenue.
b/ 11% share of VAT which goes to social security in 1992 in turn is split 90% to SSS, and 5% to provinces
   and national administration.   In 1993, an additionnal US$1,836 million are transferred from the National
   Administration to Provinces in order to finance the transfers of education and health responsabilities and the
   coparticipation fund of US$43 million per month.
c/ In 1993, 14% of income tax is directly alotted to provinces; remainder follows 57.66% rule.
d/ 50% of assets is for education fund, of which 65% goes to provinces in 1992; remainder follows 57.66% rule.
e/ 40% of provinces' 53% share goes to FONAVI.
f/ Consists of financial services, bank debit, tax arrears payments, and others; bank debit and financial services
   taxes.
g/ Includes fixed-rate deposit tax , provincial deficit fund, electricity, and others; fixed-rate and provincial deficit fund.

   Source: Government of Argentina, Ministry of Finance.

44.   Reducing the payroll tax through reduction of health funds contributions, which are fully deductible from the base of the personal income tax, will automatically increase the base of the personal income tax. Lower contributions can lead to an increase in after-tax wages since a reduction in labor cost leads to an increase in labor demand, which in turn affects positively real wages (and can also reduce unemployment). The positive impact on real wages will be reinforced if a decline in the price level occurs. As argued by Samuelson (1966),[18] the price of capital would be positively influenced since labor costs directly affect the production cost of investment goods. Finally, simultaneous reductions in the wage tax, coupled with other reforms in service delivery, will also improve the equity of the tax system.

45.   The August 1992 agreement with provinces helps redress the earmarked imbalance between the social security system and other demands on Treasury resources fixed in the coparticipation regime. The package assigns an additional 15 percent of total coparticipated tax revenues to the social security system, but does not compel provincial governments to adjust as much (as originally intended by the Government). Tax revenues allocated to provinces are projected to increase by about US$3.8 billion between 1992 and 1993. The agreement left in place less effective transfers, such as FONAVI. Transfers other than coparticipation should be considered as an instrument of structural adjustment and in that sense should be linked to improvements in the fiscal performance of the provinces.

---

18   Samuelson P.A., "A New Theorem on Nonsubstitution", in *The Collected Scientific Papers of P. Samuelson*, MIT press, 1966.

CHAPTER 4. TAX ADMINISTRATION

1.   The deterioration in tax administration has been a major reason for declining tax revenues in Argentina during the last decade. The capacity to administer efficient taxes was eroded by inattention to management and systems development. Moreover, frequent legislative changes and the imposition of new levies greatly complicated the work of the General Tax Board (DGI), resulting in the accumulation of inconsistent bureaucratic procedures. Finally, the penalties for evasion were low and loopholes proliferated. This chapter, after a brief evaluation of the sources of change in tax effort, reviews changes in the enforcement regime and loopholes, and then tax administration itself.

A. Tax Administration: Overall Evaluation

2.   The increase in tax revenues in 1986 was entirely attributable to the low level of inflation during the first year of the Austral Plan (1985) and the subsequent increase in inflation dramatically reduced tax receipts.[1] However, recent improvements appear to be more permanent. The estimated results presented in Figures 4.1-4.4 suggest that much of the increase in real tax revenues over the last two years has been attributable to a considerable improvement in tax administration.[2] To illustrate, Figure 4.3 indicates that the average monthly increase in VAT revenues over the 1989-91 period (8.15 percent) is explained by an increase in the Olivera-Tanzi effect (2.42 percent), as well as an increase in the nominal tax rate (0.84 percent) and in the tax effort (6.69 percent) and a decline in the tax base (-2.01 percent). The substantial increase in tax effort reflects the extension of the VAT's base (in particular to services), and improvement in the tax collection effort.

3.   Over the 1989-91 period, tax effort on VAT appears to have been most significant at the beginning of 1990 and during the third quarter of 1991; however, a decline occurred in the third quarter of 1990 and from December 1990 to February 1991. The same pattern was generally found for other coparticipated taxes such as the profit tax, sales tax, and assets tax. Trade tax revenues declined progressively over the 1989-91 period as a result of the trade liberalization program. Results suggest, however, that on average the authorities increased their effort via improved administration over this period.[3]

---

[1]   For a discussion of this period, see "Argentina: Tax Policy for Stabilization and Economic Recovery," pp. 12-16.

[2]   The approach is presented in detail in Annex 4.1.

[3]   This is also suggested in Table 3.1.

Figure 4.1: ARGENTINA (1989-91)
Tax Effort-Coparticipated Taxes

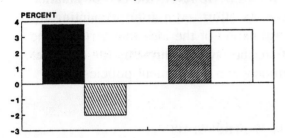

Figure 4.2: ARGENTINA (1989-91)
Tax Effort - Profit Tax

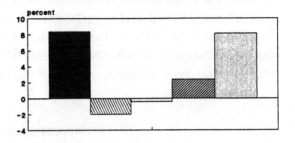

Figure 4.3: ARGENTINA (1989-91)
Tax Effort - VAT

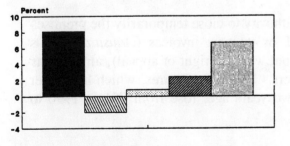

Figure 4.4: ARGENTINA (1989-91)
Tax Effort - Import Tax

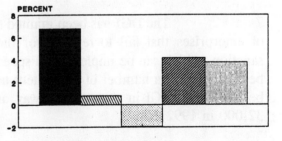

4.		Unstable economic conditions can influence revenue performance not only through the Tanzi effect but also indirectly through the tax effort. To test this hypothesis, the responsiveness of the tax effort to changes in GDP growth rate and inflation rate over the last two years is examined in Annex 4.1. The results suggest that the variations in tax effort are more likely to be the consequence of political and institutional changes, such as the reduction in exemptions, and not solely or even primarily a consequence of macroeconomic conditions.[4] However, the rate of inflation exerted a significant and negative influence on the tax effort--even after accounting for the Olivera-Tanzi effect. This represents some estimation of the idea that a rise in the rate of inflation can influence the efficiency of the tax system through, for example, changing taxpayer attitudes or loss of public confidence in government policies.

B. Enforcement and Tax Expenditures

5.		Creating a culture of tax compliance in a country where evasion has been the norm has been a major focus of President Menem personally as well as his Administration. To reduce the degree of tolerance for tax evasion, the Menem Administration has focused on increasing tax penalties, reducing tax amnesties, and (more recently) controlling industrial promotion.

Penalties for Tax Crimes

6.		Among the many strategies adopted by the tax administration has been the reactivation of existing and newly created legal capacities to enforce compliance. A new penal law, which established stiff penalties for offenders, was signed by the President in February 1990. The Law has strengthened the hand of the authorities in prosecuting tax evasion and fraud, mainly by reducing the burden of evidence required before the Government can proceed with penalties.

7.		The DGI has been granted the authority to close temporarily the premises of enterprises that fail to register for the VAT or to issue invoices (*clausura*). This sanction, which can be implemented speedily (but with the right of appeal), already has been applied to a number of delinquent taxpayers. Business closures, which had never been used by DGI in a systematic way until two years ago, rose from 751 in 1990 to 32,000 in 1992.

8.		In addition, Law 23,771, which became effective on March 8, 1990, provides a special procedure for crimes involving fraud, evasion, and omission regarding both taxes and social security contributions. It applies to infractions committed both by taxpayers and public officials, and sets forth the applicable judicial procedure. Some of the penalties provided are fines, but most are imprisonment for terms of up to eight

---

4		The impact of GDP growth did not appear significant on tax effort even if a positive relationship between GDP growth and tax effort should result from most marginal tax rates being higher than the average. The explanatory power (adjR^2) of the regressions is very low except for the value added tax.

years. DGI has been actively submitting to the courts proposals for detention on the grounds of tax evasion. Since the law was enacted, it led to 541 proposals to the courts, 76 actual detentions, and 40 fines with tax credits.

Amnesty Policy

9.   Tax amnesties are transitory suspensions of procedural law and the creation of alternative, temporary compliance rules. Even though tax amnesties may generate temporary revenue, they ultimately tend to undermine compliance with the tax laws--since taxpayers prefer to postpone paying taxes as much as possible in the expectation of a future amnesty. Repeated tax forgiveness has become a feature of the Argentine tax system, with 16 separate tax amnesties granted over the last 33 years (an average of one every two years) in the form of forgiveness, moratoria, and ready compliance schemes.[5] Under the Menem Administration, the decrees regarding tax amnesty policy are Decree No. 292/91, published in March 1991; Decree 1646, published in August 1990; and Decree No. 1299, published in September 1989.

10.   The generic term for these decrees, which all contain similar provisions, is "spontaneous presentation." However, it is not clear how spontaneous this presentation is because in many cases taxpayers taking advantage of amnesties are already under investigation by DGI. The decrees specify that if DGI has initiated procedures for criminal penalties, or has formally initiated an investigation of the taxpayer, then the amnesty does not apply; however, there are a number of loopholes in these rules that in practice allow many taxpayers to claim the amnesty--even if they are under investigation. An example of these loopholes is the following: if 30 days have elapsed between the "last intervention" of DGI and the taxpayer's presentation, the amnesty is available, even if DGI has been investigating the taxpayer; the amnesty is unavailable only with respect to the tax and the period under investigation.

11.   In November 1991, a decree on tax amnesty was published covering tax obligations up to January 31, 1991. The amnesty decree provides for forgiveness of penalties and interest, but not the underlying tax obligation or its indexation for inflation. The forgiveness of penalties and interest is a significant benefit, and generally taxpayers are better off than if they had paid their tax when due.

12.   Amnesties constitute an admission of policy failure on the part of the tax administration. Increased DGI efficiency will be required to preclude the need for future amnesties.

Industrial Promotion

13.   The Bank estimates that subsidies to industry through promotion regimes amounted to US$2.2 billion in 1989 or more than 1.8 percent of GDP. More

---

5   Amnesties cancel taxes and penalties due to evasion in exchange for reduced compensatory tax; moratoria are restricted to interest due and inflation adjustments of taxes in arrears; and ready compliance gives more time to taxpayers and may reduce the inflationary adjustment of the amount due.

importantly, because of exemptions already granted to future projects as well as pending legislation to increase the program, the fiscal cost would have been over US$3.0 billion in 1992 if policies to curtail the program were not adopted (see Table 4.1). Reducing the fiscal costs is not easy because the Government, during the mid-1980s, granted legally binding contracts with tax exemptions for up to 15 years.

14.   At the beginning of its tenure, President Menem's Government adopted emergency measures to limit the flow of industrial promotion costs. The Emergency Law of July 1989 deferred 50 percent of industrial promotion benefits for one year beginning in August 1989 in exchange for a tax credit to be paid 24 months later (though none has been issued). Since March 1990, several additional measures have been taken. The Secretary of Public Revenue canceled the benefits of 43 firms. Decrees 435 of March 1990 and 612 of April 1990 transferred authority for industrial promotion from provincial administrations and Tierra del Fuego to the Secretary of Public Revenues, under the Ministry of Economy. This changed the incentive system governing the granting of these benefits, since provincial authorities previously had been able to, in effect, give away federal revenues. In addition, the Government replaced the provisions that allowed beneficiaries to deduct their full costs rather than value-added from taxes. Finally, the Government issued a decree canceling all extant contracts not yet in force and canceled rights to renew existing contracts.

15.   The Government also decided to step up the monitoring of the companies promoted in light of the high tax-evasion rate generated by the promotional scheme. With this objective in mind, Decree 1355/90 (August 1990) required a series of data from the companies about their original commitments--investment, employment, and production, and the extent to which they had complied with these commitments--together with the use they made of the tax benefits. About 2,400 projects had complied with this requirement by January 31, 1992. This information will provide the basis of the tax credit program.

16.   **Tax Credit Program**. To close the industrial promotion loophole, the Government decided to replace the self-monitored tax deductions with a tax credit program. Delayed several times as the consequence of administrative problems in the review process, political pressures, and unclear relationships between the federal and provincial Governments, the program was launched in November 1992 with Decree 2054/92. Adequate control of tax expenditures for industrial promotion was estimated to produce fiscal savings of about US$900 million in 1993, and cap the total cost of the industrial program at US$1.4 billion (Table 4.1).

Table 4.1 - INDUSTRIAL PROMOTION: Estimated Fiscal Costs and Savings of Reform Program
(In US$ million)

	1990	1991	1992	1993	1994	1995
Tax Expenditures Before Reforms (Projected) a/	3012	3269	3491	3945	3675	3719
Industrial Promotion	2661	2888	3085	3521	3232	3256
Existing Projects b/	2451	2468	2455	2681	2182	1996
Law 23614 (Projected) c/	210	420	630	840	1050	1260
Tierra del Fuego d/	351	381	406	424	443	463
Savings from Policy Reforms	528	822	828	2382	2256	2335
Industrial Promotion	518	760	630	2118	1929	1910
Suspension of Promotion for New Projects e/	210	420	630	840	1050	1260
50 Percent Benefit and IVA Compras Suspension f/ g/ h/	308	340	0	0	0	-172
Penalties for Non-Compliance with Emergency Law i/	0	0	0	353	0	0
Reduction in Benefits - Decree 2054 j/	0	0	0	925	879	822
Tierra del Fuego k/ l/	10	62	198	264	327	425
Fiscal Cost After Reforms	2484	2447	2663	1563	1419	1384
Industrial Promotion	2143	2128	2455	1403	1303	1346
Tierra del Fuego	341	319	208	160	116	38

a/ Includes SICE and Four Provinces programs.   Based on February 1993 information.
b/ Equal to "Costo Fiscal Utilizado".
c/ Includes US$ 210 million per year of new projects, as provided in law 23614 of September 1989, but not yet in force.
d/ Production and import levels are assumed to increase at a 4.5 percent rate after 1992.
e/ Savings from suspension of Law 23614 (footnote b).
f/ Suspension of 50 percent of benefits by the Emergency Law. Only 20 percent of the tax obligation
   is estimated to have actually been paid.
g/ It is assumed that only 50% of the IVA Compras was actually collected during 1990 and 1991. In
   1992 a judicial decision suspended the collection of the IVA Compras.
h/ The refund of the IVA Compras paid during April 1990 to December 1991 starts in 1995.
i/ It is assumed that during 1990 and 1991, only 20 percent of the tax liability from the 1989 Emergency Law
   was actually paid. This amount was announced to be paid in 1993, as a consequence of audits, including a penalty
   of 100 percent as provided by law. The refund of the original payment, as provided by Law, will also come in 1993.
j/ This measures the fiscal savings from the bond substitution process started in December 1992 (decree 2054).
k/ Includes suspension of reimbursements to the continent (June 1990).
l/ Includes 1991-92 fiscal savings from reduction in the domestic sales tax (impuestos internos); also includes 1993-95 savings
   from decree 1998/92 (November 1992), assuming a yearly percent fall of 8 % in production and import levels after 1992.

17.   Under the Decree, each beneficiary was fully audited for compliance against its original contract. Those passing the audit received nontransferable fiscal tax credits redeemable against taxes in the year of the tax collection. Those failing to reach the employment, investment, or production levels stipulated in their original contracts received a credit of sharply reduced value in proportion to their noncompliance and will be audited for back taxes. This criterion was applied on a sliding scale, according to which the greater the noncompliance the larger the number of tax credits forfeited.[6]

18.   The criterion for penalization is applied across the board to minimize the need to study each case separately. The tax credit program is based on the following principles: (i) The credit is calculated on the basis of the theoretical fiscal cost that was calculated by the authorities when the projects were originally approved. The Government is also using the information obtained by Decree 1355 for reference purposes; (ii) the credits are nontransferable and registered. They are subdivided by type of tax instead of issuing an all-purpose tax credit suitable for meeting any of the fiscal obligations of the promoted project; (iii) the original theoretical fiscal cost are adjusted by the subsequent reduction in the profit tax (from 33 percent to 30 percent) and in VAT (18 percent compared to rates between 16 and 20 percent); (iv) the credits should be issued once a year, but only after the authorities confirm that there has been no reduction in employment or production and the firm has paid all taxes due; (v) contractual commitments are measured in physical terms and the data for three years should be averaged to ensure more equitable treatment; and (vi) if projects fail to meet the startup deadline, all promotional benefits were to be eliminated.

Tierra del Fuego

19.   Exemptions granted to producers in Tierra del Fuego also constituted a source of fiscal loss--estimated to be about US$600 million in 1992 if the regime had been maintained (Table 4.1).[7] Phasing out tax expenditures to support Tierra del Fuego is necessary for both fiscal and resource allocation reasons. The electronics industry--

---

6   The tax credit reduction scale was defined as follows:

Percent Average Noncompliance	Criterion	Percent Credit Reduction
Less than 5%	No penalty	0%
Between 5% and 10%	1 for 1	Between 5% and 10%
Between 10% and 20%	1.2 for 1	Between 12% and 24%
Between 20% and 30%	1.4 for 1	Between 28% and 42%
Between 30% and 40%	1.6 for 1	Between 48% and 64%
Between 40% and 50%	1.8 for 1	Between 72% and 90%
More than 50%	2.0 for 1	100%

7   Originally, the Law 19640/72 and Decrees 1139/88 and 1345/88 provided to industrial activities located in Tierra del Fuego: (a) exemption from the VAT, (b) exemption from import tariffs (on imported inputs only), (c) subsidies exports from Tierra del Fuego to the mainland, (d) subsidies exports from Tierra del Fuego to abroad, (e) exemption from domestic sales tax, and (f) exemption from the income tax.

previously located primarily in Tierra del Fuego--has partially shifted to the mainland where costs are lower to compete with Brazil in the regional trade area, MERCOSUR.

20.   In 1991 and 1992, the Government progressively reduced the fiscal cost of the Tierra del Fuego regime. First, the Government eliminated the domestic sales tax on electronic products in November 1991 and, with it, took away the value of the exemption for Tierra del Fuego producers. Second, tax rebates on export from Tierra del Fuego to the mainland and abroad were virtually eliminated by the Decree 888 in June 1992. Finally, the Government decided the progressive elimination of the VAT exemption (Decree N.1999/92, November 1992) by enacting the following schedule: the promoted industries will pay 25 percent of the existing VAT rate in 1993, 50 percent in 1994, 75 percent in 1995 and 100 percent in 1996.

21.   With the progressive elimination of the exemption on the VAT, the major benefits for industries located in Tierra del Fuego will remain the exemption from import duties--that represented a fiscal cost of about US$80 million in 1992--and the exemption from the income tax--about US$20 million. Accordingly, the total fiscal cost of the Tierra del Fuego regime will by 1995 be reduced to a tenth of its original projected value.

C. Administrative Developments: DGI, Customs and Social Security

22.   Improved tax administration has occurred in several agencies charged with collecting national taxes: DGI, the National Customs Administration (ANA), the Social Security Administration, and other bodies. DGI is the most important of these agencies, both in revenue collected and with respect to its auditing and prosecuting powers. In 1990, DGI collected 58 percent of national revenues, Social Security 29 percent, and Customs 13 percent.   This section reviews the operational and administrative developments that have taken place in DGI and ANA. Social Security administration is discussed in Chapter 11.

DGI Administration

23.   DGI administration has improved during the Menem Administration. In 1989, a unified taxpayer identification number was developed, and in 1990 the implementation of a large taxpayer current account software was initiated. The current strategy seeks to enhance simultaneously computerization and human resources development. The administration has attempted to reactivate its managerial capacities through actions in the areas of collection management, audits and internal control, and personal policy. The DGI has markedly increased the number of audits, closures and detentions (Table 4.2). It has also developed a computer system in DGI agencies across the country.

24.   **Collection Management**. The primary functions of DGI--facilitating and monitoring taxpayer compliance and preventing taxpayer non-compliance--have until recently operated very inefficiently. The tax roster was allowed to deteriorate, while the collection system was designed to operate centrally; additionally, data were collected manually but input centrally, with a high percentage of error. The various systems used

over 2,000 programs in old, difficult to modify languages, which made their modification cumbersome and information retrieval extremely slow. Recently, the DGI administration attempted to increase the efficiency of tax collection through the use of computer software. In January 1991, this software was tested at the National Agency for Large Taxpayers in Buenos Aires and at the end of 1992 was operational in 80 other agencies. The immediate validation of the tax return against payments and the up-to-date information on collections by tax and payments decreased the number of errors by 40 percent during the first month of operation. In the medium-term, the success of this operation should lead to a reduction in errors to the level reached in countries like Mexico and Spain.

Table 4.2: Tax Administration, Indicators of Collection Effort (1987-92)

	1987	1988	1989	1990	1991	1992 a/
Collection Orders	9,668	15,137	15,841	13,089	69,548	48,708
Control						
Closures	0	0	0	751	8,157	32,000
Effective Closures	0	0	0	n.a.	5,466	17,184
Fines	n.a.	n.a.	n.a.	n.a.	40,933	n.a.
Audits and Indictments						
Indictments Initiated	20,903	33,770	25,286	39,138	179,452	n.a.
Indictments Pending	n.a.	n.a.	n.a.	n.a.	116,084	197,332
Internal and External						
Audits	25,955	21,310	13,864	20,845	41,313	n.a.
Preventive Audits	n.a.	40,475	38,483	119,969	228,821	n.a.

a/ Estimates based on first quarter of 1992 only.

Source: DGI and World Bank staff estimates.

25.   The DGI Administration seeks to duplicate this software in their 40 largest agencies, covering the largest 30,000 taxpayers responsible for about two-thirds of all revenue. Because the technology used can be adapted for use by all computers--from microcomputers to mainframes--this system can be readily disseminated to collection agencies. The 1993 objective of the Government will be to extend the system to all DGI agencies (approximately 150) and 300,000 taxpayers.

26.   In the meantime, DGI has attempted to compensate for the absence of automated systems for collection and taxpayer auditing through several local initiatives, some of which have had notable success. The LoterIVA, a lottery based on VAT receipts, has been well received, and has increased registration of transactions. Also, legal modifications have allowed more flexibility in the application of fiscal secrecy, permitting DGI to publish in newspapers lists of defaulting taxpayers, which has also curtailed fraud. Recently, performance indicators have been developed to assess critical areas of DGI actions. The system, implemented manually, collects information such as criminal cases, closure resolutions, or court appeals. This information is crucial to determine the effectiveness of the recent effort of DGI concerning tax penalties as well as to evaluate the internal performance of the agency.

27.　　　　Increased public information is necessary to improve compliance and to introduce a sense of participation, which was lacking in both instances. Current DGI efforts place more emphasis on participation and cooperation; also, semi-annual surveys of major taxpayers will be carried out and the results disseminated to the general public. Based on the results of the surveys, a plan of action will be developed to improve services. Some measures--such as better access to taxpayer current account or legislative database--are already under discussion.

28.　　　　Another aspect of the tax administration system that facilitates taxpayer compliance is the expense and degree of difficulty involved in preparing tax forms. DGI simplified the tax forms in 1992.

29.　　　　**Inspection and Audit**. Taxpayer inspections and audits have been one of the most serious prominent problems of tax administration over the last decade. The fact that audit cost exceeded revenues suggests serious problems with the auditing program. For example, between 1986 and 1989, collected revenue per audit fell from US$126 to US$34, while the average cost per audit increased from US$278 to US$838. For a long time, DGI management was unable to generate from within the necessary changes to strengthen and consolidate any long-term strategy for improving productivity. Since 1989, however, many of the problems that plagued the institutional infrastructure of tax administration have been identified, as explained below.

30.　　　　Under the current administration, DGI has addressed the audit and inspection problems by launching an extensive audit of industrial promotion beneficiaries and making a census of VAT taxpayers (*Operacion Rastrillo*). The VAT census was successfully completed in April 1991. This operation provided an impressive amount of information about potential taxpayers; moreover, the presence of DGI officials all over the country had a deterrent impact on VAT noncompliance. (To carry out the operation, DGI worked with a team of more than 3,000 agents in the field.)

31.　　　　The DGI effort and the impact of *"Operacion Rastrillo"* is summarized below:

Number of visits:	489,716
New taxpayers enlisted:	164,447
Additional registrations (spontaneous):	135,714
Presumption of evasion:	140,000
VAT errors detected:	134,601

32.　　　　The strategy also focuses on the improvement of DGI's audit capacity. This includes the development of a computer program and the use of new tax audit procedures for selected economic firms in different sectors. The recent results appear encouraging in the petrochemical and metal mechanic sectors. The administration has been able to detect interruptions in the VAT chain and to develop indicators of critical inputs to estimate taxable bases.

33.　　　　Finally, the effectiveness of DGI's inspections and audits is closely linked to the improvement of the National Tax Court operations. Taxpayers can appeal a DGI tax or penalty by lodging a formal appeal with the National Tax court. The efficiency of the court is low, in that the average waiting period for a case is almost 3 years, the court is about 8 years in arrears, and the number of pending cases increases by an average of 15 percent yearly. The perceived inefficiency of the court also plays a role in decreasing voluntary taxpayer compliance, since it provides an easy way to defer or even eliminate payments.

34.   **Personnel Policy and Training**. DGI operates independently of general public sector personnel regimes. This allows it to offer somewhat more attractive working conditions than other government bodies. However, existing union contracts have demanded a flat compensation curve, as well as ensuring job security, which make it difficult for management to improve the quality of the work force. Qualified staff were difficult to attract and retain, morale was low, and staff usually held more than one job to compensate for low wages. For a long time, DGI management was unable to plan or carry out reforms to improve productivity. Until 1990, the high turnover in the position of Director General of DGI aggravated this situation.

35.   A new general organizational structure for DGI was approved by Presidential Decree in June 1991. This new classification is in line with modern managerial concepts (e.g., planning, operations, and support) and should function well with minor lower-level modifications.

36.   Nonetheless, labor agreements continued to impede DGI management then making changes in staff necessary to improve productivity. Remuneration, career path, and other human resource issues of the proposed structure were reviewed and embodied in a Collective Work Agreement between DGI and its union, AEDGI, to which most DGI staff belong. DGI management refused to renew a Collective Work Agreement which provided job security and the excessively generous leave policy. The Ministry of Labor was asked to arbitrate; the verdict was not accepted by the union, which appealed to the Labor Chamber at the Appeals Court. The verdict of the Chamber favored DGI, with the union's only recourse now being the Supreme Court. The Chamber's verdict was unanimous, so it is expected that DGI's version of the Collective Work Agreement will be signed. This new agreement established incentives including promotion procedures to increase productivity.

37.   Training recently has become an area of concern for DGI. Increased training and managerial attention to staff is required to improve the culture of the organization. A training program has been developed with the University of Buenos Aires[8] and an impressive number of internal courses have been implemented--903 courses attended by 15,300 agents. About 70 percent of the courses were technical while the rest were introductory classes for new agents. The Department of Training offers courses in accounting, auditing, and general tax legislation. Finally, the long-

---

8   The classes scheduled for 1991 were attended as follows:
Information System Auditing: 30 agents.
Audit Programming: 35 agents.
Inspectors/Auditors Program: 240 agents.

neglected Research Department is expected to be strengthened in the short run. Lack of long-range planning has been a chronic deficiency at DGI, with monitoring and decision-making more difficult because of the paucity of appropriate information available to management. Modern technology and management information systems must be introduced. For example, there is only one computer in the Analysis and Statistical Department (with a staff of about 25 people).

Customs Administration

38. The closed economy of the last decades granted ANA enormous operational discretion and intervention capacity. However, the impressive trade liberalization of 1988-91 changed the ANA's role. Instead of collecting trade duty revenues, the main task of this agency is now to collect VAT and import excise taxes.

39. In response to this modified role, the Menem Government has begun a reform of the customs administration. The official strategy is based on the revision of operational norms and laws as well as the development of the managerial capacity of the administration. The objective is to eliminate the legal and operational limits of the existing system through the simplification of the legal framework, the harmonization of the classification code, and the development of a computer system.

40. In Argentina, tax evasion and exemptions have been traditionally widespread. Although there is no way of quantifying tax evasion with precision, a recent examination revealed the existence of more than 6,400 fraudulent transactions for an estimated value of US$500 million between 1986 and 1988. In Table 4.3, the ratio of the effective import tax rate to the nominal tax rate indicates the extent to which exemptions have cut the revenue base of import taxes. Over the 1989-91 period, exemptions on average were about 39.3 percent. The proportion of exempt imports however decreased from 49.2 percent to 39.1 percent between October 1988 and October 1991. This decline is the result of an increased effort by the customs administration as well as the reduction of legal tax rates. The lighter burden on local firms reduces the incentive to seek exemptions on imported inputs.

41. To demonstrate its determination against the widespread use of exemptions and fraud, the Menem Administration's first action was to apply the existing tax laws to a number of fraud cases--which had been a US$200 million scandal during 1986/87. Customs authorities recently confiscated merchandise and vehicles used for fraudulent operations. At the same time, the authorities attempted to reduce corruption. Special monitoring of operations at the Ezeiza International Airport led to the discovery of more than 1,000 cases of fraud resulting in the indictment of 15 former customs officials--including one former customs administrator.

42. The complexity of the customs codes also led to pervasive fraud and abuse. The complexity of the tax structure in Argentina originates in the multiplicity of rates and the number of products classified in the export and import Codes. The number of tariff codes increased over the years to shelter individualized benefits within the customs codes. The import and export codes delineated 12,000 and 7,000 products, respectively. The reduction in the number of rates to three in February 1991 (expanded

to 4 a year later) and the application of a reduced products list (8,000) and unified external trade code in January 1992 have simplified customs administration considerably.

43.　　　　The valuation of goods is also crucial for the smooth functioning of the trade tax system. Recently, the authorities have proved that undervaluation in customs was one the major contributors to the loss of VAT revenues. Because the technology used by ANA at the beginning of the 1990s was almost the same as in the 1930s, the strategy also focused on the development of an efficient automated system for trade taxes. Argentine authorities elected to proceed with an adapted version of the integrated customs administration software developed by the French customs administration (SOFI)--called MARIA in Spanish. The Government began to implement this software in mid-1991 and expects it to be operational by mid-1993 in the Ezeiza Airport, and during 1994 in the rest of the customs offices. In addition, the registration of documents and operational procedures has been simplified by the new administration.

44.　　　　Finally, ANA is developing a new personal policy. The major goal is to establish a clear distinction between the managerial and operational functions of the administrators. This effort allowed the firing of corrupt personnel, and strengthened management. However, the current, highly concentrated decision structure should be replaced by a more effective division of work. Recently training also has become an area of concern within ANA.

Table 4.3: Import Taxes, 1988-91 a/

Period b/	Average Nominal Rate (1) c/	Average Effective Rate (2) d/	Tax Exemption (1)/(2) e/
Oct. 21, 1988 - Oct. 27, 1989	22.26	12.20	1.82
Oct. 19, 1989 - Dec. 15, 1989	24.06	12.24	1.97
Dec. 15, 1989 - Jan. 10, 1990	17.17	9.64	1.78
Jan. 1, 1990 - Apr. 20, 1990	13.84	8.14	1.70
Apr. 21, 1990 - Jan. 1, 1991	13.61	9.66	1.41
Jan. 5, 1991 - Apr. 4, 1991	12.76	9.23	1.38
Apr. 2, 1991 - Oct. 30, 1991	8.41	5.13	1.64

a/　　Based on a sample of imported products representing about 25 percent of total imports.
b/　　Each period corresponds to a change in the trade regime.
c/　　Weighted legal tax rates.
d/　　Total actual import tax collection divided by total imports.
e/　　The difference between (1) and (2) can be explained by the exemption of certain imports from taxes and by the failure to collect taxes when legally due.

Source: Argentine Customs and Bank staff estimates.

45.　　　　Collections from import taxes have tripled as a share of GDP from 1990 to the first semester of 1992. Because the changes in the legal framework have been so important during the last two years, it is difficult to evaluate the improvement in customs administration. However, the results presented in Table 3.1 suggest that the efficiency of customs administration has increased between 1989 and 1991. The ratio of the nominal rate of import tax to the effective rate decreased from 1.82 percent in 1989 to 1.64 percent in October 1991 (see Table 4.1). The highest level of efficiency appears to have been reached in the first quarter of 1991.

D. Recommendations

46.　　　　Improvement of the tax administration has been a major factor in the recent good performance of the tax system. This effort was possible largely owing to the coincidence of two factors that had not existed in Argentina for many years. The first was a commitment to improve tax collections by both top political leaders and the newly-appointed top managers of the tax system. The second, equally important factor was the capacity of the tax administration to respond to these new directives in an effective way.

47.　　　　The analysis suggests that tax administration reforms have been permanent and a major cause for the revenue improvements to date. Nonetheless, the Government should accelerate efforts to establish firm control over revenue streams.

48.　　　　**Industrial Promotion.** The Government as priority renewed efforts to control industrial promotion through the tax credit exchange program. To complete the program, the Government should: (i) reinforce the industrial promotion team at DGI with additional resources and managerial attention; (ii) grant no waivers for the starting dates, by which time a firm would have to be producing at contractual levels to receive benefits, regardless of investment made; (iii) devote the necessary resources to audit firms that did not pay taxes during the suspension of benefits in the year following the Emergency Law, a process that has achieved only 50 percent of its targeted audit rate thus far, but could yield revenues of more than US$300 million. It should also (iv) make permanent the suspension of the new Industrial Promotion Law, whose suspension expires at end-1993.

49.　　　　**Internal DGI Administration.** Other DGI actions could also strengthen the Government's control over revenues. The DGI should (i) accelerate cross-checks between the DGI and the social security institute (DNRP), with the objective of unifying the two collection systems in the coming 6-12 months. The eventual effort should conclude in giving the DGI control over Social Security collection. Furthermore, it should (ii) capitalize on its recent success in modifying labor agreements by replacing incompetent tax inspectors and auditors, and more importantly installing a modern personnel system with systematic recruitment, training and career development, together with performance-based incentives systems, even possibly including commissions on revenues from audits. DGI also (iii) needs to improve other basic management systems, including internal budgeting, procurement, payroll administration, and asset management. The Government already plans to (iv) transfer to regional offices the tax audit software to control the largest 1,000 taxpayers at the regional level. Administratively, DGI should (v) give auditing the same emphasis as collections through the development of a computerized support; and (vi) DGI should start producing the necessary information to determine the coefficient of effective collection of tax assessments--to provide DGI management with a reliable indicator of its own performance.

50.　　　　**Tax Court.** It is also important that the relationship between the tax administration and the judicial power be simplified and that the role of the Fiscal Tribunal be strengthened. The effectiveness of DGI's inspections and auditors is closely linked to improvements of the National Tax Court operation. Taxpayers can appeal a DGI tax or penalty determination by lodging a formal appeal with the National Tax Court. The perceived inefficiency of the court also plays a role in decreasing voluntary taxpayer compliance, as it presents an easy road to deferral or even elimination.

51.   **Customs Administration**.   Regarding the improvement of Customs Administration, the Government should also accelerate its efforts since the implied revenue losses are still high.   This would include the revision of the legal norms governing trade transactions and implementation of the computerized control system. The Government also should accelerate the revision of the agreement between ANA and the Association of Customs Agents, which has to be approved by the Tribunal de Cuentas, so as to proceed expeditiously with the implementation of the MARIA software.

CHAPTER 5. HEALTH

A. Overview

1.   Argentina spends nearly 10 percent of its GDP on health. Of this about 60 percent is spent through the public sector, roughly one-third through federal and provincial budgets and two-thirds through the quasi-public health funds (*obras sociales*) (Table 5.1). Expenditure on health care in Argentina increased from around 7 percent of GDP in 1970 to nearly 9 percent in 1986, the most recent year for which data are available. The share of public spending through the budget, after an increase during the 1970s, has fallen back to the level of 1970, about 22 percent, while the *obras*' share grew from 26 percent to 36 percent during the 1970s, and has been nearly constant since. Most observers agree that present expenditures entail serious deficiencies.

Health Situation

2.   While Argentina has made notable progress in improving health status, infant mortality was still high at 25.7 per 1,000 live births in 1988, slightly higher than the levels estimated for Mexico (23.6) and Brazil (24.8) and much higher than in neighboring Uruguay (21.0) or Chile (18.9). Seventy percent or more of all deaths before the age of 28 days are preventable with adequate medical care during pregnancy and at birth; yet this share has not changed since 1980. Just under 60 percent of infant deaths in the subsequent 11 months of life could easily have been prevented. For children aged 1-4 years, the largest single cause of death (other than accidents and violence) is infectious and parasitic diseases, influenza and pneumonia, and nutritional deficiencies--all of which are largely preventable.   Matters   may   be worse at later stages of life. Compared to the standardized mortality rate in Cuba and Costa Rica, Argentina's situation, while comparatively better for young children (even though it is not satisfactory in the first year of life), is considerably worse for those between 40 and 64 years old, with 8.7 deaths per thousand versus a comparator value of 7.6. Fully 60 percent of the additional deaths in this age group are due to diseases of the circulatory system, and are therefore presumably caused mostly by diet and other lifestyle factors. A better health care system could reduce deaths among infants and children, and could probably improve health status for the age 40-65 group.

Institutional Financial Structure

3.   Argentina's health care delivery and financing system comprises three subsectors: public expenditures through the budget, the quasi-public health insurance funds (the *obras sociales*), and the private sector.

4.   **Public Spending through the Budget**. The public sector provides health resources through the Treasury--including the Ministry of Health as well as other ministries--and the provinces. The great bulk of public health care now is the responsibility of provincial governments. The national Ministry of Health and Social Action (MHSA, *Ministerio de Salud y Acción Social*) formerly operated a large number

of hospitals and clinics, but most of these have been transferred to provincial administrations and nearly all the remainder are scheduled to be similarly transferred during 1992. MHSA therefore administers only those programs that do not require hospitals or clinics and that generally do not reach individual patients.

Table 5.1: Health Expenditure, 1970-86
(in US$ millions and shares of GDP
and of total spending on health)

| | | Public Sector | | | | |
	Federal	Provincial & Municipal	Obras Sociales	Total	Private Sector	Total
1970						
Million US$	107	439	624	1,170	1,215	2,385
Percent GDP	0.3	1.4	1.9	3.6	3.8	7.4
Percent Total	4.5	18.4	26.2	49.1	50.9	100.0
1986						
Million US$	256	1,292	2,617	4,165	2,884	7,049
Percent GDP	0.3	1.6	3.3	5.3	3.7	9.0
Percent Total	3.7	18.3	37.1	59.1	40.9	100.0

Source: Fundación de Investigaciones Económicas Latinoamericanas (FIEL),
          *El Sistema de Obras Sociales en la Argentina: Diagnóstico y
          Propuesta de Reforma*, Buenos Aires, August 1991.

5.   In recent years, the MHSA almost ceased to function and failed to provide even minimal services to the population under its care. An accumulated deterioration over many years was aggravated by the hyperinflation of 1989-90, to the point that in the latter year the Ministry could not buy vaccines, and maintenance of this crucial program depended on emergency help from UNICEF. The Ministry employed 30,000 people but produced no services. That staff has been cut to about 9,000, with 2,000 of the reduction coming at the central level. The statistical service of the Ministry has continued to function, but there is no evidence of these data being used to guide budgeting or operations.

6.   **Obras Sociales**. Both the public sector and the quasi-public *obras* sociales operate at all three political levels of the country--national, provincial, and municipal. The *obras sociales*, which have no exact counterpart in other countries, are obligatory health insurance schemes financed by a 9 percent wage tax with a 3:6 contribution ratio for employees and employers, respectively. By law, at least 80 percent of these funds are to be spent on members' health care, and no more than 8 percent on administration; an *obra* is free to spend the remaining 12 percent as it pleases. This provision often has been violated, which is one of the reasons for the *obras'* financial difficulties.

7.   Originally independent of the government, the *obras sociales* have been brought increasingly under public control, in some cases by direct intervention and in others by various limitations on their funds and expenditures. Most recently, the Deregulation Decree 2284 of 1991 centralized the collection of the wage tax along with social security and family allowances. Ten percent of *obra* wage funds (and 50 percent

of their other revenues) go to the National Administration of Health Insurance (ANSSAL), which is empowered to use them as subsidies to *obras* in financial difficulty or which are too poor to provide adequate medical care to their members, or to finance and enforce plans for cleaning up an *obra's* debt and rationalizing its administration. The first of these possible uses clearly represents a socialization of the tax pool across income classes; the second is a regulatory function. Since ANSSAL's use of funds is controlled by the MHSA budget, in principle it returns funds unspent by the *obras*' to the Treasury.

8.   Employed contributors to an *obra* also pay into the Institute of Health Insurance for Retirees and Pensioners (INSSJP), which operates the Program of Integral Medical Care (PAMI) to provide medical care to the elderly. In addition to separating the elderly from those of working age, PAMI acts as a residual or last-resort *obra* for certain other categories of the population, including some who are indigent.

9.   **Private Sector**. Private providers of health care (and other medical goods and services) sell directly to the public, but depend for most of their revenue on contracts either with the *obras sociales* or with prepaid medical plans or other kinds of private insurance. The latter two categories represent out-of-pocket family expenditures or employer subsidies, and together constitute the largest form of private expenditure. At low levels of family income out-of-pocket expenses pay primarily for medicine according to a 1989 survey in nine areas of the country. At higher incomes households begin to spend more on pre-paid health plans and direct payments to private doctors or dentists.

Infrastructure and Other Inputs

10.   Hospitals operated by provinces and municipalities account for 56 percent of the beds. The *obras sociales* contract most of their services with private facilities for the care of their members and account for about 5 percent of the beds. The private sector accounts for the remainder. Average occupancy is quite low, only 59.2 percent of disposable bed-days, although other limiting factors--shortage of medicines and other inputs, inoperable equipment and absenteeism by doctors--may mean that real delivery capacity is more constrained than bed-days would indicate. Long-stay beds, in chronic-care facilities, are found almost entirely in the public sector. It appears that average length of stay in hospital has been cut slightly since 1985, to 9.4 days, with reductions in almost all provinces, possibly reflecting increased efficiency.

B. Federal Expenditures in 1992

11.   Health programs represent over one-quarter of the MHSA budget, of which half is represented by the budget of ANNSAL, mostly for subsidizing financially weak health insurance funds (Table 5.2). Most of the remainder is for six programs.

12.   The most important is Preventive Health which absorbs US$127 million and covers primary health, including maternal-child health care; epidemiology, including the relevant institutes; vaccination programs; and health education programs. Prevention

of communicable disease and surveillance activities involve large externalities and are appropriately undertaken by the Federal Government. If they are successful, they can also save resources that the provinces would otherwise have to spend on curative care. Other preventive efforts by the Federal Government include programs to slow the spread of AIDS or reduce the health damage from accidents, smoking, or other behavior-related problems. General health care absorbs US$46 million and at present covers drug banks, implants, cancer, surgical procedures, and rehabilitation. Preventive Environmental Health absorbs US$25 million and covers detection and care of endemic diseases, and the control of environmental health conducted at the federal level. Hygiene control absorbs US$10 million and consists of regulation, inspection, and vigilance in processing and transportation of drugs, pharmaceuticals, and food, especially in the border areas. Health infrastructure absorbs US$11 million and covers construction of 4 new hospitals in the provinces with IDB financing. National health policy absorbs US$32 million and covers the administration and technical support for the health programs.

13.   The health status data suggest that the Government should be focusing its efforts at the national level on infant mortality, reducing smoking-related deaths, and preventive medicine (including vaccines, AIDS prevention, etc.). How much to spend relative to the size of the problems needs further evaluation. Savings might be achieved through consolidation of the Formulation and Implementation Programs at the Ministry level, and better coordination of the health prevention programs at the provincial and federal level.

Housing and Other Social Welfare

14.   Just under two-thirds of the MHSA budget is allocated to housing; over one-half to a single program of loans to the provincial governments for subsidized housing. Non-health expenditures other than housing consist of eight percent of the MHSA budget; this has been reduced compared to previous years mostly due to the transfer of two nutrition programs and consolidation of the remaining programs. PAN, a consumption maintenance program undertaken between 1984-89, was phased out and the Social Nutrition Program, a school and infant feeding program, was reduced from 7.8 percent of the MHSA budget to just 1.2 percent. The remaining funds were mainly allocated for supervision of these programs at the federal level. While the responsibility for other social welfare programs (such as Minors and Family Institutions) has been transferred to the provinces, the remaining consolidated programs that involve formulation of policy, supervision, and coordination need to be evaluated for possible reduction.

Table 5.2: Argentina - Federal Government Expenditures in Health, Housing, and Welfare, 1992
(US$ millions)   9-Nov-92

	Total	National Administration			Transfers
		Total	Current	Capital	
Health	631.6	317.2	302.9	14.3	314.4
Ministry of Health and Social Action (MHSA)	476.1	223.4	210.6	12.9	252.7
National Health Policy	32.0	27.7	27.3	0.4	4.3
Hospital Infrastructure	10.7	8.8	0.5	8.3	1.9
Health Clinic Construction	2.1	1.9	0.3	1.6	0.1
General Health Care	45.8	17.3	15.6	1.7	28.5
National Health Insurance (ANSSAL)	217.4	6.3	6.3	0.0	211.1
Preventive Health	128.7	127.2	126.7	0.5	1.6
Hygiene Control	9.7	9.7	9.4	0.2	0.0
Provincial Aid for health care	2.5	0.0	0.0	0.0	2.5
Preventive Environmental Health	24.6	24.6	24.5	0.1	0.0
Social Coverage in Health	2.6	0.0	0.0	0.0	2.6
Other Jurisdictions	155.5	93.8	92.3	1.5	61.8
Congressional Medical Plan	14.8	14.8	14.8	0.0	0.0
Ministry of Defense and Armed Forces	39.1	39.1	39.0	0.1	0.1
Army Sanitation	2.7	2.7	2.7	0.0	0.0
Navy Sanitation	24.4	24.3	24.3	0.0	0.1
Air Force Sanitation	11.9	11.9	11.9	0.0	0.0
Air Force Hospitals	0.1	0.1	0.1	0.0	0.0
Others	101.6	39.9	38.5	1.4	61.7
Ministry of Interior, Sanitation	2.0	2.0	1.9	0.1	0.0
Potable Water Council	29.0	6.4	5.5	0.9	22.6
Ministry of Education, Student Health Programs	48.4	9.2	8.9	0.3	39.1
Treasury Transfers for MHSA salary enhancements	22.2	22.2	22.2	0.0	0.0
Housing	1103.9	23.4	22.9	0.5	1080.5
Ministry of Health and Social Action	1100.0	19.5	18.9	0.5	1080.5
FONAVI a/	934.3	15.9	15.9	0.1	918.3
Urban Development	80.3	0.8	0.5	0.3	79.5
World Bank Housing	85.4	2.7	2.6	0.2	82.7
COVIARA - Defense Housing b/	3.9	3.9	3.9	0.0	0.0
Welfare (Social Action) c/	386.3	120.3	102.3	18.0	266.0
Ministry of Health and Social Action	141.1	59.4	41.5	17.9	81.7
Social Nutrition Program and PAN	22.1	0.7	0.7	0.0	21.3
Social Welfare Coverage	24.7	6.2	6.2	0.0	18.5
Human and Family Development	62.2	23.9	17.1	6.8	38.4
Social Action Policy and Construction	28.3	24.9	14.0	10.9	3.4
Adolescent Half-way House	3.7	3.7	3.6	0.1	0.0
Other jurisdictions	245.2	60.9	60.8	0.1	184.3
Congressional Social Aid Programs d/	6.0	0.0	0.0	0.0	6.0
Presidency's Sports Fund and Policy	6.9	2.9	2.8	0.1	4.0
Ministry of Labor and Social Security e/	201.7	27.4	27.3	0.1	174.3
Treasury f/	30.6	30.6	30.6	0.0	0.0
Memo					
Total expenditures of MHSA	1717.2	302.3	271.0	31.3	1414.9

a/ National Housing Fund and housing policy administration.
b/ Treasury transfer; does not include US$50 million received through FONAVI.
c/ Does not include social security transfers.
d/ Senate and Lower House grants to non-profit organizations.
e/ Includes all expenditures of Ministry of Labor and Social Security.
f/ Consists of funding of the "Worker's Telegram" and salary enhancements in the Ministry of Labor and Social Security.

Source: 1992 Budget (February 1992) and Contaduria General de la Nacion.

C. The Role of Health Insurance Funds (*Obras Sociales*)

Historical and Legal Background

15.   Most public expenditures on health are through the *obras sociales*. These insurance institutions originated with various labor unions offering medical care services to their affiliates and their families around 1910; they formed "funds" based on employee-employer agreements to pay for these services. The *obras sociales* received major encouragement during the Peronist Government (1946-52) as part of a political project to foster strong trade unions. Because of the close association between the *obras sociales* and the unions, the health insurance system was both highly politicized and heterogeneous, and the quality of the service varied with the economic situation and power of the individual union. Each union served to pool risk among its members, but there was no pooling across unions, sectors, or professions, and thus no subsidy from better-paid to poorer-paid workers. Until 1970, successive governments left the unions to manage their own *obras*. During this period the *obras* increased in number, until by 1990 there were a total of 336; 291 of these are federally coordinated and legally able to operate in more than one province, while an additional 45 enrolled the public employees of provinces, municipalities, and the federal Judiciary, Congress, and the Armed Forces.   (Provincial governments have powers to regulate only those *obras* composed of their own employees or those of municipalities in the province.) The *obras* also expanded into other activities. These include tourism, vacation resorts, recreation and sports centers, warehouses, legal services, libraries, technical schools, and workplace restaurants, among others. It was not always possible to distinguish between the activities that belonged to the union and those of the associated *obra social*.[1] Today, the 5 largest *obras* account for nearly half the total membership and the top 15 account for over 90 percent of membership, while the 15 smallest together hold fewer than 4,000 members (Table 5.3). The total beneficiary population grew by almost 1.3 million, following the restoration of civilian government in 1984, and has been nearly constant since then, at about 17.5 million.

16.   Public discontent with service quality eventually led to Law No. 18610 of 1970. This law dictated that at least 80 percent of the *obras*' resources from employer and employee contributions be used to provide medical services, and that not more than 8 percent be spent on administration, with freedom to spend the remaining 12 percent or more as the *obra* wished. It also established the National Institute of Social Insurance (INOS) to regulate the financial and medical management of the *obras*. INOS' functions were to promote development of the medical services and to use part of the resources of the financially stronger institutions to subsidize the weaker and poorer *obras*. INOS' functions were financed by 10 percent of the total wage contributions and 50 percent of all other income of the *obras sociales*. In 1971, two further laws established the

---

1   In addition to the union-based institutions, there grew up some 1,000 nonprofit mutual assistance organizations, which offer health care plans funded by individual contributions from the workers in a sector, profession, or other group. Unlike the obras sociales, these institutions do not receive financing from employers, and the workers' contributions are not legally mandated.

Institute of Health Insurance for Retirees and Pensioners (INSSJP). Employed beneficiaries of *obras* were thenceforth required also to contribute to financing this Institute. In 1989, Law No. 23660 reestablished the obligatory affiliation of workers and increased the contribution of the employers to 6 percent, but left the workers' contributions unchanged at 3 percent. The National Administration of Health Insurance (ANSSAL) replaced INOS in managing the new system; since then ANSSAL has carried out INOS' functions with respect to the *obras sociales* but without any fundamental reforms such as extending the system to cover the self-employed and the indigent.

Table 5.3: Distribution of Obras Sociales and their Membership by Size and by Type of Ownership or Affiliation, 1990

Classification	No. of Entities	% of Total	Total No. of Beneficiaries	% of Total	Average No. of Beneficiaries
Trade-Union Related	201	69.1	7,014,977	39.9	34,900
State (Public)	15	5.2	765,927	4.4	51,062
"By Agreement"	31	10.7	233,471	1.3	7,531
Management Staff	24	8.2	979,109	5.6	40,796
Mixed Administration (Partly Trade Union)	12	4.1	8,426,827	48.0	702,235
Voluntary Affiliation	3	1.0	59,321	0.3	19,733
Other	5	1.7	86,602	0.5	17,320
Total	**291**	**100.0**	**17,566,234**	**100.0**	**60,365**
5 Largest	5	1.7	7,924,212	45.1	1,584,842
10 Largest	10	3.4	10,160,518	57.8	1,016,052
15 Largest	15	5.1	11,670,725	66.4	778,048
15 Smallest	15	5.1	3,790	0.0	253

Source: Fundación de Investigaciones Económicas Latinoamericanas (FIEL), *El Sistema El Sistema de Obras Sociales en la Argentina: Diagnóstico y Propuesta de Reforma*, Buenos Aires, August 1991.

Principal Issues and Problems

17.   The *obras sociales* are at the heart of the Argentine health system given the complexity of their relations to producers and consumers of health care and to other sectoral institutions. One issue of debate is whether the share of wages that is paid into *obras* is a **tax**, no different from any other publicly-enforced, obligatory payment, or is a private **contribution** by a free association of workers in a given industry, firm or occupation. The *obras* themselves naturally defend the second interpretation, referring both to the historical development of the institutions and to the general orientation of the government toward privatization and deregulation. The government takes the position that *obras* monies are legally "funds of public interest" and their payment is involuntary;

thus, the *obras* themselves are simply private collectors of a public tax. These legal issues must be resolved.

18.   There are actually three mandatory elements in the *obras* system. The first is the payment of the wage share. The second is the obligatory affiliation with a particular *obra*, about which the worker has no choice (even though he is free to join or leave the labor union with which the *obra* is affiliated). The third, and arguably the least important, is the limitation on choice of medical providers with which the *obra* contracts; an insured member generally has less choice than under a private insurance plan, unless the latter is an HMO where the providers are also the insurers. For a large *obra* with substantial bargaining power, it is possible both to negotiate below-market costs and provide access to a large group of providers.

19.   There is some consensus that relaxing the second limitation--the lack of choice as to one's insurer--would compensate for the tax-like character of the payment. Under this regime, *obras sociales* would be forced to compete for their members' loyalty and money, but could then design or buy the health plan they wanted with a minimum of further government intervention.

20.   The ANSSAL system of cross-subsidies is also plagued with problems. First, the 10 percent of wage contributions (and 50 percent of other revenues) that *obras* are required to pay to ANSSAL is in principle available for subsidies to poorer *obras* to enable them to buy better health care for their members. However, there are no rules governing such transfers, and in the past these funds were used more for political rewards than anything else. Even without any political or financial corruption, the ANSSAL mechanism is an inefficient way to provide for subsidies across income levels, because it involves administrative costs and because the contribution of a particular *obra* depends on the composition of its revenues (wage contributions versus other sources) and not only on their level.

21.   Second, ANSSAL has to finance reform plans to pay off the institutions' debts, scale down their administrative expenses, and restore them to financial health. An *obra* must submit such a reform plan and have it approved by ANSSAL just to be eligible for a share in the "Redistribution Fund." Six such plans had been approved by late 1991, and 17 more were under discussion. At US$400 million, the total debts of the system are small compared to the sums received each year by ANSSAL, and could be fully paid with less than two years of current revenues. However, this would require at least a transitory reduction in health care spending by the *obra*, unless other expenses could be cut sufficiently; importantly, it would require that all of ANSSAL's receipts be used for this purpose but nothing could be used for subsidies. While these flows are a relatively small fraction of all revenues of the *obras*, they are large compared to the revenues of the numerous small institutions, and compared to the debts of most of them. Total resources managed by ANSSAL are some 18 percent of the total wage-based contribution by workers and employers. This is much larger than the 10 percent rate applied to these contributions because of the 50 percent rate applicable to other income of the *obras sociales*, and because ANSSAL also earns 10 percent of its total revenue in the form of interest on the funds it controls. Fully 90 percent of the agency's revenues return to the *obras* in the form of subsidies and support for

restructuring, 9 percent are used to help finance federal hospitals, and only 1 percent is required for administering the system. The real value of these flows appears to be less than it was in 1986 (see Table 5.1), presumably because the combination of recession and hyperinflation both reduced the real wage bill, and, by delaying contributions to the *obras* and to ANSSAL, further reduced the value of these contributions. The estimates for earlier years also may be partly derived using different methods; for 1990, the structure of the transfers is more trustworthy than the amounts.

22.   Third, the ANSSAL has inadequate information on which to base its cross-subsidy decision. This is owing in part to the poor records and control system of the *obras* themselves.

23.   The subsector has other problems as well:

o   The economic recession of the 1980s has reduced real revenues for many *obras*, both because of lower real wages and because of the loss of formal sector employment and the growth of informal jobs from which no insurance contributions are paid. ANSSAL's information system is inadequate to trace and recover non-payment.

o   While the health insurance plan for retirees and pensioners (PAMI) has some four million affiliates and several other *obras* are very large, some of them are too small to be viable. They do not benefit from economies of scale, and as insurers they are exposed to high risks. A free-market solution would undoubtedly involve the disappearance of many small organizations or their merger into a smaller number of larger, economically viable *obras*.

o   Meanwhile, medical costs continue to rise in Argentina as in other countries. The bargaining power of the *obras* may hold costs below what they would be in a completely free, fee-for-service market, but it cannot readily cope with overbilling for nonexistent or superfluous services or with the introduction of cost-increasing procedures. *Obras* plans typically do not cover much preventive care--that is left to the public sector--and do not provide adequate incentives to avoid costly curative care. While providers of medical care compete for *obras* contracts, this competition does not extend to choices by individual beneficiaries.

D. Prospects and Recommendation for Reform

Federal Policy and the Ministry of Health

24.   The health status of Argentina and the problems affecting its health care system are sufficiently worrisome that health should take priority over more general social welfare objectives both in the budget and the program activities of the Federal Government. With the transfer to the provinces of most social welfare programs, the federal Ministry will have a new leadership role but will execute very few programs. The Ministry must therefore reduce its size and scope to focus on a few key national objectives.

25.   The Ministry has made a good choice in the kind of programs on which to concentrate: maternal and child health, endemic diseases, and epidemiological and preventive efforts generally. However, the division of labor between the federal and provincial ministries means that no one is clearly responsible for analyzing which health expenditures have the highest return. It should be part of the Federal Government's task to evaluate the cost-effectiveness of **all** health interventions of interest to the country, including all those mostly curative efforts that are now the responsibility of the provinces and municipalities. Such analysis can extend to questions of rehabilitating, modernizing, or closing provincial health facilities, and should specifically include study and formulation of rules governing investment in the sector, particularly investment in equipment. This is consistent both with the national Ministry's job of setting policy for the public sector generally as well as the necessity of collaboration with the provinces. Showing them how to save money or lives would be the real test of whether the Ministry of Health can justify its budget.

26.   As part of its effort to change roles, the Ministry needs to examine the numerous small programs it now operates that individually absorb only small shares of the budget but which may need to be eliminated or consolidated. The school and pre-school feeding programs are worth preserving. If the provinces continue to operate those programs, there **may** be a role for federal Ministry help in evaluation and technical improvement. There is also a clear federal role for relating the maternal and child health program--which will include supplemental feeding of pregnant and lactating women and of children through age six--to other food distribution programs. The guiding principle should be to use food for health benefits, which requires integrating food supplementation with medical care and health education. There should be no Ministry participation in any program, unless it is accompanied by evaluation. The only such evaluation yet conducted in Argentina concerned the school lunch program.[2]

27.   To discipline expenditures and satisfy these objectives, the Ministry should not have access to any earmarked funds. Funds obtained from the national lottery should go straight to the Treasury and then be allocated for health as necessary. To make the health budget an effective instrument of Government health policy, in turn, will require more transparency and better coordination in setting priorities between the staff of the Ministry and the Treasury.

28.   The Ministry needs to continue to shrink its staff and increase its technical capacity and productivity. Although the administration reform did reduce personnel, a major health reform might reduce the central staff to less than 1,000. Remaining staff must be competent, well-motivated, adequately paid and work full-time. However, for those people to do their job--particularly the analytical job, which increasingly must justify the Ministry's existence--they will need a modern system for gathering and processing information: computers, software and training.

29.   Furthermore, the reformed Ministry must attend to the task of establishing norms and quality standards for medical education, medical care, drugs and equipment,

---

2   Pan American Health Organization, Evaluacion de un Programa de Alimentacion Escolar: El Caso Argentino, 1990.

and their subsequent policing. In the absence of government assumption of this role, the medical associations have set their own standards, but these are not uniform and may unduly favor the interests of doctors. Standards that are transparent and fully enforced represent a public good that only the state can provide, and it is a measure of the deplorable state of the public health system that this job has not been done adequately despite its low cost.

30.   These suggestions would create a smaller, policy-setting Ministry of Health. They would affect the relation of the public and private health subsectors by giving the state control of standards which the private sector would have to follow, and increasing its capacity to negotiate with private providers and suppliers. The remaining major responsibility of the Ministry of Health would be to oversee the transition to a new health system for the country by undertaking a substantial reform of the *obras sociales*. This topic is treated in the next and last section.

Proposed Reform of the *Obras Sociales*

31.   Public expenditures on health cannot achieve major productivity improvements--and hence improvement in health status--without a major reform of the *obras sociales*. The Government has prepared an ambitious reform, the principles of which were set forth in a Decree of January 1993 and draft law still under discussion.

32.   A draft law would establish a voucher for a universal and fairly generous health care package with an equal value for everyone, except that higher costs are allowed for (one of two age) groups, presumably the elderly. The self-employed registered with the social security system would be included and required to contribute also. Beneficiaries' contributions in excess of the minimum value would be used entirely to subsidize lower-paid contributors. Existing *obras sociales* could qualify as provider entities (*Entes Prestatarios*), along with other insurers or providers meeting a short list of conditions. Public providers would also be allowed to participate, with the requirement that they charge insurers separately for care provided under contract to a provider, and not use public funds for this purpose. Except for specified transitional costs and the coverage of indigents, everything is to be paid out of wage contributions and not from the federal Treasury. (The indigents who have contributed nothing either as employees or self-employed workers would continue to depend on provincial and municipal public services, which is why this prohibition is important to protect their access to care.)

33.   There is explicit provision for the transition from the old system to the new, with supervisory bodies created for that purpose, funds allocated from the Treasury for transitional expenses, short-term protection for beneficiaries, and a timetable of specific actions. After the transition there would continue to be both medical and financial supervision of the system, with these tasks entrusted to separate bodies but under the supervision of the Ministry of Health. These bodies would finish the job of "reconverting" *obras sociales*, which is one of ANSSAL's functions, and would continue its supervisory functions; ANSSAL itself would cease to exist. The Ministry would have overall responsibility for the conduct of the new system, which would be a *de facto* national health insurance program even if not legally so defined.

34.		The most radical change in the proposal is to introduce competition among health care plans and organizations. The reform would let beneficiaries choose their own plan after a transition period. A "plan" would cover a specified list of health care benefits and run for a predetermined period, presumably one year. Beneficiaries would be allowed to change plans during an "open" period each year.

35.		This reform would be initially cost-neutral by paying for the plans--or at least the obligatory component of coverage--out of the 9 percent wage tax. To assure that the reform would also redistribute health care spending from rich to poor, the reform would establish a minimum plan to which every beneficiary would be guaranteed access, whether or not his salary were high enough to pay for it. People whose contribution exceeded the cost of the minimum plan would have their tax used to subsidize the minimum for others. In principle, the remainder could be credited to them for the purchase of a more generous plan, or in an extreme case could be returned in cash or used to offset income tax; alternatively, it could all be used for subsidies. All these features could be incorporated in a voucher scheme, with the value of the voucher varying by level of individual contribution. However, the Government has chosen not to incorporate these refinements, but to adopt a single value for the basic health coverage only.

36.		The medical care content and the definition of beneficiaries of the minimum plan would be determined by a special Superintendency to regulate standards. The content--that is, the specification of what kinds of medical care would be covered-- should be related to the basic health needs of the population, and would implicitly reflect public priorities. Every organization offering any kind of insurance or prepaid care would have to offer this minimum. They could then be allowed to offer a variety of plans tailored to the market they want to attract, which would add features to the minimum plan. As long as the quality of medical care is adequately policed and there is protection against fraud, there would be no reason for the government to regulate these more generous packages.

37.		Given the content of the medical plan, the Government has elected not to let the market determine its price for two reasons. First, it is preferable to have suppliers compete on quality and customer satisfaction rather than risk having them cut quality in order to offer lower prices. Dissatisfaction with quality is rife, particularly among beneficiaries of the poorer *obras sociales*; competition on quality is desirable and might be worth more to consumers than a cost reduction. Offerors of unregulated, higher-priced plans would still have ample scope for price competition. Second, because the competitors in this market would initially include many *obras sociales* trying to retain their own members, and with limited resources, price competition might put many of them out of business before they could show whether they could compete or not. Many *obras* might ultimately fail the test, because they are too small in size, poorly administered, or other salient reasons; even so, they should be given a transition period to become competitive. So the Government will set the price, and may later have to adjust either the price or the content of the minimum plan as events warrant.

38.		A separate Superintendency would establish conditions of entry--primarily minimal capital requirements. The reform would **make no distinction** between insurers and insurer-providers. Either kind of organization would be allowed to offer the basic plan at the fixed price. Similarly, the Government need not regulate the **type of contract** between insurers and providers, whether capitation, fee-for-service or some other variant. However, the providers' monopolies on negotiation with doctors should and probably will be broken.

39.   Priority would be given to restoring *obras* with deficits to financial equilibrium through an initial restructuring plan for past liabilities. It is not necessary that all debts be settled before the reform goes into effect, but it is advisable that every *obra* have its current expenses under control and have some arrangement for working off its debts if they are large enough to hamper its participation in the reform. A transition program would allow for an extraordinary one-time use of resources to contract out the needed financial reviews, and/or expedite mergers and consolidations among the weaker and smaller *obras* without waiting for the market to do so.

40.   As insurers and providers compete for the pool of healthy individuals, they would also try to avoid those with existing health problems or propensities to cost more in the future--"creaming" healthy subscribers and "dumping" less healthy. Fixing the price of the minimum package, while justifiable on other grounds, exacerbates this problem. The reform is grounded on three principles that can help solve this and other problems. First, any insurer participating in the scheme could be allowed to reject an applicant for any unregulated non-minimum package, but not for the minimum; all beneficiaries must be accepted, independent of medical or financial considerations. Second, because the elderly tend to have more need for medical care, it might make sense to limit the scheme to those of working age, at least initially. That would imply retaining PAMI as the basic provider for the elderly--although a pensioner who could buy a package beyond the minimum would be free to leave PAMI. This is not ideal because it restricts freedom of choice, so the Government would define a minimum package for those over 65, at a higher price, and require PAMI to compete in that market. Third, if some people want to leave a small *obra* but others are content to stay, a previously viable *obra* might become too small to survive. There may therefore need to be some rules about minimum size, or even some restrictions on an individual's ability to leave his *obra* by himself rather than as part of a group. All such interference with the principle of free choice, however, would be transitory and phased out over a two-year period. It has not been decided how the reform will treat all these aspects.

41.   Finally, the reform of the *obras sociales* will not put an end to the relation between them and the facilities of the public sector. *Obra* beneficiaries often use public hospitals for services their organization does not provide: public hospitals will always be the providers of last resort, but they must be able to recover costs from anyone who is a beneficiary of an *obra* or similar third-party payer. Improvement of the provincial ministries' administrative capacity and information systems will also pay off here by improving cost recovery and forcing insurers either to provide services, contract them, or pay the public sector for them.

42.   Since these proposals are not yet law and may be modified before adoption, a few issues deserve mention as potential sources of difficulty:

o   It is the prerogative of provincial and municipal governments to determine how to finance coverage for their own employees; this may lead to some differences in equity, although not in the definition or price of the basic package.

o   Public facilities must recover costs from private providers with which they have contracts, but it is still not clear how to deal with patients who belong to a provider not under contract and who demand care from the public sector.

o   Because no one can be denied membership on the basis of medical condition, some providers may end up with an excess of high-cost members. This may require some pooling of (specified) high-risk conditions, reinsurance through the Ministry of Health, or other special arrangements.

o   By allowing free movement of beneficiaries, and competition on quality but not on price, the reform should reduce the need for some kinds of information about the operations of individual providers. To police quality and prevent fraud, however, the Ministry will still need a great deal of information so it will be urgent to develop a system for monitoring these matters and reacting quickly when needed. A sluggish or ill-informed supervision of the reformed system would soon increase dissatisfaction.

o   Finally, it is proposed to create a Consultative Committee drawn from all interested parties to advise on the transition to the new system but its composition and powers remain to be specified and this could generate political difficulties or obstacles to implementation.

CHAPTER 6. EDUCATION

A. Principal Educational Issues

1.   The public sector in Argentina spent an estimated 4.2 percent of GDP on education, about one-quarter at the federal level. Public education represents about two-thirds of all education spending. Austerity programs and other spending inefficiencies have undermined the quality of education and given rise to several other problems.

2.   One problem of the Argentine school system is that so few students complete primary schooling. Relatively few acquire the secondary education necessary for participation in a modern economy. Economic pressures on poor families during the 1980s undoubtedly explain some portion of high rates of repetition and drop out, particularly at the primary level.[1] However, the poor quality of instruction also contributes to the high drop-out rate.[2] The system is plagued by poor teaching, little or no evaluation of results, and generally low morale throughout the system. Salaries have fluctuated widely around a falling trend, with the consequence that few teachers work a full week--only 5 percent in 1986 at the secondary level. More than half of all secondary schoolteachers work less than 12 hours a week, and depend on other jobs to supplement their income. Furthermore, teachers are often absent, even during those few hours when they are expected to be in school. This means either that children are not taught at all, or that schools must hire substitute teachers. The results of the only national achievement test--a small-scale, standardized, uniform test of Spanish and mathematics administered to 6th and 9th-grade students in 10 provinces and the Municipality of Buenos Aires in 1991--revealed serious deficiencies in these academic subjects.

3.   Problems of low quality and inefficiency also affect the universities. Teachers at this level are poorly compensated, commonly work only part-time, and frequently miss their classes or make only minimal efforts to teach. Students enjoy tuition-free education but often take much longer than necessary to complete a course of study, or drop out before finalizing their studies. In addition, higher education is highly politicized: universities are legally autonomous, students participate in electing administrators, and schools are frequently disrupted by political confrontation among parties and interest groups.

---

1   This happens in spite of the apparent high rate of return in increased income associated with extra schooling at this level. Econometric estimates of this relation for the country as a whole and several smaller jurisdictions consistently show that primary education pays off appreciably better than secondary schooling, which in turn shows a higher return than university. The estimates for 1985 give a rate of return of 14.4 percent to primary schooling, 8.4 percent at secondary level and 6.7 percent at university. (These estimates do not distinguish the specific rate of return due to literacy, which may be the principal contribution of early primary schooling.)

2   See Norberto Fernandez Lamarra et al., *Calidad de la educacion: aportes para un debate desde la perspectiva del planeamiento*, Buenos Aires: PRONATASS, September 1991.

4.   One of the reasons for poor quality is inadequate and inefficient spending. From 1970 to the mid-1980s, public expenditure on education in Argentina varied from 2-4 percent of GDP. Much of this fluctuation reflects variation in real salaries. Some part of it also reflects expansion of higher education, where enrollments and expenditures increased sharply in 1970-75 and again in 1983-86. Since the mid-1980s, however, there has been a marked decline in real educational spending through the public sector. Even though expenditure will have to increase as part of a solution to the problems of the education sector in Argentina, spending will have to accompany institutional changes to resolve the serious problems of morale and indiscipline.

5.   The role of the Federal Government in education is undergoing change in that it will abandon almost entirely the provision of pre-university education. The role of the Ministry of Education can be much more focused on policy, leadership, and quality standards--and at a much lower level of expenditure. The 1992 budget does not reflect a new equilibrium situation at the federal level. Nonetheless, this is the first budget to take into account the impending transfer of responsibilities, and to begin to define the future role of the Ministry.

B. The Level and Structure of Expenditure in Education

Sources and Uses of Education Funds

6.   The Argentine public sector financed just under two-thirds of total education expenditure of about 7.1 percent of GDP in 1986 [3] (Table 6.1). The Federal Government spent 1.3 percent of GDP on education: of this, over 80 percent went directly to federal universities, and most of the remainder to subsidizing the private sector. Provincial and municipal governments spent another 3.2 percent of GDP on public education. Total federal and provincial subsidies to the private sector amounted to 0.3 percent of the GDP.

Federal Outlays

7.   Public spending for education grew rapidly, over 10 percent annually in the early 1960s and again in the early 1970s, but then slowed down to 1.3 percent per year during 1981-86 as a result of austerity programs and political conflict affecting the universities in the early 1980s. The Federal Government progressively transferred primary education responsibility to the provinces after 1978. Federal spending was thereafter limited to secondary and tertiary education, especially after 1985, when the transfer was completed. The federal role was again reduced as the provinces assumed responsibility for all public secondary schools.

8.   Real spending by the Ministry of Education and Culture (MEC) declined on average by about 9 percent annually during the 1987-91 period as the Government tried to come to grips with the fiscal deficit. The MEC share of GDP fell from 1.9

---

3   This is the last year for which data are available.

percent in 1987 to 1.3 percent in 1990. The advent of stabilization and improved revenues permitted a small increase to 1.5 percent in 1991.

Table 6.1: Sources and Uses of Funds in the Education Sector, 1986
(as percentage of GDP)

| Uses/Sources | Education Sector | | | | Non-Private Subtotal | Non-Educational Sector | Totals |
| | Public | | | | | | |
	Federal Establishments	Provincial Establishments	Cooperatives	Subtotal			
Federal Treasury	1.10	0.02	-	1.12	0.22	-	1.34
Provincial Treasuries a/	-	3.11	-	3.11	0.10	-	3.21
Consolidated Government	1.10	3.13	-	4.23	0.32	-	4.55
Families	-	-	0.25	0.25	0.75	1.50	2.50
Total	1.10	3.13	0.25	4.48	1.07	1.50	7.05

a/ Includes municipal taxes.

Source: "El Gasto Publico Social - Volume III: Sector Education," National Technical Assistance Program for Social Sectors of the Argentine Republic (Government of Argentina/IBRD/UNDP), Ministry of Economy, 1991.

9. In a pattern common to public sector expenditure reduction, the Ministry cut investment and maintenance to preserve salaries. Capital expenditure, which had accounted for about 13 percent of total expenditure in 1987, was crowded out by current expenditure and its share in the total was reduced to less than 5 percent in 1991. Personnel expenditure, which accounted for just over 60 percent of total spending in 1987, grew to 73 percent of the total in 1991. The reduced spending resulted in poor maintenance of the national secondary and superior non-university schools. A 1988/89 survey of the physical condition of secondary and non-university education establishments rated only about one-third in a reasonable state of repair (i.e., requiring less than US$10 per square meter of repairs). Nearly 20 percent were rated in poor condition (more than US$30 per square meter of repairs) and about 44 percent were classified as passable (between US$10 and US$30 of repairs per square meter).[4]

10. MEC is also responsible for some relatively marginal spending on culture, research, and general administration, which remained a constant share of the budget at 24-26 percent of total MEC outlays. About 11-13 percent of the budget went for subsidizing private education and about 10-11 percent for CONET technical schools.

11. The outlays also include direct subsidies to support teacher salaries in private schools. These subsidies were chiefly allocated to secondary education. A 1985

---

4   "Servicios Educativos Nacionales en Las Provincias: Informacion Basica Sobre Aspectos Financieros y Edilicios", Ministry of Culture and Education, August 1991.

study[5] found that 76 percent of all private secondary institutions received subsidies. Of these, 81 percent received between 80-100 percent of teacher salaries as subsidies, 15 percent received between 50-80 percent, and for the remainder (4 percent), subsidies covered less than 50 percent of salaries. The incidence of these subsidies was relatively regressive, mostly benefitting the richest 40 percent of the population.

The 1992 Budget

12.   Because of the transfer of secondary education to the provinces, including schools run by MEC, CONET technical schools, and publicly subsidized private institutions, the real 1992 budget is lower than 1991 by about 28 percent. The budget still includes US$218 million for secondary education. This allocation was considered necessary to help the provinces administer the newly transferred services, as only the largest provinces would have adequate capacity to deal with this additional responsibility. It is not clear, however, what the federal Ministry will do for the provinces, or whether such a large appropriation is justified. Put another way, the proposed secondary-level spending by a Ministry that will no longer administer any schools of its own is fully 40 percent of what the Ministry actually spends on running schools (US$505 million). Since the transfer of the subsidy to private schools does not involve any educational administration, there is presumably little or no need for the federal Ministry to advise the provinces on how to do it.

13.   Federal universities alone are to receive 52 percent of total MEC outlays in the form of current transfers. The budget share for teacher training has increased over previous years and now accounts for 6 percent of the total. This allocation may need further upward adjustment in view of the acute need for better-trained teachers; however, it might be wasteful to allocate more to training unless pay is raised and working conditions normalized. Administrative, health-related, and cultural spending represent another 14.3 percent of total MEC spending. This last category consists of many relatively small programs, such as Conducting Educational Policy, Hospital Services, and others, that should be reviewed in light of the Ministry's new role.

Transfer of Secondary Education

14.   The Argentine Federal Government legally transferred the responsibility for secondary education to the provinces in 1992. The formal transfer, however, will only take place as agreements are reached with the individual provinces, during the planned one-year transition period. Provinces are expected to finance the additional spending required by this transfer from the expected increase in shared revenue funds, estimated at about US$1.2 billion.[6] Operating costs of the transferred schools

---

5   Beccaria, Luis A. and Riquelme, G. *"El Gasto Social en Educacion y la Distribucion del Ingreso,"* Facultad Latinoamericana de Ciencias Sociales, 1985, in *"Analysis del Gasto Publico en Educacion,"* Ministry of Education and Culture, 1990.

6   The first 83 percent of the increase in national coparticipation revenues is distributed according to the existing coparticipation formulas; the second 8.3 percent according to the individual province expense for the transferred schools; and the rest according to the population share of each province.

(assuming no change in salaries, and including only the subsidized cost in the case of private schools) are about US$780 million. The three main components of this amount are US$258 million for the MEC-controlled schools, US$247 million for CONET facilities, and US$237 million for private school subsidies. Since the costs of the transfer for individual provinces vary with enrollment size, teacher and personnel costs, and physical state of the infrastructure in the schools to be transferred, and since the capacity to meet these costs depends in part on the existing financial conditions of the province, extensive negotiations are underway to verify the actual costs, and to determine the need for additional funding. Of the total estimated operating cost, approximately half would be borne by the capital city and the Province of Buenos Aires, which have the largest number of federal schools and teachers. The largest element of transfer cost is teacher salaries, partly because only salaries are covered by the private school subsidy, but private employers' contributions to social security are also included, so that labor costs are subsidized. To the extent that the provinces receive more than this amount of US$780 million in increased coparticipation funds, there will be a net gain for the provincial governments.[7]

15.   A special Transfer Commission in MEC was set up to address some of the complications of the transfer. There is a need to resolve issues relating to: (i) salary and quality differentials between the federal and provincial schools, for which no allowance has been made in the estimate of costs associated with the transfer; (ii) teachers' unions, to verify if they have provincial counterparts that former federal teachers can join; (iii) arrangements for teachers' retirement and social assistance, requiring legal conventions to allow the transfer of pension funds from federal to provincial institutions; (iv) the choice of social and health insurance funds (*Obras Sociales*) to which teachers will belong; more fundamental, given its potential impact on the quality of education, is (v) the issue of teacher qualification, particularly whether teachers' credentials should be determined before or after the transfer takes place, that is, under federal or provincial standards; and finally, (vi) the proportion of the additional coparticipation funds allocated to the transferred secondary schools is not fixed but is left to the discretion of the provincial governments. Financing for the schools may

---

7   However, this comparison does not include the distribution of "excess" funds--transfers from the Federal Government, beyond what it currently spends on education programs that the provinces will take over--among the provinces, which have quite different shares of federal and provincial secondary schools. Nor does it take into account the continued spending by the Federal Government for activities relevant to the secondary level, which would represent an increase in total public spending. And of course, any excess federal transfers may not look excessive at all compared to the costs of equalizing or raising pay, or improving school buildings and other inputs.

Table 6.2: Argentina - Federal Government Expenditures on Education, 1992
(US$ millions)

9-Nov-92

	Total	National Administration			Transfers
		Total	Current	Capital	
Ministry of Culture and Education	1391.2	474.0	406.0	68.0	917.2
Education Budget and Policy	106.8	105.5	43.7	61.8	1.3
Teacher Education & Training	83.0	83.0	83.0	0.0	0.0
Cultural Budget	16.0	15.9	15.6	0.4	0.0
Transfers to Universities	723.9	0.0	0.0	0.0	723.9
Financial Aid for Private Universities	30.0	0.0	0.0	0.0	30.0
High School	218.0	218.0	218.0	0.0	0.0
Agricultural Education	69.7	0.1	0.1	0.0	69.5
Technical Education Council a/	17.1	17.1	17.1	0.0	0.0
Scientific Research b/	41.7	0.0	0.0	0.0	41.7
Medical assistance for students	9.3	9.2	8.9	0.3	0.0
Hospital services c/	39.1	0.0	0.0	0.0	39.1
Public Library System	1.2	0.2	0.1	0.1	1.1
National Cinematographic Institute	6.9	4.3	3.6	0.7	2.6
Permanent Student Fund d/	6.8	6.8	4.6	2.2	0.0
Equal Opportunity Scholarship Institute	2.7	1.0	0.8	0.2	1.7
Teacher Pilot Programs	6.0	6.0	6.0	0.0	0.0
Discovery of America 1492 Fund	6.8	6.8	4.6	2.2	0.0
National Academies	6.2	0.0	0.0	0.0	6.2
Others	49.1	49.1	48.2	0.8	0.1
Congress: Public Libraries	19.8	19.8	19.2	0.6	0.0
Public Administration Institute (INAP) e/	7.4	7.4	7.2	0.2	0.0
Military Academies	21.9	21.9	21.9	0.0	0.1
Research and Development f/	174.6	99.1	91.3	7.9	75.5
INTA and INTI g/	102.3	99.1	91.3	7.9	3.2
CONICET Scholarship and Promotion h/	72.3	0.0	0.0	0.0	72.3
Total	1615.0	622.2	545.5	76.7	992.8

a/ Manages technical high schools.
b/ Research grants for universities.
c/ Grants to universities for student health and hospital services.
d/ Permanent Student Fund.
e/ Presidency-operated institute for training of civil service.
f/ Not classified by the government as "education."
g/ National Institutes of Agricultural and Industrial Technology.
h/ One of two CONICET programs operated by the Presidency.

Source: 1992 Budget (February 1992) and Contaduria General de la Nacion.

therefore vary according to the political circumstances of a particular province, and the anticipated expenditures (estimated from current federal spending) may not be realized.

16.   Points (i) through (v) of this list refer: (a) to how teachers and other staff who used to work for the Federal Government can be integrated into the pay scales, labor unions, insurance funds and other institutions to which provincial employees belong, and--in the case of salaries--(b) to whether there may also be changes in the working conditions of provincial staff. Point (vi) is quite different, since it refers to the essentially political choice of each province, whether to spend the same amount on secondary schooling as the Federal Government has been spending or to transfer resources between education and other sectors. These choices could cause educational spending per pupil to become either more or less unequal across provinces, depending on whether educational priorities are associated positively or negatively with provincial income and revenue levels.

C. University Education

17.   Universities suffer from poor quality, demoralization, and politization. They represent a difficult problem for the Government because they are legally autonomous. This implies that while money for them passes through the Ministry of Education, they are not actually controlled by the Ministry.

18.   Federal expenditure per pupil per year was **lower** for university than for secondary education in the mid-1980s, despite the intrinsically higher costs of higher education. This reflects the large number of "students" who take few classes, take many years to graduate or never do so, and generally clog the system. The lack of a system for monitoring student attendance and performance contributes to this problem; however, the fundamental difficulty is lack of standards for entering and staying in school, and lack of cost to the student for staying longer than necessary. Desertion rates typically range from 30 to 40 percent, but an even larger share of inefficiency may arise from students remaining many years at university while taking very light academic loads. The low salaries of university teachers help account for the apparently low level of spending per pupil, but do not explain why costs are no higher than in secondary schools. Low pay explains why most university teachers work only part time.

19.   Lack of serious academic entrance requirements means either that the level of teaching will fall to match students' abilities, or that the university must spend part of its resources raising students to the level of competence they should have acquired before entering. There is an even more pernicious effect of the influx of ill-prepared students in the case of public universities; those students often will resist an attempt to raise standards to protect their status at the university as students, which contributes to the politization of their institution.

20.   Public university education in Argentina is largely or entirely free. This means that the upper classes, which are better able to send their children through secondary school and to afford keeping them out of the labor market, are better placed to take advantage of the subsidy than are poorer families. Anecdotal evidence suggests that approximately 50-60 percent of the university students come from the paid, private

secondary schools. Public financing of the system is therefore regressive, despite the intention to be equitable. Proposals to introduce realistic--not necessarily full-cost--tuition have been discussed for years, but implemented only recently in such places as Cordoba. Students' interests and the autonomy and weak leadership of the universities also combine to work against it.

21. Another institutional problem is the traditional organization of higher education by discipline, under which each faculty sets its own rules--with much more laxity in some departments than others; moreover, a complicating factor is that students typically study only one subject. The "university" in effect is really merely an administrative umbrella for essentially autonomous faculties. It is plausible that the resulting narrowness of education and the very low standards in some disciplines help explain the low return to higher schooling, but one cannot conclude that definitively from available evidence. At most, a thoroughgoing reform of the universities appears necessary, including the adoption of higher, facility-wide standards, which could raise the return to schooling at their level and therefore help to justify the greater expenditure that will be needed if quality is to be raised or even maintained in some order.

22. Some initiatives to improve the educational and financial performance of the public university system have already begun. A committee made up of the Secretary of Finance, Subsecretary of Coordination of MEC, and four deans representing the universities, has been formed. Agreements were reached with each of the 29 universities on the need for university system reform. Universities were allocated a given budget to manage in 1992 and legislation was drafted that incorporated provisions for the sale of technology and research results by universities to increase their revenues; joint ventures with industry to establish a link with labor market needs; administrative and organizational reforms; and cost recovery. These proposals are all steps in the right direction; it remains to be seen how readily they can be implemented, given the extreme political sensitivity of these issues.[8]

D. Policy Options for Reform

Defining The Federal Role

23. As the Government prepares to commit another US$1.6 billion to education and research, it must reevaluate the role of the Federal Government in education. One strategy is for the Government to focus on broad policy, leadership, and communication in innovative specialized programs across provinces, and national quality standards. This would permit some reduction of funds spent on policy (US$105 million) and other programs, which would be reviewed for their effectiveness. The review should focus on the efficiency of Teacher Education and Training Programs (US$83 million), the Cultural Budget (US$16 million), Technical Education Council (US$17 million), and Scientific Research (US$42 million).

---

8 *"Private Financing of Higher Education in Latin America and the Caribbean,"* Technical Department, Latin America and the Caribbean Office, The World Bank, March 1992.

24.   Other policies that would form part of a new federal education policy include: (i) Facilitate the negotiation of *convenios* with the provincial governments, under whose terms they will take over the secondary schools, by improving estimates of province-by-province financing requirements. (ii) Improve the sectoral information system (it now has raw enrollment data only up through 1988, and analyses of data only through 1986) but mostly so it can be used to estimate efficiency. The basic data on enrollment can be turned into analyses of dropout and repetition rates and of years of effort required to produce a year of completed schooling. Even without getting into the issue of quality, this work might show how to reduce wastage in the system. (iii) On the basis of the 1991 experiment with standardized tests, develop a set of uniform national tests of learning in a few basic subjects, at least in Spanish and mathematics, and start administering them. Such tests have flaws, especially for international comparisons, but the total absence of tests is worse. This would focus attention on some of the more measurable aspects of quality, help those provinces wanting to create a better system, and provide a real learning measure to accompany the indicators of physical output. (iv) Survey the status of textbooks as to obsolescence, accuracy, etc., and prepare a plan for textbook renewal. Publishers could be expected to jump at the opportunity; individual schools reportedly have considerable freedom to order texts from an approved list, so they would not feel compelled to buy just one book in each category; and various types of technical assistance would be readily available both nationally and from abroad.   These actions are consistent with a revised federal mandate, and could markedly increase the efficiency of expenditures.

University Reform

25.   The largest potential efficiency gains in federal spending are to be found at the university level. Even the relatively high share of the budget has not been sufficient to prevent decline in the quality of public university education in Argentina.

26.   Because competing private universities can fulfill much of the demand and because subsidies to university students tend to be regressive (most graduates earn better-than-average salaries), the Government should consider a program of phased divestiture of the university system. This would allow it to concentrate its resources on selected subsidies to low income university scholarships and enrichment programs for primary and secondary education administered at the provincial level.

27.   As an interim policy, the Government should consider the establishment of a combination of user fees (i.e., tuition) and targeted subsidies (i.e., loans and scholarships for low-income, meritorious students) to enhance financing. Adopting a needs-based, targeted student loan program would ensure that low-income students would have access to university education. If the system's 700,000 students were charged a modest tuition of US$100 per term plus US$20 per month (private universities charge US$250-600 tuition plus US$300-800 month), the Government would mobilize nearly US$300 million of additional funds. Adopting a needs-based, targeted student loan program would ensure that low-income students would have access to university education.

Subsidies to Private Education

28.　　　　Private schools play an important role in Argentina, more so as the public system deteriorates. However, the quality is varied, public accountability in the use of public resources is minimal, and subsidies tend to be regressive. The Government should review the system of private subsidies and consider moving to portable subsidies to individuals rather than institutions so as to enhance competition in service delivery.

Future Spending

29.　　　　Total spending will probably have to increase--especially at the provincial level--as part of an overall reform, even after gains from reallocating existing budgets have been undertaken.

30.　　　　First, it may be necessary to equalize salaries between provincial and federal teachers, as the federal secondary schools are handed over to provincial governments. The cost of increasing the pay of the ex-federal teachers to levels in the provinces has not been calculated, although this should be of basic concern to the provincial governments, which would have to pay any such cost.

31.　　　　Second, a general salary raise for full-time provincial teachers is necessary to attract better people and to restore morale. There is no estimate of what level of pay would be sufficient or reasonable for this purpose, nor how to define "comparable" work to establish comparable pay, but clearly it would have to be large enough to put an end to absenteeism and to reduce, if not eliminate, the tendency to work very few hours a week. Any general increase would have very large fiscal implications because it would presumably have to apply to primary teachers as well (although possibly with a smaller percentage increase).

32.　　　　This cost could be at least partially offset by reducing the number of teachers, consistent with reasonable class sizes. At present student-teacher ratios are quite low (about 11) and highly variable across provinces (6-15). Also, leaves are excessive and poorly monitored. A structural reform could substantially affect costs of higher wages.

33.　　　　Third, the Government must increase expenditures on textbooks and materials as well as investment. The school system needs better as well as more books; many of those in use are reported to be decades old, and some are said to be full of factual errors. This kind of increase would also have to apply to primary schools, although the cost there would be less because of the smaller variety and lower cost of the required books and materials. Finally, physical rehabilitation of school buildings cannot be avoided.[9]

9　　　Estimates of the cost are available from a recent census of educational infrastructure carried out under Bank loan 2984-AR.

CHAPTER 7. MILITARY EXPENDITURE

A. Introduction

1.   Military expenditures are the largest category of discretionary expenditure, absorbing about one-seventh of the noninterest federal budget. Military spending (other than pensions) is less than 2 percent of GDP, about one-third the level of the early 1980s, reflecting the Government's judgment that both external and internal threats to security have abated.

2.   Abroad, considerable progress has been achieved in improving external relations. After having been on the brink of war in 1978, Chile and Argentina signed a Treaty of Peace and Friendship in 1984 which, among other things, laid the basis for ending border disputes. In August 1991, the two countries signed a series of agreements designed to resolve 24 outstanding border conflicts. The unresolved territorial dispute over the Malvinas Islands, which led to war with Great Britain in 1982, is now subject to bilateral negotiation, and Argentina has reestablished diplomatic relations with the United Kingdom. Efforts have also been made to improve relations with Brazil, particularly in the nuclear field. A series of confidence-building measures undertaken since March 1985 led to the November 1990 announcement that Argentina and Brazil were renouncing the manufacture of nuclear weapons and intend to use their nuclear technology for "exclusively peaceful ends." In December 1991, the two countries agreed to open all nuclear facilities to international inspection.

3.   There also is increasing recognition of the value of regional agreements to limit arms procurement and overall levels of military expenditure. For example, upon signing the August 1991 agreement discontinuing production of chemical and biological weapons, Argentina and Brazil acknowledged the need for an agreement with other Latin American governments prohibiting the development of weapons of mass destruction. Peru's recent initiative within the Rio Group that proposed disarmament of the Southern Cone is yet another indication of the heightened interest in regional security arrangements.

4.   At home, the improved international situation following the collapse of the Soviet Union has virtually eliminated the perceived threat of external support for armed internal insurgency groups. The return to constitutional democracy in 1983 has proved to be enduring, even in the face of the country's most difficult economic crisis in 1989. The new strategic environment implies that the military's domestic political role can be transformed into one consistent with the professional role of the armed forces in modern democratic states.

5.   In the world of the 1990s, the Government has also recognized that there is a close relationship between military and economic security. Economic growth will strengthen Argentina's ability to compete in a world which, since the demise of East-West rivalry, is increasingly characterized by economic rather than military competition. Carefully controlling expenditure--including military expenditure--can contribute to

lowering both the fiscal deficit and the rate of inflation, as well as consolidate the restoration of high rates of sustainable economic growth. Coupled with the planned restructuring of the Armed Forces, which will strengthen the military's ability to carry out the functions assigned by the Government, a strong economy will provide the foundation on which Argentina will base its future relations with other countries.

6.   The Government has recognized that adopting this strategic vision implies formulating new spending priorities. The Government wants to refocus military spending honed on a new strategy deploying fewer fiscal resources but in a more efficient manner so as to maintain or even strengthen present levels of national security. This chapter examines military expenditures under the assumption that the Government's goal is to lower the cost of maintaining its armed forces without compromising national security. This can only be accomplished through enhancing the efficiency of the military.

B. Military Expenditures in 1984-1990

Armed Forces

7.   Argentine military expenditure averaged 2.8 percent of GDP in 1984-87 as shown in Table 7.1. In 1988, expenditure rose to a high of 3.3 percent of GDP, and fell to 2.7 percent in 1989 and 2.4 percent in 1990. This represents a significant reduction from the 1970s when military expenditure averaged 4.7 percent of GDP, and the early 1980s when military expenditure averaged 6.0 percent of GDP.[1]

8.   While military expenditure fell from 1988 to 1990, current personnel costs remained at 1.0 percent of GDP and pension payments averaged an additional 0.7 percent of GDP. Thus, the entire burden of expenditure adjustment fell on operations and maintenance and capital expenditure.[2] Operations and maintenance--which consists of transportation and office expenses, personnel-related purchases of goods and services, and maintenance--fell from 1.1 percent of GDP in 1988 to 0.6 percent of GDP in 1990 while capital expenditure fell from 0.5 percent to 0.1 percent of GDP. The overall share of personnel in military expenditure rose from 55 percent in 1988 to over 70 percent in 1990; operations and maintenance fell from 32 percent of total military expenditure to 25 percent; and capital expenditure fell from 13.4 percent to 4.7 percent of military expenditure.

---

[1]   Estimates prior to 1983 are based on data from the Stockholm International Peace Research Institute (SIPRI). These years were not examined in this report.

[2]   While below we have followed the Argentine convention of distinguishing between current and capital expenditures, the IMF's Government Financial Statistics classifies all military outlays as current consumption.

Table 7.1: Ministry of Defense Expenditure, 1984-90
(in percent of GDP)

	1984	1985	1986	1987	1988	1989	1990	1991	1992
Expenditure by Category	2.85	2.50	2.72	3.00	3.25	2.68	2.36	2.56	2.40
Current Expenditure a/	2.60	2.29	2.46	2.52	2.82	2.40	2.25	2.40	2.24
Personnel	1.19	0.89	0.91	1.01	1.00	0.99	1.00	1.02	0.99
Operations & Maintenance	0.71	0.84	0.91	0.81	1.07	0.79	0.59	0.69	0.57
Military Pensions	0.71	0.57	0.64	0.70	0.75	0.62	0.65	0.69	0.68
Capital Expenditure	0.25	0.21	0.26	0.48	0.43	0.27	0.11	0.16	0.16
Procurement	0.12	0.14	0.18	0.38	0.27	0.19	0.07	0.12	0.13
Construction	0.09	0.06	0.07	0.10	0.14	0.05	0.02	0.02	0.02
Research & Development	0.04	0.01	0.01	0.01	0.03	0.03	0.02	0.02	0.01
Expenditure by Branch	2.85	2.50	2.72	3.00	3.25	2.68	2.36	2.56	2.40
MCO Administration	0.08	0.16	0.08	0.22	0.44	0.48	0.36	0.33	0.30
Army	0.67	0.55	0.60	0.60	0.66	0.52	0.45	0.45	0.45
Navy	0.43	0.34	0.40	0.46	0.42	0.35	0.30	0.30	0.26
Air Force	0.59	0.56	0.63	0.63	0.57	0.45	0.30	0.33	0.28
Paramilitary	0.38	0.32	0.37	0.39	0.41	0.26	0.27	0.46	0.41
Military Pensions	0.71	0.57	0.64	0.70	0.75	0.62	0.65	0.69	0.68
Memo:									
Total Expenditure (Excluding Pensions)	2.14	1.94	2.08	2.31	2.50	2.05	1.71	1.86	1.72
Total Expenditure (in percent of Federal Government Expenditure) b/	14.33	13.78	14.54	15.41	17.50	16.67	14.13	11.85	10.22
Total Expenditure (1991 US$ millions)	3,768	3,168	3,656	4,121	4,350	3,433	3,036	2,374	2,625

a/   In government accounts, all military expenditure is recorded as current expenditure because
military capital equipment is not growth promoting. However, for purposes of this analysis,
the current-capital expenditure dichotomy is relevant.
b/   National Administration and Social Security excluding interest.

Source: Ministry of Defense.

Defense Enterprises

9.   Some 33 public enterprises are presently under the control of the Ministry
of Defense. These companies consist of steel producers, petrochemical companies,
shipyards, and producers of civilian and military goods. In total, they employed
approximately 33,000 workers in 1991. The primary subsidy to these enterprises
incorporated in military expenditures consists of the wages paid to the 10,000 employees
of the holding company, General Directorate for Military Factories (DGFM). These
companies were originally established in the 1940s through capital infusion from the
Ministry of Defense; the Government is currently servicing their foreign debts. During
the 1960s and 1970s, an undetermined amount of funds from some of these enterprises
was diverted to military spending. Other than the wage and debt obligations, there
currently appear to be no other Government payments to these companies. The Ministry
of Defense plans to privatize 30 of these companies in 1992.

C. Personnel, Wages, Allowances, and Pensions

Military Personnel

10.   The size and structure of Argentina's military and paramilitary forces have undergone dramatic changes since 1984. In the early 1980s, officers accounted for 8.5 percent of the total force. Total military personnel fell from 188,000 in 1984 to 98,000 in 1991 (Table 7.2). However, the size of the officer corp fell only 8 percent, and enlisted soldiers 13 percent, while the number of conscripts declined by 87 percent. Thus, the ratio of soldiers to officers fell from 11 to 6.

Table 7.2: Military Personnel, 1984-91

	1984	1985	1986	1987	1988	1989	1990	1991
Officers	15,952	15,425	14,725	14,570	14,603	14,734	14,838	14,598
Lieutenant General	0	3	1	1	1	1	0	2
Major General	10	20	9	14	13	14	19	17
Brigadier General	129	124	110	119	121	124	140	122
Colonel	1,143	1,176	944	987	1,012	1,062	1,135	1,055
Lieutenant Colonel	1,899	1,873	1,877	1,873	1,897	1,876	1,825	1,826
Major	1,922	1,986	2,114	2,247	2,366	2,507	2,574	2,558
Captain	2,992	2,955	2,904	2,883	2,836	2,890	2,763	2,905
First Lieutenant 1	2,761	2,631	2,334	2,411	2,477	2,685	2,995	2,983
First Lieutenant 2	2,351	2,332	2,293	2,263	2,223	2,039	1,997	1,765
Second Lieutenant	2,745	2,325	2,139	1,772	1,657	1,536	1,390	1,365
Enlisted	82,861	78,949	75,773	72,988	72,325	70,323	72,669	71,754
Sergeant Major	3,083	2,565	2,084	2,172	2,197	2,233	2,329	2,150
Sergeant Principal	3,587	3,722	3,635	3,817	4,224	4,263	4,800	5,141
Sergeant Adjunct	7,907	7,866	8,428	8,692	9,313	9,594	10,476	10,630
Sergeant 1	10,572	10,789	11,757	11,432	11,401	12,035	12,507	13,414
Sergeant	14,260	13,117	11,894	12,555	13,766	14,628	16,165	15,952
Corporal 1	17,322	19,123	17,071	16,804	14,844	13,407	12,276	11,344
Corporal, Gendarme, Sailor & Private	26,130	22,767	20,904	17,516	16,580	14,163	14,116	13,123
Conscripts	89,441	48,540	37,692	40,821	42,290	46,755	29,685	11,826
Total	188,254	142,914	128,190	128,379	129,218	131,812	117,192	98,178
Memo: Soldiers/Officers a/	10.8	8.3	7.7	7.8	7.8	7.9	6.9	5.7

a/ Soldiers include enlisted and conscripts.

Source: Ministry of Defense.

11.   These changes in personnel have converted the structure from a pyramid to one with bulges in the middle ranks of officers and in the upper ranks of the enlisted corp.   Lieutenant colonels outnumber second lieutenants in the armed forces and sergeants outnumber or nearly equal lower-ranking soldiers in most of the services. This is the logical outcome of reducing military outlays and reducing entry at lower grades.

Civilian Personnel of the Ministry of Defense

12.   Civilian personnel employed by the Ministry of Defense decreased by nearly 25 percent between 1984 and 1990 (Table A7.1). This can be attributed to the relatively low wages paid to these workers, their low productivity, and a voluntary retirement program implemented by the Ministry in 1987. In 1984 the ratio of civilian Ministry of Defense workers to active duty servicemen was 28 percent, excluding DGFM personnel. By 1990, this ratio had risen to 34 percent.

Wages and Allowances

13.   Salaries paid by the Ministry of Defense to both military and civilian personnel are composed of a base wage (which is taxable) and several non-taxable allowances, only a portion of which are included in the calculation of pensionable income (Tables A7.3 and A7.4). Argentine military wages are significantly higher than civil service wages, and are on a par with military wages in other countries compared to private sector incomes.

14.   On average, military personnel receive higher wages than civil service personnel at roughly the same level and with approximately the same number of years of service. A colonel with 33 years of service had a net annual income in 1991 of US$23,774 compared to US$11,545 for a grade 30 civilian employee of the Ministry of Defense with 30 years of experience. Most civilian Ministry of Defense employees earned less in 1991 than the average first lieutenant. Among the enlisted ranks, a sergeant adjunct who had served 21 years earns 2.7 times the average grade 21 civilian employee with 20 years of experience.

15.   In general, the net annual income received by Argentine military personnel does not appear excessive compared to wages in the private sector or to military wages in other countries. The average skilled industrial worker received a net annual income of US$6,500 in 1991, which is comparable to that of a corporal first class. The industrial worker's supervisor earns about US$10,400, equivalent or the net annual income of a first lieutenant or a mid-level sergeant. A bilingual executive secretary earns about US$17,000, which approximates the net annual income of a sergeant major. A plant manager in the manufacturing sector earns between US$45,000 and US$65,000 (net of additional compensation), well in excess of the US$27,000 net annual income in 1991 of a brigadier general with 37 years of military service.

16.   For the higher ranks, a general with 26 years in the United States military earns 3.4 times the median family income and 1.7 times the mean family income for a family of four. In Brazil, a general who has served for 30 years earns 3.3 times the median and 1.7 times the mean income. A general who has served 40 years in the Argentine armed forces earns 3.7 times the estimated median and 1.8 times the mean income.

17.   A mid-level officer in the U.S. military with 15 years of service earns 1.6 times the median income and 0.8 times the mean income. A Brazilian major with 20 years of service earns 2.1 times the median and 1.0 times the mean income. An

Argentine major who has served 21 years receives 1.9 times the median income and 1.0 times the mean income. A U.S. warrant officer with 26 years' experience earns a salary 1.1 times the median income and 0.6 times the mean income. In Brazil, a sergeant with 21 years of service receives 0.9 times the median and 0.5 times the mean income. An Argentine sergeant with 31 years of service receives 2.1 times the median income and 1.0 times the mean income. In essence, although Argentine military wages are significantly higher than civil service wages, they are on a par with military wages in other countries compared to private sector incomes.

Pensions

18.   Military pensions are managed by the Institute for Financial Aid to Retired Military Personnel (I.A.F.). Due to the generous terms provided to the military, employer and worker contributions are not sufficient to cover current payments to the military. The I.A.F. pays from one-fourth to one-third of the total pensions out of its funds and the Treasury directly pays the remaining portion out of general funds.

19.   Military pensions are 82 percent of pensionable income and are adjusted in line with actual military pay increases. Military personnel with less than 15 years of service receive no pension, those who have served between 15 and 35 years receive 45-50 percent, and those with over 35 years of service receive their entire net pension. In contrast, to receive a pension, civilians must work 30 years. Those who retire before completing 30 years' service must work additional years in the private sector to be eligible for a pension.

20.   Unlike the civilian social security funds, there is no reciprocity between the I.A.F. and the civilian social security system. Thus, a major who serves 25 years in the military receives only half his net pension at retirement and must work an additional 30 years in the civilian sector to be eligible for a civilian pension.[3]

D. Overview of Military Expenditure: 1991-1992

21.   Military expenditure in 1991 was projected to increase to 2.7 percent of GDP from 2.4 percent in 1990 (Table A7.2 and A7.6). Most of the increase relative to GDP is accounted for in the budgets of the paramilitary forces, which rise from 0.3 percent of GDP to 0.5 percent; the budgets of the military branches and Ministry of Defense administration do not appreciably change relative to GDP. This reflects the Government's decision to expand the role of the paramilitary to concentrate efforts on border control.

---

3   The probability of achieving a civilian pension is minimal, particularly for mid- and high-ranking officers and enlisted men with many years of service. If, however, a former serviceman did complete 30 years in the civil sector, his total combined pension payments could not exceed the current salary (exclusive of non-pension supplements) received by a Brigadier General with 35 years of service.

22.　　　　The 1992 budget, submitted to Congress in September 1991, proposes that military expenditure increase by 12.8 percent, in line with expected inflation. Therefore, the real level of military expenditure is budgeted to remain constant and to fall to 2.5 percent of GDP (given the 6.5 percent real growth rate projected by the Government). The budget does not reflect 1992 restructuring of personnel and facilities. However, these measures are expected to lower expenditures only after 1992. The budget also does not reflect the recently enacted military pay increases.

23.　　　　With respect to the composition of military expenditure in Argentina, personnel costs (excluding pensions) absorb 60 percent, a disproportionately high share. In 1990, capital expenditure accounted for only 6 percent of total expenditure while operations and maintenance were 33 percent. A comparison of the composition of military budgets in other countries underscores the degree to which personnel costs absorb too large a share of the military budget. For instance, Brazil, Chile, Colombia, and Greece allocated on average 52 percent of their military budgets to personnel, 24 percent to operations and maintenance, and 24 percent to procurement, construction, and research and development in 1990.[4]

E. Personnel Retrenchment Policy Options

24.　　　　The Government recognizes that releasing civilian and military personnel is central to redressing expenditure imbalances. Reform has the potential to cut total expenditures while at the same time maintaining the level of effective security services delivered. This would be an unambiguous policy improvement from the perspective of the Government.

Civil Service Retrenchment

25.　　　　The Ministry of Defense is instituting substantial cuts in civilian personnel as part of the Government's overall retrenchment policy. As of 1990, there were 50,300 civil servants while military personnel had fallen to 117,000, producing a ratio of 43 percent. In 1991, 16 percent of civil service workers were released, and in 1992 a further decrease of 22 percent is planned. The Ministry's plan to reduce civilian workers to 27,000 by 1993 will lower the ratio to 28 percent of 1991 levels of military personnel.[5]

26.　　　　Data on the number of personnel released in each grade was not available. However, assuming the Ministry of Defense follows a pattern similar to the rest of the public sector in its 1991 retrenchments, a disproportionate number of lower grade personnel will be released. Because the remaining number of lower-level personnel will be quite small, the 1992 retrenchment program is expected to be more evenly distributed among the lower, middle, and higher grades of civil servants.

4　　Per capita income levels in Argentina, Brazil, Chile, and Colombia are in the range of middle-income developing countries. Per capita income in Greece is somewhat higher.

5　　The Ministry of Defense is contemplating reducing military personnel.

27.   The net benefits of the administrative reform program in 1991 and 1992 consist of the cost of releasing workers offset by the cost savings to the Government. The immediate cost to the Government is the severance payment. In subsequent years, the costs fall to zero until workers become eligible to receive pension payments. Beginning in 1993 the combined savings to the Government would be in the range of US$80 million per year or about 9 percent of total personnel costs. To the extent that military personnel are released, further retrenchment of civil service personnel would be warranted.

Military Personnel Retrenchment

28.   The progress being registered in releasing civil service personnel has not yet been matched by a military restructuring plan, although the Government has formally announced its intention of reducing the armed forces by 20 percent. There are three important reasons why restructuring military personnel, as is already being contemplated by the Ministry of Defense, is a necessary ingredient of the reform strategy. First, the new security environment warrants a different configuration of forces. Second, in the long run, the only method of correcting the imbalance between personnel costs and capital expenditure lies in releasing military personnel. At the present time, total expenditure stands at about 2.5 percent of GDP. If personnel costs were to remain the same, overall expenditures would have to rise to as much as 4 percent of GDP to reach a proper mix between current and capital expenditures. Such increases are clearly not consistent with Government macroeconomic policy goals.

29.   The third reason to consider retrenchment of military personnel is the imbalance in the structure of the military. Although the number of military personnel has been halved since 1984, almost all the decrease has been implemented through attrition of officers and enlisted men and by a significant reduction in the number of conscripts. These developments, while a source of important fiscal savings, have seriously altered the personnel structure of the military resulting in an officer corps structure suited to a force twice the size of the current Argentine armed forces. The only means available to correct the situation rapidly is to trim personnel from those ranks that are overstaffed, thereby reestablishing the traditional pyramid.

30.   Since detailed information on plans to restructure the Army, Air Force, and Navy is as yet unavailable, several scenarios for the Armed Forces have been examined for purposes of illustration (Table 7.3). These will indicate the costs of options available to the Government. Clearly, an optimum staff structure can be determined only in the context of a thorough review of security needs, threat analysis, force composition, the relative roles of the different branches, the functions each will be required to perform, and the implications for unit composition and equipment. Nonetheless, these scenarios demonstrate how the costs of options available to the Government may be calculated and what the magnitude of specific reductions might be.

31.   The financial consequences of various alternative policies are estimated below. The analysis proceeds in the following manner. First, the financial consequences of releasing a soldier at any given rank are calculated (Table A7.5). This enables the Government to quantify the implications of any retrenchment policy scenario

it chooses to pursue. Second, the financial impact of a retrenchment scheme consistent with a 25-percent, across-the-board reduction is evaluated. Finally, the financial implications of a retrenchment scheme that would restore the pyramid personnel structure is examined (Scenario II). Although the examination of Scenario II has some clearly beneficial efficiency attributes, the report should not be interpreted as recommending this specific policy. Furthermore, although the evaluation is made on an annual basis, there is no need to implement this scheme immediately. In fact, there may be certain financial advantages to spreading out retrenchment over two or three years because the cost savings from the initial year can be used to fund severance payments for subsequent years.

Table 7.3: Military Personnel - Retrenchment Scenarios (1984-91)

	Actual 1991	% 1991	Scenario I a/ Across the Board Reductions No. Re-trenched	Proj. 1992	% 1992	Scenario II b/ Reestablishing Pyramid No. Re-trenched	Proj. 1992	% 1992
Officers	14,598	14.9	848	13,750	18.7	8,266	6,332	8.6
Lieutenant General	2	0.0	0	2	0.0	0	2	0.0
Major General	17	0.0	0	17	0.0	9	9	0.0
Brigadier General	122	0.1	0	122	0.2	61	61	0.1
Colonel	1,055	1.1	28	1,027	1.4	791	264	0.4
Lieutenant Colonel	1,826	1.9	85	1,741	2.4	1,370	457	0.6
Major	2,558	2.6	167	2,391	3.2	1,919	640	0.9
Captain	2,905	3.0	215	2,690	3.7	2,179	726	1.0
First Lieutenant 1	2,983	3.0	227	2,756	3.7	1,939	1,044	1.4
First Lieutenant 2	1,765	1.8	79	1,686	2.3	0	1,765	2.4
Second Lieutenant	1,365	1.4	47	1,318	1.8	0	1,365	1.9
Enlisted	71,754	73.1	20,164	51,590	70.1	4,480	67,274	91.6
Sergeant Major	2,150	2.2	118	2,032	2.8	538	1,613	2.2
Sergeant Principal	5,141	5.2	673	4,468	6.1	1,285	3,856	5.2
Sergeant Adjunct	10,630	10.8	2,877	7,753	10.5	2,658	7,973	10.8
Sergeant 1	13,414	13.7	4,582	8,832	12.0	0	13,414	18.2
Sergeant	15,952	16.2	6,480	9,472	12.9	0	15,952	21.7
Corporal 1	11,344	11.6	3,277	8,067	11.0	0	11,344	15.4
Corporal, Gendarme, Sailor & Private	13,123	13.4	2,157	10,966	14.9	0	13,123	17.8
Conscripts	11,826	12.0	3,561	8,265	11.2	11,826	0	0.0
Total	98,178	100.0	24,574	73,604	100.0	24,573	73,605	100.0

a/   Scenario I lowers the force size by 25 percent. Each rank is cut in proportion to its share of the total.

b/   Scenario II also lowers the force size by 25 percent, but the distribution of personnel is altered to produce a pyramidal hierarchy.

Source: Staff estimates.

32.   The costs of releasing a soldier are the retrenchment payments and the pension payments for those who are eligible. The fiscal benefits or cost savings to the Government consist of the salary the soldier would have received, pensions that would have been paid to retiring personnel, costs of hiring replacement personnel (to maintain the same size of the military), and personnel carrying costs. The basic wage base is assumed to remain constant in real terms throughout.

33.   Scenario I shows the potential cost savings of a random retrenchment policy that lowers the total by 25 percent and each rank by its share based on a formula that reduces ranks with the largest number of personnel the most. This scenario takes no account of efficiency or the military's personnel needs. It moves the personnel structure in the direction of a similar proportion of personnel at each rank instead of a more efficient pyramid structure. The overall savings from this policy are quite dramatic. In the initial year, net benefits are positive, and in subsequent years savings amount to over US$200 million per year with a present value after four years equal to US$865 million.

34.   Scenario II is based on the objective of reestablishing a modern military pyramid. As in scenario I, the total number of personnel declines by 25 percent but the distribution is altered to produce a pyramid hierarchy, thus improving the operational efficiency of the military. The following policies were assumed. First, all conscription is discontinued in accordance with the recent trend. Although this does not help to create a pyramidal personnel structure, it coincides with policies implemented in other nations where a professional army has proven more cost effective (despite lower salary payments to conscripts). Second, all personnel in the lowest two officer ranks and the four lowest enlisted ranks are retained. Third, the top three enlisted ranks are cut by 25 percent and the middle five officer ranks by 75 percent equivalent to a 55 percent decrease of all officers and a 6 percent decrease of enlisted personnel. Fourth, the number of generals is reduced by 50 percent. Overall, costs exceed benefits by US$65 million in the first year; however, in subsequent years savings are approximately US$155 million. In total, the present value of the savings four years after program implementation is US$535 million.[6]

F. Facilities, Assets and Operations

35.   In addition to retrenching military and civilian personnel, the Ministry of Defense has begun a process of administrative reorganization and facilities restructuring designed to make the existing military personnel, plant facilities, and equipment more effective in providing national security. Administrative reorganization will consolidate activities and lead to discontinuation of certain administrative operations. Facilities restructuring involves consolidation of facilities, closure of certain facilities, and sale of redundant assets.

36.   As with personnel retrenchment, the cost of restructuring facilities is likely to exceed benefits in the early stages. Reorganization of facilities normally requires high initial outlays for the transfer of personnel and capital equipment and modification of facilities to prepare them for their new tasks. There is often a delay in asset sales, as a modification of facilities generally precedes consolidation, and generally

---

6   In contrast, the economic gains to the country will consist of the increase in national output attributed to released workers, and thus are only realized when released personnel eventually obtain employment in the private sector. To some extent, these real efficiency gains will not be reflected in an increase in measured GDP due to the accounting practice that equates government services with government expenditures.

precedes asset sales. These costs can be contained by using existing facilities to the extent possible. The initial costs will be offset in future years through decreased operating expenses and accelerated asset sales. There will also be a gain to the country from improved strategic capabilities of existing facilities.

37.   In December 1991, Congress approved a law allowing the Ministry of Defense to retain the proceeds from all asset sales under its administration. Normally, assets are not owned by an individual ministry, but instead are the property of the whole government; individual ministries are the custodians--not owners--of government property. Nonetheless, a policy of permitting ministries to retain a portion of the revenues from asset sales is desirable because it provides an incentive for ministries to vigorously pursue asset sales, and rewards them for instituting cost savings improvements. The current practice of permitting the Ministry of Defense to retain all proceeds, however, appears to be generous. The Ministry of Economy should at least monitor the disposition of these funds within the Ministry of Defense budget to ensure that they are devoted to funding structural reform measures--through canceling liabilities of the defense sector rather than funding current expenditure. To the extent that funds are not used in this manner, the Ministry of Defense should be forced to forfeit some of the proceeds.

38.   The process of facilities restructuring is still in its nascent stages and no cost assessment is possible at this time. However, the three military branches have identified certain actions and have outlined the basic direction envisioned.

39.   The *Army* recently announced broad reform measures including asset sales; elimination of some of the existing operations; consolidation of units, agencies, commands, and directorates; and building new facilities where necessary and upgrading existing ones. During the fourth quarter of 1991, a number of immediate measures were set in motion designed to produce cost savings without placing an additional burden on the budget. These include consolidation of army arsenals and sale of real estate.

40.   The *Air Force* has embarked on a plan to decrease operating costs by making better use of existing equipment thereby obviating the need to make additional purchases of spare parts by eliminating less strategically important flights and by consolidating certain administrative and educational functions.

41.   The *Navy* plans to reduce the number of departments, restructure the naval education system, and centralize educational facilities for enlisted personnel. Several commands and agencies will be transferred and consolidated.[7]

G. Conclusions

Military Expenditure in Modern Argentina

---

[7]   See Annex 7 for a more detailed description of these activities.

42.   Prior to 1984, military expenditure in Argentina was well above the world average. Since that time the Government has reduced military expenditure considerably to roughly half the world average. However, military expenditures in Argentina still remain somewhat higher than the Latin America average and are still a significant proportion of government spending and particularly of discretionary government spending. The Government's announced intention to review military expenditure policy in the context of total government expenditure policy is indeed timely and necessary.

43.   Throughout the world, a trend has been developing to lower military expenditure. Many governments are reallocating budgetary resources to higher priority areas. Even prior to the emergence of this trend, there were at least 10 countries with military expenditure of 1.0 percent or below.[8] In Latin America, countries such as Brazil, Costa Rica, the Dominican Republic, Ecuador, Jamaica, Mexico, Paraguay, and Venezuela are estimated by SIPRI to spend 1.5 percent of GDP or less on the military. Decreased tensions and the development of regional security arrangements have the potential to greatly diminish the need for security expenditures by all countries in Latin America.

Reform Principles

44.   As Argentina undertakes a reform of the military and an improvement of its overall public finances, certain principles of reform will be crucial to its success. One principle is that in modern societies, the military is subject to the same **budgetary processes and controls** as other sectors of the Government. **Public transparency**, widely regarded as a condition for a sound democratic process, substantially enhances the Government's monitoring of economic ministerial activities. For instance, the military could benefit from an assessment of proposed equipment purchases that take account of the total lifetime costs of proposed options. Such cost assessments could be an important input into a process whereby the military attempts to obtain the highest security benefits from a given military capital budget.

45.   A second budgetary principle is that all sectors of the Government should contribute to lowering the fiscal deficit. Therefore, some portion of the financial gains from reforming the military should revert back to the Treasury. Alternatively, the Treasury should be in a position to monitor closely the use of the funds by the Ministry of Defense.

46.   A third budgetary principle is that proceeds from asset sales should be used to finance structural reforms rather than pay for current operations. The present reform plans under consideration by the Ministry of Defense are likely to require substantial initial outlays that will result in reduced expenditure in the medium term. Relocation and reconfiguration of facilities requires an initial investment to prepare assets for sale and to refurbish existing facilities to prepare them for their new uses. Furthermore, the military will not likely need to acquire improved transportation equipment to perform its assigned functions. Retrenchment of certain ranks involves a

---

8   These include Costa Rica, Fiji, Ghana, Jamaica, Japan, Luxembourg, Mauritius, Mexico, Niger, and Sierra Leone; based on military expenditure estimates from SIPRI for 1988-89.

high initial outlay for severance compensation. Privatization of public enterprise also requires an initial investment before net proceeds can be realized. The Treasury should be in a position to ensure that the Ministry of Defense uses any excess funds from its reforms in this manner.

47.   Thus the proceeds from asset sales and privatization of defense industries should be allocated to pay for military personnel retrenchment, reform of military pensions, retire debt, or prepare facilities for sale. Some portion of the savings realized by the retrenchment of military personnel might be applied to operations and maintenance or capital expenditure, as well as to structural reforms. Care must be taken to establish a strong accountability mechanism and transparency to avoid misuse of proceeds.

Proposed Reforms

48.   The Government of Argentina has recognized that military expenditure in Argentina has two serious imbalances: (i) disparity exists between the level of equipment-related expenditure and personnel expenditure, which greatly diminishes the security benefits obtained from the military budget; and (ii) the other major imbalance exists in the structure of personnel. Today's strategic and economic environment has led to a 48 percent reduction in the size of the force. As a result, the military has too many officers and sergeants in proportion to the lower ranks leading to much higher personnel costs than necessary to maintain the current size of the military. The Government has proposed to correct this imbalance through major reforms of the military that focus among other things on retrenchment of military personnel.

49.   The Ministry of Defense should initiate a formal review process to examine the structure of the armed forces in light of Argentina's security requirements. A **retrenchment scheme** that decreases military personnel by 25 percent by releasing 55 percent of officers (through attrition, early retirement and compensated voluntary severance packages), canceling conscription, and releasing through a phased program 6 percent of enlisted personnel (from the ranks of upper-level sergeants) has shown that a pyramid structure can be reestablished resulting in considerable savings in the near term. The cost of this scheme in the initial year is estimated at US$65 million. In subsequent years, the annual cost savings will exceed US$150 million. A retrenchment scheme to release 40 percent of its civil service workers leads to an estimated initial net loss of US$25 million in 1991 and US$42 million from the planned retrenchment in 1992. This will result in annual savings of US$80 million in subsequent years. Therefore, the net savings from retrenching both civilian and military personnel has the potential to lower effective personnel costs by nearly 20 percent of 1991 levels.

50.   An additional method of lowering personnel costs would be to **rationalize the pension system**. Military pensions are based on earnings in one year, compared to an average of three years for civilians. We recommend that the government bring military pensions into conformity with the civil service pension system, currently under review. At the same time, we recommend that the Government allow portability between the two systems, as already occurs with the civil service and private sector pension systems. This would enable a smoother transition to a smaller force by

permitting released military personnel to incorporate their years of service into the civilian pension system. Furthermore, it could help defer pension payments to released military personnel and thereby spread out the costs of retrenchment.

51. **Military wage scales should be simplified** by incorporating pensionable allowances and the seniority premium into the taxable wage base while making appropriate adjustments to the remaining premiums. Transparency would make a higher proportion subject to income tax in line with other improvements in the tax system.

52. The Ministry of Defense has analyzed the nature and location of defense facilities and concluded that substantial **restructuring of these facilities** could greatly enhance the effectiveness of the military. This process will also release substantial assets the Ministry of Defense proposes to sell to finance its restructuring. The Government should ensure full transparency of accounting from proceeds of asset sales.

53. To facilitate the restructuring process, the Ministry of Economy should agree to allocate a fixed share of the budget to the Ministry of Defense over the medium term. This would provide an incentive to restructure by guaranteeing a specific level of expenditures for a period of years.

CHAPTER 8. THE PRESIDENCY

A. Presidency Expenditures

1.   The Presidency represents a significant proportion of government spending, averaging 8.2 percent of national non-interest expenditures since 1980 (Table 8.1).   The Argentine Constitution mandates the existence of no more than eight Ministries in the national administration, a limit recently reenforced with the administrative reform of 1991-92.   However, governments have used the Presidency jurisdiction as the sphere of Government where secretariats with Ministerial rank could be established.   This could explain the increase in current expenditures, especially the wage bill and the resulting increase in purchases of goods and services.   Current expenditures for the Presidency have averaged 3.4 percent of national administration expenditures in the period 1980-91.

2.   Capital expenditures, which doubled in 1982, have averaged 4.8 percent of national administration spending.   These expenditure patterns can be explained by the development of Argentina's nuclear energy capabilities in the 1980s, in particular the nuclear plants, Atucha I and II.[1]   Expenditures for the National Commission of Atomic Energy have accounted for a significant proportion of investment spending by the national administration.

Jurisdiction of the Presidency

3.   Recent efforts have been made to decrease the size and role of the state. One of the more comprehensive programs to achieve this objective is the administrative reform program of the public sector aimed at: (i) strengthening the Government by focusing on core functions and reducing its scope, including a substantial reduction of public employment in the Federal Government by mid-1992; and (ii) restoring incentives and flexibility in public employment by increasing the salary compression ratio (highest to lowest paid) from a low 3:1 to 10:1 by mid-1992.   Under this program, ministerial structures were reorganized to reflect a new economic role of the state.

4.   The Presidency, however, has been largely exempt from the administrative reform program.   An increasing number of Government secretariats, subsecretariats, general and national directorates, departments and units in the central administration, and decentralized agencies were placed under the Presidency jurisdiction over the last years.   The areas covered by these range from drug prevention, sports, and tourism to science, technology, and public administration.   Personnel levels for the central administration and decentralized agencies as well as the number of sub-secretariats, general and national directorates, departments and units that fall under the Presidency in 1991 are presented in Table 8.2.   The Presidency is now organized into

---

1   See chapter on investment for a complete description of the evolution and performance of these investment projects.

a score of disparate administrative units and agencies, many of which duplicate functions undertaken in the Ministries.

Table 8.1: Presidency Expenditures, 1980-91
(US$ millions)

	1980	1981	1982	1983	1984	1985	1986	1987	1988	1989	1990	1991 a/
Current Expenditures	2.6	2.0	2.3	2.5	3.3	4.3	3.6	4.2	5.0	4.4	3.3	
Wages	1.4	1.1	1.0	1.0	1.5	1.7	1.4	1.7	2.2	2.0	1.8	
Goods and Services	1.1	0.8	1.2	1.2	1.7	2.6	2.1	2.4	2.8	2.3	1.4	
Transfers	0.1	0.0	0.1	0.2	0.0	0.0	0.2	0.1	0.1	0.0	0.1	
Capital Expenditures	3.6	3.9	7.6	6.4	4.9	5.4	5.4	5.6	3.1	3.5	3.4	
Total	6.1	5.9	9.9	8.9	8.2	9.7	9.0	9.7	8.1	7.9	6.7	6.5

a/ Data not available in disaggregated form.
b/ 1992 budget submitted to Congress.

Source: General Accounting Office.

Table 8.2: Presidency Structure, 1991

	Current Staff Level a/	No. of Subsecret.	No. of General Directorates	No. of National Directorates	No. of Directorates	No. of Departments	Other Units
Central Administration	3,750	17	32	16	44	2	9
Legal & Tech. Secret.	153	2	4	0	2	0	0
Gen. Secret. of the Pres.	793	3	7	0	13	1	1
Public Affairs Secret.	330	2	4	2	0	0	0
Science & Technology Secret.	190	3	1	5	8	1	2
Drug Prevention Secret.	83	2	2	5	0	0	0
Communications Secret.	1,077	0	4	1	7	0	0
Casa Militar	211	0	0	0	0	0	3
Presidential Unit	91	0	2	0	0	0	3
Presidential Spokesman Unit	54	0	2	0	0	0	0
National Sports Agency	125	3	1	3	3	0	0
National Tourism Agency	643	2	5	0	11	0	0
Decentralized Agencies	10,274						
INAP	148						
CONICET b/	5,441						
Lillo Foundation	198						
CONFER	251						
CNEA	4,236						
Total	14,024						

a/ Structure approved in the context of Decree 2476 of November 1990.
b/ Does not include 2,789 scholarship recipients.

Source: Boletin Oficial, various issues.

5.   Of the 14,000 employees in the Presidency, 4 units account for 80 percent: the Communications Secretariat (with about 1,000 employees), the National Tourism Agency (650), CONICET (5,450), and CNEA (4,200) (Table 8.2). The Presidential Spokesman Unit is responsible for formulating and controlling the execution of communications policies, disseminating governmental actions, and managing mass media, employing 50 workers. The Official Service of Radio Broadcasting, which includes all radio stations under this jurisdiction. The National Tourism Agency (ENATUR) contributes to the development and promotion of tourism at the national and international levels and tourism of a social and educational nature. It also provides non-regular air transportation services to tourist groups on occasion. The National Council on Science and Technology (CONICET) under the Secretariat of Science and Technology promotes, coordinates, and conducts research in the pure and applied sciences. It also promotes research in laboratories and other research centers and provides subsidies and scholarships to university graduates to promote scientific research. Researchers comprise 46 percent of staff (2,516) while technical support staff represent 53 percent (2,880). There are also 2,789 scholarship recipients at home and abroad. The National Commission of Atomic Energy (CNEA) promotes and undertakes industrial activities, including electricity production, and scientific studies on nuclear energy. It also supervises the implementation resulting from this research to ensure proper procedures are followed. Some of the research applications include power generation, agriculture, biology, and industry.

1992 Budget of the Presidency

6.   Total expenditures for the Presidency was US$1.4 billion in 1992, US$886 million corresponding to current expenditures (68 percent), and US$440 million (32 percent) for capital expenditures (Table 8.3). Most central administration expenditures correspond to the wage bill and purchases of goods and services. In the case of special accounts, the wage bill for the National Intelligence System (SIDE) represents an outlay of US$110 million.[2] Under decentralized agencies, 64 percent of total Presidency expenditures are allocated to investment spending for CNEA. Capital expenditures for this agency represent 99 percent of the Presidency capital spending budget of US$440 million.

---

2   Total expenditures for this special account, whose structure is not available to the public, represent 10 percent of the total Presidency wage bill.

Table 8.3: Presidency Expenditures, 1992
(US$ millions)

	Presidency Expenditures	Total Expenditures	Presidency Exp. as % of total
Functional Classification			
General Administration	213.6	2,768.4	7.7
Defense	0.0	1,738.7	0.0
Security	0.0	1,185.8	0.0
Health	0.0	641.4	0.0
Culture & Education	7.4	1,587.1	0.5
Economic Services	847.5	4,448.4	19.1
Social Welfare	6.9	2,629.2	0.3
Science & Technology	250.8	468.6	53.5
Public Debt	0.0	2,554.3	0.0
Total	1,326.2	18,022.2	7.4
Economic Classification			
Current Expenditures	885.8	15,381.4	5.8
Wages and Salaries	338.6	4,944.1	6.8
Goods and Services	245.8	1,853.6	13.3
Interest	188.6	8,014.7	6.3
Transfers	112.8	5,569.0	2.0
Capital Expenditures	440.2	2,640.8	16.7
Capital Goods	14.1	202.3	7.0
Construction	426.1	857.9	49.7
Financial Investment	0.0	1,580.6	0.0
Total	1,326.1	18,022.2	7.4

Source: Government of Argentina.

7.   Central administration expenditures account for 9 percent of total expenditures, special accounts for 12 percent, and 79 percent correspond to decentralized agencies.[3] Expenditures for general administration (16 percent), economic services (64 percent), and research and development (19 percent) account for 99 percent of total Presidency expenditures, with CNEA expenditures for economic services and research and development representing US$800 million and US$52 million, respectively.

8.   The main proposals presented in the budget include an increased drug prevention role, the development of space technology, the continuation of atomic energy policies with the corresponding maintenance of the two nuclear plants, and the near completion of the plant to manufacture a special coolant known as heavy water.

9.   The Government intends to intensify its drug prevention efforts in 1992. The Secretariat of Programming and Coordination for Drug Prevention will support national security forces and provincial police forces in their efforts to eliminate the use and commercialization of drugs. This will entail financing of operations, procurement of equipment, and prevention and rehabilitation programs.

---

3   See Tables 8.3 and 8.4 for a complete description of 1992 Presidency expenditures disaggregated by functional classification for the Central Administration, special accounts, and decentralized agencies.

10.   On space science and technology matters, the National Commission for Space Activities (CONAE) has been created to design, execute, control, and manage space projects.   CONAE will provide space technology training to agriculture, cartography, mining, meteorology, geology, environment, medicine, communications and defense, among others. It will also be available to the private sector once permits are granted.

11.   On atomic energy issues, expenditures for CNEA include nuclear fuel, heavy water, spare parts, and services.   These expenditures are estimated to equal US$150 million, including maintenance of the two nuclear plants, Atucha I and II. Some 60 percent of the Atucha II plant was completed by beginning of 1992. The 1992 budgeted expenditure equals US$380 million to be financed by a German credit line of US$304 million (80 percent), and the remaining US$76 million by issuing of CNEA bonds (which operate as counterpart funds). CNEA has scheduled completion of this plant for 1996.

12.   The industrial plant of heavy water, with a production capacity estimated at 200 tons per year, is expected to be fully operational in 1993 (98 percent has already been completed).   This plant is located in Arroyito in the Province of Neuquen, constructed under contract to a Canadian firm.

B. Recommendations

13.   The staff under the Presidency, following a pattern in other countries, has grown steadily in recent years, perhaps reflecting political demands. The number of secretariats, subsecretariats, directorates, departments and units as well as personnel levels has increased. The recent administrative reform program, which successfully reduced personnel levels in the national administration, has not significantly affected this jurisdiction. Some changes have been enacted; however, the approved structures reflect only marginal reforms.

14.   A close examination of the agencies under this jurisdiction and their roles suggests unnecessarily high employment levels in the central administration and decentralized agencies.   Furthermore, the public sector reforms in progress render certain roles obsolete. Thus, a comprehensive program to reform civil service should be implemented for the Presidency along with a redefinition of roles for agencies under its jurisdiction. This would entail the conversion of secretariats into subsecretariats, the elimination of agencies no longer relevant in the context of the existing economic framework, the consolidation of other agencies under a general Subsecretariat of the Presidency, the transfer of agencies that oversee matters relevant to other jurisdictions, and the privatization of decentralized agencies in line with recent efforts to improve public finances.

15.   Specific proposals for the Government to consider include:

Central Administration

o   Merge and rationalize the Legal and Technical Secretariat, and the General Secretariat of the Presidency under a new General Subsecretariat of the Presidency. From current staff levels of 946 employees, the new subsecretariat would retain, say, 650, with 277 jobs eliminated, and the 19 positions for the Commission on Environmental Policy transferred to the Ministry of Health and Social Action.

o   Eliminate the Public Administration Secretariat, since its functions are already being undertaken by the Ministry of Economy. The elimination of this redundant secretariat would result in a reduction of 330 permanent positions from the public sector budget.

o   Rationalize the Secretariat of Science and Technology under a new Subsecretariat of Science and Technology to be transferred to the Ministry of Education. This would entail the elimination of 90 positions from the Presidency budget, and the transfer of the remaining 100 positions to the Ministry of Education budget.

o   Transfer the Drug Prevention Secretariat to the Ministry of Health and Social Action under a new Subsecretariat of Drug Prevention. This would entail the removal of 83 positions from the Presidency budget.

o   Eliminate the Communications Secretariat and establish a Directorate of Communications under the new General Subsecretariat of the Presidency. Eventually, the National Service of Radio Telecommunications could be privatized, removing 950 positions from public sector accounts.

o   Rationalize the National Sports Agency by establishing a National Directorate to be transferred to the Ministry of Health and Social Action. This would entail eliminating 50 positions, and transferring 75 for a net reduction of 40 percent.

o   Rationalize the National Tourism Agency and establish a new National Directorate also under the jurisdiction of the Ministry of Economy. This would result in the elimination of 500 positions, and the transfer of 143 for a net reduction of 78 percent. The privatization of the Embalse and Chapadmalal tourist complexes would be necessary to achieve these personnel levels.

16.   The Casa Militar, Presidential Unit, and the Presidential Spokesman Unit, which have personnel levels under 250 employees, could remain unaltered.

Special Accounts

17.   The Government should consider reducing employment in SIDE and transferring it to the National Directorate of Intelligence under the Ministry of Interior. Its employment could be reduced to 200 which would reduce its wage bill by US$110 million. All other special accounts under the Presidency, except those related to Presidential expenses, should be eliminated.

Decentralized Agencies

18.   The recent economic events in Argentina, in particular the privatization of several public enterprises and public sector employment rationalization, have contributed to diminishing the role of the public sector in the economy. This trend continued in 1992 as the privatization process neared its conclusion. The Government should consider revamping INAP in the context of a new training program for civil servants; upgrading the quality of the civil service is imperative, but decentralizing training budgets to ministries and having those offices then contract out individual training courses may prove more cost effective. Some of the 148 staff of INAP could be relocated to the ministries to help organize the training.

19.   CONICET and the Miguel Lillo Foundation should be privatized, resulting in 5,639 positions being abolished from the public sector budget. Research and development activities could be undertaken in public and private universities. The Government could support these activities through specific programs financed by the corresponding ministerial jurisdictions on the basis on their immediate needs and financing requirements. The Government could also consider promoting private sector research development mainly by subcontracting with current CONICET researchers to undertake studies based on jurisdictional needs.

20.   The elimination of the Communications Secretariat in the central administration as described above would result in the elimination of CONFER along with its 251 positions.

21.   The CNEA should be restructured into business and research units. The power generation should constitute one business unit under the Secretariat of Energy in the Ministry of Economy. Also, the industrial plant for heavy water after completion could constitute another business unit under the same Secretariat. Possible privatization of these units could lead to an eventual savings of 4,236 positions, at an annual cost to the public sector of US$850 million.

Fiscal Impact of Reform Proposals

22.   The rationalization of the Presidency jurisdiction would result in a net savings of US$570 million (Table 8.4). The initial savings for the central administration and decentralized agencies would equal US$813 million, excluding severance payments. If voluntary retirement is assumed to take place, with an average of 13 years of service for retiring personnel, including a 20 percent premium added over the existing benefits under current legislation, the estimated cost to the Government of the administrative reform program would amount to US$240 million during the first year of the program. The net savings in later years will be greater since all payments to voluntary retirees will be made as they leave the public sector.

**Table 8.4: Estimated Fiscal Savings of Proposed Reform
of the Presidency in 1992
(US$ millions)**

	Savings
Central Administration	49.2
Wages	35.4
Goods and Services	13.8
Capital Expenditures	0.0
Decentralized Agencies	763.7
Wages	165.9
Goods and Services	163.5
Capital Expenditures	434.3
Savings	812.9
Cost to the Government a/	240.0
Net Savings	572.9

a/   Assumes voluntary retirement takes place with an average
of 13 years of service for personnel, including a 20 percent
premium over the existing benefits under current legislation.

Source: Staff estimates.

CHAPTER 9. PUBLIC ENTERPRISES

A. Background

1.   Over the last decade, the public enterprises (PEs) were linked to other sectors of the private economy and the public administration through a complex system of transfers.   Some of these transfers were implicitly reflected in low prices to consumers of public output and high prices to suppliers of goods and services. PEs in the hydrocarbons sector paid taxes that were earmarked for the social security and the investment funds. At the same time the Treasury, previously used to finance operational deficits, has been servicing a large part of the outstanding stock of foreign debt of the public enterprises.

2.   During the 1980s, the deficit of the public enterprises before transfers ranged between 2.2 percent and 6.9 percent of GDP. These deficits represented between 40 and 60 percent of the overall nonfinancial public sector deficit. In 1989, the deficit of public enterprises became larger than the overall deficit of the nonfinancial public sector. The deficit of the public enterprises (before transfers) was 3.4 percent of GDP in 1989, slightly larger that the overall deficit of 3.3 percent (Table 9.1). The continued deficits incurred in the public enterprises were the result of several factors. First, the Government pursued pricing policies that have oscillated between providing sufficient resources to cover costs and combating inflation through lagging prices. Second, legal constraints have been imposed on public procurement through the *Compre Argentino* law, resulting in inflated costs for the acquisition of inputs from the private sector.   Third, noneconomic objectives, such as employment maintenance, shackle the sector, particularly the railways. Finally, the need of subsidies to the energy sector to cross-subsidize losses in other enterprises has aggravated pricing distortions.

3.   The budget strategy of the Alfonsin Administration after 1987 was to build barriers between the Treasury and the nonfederal public sector in an attempt to force each component of government to put itself in fiscal balance. This principle permitted a substantial reduction of the amount of transfers in 1988, limiting them to 1.1 percent of GDP. However, insulating the public enterprise sector from the central administration was accomplished by an internal cross-subsidy system, whereby the money-making enterprises (essentially the state-oil company) had to provide funds to finance loss-making ones, particularly the railways. This system was dependent on reducing the deficit of loss-making enterprises, and guaranteeing sufficiently high real prices. Other unresolved issues (such as the royalty payments from the oil company that involved a strong subsidy element) also threatened the ability to generate sufficient resources.   But the most fundamental problem with this strategy was the distortion arising from cross-subsidies, since they led to greater distortions in prices, discouraged appropriate investment levels, and affected demand arbitrarily.

Table 9.1: Public Enterprise Budget, 1989-94
(% of GDP)

	1989	1990	1991	1992a/	1993a/	1994a/
Current Revenues	9.62	9.24	7.03	6.67	3.84	3.59
Current Expenditures	11.05	9.40	7.42	6.80	3.44	2.95
Interest	0.12	1.38	0.68	0.34	0.19	0.12
Domestic Debt b/	0.00	0.05	0.00	0.00	0.09	0.10
External Debt c/	0.12	1.33	0.68	0.34	0.09	0.02
Savings	-1.43	-0.16	-0.40	-0.13	0.40	0.64
Capital Revenues	0.04	0.01	0.25	0.00	0.00	0.00
Capital Expenditures	1.98	1.32	1.22	0.99	0.68	0.58
Financing Requirement (before transfers)	3.41	1.48	1.62	1.12	0.28	-0.06
Transfers	0.83	0.70	1.12	1.54	0.50	0.20
Central Administration	0.51	0.49	0.83	1.57	0.53	0.23
Special Accounts	0.32	0.22	0.29	0.00	0.00	0.00
Others	0.00	0.00	0.00	-0.04	-0.03	-0.03
Total Revenues	10.49	9.96	8.40	8.21	4.34	3.79
Total Expenditures	13.03	10.72	8.65	7.79	4.12	3.54
Financing Requirement	2.54	0.76	0.25	-0.42	-0.23	-0.26
Memo:						
Operating Surplus (US$ m)	-665	1379	1221	2880	3397	3598
Primary Balance (US$ m)	-242	2012	2858	4865	3747	3598
Privatization Revenues (US$ m)	0	633	1637	1985	350	0

a/ On the assumption that the following enterprises are not privatized before 1992: YPF, YCF, Yacyreta, Comision de Salto Grande, ENcotel and OED.

b/ Accrued real interest payments.

c/ Accrued external interest payments.

Source: Ministry of Economy, "Budget on a Cash Basis" and "Efecto Fiscal de las Privatizaciones."

4.   The Central Government often overruled the price-setting power of institutions as part of its attempt to control inflation. The strong fluctuations in the real price of public production, induced by policy considerations unrelated to the objectives of the public enterprises, provided a highly unstable environment, and prevented the public enterprises from pursuing strategies aimed at efficiency improvements (see Table 9.2). The prices of inputs used by the public enterprises have also frequently been set by political authorities, with a disregard for the economic cost of production. Almost 25 percent of the purchases of goods and services relate to transactions among public enterprises themselves at regulated prices. For example, YPF was required to sell gas to Gas del Estado below its own production cost and to buy coal from YCF at a price three times the international price of coal in 1988. Furthermore, purchases of the rest of the inputs were regulated by the *Compre Argentino* law, which favored domestic private industry. Since most of the private sector is oligopolistic in nature, sales to public enterprises were often executed at a premium and implied subsidies to private industries. Together with other inefficiencies in the regulatory environment, this policy induced the need for transfers from the Treasury to cover operational losses.

5.   Financial distortions were particularly large in the hydrocarbons subsector, where it was estimated that subsidies cost at least US$2 billion in 1989 (see Annex 1.1). This figure includes approximately US$1 billion in subsidies to private sector entities, US$327 million to the Provinces as excess royalty payments, and US$500-600 million for costs of the "Compre Argentino" policy. This financial drain contributed to the severe financial problems of YPF and GdE, and, as a result, the country.

B. The Menem Administration Strategy

6.   To deal with these problems, the Argentine Government has recently pursued a strategy of: (i) privatization; (ii) change in pricing regulation; and (iii) strict predetermination of the rules regarding the transfers between the sector and the central administration.

Privatization Program

7.   The Government has accelerated the timetable for privatization or partial divestiture, with the objective of reducing the budgetary burden of the enterprises on the Treasury, making the firms more competitive, and increasing the volume and efficiency of new investment. The July 1989 Law on the Reform of the State made most major enterprises eligible for divestiture. The Government has sold two television stations: the telecommunications company ENTel (US$2,178 million plus US$5 billion in external debt) and Aerolineas Argentinas (US$150 million plus US$1 billion in external debt). It also has auctioned off several areas of YPF (realizing US$1,400 million). The Government started a comprehensive restructuring of the railways including the privatization of long-distance cargo lines, and the layoff, early retirement, or transfer to the National Tax Authority (DGI) of some 10 percent of the railway's workforce. Over the first semester of 1992, the Government received about US$2,177 million in privatization revenues--US$1,299 in cash and US$878 million in debt-reduction.

8.   As of October 1991, the total number of public enterprises in Argentina were about 220 with about 26 percent (57 enterprises) owned by the Federal Government and the remainder by provincial governments (65 percent) and municipal authorities (9 percent). The major enterprises were mainly concentrated in three major sectors: Hydrocarbons and Energy, Transport and Communications, and Industrial and Services sectors.

9.   A timetable has been set to privatize most of the remaining public enterprises under the ownership of the Federal Government in 1992-93, including defense industries, the nation's largest distributor of electricity (SEGBA), ports and maritime transport, reinsurance, and the entire power sector. Such a reform program will exert a significant impact on the public budget (see Table 9.1 above).[1] The deficit of the public enterprises is projected to decline from 3.4 percent of GDP in 1989 to

---

1   The figures presented in Table 9.1 are tentative. The definitive privatization schedule has not been agreed yet. In any case, this program is likely to change according to the evolution of the macroeconomic and legislative conditions.

-0.06 percent of GDP (surplus) in 1994. This dramatic decline is explained by the privatization of the major public companies, which leads to a larger reduction in expenditures than in revenues. Specifically, the surplus of the public enterprises should be the result of YPF and YCF activities. Overall, the public enterprise accounts are expected to be balanced from 1993 onwards.

Table 9.2: Real Price of Public Production
(Index: 1982=100)

	1981-85 Average	1986	1987	1988	1989	1990	1991
General Level	118.1	135.6	128.1	127.4	126.2	130.6	113.3
Fuel and Energy	128.6	151.8	140.1	144.0	120.2	127.3	104.7
Fuel	130.7	158.0	146.0	151.0	125.7	132.8	108.5
Energy	115.5	114.2	108.6	109.9	90.5	98.0	83.3
Transp. & Commun.	102.3	101.0	94.7	79.2	141.2	142.3	144.9
Transport a/	86.9	83.5	97.7	78.6	88.8	82.7	76.3
Communications b/	132.2	133.6	92.5	83.3	219.5	185.2	247.6
Industry and Services	59.7	70.1	77.0	62.0	84.5	59.9	55.4

a/ Includes Aerolineas.
b/ Excludes ENTel (privatized in November 1990) as of the first quarter of 1991.

Source: Carta Economica.

10. If the privatization program is completed on schedule, transfers from the Treasury to public enterprises would also be affected dramatically. Public transfers to public enterprises are projected to decline from 0.82 to 0.20 percent of GDP over the 1989-94 period (see Table 9.1). Transfers from the Central Administration to the public enterprises are, however, planned to be higher in 1992 than in 1991, mainly because privatization will also involve costs to the Central Government. To make the public enterprises more attractive for sale, the Government's restructuring program would involve: (i) the absorption of labor redundancies, which costs an average of about US$12,000 per worker; and (ii) the absorption to a great extent of public enterprise debt and other liabilities. Preliminary estimates show that the total labor reductions associated with restructuring are about 95,200 people, representing a reduction of about 37 percent from the June 1991 public enterprise employment level, and with an indemnity labor cost of about US$1.1 billion.

11. In addition, the composition of the transfers to public enterprises will be affected by the privatization process (see Table 9.3). In 1992, YPF and Hidronor will receive more money than in 1991, while the railways and Gas del Estado will be less privileged. This shift in favor of YPF is mainly due to the Government's plan to accelerate exploration and development for oil to increase the market value of YPF, which might be sold in 1993. In contrast, the amounts transferred to YPF are supposed to be eliminated in 1993. The railways and Yacyreta will become the main recipients.

Finally, in 1994, most of the transfers from the Central Administration will be allocated to Yacyreta.

Table 9.3: Composition of Transfers from the National Administration to PEs
(percent)

| | 1990 | 1991 | Budget 1992 | ---- Projected--- | |
				1993	1994
Electricity and Water	3.7	10.3	8.6	0.0	0.0
Railways	50.8	41.4	29.9	45.6	0.0
Gas	18.4	10.5	3.0	0.0	0.0
Hidronor	10.1	9.9	19.0	0.0	0.0
OSN	0.2	0.1	0.0	0.0	0.0
SEGBA	0.9	11.8	11.8	0.0	0.0
Yacyreta	9.2	12.3	14.5	39.6	85.6
YPF	n.a.	0.5	8.5	0.0	0.0
Others	6.8	3.1	4.6	14.8	14.4
Total	100.0	100.0	100.0	100.0	100.0
Memo: Transfers (US$ millions)	1220.9	1862.2	2025.6	816.6	385.0

Sources: Ministry of Economy, 1991 and 1992 Budgets, and the "Efecto Fiscal de
las Privatizaciones: Periodo 1992-94", January 1992.

12.   The privatization of state firms is estimated to generate important resources for the Government.   As of December 1992, the accumulated total revenues from privatization are estimated at US$13 billion both in cash and debt-reduction revenues (see Table 9.4).   In 1993, the privatization of YPF is projected to provide additional revenues for about US$4.8 billion.   This figure probably underestimates future revenues because the list of companies considered is incomplete, as it does not include Encotel, Puertos A.G., and part of the railways.

13.   A substantial amount of privatization revenues has been used to reduce both domestic and external debt, for example, in the case of Entel and Segba for a total of US$8.8 billion.   It is important that privatization revenues --which are transitory-- will continue to be used to reduce the future debt-service of the public sector.   As described in chapter 14 of the report, in absence of debt-reduction, the stock of consolidated bond, BOCON, is projected to reach US$13-17 billion, contributing to a dramatic increase in debt-service from 1997.   Assuming that the discount on this bond will have a secondary market of about 65 percent--equal to the discount obtained in the recent Brady deal--the Government would be able to reduce its debt by about US$3.6 million by using half revenues from YPF (about US$2.4 billion).

14.   At the end of the current privatization program, the total value of assets remaining in the hands of the Government is estimated at about US$6.6 billion, including parts of YPF, Yacyreta and CNEA.   Note, however, that these figures are only tentative because the market value of the public companies is likely to vary according to the success of the privatization program and the evolution of the macroeconomic environment.   In future, given the still high debt load of the

Government, resources from asset sales should only be used to reduce liabilities rather than finance current expenditures.

15.　　　In light of the above, the effect of privatization on public finances should be positive in 1992-94. First, the sales of most public enterprises provided and will continue to provide a major source of revenues for the Central Administration, even though some costs, such as indemnization, will reduce the net gains. Second, in 1993 and 1994, the public enterprise accounts are expected to be balanced, thereby affecting positively the overall budget of the nonfinancial public sector. Moreover, transfers from the Central Administration are projected to decrease from 1.5 percent to 0.20 percent of GDP between 1992 and 1994. At the end of 1994, the public enterprises remaining in state hands would be: part of YPF and of several recent privatized enterprises, Yacyreta, YCF, and the companies affiliated with the Atomic Energy Commission (CNEA) (see Table 9.4).

Pricing Regulation

16.　　　As explained above, the Government often imposed pricing decisions on the public enterprises. After a period of sharply falling real prices due to the hyperinflation of mid-1989, the Menem administration saw the need to recuperate these prices to mitigate public enterprise deficits. From the third quarter of 1989 to the fourth quarter of 1990, the public enterprise prices were at a historically high level. The deregulation of oil prices in the first quarter of 1991 to a large extent explains the decline observed in 1991 (see below).

17.　　　The privatization program will also modify the pricing regulation of former public firms. Although it is difficult to anticipate the outcome of the negotiations between the authorities and the potential buyers, the regulatory framework currently proposed by the Government suggests that the output prices should be fixed according to their international production cost. Additional instruments, such as the marginal cost and the evolution of the benefits of the former public enterprises, can also be taken into account. As an illustration, the recent increase in ENTel corresponded to the US inflation rate during the same period (1.3 percent). Clearly, this assumes that the inflation rate in Argentina will remain close to the international inflation rate. The pricing regulation is a crucial element of the privatization process, since most of these enterprises are operating in highly imperfect markets.

18.　　　Of particular importance to public finances is the reform of the energy sector. The state monopoly and the pricing policies in the energy sector created distortions that have lowered productivity and investment in what should be a leading sector in Argentina. To overcome these problems the Government has recently: (i) adjusted real prices for oil products to reflect their international opportunity cost; and (ii) adjusted taxes to remove biases against or in favor of particular products, and revamped energy-related special funds to ensure that resources mobilized are expended efficiently. In addition, the Government is changing the structure of the oil industry through the conversion of the YPF service contract areas to oil concessions or association type contracts, opening up areas formerly monopolized by YPF to private investment under joint contracts, and selling certain underexploited oil fields, as well as eliminating obstacles for a rapid approval of contracts for exploration and production.

Table 9.4: Estimated Market Value of State Assets Eligible for Privatization (US$ million unless otherwise indicated)

Enterprise Name	Projected Sale Date	Percentage Share Sold	----------- Privatization in Progress ---------			Assets in Public Sector
			Total Revenues (US$ mil)	Cash Revenues (US$ mil)	Debt Revenues (US$ mil)	
YPF			6217	1417	0	2400
Marginal Areas (56)	Oct 90	100	434	434.2	0	0
Central Areas (11)	June 91	50	560	560.1	0	280
Extentions (2)	Oct 91	40	244	243.5	0	146
Cuenca Austral I+II	Dec. 91	70	180	179.5	0	54
Others a/	Sept.93	60	4800	na	na	1920
Railways			153			75
Merchandise	Oct 92	51	153	na	na	75
Passengers	Nov 93	na	na	na	na	0
Aerolineas	Nov.90	85	1198	147	1050.8	180
Entel			7206	2178	5028	0
Zona Norte	Nov 90	60	2408	100	2308	0
Zona Sur	Nov.90	60	2834	114	2720	0
Telephonica Shares	Dec 91	30	838	838.1	0	0
Telecom Shares	March 92	30	1125	1125.4	0	0
Electric Companies			1508	264	878	3330
Segba			1120	242	878	53
Puerto Nuevo	April 92	60	92	92.1	0	37
Central Costanera	May 92	60	90	90.2	0	36
Distribution	August 92	51	938	60	878	460
CNEA & a/	na	na	na	na	na	2616
Yacyreta	na	na	na	na	na	
AyEE	na	na	167	22	0	73
Alto Valle	Aug 92	90	22	22.1	0	2
Others	na	51	145.35	na	na	71
Hidronor	na	51	220	na	na	108
Elma	na	51	114	na	na	56
Gas del Estado	Nov 92	70	1866	300	1566	560
Puertos A.G.	na	na	na	na	na	na
OSN b/	Dec. 92	0	0	0	0	na
Encotel	na	na	na	na	na	na
Military Firms	na	na	116.1	162	na	na
Others c/	na	na	129	116.5	12	na
Total			13707 d/	4585	8535	6600 e/

na = not available

a/ Figures estimated by McKinsey and do not include liabilities.
b/ The assets of OSN are not sold by the State.
c/ Includes real estate, televisions and hotels.
d/ Total revenues as of December 1992. Exclude revenues projected in 1993-94.
e/ Assuming that CNEA will remain in the public sector, but no military firms.

Sources: Ministry of Economy, "Efecto Fiscal de las Privatizaciones", January 1992 and Fiel, "La Reforma Economica, 1989-91".

New Procurement Law

19.   Following the strategy of the previous Alfonsin Administration, the Menem Government first created an Investment Fund to manage the public enterprises deficit. Basically, the Fund's role was to collect taxes from profitable public enterprises such as the energy and communication companies to pay the debt service of the public enterprise sector. In 1991, the Investment Fund was eliminated. Since then, the Government has been working on a new procurement law that would improve competition and transparency in public purchases and effectively nondiscriminatory subsidies to domestic firms.

20.   The new Law of Procurement submitted to Congress in January 1993 would establish the basis for a long-term nondiscriminatory regime for the public sector. This will allow the Executive to make public purchasing more competitive and more transparent, and to eliminate procurement subsidies, such as those contained in the Buy-Argentina Law (*Compre Nacional*). The Government has also developed a program to reduce the number of earmarked funds from over 150 in 1989 to about 75 in 1992. The Government began withholding half of all funds on an emergency basis in mid-1990; it also reduced the number of funds by one-third by 1991. In the 1993 budget, the number of earmarked funds has been reduced to 44. This will be coordinated with the administrative reform, since many of these funds provided automatic resources to selected decentralized agencies.

C. Recommendations

21.   Public enterprises accounted for one-quarter of public spending in Argentina as late as 1990; however, the privatization program has already shrunk this to 17 percent. The Government's program of public enterprise privatization has produced enormous benefits: capital revenues to support the transition to a sustainable public finance position, relief from investment demand in the sector, an end to pricing distortions, and macroeconomic shocks associated with political pricing, to name a few. Assuming that the privatization program is completed as scheduled, resources for the Government are estimated above US$18 billion in the 1990-93 years, including the privatization of YPF. While part of these revenues will be cash revenues to the Treasury according to the 1992-93 fiscal accounts figures, these revenues should also facilitate reductions in domestic and foreign debt. Additional debt-equity swaps not shown in the fiscal program may lead to a reduction of roughly US$3 billion in the stock of public debt. This application of privatization revenues is particularly important in light of the recent debt-reduction deal with commercial banks and the issue of the BOCON. At the end of the current privatization program, the total value of assets remaining in the hands of the Government is estimated at about US$6 billion, including parts of YPF, Yacyreta, and CNEA. In future, given the still high debt load of the Government, resources from asset sales should only be used to reduce liabilities rather than finance current expenditures. (These figures do not include the privatization receipts associated with the capitalization of the social security system, namely the use of YPF receipts and revenues from the income tax. This could reduce the BOCON stock by an additional US$6 billion.)

22.   Budget transfers amount to US$2 billion annually, and should be phased down in accordance with the privatization and enterprise restructuring schedule. In 1993, these should be less than US$800 million--mostly to the remaining segments of the railways and Yacyreta--and less than US$400 million in 1994, nearly all to Yacyreta. Special effort needs to be devoted to reductions in railway transfers, since they are economically inefficient and costly.

23.   A prerequisite for economic success in privatization is the enactment of a clear regulatory framework, especially for pricing in those sectors not subject to the discipline of price competition from competing sellers. In particular, output prices must be fixed according to their international production costs and not only to the evolution of the benefits of the former public firm. Finally, the new Law of Procurement must establish the basis for a long-term, nondiscriminatory regime for the public sector.

CHAPTER 10. PROVINCIAL GOVERNMENTS

A. Introduction

1.   Throughout most of the 1980s, provincial governments benefitted from increased revenues associated with coparticipated transfers from the Federal Government and transfers to fund selected programs.[1] They also received *ad hoc* discretionary grants, as well as rediscounts from the Central Bank to provincial banks (which in turn financed the deficits of the provincial governments). The availability of these resources and sources of financing created the perverse incentive to spend without raising revenues. For these reasons, provincial governments have been primary contributors to the consolidated public sector deficit since 1986.

2.   Over the last five years, the Federal Government has reduced the financing incentives that promoted fiscal indiscipline in the provinces. First, the Federal Government enacted a new Revenue Sharing law in 1987 (effective January 1988) that restricted discretionary grants to provincial governments. Then, in 1990, the Federal Government cut rediscounts to Provincial Banks from the Central Bank. The provinces, however, were still able to obtain financing through private banks and public national banks to fund their provincial (own) bank loans. The Convertibility Law of April 1991 prohibited the Federal Government from making special contributions to the provinces and also cut off financing of provincial deficits through the provincial banks. However, a sharp increase in shared tax revenues at the national level (due both to the Tanzi effect and increased efficiency of tax administration) drastically reduced the provincial government deficits, and therefore their need to increase revenues or reduce expenditures. More recently, the Federal Government has transferred additional responsibilities for health and education to the provinces (cushioning this with additional automatic revenue sharing) that will "take up the fiscal slack" from automatic revenue sharing. Even so, until full adjustment in provincial public finances puts them on sound footing, they remain a potential source of macroeconomic instability.

3.   Reducing the fiscal deficit of the provincial public sector is not the only goal. Improving the efficiency and equity of the provincial public sector cannot be neglected due to the size of the provincial public sector (expenditures of almost 12 percent of GDP for its central administration alone) and the importance of its responsibilities. With the extensive privatization of Federal Government entities and the transfer of expenditure responsibilities to provincial governments in the adjustment process, the relative importance of the provinces in Argentina's consolidated public sector is increasing rapidly. Provinces now have most responsibility for providing not only physical infrastructure, but also such social services as education, health, security, and housing. Improving the efficiency of the delivery of these provincial social services could be one of the most effective ways to improve the standard of living in Argentina, especially its lower income population.

---

[1]   This chapter is a summary of *Argentina: Towards a New Federalism*, World Bank: June 1992 (Green Cover).

B. Evolution of Provincial Government Deficits

4.　　　　In the 1980s, the average annual primary deficits of Argentina's provinces excluding discretionary grants of the National Treasury (ATN) stood at nearly 1.7 percent of GDP. The provinces contributed on average approximately 40 percent to the fiscal primary deficit of the previous decade. If discretionary Treasury grants are included, 1984, 1987, and 1988 were the worst years for the provincial deficits. However, the total deficit of provincial governments in 1990 was also high: US$1.6 billion. In 1990, as in other years, most provinces "financed" their deficits by: (i) arrears in salaries and to their suppliers; (ii) loans from provincial banks (these banks were in turn financed by rediscounts from the Central Bank); and (iii) loans from national public banks (accounting for more than 20 percent of their financial needs).

5.　　　　The provinces remained financially distressed after 1986 and were unable to recover until the second semester of 1991. Between 1981 and 1985, the annual financing requirements of provinces averaged only US$800 million. Between 1986 and 1990, this need doubled to an annual average of US$1.6 billion. Preliminary data for 1992 show provincial government deficits amounted to about US$400 million.

6.　　　　Advanced[2] provinces (i.e., those with large populations and high Gross Provincial Product GPP) were responsible for about 35 percent of the total deficit in 1990 (Table 10.1). This is about the same percentage as the total for Underdeveloped provinces (i.e., those with low per capita GPP and high poverty), although expenditures for the poor provinces are less than one-third those of the wealthier provinces. The public sectors of poorer provinces clearly did not improve their performance in 1990 in comparison to the other provinces. The highest of the average annual deficits for the 1980s (excluding ATNs) are for the provinces of: La Rioja (31 percent of GPP), Formosa (19 percent), Catamarca (11 percent), and Chaco (10 percent). The annual average for all provinces was much lower: only 2 percent or GPP, due to the relatively low deficits in the Province of Buenos Aires (1 percent) and Municipality of Buenos Aires. However, the absolute size of the deficit for the Province of Buenos Aires is by far the biggest, because its total fiscal size dwarfs that of the other provinces (total expenditures represent about a quarter of the total and are over three times larger than the next highest province). Nevertheless, tiny La Rioja's deficit totals nearly a third that of the Province of Buenos Aires.

C. Provincial Government Revenues

7.　　　　The two main sources of revenue for provincial governments are own-source taxes and transfers from the Federal Government. The Government transfers occur through two main channels: revenue sharing of taxes collected by the Federal Government and discretionary grants.

2　　Based on the Consejo Federal de Inversiones (CFI) stratification of provinces into four main groups: Advanced, Low Density, Intermediate and Underdeveloped. See the table on the following page for the groups and the provinces included in them.

8.   Tax revenue from provincial sources derive from taxes on real estate tax and automobiles (assets) that comprise 40 percent of local tax revenue and a turnover sales tax and a stamp tax (transactions) that comprise the remaining 60 percent.

Table 10.1: Population and Revenue-Sharing

	Population	Households w/ Unsatisfied Basic Needs (1988)	Secondary Distribution of Coparticipated Taxes Legal Shares (1988)	1990 Deficit (US$)
24 Provinces (million)	32609	1995		1665.2
(Percent)	100.0	100.0	100.0	100.0
Advanced	69.1	57.1	44.0	34.8
Federal Capital	9.1	3.7	-	0.7
Buenos Aires	38.6	34.6	22.0	17.1
Cordoba	8.5	7.4	8.9	10.4
Mendoza	4.3	3.5	4.2	0.9
Santa Fe	8.6	7.9	9.0	5.6
Low Density	5.3	6.5	9.3	13.9
Chubut	1.1	1.4	1.6	2.1
La Pampa	0.8	0.7	1.9	-0.0
Neuquen	1.2	1.7	1.7	1.9
Rio Negro	1.6	2.2	2.5	5.3
Santa Cruz	0.5	0.5	1.6	3.4
Tierra del Fuego	0.2	0.0	-	1.2
Intermediate	11.8	14.7	19.2	19.8
Entre Rios	3.1	3.7	4.9	4.4
Salta	2.7	3.8	3.8	4.7
San Juan	1.6	1.5	3.4	-0.1
San Luis	0.9	1.0	2.3	-0.3
Tucuman	3.5	4.5	4.8	7.1
Underdeveloped	13.8	21.7	27.5	35.5
Catamarca	0.8	1.1	2.8	3.8
Chaco	2.6	4.4	5.0	5.2
Corrientes	2.4	3.8	3.7	3.6
Formosa	1.2	2.2	3.7	5.6
Jujuy	1.6	2.4	2.9	6.5
La Rioja	0.7	0.8	2.1	6.6
Misiones	2.4	3.6	3.3	3.4
S. del Estero	2.1	3.4	4.1	0.9

9.   By far the most important channel automatic revenue transfers to the provinces is the *Coparticipacion Federal de Impuestos* (the revenue-sharing law), representing approximately 80 percent of total automatic transfers. It automatically distributes to the provinces a percentage of the revenue obtained from the following important taxes: VAT, Income and Asset, Excises, and (after 1988) the Fuel Tax. Petroleum, natural gas, and hydroelectricity royalties explain another 10 to 15 percent of all automatic revenue transfers.

10.   Besides these automatic transfers, there also are discretionary grants that in some years have accounted for more than 50 percent of provincial revenues. The most important discretionary grants are: grants from ATN, customarily used to finance local deficits, and grants from the National Housing Fund (FONAVI), which finances the construction of houses for the poor.

Own-Source Revenues

11.   Revenue from provincial sources in 1981/82 comprised 55 percent of current revenues (excluding grants), 51 percent in 1983, and 45 percent in 1990. However, the decline is more severe in the Underdeveloped provinces, whose share declined from 32 percent in 1981/82 to 12 percent in 1990.

12.   The provinces collected taxes from own-sources about US$6.4 billion in 1980 but only US$4.1 billion in 1990. The tax effort for all taxes varies among provinces. For example, in Catamarca and La Rioja the rural real estate tax is only 8 cents per hectare in production, while in other provinces located along the Andes it was much higher (e.g., in San Juan US$1.12 and in San Luis US$0.38). Chaco, Formosa, Santiago del Estero, Tucuman, Chubut, Neuquen, Rio Negro, Santa Cruz, Salta, Corrientes, Jujuy and La Pampa each collect less than US$1 a year per hectare in production for the rural land tax. For the urban real estate tax, revenue per home is only US$4 a year in Catamarca; US$7 in Formosa; US$6 in La Rioja; US$8 in Santiago del Estero; and US$5 in Tucuman, compared to an average of US$95 for the Advanced provinces. At a rate of 1 percent of property value, which is reasonable by international standards, a tax of less than US$10 per home means the average value of urban properties for tax purposes is less than US$1,000 in many Argentine provinces.

13.   Provincial tax administration performance has not been effective. Problems include overstaffing, misallocation of human resources, and lack of coordination with other public agencies.

Revenue-Sharing

14.   Law 23548 (1988) granted all provinces the largest primary share of federal taxes in Argentine history. In 1961-70, for example, the share was 39 percent, and it was as low as 29 percent in 1983, compared to 58 percent at present. The law also validated the implicit secondary distribution rule that existed between 1985 and 1988, which perpetuated the trend favoring Underdeveloped provinces, and simultaneously reduced the share of Advanced Provinces from 49 percent to 44 percent (Advanced provinces obtained 58 percent of shared taxes at the beginning of the 1970s). Underdeveloped provinces increased their share of secondary distribution from 19 percent in 1971-72 to 24 percent in 1984, and then to 28 percent in 1988.

15.   A few provinces receive substantial income from royalties for the use of exhaustible resources. In provinces like Chubut, Neuquen, Santa Cruz, and Rio Negro, the fiscal circumstances of any year are highly dependent on the status of royalty income.

Discretionary Grants

16.   The most important nonreimbursable grants are from the Treasury, which typically are used to finance provincial deficits. In 1990, these grants were only US$73 million compared to US$4,774 million in 1983. The 1988 revenue-sharing law

restricted the amount of discretionary grants to 1 percent of revenue obtained from coparticipated taxes. These discretionary treasury grants provided incentives for provincial fiscal indiscipline, as they were allocated in direct proportion to the size of the deficit. The higher the deficit, the higher the transfer to the province. Thus, this revenue sharing law was an essential first step in the direction of eliminating incentives for fiscal indiscipline in the provinces.

17. The most important "reimbursable" grant is FONAVI. Until 1991, FONAVI was financed by revenue generated from a 5 percent tax on wages and salaries. Currently, it receives 40 percent of the fuel tax.

18. FONAVI transfers to the provinces are important (although they have fluctuated widely, varying from US$900 million to US$1,400 million a year). The Federal Government provides a loan to the provinces which in turn lend the money to poor individuals. The collection from installments is supposed to be transferred back to the Federal Government. From 1978 to 1987 income recovered from outstanding loans was always below 2 percent of FONAVI total revenue. Recent provincial recovery ratios have improved to 4 percent. In summary, FONAVI operates more like an earmarked tax directed to the provinces.

Regional Distribution of Funds

19. The complicated framework that governs intergovernmental transfers in Argentina serves to obscure the relative position each province or group of provinces occupies. The 1988 revenue-sharing law is intended to redistribute income across regions; however, all other transfers have secondary distribution rules that differ from the one stipulated in this law.

20. If per capita fiscal revenues were equal across provinces, each one would enjoy the same opportunity to provide similar government services per capita. However, regional income redistribution in Argentina is highly skewed (Table 10.1). Total revenue per capita from all sources (i.e., own and federal tax and non-tax revenues plus grants) in Low Density provinces (small population and high per capita GPP) is three times higher than in the Advanced provinces (high population and high GPP); similarly, Under-developed (low per capita and high poverty) and Intermediate (intermediate population and intermediate GPP) provinces obtain approximately 50 percent more revenue per capita than the most developed (Advanced) provinces. Discrimination against Advanced provinces has led to public investment per capita in this group that is less than half the national average (US$30 compared to US$67).

21. If automatic federal transfers from all sources are divided by the number of households with unsatisfied basic needs, the discrimination against Advanced provinces is equally severe. A poor household in an Advanced province on average receives US$2,600 compared to more than US$10,000 for Low Density provinces, and around US$4,500 for Intermediate and Underdeveloped provinces.

D. Provincial Government Expenditures

22.   Expenditures related to wage and employment policies account for nearly two-thirds of all provincial government outlays. Capital expenditures, which in 1981 were US$4.6 billion, fell to only US$2.1 billion in 1990. As with the Federal Government, when provincial governments became strapped for funds, they reduced capital expenditures as a means of reducing their deficits.

Personnel Expenditures

23.   The share of each of the four groups of provinces in total personnel expenditures for all provinces generally remained constant between 1983 and 1990. This suggests that wage and employment policies in each group were "adjusted" to yield a similar increase in personnel expenditures: in other words, provinces with more personnel (Advanced and Intermediate) adjusted their wages downward compared to less personnel-intensive provinces.   Obviously, those provinces that had more public employees and reduced their real wages to "finance" overstaffing are in the worst position to initiate necessary public sector restructuring.

24.   Provincial public sector employment increased almost 40 percent in seven years between 1983-90, while the average salary fell 20 percent in real terms. An explosion in public employment occurred in Low Density provinces (almost 70 percent increase from 1983 to 1990). The public sector in many provinces is considered the employer of last resort, and politization of the provincial public sector undoubtedly accounted for some of the overstaffing.

25.   The availability of federal funds may have induced provinces to place more people on the public payroll or raise salaries. Figure 10.1 shows the relationship between the percentage change in total personnel expenditure 1981/1990 (vertical axis) and the total change in all federal transfers (both automatic transfers and grants) for all provinces. Clearly the correlation is high, showing a tendency to use the increased transfers to hire more personnel.

26.   The 1990 Census of provincial public employees undertaken by the Province of Buenos Aires revealed other problems, namely: (i) a concentration of public employees in positions with lower salaries; (ii) an excess of employees with higher education holding administrative (as opposed to technical) jobs, and low representation of employees with secondary education; (iii) an inefficient distribution of personnel (oversupply of administrators), with shortages in key areas like the police force; (iv) important differences in salaries between the central administration and decentralized agencies, which promotes continual conflicts over personnel matters; and (v) an increase in the number of teachers without tenure from 18,000 in 1983 to 26,000 in 1989 (there probably were more than 40,000 in 1991). Many of these untenured teachers are political appointees.

Figure 10.1
Change in Provincial Employment and Resources
from Federal Government

(Percent increase between 1981 and 1990)

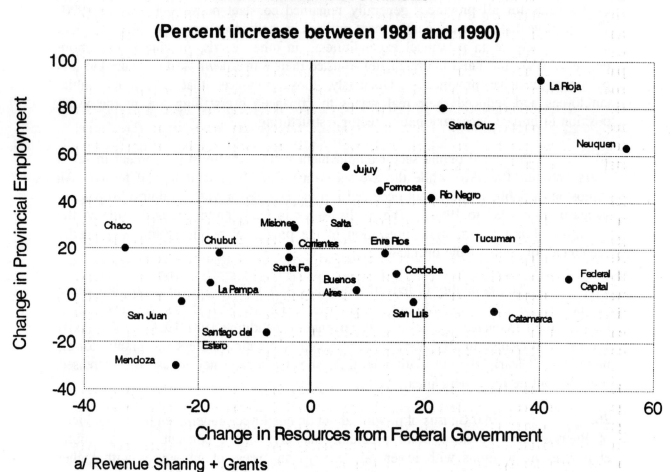

a/ Revenue Sharing + Grants

27.   There are dramatic differences in personnel expenditures across provinces.[3] The number of policemen per capita in the Province of Buenos Aires is less than two-thirds that of Cordoba, Santa Fe or Mendoza. Formosa, La Rioja, and Tierra del Fuego have three times, and Santa Cruz four times more policemen per capita than Buenos Aires. Although some of this variation is explained by the lower demographic density of these other provinces compared to Buenos Aires, part may also be due to an excess of policemen. The number of employees in the health sector in La Rioja is four times higher than the national average. In Salta, the ratio is also high and has tripled since 1984.

28.   **Education**. The 24 provinces paid almost 465,000 teachers' salaries (including non-tenured teachers). These teachers worked with 5,200,000 students, for an average ratio of 11 students per teacher. Although the data must be treated with caution, this ratio suggests tremendous overstaffing. This could be explained by the paid leaves of absence that teachers take (with substitutes hired in their place) and, in some provinces, by the politization of hiring practices in the public education sector (i.e., hiring non-instructional staff under the category of "teachers" who in reality are recipients of political jobs). Most classrooms in the country have two to three times more students per teacher, which could well reflect the large number of nonteaching staff paid out of the education budget.

29.   **Transfers**. Transfers of provinces to municipalities increased from US$844 million in 1981 to US$1,454 million in 1990. Provinces share with municipal governments the revenue they collect from own sources and from the Federal Revenue-Sharing Law. These transfers averaged 8 percent of total provincial taxes plus the tax revenue received from federal coparticipated taxes, while in 1990 the average was 14.3 percent. The extra resources transferred to municipal governments probably financed overstaffing. For example, in the Province of Buenos Aires, public employment in municipal governments increased 67 percent between 1982 and 1989, compared to 35 percent for the provincial government labor force.

30.   The larger participation of municipalities suggests that provincial governments face a problem similar to the Federal Government: higher municipal government expenditures or lower fiscal effort required increasingly higher transfers from the provincial governments. Many provinces have the same perverse incentives in their transfer systems to municipalities as those inherent in the provincial/federal transfer system before the revenue-sharing law of 1988. In these provinces, municipalities with higher deficits receive higher transfers.

31.   The financing of municipal governments varies enormously in Argentina. In some provinces (e.g., La Pampa) revenue-sharing has strong incentives for fiscal effort; in others, provincial governments make discretionary grants. Also, there is interest in decentralization of responsibilities from provincial to municipal governments to increase accountability to local users. However, this would also require reform of revenue assignment to municipalities to enable them to raise sufficient resources to provide these services. Today, municipal taxes in Argentina do not permit this. In

---

3   See *Argentina: Towards a New Federalism*, World Bank: June 1992, pp. 41-47.

many cases, municipal fees bear no relationship to the public services rendered to the community--which effectively destroys the linkage between the service and the charges used to finance it.

32. Transfers to finance public enterprise deficits are not important in the provinces. There are several possible explanations for this: (i) provincial public enterprises are basically reduced to electricity companies, and in some provinces these services are provided by decentralized agencies that are consolidated in the budget; (ii) some provincial electricity companies paid nothing for the energy they bought from the federally owned utility Agua y Energia Electrica, since they were able to transfer their problems to the Federal Government; and (iii) in some provinces the average electricity price traditionally was higher than the national average, which should give them better cash flow.

33. **Provincial Social Security Systems.** Transfers to finance the deficits of the provincial social security systems were important from 1983 to 1990, although they were reduced to US$600 million annually in recent years. This reduction in transfers to the social security system can be traced to the introduction of employer labor taxes in 1984. Moreover, most provinces require the first raise in monthly salaries to be transferred to the provincial pension system. During inflationary periods, the pension systems receive substantial inflows of additional funds from these monthly raises.

34. The provincial pension systems deal exclusively with provincial public employees; in most cases provinces also administer the pension system of the municipal public employees. The provincial pension systems are more "generous" on average than the federal system: pensions can be received earlier, the minimum number of years of contribution is lower, and pensions are fixed at 82 percent of wages. In some cases, pensions are also granted to housewives who have made no monetary contribution to the system; in addition, a significant number of pensions have gone to those who have been wrongly classified as "incapacitated."

35. The average ratio of workers to beneficiaries for the 24 provinces was slightly reduced from 2.74 in 1980 to 2.65 in 1990. For actual contributions these ratios are lower than those needed to self-finance a pay- as-you-go system, generating a deficit that is nearly 30 percent of the expenditures of the consolidated provincial pension systems. However, almost all provinces and municipalities have increased substantially the number of public employees, which makes the potential problem appear less severe. From 1981 to 1987 the number of provincial pension system beneficiaries (those retired or their survivors) grew at an annual rate of 3.1 percent, while for the Federal Pension System the rate was somewhat smaller at 2.8 percent. But after 1987 the provincial pension systems weakened. While the Federal System maintained its growth rate in total number of pensions, most provinces (except four) increased theirs. From 1987 to 1991, 7 out of 18 provinces for which data were available experienced annual growth rates of two digits or more, compared to 3 provinces out of 23 before 1987. For those 18 provinces the average annual growth rate after 1987 was 3.8 percent, compared to 2.5 percent between 1981 and 1987.

36.   If pensions continued growing at 3.5 percent a year, and employment were reduced 25 percent, the provincial pension system deficit at the end of the decade would be more than three times higher than the actual deficit (over US$1.8 billion a year compared to US$572 million in 1990).

37.   **Capital Expenditures**. FONAVI and Highway Fund transfers represented 35 percent of capital expenditures in 1983. Their share grew to 49 percent in 1990. This indicates that provinces reduced capital expenditures without earmarked financing. The average cost of a FONAVI house--calculated as the money spent by the program divided by the total number of houses built in a given year--more than doubles the cost calculated at market prices.

38.   Two other problems with capital expenditures are: (i) the decision about what investments to make is highly bureaucratic with practically no professional evaluation of the different projects; (ii) in most provinces there are rules that try to ensure that all formal controls have been invoked (although in practice they are frequently ignored), but there is essentially no control over project execution.

E. Recommendations

39.   Preliminary estimates for 1992 show that the increase in federal revenue sharing allowed the provinces to almost balance their budgets. However, failure of the provinces to maintain this balance could seriously jeopardize macroeconomic stability.

40.   The deficit is not the only problem that has to be addressed. Provincial *real* current expenditures jumped by 41 percent during the 1982-90 period, while capital expenditures dropped by 25 percent. Higher current expenditures affect not only the possibility of balancing the budget, but also tend to deteriorate the real exchange rate, since they are concentrated in non-traded goods and services; on the other hand, money collected from taxes paid by the private sector is distributed more evenly between traded and non-traded activities.

41.   The large primary share of the provinces in coparticipated taxes creates an additional problem in 1992, since provinces will be able to finance additional expenditures without paying the political cost of raising taxes. This problem was partially solved with the 1992 transfer of secondary schools and other social expenditures to the provinces; however, because of prior revenue sharing, provinces will receive more funds if the Federal Government is able to increase tax revenues, as foreseen in the 1992 budget. This will allow provinces to raise their expenditures by US$0.5 billion compared to 1991, or US$1.4 billion compared to 1990.

42.   Another problem is the inefficiency of provincial and municipal tax systems. They are characterized by highly distorting taxes, poor administration, and do not make full use of the revenue potential of local tax bases. The lack of coordination among the three levels of government leads to double or even triple taxation of the same taxpayer. Furthermore, the intergovernmental transfer system encourages free-rider behavior. The lack of transparency in intergovernmental transfers was not totally eliminated by the

1988 revenue-sharing law, since other transfers remained in place, and rediscounts and industrial promotion incentives continued to favor some provinces.

Own-Source Revenue

43.   Own-source revenues account for about 45 percent of total provincial revenues. Improvements in own-source revenues could be achieved through several actions.

44.   **Turnover Sales Tax**. The structure of the sales tax is inefficient and its cascading nature has negative consequences for resource allocation, favors vertical integration, and adversely affects exports and local industries. In the short run, the current structure of the sales tax could be improved by: (i) reducing provincial taxes on financial activities; and (ii) reducing the rate on primary and industrial activities to moderate the negative cascading effects caused by the rate structure. In the long run, the turnover tax might be replaced by a provincial sales tax on final sales. The tax base should be the same for all provinces, although the rates could vary somewhat.

45.   **Real Estate Tax**. There are three general problems with the property tax: (i) the progressive rate structure (i.e., tax rates that rise by property value brackets, which taxes larger properties and more valuable properties at a higher rate); (ii) the suboptimal use of its revenue potential in most provinces; and (iii) excessive effective rates in some provinces, including Buenos Aires and Entre Rios. Provinces and municipalities must improve their policies by: (i) simplifying building permits for new construction; (ii) compulsory updating of taxpayer data; and (iii) ensuring the requirements on notaries are met to submit data promptly and accurately. The updating of taxpayer information could be subcontracted to private enterprises along with the collection of arrears. Investment in improvements of cadastres must be part of an integrated effort to improve overall real estate tax collection, including value assessment, billing, and collection procedures. A possible second step to improve the administration of the tax would entail decentralization of the assessment process to municipalities, at least for property improvements.

46.   **Automobile Tax**. Autos are taxed several times a year to avoid the effects of inflation. In the current, more stable macroeconomic context, installments should be reduced to a maximum of two per year. This would facilitate enforcing the use of a sticker on automobiles that would ease the control of the payment of the tax.

47.   **Stamp (or Transfer) Tax**. Provinces receive 40 percent to 50 percent of the revenue of the stamp tax from financial transactions. This tax is highly distortionary. The tax should be gradually phased out.

48.   **Tax Administration**. The budget of provincial tax collection entities should be independent of the general budget, with a ceiling calculated as a percentage of tax revenue. In most provinces, tax agencies have no personnel shortages but they do need more tax auditors; the number of less qualified personnel should be reduced and the number of tax auditors increased. The director should be free to fire personnel, especially auditors. Efficiency gains in tax administration are closely related to

efficient computerization. For example, audits could be organized by computer by identifying inconsistencies in taxpayer data. The technology developed at the federal level to monitor the largest 1,000 to 2,000 taxpayers should be disseminated to the provinces. Finally, there is a strong need to coordinate the tax collection efforts of federal and provincial entities. Currently, there is little cooperation and even less cross-checking.

49.   **Revenue-Sharing with Municipalities**. Provincial government might improve service delivery and accountability by decentralizing some activities to local governments. To avoid incentives to spend without regard to revenues, decentralization might require that municipalities finance more of their expenditures out of locally generated revenue. Any revenue sharing of provincial taxes should be carefully designed to prevent municipal governments from making a large fraction of their expenditures without paying the political cost of raising the funds. In addition, municipalities should be prevented from using taxes on production that can be exported to other municipalities.

Revenues from the Federal Government

50.   During 1991 and 1992 the improved revenue performance at the federal level increased coparticipated taxes massively in real terms. In 1992, coparticipated revenues were projected to be about US$10.2 billion. To offset the one-time jump in these co-participated revenues, the Federal Government transferred social expenditures, as noted above, an action that improved the overall federalist framework. In addition to coparticipated taxes, the 1992 federal budget anticipates transfers of US$2.2 billion in resources other than co-participation through several programs earmarked to support particular spending activities. In all, federally collected revenues account for about 55 percent of all revenues spent by provincial governments.[4]

51.   Although the provincial deficit has fallen and the 1987 Coparticipation Law has made transfers less *ad hoc*, the overall incentive structure of Argentine fiscal federalism is still not optimal. By delegating to the Federal Government their taxing authority, provincial governments are less politically accountable to their immediate constituents for revenue performance. In times of revenue shortfalls, provincial authorities can assign blame to federal authorities; in times of abundance, provincial officials can spend revenues with less regard for future performance. Inefficient service delivery can be blamed on the lack of federal revenues. Moreover, the structure diverts attention of local authorities from improving their own tax and expenditure framework to lobbying at the national level to achieve a larger share of the revenue collected elsewhere.

52.   Revenue sharing also introduces some inflexibility in anticyclical fiscal policy because provincial governments are likely to spend the revenue they receive from the Federal Government. Thus, the impact of variations in tax rates for anticyclical

---

4   As described in Chapter 3, the co-participation agreement was slightly modified in August 1992.

reasons are likely to be partially offset by (automatic) variations in spreading out of coparticipated revenues.

53. Despite the problems, the 1987 Revenue Sharing Law was a major step forward in that it helped to right incentives by setting out an agreed framework that placed limits on federal responsibilities and implicitly on the potential returns to lobbying with the Federal Government for more revenues. Nonetheless, further reenforcement of the new incentive framework is necessary to ensure that provinces will make the required adjustments in spending and own-revenue performance in lieu of depending on federal revenues to finance excessive employment.

54. **Reinforcing the Incentive to Adjust.** One option to increase the incentive for provincial adjustment would be to modify the primary distribution of the Revenue Sharing Law. This would be difficult politically. It also may not be necessary insofar as overall accounts at both the federal and provincial level may be in rough--if tenuous-- equilibrium. At issue then is the marginal changes that result from improved federal tax administration or new revenue measures at the federal level.

55. This suggests a second option: seeking an accord to reduce the marginal transfers from future improvements and/or seeking to transfer additional expenditures to the provinces with projected "windfall" gains from marginal increases in future federal revenues. This is the strategy the Government has followed to date and warrants support. Universities, the federal police serving the federal capital, and Justice, and the regulations of the Ministry of Labor are good candidates to be transferred to the provinces.

56. A third option, not exclusive of the first two, is to recast the US$2.2 billion of noncopartipated transfers through the budget. The largest of these are the FONAVI housing program (US$900 million), special aid to Buenos Aires and Tierra del Fuego (two programs totalling US$300 million), the Tobacco Fund (US$100 million), and the National Highway Fund (US$100 million). With the agreement of the provinces, some or all of these resources might be consolidated into a program of block grants to be disbursed in proportion to current savings performance of provinces and/or to reimburse the cost of agreed reforms, such as severance payments to redundant workers or provincial social security reforms. This fund could be supplemented with (i) incremental improvements in aggregate coparticipated resources, and (ii) loan proceeds from international financial institutions. A fund of US$2 to 3 billion could provide a powerful incentive to adjust current expenditures and revenues and provide a continuing source of much-needed investment at the provincial level.

57. Independent of the creation of this fund, the Government should simplify the extrabudgetary transfers, allowing for a unique special regime, on top of the general revenue sharing scheme that will deal simultaneously with transfers for food to schools, regional development, or grants to finance transitory deficits. These transfers could be matching or non-matching, depending on their nature.

58. Second, the Government should consider repealing the Energy Development Fund for the Interior (FEDEI). The FEDEI was financed by resources from taxes on

fuels, electricity, and natural gas that were modified in 1991. FEDEI is expected to receive resources from a fee on wholesale electricity sales after the privatization of the electricity market. This fund was used to finance electricity projects, which in some cases were "white elephants." This fund would not be necessary if provinces privatize their electricity companies.

59.   **Secondary (Regional) Distribution**. The regional redistribution of federal revenue in favor of low-income provinces is at the expense of provinces with the largest concentration of low-income families. As a result of differences in transfers per capita of 150 to 250 percent, underdeveloped provinces have 50 to 60 percent more total government revenue per capita than the Advanced provinces and similar total revenues per poor household. (Low density provinces have by far the highest revenue per capita and per poor household, but that in part reflects oil and gas revenues.) The redistribution is mainly at the expense of Gran Buenos Aires. Such high redistribution reduces the incentive for raising own-source revenues and reduces the accountability for service delivery, because local taxpayers bear so little of the cost of services. The recent transfer of secondary schools and health services to the provinces has reduced the discrimination against the Province of Buenos Aires. This problem could gradually be reduced by reducing the disparity on federal transfers per capita to each province (aside from royalties which reflect, to some degree, local ownership of national resources in a federal system).

Expenditures

60.   **Administrative Reform**. Excessive employment is the most important expenditure problem of the provincial governments. Generalizing from a study made for the Province of Santa Fe, employment in general activities or administration could be reduced by as much as 50 percent. Employment could be reduced by eliminating overstaffing with an administrative reform similar to that of the Federal Government and privatizing some activities (like cleaning of buildings). This reduction is conservative if one considers that in Santa Fe the special labor regime for public employees allows them to work annually only half the number of days the average private employee must work--because of the 6-hour work day in this province, and special unpaid leaves. An administrative reform of the type applied at the federal level could generate savings of perhaps US$700 million annually, while allowing for a generous improvement in real wages for the remaining skilled workers.

61.   Most provinces have fewer-than-normal work days for public employees, in addition to special paid leaves for exams in the case of students or for illness of family members, as well as longer vacation periods than employees in the private sector. There is no reason to maintain such privileges, especially if salaries are raised, since in many cases they are supposed to represent compensation for lower salaries, especially for highly qualified workers, who have suffered especially from wage compression. Reduction in the provincial labor force should be followed by increases in upper-level salaries to stop outmigration of skilled personnel and to encourage the hiring of highly-qualified employees. Public employees enjoy employment guarantees, which should be reduced before salaries are improved. To avoid legal complications,

employees could be asked to opt for higher salaries but without job guarantees or job stability but limited wage increase.

62.   Administrative reform of the provincial public sector is closely related to the potential reduction in the number of teachers. Teachers account for 42 percent of total public employment, while blue-collar and administrative workers (classified in the budget under "general activities") represent another 27 percent (e.g., compared to less than 10 percent in the United States).

63.   For teachers, overstaffing is apparent from the low ratio of students to teachers. Rules that govern the labor conditions of teachers are lenient, especially regarding the granting of unpaid leave, and lack of administrative control. The approach should be to reduce the number, then increase the pay of those remaining in exchange for improvements in productivity. The public schools also need restructuring: (i) the number of classrooms need to be reviewed; (ii) the labor regime for teachers should be changed, curtailing the privileges; and (iii) the federal transfers for schools should be allocated as a function of the number of students and not of the payroll of each public school. Money spent on private education might also be allocated as a function of the number of students and not in proportion to teachers' salaries. This would introduce competition among private and public schools. It may even be useful to apply some variant of the Chilean scheme, where transfers are made directly to the schools, private as well as public; while this has generated a short run adjustment problem in Chile as students have left municipal schools, in the long run, it will dampen cost increases and improve educational quality.

64.   Hospitals could be decentralized and user fees introduced as much as possible. In the Province of Buenos Aires, user fees allowed some hospitals to become self-financing. Transfers to hospitals should be related to the number of patients and not to the size of their payrolls.

65.   A functional analysis is needed to establish the responsibilities of each provincial ministry. This analysis should lead to: (i) elimination of unnecessary agencies; (ii) listing of those agencies that could be privatized; and (iii) assessment of the optimum number of public employees for each agency. As with the Federal Government, certain administrative functions, like tax administration or regulations affecting the environment, should be strengthened.

66.   **Transfers to Provincial Public Enterprises.** Transfers from the provinces to provincial enterprises are fairly small and mostly in the province of Buenos Aires. In part, this may reflect reliance on low-cost provincial bank finance rather than transfers; such finance is drying up. Provinces should consider the Federal Government's example in changing the institutional regime for provincial public enterprises, including privatization. This would reduce public expenditures somewhat and improve service delivery.

67.   **Reforms in Provincial Pension Systems.** Provincial pension systems are in financial distress. This situation will be even worse in the future because the needed administrative reform will reduce income by reducing the number of employees paying

into the system; the high rate of growth in the number of beneficiaries will increase outlays beyond reasonable revenue expectations. Hence, part of the cost savings from adjustment and part of the "excess" of coparticipated revenues will be needed to finance provincial pension funds. At the same time, it may be necessary to reduce provincial pensions, which currently are often more generous than the federal system.

68.   The first step in reform should be careful studies of the existing provincial pension systems to: (i) project the revenues and costs of the current systems without changes; (ii) define alternative reforms; and (iii) simulate the fiscal impact of such reforms. One alternative for reform that should be analyzed and considered is that provinces move toward capitalization schemes similar to those being studied at the federal level, perhaps designing mechanisms to integrate provincial reforms into the national reform.

69.   **Deregulation.** Provinces should improve provincial laws that introduce barriers to entry into several markets or lead to higher costs. To this end, Decree 2248/91 of the Federal Government should be replicated in the provinces. There is a need for standardizing regulations so as to reduce costs fully.

70.   **Capital Expenditures.** The burden of public investment now has been delegated to the provinces. But provincial investment levels have fallen so low that essential infrastructure is deteriorating. Moreover, the provincial capacity to administer an investment program is minimal. Provinces seldom perform evaluation of their own expenditures for social projects. The introduction of this kind of analysis is urgent. It will require special staff training, since the responsibilities of local governments are concentrated on expenditures that are difficult to evaluate (e.g., education and health). The transfer of expenditure responsibilities to the provinces further intensifies this problem.

71.   FONAVI routinely spends an amount equal to one-third of all provincial investment; yet it neither efficiently allocates resources nor is it self-financing. Moreover, there is no *a priori* reason to favor investments in housing over alternative investments in health care, roads or other public services. Currently, the provincial government performs the construction of the house, selects the beneficiary, and collects the installments. However, the provincial governments usually pay higher-than-market prices for sites and construction, and then do not collect the monthly payments on the houses. The system should be reformed so that each province may keep for itself the amounts collected from old loans, while the earmarked financing of FONAVI should be gradually phased out. FONAVI funds could also be used to finance layoffs of provincial employees. Provinces could be allowed to spend the money they collect from FONAVI loans for any social expenditure. The allocation of money should be done after competing public projects have been evaluated.

CHAPTER 11. SOCIAL SECURITY (PENSION INSURANCE)

A. Overview

1.   The National Pension System (NPS) insures about 90 percent of Argentina's economically active population against the risks of old age, disability and survivorship.   The system operates on a pay-as-you-go (PAYG) basis (i.e., current contributions of active members finance current pension benefits of retired members or their dependent survivors).   Membership in the NPS or other public pension schemes is mandatory, and the payment of benefits is guaranteed by the state.   Troubled by massive evasion, the NPS has become a major problem in Argentina's public finances: in addition to absorbing significant general tax revenues and budget transfers, the system accumulates arrears with pensioners because of underpayment.   For a large share of active workers, the NPS fails to remove the prospect of dependence on private charity or public welfare in their inactive years, which is the principal rationale for universally mandating pension insurance.   It also distorts labor markets through excessive payroll deductions, and forgoes the possibility of generating long-term savings by exclusively relying on PAYG financing.   The Government has reached the conclusion that the present system requires radical reform, and has submitted to Congress a draft law for the introduction of a new, so-called Integrated Pension System (IPS).

2.   The Government's analysis adopts the principle of securing a socially acceptable level of income for all inactive workers and their dependent survivors through mandatory insurance during their active years.   The principle is efficient for countering the moral hazard problem of relying on charity or welfare; and pooling risks while avoiding the adverse selection problem of voluntary insurance.   Instead, inefficient entitlement rules, aggravated by a poorly administered supply monopoly of the state, are seen as the principal endogenous causes of the NPS' failure--in addition to the ageing of the population and macroeconomic instability which are exogenous to the system. The rules encourage evasion by delinking expected benefits from contributions at the margin; mandating a sub-optimal level of insurance; and leaving the insured uncertain about promised benefits relative to either their historical real earnings or future real wages.   Combined with weak controls, they create opportunities for fraud, in turn causing inequities.   The system also lacks an internal redistribution mechanism, exposing it to unsystematic policy interventions.

3.   The draft law would address the root causes by: (i) introducing fully capitalized and privately managed pension funds that would provide pension benefits in strict proportion to life-time contributions and investment performance; (ii) establishing a new public PAYG pension scheme that would produce a transparent redistribution by providing an essentially uniform basic pension; and (iii) defining for all workers maximum and minimum mandatory insurance levels in relation to average wage income. The law would reduce evasion further by raising Argentina's low pension requirement as to minimum years of contribution.   Combined with an increase in the minimum age

at retirement, reduced evasion would reverse a dramatic increase in the dependency ratio (pensioners/contributors) from 0.39 to 0.62 during 1980s.

4.   Prior to the introduction of the IPS--expected to occur on January 1, 1994--the Government is cleaning up the NPS, including a settlement of accumulated arrears with pensioners, improved administration of collections and benefits, and a transparent allocation of tax revenues. The main challenge of the reform ahead will be to finance the transition from a one-tier PAYG system to a two-tier system involving PAYG and capitalization. Over the next generation, the state will need to provide for pensions granted before the reform and to compensate active workers for their pre-reform contributions, but will receive contributions only in the context of the new public scheme. Since the room for additional taxation or debt financing is limited, the Government must exercise unpopular restraint in adjusting pre-reform pensions and granting compensation for pre-reform contributions; and also drastically lower the ratio of pensioners to contributors by swiftly raising Argentina's low thresholds for obtaining a pension. The second important issue is the generation of confidence in the performance of the new pension funds. This involves the regulatory framework for the pension fund managers, investment rules that exclude the involuntary purchase of public debt issues, and the establishment of a professional, non-politicized superintendency.

B. The Failure of the National Pension System

Basic Characteristics of the System

5.   **Formal Social Security**. Argentina's formal social security system comprises mandatory pension insurance, mandatory health insurance for pensioners and for active workers, family assistance, and support for low-income housing construction. Work-related risks (loss of employment and work accidents) are covered by legal compensation claims against employers; insurance against the risk of such claims is voluntary and is provided by private institutions. Pension and health insurance and family assistance are financed through payroll taxes in the form of employer and employee contributions (Appendix Table 4.3) and contributions of independent workers. Earmarked taxes complement the revenue base of pension providers, and have recently replaced payroll deductions in the financing of low-income housing.

6.   **Supply**. The state holds the supply monopoly for mandatory pension insurance.[1] The state also manages health insurance for pensioners and the family assistance and housing funds; health insurance for active dependent workers is exclusively supplied by union-held institutions. Almost 90 percent of the gainfully

---

[1]   Article 14 bis of the Argentine constitution (added in 1957) requires mandatory pension insurance to be supplied by the state with indexed benefits. The benefit and entitlement criteria have been specified in Laws 18.037 and 18.038 of 1968 and 1969 (henceforth, the pension laws) for, respectively, dependent and independent workers. The laws make pension insurance mandatory for all gainfully employed persons 16 years and older--about 10.6 million workers in 1990. Excluded are the unemployed and the non-remunerated family workers, about 900,000 and 400,000, respectively, in 1990.

employed are obligated to seek pension insurance with the NPS administration directed by the Secretariat of Social Security in the Ministry of Labor and Social Security. Of these, about two-thirds are dependent workers and one-third independent workers. Members of the police and the armed forces and provincial and municipal employees are insured by separate public institutions. Voluntary pension insurance on a capitalization basis is supplied by private institutions, so-called Retirement Insurance Companies (Seguros de Retiro).[2] While these institutions cover only 1.2 percent of the gainfully employed, they provide a repository of pension fund management expertise valuable for the future mandatory capitalization scheme.

7.   **PAYG Basis and State Guarantee**. The NPS and the other public pension institutions operate on a PAYG basis. PAYG financing was not the initial choice, however. The first pension insurance--established for public employees in 1904--was based on capitalization principles. The accumulated reserves of this and other publicly managed funds were subsequently eroded as the state expanded benefits without commensurate increases in contributions and directed investments to government debt obligations at negative real interest rates. Laws 18.037 (for dependent workers) and 18.038 (for independent workers) formally reconstituted the system on a PAYG basis in, respectively, 1968 and 1969.

8.   The pension laws call for current expenditures to be financed out of current revenues from contributions and operational returns of the system such as penalties and interest on technical reserves; tax revenues are not mentioned. Deviating from PAYG principles, however, individual benefits are not defined as shares in total current revenues, but as rights based on historical individual income (dependent workers) or politically determined minimum pensions (independent workers). Financial equilibrium therefore is not assured, making it necessary to complement the system with a state guarantee for pension payments. A shortfall in revenues would call the guarantee; and failure to transfer sufficient resources would result in arrears with pensioners. Only in the case of independent workers could the Government avoid arrears by reducing the minimum pension, though it might then fail on the objective of preventing dependence on charity or welfare. To prevent the guarantee from being called, the NPS must be able to raise contributions or add to the revenue sources enumerated in the pension laws, i.e., include general tax revenues.

Financial Disequilibrium

9.   A PAYG system without general tax revenues is in cash flow equilibrium when total annual receipts from own sources cover total annual outlays. Neglecting operating returns and administrative costs allows for a simple equilibrium condition: the *contribution rate* (contributions as a percent of average earnings of active workers) must equal the product of the *pension rate* (average pension as a percent of average pensionable earnings at retirement), the *earnings ratio* (average pensionable earnings divided by average earnings of active workers) and the *dependency ratio* (the number of beneficiaries divided by the number of contributors). All things being equal, this condition cannot be met if the dependency ratio is highly elastic with respect to the

---

2   Their operations are regulated by Resolution 19.106 of 1987.

contribution rate, i.e., when a required increase in the contribution rate, by inducing evasion of contribution obligations, would lead to an offsetting increase in the dependency ratio. This has come to be the case in Argentina.

10.   The average legal pension rate for retired dependent workers and their survivors was approximately 70 percent in 1990, excluding the effect of a two-months lag in wage indexation. The dependency ratio in that year would have been 0.33 (i.e., three workers supporting one beneficiary) had all legally covered workers actually contributed. Demographic projections--assuming constant age at retirement--suggest that the dependency ratio would increase to 0.39 over the next 20 years and subsequently remain stable. The earnings ratio would be close to unity if pensionable income were determined as the average of fully wage-indexed earnings in all years of contribution. In this hypothetical case, therefore, the required contribution rate would be 23 percent and would gradually increase to 27 percent over the next 20 years as a result of the demographic transition. In other words, the present contribution rate of 26 percent for dependent workers would be more than sufficient for the financial equilibrium of the NPS over the medium term.

11.   In reality, however, the average dependency ratio in 1990 was 0.62--1.6 workers supporting 1 beneficiary. The earnings ratio was 1.5; this excludes the effect of a wage-indexation lag. The dependency ratios were 0.48 and 1.39, respectively, for dependent and independent workers. Financial equilibrium for the NPS is clearly out of reach with the observed dependency ratio and earnings ratio. The required contribution rates would be about 50, 150 and 70 percent, respectively, for dependent workers, independent workers, and the NPS on average. The wide gap between the actual and the hypothetical ratios in Argentina is caused by entitlement rules that encourage evasion and fraud, and by weak controls allowing such responses on a large scale.

Entitlement Rules

12.   **Dependent Workers.** Law 18.037 promises dependent workers a wage-indexed regular pension (*jubilacion ordinaria*) between 70 percent and 82 percent of their pensionable earnings, defined as the average of wage inflation-adjusted monthly salaries in the three years the highest salaries were earned during the last 10 years of employment. Wage indexation is lagged by 60 days, both for the regular adjustment of pensions and for the determination of pensionable earnings on the day of retirement. The rate of 70 percent applies to male and female workers at the minimum retirement age of, respectively, 60 and 55 years. The rate increases to 78, 80, and 82 percent if retirement is postponed by, respectively, 3, 4 and 5 years. The same rates apply to disability pensions if employment has lasted, respectively, less than 3 years, 3 years, 4 years, and 5 years or more. To qualify for a regular pension, a worker must have been gainfully employed for at least 30 years, but needs to have contributed for only 15 years. Workers with at least 10 years of employment and 5 years of contribution can retire at age 65 with 60 percent of their pensionable earnings as defined above ("advanced age pension"). Widow pensions amount to 75 percent of the pension of the deceased; they are shared by the widow and all other dependents broadly defined. Since 1983, furthermore, all pensions including widow pensions and advanced age pensions

are subject to a minimum which the Government is free to set. A maximum pension was introduced in 1988 at 15 times the then applicable minimum pension, but subsequently wage-indexed.

13.   **Independent Workers**. Law 18.038 allows independent workers to choose between categories of monthly pensions. These are defined as multiples of the minimum pension ranging from 1 in the lowest category to 30 in the highest category. For independent professionals and entrepreneurs, the choice is restricted to the middle and higher categories. Monthly contributions are 21 percent of the targeted pension. The retirement age is 65 years for men, 60 years for women, and 70 years for the advanced age pension regardless of gender. Required years of contributions are the same as for dependent workers and so are the rates of disability, advanced age, and widow pensions.

14.   **Incentives for Evasion and Fraud**. The above rules encourage evasion by failing to connect expected benefits with contributions at the margin. Contributing for more than 15 years--or for more than 5 but less than 15 years--will not raise a worker's expected benefits. In all but 3 years, furthermore, dependent workers cannot raise their expected benefits by having their employers report wages in excess of what the NPS administration accepts without raising questions; employers and workers therefore have an interest in colluding to overreport wages during 3 years and underreport in all other years.

15.   For dependent workers, evasion is also a way of escaping from what--assuming low wage inflation or instantaneous indexation--appears to be an obligation to overinsure. Since pensioners are not liable to workers' contributions to pension and health insurance (16 percent of gross salary), a retiree with 82 percent of indexed gross salary is promised 98 percent of the net salary in his or her peak years of earnings--substantially more than the individual indexed average lifetime net salary. The pensioner typically has no work-related expenditures such as transport and carries a lower burden of maintaining a family than a young or middle-aged worker. Since the active worker cannot borrow against the expected pension, this imposes a sub-optimal lifetime distribution of consumption.

16.   Manipulating the pensionable income is also attractive as an individual strategy to compensate for the effects of lagged indexation in an inflationary environment. Adjustment of pensions to wage inflation occurs only 60 days after general wages have increased by more than 10 percent since the preceding adjustment and without recognition of wage inflation during the two months. Pensions therefore tend to fall significantly behind during periods of high wage inflation; while catching up during the subsequent stabilization, there is no compensation for the preceding loss. Even more pernicious for the individual pensioner is the two-months indexation lag at the day of retirement; this can reduce the individual pension base permanently in a manner he or she cannot predict.

17.   The law for independent workers might seem to avoid mandating sub-optimal insurance by giving members a choice between pension targets, the lowest of which equals the minimum pension. However, the minimum pension is not

systematically linked to a wage index or any other income indicator. In adjusting the minimum pension, the Government is therefore free to respond to various pressures, including the pressure to contain the NPS deficit. (Raising the minimum pension increases benefits and contributions of independent workers proportionally, thus magnifying any existing imbalance.) The resulting uncertainty among independent workers as to the adequacy of their expected pension creates incentives to enter the system late in working life and to select the lowest pension category, while seeking old age security by other means or relying on charity. As indicated below, this has resulted in a wide-spread underinsurance of independent workers.

18.   The strength of these incentives is reflected in evasion rates. In 1990, the NPS did not receive contributions for 33 percent of dependent workers and 63 percent of independent workers. Contributions received for dependent workers were on average more than 15 percent short of what could be expected on the basis of average wages. This is despite increased contributions in the 3 years in which salaries tend to be overreported: a check on the contribution and wage history of all new pensioners during two recent months revealed that the average real wage of the three years with the highest reported salaries was about 50 percent above the average of the last 10 years. Also, among independent workers, contributors aged 45 represented less than one-third of all contributors, whereas the age group accounts for more than two-thirds of independent workers. In addition, weak controls and opaque criteria have generated an unreasonably high share of disability pensions. In 1990, disability pensions accounted for 18 percent and 26 percent, respectively, of all pensions of dependent and independent workers; shares reached more than 60 percent in various provincial branches of the NPS administration.

Policy Responses in the 1980s

19.   **Revenues.** The financial disequilibrium of the NPS emerged in the late 1970s. Successive governments, however, shied away from addressing the fundamental issue of the incentive structure. The authorities raised independent workers' contributions from 12 percent to 15 percent in 1980 and to 21 percent in 1987. In 1980, they also replaced employers' contributions (15 percent of gross salary) by an earmarked share of value added tax revenues with an insignificant net increase in NPS revenues. Employers' contributions were reinstated in 1984 at 7.5 percent, raised to 10.5 percent in the following year and to 12.5 percent in 1987, and reduced to 11 percent in 1988. Again, this yielded no net addition because revenues from the value added tax were replaced by lower revenues from other taxes (on fuel, telephones, and foreign exchange). The dependent workers' contribution rate of 11 percent remained unchanged until 1988 when it was lowered by one percentage point. These measures were insufficient to maintain financial equilibrium. Beginning in 1979, the authorities reduced pension payments substantively below legal levels, and financed the remaining flow deficit with *ad hoc* treasury transfers or Central Bank credit. The following table provides information on the extent to which these measures were taken.

Table 11.1: Policy Response to NPS Disequilibrium, 1978-91
(percent and US$ millions)

	Average Pension as Percent of Average Salary	NPS Expenditures (US$ Millions) [a]	Financing in Percent of Expenditures		
			Own Resources	Tax Revenues	Deficit
1978	65	3124	96	-	4
1980	40	4061	89	11	-
1985	36	3256	75	34	(9)
1987	25	4085	80	13	7
1988	32	3937	59	33	8
1989	31	2138	66	18	16
1990	43	4652	68	24	8
1991 [b]	40	4135	75	16	9

a/   Includes net transfers to other parts of the social security system.
b/   January-July.

Source: PRONATASS (1978-88), Macroeconomica (1989-91).

20.   **Minimum Pensions**. The NPS mitigated the impact on the poor by administering the cuts in a progressive manner; basically, pensioners received the minimum pension plus a fixed share of their residual entitlement (27 percent in 1987). This implies that more than 95 percent of independent retirees received their legal benefits as they had chosen the lowest pension category which equals the minimum pension.   A large share of dependent workers--about one-half in 1990--also received their legal benefits as wage inflation and lagged indexation reduced their entitlements. As discussed above, however, the minimum pension is not indexed.   Absent effective action against evasion and without significant measures to expand the revenue base, the authorities could contain the NPS deficit only by delaying the adjustment of the minimum pension. In percent of average salary, the minimum pension fell from a high of 48 in 1983 to a low of 16 in 1987 and has since remained below 30.   Against the background of an approximately 30 percent decline in the real average wage between 1983/85 and 1990/92, this suggests that the NPS failed to secure a socially acceptable minimum income for most retirees and their dependents.

21.   **Arrears with Pensioners**. The pension cuts generated claims against the NPS. The holders of such claims could interrupt a two-year statute of limitations only by bringing cases. About 20,000 judgments against the NPS have so far been obtained, and about 60,000 cases are pending. (Without the instrument of class-action suits, claims in Argentina have to be presented individually). To prevent the complete insolvency of the NPS, the Government suppressed their implementation through Decree 648/87 at the same time offering partial compensation against relinquishment of the claims.   In addition, Decrees 648/87 and 366/89 and Law 23.827 promised all pensioners instalment payments on a reduced amount of debt in exchange for relinquishing their claims. About 1.45 million pensioners accepted but did not receive payment. In July 1989, the new Government suspended the statute of limitations, which made the system liable for all underpayments starting in July 1987, in addition to commitments resulting from the debt exchange and from judicial sentences.

22.   The Government estimated the stock of debt as of April 1, 1991 at US$7.3 billion. This estimate includes: (i) US$5.2 billion accumulated since July 1987; (ii) US$1.7 billion reflecting the debt exchange under Decrees 648/87 and 366/89 and Law 23.827; (iii) US$0.3 billion on account of judicial sentences already obtained; and (iv) US$30 million reflecting unmet obligations under special laws for privileged pensions. The NPS has accumulated arrears at a monthly rate of about US$200 million through August 1992, when the Government raised pensions using coparticipation resources.

C. Restoring a Viable Pension System

23.   In late-1990, the Government acknowledged that the NPS as established by the pension laws would never be able to meet its objectives. A reform strategy was then developed in stages. At years-end the Government rejected a seriously deficient proposal from within the NPS administration and began reviewing reform options. A new economic policy team reached the basic decision on the introduction of a two-tier system in March 1991. A group of experts then worked out key parameters of the new system that would allow for a fiscally sustainable transition path. On that basis, the Government submitted the first draft of a reform law to Congress in June 1992. The subsequent public discussion motivated the Government to present a second draft in August 1992 and introduce modifications in December. The law is expected to pass in early 1993, and to take effect in early 1994. In 1991, the Government also began cleaning up the NPS, which will remain responsible for the benefits of existing pensioners and workers retiring prior to the establishment of the IPS in early 1994. This involves the settlement of debt with pensioners, revenue enhancements--improved collections and additional tax revenues--allowing for an end to underpayments, and measures to slow new entries to the pool of beneficiaries.

Reform Options

24.   **Principal Options.** The Government weighed the principal reform options of: (i) rebuilding a publicly supplied system on strict PAYG principles defining individual benefits as shares in total current revenues; and with rules establishing a credible link between expected benefits and contributions at the margin, a transparent internal redistribution mechanism, reduced uncertainty about expected benefits relative to general wage development, and a lower level of mandated insurance; (ii) providing a uniform social minimum pension on a PAYG basis, while leaving the attainment of higher post-retirement income objectives to private initiative; and (iii) following the Chilean example of a one-tier mandatory private system based on capitalization principles. The first option would require high contribution rates--in addition to significant tax financing--and offer low returns to young and middle-aged workers. It would, thus, continue to depress labor demand in the formal sector and provide incentives for staying out of the system. A minimum pension scheme would allow for lower contribution rates only if the evasion problem could be addressed by other means as it would not establish a link between expected benefits and contributions at the margin. Even then, contribution rates could be reduced only in the long-term because the system would remain liable for pensions already granted, and would also have to

compensate middle-aged and older workers with average-to-high earnings which--relying on the promise of proportional pensions--had not saved for retirement.

25.   A privately supplied pension fund scheme would avoid the evasion problem provided it was considered credible, i.e., funds were managed professionally, fund managers exposed to competition, forced investments in Government titles ruled out, and a competent superintendency installed.   As evidenced by the Chilean experience, furthermore, mandatory capitalization schemes promise important benefits for the economy by generating long-term domestic savings and promoting capital market development.   This option, however, would require the Government to mobilize, for an extended transition period, more than 6 percent of GDP for paying existing pensioners and compensating workers for contributions already made.   Additional tax revenues in that amount would be unattainable under present circumstances.   In practice, the authorities would have to direct pension fund managers to invest in Government titles, thus undercutting the credibility of the reform.   Further considerations relate to social equity objectives and constitutional constraints.   A private pension fund scheme obviously will provide benefits only in strict proportion to contributions; and will not fulfill the state's constitutional obligation to provide indexed pension benefits.   A mandatory private pension fund scheme would, therefore, need to be restricted in size and be complemented by a public PAYG scheme with a strong redistributive component.

26.   These considerations resulted in a reform concept that combines the principal options.   In the first draft reform law, the Government proposed a strict PAYG scheme for older workers (i.e., born before 1947; this would be achieved by appropriate changes in the existing pension laws which, however, would not affect pre-reform pensions.   Workers born in 1947 or later would be obligated to participate in each of the two schemes of a new, so-called Integrated Pension System (IPS): a public PAYG scheme offering an essentially uniform basic pension similar to the second option above, and a privately supplied scheme on strict capitalization principles along Chilean lines. However, the basic pension (about 22 percent of average salary) would be lower than the social minimum, and monthly benefits from savings in the private scheme would be modest (about 40 percent of individual real average life-time monthly earnings after 40 years of contributions on conservative rate of return assumptions of 2 percent in real terms).   Only jointly would the two schemes provide adequate pension insurance.

27.   The Government's actuarial projections indicated that the proposed reform would require tax financing on a declining basis for some 20 years, beginning with about US$4 billion (less than 3 percent of GDP) in the first year. This result depended on the denial of compensations for previous contributions to workers born 1947 and later, and on restrictive entitlement rules for the older group including a regular pension rate of 70 percent instead of the famous 82 percent promised in Law 18.037.   The subsequent public discussion revealed unwillingness to accept these implications.   The Government responded by submitting to Congress a new draft law which would bring active workers of all age groups into the IPS and thereby by-pass the politically charged issue of the 82 percent.   However, it would also provide for a third, so-called compensatory pension in recognition of all pre-reform contributions.   This additional commitment makes a sustainable financing of the medium-term transition harder to obtain, requiring the Government to take a tough stance toward rates of basic and

compensatory pensions, minimum years of contribution and age at retirement, disability criteria, and adjustments for existing pensioners.

Key Characteristics of the New System

28.   The draft reform law is innovative in allocating the supply of mandatory pension insurance between private and public schemes, respectively organized on capitalization and PAYG principles. The private scheme will not be described here in detail as it closely follows the well-known Chilean model. Instead, the following focusses on the manner in which the combined system addresses the key problems of social security revealed by the failure of the old system.

29.   **PAYG Principles**. The new system links benefits of the public scheme to current contributions rather than historical income subject to a lagged wage-index (dependent workers) or politically determined minimum pensions (independent workers). The instrument for this is the so-called average mandatory workers' contribution rate (AMPO--aporte medio previsional obligatorio) defined as total current contributions to the private scheme divided by current number of contributors. The basic and the compensatory pensions are established as multiples of AMPO; and so are the minimum and maximum of earnings for which contributions are due. With the multiples defined, the dependency ratio is then left as the only determinant of the system's financial position. Lowering this ratio is of course a key objective of the reform but this cannot be obtained without significant initial tax revenues that obviate the need for higher contribution rates. Starting from a situation of severe imbalance between total contributions and expenditures, the Government hopes to progressively reduce reliance on general tax revenues and excessive employers' contributions.

30.   **Contributions**. Contributions are proportional to monthly earnings within a band. Earnings of dependent workers include gross wages and other payments in cash or kind including fringe benefits, but excluding severance pay and other formal social security benefits such as family assistance. Earnings of independent workers are estimated. Dependent and independent workers contribute 11 percent to their private pension fund; employers and independent workers contribute 16 percent to the public scheme. The total contribution to the IPS is therefore a uniform 27 percent for all workers compared to 26 percent of gross salary for dependent workers and 21 percent of the target pension for independent workers in the NPS. Contributions must be made for monthly earnings of at least 3 AMPOs; but are not mandatory for the part of earnings that exceeds the equivalent of 60 AMPOs. The AMPO is 11 percent of average reported or estimated earnings within this band; this average is likely to be close to the average wage. The new system therefore obligates all workers to contribute--personally or through their employers--27 percent of their earnings within a band of 33 percent to 660 percent of the average wage.

31.   **Integration of Independent Workers**. As discussed above, the separate treatment of independent workers through Law 18.038 left about one-third of the workforce grossly underinsured and dependent on minimum pensions equivalent to 16-30 percent of average wage in the 1980s. The draft law eliminates the separation from dependent workers. While practical difficulties of estimating their earnings are likely

to result in the majority contributing only the minimum, this would still insure them on a basis of about 33 percent of average wage; as shown below, internal redistribution raises the expected total pension benefits of young independent workers to about 45 percent of average wage.

32.   **Pension Requirements**. A sharp tightening of qualifications for obtaining a public pension is critical for reversing the increasing trend of the dependency ratio. The draft law raises the minimum years of contributions from 15 to 30; and the minimum age at retirement to a uniform 65 years from 55 years for dependent women and 60 for dependent men and independent women. It also eliminates the possibility of obtaining an advanced age pension after only 5 years of contributions. The immediate application of these requirements would deprive many older workers which evaded contributions in their young and middle years from any chance to obtain a pension. The draft law therefore contains a set of transitory regulations which effectively allow such workers to meet the qualifications at age 70. An estimate of the effect of these measures on the dependency ratio is presented in the context of the medium-term transition discussed below.

33.   Public disability benefits require the existence of a private disability pension. The private pension funds purchase disability insurance for their affiliates from life insurance companies. The right to a transitory disability pension--up to 3 years but not more than years of previous contribution--is established if an independent medical commission confirms a work incapacity of at least 66 percent; and is extended to life if the commission reconfirms the finding after 3 years. The affiliate, the pension fund manager, and the life insurance company can each appeal the finding to a central medical commission appointed by the superintendency for pension funds.

34.   **Expected Benefits**. The draft law--as modified in December 1992--promises a uniform basic pension of 2.5 AMPOs (about 27.5 percent of average current wage) after 30 years of contributions. The pension increases by 2 percent of this amount for each additional contribution year up to a maximum of 45 years, i.e., to at most 3.25 AMPOs (about 36 percent of average current wage). The law also provides for a compensatory pension for dependent workers in recognition of their pre-reform contributions. This amounts to 1 percent of their pension base for each pre-reform year of contribution up to at most 30 years. The pension base is defined as the average wage-indexed monthly salary in the last 10 years before retirement; this effectively eliminates the pension base manipulation described above.

35.   The private pension fund offers the retiree a choice between a programmed withdrawal from the individual capitalization account and an indexed annuity to be purchased from a commercial insurance company. The resulting pension obviously depends on the individual contribution history and the investment performance of the fund. The share of contributions going to the individual account can also differ between funds, because fund managers are free to set the management fee. Since workers can freely switch their accounts between funds, however, competition is expected to limit variations. The fee must also cover the cost of disability insurance, which managers must purchase for fund members. It is expected to amount to about 3 percentage points

of the 11 percent contribution, leaving 8 percent for the individual capitalization account.

36.   Total expected benefits for workers entering the new IPS in early 1994 will differ according to their age, years of previous contributions, and expected future contributions to the private scheme; but also with respect to their fund's investment performance. To allow for a comparison of main cases, Table 11.2 calculates expected benefits for workers earning the average wage, which is also assumed to remain constant throughout. The workers are young (25 years), middle-aged (45 years) or close to retirement (65 years); they have either 30 or 40 years of contribution at retirement, and the real rate of interest achieved by their fund is either 2 percent or 4 percent.

Table 11.2: Total Expected Benefits at the Start of the Reform
(In percent of average salary)

Age at Entry	Years of Contribution at Retirement a/	Basic Pension	Compensatory Pension	Pension Fund Benefits; RRI b/ 2%	4%	Total Benefit
25	40	33	0	38	68	71 - 101
45	40	33	20	14	21	67 - 74
65	40	33	30	0	0	63
25	30	28	0	24	40	52 - 68
45	30	28	10	14	21	52 - 59
65	30	28	30	0	0	58

a/ Retirement at age 65.
b/ Real Rate of Interest.

Source: Secretariat of Social Security

37.   The results show the benefits of a strong pension fund performance for the young. On conservative assumptions--a real interest rate of 2 percent--the new system promises workers with a clean contribution history (40 years) benefits in a range of 63-71 percent. This is on the level of promised benefits in the existing system for dependent workers--taking into consideration the adverse impact of the indexation lag on entitlements. Central to the new system is the link between expected benefits and contributions absent from the present system, including much more stringent minimum requirements and incentives to meet obligations throughout working-life. As shown, a young worker missing contributions in 10 of his prospective 40 years prior to retirement must contend with a pension almost 20 percentage points lower.

38.   The draft law produces a transparent internal redistribution through the basic pension. The strength of the redistribution effect is apparent from Table 11.3, which shows the expected benefits of young workers with earnings ranging over the spectrum of earnings subject to mandatory pension insurance. While maximum earnings are 20 times minimum earnings, expected maximum benefits are a multiple of about 6 of expected minimum benefits.

Table 11.3: Redistributive Effect of New Pension System

Own Salary as % of Average Salary	Total Pension a/ as % of Own Salary	Total Pension a/ as % of Average Salary
33	137	46
100	71	71
660	43	284

a/   Total expected benefits for a worker entering at age 25, retiring at age 65, and expecting the pension fund to achieve a real rate of interest of 2 percent annually.

Source: Social Security Secretariat

39.   **Conclusion**. The draft law promises to address the causes for the failure of the NPS in an innovative and convincing manner within Argentina's constitutional and political constraints. It will be important, however, that the Government win Congress' approval without compromising on tough pension requirements and restrictive rates for the compensatory pension. Pressures for an extended phase-in of pension requirements--postponing the necessary reduction in the dependency ratio--and for doubling the compensatory pension must be resisted for reasons discussed below.

D. Cleaning Up the Old System

40.   The Government is settling the NPS' arrears with pensioners. The Government must also end the practice of underpayments and, in addition, move the system into surplus before the reform directs part of the contributions to capitalization accounts. To that end, the Government is reducing certain privileges, raising pension requirements, improving the collection of contributions, and earmarking tax revenues for social security.

Settling Debt with Pensioners

41.   In August 1991, Congress passed Law 23.982 on the consolidation of public debt with pensioners and suppliers accrued until April 1, 1991. The draft pension reform law requires the Government to also consolidate any later arrears before introducing the new system. The consolidation is being accomplished through the issuance of consolidation bonds (BOCONs) with a 10-year maturity and 6-year grace period on principal and interest. About US$1.7 billion had been issued by end-June 1992. Pensioners can choose between instruments issued in pesos at the average interest rate of the public savings bank or in US dollars at LIBOR. The bond is freely negotiable. The state accepts the bonds at par value for specified purposes. Bond holders will be allowed to apply the paper to obligations against the NPS that were due prior to April 1, 1991. The original subscribers, i.e., the pensioners, can also use the paper for canceling any other obligations against the state they may have, under conditions to be specified in a special law. In addition, any holder is allowed to settle disputed tax obligations that were due prior to April 1, 1991.

42.   The Government intends to repurchase a major share of the BOCONs at their market value, currently about 70 percent of face value. To that end, the Federal Government's share in the proceeds from the sale of shares of the state oil company (YPF) (about 51 percent with the rest going to the provinces and workers) have been earmarked for the public pension system, in addition to 20 percent of revenues from the income tax. The proceeds from the sale of YPF shares are difficult to project, but it appears likely that at least US$4 billion will be made available to the NPS. The income tax share is expected yield about US$1.2 billion in 1993. This suggests that most, if not all, BOCONs to be issued to pensioners could be retired within the six-year grace period.

Streamlining the NPS

43.   **Reducing Privileged Pensions.** The preferred treatment of legislators, judges, and leading members of the executive branch has become a symbol for the inequities of the NPS. Through Decree 1324/91, the Government removed all privileges. Congress ordered non-effectiveness of the decree through a provision in Law 23.966. However, other provisions of this law curbed abuses by tightening pension requirements: beneficiaries must have held public office for at least 2 years (legislators) or 4 years (executive branch) and must meet the general qualifications for access to NPS pensions as to minimum years of contributions and age at retirement. The law also enabled the Government to reduce privileged pensions for 5 years by declaring a "pension emergency".

44.   **Raising Pension Requirements.** The number of pensioners has been growing at an annual rate of about 3 percent over the last decade. The prospect of a reform with more stringent entitlement criteria, furthermore, could lead to a pre-reform rush into retirement. Through Decree 2016/91, the Government has therefore increased the minimum years of contributions from 15 to 20 years. The NPS administration is also conducting an audit of disability pensions concentrating on provinces with an excessive share of disability pensions in total pensions. The draft reform law, furthermore, tightens requirements for retirement between its promulgation--expected for February, 1993--and the establishment of the new system in early 1994: minimum years of contributions increase by a further 10 years and minimum age at retirement by 2 years. These actions are expected to stabilize the total number of pensioners at about 3 million, allowing the dependency ratio to fall as the number of contributors increases.

45.   **Higher Contributions.** Revenues from contributions increased by about 90 percent between the first quarter of 1991 and the fourth quarter of 1992, compared to an increase of about 40 percent in the average industrial wage. This reflects both higher contribution rates and improved collection efforts. Law 23.966 increased the employers' contribution rate by 5 percentage points while abolishing employers' contributions to the housing fund. The combined contribution rate of dependent workers and their employers therefore increased from 21 percent to 26 percent of gross salary. No less important, the unification of collections for all components of the social security system--including health insurance and the family fund--under the Secretary of Social Security in October 1992 strengthened administration and reduced evasion; contributors want to make health insurance payments because they are linked to benefits, and

unification thus compelled contribution to social security. With the rapid improvement in the performance of the general tax office (DGI), it has also become possible to systematically cross-check social security and corporate and income tax collections--a task still not yet done.

46.   **Adjusting Pensions**. Following a financing agreement with the provinces in August 1992 described below, the Government has ended the underpayment of pensions. This is estimated to increase total payments by about 30 percent. About one-half of all pensioners--including nearly all retired independent workers--cannot benefit from the adjustment because their entitlements are not higher than the minimum pension. Raising also the minimum pension by 50 pesos per month would increase total payments by about 40 percent. The Government is under political pressure in this regard, because the sharp increase in the pensions of dependent workers with higher claims, which also receive consolidation bonds for past underpayment, is seen as a gross inequity. The adverse distribution effect of complying with the existing pension laws, however, only brings into the open the old system's defects of severe underinsurance for independent workers and the capricious redistribution caused by the wage-indexation lag for the pension base of dependent workers. The reform will eliminate these effects for the affiliates of the IPS. The Government's position is that the new system must not be burdened with legacies of the old system. Instead, any payments in excess of legally mandated levels should be on a welfare basis; targeting would then allow for lower overall payments because retired independent workers which opted for the lowest pension category need not be poor.

Tax Financing

47.   In the first semester of 1991, the NPS administration received monthly contributions of US$403 million and made monthly payments (including administrative expenses) of US$528 million. The monthly "system deficit" (contributions minus expenditures) therefore was US$125 million. The administration received shares of the fuel, gas, telephone and foreign exchange taxes amounting to about US$85 million monthly. The overall deficit of US$40 million per month was financed by transfers from the Treasury.

48.   In August 1991, Law 23.966 shifted the NPS' tax revenue base to a 10 percent share of VAT revenues (ahead of coparticipation with the provinces) and to 100 percent of a new tax on so-called unproductive goods of personal wealth (personal goods tax). The initial yield of the new tax base was slightly lower than revenues from the old sources. However, the change was significant because VAT revenues were poised to grow rapidly as a result of improved tax administration and economic growth, whereas the old taxes would eventually be removed in the context of privatization and tax reform. Temporarily, the NPS also received a 30 percent share of all privatization proceeds, later replaced by the YPF law which, as mentioned above, allocates proceeds for the retirement of debt with pensioners. With these measures, the Government was able to increase the minimum pension from 120 pesos to 150 pesos per month, while also moving the overall balance of the NPS into a small surplus.

49.   In August 1992, the Government entered an agreement with the provinces on the provisional allocation--until end-1993--of 15 percent of all coparticipated revenues to social security (see Chapter 3). Included in this share is the reimbursement of the provinces for the DGI's cost of collecting the shared taxes in an unspecified amount. The agreement is to be replaced by a new agreement or new law on federal-provincial revenue sharing. Subsequent to the agreement, the Government ended the underpayment of pensions mandated by the existing pension laws. Table 11.4 shows estimates for contributions, expenditures, and revenues from the various taxes for 1993, expected to be the last year before the reform. Included is also the surplus of the family assistance fund, which the Secretariat of Social Security appropriates for pension payments.

Table 11.4: Estimated NPS Finances for 1993 and 1994-97

(In US$ millions)

	1993	Scenario I Avg. 1994-97	Scenario II Avg. 1994-97
Contributions (Wage Tax)	9,260	9,152	7,618
Family Fund Surplus and Other Income a/	622	1,065	1,065
Expenditures	12,305	15,804	15,725
Old System	11,952	13,542	13,542
Integrated System		1,896	1,817
Basic Pension		1,141	1,062
Compensatory Pension		755	755
Admin. Costs and Provincial Transfers	353	366	366
System Balance	(2,423)	(5,587)	(7,042)
Tax Revenues b/	6,116	7,703	7,703
Value-Added (10%)	1,813	2,230	2,230
Coparticipated (15%)	3,178	4,068	4,068
Personal Goods (100%)	104	147	147
Income (20%)	1,021	1,258	1,258
Income for Military Pensions and PAMI c/	3,369	3,977	3,977
Other Expenditures	5,383	5,495	5,495
PAMI and Military Pensions c/	4,525	5,126	5,126
Other Transfers	858	369	369
Overall Balance	1,679	598	(857)
Assumptions			
Rate of Growth of Contributors		5.5%	1.5%
Rate of Growth of Average Salary		10.3%	8.1%

a/ Fund for dependents.
b/ Percentages represent amount of tax earmarked for social security.
c/ PAMI is a publicly-financed health plan for retirees.

Source: Ministry of Finance and Bank staff estimates.

50.   For 1993, the system balance--contributions net of expenditures--is in surplus by US$1.7 billion. This is because the general tax revenues more than offset the system deficit, and because the system still retains the share of contributions that, beginning in 1994, will go into the privatized system.

E. Managing the Medium-Term Transition

51.　　　　Reducing Argentina's excessive dependency ratio of .62 is the key to the success of the pension reform. In the long-run, a ratio consistent with the projected age structure--about .32--will allow the public scheme to finance a basic pension with a modest contribution rate and without tax revenues. Contributions, however, will fall at the beginning of the reform to allow workers to save through their individual capitalization accounts. Over the next generation, furthermore, the public sector must provide for the benefits of pre-reform pensioners; for an even longer period it must also compensate workers for their pre-reform contributions.   The task of managing the long transition is easier the more rapid is the initial reduction in the dependency ratio; and of course the less generous pre-reform pension adjustments and compensations for pre-reform contributions.

52.　　　　**Dependency Ratio Projections**. Without a change in the existing pension laws, the number of beneficiaries will continue to grow at a higher rate than the number of contributors. Even without an increase in evasion, this would result from the aging of the Argentine population. Column A in Table 11.5 depicts the projected development of the dependency ratio on this assumption; it shows that the ratio would rapidly increase in the next few years and at a smaller rate in the following decade, before levelling off at about .68. This underlines, if at all necessary, the case for the reform.

53.　　　　The direct instruments of the reform law for reducing the dependency ratio are increases in, respectively, the minimum age at retirement and the minimum years of contribution; the indirect instrument is the attraction of pension funds to younger workers and of the basic pension for independent workers and low-wage dependent workers. The effect of raising the minimum age at retirement by 5 years is depicted in Column B of Table 11.5. The measure is shown to do no more than stabilize the existing dependency ratio.   This reflects an already relatively high average age at retirement (about 64 years for men) in Argentina in response to incentives in the existing laws such as raising the pension rate from 70 percent to 82 percent by delaying retirement or receiving an advanced age pension after only 5 years of contribution. More important is the increase in minimum years of contributions introduced by Decree 2016/91 and extended in the draft law. Column C of Table 11.5 shows a steep decline in the dependency ratio already in the first few years. Since the old rules had encouraged active workers to evade contributions until 15 years prior to expected regular retirement (or 5 years prior to an "advanced age" retirement at 65), the measure compels a significant share of workers to postpone retirement until age 70. However, many of these workers are likely to seek loopholes in the transitory regulations, challenge the reliability of the NPS records or claim disability. Projections in Column D assume that flexibility in the system will enable 10 percent of those affected to receive a pension with less than the required years of contribution. The most optimistic assumption is that the attractiveness of the new system will soon begin to reduce evasion and add to the impact of stricter pension requirements. On this basis, Column E shows the dependency ratio to decline to about .52 and .44, respectively, already in 1995 and 2000.

54.   The following considerations on the financial transition are based on the more conservative dependency ratio projections in Column D. An alternative projection of the implications of the reform for the budget of the public pension system based on Column E is also discussed.

Table 11.5: Projected Dependency Ratio Under Alternative Policies

	No Policy Change a/	Raising Retire- Age b/	Increasing Years of Contribution c/	Flexibility d/	Reform Plus Reducing Evasion e/
	A	B	C	D	E
1990	.62	.62	.62	.62	.62
1995	.66	.62	.55	.57	.52
2000	.66	.60	.49	.51	.44
2005	.67	.60	.44	.48	.38
2010	.68	.61	.40	.45	.35
2015	.68	.61	.38	.44	.33
2020	.68	.62	.37	.43	.32
2025	.69	.63	.36	.43	.32

a/   No change in policies.
b/   Normal retirement age raised to 60 for women and 65 for men without exception; advanced
      age-retirement is 5 years older.
c/   Retirement age as in b/; minimum years of contribution raised to 30 years.
d/   Retirement age and years of contribution as in c/; some flexibility in the granting of
      regular pensions.
e/   Retirement age and years of contribution as in c/; decreasing rate of evasion.

Source: Secretariat of Social Security.

55.   **Budget Projections**. In projecting the implications of the reform for the public pension system, assumptions must be specified for the growth of the nominal average wage (determining contributions and pensions) and for the growth of nominal GDP (determining tax revenues). A more rapid growth of GDP relative to average wage would be salutary as tax revenues would grow at a higher rate than the system deficit, i.e., the balance of contributions and expenditures. Higher wage growth would have the opposite effect. Absent a firm basis for assumptions either way, the following assumes them to grow at the same rate. Without loss of information, the growth rate can be assumed to be zero. Tax revenues are then also constant and can be directly compared to the system balance.

56.   The system balance is projected in Table 11.4 based on the Government's projection of old and new pensioners, the dependency ratio projection in Column D of Table 11.5, and nominal wages that rise faster than GDP. An average of 35 years of contributions is assumed for new pensioners. For the basic pension, this results in a rate of 30 percent of average salary; for the compensatory pension the implication is a rate of 30 percent of the average indexed wage of the last 10 years until 1999, followed by a decline of one percentage point annually as new pensioners show fewer pre-reform years of contribution than the maximum established in the draft law.

57.　　　　The projected system balance shows a deficit of US$5.6 billion in 1994-97 Scenario I (Table 11.4). The deficit remains stable for 4 years before it begins a slow decline at a rate of US$150-200 million annually. The main reason is nearly constant expenditures as the increasing number of basic and compensatory pensions balances the reduction in the population of pre-reform pensioners. A less optimistic dependency ratio and slower growth rate in nominal wages is shown in Scenario II (Table 11.4). Assuming that average wages increase at the same rate of nominal GDP and that the rate of growth of contributors is 1.5 percent, the system would show an average deficit of US$7 billion per year, and an overall deficit of US$850 million. The magnitudes underscore the importance of lowering the dependency ratio, restraining pension increases and securing general tax revenues to cover the system deficit.

58.　　　　**Pension Fund Savings.** The affiliates of the mandatory pension funds are expected to save an average of 8 percent of current earnings on their individual capitalization accounts--one-half of the contributions to the public scheme shown in Table 11.6. Following retirement, the savings will on average be drawn down over about 15 years, which is the approximate life expectancy at age 65 in Argentina. Assuming wages to grown in line with GDP and the nominal interest rate to exceed the growth rate of nominal GDP, the accumulated savings will grow as a share of GDP over several decades, though at a gradually declining rate as the young workers of 1994 enter retirement. Table 11.6 indicates the order of magnitude: about 13 percent in 2000, 25 percent in 2005, and 50 percent in 2015. These savings, which are of long-term nature, represent a source of demand for Argentine debt paper with extended maturities-- expected to be supplied by the privatized infrastructure companies seeking investment finance, other highly rated companies and the Government. The draft law also allows a maximum of 10 percent of the funds' portfolio to be invested in foreign financial instruments.

Table 11.6: Estimated Pension Fund Savings a/

Year	Active Affiliates	Retired Affiliates b/	Total
1995	3.46	0.12	3.58
2000	12.41	1.05	13.47
2005	21.83	2.78	24.61
2010	31.76	5.21	36.97
2015	42.20	8.25	50.44
2020	53.13	11.83	64.95
2025	64.54	15.89	80.43

a/ Assuming growth rate of 8 percent for nominal wage and nominal GDP, nominal interest rate of 10 percent, and retirement rate (new retirees/active affiliates) of 2.5 percent (all annual).

b/ Assuming programmed withdrawal over 15 years.

59.   A major part of the mandatory contributions to the private system is likely to add to Argentina's aggregate private savings; a smaller part will be offset by reductions in voluntary savings made previously in the expectation that the old PAYG system would not adequately secure pensions. Public savings will be adversely affected only to the extent the Government fails in its intention to finance the transition with tax revenues rather than debt issues. Overall, the reform is therefore likely to increase domestic savings significantly.

60.   **Risks**. The main risks to the reform--in addition to legislated additional pension increases discussed above--are: a slower decline of the dependency ratio, lack of confidence in the private pension fund system, and unsettled problems of the provincial pension schemes that remain outside the new IPS. The conservative dependency ratio projection underlying the base case assumes that the restrictive rules of the draft law regarding the transition to higher minimum years of contribution will be confirmed; and that the administration will allow for only a modest degree of flexibility in their implementation. Older workers with insufficient years of contribution will therefore have to delay retirement until age 70.

61.   Confidence in the private pension fund scheme depends on a coherent set of rules, and on the credible policing of the rules by a professional supervisory body free of conflicts of interest and political intervention. The draft law presents a consistent set of rules for pension fund managers (AFJP--Administradoras de Fondos de Jubilaciones y Pensiones) and the obligations and rights of the superintendency. The Government has rightly resisted an attempt by the unions, which may set up AFJPs, to restrict the rights of affiliates to transfer their accounts to another AFJP. As it stands, unions may set up AFJPs, but must compete with other private insurers. The draft law also prohibits any minimum investment requirements, which would have reduced confidence in the performance of the funds.

62.   The draft law, however, lacks rules on the composition of the superintendency. In this regard, a recent agreement between the Government and the unions would staff the superintendency with representatives from the state, the unions, employers, and the affiliates. This arrangement might be seen as a throw-back to the days of corporatism in Argentina, and undermine confidence that all AFJPs will be held to the strict standards of the law including application of the ultimate sanction, i.e., -revocation of the AFJP license and transfer of the pension fund to other AFJPs. The Chilean experience has shown the key importance of a professional and effective superintendency for the viability of a mandatory private pension fund system; a weak superintendency risks that the state guarantee for a minimum fund performance will be called.

63.   A different type of risk is generated by a number of provincial public sector pension schemes that promise benefits even more generous than promised by the existing national pension laws. As these comparatively young PAYG systems mature, they are likely to generate an increasing fiscal burden for the provinces--curtailing provincial public investments and public services, and eventually requiring a federal bailout. While the draft reform law would permit the voluntary affiliation of provincial public employees in the IPS, the offer is unlikely to be taken up by a large number

because of the superior promises of the provincial laws. The problem is aggravated by the transfer of secondary schools and public hospitals to provincial jurisdictions. A similar problem exists with the pension systems of the armed forces, which are also independent of the proposed IPS.

F. Recommendations

64.   The reform project promises to create an efficient pension insurance system for Argentina, free of the serious defects of the existing system. The transition to the new system, however, is burdened by the legacies of the old system, a looming insolvency of provincial pension schemes, and attempts of interested parties to gain political control over the new private pension scheme. To secure a successful transition, the Government may want to consider the following recommendations:

(i)   protect the new system against demands that it raise benefits for pre-reform pensioners beyond levels mandated by the old laws; poverty among pre-reform pensioners results from defects of the old laws that allowed for the under-insurance of independent workers and for unintended distribution effects through the wage-indexation lag; it should be addressed in the context of the Government's new social assistance policy;

(ii)   resist demands for raising the compensatory pension above levels established in the December modification of the draft law;

(iii)   lower the average level of pension insurance--projected to be about 70 percent of average wages--to 55-65 percent, levels common in Western Europe; a reduction by 6 percentage points could be achieved by lowering the basic pension after 30 years of contribution from 2.5 AMPOs to 2 AMPOs;

(iv)   resist pressure for weakening the rules for the transition to higher minimum years of contribution and age at retirement; instead, allow workers not qualifying under the rules to retire at age 65 or later with actuarially fair deductions from their pensions;

(v)   strengthen the audit program for disability pensions;

(vi)   further strengthen social security collections through systematic cross-checks with the DGI;

(vii)   extend mandatory affiliation with the IPS to all economically active, including provincial and municipal public employees; at a minimum require provincial and municipal schemes to adopt the same criteria as to minimum years of contribution and age at retirement; and

(viii) establish a professional superintendency for AFJPs based on a review of the Chilean experience.

CHAPTER 12. PUBLIC INVESTMENT

A. Capital Stock and Recent Trends in Investment

1.   Total gross investment fell in the late 1980s to levels roughly half those of the 1970s (Figure 12.1). Investment rates fell so low that they did not even cover the rate of depreciation on existing capital, implying a decrease in the country's capital stock. Total investment fell to 8.7 percent of GDP in 1989, and then to a mere 8.1 percent of GDP in 1990, the lowest level in the recorded history of the country, while depreciation was estimated at 9.9 percent and 9.4 percent of GDP, respectively. According to the Secretariat of Planning, the reduction has been most dramatic in the most dynamic items in the capital stock: machinery and equipment, especially transport equipment. For these categories, the shrinkage in capital stock began in 1984. The lack of new investment also has increased the average age of the country's physical assets, which further widened the technological gap between Argentina and the rest of the world.

2.   Public investment, under the weight of budgetary stringency and the increased interest bill, virtually collapsed in the early 1980s. The collapse of public investment also contributed significantly to the reduction of private investment. The decrease in public investment reduced the demand for goods and services produced by private suppliers and had an impact on the level of economic activity. On the supply side, a lower level of public investment eroded the quality of the services produced by the public sector, which in turn increased production costs for the private sector. Lower demand and higher production costs undermine private investment.[1] More importantly, the extremely unstable macroeconomic policies and the effects of external shocks gave rise to a high and variable inflation that deterred investment. Thus, private investment declined sharply as well during the 1980s, though less sharply than public investment. In 1990, private investment was less than one third of its 1980 level.

3.   The situation changed significantly in 1991 when, for the first time in several years, investment levels were estimated to have recovered to 12.5 percent of GDP (measured at current prices).[2] All of the increase is due to a major rise in private investment. Total savings has also increased sharply, led by foreign and public savings. Much of the foreign savings probably is the repatriation of previous domestic savings. These developments are mainly due to a perception that the 1991 economic reforms are permanent.

---

1   International empirical evidence reinforces this conclusion regarding the complementarity between public and private investment. See two interesting pieces by David Aschauer: "Is Public Expenditure Productive?" *Journal of Monetary Economics*, March 1989; and "Does Public Capital Crowd Out Private Capital?" *Journal of Monetary Economics*, October 1989.

2   The investment surge was almost 50 percent in real terms. Preliminary estimates indicate that fixed capital formation reached 10 percent of GDP in 1991 at constant prices.

Figure 12.1:

Public and Private Investment
(% of GDP, current prices)

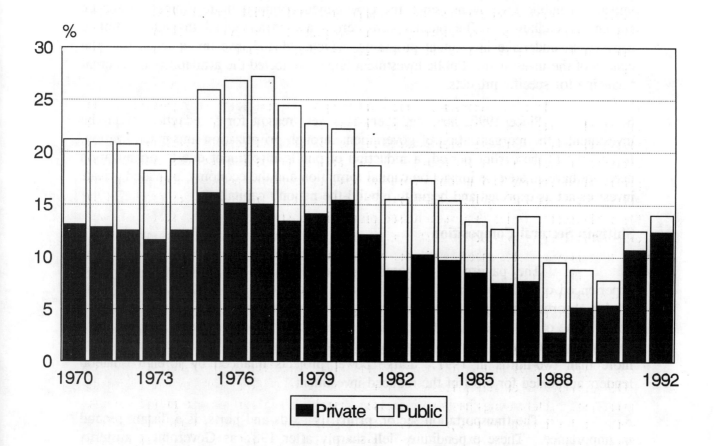

B. Recent Trends in Public Investment

Aggregates

4.   Public investment--investments undertaken by the Federal Government and public enterprises--increased considerably during the 1970s, reaching a historic peak of 11 percent of GDP in 1977, the high water mark for the expansion of the state generally. This increase was followed by a major collapse in the 1980s. By 1990, for example, public investment was less than 20 percent of its 1977 level as a proportion of GDP. Estimates for 1991 show public investment at around 1.8 percent of GDP.

5.   There are several reasons for the plunge in public investment. First, the reduction in foreign financing at the beginning of the 1980s led to a significant reduction in public expenditures. Stabilization programs during the 1980s had a disproportionate impact on public investment, since the Government found it more difficult to reduce current expenditures.[3] The public sector crisis also deteriorated the administrative capacity to undertake investment programs, which reduced investment levels and the quality of the investment. Public investment largely reflected the availability of external financing for specific projects.

6.   Since 1990, however, there is a new reason for a reduction of public investment: the reorganization of government through privatization and federalization. In contrast to the earlier period, a reduction of public investment due to privatization need not have an adverse impact on capital formation and the economy, provided private investors act as expected and begin to rebuild the nation's capital.

Shifts in Sectoral Composition

7.   The pattern of sectoral distribution of public investment has also experienced considerable variations in the last two decades (Table 12.1). Energy and mining absorbed most public investment, especially since the mid-1970s. Although the dollar value of this investment has declined considerably since the early 1980s, energy and mining have gone from less than one-third of total public investment in 1980 to more than two-thirds in 1991. Large power projects financed by foreign bilateral lenders accounted for most of the reduced investment.

8.   The transportation sector, primarily roads and ports, is a distant second in importance. These expenditures fell sharply after 1987 as Government austerity programs led to a lack of new investment and a fall-off in attention to maintenance of vital infrastructure.

---

3   Investment has tended to suffer larger cuts than current spending during stabilization programs in Latin America in the 1980s. See, for example, the evidence in F. Larraín and M. Selowsky, *The Public Sector and the Latin American Crisis*, ICS Press, San Francisco, 1991.

Table 12.1a: Public Investment by Sector
(Percent of GDP)

	1980	1981	1982	1983	1984	1985	1986	1987	1988	1989	1990	1991	1992
Economic Sectors													
Agriculture	0.0	0.0	0.0	0.0	0.0	0.1	0.1	0.1	0.1	0.1	0.0	0.0	0.0
Communications	0.6	0.6	0.5	0.5	0.3	0.2	0.4	0.7	1.7	0.5	0.1	0.0	0.0
Energy and Mining	2.2	2.1	2.3	2.5	2.1	2.3	2.0	2.2	2.5	1.6	1.6	1.3	1.1
Manufacturing a/	0.8	0.8	0.9	0.7	0.9	0.5	0.9	1.1	0.6	0.0	0.0	0.0	0.0
Transportation	1.3	1.0	1.1	1.2	1.3	0.9	0.9	0.8	0.8	0.7	0.4	0.2	0.2
Social Sectors													
Education	0.0	0.0	0.0	0.0	0.1	0.1	0.2	0.3	0.2	0.1	0.0	0.1	0.1
Health b/	0.3	0.1	0.1	0.1	0.1	0.1	0.1	0.1	0.1	0.1	0.0	0.1	0.1
Housing	0.0	0.0	0.0	0.0	0.0	0.0	0.0	0.0	0.0	0.0	0.0	0.0	0.0
Social Security & Welfare	0.0	0.0	0.0	0.0	0.0	0.0	0.0	0.0	0.0	0.0	0.0	0.0	0.0
Others													
General Admin.	0.6	0.7	1.1	1.2	0.7	0.6	0.6	0.6	0.5	0.5	0.1	0.0	0.1
Defense & Sec.	1.0	1.3	0.8	0.9	0.2	0.2	0.2	0.3	0.2	0.1	0.0	0.0	0.1
TOTAL	6.8	6.6	6.8	7.1	5.7	4.9	5.2	6.2	6.7	3.6	2.4	1.8	1.8

a/ Military factories, petrochemical plants, iron and steel factories.
b/ Includes Public Works and Services.

Source: Contaduria General de La Nacion.

Table 12.1b: Public Investment of the Federal Government BY SECTOR
(US$ million)

	1980	1981	1982	1983	1984	1985	1986	1987	1988	1989	1990	1991	1992
Economic Sectors													
Agriculture	3	0	0	0	45	71	82	77	99	70	8	32	56
Communications	807	729	656	672	331	304	484	983	2311	589	174	6	3
Energy & Mining	3035	2005	2882	3250	2765	2927	2651	3091	3410	2077	2097	1790	1746
Manufacturing a/	1177	1024	1101	935	1211	640	1210	1554	773	21	4	0	0
Transportation	1794	1374	1361	1546	1703	1079	1148	1091	1127	935	521	296	294
Social Sectors													
Education	2	1	0	0	136	152	204	350	248	153	47	163	163
Health b/	378	162	126	141	137	106	86	101	81	68	18	91	99
Housing	1	0	0	0	0	0	0	0	2	1	0	0	0
Social Security & Welfare	28	33	30	44	13	13	15	13	13	10	9	0	0
Others													
Gen. Admin.	810	955	1330	1493	922	711	825	826	630	585	104	56	194
Defense & Sec.	1426	1645	1037	1104	295	192	260	380	295	113	36	4	122
TOTAL	9462	8628	8524	9184	7559	6195	6965	8466	8989	4622	3017	2438	2677

a/ Military factories, petrochemical plants, iron and steel factories.
b/ Includes Public Works and Services.

Source: Contaduria General de La Nacion.

9.   The third largest sector was defense. After a significant increase in the 1970s, the trend peaked with the South Atlantic War in 1982. The return to civilian government brought steep initial cuts in defense investment. There was a rise in the 1987 election year but this was followed by heavy cuts through 1990.

10.   Manufacturing is another sector whose importance has greatly diminished. These activities include the petrochemical, steel and military companies. At the beginning of the 1970s, this sector accounted for 12 percent of public investment. At the beginning of the 1990s, public investment in manufacturing had virtually stopped.

11.   Investments in the social sectors (health, housing, education and social security) increased after the return to constitutional democracy in 1983, primarily through the expansion of education and health. This pattern was halted after 1987, when austerity forced expenditure compression across the public sector. In 1990, investment in the social sectors was reduced to its minimum of the decade (only US$74 million), and its share of total public investment dropped to 2.5 percent.

C. Public Investment Programming Mechanism and Project Selection

12.   The investment programming mechanism has never been strong in Argentina. Each agency with a significant investment capacity has defended its autonomy for investment decisions, usually supported by interested parties such as suppliers and contractors.

13.   Article 13, Law 21550 of 1977, provided the basis of a modern public investment process. It established the joint responsibility between the Ministry of Economy and the Secretary of Planning for the definition of priorities for public investment. At the same time, it also established the need to obtain approval of projects that exceeded US$5 million. The National Directorate of Projects under the Secretary of Planning, by law, was to approve technical and economic matters relating to these projects. This approval was to be based on an adequate project formulation, basic requirements for economic evaluation, and to some extent on the consistency between the project and the government's political and development strategy. The National Directorate of Budgeting under the Ministry of Economy would approve the formulation and financial analysis of projects. If appropriate, the Subsecretary of Public Enterprises would approve projects relating to public enterprises.

14.   Article 13 was applied strictly only until 1981. Only 90 projects of 223 projects presented during 1977-83 were approved. However, during the high inflation and unstable political conditions of the 1980s, it became virtually impossible to implement the project review system envisaged in the law. From 1981 to 1984, agencies with significant investment capacity found legal and quasi-legal ways to prevent the Secretary of Planning from reviewing their projects. As a result, the number of projects analyzed gradually decreased: fewer projects were presented--reaching a low of only 4 during 1988-89--and a smaller percentage was rejected. The authority of the Secretary of Planning also decreased. Strategies used to avoid the review required by

Law 21550--77 included the disaggregation of a large project into many small projects whose amounts fell under the legal minimum. The National Directorate of Roads used this strategy extensively and convinced the President to use his power to approve financing of projects that had not undergone review by the Secretary of Planning. The National Commission on Atomic Energy (CNEA) used its location in the Presidency to have Atucha II approved. In other cases, executing agencies started projects that enjoyed strong political backing without approval from the Presidency and/or the Secretary of Planning. Projects, once started, were difficult to cancel on rate of return criteria because of the cost of contract cancellations. Sometimes foreign financing from suppliers was sufficient to begin a project, later notifying the Secretary of Planning. Executing agencies were not held legally accountable.

15.   By the late 1980s, the investment programming process had completely disintegrated. Projects submitted in many cases lacked revenue and expenditure forecasts. Costs were also underestimated as a result of underestimated physical and economic risks. Benefits were routinely overestimated. Delays in project execution led to increases in real costs. Problems in project preparation were caused not only by the lack of efficient personnel training. Suppliers with political influence sought to shield institutions from involvement by the Ministries of Planning and Economy to avoid the risk that their project might be delayed or vetoed. In the absence of a capital budgeting process, expenditure compression was distributed proportionally to all projects without considering which projects had the highest social benefit or were close to completion. As a result, several projects were funded that eventually became inoperative, not fostering economic growth or goals and wasting scarce resources.

16.   Special earmarked accounts, such as the Energy Fund, the Fund of Hydroelectric Works, and the Electric Fund, kept many projects alive. A decree established a unified investment fund in October 1989, but only 50 percent of this fund was to be used for investment, the other 50 percent being used by the government to reduce the deficits. The pressure to increase its primary surplus in 1990 compelled the Government to use most of the fund to cover current expenditures. This caused several projects to be stopped for lack of resources. Due to the lack of counterpart funds, multilaterals and bilaterals have not disbursed funds for some projects already approved.

D. Public Investment--1992 and Beyond

17.   The Government began to reconstruct the public investment process in late 1990 and produced its first public investment program in a decade for 1991. The program contained sectoral amounts, project amounts, and financing requirements, together with prospective financing, although the links with the budget were weak and there was little, if any, project selection. During 1991, the Secretariat of Planning was strengthened yet further. The strategy was to first strengthen the Ministry's knowledge of existing projects, better coordinate projects under execution, focus on those with external finance, and issue adequate guidelines for the preparation of the 1992 program. The execution of the program would be monitored through the budget process.

18.   The redefinition of the role of the public sector in the economy and the reorganization of public finances had a major impact in the composition, absolute value, and financing of public investment. Many of the functions previously held by the Federal Government will be transferred to the provinces. Most hospitals and schools fall under the latter category. The social security system will be privatized. Most public enterprises will be privatized, and thus investments in these sectors will be phased out as soon as the Federal Government divests the assets and transfers the functions. There remains a question, however, about the access of private producers to financing and how, if at all, the Government should or could aid that access.

19.   The Secretary of Planning produced the 1992 investment program in time to be integrated into the 1992 budget. The program foresees investment of US$2.6 billion in 1992 (Table 12.2). Of this, about US$700 million would be financed through Treasury savings, US$1.0 billion from savings of the executing agencies, and the remainder from foreign and domestic borrowing.

20.   The 1992 program raises several important issues. First, the Federal Government is financing a large proportion of its investment from domestic savings, either mobilized through the Treasury or through savings of executing units. Aside from savings mobilized through YPF, the major sources of domestic savings are the Treasury and the wage tax to support housing. Domestic savings leverage relatively low levels of foreign borrowing: every peso of domestic savings mobilizes only A$0.55 cents of foreign resources, even though most foreign loans require a much lower effective level of counterpart governmental savings. Since the "scarcity" factor from the vantage point of the Government is its own savings--not the availability of total savings--projects that do not lever foreign savings or lever a relatively low amount, should be carefully compared to those that do, in terms of rate of return, revenue generation, and cost of capital (including appropriate adjustment for exchange risks).

21.   Second, the Federal Government mobilizes US$1.1 billion in savings which it passes through to the provinces for their investment. The most notable is the housing program through FONAVI. This program mobilizes little if any foreign finance (the World Bank has canceled its loan), and yet it represents 40 percent of all domestic savings at the federal level.

22.   Third, within the category of foreign finance, the Government is using 60 percent of its borrowing capacity to borrow from expensive sources of credit other than the IDB and the World Bank--primarily suppliers' credits or other forms of tied loans. Nearly half of the US$639 million is a loan from the German government to support purchases for Atucha II from Siemens, the German heavy electrical equipment supplier. Of the US$2.6 billion, roughly half (US$1.2 billion) would be allocated to the power sector, about one quarter (US$0.6 billion) to hydrocarbons, and about 5 percent (US$100 million) to transport. The remainder would be divided among other infrastructure projects on a smaller scale.

Table 12.2: ARGENTINA: Public Investment Program and Financing, 1992
(US$ Million)

12 May 1992

	Investment	Domestic Savings			Domestic	Foreign Borrowing			Total
		Treasury	Executing	Total	Borrowing	IBRD	IDB	Other	
Legislative and Judicial Branches	29	21	8	29	0	0	0	0	0
Senate and Congress	3	3	0	3	0	0	0	0	0
Judiciary	26	18	8	26	0	0	0	0	0
Presidency and Foreign Ministry	480	43	36	79	85	0	12	304	401
CNEA ª/	426	25	12	37	85	0	0	304	389
Science and Technology	19	7	0	7	0	0	12	0	12
Foreign Ministry	29	5	24	29	0	0	0	0	0
COMIP	6	8	0	6	0	0	0	0	0
Ministries of Interior and Justice	52	35	8	43	0	0	0	9	9
Defense	92	33	59	92	0	0	0	0	0
Social Sectors	1246	127	968	1095	0	57	94	0	151
Education	146	109	2	111	0	0	35	0	35
Health and Social Action	38	18	17	35	0	0	3	0	3
Housing	1062	0	949	949	0	57	56	0	113
Labor	0	0	0	0	0	0	0	0	0
Economic Sectors	380	259	42	301	0	24	32	23	79
Tax and Customs Administration	15	1	14	15	0	0	0	0	0
Highway System	197	197	0	197	0	0	0	0	0
Agriculture	57	2	28	30	0	13	14	0	27
Architecture ᵇ/	71	37	0	37	0	11	0	23	34
Subsecretary of Industry and Trade	2	2	0	2	0	0	0	0	0
Water Treatment	38	20	0	20	0	0	18	0	18
Public Enterprises	1644	306	853	1159	-45	202	25	303	485
Yacyretá	339	93	1	94	-85	200	0	130	245
Hidronor ᶜ/	340	203	0	203	-17	0	5	149	137
AyEE	81	0	38	38	33	0	10	0	43
SEGBA ᵈ/	91	0	63	63	4	0	0	24	28
YPF	488	0	488	488	0	0	0	0	0
YCF	10	10	0	10	0	0	0	0	0
GdE	143	0	123	123	20	0	0	0	20
FA	57	0	57	57	0	0	0	0	0
FEMESA	30	0	30	30	0	0	0	0	0
AGP	12	0	12	12	0	0	0	0	0
ELMA	2	0	2	2	0	0	0	0	0
OSN	48	0	36	36	0	2	10	0	12
Encotel	3	0	3	3	0	0	0	0	0
Total	3923	824	1974	2798	40	283	163	639	1125
Memo:									
Total Investment, excl. Provinces ᵉ/	2647	674	1025	1699	40	226	43	639	948

a/ Other foreign financing includes financing from Germany.
b/ Other foreign financing includes US$23 million from the former Soviet Union.
c/ Other foreign financing includes US$140 million from Brazil.
d/ Other foreign financing includes US$24 million from Italy.
e/ Excludes FONAVI, Provincial Highway Departments, Water Treatment, and US$93 million for education.

Source: 1992 Investment Plan (September 1992).

Sectoral Issues

23.   **Electricity**.   This sector is undergoing a total restructuring aiming at divestiture of the national utilities and concentration of the role of the State in regulation. A new electricity law was enacted in January 1992, providing the basic rules for functioning of the power sector and facilitating the participation of private capital. A regulatory agency is being formed; the public contest for selection of its five members is underway. Procedures established by the Secretariat of Electric Energy (compatible with the new law) define the tariff for bulk sale transactions in accordance with marginal cost principles.   The law also has provisions for adhesion of the provinces to the centrally regulated system, which would help solve the tariff distortions of the provincial utilities. Eight percent of SEGBA generation amounting to over 2000MW have been sold to two private groups; SEGBA's distribution is slated for privatization in August 1992. AyEE generation will be partly privatized and partly transferred to the provinces. The HIDRONOR and AyEE high voltage transmission systems are being unified for future privatization. The resulting HIDRONOR (all hydrogeneration) will be listed in the stock market and progressively sold.

24.   The investment consequences of the Government's policy stated above is that the Government will only commit its own fund to help complete the four projects which are under its own funds to help complete the four projects which are under construction: Piedra del Aguila, Yacyreta (including the first phase of the transmission system), Atucha II and Pichi-Picun-Leufu, the three former being the largest projects in execution in the country. The second phase of the Yacyreta transmission system and the generation expansion beyond completion of the ongoing projects are expected to be carried out by the private sector. The two large hydro projects (Piedra del Aguila, 1400MW, and Yacyreta, 3100MW) have very high rates of return for their completion, and thus the required Government contributions are warranted. Furthermore, in the case of Yacyreta they are essential to ensure further financial participation of the World Bank and the IDB, and new export credits. Pichi-Picun-Leufu completion has to be analyzed under the extremely favorable terms of financing provided by Brazil for the civil works. Since credits for electromechanical equipment can be obtained at standard terms, the Government contribution for completion of Pichi-Picun-Leufu will be minimal. While this project failed to meet the least-cost expansion criterion, the Bank gave the no-objection to the Argentine Government in 1990 for its construction, on the basis of an economic analysis that included both investment and the specific, earmarked financing. Under a similar approach, the completion of Pichi-Picun-Leufu is now justified, notwithstanding an ERR below the threshold level of 12 percent.

25.   The completion of Atucha II has to be analyzed taking into account its economic merits and the financial burden on the Government.   Considering the investments up to the end of 1991 as sunk costs and the proxy for benefits estimated at the current values of long term marginal costs at the grid level, the ERR would be slightly over 12 percent, marginal with respect to the usually acceptable opportunity cost of capital for long-maturity projects in Argentina. From a financial standpoint, it would require, under the most unfavorable scenario for obtaining new sources of financing, some US$700 million from Government contribution. This would seem an excessive

financial burden to the completion of the plant, at the earliest possible date, 1997.[4] Recent Bank analysis of the energy balances for the end of the decade show that Atucha II could be delayed by some two years, under a low demand growth with negligible risk for the supply; even for the high demand growth the risks of decreasing the quality of the supply are reasonably affordable. The completion of Atucha II should be tied to a low Government contribution during the next few years, when Government is already making a considerable effort for completion of the two huge (and more priority) hydro projects. It would be reasonable to consider the use of the revenues generated by CNEA from power sales for financing of Atucha II. This would be possible if energy sales rate for Embalse and Atucha I were all directed to CNEA, instead of only the portion to cover O&M costs.[5] However, this possibility should be considered jointly with the establishment of a free-standing power business unit in CNEA, which would depend upon its restructuring (see Chapter 8, para. 21).

26. **Hydrocarbons**. This sector has two important enterprises: Yacimientos Petroliferos Fiscales (YPF) and Gas del Estado (GE). GE is in the process of being privatized, a process that should be completed in 1992. YPF is the largest enterprise in the country. Some oil fields have already been privatized (the so-called "marginal areas"), but it is likely that privatization during 1991 and 1992 will affect over 25 percent of the company's productive capacity.

27. Annual YPF investment in exploration of gas and petroleum is approximately US$500 million. To increase current production and maintain petroleum exports, this investment will need to increase by some US$300 million per year; that is, including private investment, exploration resources should be about US$800 billion per year. Such a program would have high returns: even assuming a price of US$11/barrel of petroleum and high relative costs, the present net value would be about US$1 billion. If the price of the petroleum were US$16, and the costs were reduced 40 percent (the replacement of the "Buy Argentina" Law with a modern procurement law would reduce costs by this magnitude), the NPV of YPF investments would be six times higher. The current price of petroleum is about US$19/barrel. Thus, investment in exploration appears to be highly profitable both for YPF and private sector operations.

28. Since Gas del Estado is to be privatized, it makes little sense to invest US$53 million in transport equipment and US$9 million in storage facilities. These funds should be reallocated.

29. **Roads**. The national trunk road network (38,000 km) is administered by the National Highway Administration (DNV); the Provincial Highway Administrations (DPVs) are responsible for about 170,000 km of provincial roads, and a third level (municipal authorities) manages tertiary roads and urban streets. There is widespread agreement that the manner of splitting the responsibilities for similar highway activities between the three levels is currently inefficient, resulting in unnecessary duplication,

---

4   Bank's assessment; official CNEA plans call for plant commissioning in 1996.

5   As per the existing electricity law and common to all national utilities, the balance goes to the Secretariat of Electric Energy which, in turn, directs these funds to the sector projects.

inadequate planning, suboptimal use of resources, and lack of coordination. Since DNV and the DPVs (and to some extent the municipalities) perform and manage similar functions, the potential increase in cost effectiveness through delegation of work and responsibility is high. Decree 616/92 (issued on April 10, 1992) established that the role of DNV will be limited to national road planning, technical leadership, assignment and auditing of financial resources to DPVs, road research, environmental analysis of road projects, standardization of road maintenance and construction, and transfer of technology to DPVs. While the jurisdiction of the national network will remain with DNV, it will delegate the execution of road works to the DPVs. The transition to this scheme will take years to materialize, given the current low capacity of most of the DPVs.

30. Roadways have also suffered from the drastic cut in funds that affect all sectors. As a consequence, no new road construction is underway, and maintenance has been cut sharply. The existing network satisfies the demand for road transport in length, but its condition is, in general, unsatisfactory and deteriorating rapidly, making road maintenance the highest priority in this sector. The criterion for fund allocation to DPVs is not based on demand, but rather on formulas of doubtful value with little regard to road requirements. The DVPs need technical assistance to play a more significant role in road activities. Also, engineering methods are not being used to increase the safety of traffic and to make traffic operate more efficiently. The use of such methods would create information that would permit an improvement in future decision-making. The personnel of the DNV, just as in the DVPs, suffer from the same problems that exist in the other sectors: low wages, low morale, and lack of motivation.

31. Due to the problems indicated, the Federal Government has decided to privatize not only road construction but maintenance as well. The Province of Buenos Aires is pursuing a similar course of action. Nonetheless, the implementation of the concession system is incipient (started in early 1991), and needs reinforcement of the technical and financial oversight by DNV to avoid disputes that may arise due to work done by the contractors. Nor is there a relationship between the contractor's profits and the level of activity in the economy (this naturally being reflected in the volume of traffic), which can result in a lower return than expected, with negative consequences in the effected maintenance.

32. The Government currently plans to improve administrative and executive efficiency and restore routine maintenance of the national and provincial road networks. The central idea is to merge the DNV and the DVPs. The program would, among other things, initiate a pilot program to monitor vehicle weight per axle so as to enforce weight limits on roads.

33. **Health**. With the transfer of 12 hospitals to provincial management, the Federal Government has sought to disengage itself from direct managerial and delivery responsibilities in the sector. Nonetheless, it has a project for US$38 million which is designed to build 5 new hospitals. The project is financed by an IDB loan, US$3 million of which would be disbursed in 1992; the remaining financing would come from the Treasury (US$18 million) and Ministry of Health (revenues from the national lottery). Because of the excess capacity that exists in the sector (discussed in Chapter

4), and the deteriorated state of that capacity, the returns to investments in rehabilitation projects are much higher if combined with a reorganization of health care provision. For these reasons, the Government has already downsized the project.

34. The World Bank has a loan in execution, the Social Sector Management Loan, which includes some aspects of public health. If potable water and sewage are considered as part of health, there is an IBRD loan that is about to be completely disbursed, although US$47.3 million is yet to be issued; and there is another IDB loan that still has US$64 million undisbursed. Furthermore, the IBRD has approved loans for potable water and sewage and flood rehabilitation. In total, these loans require local counterpart funds from the Government of less than US$1 million annually.

35. **Housing**. About 12 percent of the population live in unsafe housing and another 24 percent live in overcrowded conditions (3 to 4 people in a room). The housing deficit is estimated to be increasing by 115,000 units annually (100,000 new units are built each year, demand is 125,000, and 90,000 become unlivable). These needs are not met by the current system.

36. There are two entities at the federal level that participate in the supply of housing: the Fondo Nacional de la Vivienda (FONAVI), dependent on the Secretary of Housing (SVOA) in the Ministry of Health and Social Action, and the Banco Hipotecario Nacional (BHN). SVOA defines and executes national housing policy, and assigns the resources of FONAVI among the provincial housing institutes (IPV). FONAVI, originally funded with a tax of 5 percent on salaries and wages, has been funded by 40 percent of the fuel tax since late 1991 and was intended to be a revolving fund based on recovery of market-term loans to housing beneficiaries. The total of all funds constituted 60 percent of all resources mobilized for public housing and amounted to between one-half and 1 percent of GDP in the 1985-90 period. This is the largest category of investment without foreign finance.

37. Both the FONAVI and BHN programs entailed massive subsidies to the middle class. FONAVI has built middle-class housing rather than housing for the poor and has failed to collect on its portfolio. During the first half of the past decade, the annual income of FONAVI fluctuated around US$500 million. With these funds, FONAVI produced approximately 20,000 housing units per year. The monthly quotas were only partially inflation-adjusted. However, the main factor in the revenue decline was that purchasers were not paying their quotas. FONAVI, for its part, did not demand the payments, assuming that the beneficiaries were among the poorest members of society. The result was that the revenue in 1985 from quota payments of purchasers was 0.07 percent of the accumulated cost of the houses constructed between 1972 and 1985. The recovery rates on FONAVI loans are estimated to be around 2 percent in 1988 and 1989; while they have gone up in 1990 and 1991, they are yet to reach 5 percent.

38. Like FONAVI, the BHN has serious financial problems due to the lack of adjustment for inflation and poor collection efforts. The majority of financing for operations used to be provided by the Central Bank via rediscounts, but these have been cut off, and the BHN has no sources of financing. The BHN produced some 15,000

housing units per year for the lower-middle and middle classes, 500 units of which were for the poor during the 1980s.

39.   The framework for housing financing is undergoing change. FONAVI assigns resources to the provinces, and also influences strongly how these funds are used (in particular, to which firms contracts will be granted). The builders initiate contact to obtain the contract with strong support from their business associations (camaras) and from the unions. Pressure is exerted on the SVOA, which in turn pressures the Provincial Housing Institutes (IPVs). The result is that there is a wide margin for overpricing. With the same resources, FONAVI should be able to provide three to four times its present production of housing units. If loan contracts were truly enforced, this number would be between seven and eight.

40.   However, the change in the sector should be more profound than simply cutting costs and improving collection rates. First, public investments in housing are probably too large relative to other sectoral needs. Second, the orientation to channel subsidies to the middle class through the FONAVI program seems out of step with the Government's program of directing subsidies to the relatively poor while reducing aggregate subsidies in the economy. Third, the program has been unable to mobilize effective support from low-cost international lenders because they do not fund subsidies generally, but especially directed to the middle class; hence, FONAVI resources consume an appreciable portion of government savings that could otherwise be used to leverage a much larger investment program through foreign borrowing. Finally, the return to price stability offers the opportunity to facilitate the entrance of private banks into housing lending, and thus effectively privatize the provision of housing finance.

41.   **Defense**. Most investment in the sector occurred through enterprises under the Ministry of Defense, notably the General Mosconi and Bahia Blanca petrochemical plants, the steel company SOMISA, and the Military Factories complex (which includes various smaller enterprises). A recent decree established that all of these firms should proceed towards privatization, and this process would be supervised by the Ministry of Defense, reporting to the Ministry of Economy. It also established that all investment already being executed would be suspended--with some exceptions for important allocations; therefore, there will no large investments in 1992, other than US$92 million maintenance. Recently, the Ministry announced that it would buy new military fighter aircraft; though cost data are not available, these investments should be carefully reviewed to ensure consistency with the defense strategy.

The Public Investment Program Beyond 1993

42.   The sharp decline of public investment to unsustainably low levels by the end of the 1980s underscores the need for a recovery of public investment. On the other hand, the reorganization of government through the privatization and federalization programs reduces the demand for publicly provided goods at the federal level.

43.   Decentralization of responsibilities in the provision of public services affects public investment, especially the Federal Government. Hospitals and schools will be transferred to the provinces. The administration of most ports will also be handed over

to the provinces, affecting the ports of Buenos Aires, Entre Rios, Rio Negro, Chaco, Corrientes, Chubut, Santa Cruz, Formosa, Misiones, Santa Fe, and Tierra del Fuego. This will relieve the Federal Government from the pressure of devoting the necessary resources to recover the badly run-down infrastructure.

44.   Privatization will obviously reduce investment through the public enterprises, and implies that resources freed could be allocated to other areas of greater social priority. The new private firms will be free from the financial constraints faced by the public sector, and thus could increase investment and improve the quality of goods and services they produce.   The privatization of ENTEL and Aerolineas Argentinas, for example, has liberated important government resources since 1991; these two companies together invested an average of US$750 million during the 1980-90 period, an obviously insufficient amount, and new, higher levels of investment are now the responsibility of the private sector. By the end of 1993, almost all public firms will have been sold. Only YPF, Yacyretá, and the companies related to CNEA would remain in state hands in the power sector. If this program is completed on schedule, the investment needs of public enterprises from 1993 would be about US$2 billion, US$3 billion in 1994, and US$3.5 billion in 1995 and beyond.

E. Recommendations

Evaluating and Programming Public Investment

45.   While the Government of Argentina has made significant progress in the planning of public investment with the appearance of public investment plans for both 1991 and 1992, the process of capital budgeting can be greatly improved, thereby increasing the efficiency of public investment. A serious shortcoming in the public investment process is the absence of a consistent mechanism of project evaluation that can guide investment decisions of the authorities. There is no data bank of public investment projects. Out of more than 20 investment projects of over US$5 million identified, economic evaluations would be found for only a few (and then, mostly from sources in international financial institutions). Moreover, the government lacks a technical group with the capacity to conduct proficient economic evaluations, or even to review the evaluations made by third parties (i.e., the international lending institutions, which require an evaluation for every project they finance). Neither does the government have a set of relevant social prices to be used in all these evaluations.

46.   It is then essential that the government start a serious effort to implement a modern project evaluation mechanism to guide public investment decisions. To do this, it is necessary first to strengthen the technical group under the Secretaría de Programación Económica that centralizes all evaluation of public investment

programs.[6] Also, it is necessary to implement an evaluation methodology that will be common throughout the public sector. A first criterion is that all investments should undergo an economic evaluation, independent of the sector to which they belong, as it is possible to evaluate almost all conceivable projects. A second criterion is that no project with a negative net present value at social prices should be carried out. Moreover, projects currently underway should be reevaluated to determine whether or not society benefits from their continuation. This highlights the need to have good estimates of the key social prices such as the discount rate, the exchange rate, and the wage rate, which are unavailable now. Given the importance of these prices (which should be used in all project evaluations), their calculation should be made by a highly competent team, or assigned to a reputable institution.

47. Having a positive net present value at social prices is a necessary, but not a sufficient condition to go ahead with an investment project. In Argentina, where the public sector faces significant financial constraints, it may be impossible to finance all projects with a positive net present value. Thus, a project ranking is needed measuring the net present value per peso of investment. The economic criteria would then be to use the resources from the highest ranked project down until they are exhausted.

48. A final consideration relates to the desirability of going towards multiyear investment plans, especially in light of the changes in the public sector over the period 1991-93. The recent yearly investment programs mark an important step forward. These could be improved by casting investment in a three-year framework. The definitions of the macroeconomic parameters in the context of the recent EFF make this possible. This would help to identify capital shortages or any shortages in economically sound projects.

Ranking Present Investments: An Illustration

49. The social return to finishing the projects in execution is high, with a few notable exceptions mentioned below. This is because the economic cost of continuing with a project should not reflect the past investment (which is a cost already incurred), but rather the future investment and the recovery value of selling the project in its current state. Thus, the net present value (NPV) of a project in execution tends to be significantly higher than the NPV calculated when the project was initiated, and this former NPV will tend to be greater the more advanced the project is. It is quite likely then that an appropriate economic evaluation will show that investment in projects close to completion has a high NPV. It is also probably profitable to invest in rehabilitation

---

6   This is a better alternative than decentralized evaluation (at the level of each ministry or entity) for at least two reasons. First, it avoids conflict of interest as each entity has the incentive to make a very optimistic evaluation of its own projects. Second, it guarantees that the same criteria and parameters are used in the evaluation of all investment projects within the public sector; and it is probably the most cost-effective option. Within the technical group, it is desirable that experts could specialize in different sectors (health, education, transportation, housing, energy, etc.). If the human resources to form this technical group are unavailable in the public sector, we strongly suggest sending new and old personnel to training courses in academic institutions recognized for their excellence in project evaluation.

and maintenance of existing assets and in the completion of most existing projects (especially those well advanced).

50.　　　　An economic evaluation of public investment projects affords more in-depth criteria than these simple (but important) guidelines. Of the 20 or so investment projects reviewed, only 11 had sufficient information on costs and benefits to attempt an economic evaluation. Table 12.3 presents a ranking of profitability for the public projects in 1992 where information was available. The criteria used was the NPV per dollar of investment to be executed from 1991 onward (also in present value). As discussed, this is the appropriate criteria for elaborating such a ranking when there are significant restrictions on resources. Of the largest ongoing projects, high priority should be given to Piedra de Aguila, Yacyretá, and the projects in the fuels sector. On the other extreme, Atucha II and Pichi Picún Leufu have a negative NPV at discount rates above 12 percent. The criteria for the internal rate of return give a similar ranking for NPV per dollar invested, as indicated in column three of Table 12.3.

Potential Savings

51.　　　　The annual investment budgets for 1992 of Atucha II and Pichi Picun Leufu are US$395 million and US$146 million, respectively. Taken together, the two absorb over 20 percent of the total investment budget of the national government (including central administration, special accounts, decentralized agencies, and public enterprises), which is US$2.6 billion for 1992. Both of these projects have negative NPVs at any discount rate over 12 percent. In the case of Pichi Picun Leufu, however, Government financing is negligible.

52.　　　　Besides these two projects, the FONAVI housing program also merits serious reservations. Although no economic evaluation is available, there is good reason to believe that its NPV would be negative at reasonable discount rates. The program absorbs over US$900 million of resources in the budget for 1992, and has some serious flaws.

53.　　　　If the Government wants to attain the highest social benefit from the use of its scarce resources, it should carefully reevaluate the investment schedule for Atucha II and adjust it by considering a later commissioning date and minimizing the burden on the Treasury during the next 3 years. In the case of FONAVI, an attractive and feasible option may be to phase out the program over the next two to three years. Table 12.4 shows the potential savings that could be attained from these projects, which is nearly US$1.3 billion in 1992. Moreover, these funds have a high government savings component, mainly because the FONAVI program does not attract outside financing. By any measure, the resources saved could be significant.

Table 12.3: Ranking of Selected Public Sector Projects

Project	Sector	Internal Rate of Return	Net Present Value Per Dollar Invested From 1991 On (NFV/NPI) a/
1. Refinery Conversion	Fuels	83.0	21.81
2. Compressed Gas for Vehicles	Fuels	70.0	4.88
3. Piedra del Aguila	Electricity	49.5	2.27
4. Despacho Regional de Carga Cuyo	Electricity	23.0	2.23
5. Interconexcion Norte y Sur con Brazil (Mosalidad II)	Electricity	32.0	1.98
6. Puerto Bahia Blanca	Transportation	40.0	1.76
7. Yacyreta	Electricity	21.6	0.51
8. Despacho Regional de Carga Noroeste			
9. Atucha II	Electricity	9.9 b/	-0.33
10. Pichi Picun Leufu	Electricity	8.1	-0.42

a/ Discount rate used: 15 percent.
b/ The IRR, considering investments from 1992 onwards, and updated long-term marginal costs would be 12 percent.

Source: Bank staff, 3, 7, 9, 10: N. De Franco, mimeo, November 1991.
Others: C. Tobal, Appendix A1 in F. Larrain and C. Tobal's "Inversion Publica en Argentina," mimeo, January 1991.

Table 12.4: Potential Savings in the 1992 Investment Plan (US$ million)

	Total	Financing	
		Foreign	Govt. Saving
Investment - 1992 Budget	2601	1895	706
Current Transfers (FONAVI)	903	0	903
Total Investment	3504	1895	1609
Projects for Reevaluation a/			
Atucha II b/	395	304	91
FONAVI	903	0	903
Potential Savings by Reallocation	1298	304	994

a/ Projects with negative social rate of return or possible low need; Pichi-Picun not included because Government savings would only be US$6 million and the project has US$140 million of tied financing under favorable terms.
b/ Includes heavy water plant.

Source: Bank staff estimates.

Transitional Problems for Privatized and Decentralized Activities

54.   Many public enterprises slated for privatization are undertaking investments that might otherwise be deferred until after divestiture. The lack of clear instructions to the executing units has created unnecessary uncertainties. Investment programs of state-owned companies scheduled to be partially privatized therefore deserve careful analysis. Not always does privatization imply a reduction in investment; YPF, for example, will retain some 75 percent of its original monopoly as a concession. Investment plans of YPF for 1992 show a significant increase of US$130 million over 1991. Any such plans should be subject to detailed evaluation.

CHAPTER 13: THE CENTRAL BANK AND
QUASI-FISCAL EXPENDITURE

A. The Quasi-Fiscal Deficit

1.   The Central Bank has been a major source of instability in Argentina. Numerous subsidies and the absorption of the internal and external debt by the public sector severely undermined the balance sheet of the Central Bank during the 1980s. The principal losses were attributable to capital and foreign exchange rate losses associated with the takeover of foreign debt, the uncovered debt from banks liquidated after the collapse of the domestic financial system in 1980-82 as well as later, disguised fiscal expenditures through the Housing Bank (BHN), and, to a lesser extent, the Industrial Development Banks (BANADE), especially in 1986-87. The net worth of the Central Bank (BCRA) was always negative during the 1985-91 period, and the cumulative quasi-fiscal losses of the Central Bank were about US$15 billion by end-1989 (Table 13.1).[1]

2.   The Central Bank recorded the accumulated "assetized" losses and subtracted the losses from capital and reserves and recorded an offsetting credit in the Monetary Regulation account.[2] The capital position therefore became negative. The losses first emerged after the 1977 attempts to liberalize the heavily intervened financial system[3] by paying interest on reserves held by the BCRA. Later, the Central Bank started to sterilize liquid funds by issuing a variety of short-term liabilities that included short-term CDs and lump-sum mandatory deposits that absorbed part of the commercial banks' liquidity. The Central Bank also experienced large losses derived from swaps and different exchange insurance mechanisms in 1982-85 associated with the assumption of the foreign debt.

3.   In the mid-1980s, aside from the substantial straightforward losses incurred through rediscounts to the public banks to subsidize housing and industry, a dynamic and procyclical component of the deficit was unleashed in 1985 when there was

---

1   Technically, the quasi-fiscal deficit is the difference between interest on the Central Bank's liabilities and interest on the Central Bank's assets, less the gain received by the Central Bank to the extent inflation reduces the real value of its net liabilities. The methodology used to estimate losses is discussed in Annex 13.1.

2   Some figures indicate that the total gross losses of the Central Bank from 1980 to 1989 were about US$48 billion (in 1989 dollars). About 70 percent of this total appears in the Bank Regulation Account system, 22 percent is due to the uncovered debt of banks in process of liquidation, and 8 percent from loans to the Banco Hipotecario.

3   In a compromise between liberalization and the need to establish monetary control, the authorities settled on the required-reserve ratio of 45 percent in the 1977 reform. To minimize the effect of the reserve requirements on borrowing-lending spreads, the Central Bank was directed to pay interest on commercial banks' required reserves. In turn, the Central Bank started to collect interest on the fraction of reserve requirements that corresponded to non-remunerated bank deposits. The balance of these operations was designated as the Monetary Regulation Account; however, it became a source of deficit, as the interest paid exceeded the interest collected.

an attempt to revitalize the banking system as part of the *Plan Austral*. The reform created "forced investments" designed to capture resources that might otherwise have remained in the market to finance public sector deficits. The major difference between forced investment and reserve requirements was that forced investment balances generally would be unavailable to the banks even when their deposits declined. Forced investments were also remunerated with an interest rate linked to the banks' average cost of funds, plus a generous spread. At the same time, the average interest rate on assets of the Central Bank were delinked from market rates because a large portion carried fixed rates or were based on LIBOR. This system exposed the Central Bank to enormous losses and required emission whenever domestic rates rose sharply compared to LIBOR (adjusted for devaluations).

Table 13.1: Summary of Public Sector Operations, Cash Basis
(in percent of GDP)

	1985	1986	1987	1988	1989	1990	1991	1992
NFPS Primary Balance	0.8	1.8	-1.4	-1.8	-0.3	1.9	2.4	3.2
NFP2.2S Interest a/	5.9	4.3	4.5	3.7	6.3	4.0	3.7	2.2
NFPS Overall Balance	-5.1	-2.5	-5.9	-5.5	-6.6	-2.1	-1.3	1.0
Quasi-Fiscal Balance b/	-2.8	-1.6	-3.4	-1.4	-5.8	-1.0	-0.6	-0.2
Overall Balance of the Combined Public Sector	-7.9	-4.1	-9.3	-6.9	-12.4	-3.1	-1.9	0.8

a/ From 1985 to 1989 only includes real interest components of domestic debt. Foreign interest is treated on accrual basis.

b/ IBRD definition: IMF definition adjusted for overall inflation, interannual inflation, and BHN provisioning.

Source: IMF (1992) and Ministry of Economy.

4.   The vulnerability of the Central Bank to interest losses was especially dramatic after 1987, when domestic interest rates were liberalized. In 1988, toward the end of the Primavera Plan, the high domestic interest rates required to support the fixed exchange rate drove up the Central Bank's interest bill. This created an unsustainable financial cycle in which the Central Bank had to create money to pay its own interest bill and then had to borrow back the australes to sterilize the endogenous monetary expansion. During the hyperinflation of the second quarter, the quasi-fiscal deficit reached the unprecedented level of 25.3 percent of GDP. The cycle was repeated at the end of the Plan Bunge y Born (July-December 1989). As markets moved against the austral in early December 1989 and interest rates skyrocketed, the quasi-fiscal deficit rose dramatically and the program finally exploded.[4]

5.   On January 1, 1990, faced with the loss of macroeconomic control and a skyrocketing interest bill, the Government announced the BONEX conversion plan to reduce domestic liquidity and eliminate the domestic component of the quasi-fiscal deficit. The authorities convert by fiat virtually all domestic commercial bank 7-day

---

4   See Paul Beckerman "Public Sector 'Debt Distress' in Argentina, 1988-89," World Bank Policy Research Paper, WPS 902, May 1992.

time deposits (worth about US$3.5 billion) and the bulk of the Central Bank and Treasury's outstanding austral debt that the deposits financed into 10-year, dollar-denominated BONEX. This measure directly halved the liquid stock of financial assets and penalized savers, but stopped the incipient hyperinflation. Moreover, it eliminated the destabilizing internal component of the quasi-fiscal deficit of the Central Bank by reducing sharply the Central Bank's interest costs. The quasi-fiscal deficit declined to 1 percent of GDP in 1990 from 6.2 percent in 1989 (Table 13.1).

6.   In April 1991, the Government implemented the Law of Convertibility. The law legally fixed the exchange rate (upper limit) at A$10,000 to the US dollar, formally deindexed most contracts and facilitated the use of the US dollar in transactions. With some US$4.8 billion in international reserves (including US$1.5 billion in gold and about US$200 million in Government dollar-denominated bonds) and a monetary base of the same size, the new law guaranteed full convertibility of the austral at A$10,000.[5] It also put a tight limit on Central bank monetary emission by requiring that international reserves be at least equal to the money base. Hence monetary emission was effectively eliminated, and a monetary discipline equivalent to a currency board was imposed on the Central Bank.[6] The quasi-fiscal deficit of the Central Bank was almost eliminated in 1991 (0.5 percent of GDP) and a dramatic change in the sources of financing of the public sector was generated. With the issuance of Communication "A" 1881-1882 (October 11, 1991), the Central Bank restricted its insurance on deposits in local currency to the first A$1,000 of each deposit, to a total amount of A$50 million in BONEX.

B. Sources of Financing of the Public Sector

An Overview

7.   In every year of the 1985-91 period the overall balance of the public sector was negative, meaning that there has always been the need to print money or issue financial liabilities in order to finance the combined deficit of the public sector (Table 13.2). According to the official data, there was no financing of the public sector deficit from the Central Bank in the 1986-88 period. In fact, the Central Bank provided disguised financing to the Non-Financial public sector that did not appear in the accounts. The NFPS borrowed from the Central Bank by obtaining rediscounts for public banks and other public enterprises (most of which were not repaid), by monetizing net amortization on bonds issued after 1985, and financing the social security float. The NFPS also placed dollar-denominated Treasury Bills at the Central Bank in exchange for local currency, an operation that was close to printing money, particularly

---

5   The Law of Convertibility was feasible, ironically, because the Bonex Plan has so discouraged money- holding that the monetary base was less than the Central Bank's international reserves.

6   The Central Bank differs from a true currency board since monetary emission can be undertaken to the extent that reserves exceed the monetary base, and the Central Bank can vary reserve requirements and thus the ratio of base to demand financial assets. In addition, international reserves are defined to include foreign currency liabilities of the Government (limited however to 10 percent of total reserves).

because these dollar-denominated Treasury bills were never redeemed. Finally, the Central Bank became the repository of a large fraction of the service of the foreign debt as a consequence of the 1984-87 rescheduling with commercial banks and the Paris Club, although the cash flow problems from these transactions were reduced by the arrears.

Table 13.2: Public Sector: Sources of Financing
(in percent of GDP)

	1985	1986	1987	1988	1989	1990	1991	1992 b/
Financing Requirements	7.9	4.1	9.3	6.9	12.4	3.1	1.6	-0.8
Domestic Financing	7.0	3.1	6.1	4.2	4.9	-0.3	-0.6	-1.0
of which:								
Net Borrowing	1.3	1.8	3.7	4.7	3.5	-0.4	-0.4	1.7
Central Bank	6.9	0.0	0.0	0.2	1.3	0.6	0.0	0.0
Other a/	-1.2	1.2	2.5	-0.6	0.3	-0.5	-0.3	-2.7
External Financing	0.9	1.1	3.2	2.5	7.9	3.4	2.2	0.2
Arrears	0.0	0.0	0.8	3.1	6.6	3.5	2.0	0.8
Memo:								
Revenues from Privatization						0.6	1.1	1.2

a/   Includes increase of net financial liabilities, net use of advances from suppliers, and net credit from the financial domestic system (excluding the Central Bank).

b/   Preliminary.

Sources: IMF, Ministry of Economy and Central Bank.

Monetary Financing

8.   Monetary emission was an important source of public sector financing in Argentina during the 1980s, despite the official figures. However, the secular demonetization process dramatically reduced revenues from money creation for the Government over the decade. The ratio of M1 to GDP declined from 8.3 percent at the end of 1980 to under 3 percent in 1989. Moreover, this ratio was volatile: as high as 7.5 percent in January 1986 and as low as 1.7 percent in July 1989. The return to price stability increased the ratio to 5.3 percent in February 1992.

9.   The fraction of the deficit that was financed with printing of money is derived from the accounts of the monetary sector.[7] The revenue from monetary creation has been calculated as the monthly change in the monetary base divided by the exchange rate for the dollar in the free market. This provides a monthly series of dollar revenue from money creation. Since the Central Bank intervened in the foreign exchange market by buying or selling foreign exchange, in many instances the changes in the monetary base are due to variations in money demand that are provided by purchases of international reserves. Therefore, reserve purchases or sales due to private sector operations have been subtracted from the series of revenue from monetization. Figure 13.1 illustrates the evolution of monetary financing over the 1988-91 period.

---

7   This is based on information from the Monetary Program.

Even if the inflation tax has been important during period of high inflation, its benefit for the public sector was nearly offset by the decline in money demand.[8]

10.   Revenue from monetary financing went through sharp cycles as a result of changes in real money demand and in the rate of inflation. Monetary theory suggests that through the variability of the inflation rate, a government can maximize revenues from monetary financing. A government must sell money when the rate of inflation is decreasing and "look the other way" when the rate is increasing. This mechanism functioned well in Argentina during most of the 1980s. Traditionally, Government finances underwent severe pressure at the end of year because of seasonal factors such as payments of the extra-month salary (the *aguinaldo*) and social security payments. The public accounts' deterioration induced the private sector to shift from the local currency into US dollars.[9] To collect revenues from monetary financing, the rate of inflation needs to increase dramatically (see Figure 13.2). In the end, the costs associated with high inflation and demonetization forced the Government to start an adjustment program. This new program was generally accompanied by a change in administration so that the public was uncertain about its true preferences; that is, whether this was a no-nonsense Government or one merely pretending to tackle the serious fiscal problems. In fact, the Government appeared tough for some time which sustained public confidence and increased the confidence of the private sector, fueled money demand, and thus momentarily postponed the eventuality of a tremendous inflationary surge.

---

8   Following the method outlined in the World Bank's *Macroeconomic Assessment* (March 1991) and developed further in Annex 12.1, total monetary financing between periods 0 and 1 can be expressed as:

(1) $\triangle H/P_0 = H_1/p_0 - H_0/p_0$

where H is the monetary base (adjusted for the changes in international reserves due to the private sector operations) and p the price level.
By definition, the rate of inflation is:

(2) $\pi = (p_1 - p_0)/p_0$

Substituting (2) from (1):

(3) $\triangle H/P_0 = [h_1 - h_0] + [\pi h_1]$

The first term in parentheses represents the fraction of monetary financing owing to the monetization process and the second term is the inflation tax. Remonetization is revenue (or losses) from changes in the willingness of the public to hold Central bank paper and the inflation tax is revenue from money emission to replace inflation-induced erosion in the real value of the peso holdings of the general public; this is estimated by multiplying the inflation rate times the real money base.

9   Other seasonal factors such as summer vacations can be explained by the private sector's portfolio shift.

Figure 13.1 : Monetary Financing
Q2/1988-Q4/1991

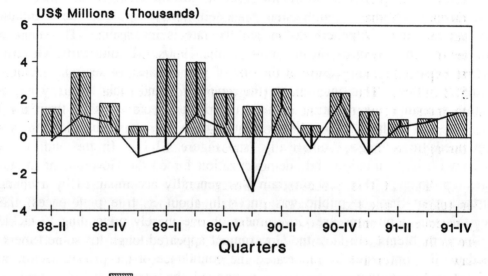

Monetary Financing ▪ Monetization
✦ Inflation Tax

Figure 13.2 : Inflation; Combined Index
Q2/1988-Q4/1991

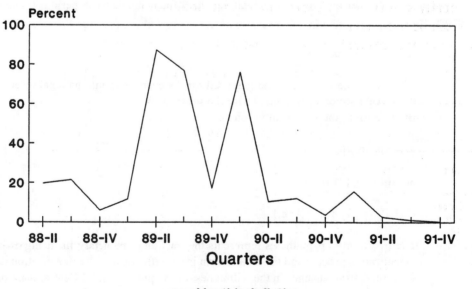

11.　　　　However, because the above mechanism was repeated over time, it became more and more difficult to convince the public that any change had taken place. The reputation of the Central Bank was declining and the public similarly adjusted its expectations downward. By end-1989, the reaction of private agents to the prospect of any inflation tax became so rapid and sophisticated that even small fiscal gaps--or other shocks--produced steep declines in money demand. The demonetization process was so intensive during 1989 that the authorities needed extremely high inflation to collect the inflation tax revenues. Although the monthly inflation rate reached 75 percent in the first quarter of 1990, revenues from monetary financing were only half those collected in the first hyperinflationary episode of 1989. Money demand actually dropped by almost US$2 billion. The Government progressively realized that financing its deficit by printing money resulted in an increase rather than a decrease in the fiscal gap. Revenues from monetary financing were not able to compensate for the loss in fiscal revenues through the Tanzi effect and the increase in real interest payments.

12.　　　　To halt this process, the Government first proceeded to the Bonex conversion (para. 5) and then initiated an adjustment program in March 1990. Since, monetary revenues are only slightly lower than during the first quarter of 1990, despite the decline in the inflation rate from 75 percent to below 3 percent. The implementation of the Law of Convertibility improved the credibility of the Government program, thereby enhancing the remonetization of the economy. However, under the law of Convertibility regime, most monetary revenues are compensated by a simultaneous increase in international reserves. In effect, the Central Bank's ability to carry out monetary policy is severely limited because of the requirement that the money base be fully backed by international reserves. The Central Bank could still undertake these functions to the extent that international reserves exceed the money base. In that sense, it is worth noting that even though the Government does not benefit immediately from the remonetization, in the long run, the increase in reserves that are invested internationally contribute to Bank profits and liquid reserves; moreover, these small amounts can be used later for monetary financing. This assumes that the public initially generated the reserves and that a run against local currency will not occur.

Table 13.3:　Sources of Financing
(US$ millions)

| | 1990 | | | | | 1991 | | | | |
	IQ	IIQ	IIIQ	IVQ	1990	IQ	IIQ	IIIQ	IVQ	1991
Financing Requirement	873	629	949	767	3218	1276	712	344	-212	2121
Net Foreign Borrowing	1164	1394	497	942	3997	305	718	1014	845	2882
Commercial Bank Arrears	970	1082	817	803	3672	800	789	556	449	2594
Net Domestic Borrowing	0	-74	-132	-200	-406	35	-98	-168	-222	-454
Central Bank Lending a/	-291	-691	585	24	64	937	92	-502	-835	-308
Monetary Financing	1427	1822	939	1927	6115	1271	1306	676	491	3744
Remonetization	-3934	1180	-371	1430	-1695	-805	955	496	449	1095
Inflation Tax	5362	642	1309	497	7810	2075	351	180	42	2649
Change in Reserves	1718	2513	354	1903	6051	334	1214	1178	1326	4051
Memo: Privatization	16	22	192	348	578	293	344	510	540	1687

a/　　Central Bank lending is defined as the variation in the monetary base less the variation in international reserves.

Source:　Annex 13.1.

Table 13.4: Sources of Financing
(in percent of total financing)

| | 1990 | | | | | 1991 | | | | |
	IQ	IIQ	IIIQ	IVQ	1990	IQ	IIQ	IIIQ	IVQ	1991
Financing Requirements	100	100	100	100	100	100	100	100	100	100
Net Foreign Borrowing	133	222	52	123	111	24	101	295	399	136
Commercial Bank Arrears	111	172	86	105	114	63	111	162	212	122
Net Domestic Borrowing	0	-12	-14	-26	-13	3	-14	-49	-105	-21
Central Bank Lending a/	-33	-110	62	3	2	73	13	-146	-394	-15
Monetary Financing	163	290	99	251	190	100	183	196	232	177
Remonetization	-451	188	-39	187	-53	-63	134	144	212	52
Inflation Tax	614	102	138	65	243	163	49	52	20	125
Change in Reserves	197	400	37	248	188	26	170	342	625	191
Memo:										
Privatization	2	4	20	45	18	23	48	148	255	80

a/   Central Bank lending is defined as the variation in the monetary base less the variation in
       international reserves.

Source: Annex 13.1.

Recent Changes in Financing

13.   The Law of Convertibility induced a notable shift in the sources of financing in the public sector. From the first quarter of 1990 to the first quarter of 1991, the inflation tax provided by far the largest source of support: it is estimated that this source of financing represented about 216 percent of total financing.   The Government also relied on external debt arrears (107 percent of total financing) as well as financing by public banks. In contrast, since the second quarter of 1991, the inflation tax has been virtually eliminated (about 40 percent of total financing). If external debt arrears continue to be used as a source of financing (161 percent), in sharp contrast to the Plan Primavera, the fall in the inflation tax would be compensated by alternative sources of financing.   The combined public sector borrowing requirements have been mostly financed by revenues from privatization and asset sales, which have represented about 150 percent of total financing since the second quarter of 1991 (compared to about 17 percent in 1990). Since the Government no longer needs to finance its deficit though the inflation tax, the monthly rate of inflation dropped from 27 percent in February to 0.7 percent in May 1992, and its creditworthiness improved.

14.   The analysis also underscores the fragility of financing. The revenues from privatization and asset sales are transient since the privatization process is planned to be accomplished at the end of 1993.

C. Strengthening the Monetary Authority

15.   To reduce the danger of future inflationary finance even further, the authorities intend to implement a new Central Bank Charter that would (among other things): (i) provide the Central Bank directors with sufficient independence to manage the institution with the objective of preserving the value of the currency; (ii) restrict Central Bank financing for the public sector to open market purchases of government securities within specified legal limits; (iii) remove functions from the Central Bank not directly related to its fundamental function of maintaining a stable currency, including removal of the trade credit function from the present Central Bank; and (iv) restrict Central Bank credit to commercial banks to liquidity rediscounts in cases of emergency-- and this only when pledged against bank capital and for a limit of 15 days.

16.   The new draft Charter should be implemented as soon as possible for at least three reasons. First, it will enhance the independence of the Central Bank through its legal constitution and financial autarky. Second, it will clarify the relations between the Central Bank and the rest of the financial system (e.g., Superintendency of Banks and credit to commercial banks). Finally, the Charter will provide a second legal pillar supporting monetary control in addition to the Law of Convertibility, which will provide assurances to investors that fear change in the exchange rate regime.

17.   In addition, other institutional changes are necessary to resolve problems associated with the new Charter, including administrative and accounting, the removal of the liquidation function, trade financing, and the reorganization of the Superintendency.

Administrative and Management Problems

18.   Over the course of 1990, successive Central Bank administrations struggled with the issue of reorganization. In April 1991, the Central Bank's directors began to carry out another reorganization, using the internal administrative powers at their disposal. This effort, including streamlining, will result in a reduction of about 25 percent of its employees in 1992 (from 2,398 to 1,782 workers). Because of the reliance on voluntary retirement and resignations to achieve staff reductions, the technical competence of the organization is an issue. Senior management of the Central Bank will have to work to strengthen the staff. Recent salary increases may help to attract high-quality personnel.

Accounting Problems

19.   By reducing the Central Bank's interest-bearing liability position and transferring it to the Treasury, the BONEX conversion constituted an important initial step in the process of recapitalizing the Central Bank. The conversion virtually eliminated the Central Bank's interest-bearing domestic liabilities, and ended the Central Bank borrowing requirement derived from the flow of net interest payments on the accumulated debt.

20.　　　　　It is crucial to determine an accurate balance sheet of the Central Bank for at least two reasons. First, reconstitution of the monetary reporting and accounting systems are essential prerequisites for development of the Central Bank's ability to generate accurate statistics for policy- making, and second, the new Charter requires the balance of the Central Bank to be accurate.[10] The current balance sheet of the Central Bank contains several weaknesses that are important to overcome as soon as possible. A partial list includes the following: (i) the Central Bank has to rely on foreign creditor claims because it has no means to provide evidence of its own about external debt statistics (this is being addressed by an audit undertaken in conjunction with the debt-reduction deal); (ii) the Central Bank is unable to determine the precise amount of domestic credit extended to the financial sector because interest due is aggregated in one global account without discriminating between debtors; (iii) several operations have been regrouped into provisional accounts without specific denominations; and (iv) there is no precise information on the use of reserves.

21.　　　　　The Central Bank made progress in auditing and adjusting its balance sheet for 1990. It ended the Monetary Regulation Account and other systems by which Central Bank losses were accumulated as "assets." The Central Bank also carried out an exhaustive revision of its external assets and liabilities, valuing them at appropriate exchange rates. Toward the end of 1990 it produced a closing balance sheet for 1989 incorporating these changes.[11]

22.　　　　　The Central Bank's accounting system is deficient in many respects. Some of the problems are conceptual in nature (as discussed above), other are technical, such as the data processing hardware. The Central Bank's data processing hardware is inadequate, at least a decade out of date. At times in recent years the Central Bank has transacted extensive open-market and exchange-market operations; however, it lacks an information system capable of performing such operations efficiently.

The Liquidation Function

23.　　　　　In the past, Argentina's Central Bank attempted to act far beyond its expected role which is one reason why it performed inadequately. Bank liquidation, in particular, has consumed and continues to consume massive time and in many instances

---

10　　Article 5 of the new Charter stipulates that "*El capital del Banco quedara establecido en el balance inicial que se presentara al momento de promulgarse la presente ley*".

11　　This turned out to be a complicated exercise for several reasons. First, existing law is understood to imply that Argentine accounting statements may not declare public sector obligations to be value-impaired. The Central Bank is accordingly unable to classify its holdings of non-marketable public sector obligations (notably the holdings of the housing bank) realistically. Second, delicate questions arose regarding some of the Central Bank's holdings of private sector commercial bank obligations. These holdings include obligations of the nearly 200 entities in liquidation. Some of these were "rediscount" operations carried out when the solvency of the banks in question was clearly doubtful. Third, the Central Bank's accounting system has simply failed to reflect true transaction values. This is particularly the case for external transactions, for which the problems of assigning correct exchange rates and counterpart accounts overwhelmed the accounting system.

producing financing pressures that generate money creation. For these reasons, the Government has begun institutional reforms to separate the liquidation function from the Central Bank.

24.   The Central Bank has been directing the liquidation of some 200 failed banks. Most of the banks that went into liquidation in the early 1980s remain in liquidation, and there are some banks whose liquidation proceedings began even earlier (one as far as 1961). The Central Bank has contracted some 1,400 people to manage the defunct banks. However, the number of staff associated with the liquidation of closed banks declined over the last two years. The total number of permanent and temporary staff employed in bank liquidation activities was reduced from 309 to 246 between December 31, 1990 and February 10, 1992. In fact, this process is part of the global strategy of the authorities to reduce the number of employees in the Central Bank. While the staff associated with bank liquidation activities declined about 20 percent, the total number of employees in the Central bank declined about 25 percent from December 31, 1990 to February 10, 1992.

25.   The main difficulty associated with the removal of Central Bank liquidation activities is that the Law on Financial Companies (*Entidades Financieras*) will need to be modified by Congress. Legal complications clearly have been an impediment to the conclusion of liquidation proceedings, but the management of the process has been wasteful and inefficient. While there is disagreement over whether the liquidation process would be best managed by a liquidation institute or by the judiciary, no one doubts that continued management of the process by the Central Bank would be inappropriate.

Trade Financing

26.   By the late 1980s, the Central Bank took on a significant role in financing external trade. The basic objective was to promote exports and to make working capital available to exporters, but in practice the Central Bank's export finance became highly distorted. Like many other central banks, Argentina's rediscounted export documents at rates ranging from subsidized to highly favorable. Moreover, the Central Bank's financing activity in this area went well beyond simple pre- and post-shipment export working-capital finance. By the late 1980s, it was fair to say that the Central Bank was running an export-import bank. Term credit to foreign importers under special trade agreements came to constitute a large proportion of this activity: this credit accounts for a significant part of the Central Bank's value-impaired external asset holdings. In particular, the system of export pre-financing was abused during 1988 and 1989 when the Primavera and Bunge y Born plans sought to stabilize the exchange rate by forcing up interest rates; many exporters, who in reality had little need for working capital credit, nevertheless took it against anticipated exports at favorable rates and placed the proceeds on deposit at high domestic rates. The Central Bank's rediscount program (in addition to the relative security of most export credit) made commercial banks willing to provide trade credit; other kinds of credit tended to be unavailable. The Central Bank largely discontinued new export financing operations after the BONEX conversion. During 1990 and 1991, the Central Bank worked to set up a new trade financing

institution, the Bank of Investment and External Trade (BICE). This new institution is expected to begin operations in 1992 or 1993.

Superintendency of Banks

27.   A reform of the Superintendency of Banks has been included in the proposed Charter of the Central Bank. The scope of the Superintendency will be enlarged within the Central Bank and the status of the Superintendent enhanced by having him or her confirmed by Congress. Over the last two years, some progress has been made regarding the supervision function of the Superintendency. The interval between each visit to financial firms has been compressed from an average of 24-36 months to 12-15 months. However, the Superintendency remains basically a weak institution and effort must be intensified to strengthen it. Unfortunately, such efforts have been delayed by changing managerial mandates, delays in approving new salary and organizational structures, and low staff morale associated with staff reductions. Given the existing policy framework, the recovery of bank lending volume and the emergence of the domestic stock market, it becomes urgent that the Superintendency be technically upgraded to fulfill its expanded functions.

D. Recommendations

28.   In an economy like Argentina's, the confidence of the private sector is closely linked to the elimination of the inflation tax. The commitment of the public sector to the Law of Convertibility, with monetary financing explicitly prohibited, is one factor explaining the success of the current adjustment program. An increase in monetary financing would therefore be perceived by the private sector as a reduction in the willingness of the Government to adjust and would lead to a decline in money demand and a sharp increase in the rate of inflation.

29.   After 1988, the Government progressively realized that the revenues derived from the inflation tax was almost offset by demonetization. In these conditions, the revenues from monetary financing did not compensate for the costs of high inflation, which reached about 75 percent per month in early 1990. Losses in tax revenues due to the Tanzi effect and higher interest payments contributed to the explosion of the overall fiscal deficit. At end- 1989, a jump in inflation led to an increase rather than a reduction in the fiscal gap. Therefore, the Government had no alternative but to reduce the fiscal deficit. The first measure was to reduce the quasi-fiscal deficit by the Bonex conversion. The Government also accelerated the adjustment effort begun timidly in the waning years of the previous administration, which reduced dramatically the public sector deficit in 1990 as well as the rate of inflation. The overall deficit of the public sector reached the lowest level of the last two decades--1.6 percent of GDP in 1991. At the same time, the Government relied on a new source of financing, the revenues from privatization and asset sales, which represented about 1.1 percent of GDP in 1991.

30.   The elimination of the quasi-fiscal deficit and the new monetary framework have given the Central Bank the opportunity to become a modern monetary authority.   Nevertheless, significant operating and administrative flaws continue to hamper the Central Bank operations.   These flaws have been magnified by the absence of a clear vision on the role of the Central Bank.   The Convertibility Law sharply reduces--but does not eliminate--the scope for an active monetary policy.   The elimination of the extraneous functions (e.g., guarantor of last resort) would also reduce the raison d'être of a Central Bank.   Along these lines, the Central Bank would be converted in a simple currency board.   On the other hand, any eventual departure from the fixed exchange rate regime may lead to an active monetary policy, thus reinforcing the role of the Central Bank.   In that case, the Government should take actions in the following areas.

31.   **Administration and Management**.   Management should revamp the structure of the Board of Directors to relieve them of operational line responsibilities. As it stands, Board members play both roles of supervising the President and carrying out his mandate.   This dilutes responsibility and compromises the advice a Board member must give its President.   The Government should use the opportunity presented by the Charter to appoint people of stature in the financial community and invest them with the responsibility of ensuring that the goals of the Charter are faithfully attained by the President and his management.   The management must also devote special attention to tasks that have a high cost if not handled properly and immediately, most notably the reconciliation of the balances with external creditor banks.

32.   **Accounting**.   Many changes carried out in recent years have significantly improved the Central Bank's accounting system.   In particular, the recalculation of the end-1989 balance sheet and the elimination of forced investments and of the Monetary Regulation Account helped to simplify the accounting system.   Nevertheless, the present system is still severely deficient.   Reconstitution of the accounting system must move in parallel with the reorganization process.   The reconstitution of the accounting system must also be carried out with a view to ensuring that it generate the appropriate statistics for the Central Bank's new responsibilities in a timely way.   The Central Bank's operations must be defined precisely along with the specific ways and means by which data will be entered into the accounting system.   Specific personnel would then be responsible for recording designated transactions.   The fundamental question is whether the present system can be salvaged or if the system should be entirely replaced.   Along these lines, it is noteworthy that an external audit of Central Bank accounts will be required by the new Charter.

33.   **Liquidation Function**. The Government in September 1992 modified the Financial Entities Law to require that all future liquidation of bankrupt financial institutions be handled directly by the court system.   This leaves on the on-going liquidations with the Central Bank, many of the liquidations are more than a decade old, yet are still time-consuming and costly.   The Central Bank should accelerate efforts to finish the process as soon as possible.

34.   **Superintendency**. Consistent with the new Charter of the Central Bank, the Government should: (i) consolidate the reform of the Superintendency of Banks by

ensuring greater administrative independence and enactment of its upgraded salary and organizational structure; (ii) assign responsibility for issuing norms pertaining to banking regulation; and (iii) assign responsibility for the timely publication of financial indicators, including the balance sheets and income statement information as well as portfolio classification of banks. Also, (iv) the management relations between the Central Bank and the Superintendency should be made clearer and more predictable; (v) more enforcement power should be attributed to the Superintendency; and (vi) instruments used to evaluate commercial bank activities should be revised. Of particular concern is the need to reduce the incentives for large banks to take too many risks (too-big-to-fail policy). One possibility may be to tie bank supervision more directly to the amount of bank capital. Well-capitalized banks would be allowed to be the most diversified in financial services, since increasing the bank's own capital requirements is probably the most effective way of reducing moral hazard incentives.

CHAPTER 14. PUBLIC FINANCE AND THE FUTURE OF PRICE STABILITY

1.   The last three years have witnessed impressive improvements in public finance, price stability and growth. The Government has made steady progress in reducing the deficit (Figure 14.1). In 1992, the nonfinancial public sector will probably register an overall surplus for the first time in decades. Equally important, the Government achieved this turnaround through structural changes that, in contrast to temporary and often inefficient measures that merely suppressed the deficit, were efficient and relatively enduring.   For example, the Government rebuilt the tax system by replacing tax handles with the VAT and income taxes; it contained the wage bill by reducing employment and increasing average wages and

Figure 14.1

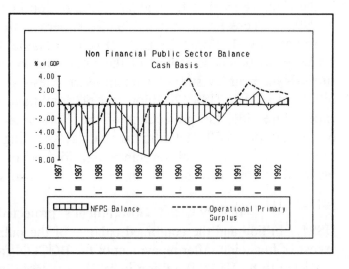

wage dispersion; it reduced public expenditures through divestitures of public enterprises and a new (if yet incomplete) federalism.

2.   Nonetheless, the Government still faces near-term and medium-term challenges that revolve around public finance and macroeconomic management. In particular, the process of adjustment has given rise to new demands on public resources, such as servicing previously accumulated liabilities, the reform of the social security system and increasing expenditures for investment and the social sectors. Moreover, if the economy does not grow as anticipated, projected revenues would not materialize. Such pressure may put new strains on public finance in the future. Several new policies and reforms, based on the recommendations of this report, would help consolidate the considerable progress to date and provide a cushion to meet these new demands with further reductions in the structural deficit.

3.   Since public finance is central to the medium-term growth prospects of Argentina--and vice versa--this chapter analyzes the Government's fiscal forecasts in light of available financing to its deficit, and objectives for inflation and growth. A first section discusses fiscal and monetary policy and their implications for prices, output and the balance of payments. A second explores medium-term demands on fiscal resources that may require adjustment over and above the Government's medium-term projections. A third quantifies the potential savings emanating from the recommendations in this report.

A. Macroeconomic Projections

Fiscal Policy

4.   The current adjustment program involves efforts to raise the primary surplus to levels compatible with projected net external financing and interest payments without incurring large amounts of new debt or recourse to the inflation tax. In the Government's medium-term program of January 1992, this translated into an increase in the primary balance from about US$2 billion in 1990 to more than US$5.0 billion in 1992.[1] Thereafter, over the 1993-2000 period, the Government projected on average a primary fiscal surplus of US$5.0 billion (Table 14.1). In 1992, asset sales were projected to be about a third of the total primary surplus. However, the operational surplus--the primary surplus without asset sales--is also projected to rise from US$1.2 billion in 1991 to US$3.2 billion in 1992, and then to US$4.4 billion in 1993. On the expenditure side, the projections of the Government included a small increase (as a percentage of GDP) in traditional capital spending and some non-traditional capital spending in the form of severance pay for retiring workers; on the revenue side it included a substantial increase in federal and social security tax revenues.

5.   In 1993, the Government's projected primary surplus will be about US$4.7 billion and the combined balance of the public sector will be in surplus. The excess of financing--after repayment of the BOCON from the income tax arrangement--is projected to be US$500 million in 1993, a notable improvement over the accumulation of arrears of US$1.5 billion in 1991. Between 1993 and 2000, the Government will have a total public sector *net* borrowing requirement without identified finance averaging about US$500 million, or 0.2 percent of GDP. These levels are financeable if the Government adheres to its present policy framework and the economy experiences no unforeseen shocks.

Monetary Policy Role

6.   Monetary policy is disciplined by the Law of Convertibility. Increases in the money base would occur only through the purchase of reserves by the Central Bank. Authorities can loosen credit policy as markets demand domestic financial assets through reductions in reserve requirements to permit greater credit. In practice, since the average term of deposits has lengthened, the average reserve requirement of the deposit base has fallen because the term accounts have lower reserve requirements than

---

1   The projections in this chapter are formulated using the basic framework of the Government's three-year program as presented to the Bank and the IMF. This includes assumptions for growth, fiscal and monetary policy, and the evolution of key external variables, reflecting December 1992 information. The methodology of the projection and detailed assumptions, together with greater elaboration of the major accounts, are discussed in Annex 14.1.

Table 14.1: Argentina - Key Macroeconomic Indicators
(US$ million)

	1990	1991	1992	Average 1993-1995	Average 1996-2000
Public Finances					
Primary Surplus	2,012	2,857	5,178	4,029	5,633
Interest payments	5,459	4,586	2,731	3,847	4,453
Domestic	229	322	160	704	1,198
Foreign	5,230	4,264	2,572	3,143	3,255
Balance (- = deficit)	(3,448)	(1,729)	2,447	182	1,181
Domestic Financing	4,483	(897)	(2,563)	201	(896)
Foreign Financing	(1,036)	2,626	116	853	(284)
Balance of Payments					
Trade Balance	8,151	4,007	(1,139)	398	2,595
Current Account Balance	1,754	(2,748)	(6,779)	(5,555)	(5,766)
Foreign Financing	161	4,330	10,216	6,115	5,801
Public Sector	(1,036)	2,626	116	(383)	(284)
IBRD a/	169	138	248	675	73
IDB a/	225	242	527	460	345
Bonds	(226)	395	(233)	(548)	(164)
IMF a/	(185)	(661)	338	348	(764)
Commercial Banks	(1,289)	0	(127)	(175)	(695)
Purchase of Enhancements	0	0	0	(1,236)	0
Bilaterals, Suppliers and Others b/	270	2,512	(637)	94	921
Private Sector	1,197	1,704	10,100	6,498	6,085
National Accounts					
GDP Average Annual Growth	0.4	8.5	6.5	3.7	4.2
GDP (US$ billion)	105.5	135.4	153.2	182.6	248.6
Total Investment (% GDP)	8.4	12.5	14.0	16.0	18.0
National Savings (% GDP)	10.0	10.4	9.6	13.0	15.7
Foreign Savings (% GDP)	(1.6)	2.1	4.4	3.0	2.3

a/ Includes set-asides and additional lending in 1993 for guarantee purchases.
b/ 1993 includes lending from Japanese Export-Import Bank for guarantee purchases.

Source: Bank staff estimates; Annex 14.

other deposits. This, together with the rapid growth in dollar deposits, has fueled an expansion of domestic credit.[2]

7.   However, demand for narrow money as measured by the M1/GDP ratio, is expected to remain constant at about 7.1 percent of GDP while demand for other financial instruments, including US dollar accounts, is seen as satisfying most of the increased demand for financial assets. Under these assumptions, the money base in peso terms is expected to increase by about US$1 billion annually. Under the Law of Convertibility, this would be generated by capital inflows and would increase international reserves by the same amount each year; this growth is reflected in the balance of payments.

Prices, Output, and Investment-Savings

8.   The Government's program anticipates that this fiscal and monetary stance will reduce the annual inflation from 139 percent in 1991 to 11.3 percent in 1992. After that time, inflation is projected to fall to 4 percent--essentially international rates. The policy framework is projected to stimulate recuperation of savings, and, in turn, a strong and sustained recovery of consumption and investment. GDP would expand by nearly 5 percent annually in 1992-94 (Table 14.1).

9.   The macroeconomic logic of the program is that continuing private capital inflows would drive the recovery as Argentines repatriate part of their vast savings abroad and foreign investors enter the economy in response to the opportunities provided by privatization and domestic growth. Thus, the growth in domestic consumption fueled by expanded credit and trade liberalization that powered the 1991 recovery gradually would be supplemented by growth in demand for investment. Export growth would be maintained through supply-side measures to reduce costs and therefore (implicitly) prices measured in dollars. Thus, the main sources of medium-term growth would be domestic consumption, investment demand, and exports--both agricultural and industrial--as well as industrial production for efficient import substitution.

10.   As the public sector adjusts to a new role, the private sector would have to be a leading expansionary force. Public investment would grow, but be concentrated in fewer activities, as privatization would reduce the demand for public investment. The savings performance that emerges from the macro-consistency projections largely reflects increases in domestic public savings and repatriation of private savings held abroad. Gross national savings would increase from the extremely low rate of about 10 percent of GDP in 1990 to 12.8 percent in 1994. Public savings would lead the recovery of savings in the initial phase, and would increase by more than 3 percentage points of GDP over the 1991-94 period. Private national savings would actually decrease in 1992, and the overall marginal domestic savings rate will be quite low (less

---

2   Since reliance on BONEX to back the monetary base is permitted, the Central Bank could conceivably reduce dollar reserves (e.g., by making an amortization payment) and shift BONEX into the legal reserve base. In practice, large or sustained use of this instrument would be self-defeating since financial markets would see this as disguised financing of the Treasury and quickly move out of domestic currency.

than 12 percent in 1992). The still-low domestic private savings are more than offset by the assumption that domestic residents will chose to hold domestic financial assets rather than foreign assets, as in the past. The repatriation of Argentine earnings on capital now held abroad would be a central element in the increased foreign savings, which would grow from about 2.1 percentage points of GDP in 1990 to 3.6 percent in 1992, and then would return to the level that reflects renewed confidence in the financial system.

Balance of Payments

11.   The Government's program relies on private capital inflows and increases in private domestic savings to finance investment. Tight fiscal policy and passive but predictable monetary policy would continue to make the investment in Argentine financial and real assets attractive. Domestic interest rates would remain above international rates in real terms, and domestic investment, long with a rich unrealized potential, would offer high financial returns for years. Given the estimated US$50-60 billion in net external private savings abroad, authorities foresee as these earnings as providing a reliable source of a steady inflow of capital, though perhaps slowing in 1993.

12.   The November 1992 changes in commercial policy--which increased the price of imports and exports in pesos--would help switch demand and channel resources from nontradeables back to tradeables, and drive the convergence of domestic and international prices. Capital inflows would slow gradually. Slower growth in the domestic market would be offset by more production directed toward export as a result of deregulation measures enhancing the productivity in the tradable sector. Nominal wages in the nontradeable sectors would fall relative to those in tradeables sector. As the demand for consumer credit weakens, credit is channelled into investment in productive activities that satisfies the new demand in net exports and internationally competitive domestic activities. The change in relative prices produces a switching of resources at the same time prices in the domestic market progressively converge with international prices. This smooth process would require no realignment of the nominal exchange rate. Growth could be maintained, and tax buoyancy allows the Government to attain revenues objectives. The resulting trade balance--and real exchange rate--would be a reflection of capital inflows to finance imports and the demand for Argentine assets. Reduced capital inflows in 1993 and beyond would imply lower import demand, and be reflected in slower growth. The Government anticipates that the trade surplus will recover progressively beginning in 1993.

External Financing to the Balance of Payments

13.   The capital account in the balance of payment reflects the summation of the projected changes in the net foreign asset position of the public and private sectors. The *public sector's* net external borrowing requirement is to be financed from net increases in exposure from the international financial institutions, and partial rollovers from bondholders and Paris Club reduce their exposure to the Government. Official lenders are expected to increase their lending to the Government, save for the IMF, which would begin to decrease its exposure after the termination of the Extended Fund

Facility. Much as with Mexico after its turning point in the late 1980s, the World Bank would increase its exposure in Argentina, but not substantially after the middle 1990s, nor would the IDB. The Paris Club, anticipated to provide roughly US$500 million in new financing, would still have negative net disbursements of funds as public financing to large investment projects would not be great. Private bondholders, including holders of BONEX, will be net recipients of funds, though the Government expects to refinance roughly three-quarters of bonds coming due.

14.   Private commercial banks, as a consequence of the DDSR deal, will also be net recipient of funds because of the amortization of arrears. In December 1992, the Government achieved a debt-reduction deal with its commercial creditors, covering US$21 billion in commercial debt and about US$8 billion of arrears. The deal's main benefits are the regularization of relations with creditors and the stopping of further arrears accumulation, which is expected to simulate external inflows.

15.   The *private sector* is projected to substantially increase its net investment in Argentina. Foreign direct investment is expected to increase at about 8 percent annually, to average about US$2 billion. Private short-term capital flows would have to average about US$5 billion--about 2 percent of GDP--to finance the projected current account deficit over 1993-2000. Since the Government has identified its financing, the actual financing requirement for the balance of payments will be a function of the desired savings-investment balance in the private sector.

Alternative Scenarios

16.   The EFF scenario is attainable if the Government continues to improve its fiscal position, and if the private markets behave in such a way as to allow a smooth transition to a sustainable balance of payments and growth path. However, even with adequate *ex ante* fiscal adjustment, it should be recognized that the economic growth may not be as high as projected. Slower growth or even a recession could come about through two related mechanisms. On the one hand, an "overshooting" of capital inflows may drive up imports and domestic asset prices to unsustainably high levels, and then, as the correction ensued, private capital flows would tamper off or even reverse, pushing up domestic interest rates. (Rising international interest rates could also slow capital inflows sharply.) Resulting higher domestic interest rates would dampen or even extinguish growth. At the same time, domestic prices may prove to be sticky downwards and converge to competitive international levels only slowly. Price setters, long used to mark-up pricing in oligopolistic environments, might not cut prices in the first months of slow demand--they might even continue to increase the prices. It might take several months of slow sales for firms to begin cutting prices to the degree necessary to adjust the overall price level. Nonetheless, slower growth could eventually facilitate the price convergence necessary to sustain the exchange rate regime and rekindle export-led growth.

17.   A recession would create added fiscal pressure with unpredictable consequences. As revenues fall and the domestic interest bill rose, the speed of the central government adjustment in reducing expenditures would determine the size of any increase in the Government's net borrowing requirement. Any increase in the

borrowing requirement would make it more difficult for the Government to achieve the partial rollover of its domestic debt with bondholders in its projections. A short growth recession would probably pose no major threat to the program.

18.　　　　Even with fiscal adjustment, the ease of capital mobility between currencies and across borders, superimposed on a small monetary base, means that the economy is still vulnerable to sudden changes in private expectations and portfolio shifts. Measures taken in November 1992 allowing dollar checking accounts and equalizing reserve requirements for pesos and dollars have stabilized the financial markets by separating risk of exchange rate changes from risks of maintaining savings in the financial system. A worsening macroeconomic panorama--or even random political or international events--could trigger a speculative attack on the peso. A sudden cycle of demonetization, very high interest rates and deep recession could produce some financial turbulence and pressure on the public banks. Nonetheless, international reserves are the highest in a decade and now cover virtually all public monetary liabilities, and this deters a speculative attack on the peso. The probability of these adverse events falls in direct relation to the Government's improvement of the fundamentals of public finance.

B. Sustainability of the Fiscal Balance

19.　　　　Since the public sector's deficit is one of the principal factors influencing the expectations of the private sector, future fiscal policy will have to be consistent with availability of finance to obviate a sudden flight from the peso, new devaluation, and an outburst of inflation. The Government's projections of its medium-term outlook are based on balancing fiscal accounts, a monetary regime that provides maximum confidence by removing the Central Bank as a source of instability, and a regulatory framework that promotes greater reliance on markets.

20.　　　　Over the 1993-2000 period, the Government's desired primary surplus and the post-DDSR interest burden would eliminate the net borrowing requirement through 1996, even after amortizing the BOCON at an accelerated rate. After 1996, the net unidentified financing gap of US$1.1 billion is less than 0.5 percent of GDP. These amounts are financeable in a world of price stability, growth, and continued payment performance. Price stability and an improved payment record will improve creditworthiness. Possible sources of financing include the foreign and domestic private sector. It is probable that Argentina could return to voluntary borrowing through bond issues in international capital markets at about the time heavy amortization payments are due--provided that the other scenario assumptions of fiscal restraint and price stability hold. The Government can also expect to mobilize considerable resources through the capitalized social security system.

21.　　　　The projections also underscore the lack of cushion in the near-term, especially since they are predicated on performance growth which, while consistent with potential, Argentina has not been able to achieve since the beginning of the century. The projections of any financing gap are sensitive to the continued willingness of present creditors to maintain Argentine exposure. The *gross borrowing requirement*--the total borrowing requirement of the public sector plus amortizations--would average US$5.9 billion in 1993-2000 or 2.5 percent of GDP. The decision by major creditors to reduce lending levels would require additional public sector adjustment. This is particularly true in the next three years, when the gross borrowing requirement is 3 percent of GDP and the transition to stability remains vulnerable to policy mistakes or external shocks.

22.   The financing gap to the public sector may well turn out to be larger than these projections. This shortage could result from five major factors: (i) the uncertainties about tax revenues associated with assumptions for growth, prices, and the exchange rate as well as tax policy framework; (ii) the increasing pressure on the Government to spend more on social sectors and investment; (iii) the uncertain costs of transition to the capitalized social security system; (iv) the near-term heavy indebtedness even after the debt-reduction deal and the continued vulnerability to interest rate surges; and (v) the settlement of domestic and pensioner arrears through the issue of new bonds (BOCON).

Revenues

23.   Uncertainty over revenue projections arise from both policy and macroeconomic assumptions. The Government tax revenue projections are based on channeling 15 percent of co-participation receipts to social security in 1993, and higher amounts in 1994. The employer's contribution to the Social Security System may be made deductible from VAT payments as revenues permit. Meanwhile, the Government has taken alternative measures that will affect positively tax revenues.[3] The main policy uncertainty is that Congress may substantially alter or delay approval of the revenue measures associated with social security.

24.   A second set of uncertainties arises from the favorable medium-term macroeconomic assumptions of the Government's projections. Slower growth would undoubtedly affect revenue buoyancy and require serious expenditure efforts at all levels of Government. More important, the grasp the Treasury has on revenues in the event of a recession may weaken as financial pressures to evade taxes rise. Since the elasticities of tax revenues are heavily affected by improvements in tax administration, it is not possible to estimate with any certainty the revenue losses if GDP growth falters; Table 14.2 presents a sensitivity analysis which relates lower-than-projected GDP growth (about 4.5 percent) with increases in the deficit, assuming that expenditures--other than formula-based transfers to the provinces--remain the same. A reduction in growth from 4.5 percent to 2.5 percent with an assumed elasticity of 1.5 would mean that the deficit would increase by US$1.4 billion.

---

3   As discussed in Chapter 3 these include: (i) the increase in the VAT rate from 16 percent to 18 percent; (ii) the increase in the tax rate of the corporate income tax from 20 percent to 30 percent; and (iii) the suspension of accumulated loss carryovers by a bond exchange program.

Table 14.2: Estimated Impact of Slower Growth on NFPS Deficit a/
(in US$ billions)

Tax Elasticities	Percent Deviation from Projected Growth b/			
	-1.0	-2.0	-3.0	-4.5
1.5	0.46	1.37	2.89	4.74
1.0	0.30	0.91	1.94	3.22
0.5	0.15	0.46	0.98	1.64

a/ Assumes that 85 percent of non-coparticipation revenues are
allocated to the Central Government.
b/ Based on 4.5 percent of GDP growth assumption in 1993 Federal Budget.

Source: World Bank staff estimates.

25. Similar problems would result from a resurgence of inflation or a devaluation. Vulnerability to inflation has been reduced through the reduction in payment lags, and the improvements in tax control systems, inspection and sanctions. But history dictates a cautious stance.

Expenditures

26. Overall public expenditures as a share of GDP, contrary to popular assertions, are not excessive. As noted in Chapter 1, public expenditures, equal to 22 percent of GDP at the federal level and 40 percent for total public expenditures, are below the average for the industrial countries' adjustment program--notably the administrative reform and the privatization program--have brought down federal public expenditures to levels that are a tolerable burden on the economy. However, the productivity of public expenditures probably has declined at a time when sustaining the recovery in the private sector requires an efficient public sector. The major expenditure problems of Argentina, therefore, are: first, to *enhance control*; second, to *improve the productivity* of both federal and provincial expenditures through improved allocation and program targeting; and third, to *reduce and reallocate spending at the provincial level*, since many provinces have yet to begin the adjustment needed to balance their budgets in a sustainable way.

27. This report has suggested expenditure reductions in selected areas in order to free up resources to meet demands for increased expenditures in health and education, which have been neglected over the last decade. The national Government may have to increase spending on national health insurance, while the provinces may have to increase expenditures associated with direct service delivery. In education, the provinces will not only have to expand educational spending on teacher salaries, but also improved teaching materials, facility maintenance, and school rehabilitation. To some extent, these could be financed through savings from reallocation within the provincial budgets and increases in coparticipation revenues. Also, scholarship spending at the national level should be increased to offset the impact of tuition increases on university students.

28. Future investment spending must make up for a decade of public disinvestment in those sectors remaining under the public domain for the foreseeable

future--roads, power, some hydrocarbon development, and social infrastructure. Investment at the federal level should increase by about US$1.5-2 billion by 1994 to maintain infrastructure and avoid constraining private growth.

Social Security

29.   The projections in the preceding section assume that the social security system reform will be passed with sufficient allocation of general revenues to cover large transitional deficits in the pension system itself. The social security reform will entail substantial transition costs since the Government has to pay the full pension of older workers along with present pensioners, while most of the contributions of younger workers are channelled into the new, capitalized system. The Government estimates the deficit of the system proper--before financing from general revenues--in the early years to be about US$5-7 billion. The system deficit would decline by about US$200 million per year thereafter. However, the amounts could be much larger depending on the final architecture of the program as approved by Congress. Reducing the minimum mandatory number of years of contribution, overly generous indexing, providing more benefits for workers between ages 35-45, or even failing to make projected improvements in evasion rates will markedly increase the fiscal costs of transition.

Financing: The Debt-Reduction Agreement

30.   The above projections include the effects of the recent debt-reduction deal between the Argentine Government and the commercial banks. At the end of 1991, Argentina's external debt was approximately US$61 billion, about 47 percent of GDP, and external interest and gross amortization due (including BONEX) still represented about 6 percent of GDP. An estimated US$33 billion represented medium-term commercial bank debt, including about US$8 billion of arrears. In December 1992, the Government singed a debt-reduction deal with its commercial creditors. The deal's main benefits are the regularization of relations with creditors and preventing further arrears accumulation, which is expected to simulate external inflows. The debt deal will substantially decrease accrued debt service payments to US$1.4 billion on average for the 1993-95 period, rising to US$3 billion by 2000, reflecting the rise in amortization of the arrears bonds to US$1.3 billion annually.

31.   The debt deal substantially improves the creditworthiness of the country by regularizing relations with creditors and by fixing the interest rate of about US$15 billion of debt. Nonetheless, interest rates on most domestic debt and on about half of commercial bank debt (including the restructure arrears) are linked to LIBOR. A one percentage point increase in LIBOR, other things being equal, would require a 4 percent contraction in Treasury spending to avoid a larger deficit. The situation will be further complicated by the fact that most of earning capacity for foreign exchange was (and continues to be) in the private sector. Under these circumstances, the major problem will not be achieving an external surplus but transferring this surplus from the private to the public sector.

Financing: the BOCON and Privatization Revenues

32.   Over the last few years, the Government has accumulated arrears with pensioners and domestic suppliers. In addition, the Government, as part of its income tax reform, suspended the poorly designed loss-carry-forward deductions for the corporate income tax, with the agreement to issue some US$4 billion in compensatory bonds. In addition, settling arrears between the health funds (*obras sociales*) and their providers will also result in additional issues.

33.   To settle problems with suppliers and pensioners, the authorities were authorized to issue a consolidation bond on May 1, 1992 (BOCON). This bond is projected to be allocated in 1992 and the beneficiaries will have the choice between a bond denominated in local currency with a domestic interest rate and a bond denominated in US dollars with the LIBOR. The service of the debt will be capitalized for the first six years (from May 1991), but debt service payments on the order of US$5.3 billion will be required in this decade between 1997 and 2000. It is noteworthy that these figures were obtained assuming that the private sector will be able to refinance voluntarily about US$2 billion of the bonds coming due. To avoid a fiscal shock, the Government should use part of the privatization revenues to reduce its stock of foreign and domestic debt. The analysis developed in Chapter 9 shows that such allocation of privatization revenues may lead to a reduction in the debt stock of about US$6 billion, representing a yearly savings in interest payments of US$400 million.

C. Savings from Recommended Reforms

34.   Because of the continued vulnerability to macroeconomic events outside its control, the Government must continue to improve the structural underpinnings of public finances. This report has identified several measures--summarized in the Executive Summary--that could provide additional savings and enhance the efficiency of the public sector. The different measures would reduce the public sector structural deficit between 1.2 percent and 1.4 percent of GDP in 1993-95,[4] and provide for increased spending where necessary to improve overall productivity. Savings from the recommended measures are presented in Table 14.3 in comparison with the baseline scenario proposed in the Extended Fund Facility Program (March 1992).

35.   The total savings for the consolidated public sector of the proposed measures is about US$2.2 billion for 1993, US$2.1 billion for 1994, and US$2.6 billion for 1995. These results would be sufficient to generate the resources necessary to accommodate the new demands on public resources and available sources of financing. Moreover, the efficiency of the Government with respect to tax revenues and investment should be enhanced through additional investment in social sectors at the federal and provincial levels in 1994 and 1995. While most savings in 1993 would be generated by privatization and assets sales, the gains in 1995 would only come from an increase in the efficiency of current revenues and expenditures.

---

4   The major recommendations are presented at the end of each chapter and summarized in the Executive Summary of the report.

Table 14.3: Argentina: Cummulative Savings from Public Sector Reforms
(Savings compared to policies assumed in 1992 EEF)
(In US$ Millions)

	1993	1994	1995
Total Savings from Recommendations	2,238	2,102	2,654
Federal Government	1,670	1,200	1,650
National Administration	3,870	3,200	3,450
Total Revenues	2,400	1,800	1,800
Current Revenues	2,000	1,800	1,800
Tax Administration a/	800	900	1,000
Industrial Promotion b/	1,200	900	800
Privatization c/	400	0	0
Total Expenditures	1,470	1,400	1,650
Current Expenditures	1,070	1,600	1,850
Wages d/	200	300	350
Earmarking e/	200	200	200
Education & Health f/	200	400	450
Defense g/	150	300	400
Presidency h/	320	400	450
which: Privatization of CNEA	300	100	0
Capital Expenditures i/	400	(200)	(200)
Social Security	(2,200)	(2,000)	(1,800)
Public Enterprises	0	0	0
Provincial Government	0	600	900
Total Revenues	800	1,100	1,000
Current Revenues j/	600	800	1,000
Capital Revenues	200	300	0
Total Expenditures	(800)	(500)	(100)
Current Expenditures k/	(500)	(200)	200
Capital Expenditures l/	(300)	(300)	(300)
Financial Public Sector	568	302	104
Central Bank m/	18	22	24
Provincial Banks n/	550	280	80
which: Privatization	500	200	
Memo :			
Total Current Savings	738	2,002	3,154
Total Capital Savings	1,500	100	(500)
Total Savings-Percent of GDP	1.3%	1.2%	1.4%
Federal Savings o/	1,670	1,200	1,650
Net Federal Savings p/	517	162	612
Provincial Savings p/	1,153	1,638	1,938

a/ Includes improvement in DGI and Customs administrations of about 0.5 percent of GDP.
b/ Assumes the implementation of the bond exchange program in mid-1992.
c/ Includes the privatization of companies which are not included in official projections.
   of US$300 million in 1993.
d/ Includes the developement of a computerized check payment system.
e/ Assumes the elimination of the Tobacco Funds and the reduction of the Grain Comission.
f/ Includes a reduction of 10 percent of National Health Insurance Budget and
   a reform of Universities financing based on a system of fees.
g/ Includes retrenchment at the 20-25 levels of about 25 percent.
h/ Includes the progressive elimination of Funcion Publica and transfers of some activities
   to other Ministeries.
i/ Includes modifications in Atucha II, Pichi Picun Leufu and the Fonavi Housing Program.
   Simultaneously an Investment Fund is created generating an increase in public investment
   of 0.5 percent of GDP.
j/ Transfers of DGI administration to provinces.
k/ Assumes that 100,000 workers leave provincial employment in 1993 and 100,000 in 1994. The savings
   will be used to pay indemnization costs and wage increases (about 10 percent on average).
l/ Assumes that provincial investment increases by 20 percent.
m/ Includes Administrative Reform, removal of liquididtion function and the stengthen of
   the Superintendency of banks.
n/ Gains equal to the Provincial Banks deficit in 1992.
o/ Before Revenue Sharing.
p/ After Revenue Sharing.

Revenues

36.   **Current Revenues**.   Although some tax policy changes have been recommended (see Chapter 3), no additional savings have been projected for 1993-95. Improvements in income tax receipts beyond those projected by the Government could be used to offset reductions in the payroll taxes.   Two measures that would affect the revenue side of public finances significantly are: the improvement of the tax administration and reform of the Industrial Promotion Program.   Regarding the tax administration, projected additional reserves are assumed to be 0.5 percent of GDP in 1993 and less than 0.1 percent of GDP in 1994 and 1995.   These figures can be compared to the results achieved in 1991, which is estimated to be above 3 percent of GDP.   Although the DGI has made substantial improvements in tax administration in the last 12 months, continuation of these improvements would yield significant external revenues.

37.   The Government has taken measures to control industrial promotion through the tax credit program, cancellation of benefits not yet activated, and careful auditing of existing beneficiaries with a view toward cancellation of benefits (Chapter 4).   The additional revenues are estimated at US$1.2 billion in 1993, US$900 million in 1994, and US$800 million in 1995.   These figures take into account the benefits from the audit of firms but paid no taxes during the suspension of benefits in 1990.   This process could yield revenues of more than US$300 million.

38.   **Capital Revenues**. Assuming that the privatization program is complete as scheduled, cash resources are estimated at US$350 million in 1993 according to the Government's January program.   However, this projection does not include the privatization of Encotel, AGP (Port Authority), OSN, and part of the railways.   This additional source of capital revenues would generate US$400 million in 1993.   These do not include the privatization receipts of Gas del Estado, YPF, or other remaining asset sales the Government intends to use to reduce its liabilities.

Current Expenditures

39.   **Wage Bill.** The Government's projections of the wage bill in the budget provide for three consecutive years of 10 percent annual increases, assuming no change in public employment.   Several measures have been recommended in this report, including the completion of the restructuring process in all Government agencies, the development of a computerized registry of civil service, the centralization of the payment function directly or through ministerial accounts in line with the new law of Public Finances, and the implementation of a computerized check-payment system through the banking system to control the wage bill.   Only the impact of the last measure has been included in 1993 in the projected additional savings.   Preliminary estimates indicate that as much as US$200 million can be saved from administrative costs and from reductions in wages to nonexistent workers.   In 1994 and 1995, additional savings will be provided by the extension of the restructuring process to all official agencies.

40.   **Health and Education**. In health, the Government's enactment of the planned reform of the social insurance funds would improve the quality of health care and reduce the substantial inefficiency of health insurance in the sector. This could provide both a source of additional savings in 1993 as well as major improvements in the productiveness of health care expenditures. This measure is projected to reduce the National Health Insurance budget by about 10 percent more. On the other hand, the decentralization of health care provision to the provinces will require increased spending at the subnational level (see below). Concerning the subsidies to universities, an interim policy option would be to establish a combination of user fees--i.e., tuition and targeted subsidies (e.g., loans and scholarships for low-income, meritorious students) to enhance financing. If the system's 700,000 students were charged a modest tuition of US$100 per term plus US$20 per month (private universities charge US$250-600 in annual tuition plus US$300-800 month), the Government could mobilize nearly US$300 million of additional funds. Adopting a needs-based, targeted student loan program would ensure that low-income students would have access to a university education. In Table 14.3, the combination of the two measures is projected to provide an additional savings of US$200 million in 1993.

41.   **Military Expenditures**. The Government has launched an ambitious program to restructure the military and Ministry of Defense. The reductions in civilian employment in the Estados Mayores has substantially offset the cost of recent wage increases. The program of restructuring the defense establishment should be used, at least partially, to provide severance payments and adjustment assistance as well as reform for the military pension system. However, Chapter 7 estimates that retrenchments at levels 20 to 25, if they become policy, could provide about US$150 million annually in additional savings after the first year, which also gives some scope for pay increases at higher levels.

42.   **Presidency**. The Administrative Reform should be extended into the Presidency as it has been implemented in other governmental agencies. In addition, some activities (such as sports or tourism) will need to be transferred to their respective provinces. The downsizing of the Civil Service Office (*Funcion Publica*) and return of its functions to the Ministry of Economy could save about US$150 million. Finally, the privatization of some parts of CNEA, e.g., commercial activities, would provide additional net savings of about US$300 million. Conservatively, these measure are supposed to reduce the expenditures of the Presidency by about US$320 million in 1993, of which US$300 million will come from the partial privatization of the nuclear agency.

43.   **Capital Expenditures**. The Government projects an increase in public investment of more than 100 percent by 1994 relative to 1991. In the wake of a decade-long decline in public investment, deterioration in basic infrastructure, and possible shortages of basic, publicly provided inputs (such as electricity) in the second half of the 1990s, increased investment is economically desirable.

44.   Nonetheless, the projected investments and their allocation merit some discussion. Two major projects should be reviewed to determine if they are consistent with the Government's medium-term investment strategy: Atucha II and the FONAVI housing program. Possible savings from these measures would amount to nearly

US$1.4 billion in 1992, and could be used for investments in road maintenance, acceleration of Yacyreta and Piedra de Aguila hydropower schedules, and increased investments in critical provincial health and education projects. To incorporate these two opposite tendencies, capital expenditures are first projected to decline by an additional US$400 million in 1993, and then to increase by US$200 million in 1994 and 1995.

Social Security

45.   The Government in its initial June 1992 projections for 1992-94 has assumed that the social security system, after financing from general revenues, will produce a surplus sufficient to buy back US$1 billion of BOCON in 1993 and US$750 million in 1994. However, the costs of the reform could rise substantially if Congress modifies the proposals. These could include changes in the indexing system for the transition, minimum years necessary to contribute (proposed to be 30), and the pension benefits for present contributors. For these reasons, we have allocated an additional cost of US$2 billion in 1993-95 in Table 14.3.

Provinces

46.   The new concept of Argentina's public sector requires provincial governments to play important roles as providers of services formerly offered at the national level--health, education, water, electricity distribution, and local road maintenance. Although these new responsibilities are supposed to have been taken into account in the 1992 budget, they will induce additional pressure on provincial expenditures. Administrative reforms similar to that designed at the national level to reduce employment in many provinces also is expected to reduce the wage bill. However, these savings could finance an increase in wages of about 15 percent. In addition, current spending on health care programs might actually rise beyond savings from a much-needed administrative reform. Public investment at the provincial level is projected to increase by 10 percent from 1993 onwards. On the revenue side of provincial finances, the privatization of several public enterprises will provide additional savings in 1993 and 1994. The transfer of the tax administration systems now in operation at DGI and improved collections of sales and land taxes should improve the efficiency of the tax administration. The improvement of the provincial tax system is assumed to be about 5 percent of total revenues in 1993, 1.5 percent in 1994, and 1.3 percent in 1995. Note that these figures are significantly lower than the recent results obtained at the federal level.

Financial Public Sector

47.   **Central Bank.** Chapter 13 recognizes the complexity of implementing a major reorganization of the Central Bank in the context of Argentina's complex labor legislation and powerful unions, and in the midst of other major reforms of the financial system. Nonetheless, it is critical to accelerate the removal of the liquidation function from the Central Bank. While these measures are likely to reduce the size of the Central Bank, the authorities should simultaneously reinforce the Superintendency of Banks by ensuring greater administrative independence and enactment of its upgraded

salary and organizational structure. This should provide an additional savings of about US$18 million in 1993, US$22 million in 1994, and US$24 million in 1995.

48.   **Provincial Banks**.   The privatization and the merger process which already began in some provinces is assumed to spread to others.

D. Conclusion

49.   The efforts of the Government over the last three years have been the basis of the present price stability and economic expansion.   The primary surplus increased sharply since 1990 and the efficiency of the public sector has been improved by several policies.   The Government program for the rest of the decade appears consistent with the macroeconomic objectives, since a further adjustment effort of the public sector is projected over the rest of the decade; the primary surplus is expected to increase in 1993-95.   However, the sustainability of the Government program may be endangered by at least five factors: (i) the uncertainty of macroeconomic and policy assumptions and their effects on revenue collection; (ii) the increasing pressure on the Government to spend more on social sectors and investment; (iii) the costs of transition to the capitalized social security system; (iv) vulnerability of the fiscal accounts to interest rates rises in the short term; and (v) the settlement of domestic and pensioners arrears through the issue of new bonds (BOCON).

50.   The Government thus needs to sustain the efforts it already has taken. Based on the recommendations of this report, several measures could provide additional savings to provide a cushion and offset any negative impact of new demands on public resources.   These measures would reduce the overall deficit of the public sector between 1.2 percent and 1.4 percent of GDP over the next three years.   In addition, the efficiency of the public sector would be enhanced since public investment at the federal and provincial level are projected to increase in the social sectors (e.g., education and health) and in infrastructure (e.g., road maintenance).   This effort will contribute to increasing the long-term growth of the economy.

ANNEX 1.1

SUBSIDIES TO THE PRIVATE SECTOR

A. Overview

1.   Subsidies were widely used in Argentina during the 1980s. Subsidies can be divided into four groups: (i) direct Treasury expenditures which are explicitly specified and budgeted; (ii) tax exemptions and tariff incentives which, in general, are not an explicit entry in the public budget; (iii) public tariff regulations resulting in pricing policies that transfer benefits across various sectors of the economy; and (iv) Central Bank policy that favors certain sectors through rediscounts and subsidized interest rates.

Table A1.1.1: SUBSIDY OVERVIEW
(US$ million)

	1987	1988	1989	1990	1991
Explicitly Budgeted Expenditures	1062	919	884	1036	661
National Feeding Plan (PAN)	-	-	208	-	-
Private School Subsidies	191	201	120	222	249
Emergency Feeding Plan	-	-	60	-	-
National Housing Fund (FONAVI)	864	603	428	810	411
Export Promotion Fund	7	9	8	-	1
Tax Rebates & Treasury Endorsements		106	60	4	--
Tax Exemptions and Promotion Regimes	4658	5466	3147	3766	3821
Export Expenditure Supplement	20	140	-	-	-
Import Expenditure Supplement	-	368	-	-	-
Special Combustible Plan	321	388	79	17	-
VAT Exemptions	2822	2808	1610	1720	2100
Income Tax Exemptions	-	105	-	63	21
Industrial Promotion	817	775	868	1123	1928
Mining Development	18	12	-	-	-
Overpricing of State Purchases due to Tariff Protection	660	870	590	734	572
Agricultural Regulations	295	452	241	82	221
Special Tobacco Fund	93	67	97	77	126
Sugar System	194	373	136	5	94
Winery Development	8	12	8	-	-
Public Tariffs	1808	352	1606	-124	-702
Petroleum Products	1107	218	775	-	-
Natural Gas	234	-32	527	-124	-702
Electricity	467	165	304	n.a.	n.a.
Central Bank Rediscounts	n.a.	864	2102	-438	412
Total	7929	8007	7924	4308	4413

Source: Staff estimates.

2.   This paper focuses only on those subsidies that were significant in terms of the estimation of their cost. Table A1.1.1 provides a summary of these subsidies. There are three qualifications worthy of recognition before proceeding with the details about Argentine subsidies. First, the focus is on subsidy expenditure, rather than a

cost-benefit measure of their effectiveness. Benefits have to be considered when evaluating any subsidy program, they are much more difficult to quantify. Second, estimation of subsidy cost is based on economic criteria. For example, under the feeding programs the estimated subsidy coincides with budgeted expenditures for the program. This contrasts with the calculation of Central Bank rediscount subsidies where the state should recover some of its expenditure. In other cases the methodology is even more complex; public tariff subsidies (combustibles) are calculated with reference to prices of substitutes, and tax exemptions require estimates of fiscal costs.

B. Direct Treasury Expenditures

3.   In 1987-89, there were a plethora of directly budgeted subsidies. They range from the provision of housing to the funding of domestic cinematographic activity. As Table A1.1.1 shows, many of these subsidies were gradually phased out during 1990 and 1991. Of these subsidies we can identify five programs which are important in terms of the proportion of budgeted funds they command.

Table A1.1.2: SUBSIDIES WHICH ARE PART OF BUDGETED EXPENDITURE
(US$ million) a/

	1987		1988		1989		1990		1991	
	Amount	% of Total	Amount	% of Total	Amount	% of Total	Amount	% of Total	Amount	% of Total
National Feeding (PAN)	-	0.0	-	0.0	208.0	30.6	-	0.0	-	0.0
Medical	0.6	0.0	-	0.0	-	0.0	-	0.0	-	0.0
Private Schools	191.6	15.6	201.0	20.5	120.1	17.8	221.8	21.4	249.2	37.6
Emergency Feeding Bonds	-	0.0	-	0.0	60.0	8.9	n.a.	n.a.	n.a.	n.a.
Housing (FONAVI)	864.0	70.5	603.0	61.6	428.0	63.6	809.8	78.3	411.3	62.0
Civil Aeronautics		14.0	1.1	11.0	1.1	10.0	1.5	1.4	0.1	-0.0
Transportation	4.0	0.3	4.0	0.4	4.0	0.6	1.0	0.1	0.5	0.1
Merchant Marine	5.5	0.4	43.6	4.6	26.7	4.0	-	0.0	0.3	0.0
Educ.& Coop Promotion	-	0.0	1.1	0.1	0.9	0.1	-	0.0	0.1	0.0
Cinematography	15.0	1.2	5.0	0.5	5.0	0.7	1.4	0.1	0.6	0.1
Export Promotion	7.5	0.6	9.1	0.9	8.1	1.2-	0.0	0.0	0.5	0.0
Forestry	17.0	1.4	11.0	1.1	6.1	0.9	0.1	0.0	0.3	0.0
Tax Rebates & Prom. Notes	106.0	8.7	90.8	9.3	4.5	0.7	-	0.0	-	0.0
Total	1225.2	100.0	979.6	100.0	881.4	100.0	1035.5	100.0	662.8	100.0

a/ Official exchange rate.

Source: Staff estimates.

National Feeding Plan and Emergency Feeding Bonds

4.   These two programs, along with the medical assistance fund, are a reaction to the social shortcomings identified in the 1984 census. Both are direct programs in the sense that the state pays the beneficiary in order to reduce the price of the service in question.

5.   The national feeding plan (PAN) was created in 1984 for two years and extended for another two. The program had annual budgeted expenditures of US$200 million, of which 90 percent was allocated for the purchase of foodstuffs, and the remainder for administration, packaging, and delivery. The plan purchased foodstuffs at a discount of about 40 percent of the retail price.

6.   Criticisms of the plan, which led to its reorganization, included the determination and selection of aid eligibility (said to be highly politicized), the lack of evidence that the plan is producing benefits (another census may be required before the plan can be fully evaluated), its limited scope (concerned only with foodstuff disbursement, not with sanitary conditions, health, etc.), and an excessively centralized bureaucracy with little direct provincial participation in implementation or decision making.

7.   As a result the emergency bonds plan was created by the 1989 government to overcome the inefficient bureaucracy of PAN by means of more direct participation of provinces and municipalities. The Government issued bonds to municipalities, which in turn could be exchanged for explicitly listed foodstuffs. The method of assigning funds, determining eligibility, etc., were again criticized. As a result, the foodstuff subsidy program was drastically reduced to US$22 million in 1992.

Private School Subsidies

8.   In Argentina the public sector spends roughly 3 percent of GDP on education combined with additional contributions of less than 2 percent of GDP from the private sector. Part of this public sector expenditure (20 percent) goes to reimbursing private schools for their faculty payroll.

9.   The program is perceived as a subsidy for the relatively wealthy, who can afford private schools. This may not be the case when considering the increase in expenditures necessary to educate these students if they were in public schools. Moreover, higher quality education is perceived to be provided in private schools. To ensure this quality a method could be devised where students themselves receive a subsidy to be redeemed by their school and thus are allowed to "vote with their feet." Such is the case in Chile.

National Housing Fund (FONAVI)

10.   Managed by the Ministry of Urban Development and Housing, FONAVI is a complement to the Banco Hipotecario Nacional (National Mortgage Bank). The fund has a multiple role: its primary function is the construction of housing for those segments of the population identified by their inability to afford it; however, it is also involved in subsidized loans as well as selection of beneficiaries.

11.   As is evident from the table, a minimum of FONAVI funding comes from the repayment of loans. The main problem is that the fund has no well-established means to enforce repayment. Thus, the predominant source of finance was, until 1992, a 5 percent payroll tax; since then, it has been earmarked from the fuel tax.

12.   FONAVI purchases materials and supervises the construction of housing, which guarantees that the funds are spent for their intended purpose. The efficiency of this centralized management is offset by improprieties associated with procurement--evident in the average costs per unit, which are more than two times the "real" cost. Assignment of funds across provinces could be more efficient as well; no consideration is given to those provinces that are more diligent in recovering funds. Moreover, the provision of funds operates as a substitute for private savings when it should be a complement.

13.   When choosing FONAVI alternatives to achieve greater efficiency, the key is permitting individual incentives and eliminating the role of the state in construction. Local government could be responsible for beneficiary selection and private banks could take over the management of loans. Instead of actually disbursing loans, FONAVI could make up the difference between the market rate of interest and the subsidized rate it desires. Finally, if the individual is allowed to select his/her own housing from the marketplace, this would lead to a reduction in costs. It is believed that these measures would lead to a 50 percent savings of resources, which would allow the plan to broaden its scope.

Tax Rebates

14.   A program that has enjoyed widespread use since the beginning of the 1970s is the return of state taxes to contractors and suppliers that worked on projects considered in the national interest, or which participated in international bidding. The terms of eligibility were quite specific and focus on the level of domestic content. These expenditures were practically eliminated after 1989.

Table A1.1.3:   FONAVI - COMPLETED HOUSING AND LOAN RECOVERY
(US$ million) a/

Year	FONAVI Sources	In US$	Loan Recovery		Housing Units Completed b/	Cost per Unit (US$ thousands)
			% of Sources	FONAVI Investments		
1978	681.1	-	-	618.9	11585	53.4
1979	761.3	0.8	0.1	558.6	16086	34.7
1980	790.2	8.4	1.1	578.6	31506	18.4
1981	458.6	13.7	3.0	597.1	27130	22.0
1982	579.8	11.1	1.9	540.1	34636	15.6
1983	550.1	5.5	1.0	506.6	39516	12.8
1984	458.7	3.5	0.8	400.1	20371	19.6
1985	583.2	2.7	0.5	396.3	20316	19.5
1986	890.0	8.7	1.0	585.1	21134	27.7
1987 c/	823.4	8.0	1.0	958.7	36223	26.5
Average	657.6	6.2	.95	564.0	25750	21.9
Total	6576.4	62.4	.95	5640.1	257502	21.9

a/ Official exchange rate.
b/ FONAVI constructs multifamily public housing.
c/ As of November 30.

Source: Secretary of Housing, Information Bulletin.

Promissory Notes

15.   Another popular mechanism is the use of guarantees and Treasury endorsements to facilitate the access of Argentine businesses into private or international capital markets. Eligible industries include those in the special tax rebate sectors and public enterprises (which were given special political consideration). As a result of mismanagement and moral hazard on the part of the participants, a large proportion of the guarantees were funded directly via Treasury resources (see Table A1.1.5). Law 23,659 was enacted in 1988 in response to expressly prohibit the granting of these notes by executive decree.

Table A1.1.4: FISCAL EXPENDITURE ON THE REBATE OF TAXES
FOR SPECIFIC NATIONAL PROJECTS
(US$ millions) a/

Benefit	1984	1985	1986	1987	1988	1989b/
Certificates of tax rebates issued by the National Treasury	24.4	3.0	3.0	14.0	16.0	1.0
VAT (IVA) Rebates	24.0	2.7	2.7	13.6	15.0	1.2
Draw Back (By the Treasury) c/	-	3.9	9.2	8.8	4.5	0.4
Total	48.4	9.6	14.9	36.4	35.5	2.6

a/   Official exchange rate.
b/   1989 rebates were calculated until September, at which time they became limited.
c/   A restricted form of import tax rebates (discussed in the next section).

Source: Staff estimates.

Table 1.1.5: PROMISSORY NOTES GRANTED TO PRIVATE INVESTMENTS
AND CHARGED TO THE TREASURY
(US$ million) a/

Activities	Notes Granted 1976-88	Notes Charged b/						
		1985	1986	1987	1988	1989	1990	1991
Celluloid and Paper	1481.6	41.2	45.3	49.4	-	-	-	-
Shipping	371.9	15.8	5.6	1.9	23.4	1.6	-	-
Chemical/Petrochemical	490.7	15.4	4.6	1.7	-	-	-	-
Steelworks/Metallurgy	355.2	2.4	3.5	2.5	0.2	-	-	-
Fishery	76.4	-	1.2	-	-	-	-	-
Refrigeration	74.2	-	1.7	2.3	-	-	-	-
Others	217.7	22.1	0.9	11.0	0.2	-	-	-
Total	3067.7	96.9	62.8	68.8	23.8	1.6	-	-

a/ In constant US dollars--deflated via US GDP deflator.
b/ Law 23,669 in 1988 restricted executive power to grant endorsements.

Source: Ministry of Economy.

16.   It is uncertain whether the overall decline in expenditures during 1985-89 has resulted due to a drop in participation, new (and stricter) definitions of eligibility, changes in Argentine debt servicing policy, different methods of financing, or the impact of inflation.

C. Tax Exemptions, Tariff Incentives and Development Regimes

17.   Until 1990, Argentina had simultaneously engaged in import substitution and export promotion to increase its industrial base.

Import Incentives

18.   A method does not exist to disaggregate the various contributions of protectionist concepts, but an overall estimate is given in Table A1.1.6. In addition, the level of protection becomes higher when one considers the arduous bureaucratic barriers, which are impossible to measure.

Table A1.1.6: 1988 IMPORT EXEMPTIONS
(US$ millions)

	1988	1989	1990
Via tariffs	620.0	585.1	57.5
Latin American Integration Association (ALADI)	356.0	276.9	384.5
Tierra del Fuego	280.9	290.7	280.9
Industrial Promotion	334.5	267.6	208.7
Temporary Exemption	191.0	229.0	279.8
Steelworks	413.6	305.0	295.9
Other	195.4	151.2	197.1
Total Exemptions	2391.3	2105.5	1704.4
Total Imports from these Sectors	5322.0	4203.2	4079.0
Exemptions as a percentage of Imports	44.9	50.1	41.8

Source: Ministry of Economy.

19.   This sort of protection supported industries which are not disciplined by the rigors of international competition and can therefore lead to inefficiency. Moreover, while the opening of certain domestic markets to ALADI imports has the potential to be beneficial, it may not be the most suitable mechanism: goods from the ALADI countries may as well be produced inefficiently. Another complication of the import incentive program is that when 40 to 50 percent of imports enter the country duty free, this greatly increases the level of effective protection the import sector receives and significantly adds to the indirect costs placed on the export sector.

Export Benefits

20.　　　　Subsidies are needed in the export sector to remove the bias against exporters inherent in Argentina's import substitution program and tax policy. These subsidies serve a dual purpose of export promotion and the development of specific regions within Argentina.

21.　　　　Complete or partial refund of internal and export taxes are available to most exporters of industrial goods. Rebates on domestic taxes apply to Argentine goods used in the export production process. A considerably higher rebate for unreported intermediate goods and overall export taxes can be achieved via the Draw Back promotion plan for those producers who can validate significant value-added.

Table A1.1.7:　COST OF THE PREFERENTIAL EXPORT PROGRAM
(US$ millions)

	1987	% of Total	1988	% of Total	1989	% of Total	1990	% of Total
Total Tax Rebates a/	333.7	56.6	380.0	54.2	595.0	85.9	550.8	87.2
Trade Rebates b/	104.0	17.6	320.0	45.6	340.2	49.1	295.3	46.7
VAT and Other Tax Refunds	131.0	22.2	-	0.0	237.5	34.3	249.0	39.2
Tierra del Fuego	98.7	16.7	60.0	8.6	17.3	2.5	6.5	1.2
Special Promotion Regimes	113.C	19.2	173.3	24.7	98.0	14.1	81.2	12.8
Industrial Promotion	26.4	4.5	39.0	5.6	41.4	6.0	21.7	3.4
Patagonian Ports	16.8	2.8	19.0	2.7	21.5	3.1	26.0	4.1
Other Refunds	1.0	0.2	59.0	8.4	33.3	4.8	2.6	0.4
Special Export Programs	68.8	11.7	56.3	8.0	1.8	0.3	30.9	4.9
Income Tax Deduction c/	77.0	13.1	85.0	12.1	0.0	0.0	632.0	0.0
Total Tax Subsidies	523.7	88.8	638.3	91.1	693.0	100.0	632.0	100.0
Total Finance Subsidy d/	66.0	11.2	62.7	8.9	-	0.0	-	0.0
Total	589.7	100.0	701.0	100.0	693.0	100.0	632.0	100.0

a/　　Replaced by two-year bonds in 1989.
b/　　After 1988, trade rebates include VAT and other tax refunds.
c/　　Selected industries enjoyed a deduction of up to 10 percent FOB on exported goods.
d/　　BCRA figures.

Source: Ministry of Economy.

22.　　　　Regional development was also promoted via additional rebates for businesses whose exports originate in special areas and are shipped from ports or pass through customs in these locations. Examples of special areas included ports located south of the Colorado river (Patagonian Ports) and the provinces of Salta, Jujuy, and Tucuman.

23.　　　　The Central Bank also provided export incentives by rediscounting loans to exporters (either prefinancing or postfinancing). The loans commanded annual interest rates of around 5 percent (in dollar terms), and for durations that varied between 180 days and 3 years. The program was eliminated under the monetary reforms of March 1990.

24.   Although the subsidies were popular with exporters, it is uncertain whether or not they are effective in removing the indirect bias against them. To be effective the subsidies need to exceed these indirect taxes, estimated by the IMF to be around 19 percent.

25.   Another critique of the export subsidy program was that it favored industrial sector exports over agricultural ones. The preference was justified on the grounds that export taxes reflect the most efficient use of land.[1] This occurred via the conversion of agricultural land, which requires a high degree of capital intensity, into land for industrial purposes which is capital intensive.

26.   The special promotion regimes were eliminated under the economic emergency law of 1989, and the tax rebates were transformed into two-year bonds.

Compensation for the Import Tax on Combustibles

27.   In the 1980s, the Argentine state fixed the price consumers pay for all petroleum products, controlled the import and export of petroleum products, and was a direct participant in supply through its monopoly on crude and 60 percent market share of derivatives. In most cases the subsidy was the difference between the input price and actual cost, which in some cases was negative. Principal subsidies were the Alconafta Plan (suspended in 1988), royalties paid to provincial governments (frozen by the emergency laws in 1989), and preferential prices to petrochemical industries that were above comparable international grades. The complex system of compensation was eliminated with the deregulation of the petroleum industry in 1991.

Table A1.1.8: COMPENSATION FOR TAX ON COMBUSTIBLES
(US$ million)

Method of Compensation a/	1987 Expend.	1987 Subsidies	1988 Expend.	1988 Subsidies	1989 Expend.	1989 Subsidies	1990 Expend.	1990 Subsidies	1991 Expend.	1991 Subsidies
Petrochemicals	65.6	62.7	86.5	85.0	35.2	62.1	-	-	-	-
Contracts	40.3	-	57.3	-	124.5	-	82.1	-	13.8b/	-
Production	24.4	-	7.9	-	29.3	-	10.6	-	-	-
Kerosene	2.6	3.0	2.7	3.5	1.6	2.0	-	-	-	-
Alconafta	80.0	80.0	20.0	20.0	-	-	-	-	-	-
Royalties	336.7	174.8	443.1	279.8	206.3	14.9	99.6	16.7	28.7	-
Solvents	-	-	-	-	-	-	108.8	108.8	n.a.	-

a/   Subsides are valued with reference to the international price of the respective byproduct.
b/   Eliminated in February 1991.

Source: Staff estimates, Ministry of Economy, and Secretary of Energy.

---

1   Land is considered as an input equal to any other for export tax purposes.

Table A1.1.9: PREFERENTIAL INPUT TARIFFS ON PETROCHEMICALS
(US$ per unit)

	August 1987	July 1988	Sept. 1989
Naphta (cu m)			
Subsidized tariff	89.4	96.0	115.0
Wholesale price	160.3	155.8	115.0
International price	155.0	140.0	115.0
Propane (ton)			
Subsidized tariff	86.5	74.1	81.0
Supply price	153.3	140.5	81.0
International price	143.0	175.0	120.0
Butane (ton)			
Subsidized tariff	79.4	67.3	70.8
Supply price	118.3	140.5	70.8
International price	143.0	162.0	130.0
Ethanol (ton)			
Subsidized tariff	84.6	66.4	73.0
Supply price	121.8	125.8	73.0
International price	120.0	150.0	130.0

Note: The subsidized tariff reflects the price at which the Argentine Government
sells derivatives to domestic petrochemical enterprises.

Source: Staff estimates.

Various Agricultural Subsidies

28.   A majority of Argentina's agricultural industries existed in an environment biased toward the industrial focus of import substitution and export promotion regimes. However, several sectors enjoyed subsidies through price supports above international averages. The most important cases were the Special Tobacco Fund (FET) and the sugar system. Tobacco subsidies were mainly financed by cigarette taxes to duplicate the per kilogram income received by producers in neighboring Brazil. Eighty percent of the fund's resources are distributed to provinces according to their share in production, with the remaining 20 percent used by the fund to supplement collection shortfalls and address concerns in the various tobacco zones. Sugar is subsidized through import restrictions and domestic production quotas that limit arbitrage opportunities. The Emergency Laws of 1989 did not suspend these subsidies, but in 1992 the Treasury retained 30 percent of the Tobacco Fund.

Table A1.1.10: VARIOUS AGRICULTURAL SUBSIDIES
(US$ millions)

	1987	1988	1989	1990	1991
Special Tobacco Fund (FET)	93.0	67.0	97.0	76.7	126.3
Fund for the Formation of Wineries	8.0	12.0	8.0	-	-
Sugar System	194.0b/	373.0b/	136.0c/	5.4d/	94.3e/
Mate a/	0.4	0.3	0.2	-	-

a/ Defined as total income for the Mate regulatory commission.
b/ Calculated with reference to an international price of US$250 per ton.
c/ Calculated with reference to an international price of US$315 per ton.
d/ Calculated with reference to an international price of US$382 per ton.
e/ Calculated with reference to an international price of US$295 per ton.

Source: Staff estimates and Ministry of Economy.

VAT Exemptions

29.   The number of goods exempt from Argentina's value-added tax has varied substantially throughout the 1980s. In the reforms of 1981, the tax was extended to basic necessities; later these received exemptions. At present not only has the tax been reextended to these goods but also includes services as well. Nevertheless, exemptions did not vary substantially between 1987 and 1989 (see table below).

Table A1.1.11: SECTORS EXEMPT FROM THE VALUE-ADDED TAX, 1987-89

Sector	Percentage of GDP
Services	20.4
Agricultural Products	9.0
Combustibles	8.0
Construction	2.1
Tobacco	1.0
Printing	0.8
Other	7.8
Total	49.1

Source: Staff estimates.

30.   To calculate the subsidy, input-output tables were used to adjust the exempted base for the possibility that exemptions granted to these sectors are recovered elsewhere along the production line. A significant amount of exempt products were either inputs for, or require inputs of, sectors which are not exempt. Nevertheless an adjusted exempted base of 49.1 percent of GDP creates an immense burden on those sectors to which the VAT applies.

31.   The cost of these exemptions was calculated as the proportion of the VAT that would apply to the exempted base (in percentage of GDP). It is estimated that

exemptions had a fiscal cost of US$6 billion[2] in 1987, US$6.4 billion in 1988, US$4.3 billion in 1989, US$3.4 billion in 1990, and US$4.2 billion in 1991. These estimates are sensitive to assumptions that agents in the exempted sectors will pay punctually and without significant evasion.

Development Regimes

32.   The provinces of La Rioja, Catamarca, San Juan, and San Luis manage their own industrial promotion regimes while the remaining provinces are centrally administered by the Ministry of Industry and International trade. The regimes have undergone several important adjustments in recent years: in 1988 Congress severely limited the benefits firms could receive by estimating the theoretical opportunity cost of fiscal incentives and coordinating them with strict accounting measures which were applied only at the end of 1992 (see Chapter 4). The purpose of this program was to limit any possibility of dual benefits by means of legal fiscal exemptions and illegal evasion. In 1989 the emergency laws further reduced all previous benefits granted by 50 percent for two years.

33.   In addition to regional policies of development, Argentina has targeted several industries for special consideration. Mining has been generously promoted by the National Secretary of Mining, but only 19 firms participated in their tax deferral plan. Procurement was promoted through the Compre Nacional Plan. The regime established a buffer between international and local prices under which Argentine firms were able to compete for government contracts. In 1990, the buffer was limited to 15 percent, with the objective of dealing with rising procurement costs, and in 1991 the regime was suspended with the Deregulation Decree 2284 in October.

Table A1.1.12:   FISCAL COST OF INDUSTRIAL PROMOTION
(US$ million) a/

	1987	1988	1989	1990	1991
VAT, Profit, and Capital	594	668	868	1123	1928
Investment Deferment	181	64	n.a.	n.a.	n.a.
Mining	17.8	11.8	n.a.	n.a.	n.a.
Procurement	660	870	590	734	572

a/ Official exchange rate.

Source: Staff estimates.

---

2   Official dollars.

D. Public Tariff Subsidies

34.   The alternatives for measuring subsidies are discussed with a distinction drawn between those goods for which an international price exists, and those for which no substitute (either import or export) can be defined. In the first case, the opportunity cost is obvious: it is the difference between the domestic and international price. The second case is more difficult since the definition of acceptable substitutes and estimate actual production cost must be broader.

35.   **Goods for Which Well-Defined [3] Substitutes Exist**. A general method for quantifying such subsidies is to multiply the difference between the domestic and international price and the quantity consumed by period. International price corrections are made to compensate for the tax component of prices.[4] Complications arise when the methodology is applied to gas oil because domestic tax policy effectively overtaxes gasoline to facilitate an additional subsidy on gas oil through a lower tax component. To correct this, an alternative method for calculating the gas oil subsidy is suggested: because gas and fuel oil derivatives have similar international prices, eliminating the tax subsidy between them should make their domestic prices roughly equivalent. Therefore, another measure of the gas oil subsidy is the difference between the domestic prices of gas oil and regular gasoline multiplied by the quantity consumed.

36.   In addition, certain industries (fishing and electric power) and the southern zone of Argentina pay reduced prices for these inputs, which are set roughly at the cost of production.

37.   To reiterate, the technique used here measured the impact of artificially low prices in relation to their opportunity cost, independent of tax differences. In contrast, the subsidies in the petrochemical industry supported by the *Treasury* (discussed in previous sections) were counted against tax obligations; in this way producers recover from low selling (or high purchase) prices.

Natural Gas

38.   From Table A1.1.13 it is evident that the largest public tariff subsidies are those pertaining to the state's provision of natural gas to industry and consumers. The method for quantifying this subsidy is severely complicated by the fact that there is no obvious substitute available competitively. It is suggested that fuel oil is a reasonable substitute because many industries can easily adapt to it.

---

3   Here "well-defined" means that the good is readily available in an international (competitive) market.

4   For example, in a deregulated world a tax would continue to apply to gasoline and gas oil; thus, using tolls to finance roadway construction and maintenance would quickly prove to be unfeasible. In this specific case, the national transportation plan of 1978 specifies that these taxes should generate revenue of no less than 2 percent of GDP.

Table A1.1.13: PUBLIC SUBSIDIES ON FUEL TARIFFS
(US$ million) a/

	1987	1988	1989	1990	1991
Fuels					
Final Product b/	1107.4	218.0	774.7	0.0	0.0
c/	1746.4	1417.0	744.7	1203.0	1745.0
Gasoline (Super)	0.0	0.0	0.0	0.0	0.0
Gasoline (Regular)	0.0	0.0	61.0	0.0	0.0
Gas Oil					
First Alternative d/	988.0	139.0	615.0	0.0	0.0
Second Alternative e/	1827.0	1338.0	806.0	1203.0	1745.0
Fuel Oil	0.0	0.0	0.0	0.0	0.0
Diesel Oil	31.1	0.0	8.7	0.0	0.0
Kerosene	88.3	79.0	70.0	0.0	0.0
Preferred Consumers f/					
Electric Powerplants	106.0	199.0	110.0	0.0	0.0
Commercial Fishing	30.0	42.0	41.0	47.7	33.6
Southern Zone	14.3	16.9	8.8	0.0	0.0
Natural Gas					
Method I: no taxes	363.8	71.0	789.2	474.0	60.5
Domestic	100.3	4.1	269.7	110.0	-68.0
Electric Powerplants	88.1	1.6	223.0	210.0	120.1
Other	175.3	1.4	276.6	154.0	9.4
Method II: Including Taxes	233.8	-31.5	527.3	-124.5	-701.7
Domestic	83.0	-8.4	243.4	-63.4	-371.0
Electric Powerplants	63.3	-8.9	163.9	91.7	66.0
Other	107.5	-16.3	130.1	-152.8	-396.7
Method III: with VAT g/	451.7	91.3	887.4	536.9	69.8
Domestic	125.6	5.0	311.1	124.3	-80.6
Electric powerplants	108.7	2.1	267.0	238.0	138.2
Other	217.4	20.0	319.3	174.6	12.2

a/   At average official exchange rate.
b/   Total as calculated using Gas Oil alternative 1.
c/   Total as calculated using Gas Oil alternative 2.
d/   Opportunity cost is international price plus required tax component.
e/   Opportunity cost is domestic price of regular gasoline.
f/   Alternative price for comparison is local non-subsidized price.
g/   Method I with a 15 percent VAT added.

Source: Staff estimates, Secretary of Energy, Platt's Oilgram, and information bulletins of
          various state enterprises.

Table A1.1.14: ELECTRICITY SUBSIDIES
(US$ million)

Consumer	SEGBA	AyEE	DEBA	EPEC	Total
Residential					
1987	198	21	13	10	242
1988	118	15	5	3	141
1989	280	39	-4	8	323
Commercial					
1987	22	-3	-1	-12	6
1988	-19	-8	-9	-27	-83
1989	8	-1	-4	-29	-28
Industrial					
1987	91	126	10	-20	208
1988	41	109	-31	-38	81
1989	45	119	-76	-100	-12
Public Lighting					
1987	14	-1	-	-	13
1988	9	-3	-	-	6
1989	17	2	-	-	19
Total	824	414	-97	-205	938
1987	325	143	22	-22	468
1988	149	113	-35	-62	165
1989	350	159	-84	-121	304

Source: Staff estimates.

39.   The alternatives for estimating natural gas subsidies can be partitioned into those where the tax component is included in the price, and others where taxes are omitted. Subsidies under the first method reflect the difference between the international price of fuel oil and "tax free" natural gas. Method II is identical to the first with the exception that taxes remain. The third method includes a VAT of 15 percent on natural gas rather than the actual tax component.

Electricity

40.   The nontradable nature of electricity contributes to the complexity of subsidy quantification. Any attempt at evaluation must involve a comparison between the actual tariff per kilowatt hour and an estimate of marginal cost. Unfortunately, no details are provided with respect to the method used to estimate marginal costs.

41.   The various enterprises included in the summary of electric subsidies (Table A1.1.14) provide approximately 66.5 percent of residential, 68.4 percent of commercial, and 75.9 percent of industrial electricity sold in Argentina.

E. Central Bank (BCFA) Financial Subsidies

42.   Argentina's Central Bank provided rediscount subsidies to the financial sector in a multitude of ways until their effective elimination during the monetary reforms of 1990. Although the flow of rediscounts was stopped in 1990, a subsidy continues because the interest rate on the stock of rediscounts is lower than the

opportunity cost for the government (BIC Treasury bond rates).[5] The most predominant subsidy was the large percentage of rediscounts granted to public banks (approximately 78.5 percent). Another more subtle mechanism is that in which the BCRA indexed its rediscounts with a 45 day lag while liabilities carried a 2 day lag.   Under a hyperinflation this difference alone produced a considerable deterioration in the BCRA balance.   This was aggravated by shorter term lengths on liabilities, smaller relative spreads on rediscounts, and failure of public banks to repay rediscount obligations.   At the onset of 1990 the government was obliged to exchange deposits for BONEX in order to delay and supplement its rediscount income.   This procedure will lose its effectiveness once the BONEX mature.

Table A1.1.15:   REDISCOUNTS VERSUS CENTRAL BANK LIABILITIES
(US$ millions) a/

		Rediscounts Granted b/ (1)	BCRA Liabilities Remunerated (2)	in % (1)/(2)
1987	I	4094	4943	82.8
	II	4533	5197	87.2
	III	3787	3863	98.3
	IV	4013	3729	107.6
1988	I	4377	4309	101.6
	II	4081	4219	96.3
	III	5069	6277	80.8
	IV	6808	7303	93.2
1989	I	3756	3996	94.0
	II	1614	1695	95.2
	III	4990	5065	98.5
	IV	3836	3964	96.8
Average		4245	4548	93.4

a/   Current dollars.
b/   National and provincial banks participate in roughly 78.5 percent of the total stock
     of rediscounts.

Source: Staff estimates.

43.   These complications imply that any valuation of Central Bank subsidies will be both complex and subject to several different methods of interpretation. Suggested alternatives are given in Table A1.1.16.

---

5   The interest rate on the BIC bonds are paid by the Treasury. However, these bonds were issued when the monetary reform of 1990 was decreed; these bonds have replaced remunerated legal reserve requirements.

Table A1.1.16: IMPLICIT BCRA REDISCOUNTING SUBSIDIES
(US$ millions) a/

			Alternatives				
		A	B1	B2	C	D	E
1988	I	142	446	612	158	-98	422
	II	120	199	300	182	54	127
	III	-1130	-529	-409	-1065	612	-647
	IV						
1988	Total	-2169	381	864	-1925	899	-120
1989	I	6558	1903	2116	6653	-312	1920
	II	2740	1853	1902	2760	-1006	3307
	III	-2804	-2449	-2402	-2779	2137	-2321
	IV	1845	375	486	1905	-63	133
1989	Total	8339	1682	2102	8539	756	3039
1988/89 Total b/		6170	2063	2966	6614	1655	2919
1990		n.a	n.a	-438	n.a	n.a	n.a
1991		n.a	n.a	412	n.a	n.a	n.a

Note: Rediscount opportunity cost definitions:

A   LIBOR plus a 4 percent annual spread.
B1   Weighted average of BCRA rates on various issues, forced savings, Cedeps, and a 1 percent monthly spread.
B2   Identical to B1 but with a 2 percent spread.
C   Yield on 10 year government debt issues.
D   Weighted average of price indices plus a 2 percent monthly spread.
E   Identical to B1 with spread determined via adjustment for size of the monthly borrowing requirement.
F   Official exchange rate.

a/ Official exchange rate.

Source: Staff estimates.

44.   Each alternative is distinguished by a different measure of opportunity cost. To calculate the subsidy for each period, we multiply the stock of rediscounts in period t by the difference between the actual index used for the rediscounts and the opportunity cost specified, and divide the product by the official exchange rate for that period. Then sum the various periods for the lifetime subsidy of the rediscount.

ANNEX 2.1

THE PUBLIC SECTOR: BUDGETING CONCEPTS
AND THE STRUCTURE OF THE FEDERAL GOVERNMENT

1.   With perennial public sector deficits, and the ensuing circularity of deficit financing and inflation, Argentina's accounting of its fiscal accounts has depended greatly on the methods used to measure revenue and expenditure. Depending on the methodology employed, differences in the calculated combined public sector deficit have been as high as 2.5 percent of GDP for accrual and cash bases budgets in years such as 1990. Understanding the different budget concepts is important in order to properly measure the obligations of the public sector, how the deficit is financed, and how programs are budgeted and executed. Annex Table 2.1.1 illustrates the variance between concepts for 1991, a relatively stable year.

2.   There are two entities that measure public expenditure and revenue: the Treasury (relying on Tax Administration data) and the General Accounting Office, both of which are dependent of the Ministry of Economy. The Treasury exercises the more influential role, as it coordinates planning assumptions not only for the National Administration, but also the Social Security system, Public Enterprises, and the relationship of the national government with the provinces. The Accounting Office records information of the National Administration only.

3.   The Treasury works with two principal definitions of the budget: cash and accrual. When looking at years already executed, the concept of "execution" replaces accrual. Cash basis accounts reflect all those revenues that are expected to be received effectively, and all those expenditures assumed as obligations and paid in the year of the budget. Cash basis reflects actual movement of funds to and from the Treasury.

4.   Accrual basis (also budget basis) reflects revenues that may presumably be received, and expenditures that are expected to be made. Rather than actual movements in the balance of the Treasury, these numbers reflect, for example, actual (or expected) contractual obligations that are authorized by Congress to be assumed by the executing agency. The executed basis reflects the contracts and obligations made in the course of the fiscal year, regardless of disbursement of funds from the Treasury. One common discrepancy in the past few years between cash and accrual has been the government's ability to pay the end-of-year, "thirteenth" month wage bonus (aguinaldo). If the government had to move the payment to January, the cash basis deficit in year 1 will be lower than the accrual basis deficit; but the following year's cash basis deficit will be higher, given that the government will still have to pay this obligation.

5.   The cash basis concept is the most simple, and allows the budget exercise to be measured day-to-day, as it is always registering flows in the Treasury balance as they occur. The Accounting Office is charged with the registering of the more complicated bases that define expenditure in its various stages once credits are created in the budget.

6.   Credit basis, as mentioned previously, reflects the authorization of funds as approved by the budget. These resources are allotted to the final level of execution, the programs themselves. At this point, the executing agencies (jurisdictions) review the programs and given the constraints of project implementation, make obligations to contractors, suppliers and personnel. Once the contracts are made, the budget concept "compromiso," i.e., commitment/executed basis, is validated. This "commitment" or contract will only be fulfilled once the executing authority agrees that the terms have been met.

7.   Once the government agency agrees that the terms of the contract have been met, the executing jurisdiction sends a payment order to the Treasury. Once this order is processed, the expenditure concept is called "sent for payment,"(mandado a pagar). This also refers to the moment revenues are sent to the Treasury (e.g. charges collected by the Civil Registry for license plates); in the case of expenditure, this order of payment, although received by the Treasury, is not necessarily paid. Depending on the Treasury's reserves, it may not be able to disburse funds for payment.

8.   "Paid" (pagado) refers to the final stage of expenditure classification by the Accounting Office. It is the disbursement of funds either directly to the creditor or to the payment office of the executing ministries, based on the amount fixed by the executing power in each jurisdiction. Whatever portion of the "sent for payment" amount is not "paid" is carried over to the next year's exercise as a "residual liability" (residuo pasivo).

9.   Typically, about 70-80 percent of the amount of credit is contracted (compromiso), whereas the amount sent for payment is close to 100 percent of the amount contracted. If the Treasury decides to withhold funding of a program, it may do so at various points in the budgeting process. The most favorable, of course, is before the commitment (compromiso) is made. Thus no creditor has a claim on the government. Once the contract is made however, the Treasury can avoid payment of the contract by delaying processing of the services rendered, or can simply allow the obligation to fall into arrears.

A. Effects of the Administrative Reform on the Budgetary Process

10.   As numerous levels of bureaucracy have been eliminated and executing authority has been consolidated, the ability of the Treasury to manage expenditures has increased. As discussed previously, once a credit has been created in the budget, the executing agency is authorized to make commitment funds through the programs. To the extent that executing power has been reduced, i.e. the number of jurisdictions and special accounts have been cut, cabinet level control over programs has been increased. Previously, some subsecretaries had been considered jurisdictions, and with this position they had been able to manage and execute programs without any but token supervision

from the ministerial level. As the government moves to eliminate all special accounts from the budget for the 1993 exercise (and their earmarked revenues), even more auditing and executing authority will fall on the central administration.

B. Categorizing Expenditure in the 1992 Budget

11.   Expenditures of the Argentine Non-financial Federal Public Sector as presented in the budget are classified in two major categories: institutional and functional. The institutional representation indicates the administrative bodies which execute the expenditure, and the latter representation indicates the purpose of the expenditure.

12.   **Institutional Representation.** The institutional hierarchy has been affected dramatically by the administrative reform over the last two years. Central control of expenditure has increased greatly as bureaucratic divisions have been eliminated or consolidated. Table A.1 displays the reductions in administrative bodies at the jurisdictional level. The importance of this to budget execution is that because only jurisdictions may authorize the commitment of resources allocated by the budget, by eliminating subsecretaries as jurisdictions, higher levels of administration have greater control over programs. The following flow chart indicates the channels of budget execution.

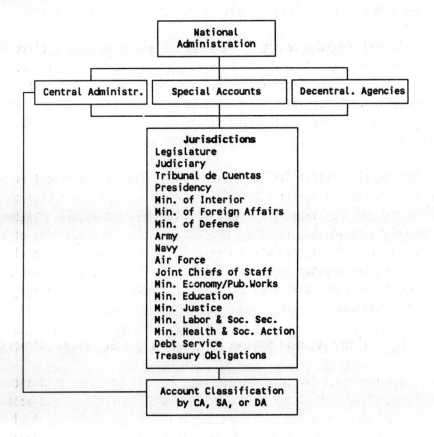

13.   The National Administration is separated into three divisions which define the general administrative "type" of expenditure. Decentralized agencies, such as the Nuclear Commission (CNEA) and the National Highway Board (DNV), are allotted funds without direct administrative control by the overseeing jurisdiction (usually a

ministry, or in the case of CNEA, the presidency). The expenditures made by the Central Administration, for example, would entail the actual administrative costs of the national administration, whereas those made through special accounts and decentralized agencies, aside from being more difficult to make accountable, are outlays to other organizations, often outside the national administration. Such large special accounts as the Tobacco Fund and FONAVI are, in fact, simply transfers to provincial governments.

14.   **Functional Representation**. There are three hierarchical distinctions made when classifying expenditure in this way. The most general being what the government calls "finalidad." The finalidades each have a unique subset of "funciones." The program itself is the final category when defining expenditure by function.

Finalidad 1: General Administration

Funciones: Policy/Administration, Fiscal Administration, Legislation, Justice, Foreign Affairs, Protocol, Provincial Aid, and Miscellaneous

Finalidad 2: Defense

Funciones: Army, Navy, Air Force, and Miscellaneous

Finalidad 3: Security

Funciones: Police, National Guard, Coast Guard, Penal System, and Miscellaneous

Finalidad 4: Health

Funciones: Medical Care, Environmental Health, and Miscellaneous

Finalidad 5: Education

Funciones: Culture, Elementary Education, Secondary Education, Universities, and Miscellaneous

Finalidad 6: Economic Development

Funciones: Subsoil Irrigation/Drainage, Agriculture/Livestock/Natural Resources, Energy & Fuel, Mining, Industry, Tourism, Railways, Roads, Waterways, Airways, Communications, Trade & Storage, Insurance & Finance, and Miscellaneous

Finalidad 7: Welfare

Funciones: Social Security, Labor, Housing and Urban Development, Social
                   Assistance, Sports and Recreation, Social Promotion, and
                   Miscellaneous

Finalidad 8: Science and Technology

Funciones: Promotion and Scholarship, Research and Development, and
                   Miscellaneous

15.   **Understanding Categorization of Expenditure: An Example.** With
many groupings which share names (for example the funcíon "labor" is also the name
a ministry), it is difficult to measure and analyze government expenditure by both its end
and its executor. The case of the FONAVI housing program is an example of many
"misplaced" programs, programs which do not follow transparent lines of administration
because of shifting roles of ministries. By functional grouping, FONAVI is clearly
defined: welfare "finalidad," and housing "funcíon." However, institutionally, it is a
special account administered by the Ministry of Health and Social Action. Due to its
size, of course, it is not hard to find in the Budget, but there are many smaller programs
which have similar functions which are operated by different ministries.

16.   Direct links between the functional representation to the institutional
representation are not easily made in most cases. The "finalidad" health envelopes all
expenditures on health programs, but cannot be equated to expenditures of the Ministry
of Health and Social Action because many different jurisdictions manage programs in
the health function; likewise, the Ministry of Health spends the majority of its budget
on non-health programs. There are separate research and technical education programs
(education and science & technology "finalidades") being managed by the Presidency,
the Ministry of Economy and Public Works, the Armed Forces, and the Ministry of
Education. Table [], in Chapter 1, displays in matrix form, the institutional and
functional classification of expenditure.

Table A2.1.1: ARGENTINA: Fiscal Accounts: Cash and Accrual
(as percednt of GDP)

	1987			1988			1989			1990		
	Accrual	Cash	Diff.	Accrual	Cash	Diff.	Accrual	Cash	Diff.	Accrual	Cash	Diff.
Current Revenue	19.6	18.8	0.8	18.3	17.6	0.6	17.0	17.6	-0.7	17.7	18.1	-0.4
Tax Revenue	18.1	17.2	0.9	16.9	16.3	0.6	15.8	16.3	-0.5	16.8	16.8	-0.1
DGI and Customs	14.0	13.2	0.8	12.1	11.5	0.6	12.5	12.9	-0.4	11.6	11.6	0.0
Social Security	4.1	4.0	0.1	4.8	4.8	0.0	3.3	3.4	-0.1	5.2	5.2	0.0
Non-tax Revenue	1.5	1.6	-0.1	1.4	1.3	0.1	1.1	1.3	-0.2	0.9	1.2	-0.3
Current Expenditures	23.4	22.1	1.3	23.0	21.4	1.6	19.5	17.1	2.4	21.8	18.4	3.4
Personnel	4.1	3.6	0.5	4.1	3.7	0.4	3.4	3.1	0.3	4.1	3.1	1.0
Goods and Services	2.1	1.3	0.7	2.0	1.2	0.8	1.6	1.1	0.6	1.4	1.0	0.4
Transfers	13.8	13.4	0.4	14.1	12.6	1.5	11.6	11.5	0.1	13.2	11.8	1.4
Provinces	6.6	6.6	0.0	6.8	5.9	0.9	5.9	6.4	-0.5	5.6	5.1	0.5
Social Security	5.9	5.6	0.2	6.1	6.0	0.1	4.3	4.3	-0.1	6.5	6.2	0.3
Others	1.3	1.2	0.1	1.2	0.7	0.5	1.5	0.8	0.7	1.1	0.5	0.6
Interest Payments ᵃ/	3.5	3.9	-0.4	2.8	3.9	-1.1	2.9	1.4	1.5	3.1	2.5	0.6
Domestic ᵇ/	0.5	0.4	0.2	0.4	0.7	-0.2	0.1	-2.0	2.1	0.5	0.4	0.1
External	3.0	3.5	-0.6	2.4	3.3	-0.9	2.7	3.4	-0.7	2.6	2.2	0.4
PE Non-interest Savings	1.8	1.2	0.6	1.0	-1.8	2.8	0.9	-1.3	2.2	1.2	-0.2	1.4
Savings	-2.0	-2.1	0.1	-3.8	-5.6	1.8	-1.6	-0.7	-0.9	-2.8	-0.5	-2.4
Capital Revenue	0.2	0.3	-0.1	0.4	0.2	0.2	0.6	0.3	0.3	0.3	0.6	-0.3
Capital Expenditures	5.3	3.9	1.4	6.0	3.4	2.6	3.9	2.8	1.1	2.6	1.9	0.6
General Gov't.	1.7	1.0	0.7	1.5	1.0	0.6	1.0	0.6	0.4	0.7	0.6	0.1
Public Enterprises	3.6	2.9	0.7	4.5	2.4	2.1	2.8	2.2	0.7	1.9	1.3	0.5
NFPS Balance	-7.1	-5.8	-1.4	-9.4	-8.8	-0.6	-4.9	-3.2	-1.7	-5.1	-1.8	-3.3
Memo:												
Primary Surplus	-3.6	-1.9	-1.7	-6.6	-4.9	-1.7	-2.0	-1.8	-0.2	-2.0	0.8	-2.8

a/ Interest payments alwasy registered on accrual basis.
b/ Real component of domestic interest payments only.

Source: Secretary of Finance

Table A2.1.2: Budget Concepts of the National Administration, 1991
(as percent GDP)

	Credit [a] Presupuesto	Accrual [b] Compromiso	Sent for Payment [c] Mandado a Pagar	Paid [d] Pagado	Cash [e] Caja
Current Revenue	15.5	14.3	14.3	14.3	14.9
Tax	14.2	13.1	13.1	13.1	13.6
Non-tax	1.3	1.2	1.2	1.2	1.3
Current Expenditures	16.5	14.5	14.2	13.5	14.2
Personnel	4.1	3.0	2.9	2.7	3.5
Goods and Services	1.3	1.0	0.8	0.7	0.9
Interest Payments	2.2	1.8	1.8	1.7	1.7
Domestic	0.3	0.4	0.4	0.4	0.3
External	1.9	1.4	1.4	1.3	1.5
External of the Treasury	0.0	0.0	0.0	0.0	0.0
Other Current Expenditures	0.0	0.0	0.0	0.0	0.0
Transfers	9.1	8.7	8.7	8.4	7.9
Provinces [f]	7.3	7.3	7.3	7.3	6.3
Social Security	0.8	0.9	0.8	0.7	0.8
Private Education	0.2	0.2	0.2	0.2	0.2
Others	0.8	0.3	0.3	0.2	0.6
Current Deficit of Public Enterprises	0.0	0.0	0.0	0.0	0.0
Extrabudgetary Expenditures	-0.1	0.0	0.0	0.0	0.1
Savings	-1.0	-0.2	0.1	0.8	0.7
Capital Revenue	1.2	1.1	1.1	1.1	1.0
Capital Expenditures	0.7	0.7	0.7	0.5	0.5
Residual from Previous Year	0.0	0.0	0.0	0.0	0.0
Economic Emergency Financing	0.0	0.0	0.0	0.0	0.0
Intra-government Transfers Received	2.1	0.0	0.0	0.0	1.5
Intra-government Transfers Paid [g]	3.9	0.6	0.6	0.5	2.6
Financing Requirement (+ = deficit)	2.3	0.5	0.1	-0.9	-0.1
Memo:					
Primary Surplus of Nat'l Admin.	-0.1	1.3	1.7	2.6	1.9
GDP (Pesos Millions)	127.3				
Operating Surplus of PEs	-0.3				0.5

Sources:
Cash basis 1991 comes from an Esquema Ahorro-Inversion August 15, 1992.
Budget basis 1991 is from the 1992 budget report recently received (September 26, 1991).
Compromiso, Mandado a Pagar, Pagado versions from Accounting Office.

a/ Budget authorization by Congress/Presidency.
b/ Revenues accrued to government upon due date of taxes; expenditures committed by spending jurisdiction.
c/ Spending jurisdiction receives revenue and sends payment voucher to Treasury.
d/ Payment made.
e/ Revenue deposited in the Treasury and expenditures debited.
f/ Transfers to provinces by coparticipation unavailable for Accounting Office; Budge data used.
g/ For Accounting Office concepts, these transfers are to public enterprises.

Table A2.1.3: Argentina - Reductions in Government Expenditure Jurisdictions

Juris. Number	1990	1991	1992
1	Legislature	Legislature	Legislature
5	Judiciary	Judiciary	Judiciary
10	Tribunal de Cuentas	Tribunal de Cuentas	Tribunal de Cuentas
20	Presidency	Presidency	Presidency
30	Interior Ministry	Interior Ministry	Interior Ministry
35	Foreign Ministry	Foreign Ministry	Foreign Ministry
40			Justice Department
45	Ministry of Defense	Ministry of Defense	Ministry of Defense
46	Army	Army	Army
47	Navy	Navy	Navy
48	Air Force	Air Force	Air Force
49	Joint Chiefs of Staff	Joint Chiefs of Staff	Joint Chiefs of Staff
50	Ministry of Economy	Ministry of Economy	Ministry of Economy and Public Works
51	Secretary of Domestic Commerce		
52	Subsecretary of Hacienda	Subsecretary of Hacienda	
53	Secretary of Mining		
54	Secretary of Regional Development		
55	Subsecretary of Public Finance	Subsecretary of Public Finance	
57	Subsecretary of Industry and Commerce	Subsecretary of Industry and Commerce	
58	Subsecretary of Agriculture and Livestock	Subsecretary of Agriculture and Livestock	
60	Subsecretary of Public Works	Subsecretary of Public Works	
61	Secretary of Communications		
63	Subsecretary of Transportation	Subsecretary of Transportation	
64	Subsecretary of Electric Energy	Subsecretary of Electric Energy	
65	Secretary of the Merchant Marine		
66	Ministry of Education and Justice	Ministry of Education and Justice	
67	Subsecretary of Education	Subsecretary of Education	
68	Secretary of Science and Technology		
69	Justice Department	Justice Department	
70	Subsecretary of Culture	Subsecretary of Culture	Ministry of Culture and Education
75	Ministry of Labor and Social Security	Ministry of Labor and Social Security	Ministry of Labor and Social Security
77	Subsecretary of Social Security		
80	Ministry of Health and Social Action	Ministry of Health and Social Action	Ministry of Health and Social Action
81	Subsecretary of Health	Subsecretary of Health	
83	Secretaries of Sports and Social Promotion		
84	Subsecretary of Human Development	Subsecretary of Human Development	
85	Subsecretary of Housing and Environment	Subsecretary of Housing and Environment	
90	Public Debt Service	Public Debt Service	Public Debt Service
91	Treasury Obligations	Treasury Obligations	Treasury Obligations
Total	39	30	18

ANNEX 4.1

A SIMPLIFIED APPROACH TO MEASURING TAX EFFORT

1.   The purpose of the approach presented in this Annex is to identify the main factors that influence tax revenue fluctuations in a country like Argentina. In particular, we need to elaborate on the meaning of tax effort in the context of the paper, as this concept is used in a somewhat unconventional way. As a starting point, tax receipts collected by the tax administration can be defined as:

(1) $T_t = t_t B_t$

where T_t is tax revenues collected at time t by the administration, t_t the average nominal tax rate, and B_t the tax base.

2.   Since the inflation rate has been high and very volatile in Argentina, the Olivera-Tanzi effect should be included in equation (1). As suggested by Olivera [1967] and Tanzi [1978], tax revenues are influenced negatively by the rate of inflation. "Given that taxes are collected with a certain lag, the real value of taxation will be reduced if, during the period between accrual and collection, prices or real GDP increase" (Argentina's Tax Report (1990), p.4). Following these authors, tax revenues can be expressed as follows :

(2) $T_t = t_t [B^*_t / [(1 + \Theta g_t)(1 + \Theta \pi_t)]]$

where B^*_t is the tax base adjusted for the Olivera-Tanzi effect, Θ the estimated delay in collection (days), g_t the growth rate of the tax base and π_t the inflation rate.

3.   Equation (2) states that tax revenues depend on the average tax rate and the potential tax base adjusted for the Olivera-Tanzi effect. Using this equation, we can determine the factors explaining the variation in tax revenues over time. Rewriting equation (2) in a log difference form, we get:

(3) $\triangle \ln T_t = \triangle \ln t_t + \triangle \ln B^*_t - \triangle \ln(1 + \Theta g_t) - \triangle \ln(1 + \Theta \pi_t)$

4.   The percentage change in tax revenues depends on the percentage changes in the theoretical tax base, on average nominal taxes, and in the Olivera-Tanzi effect.

5.   Equation (3) can be used to derive the theoretical tax base, which is the only variable not directly observable. Moreover, assuming that the variations in the tax base are attributable to changes in economic conditions or in tax administration, we can write the following equation:

(4) $\triangle \ln B^{*}_{t} = \triangle \ln V_{t} + \triangle \ln E_{t}$

where $\triangle \ln V_{t}$ is the percentage change in the tax base owning to variations in the economic environment and $\triangle \ln E_{t}$ the percentage change in the tax base derived from improvements in tax administration. As an illustration, $\triangle \ln V_{t}$ can be defined as GDP growth for sales taxes or import growth for import duties and $\triangle \ln E_{t}$ refers to greater effort in tax collection or reduction in the level of exemptions. The resulting change in the theoretical tax base is therefore the summation of both effects. Substituting equation (4) into equation (3), the percentage change in tax administration's effort equals:

(5) $\triangle \ln E_{t} = \triangle \ln T_{t} - \triangle \ln t_{t} + \triangle \ln(1 + \Theta g_{t}) + \triangle \ln(1 + \Theta \pi_{t}) - \triangle \ln V_{t}$

6.   The percentage change in tax effort is therefore defined as the change in tax revenues that is not explained by variations (i) in nominal tax rates; (ii) in the Olivera-Tanzi effect; and (iii) in the tax base owning to changes in economic conditions. The variable $\triangle \ln E_{t}$ is assumed to reflect important changes in tax legislation (except the changes in nominal taxes), in tax administration and in individuals' attitudes toward tax evasion. While the results of such a simple accounting approach should be interpreted with care, they nevertheless offer a framework in which to appraise comparative tax effort over a period of time.

7.   The above approach has been applied to the case of Argentina over the 1989-91 period. The main results are summarized in Figures 4.1-4.4 of the Report. Note that more detailed results are presented in the study "Macroeconomic Instability and the Efficiency of the Tax System in Argentina." The data on tax revenues, GDP, the rate of inflation and the exchange rate was obtained from the Government. We also used the data collected by the IMF and the World Bank. Because the data were not available, the average delay in tax collection was equal to 1 month from August 1989 to February 1990, 15 days from March 1990 to February 1991, and 10 days from March 1991 onwards. The progressive reduction in collection delay over the period reflects the successive tax reform packages implemented between 1989 and 1991. Finally, we defined the percentage change in the tax base owning to variations in economic factors as real GDP growth for all coparticipated taxes and as import and export growth for import and export taxes, respectively.

8.   Unstable economic conditions may influence the tax collection effort and the level of exemptions, therefore affecting indirectly tax revenues. In order to test this hypothesis, we examined the responsiveness of the tax effort to changes in GDP growth rate and in the inflation rate over the last two years. Identification of such influences, if any, on the effort in tax administration may confirm that macroeconomic conditions are partly reflected in the volatility of the tax effort.

9.   The preliminary results presented in Table A4.1.1 suggest that the variations in tax effort are more likely to be the consequence of political and institutional changes, such as a reduction in exemptions, rather than the consequence of macroeconomic conditions. The estimated results indicate, however, that the rate of inflation exerted a significant and negative influence on the tax effort, even after discounting for the "legal" Olivera-Tanzi effect. This result suggests that an increase in the rate of inflation can influence the efficiency of the tax system through, for example, modifications in the collection mechanisms. In the case of VAT, the rate of inflation appears to exert a positive impact on the tax effort, but the influence of uncertainty (measured as the percentage change in the rate of inflation) is clearly negative. The tax reform packages introduced in February 1990 (DUM1) such as the extension of VAT to all goods and the simplification of the profit tax influenced positively tax effort. Similarly, the extension of the VAT to services in September 1990 (DUM2) exerted a positive impact on the effort of the tax administration.[1]

Table A4.1.1: Relationship Between Macroeconomic Variables and Tax Effort
(1989:10-1991:9)

Dependent Variable	ΔE_{cop}	ΔE_{pr}	ΔE_{VAT}	ΔE_{imp}	ΔE_{tot}
Constant	6.545	19.784	-3.942	5.954	8.184
	(1.44)	(1.39)	(-0.84)	(0.53)	(2.01)
g	-0.083	-3.392	-3.945	2.514a/	-0.260
	(-0.08)	(-1.12)	(-3.77)	(1.06)	(-0.29)
π	-0.376	-1.007	0.451	-0.617	-0.372
	(-1.94)	(-1.63)	(2.56)	(-1.28)	(-2.09)
$\Delta\pi$	-	-	-9.334	-	-
			(-2.86)		
DUM1	28.370	98.806	-	159.401	28.109
	(1.27)	(1.39)		(2.87)	(1.372)
DUM2	36.097	-	16.797	-	-
	(2.12)		(1.97)		
adjR²	0.199	0.013	0.639	0.236	0.067
DR	1.95	2.57	2.47	2.12	2.36

Note: ΔE_{cop} = coparticipated taxes effort, ΔE_{pr} = profit tax effort, ΔE_{vat} = VAT effort, ΔE_{imp} = import duties effort, ΔE_{tot} = total tax effort, g = GDP growth rate, π = rate of inflation, $\Delta\pi$ = volatility of the rate of inflation, dum1 = dummy variable which accounts for the policy changes of February 1990 and DUM2 which accounts for the policy changes of September 1990.

a/   For import duties, g is the growth rate of imports rather than the GDP growth rate.

---

1   On the contrary, the impact of GDP growth did not appear significant on tax effort even if a positive relationship between GDP growth and tax effort should come from the fact that for most taxes marginal rates are higher than average ones.

ANNEX 4.2

HIGHLIGHTS OF LEGISLATION UNDER
THE MENEM ADMINISTRATION

1.   This Annex reviews the highlights of tax legislation during the 1989-91 period.

A. Gross Assets Tax

2.   The first major piece of tax legislation during the Menem administration was Law 23,760 of December 7, 1989. This law replaced the Impuesto sobre los Capitales, which had been based on net assets, with a tax on gross assets (Impuesto a los Activos), effective as of January 1, 1990. The rate of tax was set at one percent. The tax was initially made creditable against the income tax. In this sense, the tax functions as a minimum income tax, the amount of liability being the greater of the assets tax liability and the income tax liability. The tax applies generally to domestic companies, to permanent establishments of foreign companies, and to businesses operated by individuals. The rate of tax was subsequently raised to 2 percent, effective for the first taxable year of a company closing after February 18, 1991. For taxable years closing after February 18, 1992, the rate goes back to one percent.[1] In 1991 the Government reversed the deduction method and made the income tax deductible from the asset tax thereby addressing concerns about qualification of the income tax for the foreign tax credit in the U.S. and other countries with similar systems.

B. Tax on Debits

3.   Law 23,760 also revised the Tax on Bank Debits, renaming it the Tax on Debits to Current Account and Other Operations ("Tax on Debits") and fixing the rate at 3 per mil, effective as of January 1, 1990. In general, this tax applies to bank checks and similar transfers effected by any person, including both individuals and businesses.[2] As of February 21, 1991, the rate of tax was raised to 12 per mil, with 9 points of the tax being creditable against the taxpayer's income tax and VAT liability (half against each).[3] As of February 21, 1992, the rate goes back down to 3 percent, with no portion being creditable against another tax.

---

1   See Law 23,905 (Feb. 18, 1991).

2   This is a general description of the tax; a fully accurate description would require entering into details that are not necessary to the analysis of this paper. See Law 23,760, Title II.

3   See Law 23,905 (published Feb. 18, 1991), art. 1. Under Law 23,549 (Tax on Bank Debits), which had been in effect through 1989, 70 percent of the tax had been creditable against the income tax.

C. Income Tax

4.   Law 23,760 (December 7, 1989) made major changes to the income tax. The taxation of capital gains was repealed effective January 1, 1990. The general rate of tax on corporations was lowered from 33 percent to 20 percent. Dividends were generally excluded from the calculation of taxable income; however a withholding tax was imposed at a rate of 10 percent for resident individuals, and 20 percent for shareholders who did not identify themselves and for foreign shareholders. (Accordingly the maximum rate of tax on distributed corporate income is 28 percent for resident individuals and 36 percent for foreign shareholders.) The rates applicable to individuals were also reduced, the maximum marginal rate being lowered from 35 to 30 percent. Law 23,871 allowed an immediate income tax deduction for the cost of depreciable personal property acquired within the two-year period following the publication of the law (October 31, 1990).

D. Value Added Tax

5.   Law 23,760 established a tax on financial services, based on value added calculated under the addition method. While this is not formally part of the VAT, it fulfills the functional role of taxing VAT of the financial sector under an alternative, more administrable, method.

6.   Law 23,765 generalized the VAT on goods and changed the regime for small taxpayers, establishing the concept of non-registered responsible persons, effective as of February 1, 1990. Law 23,765 also allowed taxpayers to immediately use the credit for purchases of capital goods.

7.   Law 23,871, adopted September 28, 1990, broadened the base of the VAT to include most services. Previously, the VAT had been applicable only to those services specifically listed in the law.

8.   Law 23,905 raised the general VAT rate from 15.6 to 16 percent, effective February 1991. In the case of sales of gas, electricity, water, and other public utilities (except sales to residences), where the individual purchaser is registered (or a non-registered), the tax rate is 25 percent. An 11 percent rate applies to the provision of telephone services to final consumers.

E. Tax on Wealth of Individuals

9.   Law 23,769 (December 7, 1989) repealed the tax on net wealth of individuals (Impuesto sobre el Patrimonio Neto), effective as of December 31, 1990. Since this tax was based on wealth as of December 31 of each year, the last time this tax was payable was with respect to wealth as of December 31, 1989. A new tax on individual wealth (Tax on Personal Goods not Incorporated in the Economic Process) was created by Law 23,966 (August 1, 1991), effective with respect to wealth as of December 31, 1991, and December 31 of the subsequent eight years. The tax base generally includes assets that are not subject to the Impuesto a los Activos. It is noteworthy that assets located abroad are included in the tax base. Home mortgage debt

is deductible, but other debt is not. The rate is one percent of the excess of the tax base over the equivalent in australes of about US$100,000.

F. Miscellaneous Taxes

10.   Law 23,740, which was enacted in October 1989, established a one-time tax known as the "contribución solidaria," which was based on receipts obtained in 1988.

11.   Law 23,760 imposed an emergency tax on the ownership of automobiles, yachts, and airplanes as of October 31, 1989, as well as an emergency tax on the profits of financial entities for the year ending on September 30, 1989.

12.   Law 23,905 established a tax on transfers of real property by individuals at a rate of 1.5 percent, applicable where the transfer is not subject to income tax.[4] Sale of the taxpayer's only residence is not taxed if the proceeds are used to purchase a new residence.

13.   Most recently, Decree No. 2284/91, which dealt with deregulation of the economy, also made modifications to the tax laws. This decree repealed the taxes on transfers of equity[5] and debt[6] instruments. It exempted from income tax any gains realized by foreign persons from the sale of shares in domestic companies. It exempted the issuance of certain securities from the stamp tax. It repealed the 3 percent tax on exports (so-called statistical tax). It also repealed a number of miscellaneous taxes on specific products the proceeds of which were designated for specific funds dealing with trade regulation and promotion.

14.   The decree also repealed the withholding tax on dividends (i.e., 10 percent on dividends paid to residents and 20 percent for dividends paid abroad), although the drafting of the decree is somewhat unclear about the scope of this measure.[7] This aspect of the decree was apparently not well thought through, and was removed by Decree 2424/91, published on November 14, 1991.

G. Penalties for Tax Crimes

15.   Law 23,771, which became effective on March 8, 1990, provides a special procedure for crimes involving fraud, evasion, and omission regarding both taxes and social security contributions. It applies to infractions committed both by taxpayers and by public officials, and sets forth the applicable judicial procedure. Some of the penalties provided are fines, but most are imprisonment for terms of up to eight years.

---

4   Unless the taxpayer is a dealer, such transfers will not be subject to income tax, since capital gains are not taxed.

5   Impuesto Sobre las Ventas Compras, Cambio, o Permuta de Divisas.

6   Impuesto a la Transferencia de Títulos Valores.

7   See Decree 2284/91, article 79, last sentence.

ANNEX 7.1

MILITARY FACILITIES, RESTRUCTURING
AND ANNOUNCED ACTIONS

1.   However, the three Armed Forces have outlined a number of proposed reforms, some of which are already underway. A number of immediate measures have been set in motion by the Ministry of Defense that are designed to produce cost savings without placing an additional burden on the budget.

2.   The measures include the retirement of 11 Army generals and 74 Army colonels in early November 1991, a decline in the number of civilians employed by the Ministry of Defense, a reduction in the number of new recruits accepted by the service academies and the replacement of civilian teachers at these academies by military personnel, and the consolidation of army arsenals, involving the sale of property and real estate.

Army

3.   The new Army Chief of Staff has recently announced broad reform measures including asset sales, elimination of some of the existing operations, consolidation of units, agencies, commands, and directorates and building new facilities where necessary, as well as upgrading existing ones.

4.   Technical-professional training is expected to be strengthened within the existing budgetary limits, with training and specialized courses continuing on a limited basis. Future financial aid for courses taken in civilian institutions by military personnel will be suspended. Reorganization of the system of personnel mobilization will involve the transfer of 10 of the military districts to existing barracks, and 14 of them will become delegations.

5.   The current policy of self-financing of "liceos" will continue. These elementary and secondary institutions, which provide schooling to children of military and civilian personnel of the Ministry of Defense as well as to other civilians, are managed and financed through user fees by parents associations. The Army provides them with trained teachers from its force to serve as instructors.

6.   Other proposed measures include a review of the merit-based promotion system, the elimination of the National Directorate of Logistics along with the disposal of its existing assets and facilities and the rationalization of financial services.

7.   The Army proposes to continue to provide several services to the community including national health campaigns, construction of roads in remote areas, installation of emergency communication networks, and allowing civilians to attend the Army Engineering School and the Army Advanced Technical Institute. Greater coordination

with the Ministries may be sought in order to increase the effectiveness of these efforts. The Army will also transfer existing technology of national interest to the private sector.

8.   Other proposed measures include the transfer of Army facilities from Palermo and Campo de Mayo in Buenos Aires to the province of Corrientes, the sale of housing previously occupied by the Army Chief of Staff, the sale of property abroad used by Argentine military attaches, the consolidation of military attache posts, an 83 percent reduction in the relocation allowance previously allotted to Argentine military attaches serving abroad, and the dissolution of the command unit of the 4th Army Corps.

Air Force

9.   The Air Force has embarked on a plan to decrease operating costs by making better use of existing equipment and thereby obviating the need to make additional purchases of spare parts, by eliminating less strategically important flights, and by consolidating certain administrative and educational functions. In recent months, the Air Force has made progress in obtaining necessary spare parts from non-functioning equipment. Excess spare parts will be sold in the future.

10.   The Air Force is conducting a review of flight hours and will decrease or eliminate flights of the Air Force Service on behalf of the Army and charge fees to the Army for future flights. In addition, operations of the commuter carrier will be funded entirely by user fees as will flights to remote areas of the country, to the extent possible.

11.   Budgetary support for the Air Force secondary schools (Liceos Aeronauticos Militares) located in the provinces of Santa Fe and Cordoba has been cut in half, and they will become entirely self-financed in the future. Training courses provided by the National Institute of Civil Aeronautics will be eliminated and instead commercial airlines will finance training of their own pilots. Employment at the small Marambio base, located in Antarctica, will also be reduced.

Navy

12.   The Navy plans to reduce the number of departments, restructure the naval education system, and centralize education facilities for enlisted personnel. Several commands and agencies will be transferred and consolidated including the exploration company, electronics workshop, and the Alfa floating dock. Others include the transfer of the Navigation Tribunal and the General Archives to the Libertad building located in downtown Buenos Aires. Buildings previously used for agencies currently being phased out will be used.

13.   The Naval Transport Command, the Lifeguard Service, and the National Directorate of Naval Material will restructure their existing operations. The Hydrographic Services of the Navy, which provides public services to the community, will be reorganized along with an administrative simplification. No specific details on these proposals have been provided, but minimal savings are estimated.

14.   Taken together, the proposals presented by the Navy do not seem to imply cost savings, and therefore should be carefully reviewed in the context of the reform process. While some outlays may be desirable, for example procurement of spare parts to increase operational capacity, other significant capital expenditures may not be feasible within the current budgetary constraints.

<u>Table A7.1</u>: MINISTRY OF DEFENSE CIVILIAN PERSONNEL, 1984-90

	1984	1985	1986	1987	1988	1989	1990
MOD Administration	14,921	14,638	13,781	12,277	12,425	12,306	11,672
of which: DGFM <u>a</u>/	12,977	12,719	11,935	10,882	11,056	10,872	10,268
Army	12,211	11,847	10,777	9,491	9,827	9,428	10,331
Navy	15,837	15,089	14,530	14,039	11,544	11,086	10,743
Air Force <u>b</u>/	22,000	21,200	19,900	18,500	16,800	16,700	16,571
Prefectura	595	562	566	494	426	398	436
Gendarmerie	655	702	661	527	515	497	500
Total	<u>66,219</u>	<u>64,038</u>	<u>60,215</u>	<u>55,328</u>	<u>51,537</u>	<u>50,415</u>	<u>50,253</u>
Memorandum:							
Civilian/Military	0.35	0.45	0.47	0.43	0.40	0.38	0.43
Civilian/Military <u>c</u>/	0.28	0.36	0.38	0.35	0.31	0.30	0.34

<u>a</u>/   A small fraction of which may be military personnel.
<u>b</u>/   Staff estimates for 1984-89.
<u>c</u>/   Excludes DGFM civilian personnel.

Source: Ministry of Defense, Ministry of Economy and staff estimates.

<u>Table A7.2</u>: MILITARY EXPENDITURE BUDGET, 1991-92

| | -------- 1991 -------- | | -------- 1992 -------- | |
	US$ million	% of GDP	US$ million	% of GDP
Expenditure by Category	3,255	2.56	3,669	2.40
Current Expenditure	3,057	2.40	3,422	2.24
Personnel	1,303	1.02	1,512	0.99
Operations and Maintenance	873	0.69	866	0.57
Military Pensions	881	0.69	1,044	0.68
Capital Expenditure	198	0.16	247	0.16
Procurement	156	0.12	205	0.13
Construction	22	0.02	30	0.02
Research and Development	20	0.02	12	0.01
Expenditure by Branch	3,255	2.56	3,669	2.40
MOD Administration	418	0.33	461	0.30
Army	571	0.45	695	0.45
Navy	382	0.30	404	0.26
Air Force	420	0.33	431	0.28
Paramilitary	582	0.46	634	0.41
Military Pensions	881	0.69	1,044	0.68
Memorandum:				
Total Expenditure (excluding pensions)	2,374	1.86	2,625	1.72
Total Expenditure (in percent of Central Government Expenditure) a/	11.85		10.22	

<u>a</u>/　　　National Administration and social security excluding interest.

Source:　Ministry of Defense and staff estimates

Table A7.3: MILITARY WAGES, ALLOWANCES, AND PENSIONS (OCTOBER 1991)
(US$)

	Base Wage	Allowances a/	Monthly Wage b/	Seniority Premium c/	Pensionable Income d/	Worker Contrib. e/	Residency Premium f/	Special Premiums g/	Net Income (monthly) h/	Net Income (annual) i/	Employer Contri. j/	Total Cost (annual) k/	Net Pension l/	Avg. Number of Years Served
Lieutenant General	436	654	1,090	872	1,963	412	382	403	2336	29,579	707	44,123	1,609	40
Major General	431	646	1,077	840	1,918	403	377	399	2291	29,004	690	43,215	1,573	39
Brigadier General	418	626	1,044	773	1,816	381	365	386	2187	27,675	654	41,135	1,490	37
Colonel	370	555	925	611	1,536	323	324	342	1880	23,774	553	35,158	1,260	33
Lieutenant Colonel	308	461	769	415	1,184	249	269	285	1489	18,806	426	27,582	971	27
Major	265	398	663	279	942	198	232	245	1221	15,401	339	22,379	772	21
Captain	228	341	569	171	740	155	199	210	994	12,510	266	17,990	606	15
First Lieutenant 1	198	297	495	109	605	127	173	183	834	10,489	218	14,969	496	11
First Lieutenant 2	174	261	435	70	505	106	152	161	712	8,940	182	12,679	414	8
Second Lieutenant	147	221	368	37	405	85	129	136	585	7,337	146	10,337	332	5
Sergent Major	264	395	659	409	1,068	224	231	244	1318	16,658	288	23,320	875	31
Sergent Principal	229	343	572	298	870	183	200	212	1099	13,876	235	19,303	713	26
Sergent Adjunct	205	308	513	216	729	153	180	190	946	11,924	197	16,473	598	21
Sergent 1	162	243	405	138	543	114	142	150	721	9,079	147	12,468	445	17
Sergent	148	222	369	81	450	95	129	137	622	7,816	122	10,627	369	11
Corporal 1	128	192	320	45	365	77	112	118	518	6,506	98	8,781	299	7
Corporal	121	182	303	24	327	69	106	112	477	5,977	88	8,018	268	4
Volunteer 1	110	165	276	11	287	60	96	102	425	5,326	77	7,115	235	2
Gendarme	118	177	294	24	318	57	103	109	473	5,808	86	7,792	261	4

Source: Ministry of Defense; staff estimates.

a/ One hundred and fifty percent of base wage.
b/ Base wage plus allowances.
c/ Two percent of monthly wage times the number of years served.
d/ Monthly wage plus seniority premium.
e/ Twenty one percent of pensionable income.
f/ Thirty five percent of monthly wage.
g/ On average 37 percent of monthly wage ranging from 10 percent for the Navy to 110 percent for the Gendarmerie.

h/ Pensionable income less worker contribution plus residency and seniority
i/ Monthly net income times 12 plus the 13th income paid in equal installm in June and December, consisting of pensionable income less worker cont
j/ Thirty six percent of pensionable income for officers and 27 percent of income for enlisted soldiers.
k/ Net annual income plus worker and employer contributions times 13.
l/ Eighty two percent of pensionable income times 13.

Table A7.4: MINISTRY OF DEFENSE CIVIL SERVICE WAGES, ALLOWANCES, AND PENSIONS, OCTOBER 1991

(US$)

Grade	Years of Service	Base Wage	Allow-ances a/	Monthly Wage b/	Senior Prem. c/	Education Sup. d/	Pension Income	Worker Contr. e/	Net Income	Employer Contr. f/	Total MOD Costs g/	Pension h/	Annual Net Income i/
30	25	240	359	599	300	150	1,048	220	828	254	1,305	524	10,766
29	24	215	322	537	258	134	928	195	733	225	1,156	464	9,532
28	24	195	292	487	234	122	842	177	665	204	1,048	421	8,649
27	23	178	267	446	205	111	762	160	602	185	949	381	7,827
26	23	163	245	409	188	102	699	147	552	169	870	349	7,176
25	22	153	229	381	168	95	644	135	509	156	802	322	6,618
24	22	140	210	350	154	87	591	124	467	143	736	296	6,071
23	21	130	195	324	136	81	542	114	428	131	674	271	5,562
22	21	122	183	305	128	76	510	107	403	124	635	255	5,236
21	20	116	174	290	116	73	479	101	378	116	596	239	4,916
20	20	111	167	279	111	42	432	91	341	105	538	216	4,436
19	19	107	161	268	102	40	410	86	324	100	511	205	4,214
18	18	103	154	257	93	39	389	82	307	94	484	194	3,990
17	17	100	150	250	85	38	373	78	294	90	464	186	3,827
16	16	97	146	244	78	37	358	75	283	87	446	179	3,676
15	15	95	142	237	71	36	344	72	272	83	428	172	3,534
14	14	93	139	232	65	35	331	70	262	80	412	166	3,401
13	13	90	136	226	59	34	319	67	252	77	397	159	3,276
12	12	89	133	221	53	33	308	65	243	75	383	154	3,159
11	11	87	130	217	48	33	298	62	235	72	370	149	3,056
10	10	85	127	212	42	21	276	58	218	67	343	138	2,833
9	9	83	125	208	37	21	266	56	210	65	332	133	2,736
8	9	82	122	204	37	20	261	55	206	63	325	131	2,683
7	8	80	120	200	32	20	252	53	199	61	314	126	2,592
6	8	79	119	198	32	20	249	52	197	60	310	124	2,557
5	7	78	117	195	27	20	242	51	191	59	301	121	2,485
4	7	77	116	193	27	19	239	50	189	58	297	119	2,454
3	6	76	114	190	23	19	232	49	184	56	289	116	2,386
2	6	75	113	189	23	19	230	48	182	56	286	115	2,362
1	5	74	110	184	18	18	221	46	174	54	275	110	2,268

a/ Allowances are 150 percent of base wage.
b/ Base wage plus allowances.
c/ Two percent of monthly wage times number of years of service.
d/ ten percent of monthly wage for a secondary school degree, 15 percent for a technical degree, and 25 percent for a university degree.
e/ Twenty-one percent of pensionable income.
f/ Twenty-four and one half percent of pensionable income.
g/ Net income plus worker and employer contribution.
h/ On average, 50 percent of pensionable income with a range of 40 to 60 percent.
i/ Includes the thirteenth monthly salary (net income) paid in equal installments in June and December.

Source: Ministry of Defense and staff estimates

Table A7.5: ANNUAL NET BENEFITS PER PERSON FROM RETRENCHMENT
(US$)

Rank	Year 0	1	2	3	4	Total Present Value
Lieutenant General	(36,841)	11,109	10,402	9,632	8,800	1,264
Major General	(34,963)	11,308	11,017	10,684	10,310	6,315
Brigadier General	(30,915)	11,110	10,861	10,568	10,233	9,838
Colonel	(22,547)	10,368	10,606	10,816	10,997	18,173
Lieutenant Colonel	(11,152)	15,330	15,449	15,550	15,635	47,839
Major	(5,256)	13,398	13,917	14,436	14,956	48,691
Captain	358	11,550	12,143	12,745	13,356	47,714
First Lieutenant 1	3,540	12,157	12,605	13,059	13,519	52,382
First Lieutenant 2	6,569	11,598	11,960	12,326	12,697	52,792
Second Lieutenant	6,802	9,905	10,363	10,733	10,733	46,512
Sergeant Major	(14,059)	7,916	8,504	8,504	8,749	17,980
Sergeant Principal	(7,386)	11,659	11,765	11,857	11,935	37,562
Sergeant Adjunct	(3,697)	10,460	10,568	10,664	10,748	36,704
Sergeant 1	407	9,643	10,202	10,770	11,347	40,308
Sergeant	3,236	9,604	10,294	10,588	10,884	42,588
Corporal 1	5,604	8,964	9,226	9,490	9,757	41,225
Corporal	6,150	8,316	8,455	8,595	8,595	38,477
Gendarme and Sailor	6,036	8,253	8,497	8,741	8,985	38,841
Conscripts	3,500	3,500	3,500	3,500	3,500	16,830

Source: Staff estimates.

Table A7.6: NOMINAL MILITARY EXPENDITURES, 1984-1992
(US$)

	1984	1985	1986	1987	1988	1989	1990	1991 Proj.	1992 Budget
	------------Million Australes----------				Billion Australes		Trillion Australes		Million Pesos
Personnel	62.7	351.3	677.1	1754.9	7.9	253.2	5.1	13.0	1511.9
MOD Administration	0.4	5.6	25.6	69.9	0.19	34.8	0.90	1.22	106.8
Army	23.8	127.0	249.6	599.5	2.8	81.3	1.5	4.1	541.0
Navy	14.1	76.2	135.2	393.1	1.7	49.7	1.0	2.6	303.7
Air Force	14.2	83.5	149.0	405.5	1.8	48.3	0.8	2.2	228.5
Paramilitary	10.1	58.9	117.7	286.8	1.4	39.1	1.0	2.9	331.9
Operations and maintenance	37.3	332.1	647.2	1402.6	8.38	202.3	3.05	8.73	865.8
MOD Administration	0.7	28.8	22.1	60.1	2.06	55.4	0.76	1.55	198.4
Army	10.0	84.0	166.3	343.2	1.77	48.8	0.81	1.55	145.7
Navy	5.4	45.4	109.4	265.6	1.12	30.6	0.47	1.18	82.7
Air Force	11.6	108.4	226.8	396.2	1.70	42.5	0.66	1.59	142.9
Paramilitary	9.7	65.4	149.5	337.5	1.73	25.1	0.36	2.87	296.1
Procurement	6.6	53.8	133.8	649.5	2.09	48.8	0.37	1.56	205.1
MOD Administration	1.2	24.6	2.1	238.7	0.76	23.3	0.10	1.24	144.5
Army	0.4	2.2	15.5	51.6	0.23	0.8	0.01	0.03	2.4
Navy	2.7	11.5	53.8	129.8	0.49	8.1	0.10	0.05	15.6
Air Force	2.1	12.6	52.9	195.8	0.53	14.7	0.12	0.20	36.8
Paramilitary	0.2	3.0	9.5	33.6	0.08	1.9	0.03	0.04	5.8
Construction	4.5	24.2	51.1	165.1	1.10	13.3	0.10	0.22	30.2
MOD Administration	0.0	0.1	0.3	8.8	0.29	2.6	0.02	0.02	4.1
Army	1.1	5.1	14.3	52.8	0.36	2.0	0.01	0.01	6.1
Navy	0.4	0.1	1.3	2.0	0.01	0.0	0.00	0.00	0.0
Air Force	2.9	17.6	33.7	89.1	0.42	8.7	0.07	0.17	19.8
Paramilitary	0.1	1.3	1.6	12.4	0.03	0.0	0.01	0.01	0.1
Research and Development	1.9	5.0	8.5	20.9	0.22	7.9	0.11	0.20	11.7
MOD Administration	1.7	3.7	6.1	6.40	0.15	6.6	0.08	0.15	6.8
Army	0.0	0.0	0.0	.0	0.00	0.0	0.00	0.00	0.0
Navy	0.0	0.0	0.0	3.0	0.01	0.3	0.01	0.01	2.2
Air Force	0.2	1.3	2.4	11.5	0.06	1.0	0.02	0.03	2.6
Paramilitary	0.0	0.0	0.0	0.0	0.00	0.0	0.00	0.00	0.0
Pensions	37.6	224.3	474.3	1203.1	5.9	159.4	3.3	8.8	1044.1
Total	150.5	990.7	2019.0	5196.0	25.5	685.0	12.1	32.6	3668.8
MOD Administration	4.0	62.7	56.2	383.9	3.4	122.7	1.9	4.2	460.7
Army	35.2	218.3	445.7	1047.0	5.2	132.9	2.3	5.7	695.2
Navy	22.7	133.3	299.7	793.5	3.3	88.7	1.6	3.8	404.2
Air Force	31.0	223.5	464.8	1098.2	4.5	115.1	1.6	4.2	430.6
Paramilitary	20.1	128.6	278.3	670.4	3.2	66.1	1.4	5.8	633.9
Memorandum: Total (excluding pensions)	112.9	766.4	1544.7	3992.9	19.64	525.6	8.77	23.74	2624.7
Pensions Payments	37.6	224.3	474.3	1203.1	5.9	159.4	3.3	8.8	1044.1
I.A.F.	30.7	183.5	383.5	978.4	4.8	129.1	2.6	6.7	800.2
Treasury payments	22.6	124.0	261.7	664.0	3.3	90.4	2.0	4.6	555.7
Fund payments	8.1	59.5	121.8	314.4	1.5	38.7	0.7	2.0	244.4
Paramilitary	6.9	40.8	90.7	224.7	1.1	30.3	0.7	2.1	244.0
Treasury payments	5.1	29.6	64.7	165.2	0.8	22.0	0.5	1.6	183.5
MOD payments	1.8	11.2	26.1	59.5	0.3	0.3	0.2	0.5	60.4
Memorandum: Ministry of Defense									
I.A.F. Contributions a/	9.2	52.7	98.5	261.8	1.2	33.3	0.7	1.9	212.9
Army	3.5	19.1	34.1	97.6	0.4	12.3	0.2	0.6	73.0
Navy	3.3	19.5	35.6	95.0	0.4	11.5	0.2	0.6	61.4
Air Force	2.4	14.0	28.8	69.3	0.3	9.5	0.2	0.7	78.5
Interest and Amortization	26.2	238.8	299.0	719.5	2.4	106.9	0.4	3.2	323.2

a/ Worker and Employer Contributions

ANNEX 13.1

THE SOURCES OF FINANCING OF THE COMBINED PUBLIC SECTOR: A MACROCONSISTENCY FRAMEWORK

1.   The objective of this annex is to examine the consistency between consolidated public sector borrowing requirements and financing. As a starting point, the budget constraint for the public non-financial sector (NFPS) can be expressed as:

$$(1) \qquad G + I_g + iB_g + i^*B^*_g = T + \triangle B_p + \triangle B_f + \triangle L_g + \triangle B^*_g + \triangle R_g$$

where

G	=	public current expenditures
I_g	=	public investment
iB_g	=	net interest payments on domestic debt paid by the NFPS
i^*B_g	=	net interest payments on foreign debt paid by the NFPS
T	=	public revenues
$\triangle B_p$	=	domestic bonds issued to the private sector
$\triangle B_f$	=	domestic bonds issued to the Central Bank
$\triangle L_g$	=	change in domestic credit extended by the Central Bank
$\triangle B^*_g$	=	change in foreign credit to the NFPS
$\triangle R_g$	=	net change in foreign reserves of the NFPS

Equation (1) states that the non financial public sector can finance its expenditures, which consists of purchases of domestic goods for consumption and investment purposes and interest payments on domestic and foreign debt through taxes, sales of public bonds, borrowing from the Central Bank and external debt. The net change in international reserves is influenced by the revenues from privatization and by the use of these revenues.

2.   The budget constraint of the Central Bank is:

$$(2) \qquad \triangle R_p + \triangle R_g + i^*B^*_f + iB_f - \triangle B^*_f + \triangle L_p + \triangle L_g + \triangle B_f = \triangle H$$

where

$\triangle H$	=	change in monetary base
iB_f	=	net interest payments on domestic debt paid by the Central Bank
i^*B_f	=	net interest payments on foreign debt paid by the Central Bank
$\triangle R_p$	=	change in foreign reserves (derived from operations with the private sector)
$\triangle R_g$	=	change in foreign reserves (derived from operations with the public sector)
$\triangle L_p$	=	change in credit to the private sector
$\triangle L_g$	=	change in credit to the public sector
$\triangle B_f$	=	change in public bonds held by the Central Bank

The principal assets of the Central Bank are net international reserves, domestic credit, and public bonds. These assets are backing the monetary liabilities of the Central Bank, i.e., the monetary base.

3.   The budget constraint of the consolidated public sector is the summation of equations (1) and (2):

$$(3) \quad [G + I_g - T] + [iB_g + i^*B^*_g] + [i^*B^*_f + iB_f] + \triangle R_p + \triangle L_p = \triangle H + \triangle B_p + \triangle B^*_g + \triangle B^*_f$$

The first bracket represents the primary deficit, the second net interest payments paid by the non-financial public sector, and the third interest payments paid by the Central Bank.[1] The summation of these three brackets represents the consolidated public sector balance. To arrive at a borrowing requirement for the combined public sector, we add to the above balance the variations in international reserves and the net lending to the private sector. The consolidated public sector deficit can be financed through monetary creation ($\triangle H$), external financing ($\triangle B^*$), and sales of public bonds to the private sector (including commercial banks). Note that the changes in the monetary base have been decomposed into remonetization and the inflation tax (see footnote 5 in chapter 13).

4.   The framework developed above has been applied to years 1990 and 1991 on a quarterly base. The first objective consists in reconciling the ex-post accounts of the public sector. The results are presented in Tables 13.3 and 13.4 of the report. In general, the results are satisfactory in the sense that the discrepancy between the sources of financing and the financing requirements of the consolidated public sector is relatively small. Several factors may explain the existence of this discrepancy: (i) the quality of the data; (ii) the heterogeneity of the sources used; (iii) the high inflation rate during 1990 and the first quarter of 1991; and (iv) the variation in the exchange rate during 1990 and the first quarter of 1991.

5.   The data has been obtained from the budget published by the Ministry of Economy, the Monetary Program of the Central Bank, and the IMF. Interest payments are presented above the line on an accrual basis. Therefore, arrears appear below the line as a source of financing. The real interest payments have been used since there are no other statistical information available. The overall deficit is therefore defined as the operational deficit, which omits the inflation-induced portion of interest payments from the deficit calculation. However, this measure is likely to underestimate the revenues from the inflation tax.[2] As the results are expressed in US dollars, the values expressed in local currency have been divided by the monthly average nominal exchange rate for each quarter.

---

1   Foreign interest payments are shown on an accrued basis, and domestic interest payments are shown on a nominal basis. Arrears on external debt service are included in net foreign borrowing.

2   For a discussion, see M. Blejer and A. Cheastny, "The Measurement of Fiscal Deficits: Analytical and Methodological Issues," *Journal of Economic Literature*, December 1991.

6.   The most interesting aspect of these results is the shift in the sources of financing used by the public sector between 1990 and 1991. This shift is described in detail in Chapter 13 of the report. The primary surplus is projected to increase from US$2,002 million in 1990 to US$2,960 million in 1991. In fact, this improvement is largely due to the excess revenues provided by the privatization (about US$1,687 million in 1991). Note, while (accrued) external nominal interest of the public sector is slightly lower in 1991 than in 1990, domestic interest payments increased over the last 12 months. The sum of the above resulted in a consolidated public deficit of about US$3,218 million in 1990 and US$2,121 million in 1991. Note, however, that about 50 percent of the total deficit in 1991 comes from the bad results of the first quarter and that the consolidated public sector balance is projected to be positive in the last quarter of 1991. Since the second quarter of 1991, the most important part of the fiscal deficit consists in the interest payments and the amortization of domestic debt. Including the Bonex, this represents about 32 percent of the total deficit of the consolidated public sector. This illustrates the fact that Argentina's government wants to preserve its creditworthiness, at least in the domestic market. In order to determine the financing requirement of the combined public sector, we included the variation in international reserves (derived from operations with the private sector) and lending extended by the Central Bank to the private sector. The net accumulation of reserves appears to be lower in 1991 than in 1990. But, this result is mostly attributable to the first quarter of 1991. Overall, the borrowing requirements declined from US$9,073 million in 1990 to US$6,494 million in 1991.

ANNEX 14.1

GENERAL DESCRIPTION OF THE PROJECTIONS

1.   The general purpose of the projections is to assess whether the proposed fiscal and monetary policy and major macroeconomic targets for inflation, reserve accumulation, and growth, are consistent with available financing for the public sector and the balance of payments. The projections are derived from a two-gap model that integrates the public sector and financial sector into a variation of the Bank's Revised Minimum Standard Model-Extended (RMSM-X). The model consists of: (i) a set of consistent macroeconomic statistics for the base year 1990 that includes public finances, balance of payments, national income accounts, the financial sector, and external and domestic debt; (ii) a series of exogenous variables and parameters which consist of assumptions based on past performance or targets; and (iii) equations describing the relations among the variables that permit the projection of a consistent set of accounts.

2.   Because of the strong relation between public sector deficits, inflation, and poor macroeconomic performance, this model differs from most Bank models by placing the public sector at the center of the analysis. The central macroeconomic issue in Argentina, especially after the assumption of external debt of the private sector, is the internal transfer problem. The model is therefore constructed so that the primary gap is in public finances rather than in the balance of payments. While the gaps are in theory closely related, positioning the gap in the public sector allows a more direct focus on public sector financing requirements, and allows the balance of payments gap to close through private capital flows that finance the residual savings-investment balance of the private sector.

3.   As with other RMSM-X models in the Bank, the model for Argentina has three basic markets summarized in the equations for GDP growth, money market equilibrium, and the market for foreign-denominated securities. The goods and services market equilibrium as presented in the national accounts--the major aggregates being investment, consumption, and the trade balance--are a function of the rate of GDP growth. The flow equilibrium in financial markets is a function of the *ex ante* supply of base money--the result of the supply of credit to the private sector and the Government as well as reserve increase--balancing with the demand for money, which is a function of inflation and growth. The third market, that of foreign denominated securities, is a function of demand for foreign savings to finance the domestic savings-investment balances of the public and private sectors. These are described in separate sections below dealing with national accounts, the public sector, the balance of payments, financial markets, and debt stocks.

A. National Accounts

4.   The national accounts are derived as in the conventional RMSM-X models in the Bank.

(1) $GDP = C + I_{pr} + I_g + G + (X - M)$

Private consumption (C) and investment (I_{pr}) and the resource balance (X - M) are functions of the growth rate of GDP. Public consumption (G) and public investment (I_g) are policy variables and considered in the first two years--19091-92--to be exogenous. The public sector and resource balance are discussed further below.

B. Public Sector

5.   Revenues (T) less noninterest expenditures (G + (I_g)) equal the primary deficit (D). Revenues are a function of assumed elasticities of various taxes times their respective macroeconomic variables (e.g., trade taxes for import-exports, VAT for GDP, etc.). Expenditures for wages and goods and services, after adjustments for anticipated policy changes in 1991-92, are assumed constant as a share of GDP. Transfers to the provinces and social security are a function of revenues in the same period. The social security flow deficit is assumed equal to zero.

6.   To the primary deficit (D) of the consolidated nonfinancial public sector can be added the public sector interest bill--domestic and foreign--to project the financing requirement after interest payments:

$$(2) \quad D + iB_g + i^*B_g^* = \triangle B_g + \triangle B_g^* + \triangle C_g$$

As outlined in the 1989 Country Economic Memorandum[1], equation 2 is the deficit and financing equation for the nonfinancial public sector, and states that the primary deficit (D) plus domestic (iB_g) and foreign ($i^*B_g^*$) interest payments on public debt are financed through increases in domestic ($\triangle B$) and foreign borrowing ($\triangle B^*$) and credit to the Government from the Central Bank. Equation 3 is the nominal quasi-fiscal deficit of the Central Bank (QFD_{ob}), given by the difference between earnings on its assets and interest expenses.

$$(3) \quad QFD = (\triangle C_g + \triangle C_{is} + \triangle R) + \triangle MB$$

The nominal quasi-fiscal deficit is financed through increases in the Central Bank's foreign and domestic liabilities; as noted below, because the domestic interest payments are zero and we have consolidated all non-IMF foreign debt with the Treasury, the quasi-fiscal deficit is equal to earnings on reserves less IMF charges.[2]

7.   Equation 4 represents the consolidation of the accounts.

$$(4) \quad d + iB_g + i^*B_g^* + QFD = \triangle B_g + \triangle B_g^* - \triangle C_{is} - \triangle R_{ab} + \triangle MB$$

---

1   See also Anand and van Wijnbergen (1988) and Barbone and Beckerman (1989).

2   Also, the Central Bank is no longer issuing interest-bearing liabilities, so the terms for other nonmonetary liabilities in the 1989 CEM consistency framework have been dropped.

Since in theory and by law the Government has to ensure that the money base is fully backed by international reserves, the only way money can be created is through purchases of reserves.[3] This forecloses the collection of the inflation tax because:

(5) $\triangle MB + \triangle R_{ab}$

The change in the monetary base is therefore used to purchase reserves, and the last two terms are assumed equal to zero. Credit from the Central Bank to the financial system (C_{is}) is also assumed to be equal to zero--otherwise net domestic asset creation would soon result in inflationary pressures that would violate the model. In practice, some small net credit creation is likely to support the unconsolidated public financial system; however, if strictly defined convertibility is to be maintained--i.e., the ratio of reserves to money base is not to be violated--then the resulting quasi-fiscal deficit will have to be financed through a higher primary surplus or increased borrowing. This may prove to be the achilles heel of the model. Finally, domestic borrowing $(\triangle B_g)$ is constrained to zero so as to relieve pressure on financial markets to lend to the Government. This means that the financing requirement is assumed to be solely financed through the accumulation of arrears ("unidentified financing"). This then is the gap that must be filled to achieve macroeconomic consistency at international rates of inflation. The detail of the fiscal accounts is shown in Table A14.1.1.

8.   The main assumptions for prices, interest rates, and exchange rates are shown in Table A14.1.2.

C. Balance of Payments

9.   The general balance of payments is the conventional relation given in Equation 6:

(6) $\triangle R = X - M + i^* B^* + I^* + \triangle B^*$

The current account in the balance of payments is determined as a function of several exogenous variables: export and import prices, export growth rates, import elasticities, and international interest rates (LIBOR, i^*). The real value of imports is a function of import elasticities times the relevant national accounts variables--GDP, private consumption, and investment. the interest bill is the product of the interest rate times the foreign debt stock as well as dividends on the stock of foreign direct investment. The price volumes and elasticity assumptions for the trade accounts are given in Tables A14.1.3 and A14.1.4.

---

3   In practice, the law counts as reserves dollar-denominated Government securities (BONEX), and in any short period the Government can increase or decrease the BONEX backing of the base by some small portion. However, the BONEX component of the reserve backing has consistently been less than 10 percent, and any large increase would trigger a portfolio shift in financial markets.

10.   The capital account incorporates the projected foreign direct investment (I^*) as well as debt flows based on amortization schedules and projected disbursements (including extant and projected new commitments). Finally, the capital account in the balance of payments incorporates the results of the unidentified financing provided to fill the internal gap in public finances as a capital inflow; this in effect partially offsets accrued interest and amortization obligations to commercial banks.

11.   Because the model links reserve accumulation to the money supply process (equation 5), reserve increases reflect the public's willingness to hold domestic currency, and are estimated as a function of money demand (see below).

12.   Since the unidentified financing gap closes through the fiscal accounts instead of through the traditional balance of payments and because reserve changes are linked to money demand, the balance of payments can close through adjustments in the current account or in the capital account. The current account could close the model through adjusting import levels (either as a function of changes in the GDP growth or import elasticities with respect to GDP, implying movements in the real exchange rate). The capital account could close via assumptions of changes in private, non-debt creating capital movements. We have chosen the second alternative since the scenario makes no assumption about the real exchange rate that would alter the elasticities; in any event, we wish to know the magnitudes of necessary private savings to close the macroeconomic accounts. The detailed balance of payments is shown in Table A14.1.5.

D. Financing Sector

13.   The flow equilibrium in financial markets is established by the interaction of supply and demand for base money. The creation of *ex ante* base money almost exclusively through the balance of payments (since credit to the Government and financial system are, by construction, foreclosed); demand is the reflection of growth and the rate of inflation. Credit expansion was then a function of private demand for financial assets estimated on the basis of past performance of economic growth and inflation, and has a counterpart either as private foreign liabilities or remonetization and accumulation of reserves.

14.   The financial sector accounts are given by the summation of the Central Bank asset and liabilities, and the rest of the financial sector. Thus, for the Central Bank:

$$(7)\quad \triangle R_{ab} + \triangle C_g \ (=0) + \triangle C_{is} \ (=0) = \triangle MB \ (g, \pi) + \triangle NW \ (=-QFD)$$

The change in assets--net foreign reserves of the Central Bank (R_{ab}), credit to the Government (G_g), and credit to the financial system (C_{is})--is equal to change in the monetary base and net worth. The change in the monetary aggregates are estimated on the basis of past willingness of the private sector to hold currency as a function of growth (g) and price stability (π). We have omitted consideration of any nonmonetary, interest-bearing liabilities of the Central Bank since the Government has opted not to resort to this instrument as a matter of policy.

15.   Changes in the net asset position of the rest of the financial system are given by:

(8) $\triangle R_{is} + \triangle R_{ASab} + \triangle C_g \ (=0) + \triangle C_{pa} =$
$\triangle B_{pa}^{*} + \triangle M4 + \triangle C_{is} \ (=0) + \triangle NW_{bs} \ (=0)$

Increased liabilities to the private sector, either from direct borrowing abroad ($\triangle B_{pa}^{*}$) or in the form of deposits (M4), are, after depositing reserves with the Central Bank ($\triangle R_{ASab}$), channeled to the private sector in the form of credit ($\triangle C_{pa}$) or maintained in foreign currency reserves elsewhere.

16.   In practice, the model works only with the consolidated financial system.

(9) $\triangle R + \triangle C_g \ (=0) + \triangle C_{pa} = \triangle M1 + \triangle QM + \triangle B_{pa}^{*}$

Capital inflows abroad find their way into the financial system as M4 (M1+quasi-money, QM)--i.e., currency, demand deposits, savings deposits, and time deposits--and have their counterpart changes in the stock of foreign assets of the banks and credit to the private sector. Private foreign liabilities to the financial system are given from the balance of payments.

E. Debt Stocks

17.   The flow equilibrium in the balance of payments and domestic financial markets also has two equations describing the evolution of foreign and domestic debt stocks:

(10) $B_{i*} = B_{t-1}^{*} + \triangle B^{*}$

(11) $B_t = B_{t-1} + D = \triangle B \ (=0, 1992\text{-}95)$

The external public and private debt stock in time t (B_t^{*}) is equal to the previous stock plus the debt-creating flows in the capital account of the balance of payments. This is the gapfill debt in the model. New domestic borrowing is in fact constrained to zero, such that the domestic debt stock is falling in the first five years of the model. In the out-years (to avoid the destabilizing debt payments associated with the Consolidation Bond) we have permitted some domestic borrowing to refinance the debt payments and left domestic debt approximately constant. The projected debt flows are shown in Tables A14.1.6 (for domestic debt) and A14.1.7 (for foreign flows).

F. Closing the Model

18.   The model can be run either with a "requirements" approach or with an "availabilities" approach. A requirement approach takes as a given the objectives of GDP growth, inflation, and external reserve accumulation, and then uses the model to ensure that the consolidated public sector deficit (including the Central Bank) and expenditures are consistent with available financing. An availabilities approach takes as a given a projected level of available external borrowing and expected demand for money, and then adjusts the growth rate, fiscal stance, and reserve accumulation to conform to projected financing and inflation objectives.

Table A14.1.1: PUBLIC SECTOR ACCOUNTS

	1991	1992	1993	1994	1995	1996	1997	1998	1999	2000	2001
National Administration Current Revenues	19,116	25,999	30,591	33,898	36,545	39,250	42,269	45,517	49,061	52,930	57,119
DGI and Customs	17,332	24,113	28,635	31,216	33,647	36,131	38,902	41,882	45,133	48,682	52,524
VAT a/	5,985	10,570	14,853	16,204	17,507	18,845	20,343	21,961	23,729	25,665	27,759
Income b/	1,747	2,420	4,851	5,394	5,773	6,153	6,571	7,015	7,495	8,014	8,598
Assets c/		692	697	748	800	853	911	973	1,039	1,111	1,192
Sales d/	1,625	2,315	2,449	2,688	2,877	3,066	3,274	3,495	3,735	3,993	4,284
Fuel	2,031	2,630	2,288	2,499	2,700	2,906	3,137	3,387	3,659	3,958	4,281
Imports e/	812	1,847	1,918	2,095	2,274	2,461	2,672	2,900	3,150	3,424	3,689
Exports e/	501	0	0	0	0	0	0	0	0	0	0
Others f/	4,631	3,640	1,579	1,589	1,716	1,848	1,994	2,153	2,326	2,516	2,722
Non Tax Revenue	1,784	1,886	1,955	2,682	2,898	3,119	3,367	3,635	3,927	4,248	4,594
National Administration Current Expenditures	20,560	23,811	25,874	28,155	31,134	33,241	35,704	37,871	40,296	42,894	45,739
W&S General Government	4,512	4,622	5,401	5,833	6,103	6,570	7,092	7,656	8,273	8,948	9,802
G&S General Government	1,198	1,796	1,841	1,915	2,087	2,119	2,288	2,470	2,669	2,886	3,247
Others	176	0	0	0	0	0	0	0	0	0	0
Transfers	10,023	14,657	15,192	16,054	18,192	19,463	20,877	22,394	24,043	25,837	27,791
Provinces	8,027	12,507	13,004	13,632	16,027	17,132	18,360	19,677	21,107	22,662	24,357
Coparticipation		10,885	11,017	11,332	13,640	14,664	15,804	17,029	18,363	19,820	21,412
Others g/		1,622	1,987	2,300	2,387	2,468	2,557	2,649	2,744	2,843	2,945
Other Transfers h/	1,996	2,150	2,189	2,423	2,166	2,331	2,517	2,717	2,935	3,175	3,434
Interest (Accrued)	4,650	2,685	3,425	4,354	4,751	5,089	5,447	5,351	5,312	5,223	4,899
Domestic	322	160	409	776	926	1,026	1,325	1,262	1,213	1,165	1,045
Foreign i/	4,328	2,525	3,016	3,577	3,825	4,064	4,122	4,090	4,100	4,058	3,854
Social Security Savings	(130)	428	(1,367)	(3,334)	(2,912)	(2,695)	(2,443)	(2,036)	(1,355)	(1,169)	(422)
Public Enterprise Noninterest Savings	363	311	827	(24)	(50)	(45)	(40)	(36)	(32)	(29)	(26)
Current Revenues		9,116	4,893	540	486	436	392	352	316	284	255
Current Non-interest Expenditures		8,804	4,066	564	536	481	432	388	348	313	281
Public Savings	(1,211)	2,927	4,177	2,384	2,449	3,270	4,083	5,574	7,377	8,838	10,932
Capital Receipts	1,637	1,976	540	0	0	0	0	0	0	0	0
Capital Expenditures	2,219	2,410	3,389	3,073	3,533	4,063	4,673	5,374	6,180	7,107	8,173
National Administration	660	1,325	2,488	2,765	3,188	3,666	4,204	4,820	5,543	6,375	7,331
Public Enterprises	1,559	1,085	901	307	346	398	469	554	637	732	842
Nonfinancial Public Sector Balance	(1,793)	2,493	1,328	(688)	(1,084)	(794)	(590)	200	1,196	1,731	2,759
Quasi-Fiscal Surplus of Central Bank q/	64	(46)	197	354	439	570	697	860	958	1,075	1,167
Overall Balance	(1,729)	2,447	1,525	(334)	(646)	(224)	107	1,060	2,154	2,806	3,926
Net External Financing	276	116	2,125	397	(426)	(1,075)	(1,441)	(852)	(1,528)	(2,498)	(2,385)
Disbursements r/	4,666	3,731	5,349	3,963	3,752	4,160	4,170	4,007	3,890	3,813	2,263
Amortizations s/	4,389	3,616	3,224	3,566	4,178	5,235	5,611	4,859	5,418	6,311	4,648
Net Domestic Financing	(897)	(573)	102	473	824	920	(1,172)	(1,392)	(1,405)	(1,434)	(1,849)
Net Borrowing	(634)	(573)	102	473	824	920	(1,172)	(1,392)	(1,405)	(1,434)	(1,849)
Borrowing	0	0	322	693	824	920	840	800	900	1,000	0
Repayment	634	573	220	220	0	0	2,012	2,192	2,305	2,434	1,849
Net Domestic Credit t/	(263)	0	0	0	0	0	0	0	0	0	0
BOCON Buybacks = Social Security Income Tax Receipts		0	0	0	0	0	0	0	0	0	0
Government Purchase of Debt Guarantees u/		0	(43)								
IFI and Japanese Guarantee Purchases		0	(2,965)								
Cash Downpayment on Arrears		0	(700)								
Budget Surplus applied to BOCON buybacks		(1,990)	0	0							
External Additional Financing	2,350	(0)	(44)	(536)	248	378	2,506	1,183	779	1,126	309
Memo:											
Primary Surplus v/	2,857	5,178	4,753	3,666	3,667	4,296	4,856	5,552	6,509	6,954	7,658
Operational Primary Surplus	1,221	3,202	4,403	3,666	3,667	4,296	4,856	5,552	6,509	6,954	7,658
Cash Surplus of Treasury w/		829									

Table A14.1.2: PRICES, INTEREST RATES AND EXCHANGE RATES

	1991	1992	1993	1994	1995	1996	1997	1998	1999	2000	2001
ER Real Index (% + = devaluation)	−15.0%	−7.3%	3.0%	0.1%	0.0%	0.0%	0.0%	0.0%	0.0%	0.0%	0.0%
ER Real Index (1987=100)	69.0	63.9	65.8	65.9	65.9	65.9	65.9	65.9	65.9	65.9	65.9
ER (pesos per 1US$)	0.954	1.00	1.00	1.00	1.00	1.00	1.01	1.01	1.01	1.01	1.01
ER (pesos per 1US$) − end of period	0.998	1.00	1.00	1.00	1.00	1.00	1.01	1.01	1.01	1.01	1.01
ER (US$ per peso)	1.049	1.001	1.000	1.000	1.000	0.996	0.995	0.993	0.991	0.989	0.987
Monthly Domestic Interest (real)	1.0%	0.8%	0.8%	0.8%	0.8%	0.8%	0.8%	0.8%	0.8%	0.8%	0.8%
Annual Domestic Interest (nominal)	169.3%	21.7%	17.7%	14.3%	14.2%	14.2%	14.2%	14.2%	14.2%	14.2%	14.2%
LIBOR for projection a/	7.3%	3.8%	4.5%	5.8%	6.15%	6.8%	7.0%	7.0%	7.0%	7.0%	7.0%
LIBOR (IMF and World Bank estimate)	6.1%	3.8%	4.5%	5.8%	6.5%	7.0%	7.0%	7.0%	7.0%	7.0%	7.0%
Population Growth	1.5%	1.5%	1.5%	1.4%	1.4%	1.4%	1.4%	1.4%	1.4%	1.4%	1.4%
Population (Mln.)	33.27	33.77	34.27	34.75	35.24	35.73	36.23	36.74	37.26	37.78	38.31
GNP per capita	2,233	2,387	2,436	2,484	2,543	2,603	2,672	2,749	2,829	2,915	3,006
MUV (Annual < >) b/	2.1%	4.3%	3.8%	1.9%	2.7%	3.4%	3.6%	3.6%	3.6%	3.6%	3.6%
MUV Index (Intl. Deflator)	115.0	119.9	124.5	126.9	130.3	134.7	139.6	144.6	149.8	155.2	160.8
Average Monthly Inflation	7.5%	0.9%	0.6%	0.3%	0.3%	0.3%	0.3%	0.3%	0.3%	0.3%	0.3%
Domestic Index (annual < >)	139.0%	11.3%	7.0%	3.9%	3.8%	3.8%	3.8%	3.8%	3.8%	3.8%	3.8%
Domestic Index	760517	846340	905539	940930	976536	1013489	1051840	1091642	1132951	1175823	1220317
Investment Index (annual < >)	139.0%	11.3%	7.0%	3.9%	3.8%	3.8%	3.8%	3.8%	3.8%	3.8%	3.8%
Investment Index	760517	846340	905539	940930	976536	1013489	1051840	1091642	1132951	1175823	1220317

a/ Period average LIBOR.
b/ 1992 figure is G−7 inflation (consumer prices).

Table A14.1.3: EXPORTS

	1991	1992	1993	1994	1995	1996	1997	1998	1999	2000	2001
1987 Real Exports (Annual <>)											
Exports of Goods	−2.6%	4.0%	8.3%	9.4%	6.6%	6.6%	6.7%	6.7%	6.7%	6.8%	6.8%
Exports of G&NFS	2.2%	1.7%	8.3%	9.2%	6.6%	6.7%	6.7%	6.8%	6.8%	6.8%	6.9%
1. Livestock	−2.0%	4.0%	6.0%	9.5%	2.2%	2.2%	2.2%	2.2%	2.2%	2.2%	2.2%
2. Cereals	−2.0%	4.0%	6.0%	9.5%	2.2%	2.2%	2.2%	2.2%	2.2%	2.2%	2.2%
3. Other Agriculture Goods	−2.0%	4.0%	9.0%	10.0%	7.5%	7.5%	7.5%	7.5%	7.5%	7.5%	7.5%
4. Fats & Oils	−2.0%	4.0%	9.0%	10.0%	7.5%	7.5%	7.5%	7.5%	7.5%	7.5%	7.5%
5. Manufac., Food & Bever.	−2.0%	4.0%	9.0%	10.0%	8.5%	8.5%	8.5%	8.5%	8.5%	8.5%	8.5%
6. Petroleum	0.0%	4.0%	6.5%	6.5%	6.0%	6.0%	6.0%	6.0%	6.0%	6.0%	6.0%
7. Chemicals & Plastics	−3.0%	4.0%	9.0%	9.0%	7.0%	7.0%	7.0%	7.0%	7.0%	7.0%	7.0%
8. Textiles	−2.0%	4.0%	9.0%	9.0%	5.0%	5.0%	5.0%	5.0%	5.0%	5.0%	5.0%
9. Other Manufactures	−4.0%	4.0%	9.0%	9.0%	8.0%	8.0%	8.0%	8.0%	8.0%	8.0%	8.0%
Non Factor Services	6.0%	−8.0%	8.0%	8.0%	7.0%	7.0%	7.0%	7.0%	7.0%	7.0%	7.0%
Exports in 1987 Mln. US$											
1. Livestock	1,018	1,059	1,123	1,229	1,256	1,284	1,312	1,341	1,371	1,401	1,432
2. Cereals	1,125	1,170	1,241	1,358	1,388	1,419	1,450	1,482	1,515	1,548	1,582
3. Other Agriculture Goods	948	986	1,075	1,182	1,271	1,367	1,469	1,579	1,698	1,825	1,962
4. Fats & Oils	1,185	1,232	1,343	1,478	1,588	1,708	1,836	1,973	2,121	2,280	2,451
5. Manufac., Food & Bever.	1,912	1,989	2,168	2,384	2,587	2,807	3,045	3,304	3,585	3,890	4,220
6. Petroleum	268	279	297	317	336	356	377	400	424	449	476
7. Chemicals & Plastics	790	822	896	976	1,045	1,118	1,196	1,280	1,369	1,465	1,568
8. Textiles	570	592	646	704	739	776	815	856	898	943	990
9. Other Manufactures	2,758	2,869	3,127	3,408	3,681	3,975	4,293	4,637	5,008	5,409	5,841
Non Factor Services	2,489	2,290	2,473	2,671	2,858	3,058	3,272	3,502	3,747	4,009	4,290
Export Price Indices (Annual <>)											
1. Livestock	3.9%	−8.3%	3.3%	1.6%	3.1%	8.5%	7.8%	7.3%	6.8%	6.3%	6.0%
2. Cereals	2.1%	−1.5%	−0.1%	3.0%	3.0%	3.0%	3.0%	3.0%	3.0%	3.0%	3.0%
3. Other Agriculture Goods	−2.5%	−6.3%	3.3%	5.8%	7.5%	4.5%	4.5%	4.5%	4.5%	4.5%	4.5%
4. Fats & Oils	2.9%	7.7%	3.8%	2.3%	3.9%	2.0%	2.0%	2.0%	2.0%	2.0%	2.0%
5. Manufac., Food & Bever.	2.1%	4.3%	3.8%	1.9%	2.7%	3.5%	3.5%	3.5%	3.5%	3.5%	3.5%
6. Petroleum	−18.4%	1.7%	−1.7%	0.6%	3.4%	7.2%	6.7%	6.3%	5.9%	6.5%	6.5%
7. Chemicals & Plastics	2.1%	4.3%	3.8%	1.9%	2.7%	3.5%	3.5%	3.5%	3.5%	3.5%	3.5%
8. Textiles	2.1%	4.3%	3.8%	1.9%	2.7%	3.5%	3.5%	3.5%	3.5%	3.5%	3.5%
9. Other Manufactures	2.1%	4.3%	3.8%	1.9%	2.7%	3.5%	3.5%	3.5%	3.5%	3.5%	3.5%
Export Price Indices (1987=100)											
1. Livestock	111.3	102.1	105.4	107.1	110.5	119.8	129.2	138.6	148.0	157.3	166.7
2. Cereals	133.8	131.8	131.7	135.6	139.7	143.8	148.1	152.5	157.1	161.8	166.6
3. Other Agriculture Goods	100.5	94.2	97.3	102.9	110.7	115.6	120.8	126.2	131.9	137.8	144.0
4. Fats & Oils	103.5	111.5	115.7	118.3	122.9	125.4	127.9	130.5	133.1	135.8	138.5
5. Manufac., Food & Bever.	119.6	124.8	129.4	131.9	135.4	140.1	145.0	150.1	155.3	160.8	166.4
6. Petroleum	100.6	102.3	100.6	101.2	104.7	112.2	119.8	127.3	134.9	143.6	152.9
7. Chemicals & Plastics	114.9	119.9	124.4	126.7	130.1	134.6	139.3	144.2	149.3	154.5	159.9
8. Textiles	114.9	119.9	124.4	126.7	130.1	134.6	139.3	144.2	149.3	154.5	159.9
9. Other Manufactures	114.9	119.9	124.4	126.7	130.1	134.6	139.3	144.2	149.3	154.5	159.9
Exports in Current Mln. US$											
1. Livestock	1,133	1,081	1,184	1,317	1,388	1,539	1,696	1,859	2,028	2,204	2,386
2. Cereals	1,506	1,543	1,634	1,842	1,939	2,041	2,148	2,261	2,379	2,504	2,635
3. Other Agriculture Goods	953	929	1,046	1,217	1,407	1,580	1,775	1,993	2,239	2,515	2,824
4. Fats & Oils	1,227	1,374	1,554	1,748	1,953	2,141	2,348	2,575	2,824	3,096	3,396
5. Manufac., Food & Bever.	2,287	2,481	2,806	3,144	3,502	3,933	4,416	4,959	5,569	6,254	7,023
6. Petroleum	270	286	299	320	351	399	452	509	571	645	728
7. Chemicals & Plastics	908	985	1,114	1,237	1,359	1,505	1,666	1,845	2,044	2,263	2,507
8. Textiles	655	710	803	892	961	1,045	1,136	1,234	1,341	1,457	1,584
9. Other Manufactures	3,170	3,439	3,889	4,318	4,788	5,352	5,983	6,688	7,475	8,356	9,340
	0.00%	0.00%	0.00%	0.00%							
Export Totals in Mln. US$											
Exports of Goods (Constant)	10,576	10,999	11,915	13,037	13,891	14,809	15,794	16,852	17,988	19,210	20,523
Exports of G&NFS (Constant)	13,065	13,289	14,388	15,708	16,750	17,867	19,066	20,353	21,735	23,219	24,812
Exports of Goods (Current)	12,107	12,828	14,329	16,036	17,648	19,535	21,619	23,923	26,471	29,295	32,423
Exports of G&NFS (Current)	14,843	15,575	17,408	19,424	21,372	23,655	26,186	28,985	32,083	35,516	39,320

Table A14.1.4: IMPORTS AND TERMS OF TRADE

		1991	1992	1993	1994	1995	1996	1997	1998	1999	2000	2001
Import Elasticities												
Imports of Goods (Annual <>)		96.7%	65.5%	1.5%	3.1%	4.7%	4.8%	4.9%	4.9%	5.0%	5.1%	3.9%
Imports of G&NFS (Annual <>)		65.7%	43.2%	1.3%	3.3%	4.6%	4.7%	4.8%	4.8%	4.8%	4.9%	4.0%
Import Elasticity (Imp. wrt GDP)		13.1	6.7	0.4	0.8	1.1	1.1	1.1	1.1	1.1	1.1	0.9
1. Food & Consumer Goods	G	37.4	4.0	0.4	0.4	0.5	1.0	1.0	1.0	1.0	1.0	1.0
2. Petroleum	G	22.0	0.1	0.1	0.1	0.1	0.1	0.1	0.1	0.1	0.1	0.1
3. Intermediate Goods	Ir	9.2	6.8	0.2	0.6	0.9	0.9	0.9	0.9	0.9	0.9	0.9
4. Capital Goods	Ir	6.2	6.7	0.2	0.6	0.9	0.9	0.9	0.9	0.9	0.9	0.9
Non Factor Services	G	4.6	−0.9	0.1	1.0	1.0	1.0	1.0	1.0	1.0	1.0	1.0
Imports in 1987 Mln. US$												
1. Food & Consumer Goods		640	806	816	829	846	881	918	956	998	1,041	1,087
2. Petroleum		348	350	351	352	353	354	355	356	357	358	358
3. Intermediate Goods		4,055	5,834	5,869	6,010	6,232	6,462	6,706	6,960	7,229	7,515	7,813
4. Capital Goods		2,123	4,866	5,003	5,223	5,569	5,933	6,321	6,729	7,165	7,630	7,933
Non Factor Services		3,255	3,070	3,079	3,202	3,334	3,470	3,616	3,768	3,930	4,103	4,283
Import Price Indices (Annual <>)												
1. Food & Consumer Goods		−2.9%	−4.7%	3.4%	4.7%	6.8%	4.4%	4.4%	4.4%	4.4%	4.4%	4.4%
2. Petroleum		−18.4%	1.7%	−1.7%	0.6%	3.4%	7.2%	6.7%	6.3%	5.9%	6.5%	6.5%
3. Intermediate Goods		2.1%	4.3%	3.8%	1.9%	2.7%	3.5%	3.5%	3.5%	3.5%	3.5%	3.5%
4. Capital Goods		2.1%	4.3%	3.8%	1.9%	2.7%	3.5%	3.5%	3.5%	3.5%	3.5%	3.5%
Import Price Indices (1987=100)												
1. Food & Consumer Goods		101.6	96.7	100.0	104.7	111.8	116.7	121.8	127.2	132.7	138.6	144.6
2. Petroleum		100.6	102.3	100.6	101.2	104.7	112.2	119.8	127.3	134.9	143.6	152.9
3. Intermediate Goods		114.9	119.9	124.4	126.7	130.1	134.6	139.3	144.2	149.3	154.5	159.9
4. Capital Goods		114.9	119.9	124.4	126.7	130.1	134.6	139.3	144.2	149.3	154.5	159.9
Imports in Current Mln. US$												
1. Food & Consumer Goods		650	780	816	868	946	1,028	1,118	1,216	1,324	1,443	1,573
2. Petroleum		350	358	353	356	369	397	425	453	481	513	548
3. Intermediate Goods		4,660	6,995	7,301	7,615	8,107	8,700	9,345	10,038	10,791	11,611	12,493
4. Capital Goods		2,440	5,834	6,223	6,618	7,245	7,988	8,808	9,705	10,695	11,789	12,685
		0.00%	0.0%	0.0%								
Import Totals in Mln. US$												
Imports of Goods (Constant)		7,167	11,857	12,040	12,415	13,000	13,630	14,300	15,001	15,748	16,545	17,191
Imports of G&NFS (Constant)		10,422	14,927	15,119	15,617	16,334	17,100	17,916	18,769	19,678	20,648	21,475
Imports of Goods (Current)		8,100	13,967	14,693	15,457	16,667	18,113	19,696	21,412	23,292	25,357	27.299
Imports of G&NFS (Current)		11,843	17,649	18,526	19,520	21,010	22,788	24,742	26,859	29,178	31,723	34,185

Terms of Trade Index (1987=100)	1991	1992	1993	1994	1995	1996	1997	1998	1999	2000	2001
Export Price Index	114.5	116.6	120.3	123.0	127.0	131.9	136.9	142.0	147.2	152.5	158.0
Import Price Index	113.0	117.8	122.0	124.5	128.2	132.9	137.7	142.7	147.9	153.3	158.8
Terms of Trade Index	101.3	99.0	98.5	98.8	99.1	99.3	99.4	99.5	99.5	99.5	99.5
Terms of Trade Index (Annual <>)											
Export Price Index	1.4%	1.9%	3.1%	2.3%	3.3%	3.8%	3.8%	3.7%	3.7%	3.6%	3.6%
Import Price Index	0.4%	4.2%	3.6%	2.0%	3.0%	3.7%	3.6%	3.6%	3.6%	3.6%	3.6%
Terms of Trade Index	1.0%	−2.2%	−0.5%	0.2%	0.3%	0.2%	0.1%	0.1%	0.0%	0.0%	−0.0%

Table A14.1.5: BALANCE OF PAYMENTS

	1991	1992	1993	1994	1995	1996	1997	1998	1999	2000	2001
Trade Balance	4,007	(1,139)	(364)	578	981	1,422	1,923	2.511	3,179	3,938	5,125
Exports of Goods	12,107	12,828	14,329	16,036	17,648	19,535	21,619	23.923	26,471	29,295	32,423
Imports of Goods	8,100	13,967	14,693	15,457	16,667	18,113	19,696	21,412	23,292	25,357	27,299
NFS Balance	(1,007)	(935)	(754)	(673)	(619)	(555)	(479)	(385)	(274)	(146)	10
Exports of NFS	2,736	2,747	3,079	3,389	3,724	4,120	4,567	5.063	5,612	6,221	6,896
Imports of NFS	3,743	3,682	3,833	4,062	4,343	4,675	5,046	5.448	5,886	6,367	6,886
Resource Balance	3,000	(2,074)	(1.118)	(95)	362	867	1,444	2,126	2,905	3,792	5,135
Net Factor Income	(5,777)	(4,656)	(4,398)	(5,286)	(5,997)	(6,818)	(7,488)	(7.918)	(8,510)	(9,048)	(9,491)
Factor Receipts	378	456	604	914	1,026	1,166	1,224	1.234	1,239	1,220	1,230
Interest on Reserves a/	378	335	604	914	1,026	1,166	1,224	1.234	1,239	1,220	1,230
Other FR	0	121	0	0	0	0	0	0	0	0	0
Factor Payments	(6,155)	(5,112)	(5,002)	(6,200)	(7,023)	(7,983)	(8,712)	(9.152)	(9,749)	(10,268)	(10,722)
Dividend Repatriation b/	(1,177)	(953)	(1,277)	(1,469)	(1,681)	(1,914)	(2,170)	(2.452)	(2,762)	(3,103)	(3,478)
MLT interest (exc. IMF)	(4,455)	(3,607)	(2,931)	(3,543)	(3,807)	(4,108)	(4,302)	(4,375)	(4,482)	(4,497)	(4,370)
IMF interest	(314)	(331)	(276)	(303)	(307)	(300)	(260)	(150)	(106)	(42)	(3)
ST interest	(166)	(220)	(518)	(885)	(1,228)	(1,661)	(1,979)	(2.175)	(2,398)	(2,625)	(2,870)
Other FP	(44)	0	0	0	0	0	0	0	0	0	0
Net Current Transfers	29	(49)	(47)	(44)	(42)	(40)	(38)	(36)	(34)	(33)	(31)
Current Account Balance	(2,748)	(6,779)	(5.562)	(5,425)	(5,677)	(5,991)	(6,082)	(5.828)	(5,639)	(5,288)	(4,387)
Net Direct Investment b/	2,481	2,481	3,240	1,925	2,118	2,329	2,562	2.818	3,100	3,410	3,751
Debt Conv. & Privatization c/	1,974	1,857	2,140	0	0	0	0	0	0	0	0
Other	507	624	1,100	1,925	2,118	2,329	2,562	2.818	3,100	3,410	3,751
Net MLT Flows	1,288	(250)	3,347	279	(157)	(544)	(512)	(259)	(527)	(1,416)	(2,438)
IBRD	138	248	738	423	235	139	137	115	8	(36)	(275)
IDB & Other Multilaterals	242	527	303	307	295	335	332	353	378	328	(172)
Bilaterals	697	(485)	0	2	(160)	(367)	(487)	(164)	(252)	26	(524)
Financial Markets	0	(127)	(143)	(205)	(178)	(358)	(378)	(435)	(767)	(1,536)	(574)
Eligible for Debt Deal		0	0	0	0	0	0	0	0	0	0
Ineligible for Debt Deal		(127)	(143)	(205)	(178)	(204)	(224)	(281)	(305)	(305)	(305)
Refinanced Arrears		0	0	0	0	(154)	(154)	(154)	(462)	(1,231)	(269)
Debt Conversion c/	0	0	0	0	0	0	0	0	0	0	0
Other	0	(127)	0	0	0	0	0	0	0	0	0
Bonds	395	(233)	(651)	(436)	(556)	(462)	(237)	(207)	79	8	(633)
Debt Conversion c/	0	0	0	0	0	0	0	0	0	0	0
Other	395	(233)	(651)	(436)	(556)	(462)	(237)	(207)	79	8	(633)
Supplier Credits	(185)	(380)	(65)	(12)	6	3	(13)	(21)	(38)	(238)	(259)
Private Non–guaranteed	0	200	200	200	200	167	133	100	67	33	(0)
IBRD, IDB, IMF & Japanese Interest Guarantees d/			2,965								
Net ST Private Flows e/	0	7,646	2,828	4,557	4,269	4,627	2,326	2,885	3,087	2,967	3.565
CAPNIE, E&O	(667)	(0)	(0)	(0)	(0)	0	(0)	0	(0)	(0)	(0)
Unidentified (Net) from Public Sector	2,350	(0)	(44)	(536)	248	378	2,506	1.183	779	1,126	309
Overall BOP Surplus	2,704	3,099	3,808	800	800	800	800	800	800	800	800
Financing:											
< > in Net Reserves (–=inc.)	(2,704)	(3,099)	(3,808)	(800)	(800)	(800)	(800)	(800)	(800)	(800)	(800)
< > in Gross Reserves (–=inc.)	(2,964)	(2,687)	(3,543)	(1,111)	(736)	(438)	4	(295)	158	392	(697)
Net IMF	(661)	338	(265)	311	(65)	(363)	(804)	(506)	(958)	(1,192)	(103)
Purchases	337	1,223	117	721	974	1,192	232	342	125	0	0
Repurchases	(998)	(885)	(382)	(410)	(1,039)	(1,555)	(1,036)	(848)	(1,083)	(1,192)	(103)
Other BCRA Reserves (–=inc.)	(400)	(74)	0	0	0	0	0	0	0	0	0
< > in NIR due to guarantees (–=inc.) f/		0	(3,008)	0	0	0	0	0	0	0	0
Memo:											
Gross Reserve Level g/	8,974	11,661	15,204	16,315	17,050	17,488	17,484	17,779	17,621	17,229	17,926
Liquid Reserves h/	5,946	9,044	9,579	10,690	11,426	11,863	11,860	12.154	11,996	11,604	12,301

Table A14.1.6: DOMESTIC DEBT
(US$ millions)

	1991	1992	1993	1994	1995	1996	1997	1998	1999	2000	2001
New Commitments/Interest Capitalization	0	16,910	322	693	824	920	840	800	900	1,000	0
BIC, BOCREX and BOCE a/ b/	0	0	0	0	0	0	800	800	900	1,000	0
Social Security Bonds c/	0	8,633	165	317	324	363	40	0	0	0	0
Suppliers Bonds	0	5,777	110	262	349	389	0	0	0	0	0
Tax Credit Bonds d/	0	2,500	48	114	151	168	0	0	0	0	0
New Issues											
Total Disbursements	0	0	322	693	824	920	840	800	900	1,000	0
BIC, BOCREX and BOCE a/ b/	0	0	0	0	0	0	800	800	900	1,000	0
Social Security Bonds	0	0	165	317	324	363	40	0	0	0	0
Suppliers Bonds	0	0	110	262	349	389	0	0	0	0	0
Tax Credit Bonds d/	0	0	48	114	151	168	0	0	0	0	0
New Issues											
Total Amortizations	606	573	220	220	0	0	2,012	2,192	2,305	2,434	1,849
BIC, BOCREX and BOCE a/ b/	606	573	220	220	0	0	0	0	0	0	0
Social Security Bonds	0	0	0	0	0	0	1,185	1,348	1,424	1,503	863
Suppliers Bonds	0	0	0	0	0	0	578	589	615	650	689
Tax Credit Bonds d/	0	0	0	0	0	0	250	255	266	281	298
New Issues											
Total Interest (Paid)	308	160	409	776	924	1,025	1,324	1,262	1,213	1,165	1,045
BIC, BOCREX and BOCE a/ b/	308	160	87	84	100	105	183	260	341	431	431
Social Security Bonds e/	0	0	165	317	324	363	365	281	193	99	26
Suppliers Bonds e/	0	0	110	262	349	389	462	421	379	335	288
Tax Credit Bonds e/	0	0	48	114	151	168	314	300	300	300	300
New Borrowings (Domestic Credit)	0	0	0	0	0	0	0	0	0	0	0
New Borrowings (Domestic Credit)	0	0	0	0	0	0	0	0	0	0	0
Disbursements			0	0	0	0	0	0	0	0	0
Amortizations			0	0	0	0	0	0	0	0	0
Total Debt	2,300	18,637	15,344	15,817	16,641	17,561	16,389	15,252	14,113	12,960	11,409
BIC, BOCREX and BOCE a/ b/	2,300	1,727	1,507	1,287	1,287	1,287	2,087	2,887	3,787	4,787	4,787
Social Security Bonds	0	8,633	5,403	5,720	6,043	6,406	5,262	3,914	2,490	987	124
Suppliers Bonds	0	5,777	5,887	6,149	6,498	6,887	6,309	5,721	5,106	4,456	3,767
Tax Credit Bonds	0	2,500	2,548	2,661	2,812	2,980	2,730	2,730	2,730	2,730	2,730
New Borrowings (Domestic Credit)	0	0	0	0	0	0	0	0	0	0	0
BOCON Cancelation (Total)		0	3,395	0							
Social Security Cash Savings (Income Tax Receipts)		0	0	0							
Face Value Of Debt Reduction		0	0	0							
Budget Surplus Buybacks		0	1,990	0							
Face Value Of Debt Reduction		0	2,341	0							
YPF Privatization Receipts f/		0	896								
Face Value Of Debt Reduction		0	1,054								
Discount (%)		15	15	10							

a/ Existing stock includes BIC and BOCE; includes 2.3 billion in dollar denominated bonds and 650 million in supplier credits in 1991.
b/ DOD in 1991 was reduced by US$606 mln. with conversion of BOCREX to BOTE.
c/ Includes SS BOCON and Obras Sociales (see below for terms).
d/ Accumulated government obligations for loss carryover of private companies.
   Commitments from 1997-2000 represent approx. 50% rollover of BOCONs
e/ Interest paid on LIBOR.
f/ 56% of US$ 1.6 billion in privatizations.

Table A14.1.7: FOREIGN DEBT
(US$ millions)

	1991	1992	1993	1994	1995	1996	1997	1998	1999	2000	2001
Total Disbursements	8,474	11,698	9,601	8,274	8,559	9,455	9,292	8,365	8,046	8,197	6,427
BONEX, BOTE, BOTESO and Eurobonds	956	1,200	960	1,200	1,200	1,125	1,500	1,000	1,000	1,000	500
World Bank	460	481	1,689	773	518	459	471	605	605	603	403
IDB & Other Multilaterals	450	748	1,000	539	500	625	756	850	950	1,000	600
Paris Club	1,122	0	1,640	670	500	700	1,150	1,150	1,150	1,150	700
Suppliers and other Bilaterals	0	200	150	150	150	150	150	150	150	150	150
Financial Markets	0	0	0	0	0	0	0	0	0	0	0
Eligible for Debt Deal	0	0	0	0	0	0	0	0	0	0	0
Ineligible for Debt Deal	0	0	0	0	0	0	0	0	0	0	0
Refinanced Arrears		0	0	0	0	0	0	0	0	0	0
Private Non–guaranteed	0	200	200	200	200	200	200	200	200	200	200
IMF	337	1,223	1,178	721	974	1,192	232	342	125	0	0
Short Term	2,800	7,646	2,828	4,557	4,269	4,627	2,326	2,885	3,087	2,967	3,565
Unidentified Sources a/	2,350	(0)	(44)	(536)	248	378	2,506	1,183	779	1,126	309
Total Amortizations	5,498	3,964	3,735	3,663	4,264	5,357	5,776	5,061	5,665	6,711	5,094
BONEX, BOTE, BOTESO and Eurobonds	561	1,433	1,611	1,636	1,756	1,587	1,737	1,207	921	992	1,133
World Bank	322	233	322	350	283	320	334	490	597	639	678
IDB & Other Multilaterals	208	221	222	232	205	290	424	497	572	672	772
Paris Club	425	485	840	668	660	1,067	1,637	1,314	1,402	1,124	1,224
Suppliers and other Bilaterals	185	580	215	162	144	147	163	171	188	388	409
Financial Markets	0	127	143	205	178	358	378	435	767	1,536	574
Eligible for Debt Deal	0	0	0	0	0	0	0	0	0	0	0
Ineligible for Debt Deal		127	143	205	178	204	224	281	305	305	305
Refinanced Arrears		0	0	0	0	154	154	154	462	1231	269
Private Non–guaranteed	0	0	0	0	0	33	67	100	133	167	200
IMF	998	885	382	410	1,039	1,555	1,036	848	1,083	1,192	103
Short Term	2,800	0	0	0	0	0	0	0	0	0	0
Unidentified Sources a/	0	0	0	0	0	0	0	0	0	0	0
Total Interest	4,934	2,955	3,725	4,730	5,342	6,069	6,541	6,700	6,987	7,165	7,243
BONEX, BOTE, BOTESO and Eurobonds	588	436	501	570	560	562	549	530	525	528	502
World Bank	209	165	228	286	329	365	369	351	355	354	344
IDB & Other Multilaterals	175	131	185	245	279	328	363	385	409	432	437
Paris Club	534	341	456	600	628	666	657	633	617	608	590
Suppliers and other Bilaterals	276	91	103	123	128	139	143	141	139	127	106
Financial Markets	1,935	1,103	1,288	1,506	1,657	1,764	1,804	1,811	1,816	1,761	1,616
Eligible for Debt Deal	1,935	1,010	797	893	1,012	1,075	1,121	1,155	1,189	1,189	1,054
Ineligible for Debt Deal	0	94	82	104	109	107	94	79	62	43	25
Refinanced Arrears	0	0	409	509	536	582	589	577	565	529	537
Private Non–guaranteed	127	136	171	232	258	295	317	325	331	334	335
IMF	314	331	276	303	307	300	260	150	106	42	3
Short Term	166	220	518	885	1,228	1,661	1,979	2,175	2,398	2,625	2,870
Unidentified Sources a/	611	0	(2)	(21)	(32)	(11)	101	199	292	353	441
Total Debt b/	65,299	73,167	75,767	80,379	84,673	88,772	92,288	95,592	97,974	99,460	100,793
BONEX, BOTE, BOTESO and Eurobonds	7,772	8,683	8,032	7,596	7,040	6,578	6,341	6,134	6,213	6,221	5,589
World Bank	2,790	3,037	4,404	4,828	5,063	5,201	5,339	5,454	5,462	5,425	5,150
IDB & Other Multilaterals	3,170	3,697	4,475	4,782	5,077	5,412	5,744	6,097	6,475	6,803	6,630
Paris Club	7,130	8,729	9,529	9,531	9,371	9,004	8,517	8,352	8,100	8,125	7,601
Suppliers and other Bilaterals	1,665	1,752	1,687	1,675	1,681	1,684	1,671	1,650	1,612	1,374	1,115
Financial Markets	27,129	23,354	28,342	28,137	27,959	27,601	27,223	26,788	26,021	24,485	23,911
Eligible for Debt Deal	22,864	20,939	18,374	18,374	18,374	18,374	18,374	18,374	18,374	18,374	18,374
Ineligible for Debt Deal	4,265	2,415	2,272	2,067	1,889	1,685	1,461	1,180	875	570	265
PDI Bond	0	0	7,696	7,696	7,696	7,542	7,388	7,234	6,772	5,541	5,272
Private Non–guaranteed	3,492	3,692	3,892	4,092	4,292	4,459	4,592	4,692	4,759	4,792	4,792
IMF	2,544	2,882	3,678	3,989	3,925	3,562	2,759	2,253	1,295	103	0
Short Term c/	1,298	8,944	11,772	16,330	20,598	25,225	27,551	30,436	33,523	36,490	40,055
Unidentified Sources a/	8,309	8,396	(44)	(580)	(333)	46	2,552	3,735	4,515	5,641	5,950
Memo:											
Public Debt	60,845	60,530	60,103	59,957	59,783	59,088	60,145	60,464	59,692	58,178	55,946
Private Debt d/	4,454	12,636	15,664	20,422	24,890	29,684	32,143	35,128	38,281	41,282	44,847

STATISTICAL APPENDIX

STATISTICAL APPENDIX

CONTENTS

Table 1.1: Argentina - Federal Non-interest Expenditures by Functional Group

(US$ million)

	Current Expenditures			
	Total	Wages	G&S	Transfers
Legislative and Judicial Branches b/	650	544	87	19
Senate and Congress	306	259	41	6
Judiciary	344	285	46	13
Presidency and Foreign Ministry	947	414	327	207
Presidency	708	339	246	123
Foreign Ministry	239	75	81	84
Ministries of Interior and Justice	893	496	130	267
Defense	2610	1791	594	225
Ministry and Joint Chiefs	992	502	265	224
Army	734	614	120	0
Navy	442	366	76	0
Air Force	442	308	133	1
Social Sectors	2144	436	268	1439
Education c/	1321	345	61	915
Health	463	47	163	252
Housing d/	37	2	17	18
Welfare	122	24	18	80
Labor	202	18	9	174
Economic Sectors	1500	751	422	327
Tax and Customs Administration	672	478	186	8
National Highway System	176	64	24	88
Agricultural e/	326	141	75	110
Others	327	69	137	121
Treasury Obligations f/	3585	397	18	3169
Salary Enhancements	355	288	0	67
Public Enterprises	1619	0	0	1619
Military Pensions	897	0	0	897
Provinces g/	421	42	0	379
Others	294	67	18	208
Total	12328	4830	1845	5653

a/ "Own" spending of national administration; transfers by economic classification ("incisos" 31, 32, and 61).

b/ Tribunal de Cuentas included in Senate and Congress.

c/ Includes US$724 million for universities.

d/ FONAVI Housing Fund administered by Ministry of Health and Social Action.

e/ Includes MOSP expenditures in INTA, agriculture policy, grain storage and veterinary medicine.

f/ Does not include revenue sharing under law of coparticipation; consists solely of jurisdiction 91.

g/ Includes aid to Tierra del Fuego and Buenos Aires and Provincial Education Fund.

Source: 1992 Congressionally-approved Budget (February 1992) and Contaduria General de la Nacion.

Table 1.2: Argentina - Expenditures of the Legislative and Judicial Branches of Government a/
(US$ million)

	Current Expenditures			
	Total	Wages	G&S	Transfers
Legislature	284	239	39	6
Senate	83	71	13	0
Congress	141	119	22	0
Publications Office	19	17	2	0
Library	19	19	0	0
Congressional Medical Plan	15	13	2	0
Senate Subsidies to Non-profit Entities	1	0	0	1
Congress Subsidies to Non-profit Entities	5	0	0	5
Court System	344	285	46	13
Supreme Court	41	41	0	0
Lower Courts b/	293	237	43	13
Court Special Investigations	8	8	0	0
National Justice Fund	2	0	2	0
Building Construction	0	0	0	0
Tribunal de Cuentas	22	20	2	0
Total	650	544	87	19

a/ Non-interest expenditures; also includes Tribunal de Cuentas, the external auditor of the Treasury.
b/ Transfers are to the court system's pensioners.

Source: 1992 Budget (February 1992) and Contaduria General de la Nacion.

Table 1.3: Argentina - Expenditures of the Presidency and Foreign Ministry

(US$ million)

	Current Expenditures			
	Total	Wages	G&S	Transfers
Presidency	708	339	246	123
Administration	49	21	22	6
Personnel Administration a/	6	5	1	0
Anti-drug Campaign	13	2	11	0
National Planning	5	3	2	0
Science & Techn. Policy Implementation	6	5	1	0
State Intelligence	115	110	5	0
Entrepreneurial Promotion b/	20	0	0	20
Statistical Service	22	8	14	0
Communications Secretariat	18	15	3	0
National Tourism Fund	30	5	24	0
Sports Promotion and National Fund	7	1	2	4
CNEA	212	68	143	1
CNEA Research and Development	29	20	8	1
CONICET Promotion and Scholarship c/	72	0	0	72
CONICET Research and Development c/	93	67	8	18
Secret Law 18.302	0	0	0	0
Immigration Office	0	0	0	0
National Public Administration Institute	7	5	2	0
Wildlife Research and Conservation	4	4	1	0
Others	0	0	0	0
Foreign Ministry	239	75	81	84
Aid to bordering countries d/	76	0	0	76
Foreign Policy	157	75	81	2
Ministry Infrastructure	0	0	0	0
Protocol	6	0	0	6
Secret Law 18.302	0	0	0	0
Total	947	414	327	207
Memo				
Salary Enhancements funded by the Treasury, of which:				
Presidency	23	23	0	0
Foreign Ministry	3	3	0	0

a/ Función Pública.

b/ Uncategorized transfers (par.principal #3199).

c/ Grants to individuals (p.p. #3150.601).

d/ Grants to various aid programs.

Source: 1992 Budget (February 1992) and Contaduria General de la Nacion.

Table 1.4: Argentina - Expenditures of the Ministries of the Interior and Justice
(US$ million)

	Current Expenditures			
	Total	Wages	G&S	Transfers
Ministry of Interior	699	396	91	212
Administration	10	4	6	0
Elections	6	3	1	2
Immigrations	8	7	2	0
Sanitation	2	0	2	0
National Census	14	7	7	0
Political Campaign Fund a/	29	0	12	17
Federal Police Force	26	20	6	0
Federal Police Retirement Fund	3	1	2	0
Regular Police Force	407	354	54	0
ATN Provincial Fund b/	192	0	0	192
Ministry of Justice	194	100	39	55
Administration	22	20	1	0
Penal System	95	77	19	0
Penal System Social Security	55	0	0	55
Car Licensing	20	2	18	0
General Inspection	2	1	1	0
National Registry	0	0	0	0
Total	893	496	130	267
Memo				
Salary Enhancement Programs c/	120	120	0	0

a/ Grants to unspecified non-profit entities.
b/ Coparticipated funds withheld to finance provincial deficits; US$6.2m is earmarked for Tierra del Fuego.
c/ Treasury-managed programs 113, 209, 247.

Source: 1992 Budget (February 1992) and Contaduria General de la Nacion.

Table 1.5: Argentina - Non-interest Expenditures of the Military

(US$ million)

	Current Expenditures			
	Total	Wages	G&S	Transfers
Ministry of Defense	989	501	263	224
Administration	76	4	71	2
National Guard	254	234	20	0
Compliance with Law 18302 "S"	32	30	2	0
Coast Guard/Naval Prefect	35	0	35	0
National Guard various	1	1	0	0
Coast Guard	180	158	22	0
Defense Industries	177	67	106	3
Defense R&D	5	3	2	0
Coast Guard Pensions	70	0	0	70
National Guard Pensions	142	0	0	142
IAF	3	1	1	0
Antarctic Plan	13	3	3	7
Army	734	614	120	0
Operations	701	603	98	0
Military Geographic Institute	4	3	0	0
Military Schools	5	5	0	0
Sanitation	3	0	3	0
Projects (Earmarked Funds)	22	3	19	0
Navy	442	366	76	0
Operations	375	316	60	0
Economic development	12	11	1	0
Special Works & Services	23	10	13	0
Sanitation	24	23	1	0
Military Schools	7	7	0	0
Air Force	442	308	133	1
Operations	319	283	35	0
Earmarked Funds for Operations	19	0	19	0
LADE	12	2	10	0
Development of Civil Aviation	2	1	1	0
Development of Air Technology	3	1	1	0
Promotion of Aerospace Industry	20	0	20	0
Airports	46	5	41	0
Hospitals	0	0	0	0
Sanitation	12	9	3	0
Education	10	7	4	0
R & D	0	0	0	0
Joint Chiefs of Staff	3	1	2	0
Total	2610	1791	594	225
Memo				
Salary Enhancement Programs*	18	18	0	0

*Treasury-managed program #182.

Source: 1992 Budget (February 1992) and Contaduria General de la Nacion.

Table 1.6: Argentina - Non-interest Expenditures of the Ministries of Health, Labor, and Education

(US$ million)

	Current Expenditures			
	Total	Wages	G&S	Transfers
Ministry of Health and Social Action	621	73	198	350
Health				
National Health Policy	32	19	9	4
Hospital Infrastructure	2	0	0	2
Health Clinic Construction	0	0	0	0
General Health Care a/	44	8	8	29
National Health Insurance (ANSSAL) b/	217	2	4	210
Preventive Health	128	6	121	2
Sanitation Regulation	9	9	1	0
Provincial Aid for health care	3	0	0	3
Preventive Environmental Health	25	5	20	0
Social Coverage in Health (lottery funded)	3	0	0	3
Housing				
Housing Policy	2	2	0	0
FONAVI c/	25	0	14	12
World Bank Housing Loan d/	5	0	3	2
Urban Development d/	1	0	0	1
Housing Assistance (lottery funded)	4	0	0	4
Welfare				
Social Action Policy	16	13	1	2
Social Action Construction	1	0	0	1
Social Nutrition Program and PAN (lottery funded) d/	22	0	1	21
Welfare Coverage (lottery funded) d/	24	0	6	18
Human and Family Development e/	55	9	8	38
Adolescent Halfway House	4	2	2	0
Ministry of Culture and Education	1321	345	61	915
Education Budget and Policy	45	14	30	1
Teacher Education & Training	83	83	0	0
Cultural Budget	16	12	4	0
Transfers to Universities	724	0	0	724
Financial Aid for Private Universities	30	0	0	30
High School	218	206	12	0
Agricultural Education f/	70	0	0	70
Technical Education Council (CONET)	17	17	0	0
Scientific Research g/	42	0	0	42
Medical assistance for students	9	5	4	0
Hospital services h/	39	0	0	39
Public Library System	1	0	0	1
National Cinematographic Institute	5	2	2	1
Permanent Student Fund	5	0	5	0
National Equal Opportunity Scholarship Institute	2	0	1	1
Teaching Pilot Programs	6	6	0	0
Discovery of America 1492 Fund	5	0	5	0
National Academies	6	0	0	6
Ministry of Labor and Social Security	202	18	9	174
Labor Policy	24	18	6	0
Non-contributory Pension System i/	176	0	1	174
Guarantee Fund	1	0	1	0
Adminstration Special Account	0	0	0	0
Nat'l. Registry of the Construction Industry	1	0	0	0
Total	2144	436	268	1439
Memo				
Salary Enhancement programs of MHSA j/	32	32	0	0

a/ Majority of transfer (US$21m) goes to Pediatric Hospital.

b/ Obras Sociales.

c/ Housing Fund; of US$903m in capital, US$50m goes to COVIARA (Navy), US$12.4m to Obras Sociales, US$841m to provinces.

d/ Transfers to provinces.

e/ Nat'l. Children's Fund, National Institute for Mutual Assistance, social emergencies program; transfers to provinces.

f/ US$34m transferred to provinces; remainder to non-profit research institutes.

g/ Transfers to universities for scientific research.

h/ Transfers to universities for student health and hospital services.

i/ Consists of pensions to Congressmen, veterans of the Malvinas war, and other special pension funds.

j/ Treasury-managed programs #36, 115, 224.

Source: 1992 Budget (February 1992) and Contaduria General de la Nacion.

Table 1.7: Argentina - Non-interest Expenditures of the Ministry of Economy and Public Works
(US$ million)

	Current Expenditures			
	Total	Wages	G&S	Transfers
Ministry of Economy and Public Works				
Ministry Policy	42	9	32	1
Fiscal Policy	22	9	6	6
National Landmark Restoration	3	2	1	0
DGI operations	279	240	39	0
DGI (earmarked fund)	102	0	97	5
DGI bonus system	84	84	0	0
Customs operations	90	89	1	0
Customs (earmarked fund)	112	60	50	2
Customs bonus system	5	5	0	0
National Seismology Institute	1	1	1	0
Potable Water Council a/	10	2	4	5
Water Conservation a/	17	0	0	16
Water Technology Institute	6	3	2	1
Energy Development Fund for the Interior a/	44	0	0	44
Grain Commission	0	0	0	0
Grain Storage	0	0	0	0
Agriculture Policy	59	36	20	4
Mercado Nacional de Hacienda	0	0	0	0
National Meat Board	0	0	0	0
Wine Institute	19	10	9	0
Veterinary Medicine	51	22	28	1
Food/Health Standards	13	6	7	1
National Fish Market	0	0	0	0
Monitoring of Exclusive Fishing Zones	0	0	0	0
National Fishing Institute	0	0	0	0
Tobacco Fund a/	102	0	0	102
Dredging (Comision Mixta del Rio Parana)	6	0	6	0
Dredging	0	0	0	0
Waterways Policy	2	1	1	0
Port Maintenance/Construction	36	10	26	0
Trade Promotion	11	7	4	0
Industrial Promotion	6	4	2	0
National Highway Policy	1	1	0	0
National Road System a/	176	64	24	88
National Transportation Fund	3	1	1	2
Air Transport Policy	2	0	0	1
National Energy Policy	34	2	31	0
Comision Nacional de Valores	1	1	0	0
Insurance Superintendency	10	2	7	1
Industrial Technology Institute b/	30	1	1	29
Agricultural Technology Institute (INTA)	94	73	18	3
National Forestry Institute	0	0	0	0
National Seed Institute	0	0	0	0
National Park Administration	7	4	2	0
National Sugar Directorate	0	0	0	0
National Yerba Mate Commission	0	0	0	0
Mining Policy	3	3	1	0
Telecommunications Regulation	4	3	2	0
Electricidad de Misiones, S.A.	7	0	0	7
Santa Cruz Electricity Fund c/	6	0	0	6
Total	1500	751	422	327
Memo				
Salary Enhancement Programs d/	42	28	0	14

a/ Transfers to provinces.
b/ Transfers to non-profit organizations in the area of science and technology.
c/ Grant to Santa Cruz for electricity distribution; Santa Cruz is not fully integrated into the national electricity network.
d/ Treasury-managed programs #127, 204, 255.

Source: 1992 Budget (February 1992) and Contaduria General de la Nacion.

Table 1.8: Argentina - Treasury Obligations

(US$ million)

	Current Expenditures			
	Total	Wages	G&S	Transfers
Nat'l. Administration Salary Enhancements a/	355	288	0	67
Presidency, Prog. 256	23	23	0	0
Customs (MOSP), Prog. 255	28	28	0	0
MOSP, Prog. 127	12	0	0	12
MOSP, Prog. 204	3	0	0	3
Foreign Ministry, Prog. 219	3	3	0	0
Defense, Prog. 182	18	18	0	0
Penal System, Prog. 247	18	18	0	0
Police, Prog. 209	89	89	0	0
Other Security Forces, Prog. 113	14	14	0	0
MHSA, Prog. 115	22	22	0	0
Ministry of Labor and Social Security, Prog. 36	7	7	0	0
MHSA, Prog. 224	2	2	0	0
Unspecified Salary Enhancements and Benefits, Prog. 114 b/	116	64	0	52
Transfers to Public Enterprises	1619	0	0	1619
Railroads, Prog. 23	606	0	0	606
Energy Sector Public Enterprises, Prog. 159 c/	922	0	0	922
Yacyreta, Prog. 20	0	0	0	0
Various Public Enterprises, Prg. 206	55	0	0	55
Argentina Televisora Color, Prg. 26	6	0	0	6
INDER, Prog. 269	0	0	0	0
Various Public Enterprises, Prg. 242	30	0	0	30
Others	1612	109	18	1484
Min. of Labor and Social Security, Prog. 171	5	5	0	0
Min. of Labor and Social Security, Prog. 191	18	0	18	0
International Organizations, Prog. 6	84	0	0	84
IAF (Military Pensions), Prog. 35	897	0	0	897
R&D, Prog. 181	13	4	0	9
Program 112	169	58	0	111
Private Sector, Prog. 41	4	0	0	4
Ed. Fund and Salary Enhance., Prog. 241 d/	238	42	0	196
Tierra del Fuego and Buenos Aires, Prog. 7	183	0	0	183
Total	3585	397	18	3169

a/ Includes personnel in "cargos criticos," SINAPA program, and other employee benefit packages.

b/ Treasury-managed program of US$64m in salary reserves and US$52m for health and dependents programs.

c/ YPF, YCF, Hidronor, Agua y Energia, Gas del Estado, and SEGBA.

d/ US$196m is the transfer for the Provincial Education Fund (Fondo Educativo); US$42m is salary reserve.

Note: university transfers and FONAVI are administered by Ministries of Education and Health and Social Action, respectively.

Source: 1992 Budget (February 1992) and Contaduria General de la Nacion.

Table 1.9: Argentina - Federal Non-interest Expenditures by Functional Group
(US$ million)

	Capital Expenditures				
	Total	Goods	Construction	< > Stock	Financial Investment
Legislative and Judicial Branches b/	45	15	14	17	0
Senate and Congress	3	2	1	0	0
Judiciary	42	13	13	17	0
Presidency and Foreign Ministry	500	44	456	0	0
Presidency	470	44	426	0	0
Foreign Ministry	30	0	30	0	0
Ministries of Interior and Justice	58	47	11	0	0
Defense	86	55	30	1	0
Ministry and Joint Chiefs	12	8	4	0	0
Army	9	2	6	1	0
Navy	9	8	0	0	0
Air Force	57	37	20	0	0
Social Sectors	1166	18	80	2	1067
Education c/	70	14	52	2	2
Health	13	3	10	0	1
Housing d/	1063	1	0	0	1063
Welfare	19	1	17	0	2
Labor	0	0	0	0	0
Economic Sectors	344	48	258	8	30
Tax and Customs Administration	16	9	6	0	0
National Highway System	145	2	124	7	12
Agricultural e/	79	24	54	0	0
Others	105	12	74	1	18
Treasury Obligations f/	481	0	0	0	481
Salary Enhancements	0	0	0	0	0
Public Enterprises	481	0	0	0	481
Military Pensions	0	0	0	0	0
Provinces g/	0	0	0	0	0
Others	0	0	0	0	0
Total	2681	226	848	27	1579

a/ "Own" spending of national administration; transfers by economic classification ("incisos" 31, 32, and 61).
b/ Tribunal de Cuentas included in Senate and Congress.
c/ Includes US$724 million for universities.
d/ FONAVI Housing Fund administered by Ministry of Health and Social Action.
e/ Includes MOSP expenditures in INTA, agriculture policy, grain storage and veterinary medicine.
f/ Does not include revenue sharing under law of coparticipation; consists solely of jurisdiction 91.
g/ Includes aid to Tierra del Fuego and Buenos Aires and Provincial Education Fund.

Source: 1992 Congressionally-approved Budget (February 1992) and Contaduria General de la Nacion.

Table 1.10: Argentina - Expenditures of the Legislative and Judicial Branches of Government a/
(US$ million)

	Capital Expenditures				
	Total	Goods	Construction	< > Stock	Financial Investment
Legislature	2	1	1	0	0
Senate	1	1	1	0	0
Congress	0	0	0	0	0
Publications Office	0	0	0	0	0
Library	1	1	0	0	0
Congressional Medical Plan	0	0	0	0	0
Senate Subsidies to Non-profit Entities	0	0	0	0	0
Congress Subsidies to Non-profit Entities	0	0	0	0	0
Court System	42	13	13	17	0
Supreme Court	0	0	0	0	0
Lower Courts b/	27	12	0	15	0
Court Special Investigations	0	0	0	0	0
National Justice Fund	10	1	7	2	0
Building Construction	6	0	6	0	0
Tribunal de Cuentas	0	0	0	0	0
Total	45	15	14	17	0

a/ Non-interest expenditures; also includes Tribunal de Cuentas, the external auditor of the Treasury.
b/ Transfers are to the court system's pensioners.

Source: 1992 Budget (February 1992) and Contaduria General de la Nacion.

Table 1.11: Argentina - Expenditures of the Presidency and Foreign Ministry
(US$ million)

		Capital Expenditures			
	Total	Goods	Construction	< > Stock	Financial Investment
Presidency	470	44	426	0	0
Administration	31	30	1	0	0
Personnel Administration a/	1	0	1	0	0
Anti-drug Campaign	0	0	0	0	0
National Planning	0	0	0	0	0
Science & Techn. Policy Implementation	0	0	0	0	0
State Intelligence	1	1	0	0	0
Entrepreneurial Promotion b/	0	0	0	0	0
Statistical Service	1	1	0	0	0
Communications Secretariat	1	0	0	0	0
National Tourism Fund	1	1	0	0	0
Sports Promotion and National Fund	0	0	0	0	0
CNEA	418	4	413	0	0
CNEA Research and Development	9	1	8	0	0
CONICET Promotion and Scholarship c/	0	0	0	0	0
CONICET Research and Development c/	8	5	3	0	0
Secret Law 18.302	0	0	0	0	0
Immigration Office	0	0	0	0	0
National Public Administration Institute	0	0	0	0	0
Wildlife Research and Conservation	0	0	0	0	0
Others	0	0	0	0	0
Foreign Ministry	30	0	30	0	0
Aid to bordering countries d/	0	0	0	0	0
Foreign Policy	30	0	30	0	0
Ministry Infrastructure	0	0	0	0	0
Protocol	0	0	0	0	0
Secret Law 18.302	0	0	0	0	0
Total	500	44	456	0	0
Memo					
Salary Enhancements funded by the Treasury, of which:					
Presidency	0	0	0	0	0
Foreign Ministry	0	0	0	0	0

a/ Función Pública.
b/ Uncategorized transfers (par.principal #3199).
c/ Grants to individuals (p.p. #3150.601).
d/ Grants to various aid programs.

Source: 1992 Budget (February 1992) and Contaduria General de la Nacion.

Table 1.12: Argentina - Expenditures of the Ministries of the Interior and Justice

(US$ million)

		Capital Expenditures			
	Total	Goods	Construction	< > Stock	Financial Investment
Ministry of Interior	32	31	0	0	0
Administration	1	1	0	0	0
Elections	0	0	0	0	0
Immigrations	0	0	0	0	0
Sanitation	0	0	0	0	0
National Census	0	0	0	0	0
Political Campaign Fund a/	0	0	0	0	0
Federal Police Force	2	2	0	0	0
Federal Police Retirement Fund	0	0	0	0	0
Regular Police Force	29	29	0	0	0
ATN Provincial Fund b/	0	0	0	0	0
Ministry of Justice	26	16	10	0	0
Administration	9	9	0	0	0
Penal System	11	1	10	0	0
Penal System Social Security	0	0	0	0	0
Car Licensing	5	5	0	0	0
General Inspection	1	1	0	0	0
National Registry	0	0	0	0	0
Total	58	47	11	0	0
Memo					
Salary Enhancement Programs c/	0	0	0	0	0

a/ Grants to unspecified non-profit entities.

b/ Coparticipated funds withheld to finance provincial deficits; US$6.2m is earmarked for Tierra del Fuego.

c/ Treasury-managed programs 113, 209, 247.

Source: 1992 Budget (February 1992) and Contaduria General de la Nacion.

Table 1.13: Argentina - Non-interest Expenditures of the Military

(US$ million)

	Capital Expenditures				
	Total	Goods	Construction	< > Stock	Financial Investment
Ministry of Defense	12	7	4	0	0
Administration	0	0	0	0	0
National Guard	3	3	0	0	0
Compliance with Law 18302 "S"	0	0	0	0	0
Coast Guard/Naval Prefect	3	2	0	0	0
National Guard various	0	0	0	0	0
Coast Guard	0	0	0	0	0
Defense Industries	5	1	4	0	0
Defense R&D	1	1	0	0	0
Coast Guard Pensions	0	0	0	0	0
National Guard Pensions	0	0	0	0	0
IAF	0	0	0	0	0
Antarctic Plan	0	0	0	0	0
Army	9	2	6	1	0
Operations	5	1	4	0	0
Military Geographic Institute	3	0	3	0	0
Military Schools	0	0	0	0	0
Sanitation	0	0	0	0	0
Projects (Earmarked Funds)	1	0	0	1	0
Navy	9	8	0	0	0
Operations	8	8	0	0	0
Economic development	0	0	0	0	0
Special Works & Services	1	1	0	0	0
Sanitation	0	0	0	0	0
Military Schools	0	0	0	0	0
Air Force	57	37	20	0	0
Operations	6	1	5	0	0
Earmarked Funds for Operations	2	2	0	0	0
LADE	0	0	0	0	0
Development of Civil Aviation	0	0	0	0	0
Development of Air Technology	0	0	0	0	0
Promotion of Aerospace Industry	22	22	1	0	0
Airports	26	12	14	0	0
Hospitals	0	0	0	0	0
Sanitation	0	0	0	0	0
Education	0	0	0	0	0
R & D	0	0	0	0	0
Joint Chiefs of Staff	0	0	0	0	0
Total	86	55	30	1	0
Memo					
Salary Enhancement Programs*	0	0	0	0	0

*Treasury-managed program #182.

Source: 1992 Budget (February 1992) and Contaduria General de la Nacion.

Table 1.14: Argentina - Non-interest Expenditures of the Ministries of Health, Labor, and Education
(US$ million)

	Capital Expenditures				
	Total	Goods	Construction	< > Stock	Financial Investment
Ministry of Health and Social Action	1096	4	28	0	1065
Health					
National Health Policy	0	0	0	0	0
Hospital Infrastructure	8	0	8	0	0
Health Clinic Construction	2	0	2	0	0
General Health Care a/	2	2	0	0	0
National Health Insurance (ANSSAL) b/	1	0	0	0	1
Preventive Health	0	0	0	0	0
Sanitation Regulation	0	0	0	0	0
Provincial Aid for health care	0	0	0	0	0
Preventive Environmental Health	0	0	0	0	0
Social Coverage in Health (lottery funded)	0	0	0	0	0
Housing					
Housing Policy	0	0	0	0	0
FONAVI c/	903	0	0	0	903
World Bank Housing Loan d/	81	0	0	0	81
Urban Development d/	79	0	0	0	79
Housing Assistance (lottery funded)	0	0	0	0	0
Welfare					
Social Action Policy	0	0	0	0	0
Social Action Construction	11	0	11	0	0
Social Nutrition Program and PAN (lottery funded) d/	0	0	0	0	0
Welfare Coverage (lottery funded) d/	1	0	0	0	1
Human and Family Development e/	8	0	6	0	1
Adolescent Halfway House	0	0	0	0	0
Ministry of Culture and Education	70	14	52	2	2
Education Budget and Policy	62	12	50	0	0
Teacher Education & Training	0	0	0	0	0
Cultural Budget	0	0	0	0	0
Transfers to Universities	0	0	0	0	0
Financial Aid for Private Universities	0	0	0	0	0
High School	0	0	0	0	0
Agricultural Education f/	0	0	0	0	0
Technical Education Council (CONET)	0	0	0	0	0
Scientific Research g/	0	0	0	0	0
Medical assistance for students	0	0	0	0	0
Hospital services h/	0	0	0	0	0
Public Library System	0	0	0	0	0
National Cinematographic Institute	2	1	0	0	1
Permanent Student Fund	2	0	1	1	0
National Equal Opportunity Scholarship Institute	1	0	0	0	1
Teaching Pilot Programs	0	0	0	0	0
Discovery of America 1492 Fund	2	0	1	1	0
National Academies	0	0	0	0	0
Ministry of Labor and Social Security	0	0	0	0	0
Labor Policy	0	0	0	0	0
Non-contributory Pension System i/	0	0	0	0	0
Guarantee Fund	0	0	0	0	0
Adminstration Special Account	0	0	0	0	0
Nat'l. Registry of the Construction Industry	0	0	0	0	0
Total	1166	18	80	2	1067
Memo					
Salary Enhancement programs of MHSA j/	0	0	0	0	0

a/ Majority of transfer (US$21m) goes to Pediatric Hospital.

b/ Obras Sociales.

c/ Housing Fund; of US$903m in capital, US$50m goes to COVIARA (Navy), US$12.4m to Obras Sociales, US$841m to provinc

d/ Transfers to provinces.

e/ Nat'l. Children's Fund, National Institute for Mutual Assistance, social emergencies program; transfers to provinces.

f/ US$34m transferred to provinces; remainder to non-profit research institutes.

g/ Transfers to universities for scientific research.

h/ Transfers to universities for student health and hospital services.

i/ Consists of pensions to Congressmen, veterans of the Malvinas war, and other special pension funds.

j/ Treasury-managed programs #36, 115, 224.

Source: 1992 Budget (February 1992) and Contaduria General de la Nacion.

Table 1.15: Argentina - Non-interest Expenditures of the Ministry of Economy and Public Works
(US$ million)

	Capital Expenditures				
	Total	Goods	Construction	< > Stock	Financial Investment
Ministry of Economy and Public Works					
Ministry Policy	0	0	0	0	0
Fiscal Policy	25	0	24	0	0
National Landmark Restoration	9	0	9	0	0
DGI operations	0	0	0	0	0
DGI (earmarked fund)	6	5	1	0	0
DGI bonus system	0	0	0	0	0
Customs operations	1	1	0	0	0
Customs (earmarked fund)	8	3	5	0	0
Customs bonus system	0	0	0	0	0
National Seismology Institute	1	1	0	0	0
Potable Water Council a/	19	1	0	0	18
Water Conservation a/	2	0	1	0	0
Water Technology Institute	2	0	2	0	0
Energy Development Fund for the Interior a/	0	0	0	0	0
Grain Commission	0	0	0	0	0
Grain Storage	37	1	36	0	0
Agriculture Policy	20	4	15	0	0
Mercado Nacional de Hacienda	0	0	0	0	0
National Meat Board	0	0	0	0	0
Wine Institute	1	1	0	0	0
Veterinary Medicine	13	12	0	0	0
Food/Health Standards	9	8	0	1	0
National Fish Market	0	0	0	0	0
Monitoring of Exclusive Fishing Zones	0	0	0	0	0
National Fishing Institute	0	0	0	0	0
Tobacco Fund a/	0	0	0	0	0
Dredging (Comision Mixta del Rio Parana)	0	0	0	0	0
Dredging	33	0	33	0	0
Waterways Policy	0	0	0	0	0
Port Maintenance/Construction	3	2	1	0	0
Trade Promotion	0	0	0	0	0
Industrial Promotion	0	0	0	0	0
National Highway Policy	0	0	0	0	0
National Road System a/	145	2	124	7	12
National Transportation Fund	0	0	0	0	0
Air Transport Policy	0	0	0	0	0
National Energy Policy	0	0	0	0	0
Comision Nacional de Valores	0	0	0	0	0
Insurance Superintendency	1	0	0	0	0
Industrial Technology Institute b/	2	0	1	0	0
Agricultural Technology Institute (INTA)	8	5	3	0	0
National Forestry Institute	0	0	0	0	0
National Seed Institute	0	0	0	0	0
National Park Administration	1	0	0	0	0
National Sugar Directorate	0	0	0	0	0
National Yerba Mate Commission	0	0	0	0	0
Mining Policy	1	0	1	0	0
Telecommunications Regulation	0	0	0	0	0
Electricidad de Misiones, S.A.	0	0	0	0	0
Santa Cruz Electricity Fund c/	0	0	0	0	0
Total	344	48	258	8	30
Memo					
Salary Enhancement Programs d/	0	0	0	0	0

a/ Transfers to provinces.
b/ Transfers to non-profit organizations in the area of science and technology.
c/ Grant to Santa Cruz for electricity distribution; Santa Cruz is not fully integrated into the national electricity network.
d/ Treasury-managed programs #127, 204, 255.

Source: 1992 Budget (February 1992) and Contaduria General de la Nacion.

Table 1.16: Argentina - Treasury Obligations
(US$ million)

	Capital Expenditures				
	Total	Goods	Construction	< > Stock	Financial Investment
Nat'l. Administration Salary Enhancements a/	0	0	0	0	0
Presidency, Prog. 256	0	0	0	0	0
Customs (MOSP), Prog. 255	0	0	0	0	0
MOSP, Prog. 127	0	0	0	0	0
MOSP, Prog. 204	0	0	0	0	0
Foreign Ministry, Prog. 219	0	0	0	0	0
Defense, Prog. 182	0	0	0	0	0
Penal System, Prog. 247	0	0	0	0	0
Police, Prog. 209	0	0	0	0	0
Other Security Forces, Prog. 113	0	0	0	0	0
MHSA, Prog. 115	0	0	0	0	0
Ministry of Labor and Social Security, Prog. 36	0	0	0	0	0
MHSA, Prog. 224	0	0	0	0	0
Unspecified Salary Enhancements and Benefits, Prog. 114	0	0	0	0	0
Transfers to Public Enterprises	481	0	0	0	481
Railroads, Prog. 23	0	0	0	0	0
Energy Sector Public Enterprises, Prog. 159 c/	171	0	0	0	171
Yacyreta, Prog. 20	301	0	0	0	301
Various Public Enterprises, Prg. 206	0	0	0	0	0
Argentina Televisora Color, Prg. 26	0	0	0	0	0
INDER, Prog. 269	10	0	0	0	10
Various Public Enterprises, Prg. 242	0	0	0	0	0
Others	0	0	0	0	0
Min. of Labor and Social Security, Prog. 171	0	0	0	0	0
Min. of Labor and Social Security, Prog. 191	0	0	0	0	0
International Organizations, Prog. 6	0	0	0	0	0
IAF (Military Pensions), Prog. 35	0	0	0	0	0
R&D, Prog. 181	0	0	0	0	0
Program 112	0	0	0	0	0
Private Sector, Prog. 41	0	0	0	0	0
Ed. Fund and Salary Enhance., Prog. 241 d/	0	0	0	0	0
Tierra del Fuego and Buenos Aires, Prog. 7	0	0	0	0	0
Total	481	0	0	0	481

a/ Includes personnel in "cargos criticos," SINAPA program, and other employee benefit packages.
b/ Treasury-managed program of US$64m in salary reserves and US$52m for health and dependents programs.
c/ YPF, YCF, Hidronor, Agua y Energia, Gas del Estado, and SEGBA.
d/ US$196m is the transfer for the Provincial Education Fund (Fondo Educativo); US$42m is salary reserve.
Note: university transfers and FONAVI are administered by Ministries of Education and Health and Social Action, respectively.

Source: 1992 Budget (February 1992) and Contaduria General de la Nacion.

Table 2.1: Argentina - Fiscal Accounts of the Consolidated Public Sector, 1983 - 1992
(Accrual basis, as percent of GDP)

	1983	1984	1985	1986	1987	1988	1989	1990	1991	1992e
Current Revenue a/	19.3	22.4	23.1	21.7	20.0	19.1	17.6	17.7	20.4	25.0
Tax Revenue	15.7	19.1	18.7	18.6	17.8	16.8	16.3	16.6	19.1	23.8
DGI and Customs Revenue	11.0	16.5	15.1	14.6	14.0	12.1	13.0	11.5	13.5	15.9
Social Security Revenue	4.7	2.6	3.6	4.0	3.9	4.7	3.3	5.0	5.7	7.9
Non-tax Revenue	3.6	3.3	4.4	3.1	2.2	2.3	1.3	1.1	1.3	1.2
Current Expenditures	28.0	24.4	25.2	23.5	23.4	23.1	19.9	21.6	21.8	23.7
Personnel	4.8	4.8	4.1	3.6	4.1	4.1	3.4	4.1	3.9	3.6
Goods and Services	2.9	1.9	2.2	2.0	2.1	2.0	1.6	1.4	1.3	1.6
Transfers	14.5	12.7	13.5	14.1	13.8	14.1	11.6	13.1	14.5	16.8
Provinces	7.6	5.9	6.1	6.7	6.6	7.0	6.1	5.7	7.0	8.2
Social Security	6.1	5.6	5.6	5.5	5.1	5.2	3.6	5.7	6.0	8.2
Others	0.8	1.2	1.8	1.9	2.1	1.9	2.0	1.7	1.6	0.4
Interest Payments b/	5.8	5.0	5.4	3.8	3.5	2.8	3.3	3.1	2.1	1.7
Domestic c/	0.9	0.8	0.7	0.3	0.5	0.4	0.2	0.5	0.3	0.1
External d/	4.9	4.2	4.7	3.5	3.0	2.4	3.1	2.6	1.8	1.6
Public Enterprise Non-interest Savings	-0.1	0.6	1.0	1.9	1.8	1.0	0.9	1.2	0.3	0.8
Current Revenues	11.0	10.5	13.6	12.1	11.8	12.8	12.8	8.8	6.7	6.0
Current Non-interest Expenditures	11.1	9.9	12.6	10.1	9.9	11.8	11.9	7.6	6.4	5.2
Savings	-8.8	-1.4	-1.1	0.1	-1.5	-3.0	-1.4	-2.7	-1.1	2.1
Capital Revenue	0.2	0.2	0.2	0.1	0.1	0.4	0.6	0.2	1.7	1.3
Capital Expenditures	6.8	5.1	4.5	4.4	5.3	6.0	3.9	2.6	2.3	1.7
General Government	2.9	1.6	1.5	1.6	1.7	1.5	1.0	0.8	0.7	1.2
Public Enterprises	3.9	3.6	2.9	2.8	3.6	4.5	2.8	1.9	1.6	0.5
Non-Financial Public Sector Balance	-15.4	-6.3	-5.4	-4.2	-6.7	-8.6	-4.7	-5.1	-1.7	1.7
Quasi-fiscal Balance of Central Bank e/	-1.1	-2.5	-2.8	-1.6	-3.4	-1.4	-5.8	-1.0	-0.6	-0.2
Overall Balance	-16.5	-8.8	-8.2	-5.8	-10.1	-10.0	-10.5	-6.1	-2.3	1.5
Memo:										
Primary Surplus	-9.6	-1.3	0.0	-0.4	-3.2	-5.8	-1.4	-2.0	0.4	3.4
Operational Primary Surplus f/	-9.8	-1.5	-0.2	-0.5	-3.3	-6.2	-2.0	-2.2	-1.3	2.1
Net Federal Expenditure g/	36.0	31.4	31.5	27.5	30.2	29.4	28.7	24.0	24.4	24.8
Provincial Revenue, incl. transfers	11.6	10.4	10.8	11.2	8.0	10.3	9.4	9.0	10.3	13.2
Provincial Expenditure	11.4	11.9	11.4	11.1	12.9	12.3	10.6	13.2	13.5	12.8
Health Funds Expenditures h/	4.4	4.1	4.3	4.4	4.6	4.7	3.8	3.8	4.2	4.7
Total Non-interest Expenditures	48.4	44.5	46.4	43.1	46.1	48.1	40.7	40.0	39.1	38.2
Total Expenditure, incl. quasifiscal balance of BCRA i/	55.3	52.0	54.6	48.5	53.0	52.3	49.8	44.1	41.8	40.1

a/ Includes coparticipated revenues.
b/ Interest payments of the entire Federal Government.
c/ Real component of domestic interest payments for 1983-1991; 1992 is nominal due to return to stability.
d/ Accrued interest due.
e/ Real earnings on assets less real interest costs; IMF definition, 1983-87; IBRD definition 1988-1992 (see Ch.13)
f/ Primary surplus less capital revenue.
g/ Includes non-interest current account of the public enterprises and quasi-fiscal balance (- = expenditure).
h/ 1983-1987 from FIEL "Gasto Público" report (1988); 1988-1992 based on Bank staff estimates.
i/ Gross expenditure of national government, public enterprises, provinces, health funds and quasifiscal balance of the Central Bank.

Source: Secretary of Finance; Executed Budgets, 1983-1991; Cash Basis, 1992.

Table 2.2: Argentina - National Administration Savings-Investment, 1983-1992 a/
(As percent of GDP)

	1983	1984	1985	1986	1987	1988	1989	1990	1991	1992
Current Revenues	14.6	19.8	19.5	17.7	16.2	14.4	14.3	12.6	14.8	17.1
Tax Revenues	11.0	16.5	15.1	14.6	14.0	12.1	13.0	11.5	13.5	15.9
Non-tax Revenues	3.6	3.3	4.4	3.1	2.2	2.3	1.3	1.1	1.3	1.2
Current Expenditures	22.0	18.8	19.6	18.0	18.4	17.8	16.4	16.0	15.9	15.5
Personnel Expenditures	4.8	4.8	4.1	3.6	4.1	4.1	3.4	4.1	3.9	3.6
Goods and Services	2.9	1.9	2.2	2.0	2.1	2.0	1.6	1.4	1.3	1.6
Interest on Debt b/	5.8	5.0	5.4	3.8	3.5	2.8	3.3	3.1	2.1	1.7
Domestic	0.9	0.8	0.7	0.3	0.5	0.4	0.2	0.5	0.3	0.1
Foreign	4.9	4.2	4.7	3.5	3.0	2.4	3.1	2.6	1.8	1.6
Other Current Expenditures	0.0	0.0	0.0	0.0	0.0	0.0	0.0	0.0	0.0	0.0
Current & Capital Transfers	8.4	7.1	7.9	8.6	8.7	8.9	8.1	7.4	8.6	8.6
Economies	0.0	0.0	0.0	0.0	0.0	0.0	0.0	0.0	0.0	0.0
Savings	-7.4	1.0	-0.1	-0.3	-2.2	-3.5	-2.1	-3.3	-1.1	1.6
Capital Revenues	0.2	0.2	0.2	0.1	0.1	0.4	0.6	0.2	1.7	1.3
Capital Expenditures	2.9	1.6	1.5	1.6	1.7	1.5	1.0	0.8	0.7	1.2
Fixed Investments	2.4	1.4	1.3	1.3	1.5	1.3	0.9	0.6	0.2	0.4
Machinery and Equipment	0.6	0.3	0.3	0.3	0.3	0.3	0.1	0.2	0.1	0.2
Construction	1.8	1.1	1.0	1.0	1.2	1.1	0.7	0.5	0.1	0.2
Changes in Inventories	0.1	0.0	0.0	0.0	0.0	0.0	0.1	0.0	0.0	0.0
Financial Investments	0.4	0.1	0.2	0.3	0.1	0.2	0.1	0.1	0.5	0.8
Economies	0.0	0.0	0.0	0.0	0.0	0.0	0.0	0.0	0.0	0.0
Total Revenues	14.8	20.0	19.7	17.8	16.3	14.8	14.9	12.8	16.5	18.4
Total Expenditures	24.9	20.4	21.2	19.7	20.0	19.3	17.4	16.7	16.6	16.7
Financing Requirement	10.1	0.4	1.5	1.9	3.8	4.6	2.5	3.9	0.1	-1.7

a/ National Administration includes Central Administration, Decentralized Agencies, and Special Accounts.
b/ Interest bill includes interest obligations of the public enterprises.

Source: Secretary of Finance Savings-Investment Plans.

Table 2.3: Argentina - Social Security Savings-Investment, 1983-1992
(As percent of GDP)

	1983	1984	1985	1986	1987	1988	1989	1990	1991	1992
Current Revenues	4.7	2.6	3.6	4.0	3.9	4.7	3.3	5.0	5.7	7.9
Tax Revenues	4.7	2.6	3.6	4.0	3.9	4.7	3.3	5.0	5.5	7.9
Non-tax Revenues	0.0	0.0	0.0	0.0	0.0	0.0	0.0	0.0	0.2	0.0
Current Expenditures	6.1	5.6	5.6	5.5	5.1	5.2	3.6	5.7	6.0	8.2
Personnel Expenditures	0.0	0.0	0.0	0.0	0.0	0.0	0.0	0.0	0.0	0.0
Goods and Services	0.0	0.0	0.0	0.0	0.0	0.0	0.0	0.0	0.0	0.0
Interest on Debt	0.0	0.0	0.0	0.0	0.0	0.0	0.0	0.0	0.0	0.0
Domestic	0.0	0.0	0.0	0.0	0.0	0.0	0.0	0.0	0.0	0.0
Foreign	0.0	0.0	0.0	0.0	0.0	0.0	0.0	0.0	0.0	0.0
Other Current Expenditures	0.0	0.0	0.0	0.0	0.0	0.0	0.0	0.0	0.0	0.0
Current & Capital Transfers	6.1	5.6	5.6	5.5	5.1	5.2	3.6	5.7	6.0	8.2
Economies	0.0	0.0	0.0	0.0	0.0	0.0	0.0	0.0	0.0	0.0
Savings	-0.9	-2.9	-1.1	-1.3	-0.9	-0.4	-0.3	-0.7	-0.3	-0.3
Capital Revenues	0.0	0.0	0.0	0.0	0.0	0.0	0.0	0.0	0.0	0.0
Capital Expenditures	0.0	0.0	0.0	0.0	0.0	0.0	0.0	0.0	0.0	0.0
Fixed Investments	0.0	0.0	0.0	0.0	0.0	0.0	0.0	0.0	0.0	0.0
Machinery and Equipment	0.0	0.0	0.0	0.0	0.0	0.0	0.0	0.0	0.0	0.0
Construction	0.0	0.0	0.0	0.0	0.0	0.0	0.0	0.0	0.0	0.0
Changes in Inventories	0.0	0.0	0.0	0.0	0.0	0.0	0.0	0.0	0.0	0.0
Financial Investments	0.0	0.0	0.0	0.0	0.0	0.0	0.0	0.0	0.0	0.0
Economies	0.0	0.0	0.0	0.0	0.0	0.0	0.0	0.0	0.0	0.0
Total Revenues	4.7	2.6	3.6	4.0	3.9	4.7	3.3	5.0	5.7	7.9
Total Expenditures	6.1	5.6	5.6	5.5	5.1	5.2	3.6	5.7	6.0	8.2
Financing Requirement	1.4	3.0	2.0	1.6	1.2	0.5	0.3	0.7	0.3	0.3

Source: Secretary of Finance Savings-Investment Plans.

Table 2.4: Argentina - Public Enterprises Savings-Investment, 1983-1992
(As percent of GDP)

	1983	1984	1985	1986	1987	1988	1989	1990	1991	1992
Current Revenues	11.0	10.5	13.6	12.1	11.8	12.8	12.8	8.8	6.7	6.0
Tax Revenues	0.0	0.0	0.0	0.0	0.0	0.0	0.0	0.0	0.0	0.0
Non-tax Revenues	11.0	10.5	13.6	12.1	11.8	12.8	12.8	8.8	6.7	6.0
Current Expenditures	11.1	9.9	12.6	10.1	9.9	11.8	11.9	7.6	6.4	5.2
Personnel Expenditures	3.0	3.2	3.1	3.0	3.2	3.2	3.0	2.3	1.9	1.2
Goods and Services	7.1	6.4	8.9	6.5	5.6	6.8	7.9	5.3	4.5	4.0
Interest on Debt a/	0.0	0.0	0.0	0.0	0.0	0.0	0.0	0.0	0.0	0.0
Domestic	0.0	0.0	0.0	0.0	0.0	0.0	0.0	0.0	0.0	0.0
Foreign	0.0	0.0	0.0	0.0	0.0	0.0	0.0	0.0	0.0	0.0
Other Current Expenditures	1.1	0.4	0.6	0.7	1.1	1.8	1.0	0.0	0.0	0.0
Current & Capital Transfers	0.0	0.0	0.0	0.0	0.0	0.0	0.0	0.0	0.0	0.0
Economies	0.0	0.0	0.0	0.0	0.0	0.0	0.0	0.0	0.0	0.0
Savings	-0.1	0.6	1.0	1.9	1.8	1.0	0.9	1.2	0.3	0.8
Capital Revenues	0.0	0.0	0.0	0.0	0.0	0.0	0.0	0.0	0.0	0.0
Capital Expenditures	3.9	3.6	2.9	2.8	3.6	4.5	2.8	1.9	1.6	0.5
Fixed Investments	3.6	3.3	2.8	2.6	3.2	4.2	2.5	1.7	1.6	0.5
Machinery and Equipment	1.7	2.0	1.3	1.2	1.4	1.9	1.1	0.8	0.6	0.2
Construction	1.9	1.4	1.5	1.4	1.7	2.3	1.4	1.0	1.0	0.3
Changes in Inventories	0.0	0.0	0.0	0.0	0.0	0.0	0.0	0.0	0.0	0.0
Financial Investments	0.3	0.2	0.1	0.2	0.4	0.3	0.3	0.1	0.0	0.0
Economies	0.0	0.0	0.0	0.0	0.0	0.0	0.0	0.0	0.0	0.0
Total Revenues	11.0	10.5	13.6	12.1	11.8	12.8	12.8	8.8	6.7	6.0
Total Expenditures	15.0	13.5	15.5	12.9	13.5	16.3	14.7	9.5	8.0	5.7
Financing Requirement	4.0	3.0	1.9	0.8	1.7	3.5	1.9	0.6	1.3	-0.3

a/ Interest obligations of public enterprises included in national administration.

Source: Secretary of Finance Savings-Investment Plans.

Table 2.5: Argentina - Tax Revenue by Source, 1970-1992
(As percent of GDP)

	1970	1971	1972	1973	1974	1975	1976	1977	1978	1979	1980	1981	1982	1983	1984	1985	1986	1987	1988	1989	1990	1991	1992e
Treasury Revenue	16.0	14.2	12.8	13.7	17.0	11.7	13.1	15.5	16.9	17.6	19.8	17.6	16.7	16.8	15.4	12.8	13.6	12.6	10.5	9.2	10.8	15.1	16.9
Coparticipated Taxes	6.4	5.7	4.8	4.7	5.6	3.5	5.2	7.0	7.5	7.3	8.6	9.6	9.0	7.9	6.0	7.7	9.1	9.5	8.4	6.1	6.3	9.6	13.4
Value Added Tax	1.8	1.8	1.4	1.2	2.1	1.9	2.7	3.3	3.4	3.6	4.3	5.1	4.5	3.7	2.9	3.3	3.7	3.7	2.7	1.7	2.8	5.1	8.6
Profit	2.3	1.9	1.6	1.8	1.7	0.8	1.2	1.8	1.7	1.2	1.6	1.7	1.4	1.1	0.6	1.2	1.5	1.9	1.3	1.0	0.6	0.8	1.8
Capital Tax	0.0	0.0	0.0	0.0	0.1	0.0	0.2	0.5	0.6	0.7	0.8	0.8	1.0	0.9	0.5	0.6	0.7	0.6	0.6	0.4	0.6	0.5	0.6
Net Worth Tax	0.0	0.0	0.0	0.0	0.0	0.0	0.0	0.0	0.0	0.0	0.0	0.0	0.0	0.0	0.0	0.0	0.2	0.1	0.0	0.0	0.0	0.0	0.0
Excise Tax	1.6	1.4	1.2	1.1	1.1	0.7	0.7	1.1	1.5	1.6	1.7	1.8	1.8	1.5	1.2	1.5	1.8	1.9	1.3	1.0	1.0	1.5	1.4
Bank Debit	0.0	0.0	0.0	0.0	0.0	0.0	0.1	0.2	0.2	0.0	0.0	0.0	0.0	0.1	0.3	0.4	0.6	0.5	0.9	0.8	0.4	1.4	0.5
Foreign Exchange Tax	0.1	0.1	0.1	0.1	0.1	0.1	0.1	0.1	0.1	0.1	0.1	0.2	0.1	0.1	0.1	0.1	0.1	0.1	0.2	0.3	0.1	0.0	0.0
Financial Services	0.0	0.0	0.0	0.0	0.0	0.0	0.1	0.0	0.0	0.0	0.0	0.0	0.0	0.0	0.0	0.0	0.0	0.0	0.0	0.0	0.1	0.1	0.1
Tax Arrears Payments	0.0	0.0	0.0	0.0	0.0	0.0	0.0	0.0	0.0	0.0	0.0	0.0	0.0	0.0	0.0	0.0	0.0	0.0	0.0	0.0	0.2	0.2	0.6
Agricultural Sales	0.0	0.0	0.0	0.0	0.0	0.0	0.0	0.0	0.0	0.0	0.0	0.0	0.0	0.0	0.0	0.3	0.3	0.3	0.3	0.2	0.0	0.0	0.0
Various Emergency	0.0	0.0	0.0	0.0	0.4	0.0	0.0	0.0	0.0	0.0	0.0	0.0	0.0	0.2	0.2	0.1	0.0	0.2	0.9	0.5	0.2	0.0	0.0
Others	0.6	0.5	0.4	0.5	0.4	0.0	0.1	0.1	0.0	0.1	0.1	0.1	0.1	0.2	0.2	0.2	0.2	0.2	0.2	0.3	0.2	0.0	0.0
Non-Coparticipated Taxes	4.1	3.7	4.0	4.1	5.2	3.6	3.9	4.5	4.8	4.5	4.7	4.7	4.7	5.6	5.8	5.1	4.5	3.1	2.0	3.1	4.5	5.5	3.5
Stamp Duty	0.4	0.4	0.3	0.4	0.4	0.2	0.2	0.3	0.3	0.4	0.4	0.3	0.3	0.2	0.2	0.2	0.3	0.2	0.2	0.1	0.1	0.2	0.3
Import Tax	1.2	1.1	1.1	0.7	0.9	0.7	0.9	1.2	1.1	1.3	1.7	1.5	1.0	0.8	0.7	1.0	1.4	1.7	1.0	0.5	0.3	0.4	0.9
Export Tax	0.7	0.6	1.2	1.4	1.0	0.8	1.5	0.6	0.3	0.2	0.2	0.2	0.6	1.5	1.2	2.2	1.3	0.4	0.2	1.6	1.3	0.2	0.0
Other Trade Tax	0.0	0.0	0.1	0.0	0.1	0.1	0.1	0.1	0.1	0.2	0.1	0.1	0.0	0.0	0.0	0.1	0.1	0.1	0.2	0.3	0.5	0.0	0.0
Oils and Fuel Tax	1.1	1.0	0.9	1.2	2.1	1.3	0.7	1.3	1.9	1.3	1.3	2.0	2.2	2.4	3.2	1.0	0.8	0.7	-0.5	0.4	0.7	2.1	1.7
Fuel	0.0	0.0	0.0	0.0	0.0	0.0	0.0	0.0	0.0	0.0	0.0	0.0	0.0	0.0	0.0	3.5	3.5	2.1	0.9	0.5	0.7	2.1	1.7
Fuel Fund Tariff	0.0	0.0	0.0	0.0	0.0	0.0	0.0	0.0	0.0	0.0	0.0	0.0	0.0	0.0	0.0	-2.5	-2.7	-1.4	-1.4	-1.0	0.0	0.0	0.0
Transfers from Fuel Fund	0.0	0.0	0.0	0.0	0.0	0.0	0.0	0.0	0.0	0.0	0.0	0.0	0.0	0.0	0.0	0.0	0.0	0.0	0.9	0.9	0.0	0.0	0.0
Forced Saving	0.0	0.0	0.0	0.0	0.0	0.0	0.0	0.0	0.0	0.0	0.0	0.0	0.0	0.0	0.0	0.6	0.6	0.0	0.9	0.1	0.0	0.0	0.0
Special Laws	0.0	0.0	0.0	0.0	0.0	0.0	0.0	0.0	0.0	0.0	0.0	0.0	0.0	0.0	0.0	0.0	0.0	0.0	0.0	0.0	1.5	0.0	0.0
Other Taxes	0.7	0.5	0.5	0.5	0.7	0.5	0.4	1.0	1.1	1.1	1.1	0.7	0.6	0.7	0.5	0.0	0.0	0.0	0.0	0.0	0.0	2.6	0.7
Social Security System	4.7	4.7	3.9	4.8	5.5	4.4	4.1	3.8	4.5	5.0	5.4	2.6	2.3	2.4	2.9	3.6	4.0	4.0	4.3	3.5	4.4	6.2	5.6
Total Revenues	15.2	14.0	12.7	13.7	16.3	11.5	13.2	15.4	16.9	16.8	18.7	17.0	16.0	15.9	14.7	16.4	17.6	16.6	14.8	12.7	15.2	21.4	22.5

Source: Ministry of Economy, National Directorate of Budgetary Programming.

Table 2.6: Argentina - Efficient Taxes and Tax Handles, 1970-1992
(As percent of GDP)

	1970	1971	1972	1973	1974	1975	1976	1977	1978	1979	1980	1981	1982	1983	1984	1985	1986	1987	1988	1989	1990	1991	1992e
Treasury	16.0	14.2	12.8	13.7	17.0	11.7	13.1	15.5	16.9	17.6	19.8	17.6	16.7	16.8	15.4	12.8	13.6	12.6	10.5	9.2	10.8	15.1	16.9
Efficient Taxes	8.0	7.2	6.3	6.0	8.1	5.4	6.4	9.1	10.1	9.7	11.3	12.9	11.9	10.4	9.1	8.6	10.1	10.6	6.4	5.0	6.3	12.1	16.0
Value Added	1.8	1.8	1.4	1.2	2.1	1.9	2.7	3.3	3.4	3.6	4.3	5.1	4.5	3.7	2.9	3.3	3.7	3.7	2.7	1.7	2.8	5.1	8.6
Bank Debit against VAT a/																						1.4	0.5
Profit	2.3	1.9	1.6	1.8	1.7	0.8	1.2	1.8	1.7	1.2	1.6	1.7	1.4	1.1	0.6	1.2	1.5	1.9	1.3	1.0	0.6	0.8	1.8
Capital	0.0	0.0	0.0	0.0	0.1	0.0	0.2	0.5	0.6	0.7	0.8	0.8	1.0	0.9	0.5	0.6	0.7	0.6	0.6	0.4	0.6	0.5	0.6
Net Worth	0.0	0.0	0.0	0.0	0.0	0.0	0.0	0.0	0.0	0.0	0.0	0.0	0.0	0.0	0.0	0.0	0.2	0.1	0.0	0.0	0.0	0.0	0.0
Import	1.2	1.1	1.1	0.7	0.9	0.7	0.9	1.2	1.1	1.3	1.7	1.5	1.0	0.8	0.7	1.0	1.4	1.7	1.0	0.5	0.3	0.4	0.9
Fuel & Fuel Fund	1.1	1.0	0.9	1.2	2.1	1.3	0.7	1.3	1.9	1.3	1.3	2.0	2.2	2.4	3.2	1.0	0.8	0.7	-0.5	0.4	0.7	2.1	1.7
Tax Arrears Payments	0.0	0.0	0.0	0.0	0.0	0.0	0.0	0.0	0.0	0.0	0.0	0.0	0.0	0.0	0.0	0.0	0.0	0.0	0.0	0.0	0.2	0.2	0.6
Excise	1.6	1.4	1.2	1.1	1.1	0.7	0.7	1.1	1.5	1.6	1.7	1.8	1.8	1.5	1.2	1.5	1.8	1.9	1.3	1.0	1.0	1.5	1.4
Tax Handles	1.9	1.5	1.4	1.5	1.7	0.9	1.2	1.8	1.9	1.9	1.8	1.3	1.3	1.6	1.5	2.0	2.2	1.6	3.8	2.6	3.1	2.9	1.0
Bank Debit a/	0.0	0.0	0.0	0.0	0.0	0.0	0.1	0.2	0.2	0.0	0.0	0.0	0.0	0.1	0.3	0.4	0.6	0.5	0.9	0.8	0.4	0.0	0.0
Various trade taxes	0.0	0.1	0.1	0.0	0.1	0.1	0.1	0.1	0.1	0.2	0.1	0.1	0.0	0.0	0.0	0.1	0.1	0.1	0.2	0.3	0.5	0.0	0.0
Forced Savings	0.0	0.0	0.0	0.1	0.0	0.0	0.0	0.0	0.0	0.0	0.0	0.0	0.0	0.0	0.0	0.6	0.6	0.0	0.9	0.1	0.0	0.0	0.0
Foreign Exchange	0.1	0.1	0.1	0.1	0.1	0.1	0.0	0.1	0.1	0.1	0.1	0.2	0.1	0.1	0.1	0.1	0.1	0.1	0.2	0.3	0.1	0.1	0.1
Financial Services	0.0	0.0	0.0	0.0	0.0	0.0	0.1	0.0	0.0	0.0	0.0	0.0	0.1	0.0	0.0	0.1	0.1	0.0	0.0	0.1	0.1	0.1	0.1
Stamp	0.4	0.4	0.3	0.4	0.4	0.2	0.2	0.3	0.3	0.4	0.4	0.3	0.3	0.2	0.2	0.2	0.3	0.2	0.2	0.1	0.1	0.2	0.3
Agricultural Sales	0.0	0.0	0.0	0.0	0.0	0.0	0.0	0.0	0.0	0.0	0.0	0.0	0.0	0.0	0.0	0.3	0.3	0.3	0.3	0.2	0.0	0.0	0.0
Various Emergency	0.0	0.0	0.0	0.0	0.0	0.0	0.0	0.0	0.0	0.0	0.0	0.0	0.0	0.2	0.2	0.1	0.0	0.2	0.9	0.5	0.2	0.0	0.0
Special Laws	0.0	0.0	0.0	0.0	0.0	0.0	0.0	0.0	0.0	0.0	0.0	0.0	0.0	0.0	0.0	0.0	0.0	0.0	0.0	0.0	1.5	0.0	0.0
Others N.E.I.	1.3	1.0	0.9	1.0	1.1	0.5	0.5	1.0	1.1	1.2	1.1	0.7	0.7	0.9	0.7	0.2	0.2	0.2	0.2	0.3	0.2	2.6	0.7
Social Security System	4.7	4.7	3.9	4.8	5.5	4.4	4.1	3.8	4.5	5.0	5.4	2.6	2.3	2.4	2.9	3.6	4.0	4.0	4.3	3.5	4.4	6.2	5.6
Total Tax Revenue	15.2	14.0	12.7	13.7	16.3	11.5	13.2	15.4	16.9	16.8	18.7	17.0	16.0	15.9	14.7	16.4	17.6	16.6	14.8	12.7	15.2	21.4	22.5

a/ Bank debit tax in 1991 is no longer considered tax handle; credit for VAT and Income Tax.

Table 2.7: Argentina - Tax Revenue by Source, 1988.I - 1992.IV

(As percent of GDP)

	1988 I	1988 II	1988 III	1988 IV	1989 I	1989 II	1989 III	1989 IV	1990 I	1990 II	1990 III	1990 IV	1991 I	1991 II	1991 III	1991 IV	1992 I	1992 II	1992 III	1992 IV a/
Treasury Revenue	11.0	11.3	10.1	10.4	8.9	7.1	9.6	14.2	9.0	12.0	10.9	11.0	9.9	15.3	14.9	16.2	15.4	17.3	17.6	17.4
Coparticipated Taxes	8.7	9.1	8.1	8.7	7.0	4.3	5.8	10.0	4.6	6.8	6.5	7.1	6.7	10.9	9.7	11.2	12.0	13.6	14.0	14.0
Value Added	2.9	2.8	2.4	2.6	1.8	0.6	1.8	2.4	1.7	3.2	3.0	3.4	3.2	5.5	5.1	6.5	6.9	9.1	9.3	9.1
Income	1.3	1.3	1.4	1.2	1.0	0.8	0.9	1.2	0.6	0.6	0.8	0.6	0.6	1.0	0.9	0.9	1.1	1.4	2.1	2.5
Capital	0.4	0.8	0.5	0.7	0.4	0.4	0.2	0.6	0.2	0.9	0.8	0.8	0.4	0.7	0.5	0.4	0.8	0.6	0.4	0.5
Net Worth	0.0	0.0	0.0	0.0	0.0	0.0	0.0	0.0	0.0	0.0	0.0	0.0	0.0	0.0	0.0	0.0	0.0	0.0	0.0	0.0
Excise	1.7	1.3	1.1	1.3	1.3	0.5	0.8	1.2	0.6	1.0	0.9	1.3	1.2	1.8	1.4	1.5	1.5	1.5	1.3	1.3
Bank Debit	0.6	1.1	1.0	1.1	1.0	0.7	0.7	1.0	0.4	0.4	0.4	0.4	0.7	1.6	1.5	1.6	1.3	0.5	0.1	0.0
Foreign Exchange	0.2	0.2	0.2	0.2	0.3	0.3	0.3	0.3	0.4	0.0	0.0	0.0	0.0	0.0	0.1	0.0	0.0	0.0	0.0	0.0
Financial Services	0.0	0.0	0.0	0.0	0.0	0.0	0.0	0.0	0.1	0.1	0.1	0.1	0.1	0.1	0.1	0.1	0.1	0.1	0.1	0.0
Tax Arrears Payments	0.0	0.0	0.0	0.0	0.2	0.2	0.2	0.2	0.2	0.2	0.1	0.2	0.2	0.2	0.2	0.2	0.3	0.5	0.7	0.6
Agricultural Sales	0.3	0.3	0.3	0.3	0.2	0.2	0.2	0.2	0.1	0.0	0.1	0.0	0.0	0.0	0.0	0.0	0.0	0.0	0.0	0.0
Various Emergency	0.9	0.9	0.9	0.9	0.9	0.9	0.9	0.9	0.7	0.2	0.0	0.0	0.0	0.0	0.0	0.0	0.0	0.0	0.0	0.0
Others b/	0.4	0.4	0.4	0.4	0.0	0.0	0.0	2.3	0.1	0.1	0.4	0.3	0.3	0.0	0.0	0.0	0.0	0.0	0.0	0.0
Non-coparticipated Taxes	2.3	2.2	1.9	1.7	1.9	2.8	3.8	4.1	4.4	5.2	4.5	3.9	3.2	4.4	5.2	5.0	3.5	3.7	3.7	3.3
Stamp	0.2	0.1	0.1	0.2	0.2	0.1	0.1	0.2	0.1	0.2	0.2	0.2	0.1	0.2	0.2	0.3	0.2	0.3	0.3	0.3
Import	1.3	1.2	0.9	0.8	0.7	0.4	0.5	0.6	0.3	0.3	0.3	0.3	0.3	0.4	0.4	0.5	0.9	1.0	1.0	0.8
Export	0.2	0.3	0.3	0.2	0.1	1.5	2.4	2.5	2.0	1.9	1.1	0.5	0.3	0.4	0.1	0.0	0.0	0.0	0.0	0.0
Others	0.2	0.2	0.2	0.2	0.3	0.3	0.3	0.5	0.3	0.7	0.5	0.4	0.3	0.6	1.3	1.7	0.0	0.0	0.0	0.0
Fuel	-0.5	-0.5	-0.5	-0.5	0.5	0.4	0.4	0.5	0.4	0.7	0.8	1.0	1.6	2.1	2.7	2.0	1.7	1.7	1.6	1.6
Fuel	1.1	0.7	0.7	0.9	0.8	0.4	0.3	0.6	0.4	0.7	0.8	1.0	1.6	2.1	2.7	2.0	--	--	--	--
Fuel Fund Tariff	-1.6	-1.2	-1.2	-1.4	-1.2	-0.9	-0.8	-1.0	--	--	--	--	--	--	--	--	--	--	--	--
Transfers from Fuel Fund	--	--	--	--	0.9	0.9	0.9	0.9	--	--	--	--	--	--	--	--	--	--	--	--
Forced Savings	0.9	0.9	0.9	0.9	0.9	0.9	0.9	0.9	--	--	--	--	--	--	--	--	0.0	0.0	0.0	0.0
5% Public Enterprise Sales Tax	--	--	--	--	--	--	--	--	--	--	--	--	--	--	--	--	0.0	0.0	0.0	0.0
Special Laws	0.0	0.0	0.0	0.0	0.0	0.0	0.0	0.0	1.3	1.5	1.5	1.6	0.5	0.6	0.5	0.5	0.6	0.7	0.7	0.6
Social Security System	4.6	3.9	4.1	4.5	5.3	2.3	2.8	3.7	2.7	4.4	5.5	5.1	5.2	5.9	6.7	7.1	6.7	6.6	8.2	8.3
Total Revenue	15.6	15.2	14.2	14.9	14.2	9.4	12.4	17.9	11.7	16.5	16.4	16.1	15.0	21.2	21.6	23.4	22.1	23.9	25.8	25.6
Memo:																				
GDP in US dollars (billions)	14.7	16.5	18.9	20.1	15.6	10.3	15.0	14.1	18.2	21.9	26.9	36.8	31.5	33.1	33.9	34.4	36.0	36.7	39.3	41.2
VAT in US dollars (millions)	425	461	444	530	284	57	273	339	312	708	811	1267	1018	1831	1722	2227	2464	3324	3644	3769
Tax Handles in US dollars (million)	786	909	994	1079	643	446	821	1219	978	1189	1244	1605	1017	1549	1301	1360	338	393	408	359

a/ 1992 fourth quarter based on preliminary data.

b/ Includes property taxes

c/ Bank debit tax in 1991and 1992 is no longer considered tax handle; credit for VAT and Income Tax.

d/ See Table 2.9 for breakdown of tax handles.

Table 3.1: Argentina - Total Federal Public Employment (1990-1993) a/

Area	April 1990	Dec. 1992 b/	- Projected - Dec. 1993	Reductions Total	Lay-offs c	Transfers d/
Total Federal Employment	1128258	528495	466602	661656	217544	444112
National Administration	671479	284215	284215	387264	103469	283795
Administrative Reform Program	341021	227677	227677	113344	90913	22431
National Administration (budgeted)	268246	184667	184667	83579	61148	22431
Central Administration	123646	61276	61276	62370	39939	22431
Decentralized Agencies	144600	123391	123391	21209	21209	...
Other National Administration	72775	43010	43010	29765	29765	...
Other Programs	330458	56538	56538	273920	12556	261364
Public Enterprises	293482	109686	47793	245689	85372	160317
Fuel & Energy	83513	27050	12773	70740	35123	35617
Transport & Communications	194901	82636	35020	159881	50249	109632
Industry & Services	84	...	...	84	...	84
Defense	14984	...	...	14984	...	14984
Public Banking	32000	22000	22000	10000	10000	...
Armed Forces and Conscripts	131297	112594	112594	18703	18703	...

Source: Bank Staff calculation based on information provided by the Government of Argentina, Office of the Budget, Ministry of Defense and SIGEP.

a/ Does not include University teachers, estimated to be around 95,000.
b/ National Administration figures are for 1993 budget.
c/ Total net lay-offs.
d/ Transfers from the National Administration are to Provinces; transfers fronm the Public Enterprises are to the private sector via the sale of the enterpises.

Table 3.2 - National Administration: Reform Program

	April 1990	1993 Budget	Reductions Total	Reductions Lay-offs a/	Reductions Transfers
Total National Administration b/	671479	284215	387264	103469 c/	283795
Administrative Reform Program	341021	227677	113344	90913	22431
National Administration (Budgeted)	268246	184667	83579	61148	22431
Central Administration	123646	61276	62370	39939	22431
Decentralized Agencies	144600	123391	21209	21209	...
Other National Administration (off Budget)	72775	43010	29765	29765	...
Other Programs	330458	56538	273920	12556	261364
Legislature	12405	12405	0	...	...
Judiciary	14053	17476	-3423	-3423	...
Nation Accounts Court	1000	1021	-21	-21	...
Teachers	303000	25636	277364	16000	261364
Memo:					
Armed Forces (A.F.) and Conscripts d/	131297	112594	18703	18703	...
National Administration and Armed Forces	802776	396809	405967	122172 e/	283795
Gross lay-offs (exc. tax agencies, Police and A. F.)				121600	

a/ Reductions in positions via lay-offs, early retirement and attrition.

b/ Does not include University Teachers, estimated to be around 95,000.

c/ Total net lay-offs. Discounting increases in the main tax collection agencies (13,300) and police (4,800),
total gross lay-offs reach 121,600.

d/ Net of civilian personnel in Ministry of Defense, included in National Administration
budget (above). Includes conscripts, which were reduced from 29,000 in 1990 to 12,000
in 1992, a reduction of 17,000.

e/ Gross total lay-offs of 121,600 (footnote c) in the National Administration plus military reductions, are 140,300.

Table 3.3 - Administrative Reform Program: Budget and off-Budget a/

	April 1990	1993 Budget	Reduction
Total Administrative Reform Program	341021	227677	113344
Budget			
National Administration	268246	184667	83579
Central Administration	123646	61276	62370
Decentralized Agencies	144600	123391	21209
Off-Budget			
National Administration	72775	43010	29765
Central Administration	0	0	0
Decentralized Agencies	72775	43010	29765

a/ National Administration covered in Decree 2476/90 and in "Hacia un Estado Moderno" report.

Table 3.4 - National Administration - Reform Program in Budget a/ b/

	April 1990	1993 Budget	Reduction
National Administration	268246	184667	83579
Central Administration	123646	61276	62370
Ministry of Economy and Public Works	11115	6978	4137
Ministry of Foreign Affairs	3082	1611	1471
Ministry of Health	44860	12022	32838
Ministry of Labor and Social Security	2874	2149	725
Ministry of Defense	41298	27020	14278
Ministry of Interior	1167	1173	-6
Ministry of Culture and Education	14157	4120	10037
Ministry of Justice	1751	1765	-14
Presidency	3342	4438	-1096
Decentralized Agencies	144600	123391	21209

a/ 1993 Budget definition; because of changes in administrative structure selected agencies have been grouped differenlty from previous layouts in order to make data comparable.
b/ Does not include Teachers and Military.

Table 3.5 - Decentralized Agencies - Reform Program in Budget a/

	April 1990	1993 Budget	Reduction
Decentralized Agencies	144600	123391	21209
INTI	271	50	221
INTA	5788	4391	1397
INIDEP	301	203	98
INPRES	125	78	47
INCYTH/CRAS	533	327	206
National Board of the Antarctic	249	209	40
CITEFA	411	1000	-589
CONICET	8162	7400	762
National Broadcasting Commitee	301	0	301
CNV	96	147	-51
National Insurance Superintendency	196	341	-145
CRPC Yerba Mate	46	0	46
Wine National Institute	1406	555	851
Sugar National Board	207	0	207
JNG	3529	0	3529
Cattle National Market	245	0	245
Meat National Board	514	0	514
Cinema National Institute	128	183	-55
National Construction Registry	72	0	72
INAM	112	84	28
INOS	228	0	228
Citizens National Registry	1088	898	190
National Pricing Court	68	51	17
COFAPYS	97	103	-6
National Public Administration Institute (INAP)	145	165	-20
Arts National Fund	88	67	21
CUDEP	199	0	199
Data Bank	137	0	137
Militar Geographic Institute	440	341	99
SIGEP	475	390	85
CONET	5762	53	5709
Miguel Lillo Foundation	147	247	-100
National Institute of Educational Credit	35	28	7
INDEC	1204	1499	-295
SENASA	3086	2884	202
National Parks Administration	584	608	-24
Forest National Institute	319	0	319
Equestrian National Institute	18	0	18
CONEA	6287	6500	-213
DNV	7366	4018	3348
Official Broadcasting Service	1244	0	1244
CENARESO	151	144	7
DGFM	13276	4456	8820
PAN	2026	0	2026
Police Pension Fund	188	155	33
Financial Aid Institute for Pension Payment	287	208	79
Social Security National Administration	15982	9405	6577
ANA	3529	6136	-2607
DGI	10445	21229	-10784
National Lottery	3388	0	3388
Federal Police	35777	40615	-4838
Federal Prison National Board	7842	7185	657
Space National Comission	0	254	-254
National Sanitary Institute of Vegetable Quality	0	578	-578
Health Insurance National Administration	0	206	-206

a/ 1993 Budget definition.

Table 3.6 - Reform Program not in Budget

	April 1990	1993 Budget	Reduction
Personnel Included in Reform Program not in Budget	72775	43010	29765
INDER	390	0	390
Horse Racing National Board	1630	0	1630
Money House	1282	0	1282
Health Insurance Funds (Obras Sociales)	32979	15010 a/	17969
National Universities (Adm. Personnel)	36494	28000 b/	8494

a/ Estimates provided by the Government.

b/ Information provided by the Federation of Associations of Workers of the National Universities (FATUN). Includes personnel working in health centers under universities jurisdiction.

Table 3.7: Argentina - Public Enterprises Personnel

Area	Dec 1990	Dec. 1991	Projected Dec. 1992	Projected Dec. 1993	Total Projected Reduction	Reductions Lay-offs a/ 1991	1992	1993	Privatized 1991	1992	1993
Public Enterprises	293482	194742	109686	47793	245689	40536	44836	...	58204	26698	75415
Fuel & Energy	83513	66459	27050	12773	70740	16574	18549	...	480	20860	14277
YPF	36935	23404	12773	12773	24162	13531	10631	...	..	...	...
Gas del Estado	10425	10094	9063	...	10425	331	1031	...	...	...	9063
YCF	2987	2756	1450	...	2987	231	1306	...	...	...	1450
SEGBA	20271	18209	0	...	20271	2062	2403	...	...	15806	...
Agua y Energia	11276	10446	2271	...	11276	350	3121	...	480	5054	2271
Hidronor	1619	1550	1493	...	1619	69	57	...	...	...	1493
Transport & Communications	194901	113299	82636	35020	159881	23962	26287	...	57640	5838	46154
Ferrocarriles Argentinos	86335	67645	48905	35020	51315	17881	18740	...	809	...	13885
Aerolineas Argentinas	10791	...	...	...	10791	...	...	...	10791	...	...
ELMA	4449	2750	2750	...	4449	1699	1056	...	...	...	1694
AGP	3080	2758	2758	...	3080	322	406	...	...	...	2352
ENTEL	46040	...	...	...	46040	...	...	...	46040	...	...
ENCOTEL	35844	32275	26330	...	35844	3569	5945	...	...	...	26330
OSN	8362	7871	1893	...	8362	491	140	...	...	5838	1893
Industry & Services	84	...	...	...	84	...	...	...	84	...	...
OPTAR	84	...	...	...	84	...	...	...	84	...	...
Defense	14984	14984	...	...	14984	...	...	...	...	...	14984
HIPASAM	1366	1366	...	...	1366	...	...	...	...	...	1366
SOMISA	11413	11413	...	...	11413	...	...	...	...	...	11413
TANDANOR	772	772	...	...	772	...	...	...	...	...	772
Petroquim. Bahia Blanca	399	399	...	...	399	...	...	...	...	...	399
Petroquim. General Mosconi	1034	1034	...	...	1034	...	...	...	...	...	1034

Source: SIGEP

a/ Includes early retirments and attrition.

Table 3.8: Argentina - National Administration Wage Bill

	1988	1989	1990	1991	1992	- Budgeted - 1993
National Administration						
Current Expenditures (Million Pesos)	2.9	72.0	1,574.7	3,389.8	3,410.7	4,965.2
Real Expenditures (1992 Million Pesos)	5,366	3,920	4,368	3,955	3,411	4,738
Expenditures (us$ Million)	3,307	1,702	3,229	3,555	3,443	4,965
Personnel Expenditures (1992 us$ Million) a/	3,953	1,941	3,493	3,689	3,443	4,738
Personnel Expenditures (Percent of GDP)	3.7	2.8	3.1	2.6	2.2	3.0
Personnel in Budget b/			736,597	583,799	360,983	341,973
Implicit Average Wage (1992 US$)			4,742	6,320	9,538	13,854
Implicit Monthly Average Wage (1992 US$)			365	486	734	1,066

Source: Executed Budgets; Fiscal Savings-Investment Accounts (1992); Ministry of Economy.

a/ Net of indemnizations, previsions for early retirement and changes in pay-scales. Includes social contributions, annual complementary salaries, and other retributions.
b/ Budgeted National Administration Personnel plus Armed Forces personnel (excluding conscripts and universities administrative personnel; including health funds until 1992).

Table 3.9: Argentina - National Administration Compensations a/
(in million Pesos)

	1991	1992	Total
Voluntary Retirement	88.39	8.53	96.92
Severance Regime b/	43.62	169.45	213.08
Temporary Staff	2.27	-	-
Total	134.28	177.98	312.26

Source: Ministry of Economy
a/ Includes Central Administration, Special Accounts and Decentralized Agencies
b/ Personnel subject to "Disponibilidad".

Table 3.10: Argentina - Total Public Sector Employment (1960 - 1992)

	National Administration a/	Public Enterprises	National Total	Provinces and Buenos Aires Municipality	Munici-palities	Total
1960	506,367	415,457	921,824	364,512	83,626	1,369,962
1961	496,010	408,193	904,203	388,937	85,671	1,378,811
1962	469,446	325,549	794,995	414,668	88,350	1,298,013
1963	456,000	302,754	758,754	425,736	89,507	1,273,997
1964	460,527	305,319	765,846	438,590	93,277	1,297,713
1965	475,217	326,776	801,993	441,122	97,006	1,340,121
1966	481,025	339,519	820,544	468,951	101,725	1,391,220
1967	483,028	333,950	816,978	475,953	107,911	1,400,842
1968	492,443	315,284	807,727	472,537	109,247	1,389,511
1969	498,077	306,323	804,400	474,928	111,199	1,390,527
1970	511,451	302,294	813,745	474,192	112,394	1,400,331
1971	524,330	303,031	827,361	483,743	116,052	1,427,156
1972	545,787	309,769	855,556	500,898	116,198	1,472,652
1973	557,976	342,848	900,824	518,029	124,296	1,543,149
1974	517,153	408,750	925,903	564,496	135,220	1,625,619
1975	558,684	429,551	988,235	630,849	151,865	1,770,949
1976	557,691	432,715	990,406	646,654	162,248	1,799,308
1977	496,276	389,360	885,636	661,067	137,377	1,684,080
1978	497,481	361,640	859,121	688,299	133,873	1,681,293
1979	481,048	347,811	828,859	726,867	140,148	1,695,874
1980	494,565	324,916	819,481	723,293	149,858	1,692,632
1981	524,109	307,947	832,056	722,234	151,111	1,705,401
1982	514,035	300,768	814,803	723,374	151,350	1,689,527
1983	538,861	312,269	851,130	753,027	157,554	1,761,711
1984	551,708	314,831	866,539	808,473	169,155	1,844,167
1985	569,481	304,930	874,411	843,485	169,259	1,887,155
1986	564,937	307,424	872,361	912,070	171,017	1,955,448
1987	561,748	305,160	866,908	913,569	171,298	1,951,775
1988	604,629	305,288	909,917	915,556	171,671	1,997,144
1989	638,054	299,385	937,439	923,619	173,183	2,034,241
1990	671,479	293,482	964,961	929,443	174,275	2,068,679
1991 b/	581,539	194,742	776,281	929,443	174,275	1,879,999
1992 b/	284,215	109,686	393,901	1,238,874	174,275	1,807,050

Source: Ministry of Economy, SIGEP, and paper by Carlos Sanchez and Osvaldo Giordano "Public Sector Employment & Wages in Argentina: Cutbacks & Alternatives" (IEERAL database).

a/ Adjusted for under-reporting of teachers for the period 1981-89.
b/ Preliminary.

Table 4.1: 1992 PRESIDENCY EXPENDITURE BY ECONOMIC CLASSIFICATION
(US$ millions)

	Wages	Goods and Services	Interest	Transfers	Capital Expenditures	Total Expenditures	As a Percent of Presid. Expend.
Central Administration	57.9	45.9	0.0	16.4	3.2	123.4	9.3
General Administration	28.6	30.9	0.0	6.4	2.3	68.3	5.1
Other General Adminis.	8.0	13.9	0.0	0.0	0.8	22.6	1.7
Tourism	2.5	0.1	0.0	0.0	0.0	2.6	0.2
Communications	12.5	0.0	0.0	0.0	0.0	12.5	0.9
Sports	1.3	0.1	0.0	0.0	0.0	1.4	0.1
Science & Technology	5.0	0.9	0.0	10.0	0.1	16.0	1.2
Special Accounts	114.8	36.4	0.0	4.1	2.7	158.0	11.9
Intelligence (SIDE)	110.0	4.5	0.0	0.0	1.2	115.7	8.7
Other Gen. Administ.	2.0	5.0	0.0	0.0	0.0	7.0	0.5
National Tourism Fund	2.8	24.1	0.0	0.1	0.7	27.7	2.1
Nat. Radiotelecom. Service	0.0	1.4	0.0	0.0	0.7	2.1	0.2
National Sports Fund	0.0	1.4	0.0	4.0	0.1	5.5	0.4
centralized Agencies	165.9	163.5	188.6	92.3	434.4	1,044.8	78.8
Nat. Inst. of Public Admin.	5.5	1.7	0.0	0.0	0.2	7.4	0.6
CNEA (Atomic Energy Comm.)	87.9	150.9	182.8	1.7	426.5	849.8	64.1
Fed. Comm. of Radiocommunic.	2.3	2.0	0.0	0.0	0.0	4.3	0.3
Nat. Council on Sci. & Tech.	66.6	8.1	5.8	18.4	7.6	106.5	8.0
Other Sci. & Tech. a/	3.6	0.8	0.0	72.3	0.1	76.8	5.8
Total	338.6	245.8	188.6	112.8	440.2	1,326.1	100.0

a/ Includes Miguel Lillo Foundation and National Council on Science and Technology.

Table 4.2: MHSA EXECUTED EXPENDITURE BY PROGRAM, 1986-90
(in constant 1991 US$ thousands)

Jurisdiction / Type of Program	1986	1987	1988	1989	1990
80-Ministry of Health & Social Action	169234.5	216427.2	166312.5	199683.3	52733.5
006 - Social Action Construction **/	5095.4	6847.0	8543.0	7077.5	2657.4
045 - Emergency Program	0.0	0.0	0.0	98713.4	29476.5
040 - Administration of Azar & Hipico Lotteries*/	137082.7	154897.2	91514.9	83743.7	0.0
001 - Conducting Health & Social Action Policy	5780.7	8703.0	38466.9	5414.4	12404.8
003 - Social Welfare Coverage	21275.6	24959.9	17185.0	4198.8	8007.9
011 - Social Justice 1/	0.0	21020.1	10602.7	535.4	186.8
81-Secretary of Health	635209.8	708862.7	473793.9	369371.1	511571.0
004 - Social Coverage in Health	0.0	0.0	8198.0	3078.7	117.5
015 - Medical Attention Service	127734.1	164791.4	84266.7	26325.7	43734.0
026 - Preventive Actions and Control of Health	33991.2	33231.8	30648.2	14131.2	22616.5
036 - Support of the Health Programs of the Provinces	129803.3	72642.4	29426.2	3364.9	198.9
044 - Assistance in Provision of Medicine	37672.1	65031.9	11002.0	1311.5	0.0
050 - Sanitary Construction	9878.9	11685.2	3135.4	3098.3	795.7
101 - Rehabilitation of the Health Infrastructure	0.0	1940.4	5276.5	7888.4	5211.2
151 - Regulation and coordination of the "Obras Sociales"	233901.6	268760.6	171391.7	193935.8	263779.4
196 - Construction of Health Centers	0.0	0.0	0.0	0.0	0.0
318, 320, 322, 324-330 Medical Attention Service 2/	0.0	0.0	34095.6	45140.5	66494.1
481, 483 - Mental Health Service 3/	0.0	0.0	15884.4	16715.0	28999.9
505 - Odontology Attention Services	0.0	0.0	0.0	0.0	0.0
616 - Psychophysical Rehabilitation Services 4/	0.0	0.0	2101.0	4231.5	6116.4
037 - Preventive Measures & Control of Environ. Health	9538.1	19396.1	16065.7	5975.0	12798.0
010 - Formulation and Implementation of Health Policy	39465.7	53819.1	46600.2	31310.0	39932.2
033 - Regulation and Control of Hygiene	11821.7	15821.6	13839.2	8841.9	16950.7
766 - Retraining of Young Drug Abusers	1403.1	1742.1	1863.1	1650.4	3713.2
069 - Recovery and Strengthening of Health Services	0.0	0.0	0.0	2372.2	113.4
83-Secretary of Sports and Social Promotion	389630.0	435763.2	302705.8	717277.8	214652.0
Of which: 060 - National Nutrition Program (PAN)	267437.3	340562.8	237550.0	658765.3	179760.3
Of which: 009 - Social Nutrition Program	104825.7	77865.4	50369.3	31815.3	25818.3
84-Secretary of Human Development and Family	57232.7	68909.3	57237.1	48506.0	85760.3
85-Secretary of Housing and Environmental Regulation	1476922.3	1582807.8	1179373.9	875737.0	1153584.2
Of which: 029 - Subsidized Housing	1472110.1	1560086.9	1126098.4	804067.9	1023752.2
TOTAL	2728229.2	3012770.1	2179423.1	2210575.3	2018301.0
Memo Item: Annual Growth Rate of Total Total Expenditure of MHSA		10.4	-27.7	1.4	-8.7

Notes:

*. After 1991 this Administration has changed into a state society & is no longer inclueded in the National Administration
**. In 1992 budget programs 006 and 050 are combined

1. In 1988 the program was named as Democracy in Action.
2. From 1988, programs 318 (Posada Hospital), 320
   (St. Lucia Hospital), and 324 (Hospital Ferrer) &
   from 1989 the programs 322 (Rivadavia Hospital), 326 (Udaondo Hospital),
   326 (Udaondo Hospital), 328 (Lagleyze Hospital)
   330 (Sommer Hospital) are included due to
   decentralization of the organizations that were
   part of program 015 in the Central Administration.
3. From 1989 include Program 485 due to decentralization of the
   "National Protected Centers for Psychiatric Rehabilitation".
4. From 1989 includes Program 610 due to the decentralization of
   "National Institute of Psychophysical Rehabilitation".

Source: Ministries of Economy and Health and Social Action

Table 4.3: SOCIAL SECURITY CONTRIBUTIONS
(in percent of gross salary)

	Employers	Employees	Total
Pension Insurance	16.0 [11] a/	10	26.0 [21] a/
Health Insurance for			
Pensioners	2.0	3	5.0
Active Workers b/	6.9	3	9.9
Family Fund	9.0	-	9.0
Housing Fund	- [5]	-	- [5]
Total	33.9	16	49.9

a/   Brackets indicate situation prior to Law 23.966, 1991.

b/   Includes 0.9 percent contribution to the Administration of health insurance institutions.

Source: Bank Staff

**Table 4.4: DISTRIBUTION FOR THE GAINFULLY EMPLOYED BETWEEN
PUBLIC PENSION INSURANCE INSTITUTIONS, 1986**
(in thousands persons)

	Contributors	Non-Contributors	Total
I. National System	5,302	3,668	8,970
Dependent Workers	4,227	1,962	5,919
Private Sector	3,465	1,692	5,157
Formal Sector	3,033	919	3,952
Rural Sector	338	259	597
Households	94	514	608
Public Sector	762	-	3,051
Independent Worker	1,075	1,976	3,051
II. Security Forces	139	-	139
III. Provincial and Municipal			
Public Administration	961	-	961
Total	6,402	3,668	10,070

Source: Secretariat of Social Security

Table 4.5: Argentina - Military Personnel, 1991

	Army	Navy	Air Force	Prefectura	Gendarmerie	Total by Rank	Percent
Total	32145	19615	16410	13162	16846	98178	100.0
Total Officers	5932	2944	2465	1437	1820	14598	14.9
Lieutenant General	1	0	1	..	..	2	0.0
Major General	8	6	3	..	..	17	0.0
Brigadier General	50	31	20	9	12	122	0.1
Colonel	442	263	178	64	108	1055	1.1
Lieutenant Colonel	884	397	207	159	179	1826	1.9
Major	1010	626	394	222	306	2558	2.6
Captain	1134	600	584	291	296	2905	3.0
First Lieutenant 1	1199	478	529	346	431	2983	3.0
First Lieutenant 2	799	266	338	144	218	1765	1.8
Second Lieutenant	405	277	211	202	270	1365	1.4
Total Enlisted	26213	16671	13945	11725	15026	83580	85.1
Sergeant Major	1298	322	132	68	330	2150	2.2
Sergeant Principal	2889	720	735	301	496	5141	5.2
Sergeant Adjunct	4583	2255	1453	1251	1088	10630	10.8
Sergeant 1	4302	2246	1997	2208	2661	13414	13.7
Sergeant	4952	2146	2171	4115	2568	15952	16.2
Corporal 1	3135	2592	1849	1714	2054	11344	11.6
Corporal	1814	1840	782	1499	2275	8210	8.4
Private 1	111	213	..	..	..	324	0.3
Private 2	129	337	..	..	..	466	0.5
Gendarmerie/Sailor	..	..	..	569	3554	4123	4.2
Conscripts	3000	4000	4826	..	..	11826	12.0

Source: Ministry of Defense

Table 4.6: Argentina - Composition of Military Expenditure for Selected Countries, 1990
(Percent of Total Expenditure)

	Argentina a/	Average b/	Brazil	Chile	Colombia	Greece
Personnel	60.7	52.6	63.1	39.9	51.7	55.5
Operations and Maintenance	33.1	23.9	30.9	28.4	20.0	16.2
Procurement/Construction/R&D	6.2	23.6	5.9	31.7	28.2	28.3
Total	100.0	100.0	100.0	100.0	100.0	100.0

Source: United Nations, Reduction of Military Budgets, Military Expenditures in Standardized Form
    Reported by States. Report of the Secretary-General, A/46/381, September 18, 1991

a/ Excludes military pensions, which are presumed to be missing from the accounts of the other countries.
   If pensions were included, the proportions would change as follows: personnel 70.1 percent,
   operations and maintenance 25.2 percent, and capital expenditures 4.7 percent.
b/ Excludes Argentina.

Table 5.1: Argentina - Domestic Debt
(US$ million)

	1989	1990	1991	1992
Total	799	2716	1562	6900
BOCREX a/	0	406	105	148
BOCE b/	364	829	73	6
BIC c/	352	1338	1369	1480
CNEA d/	71	26	0	0
BOCATE	12	26	15	8
BIC Provinces	0	91	0	--
BOCON e/	0	0	0	5258
Memo:				
Dollar Issues				
BONEX f/	5894	5668	5838	5690
BOTE and Euronotes g/	0	0	501	2857

a/ External Credit Bonds
b/ Economic Consolidation Bonds
c/ Investment and Growth Bonds
d/ Atomic Energy Commission Bonds
e/ Debt-consolidating bonds issued to suppliers and pensioners
f/ External Bonds
g/ External Treasury Bonds

Source: Central Bank of Argentina

Table 5.2: Argentina - External Debt by Creditor, 1983-1991 a/ b/
(Millions of US dollars; end of period)

	1983	1984	1985	1986	1987	1988	1989	1990	1991	1992
Total Debt	45069	46171	49326	51422	58324	58303	65511	62974	65229	73167
Medium and Long Term	36835	39601	45140	47222	54749	54803	62900	59998	63931	64223
Short Term	8234	6570	4186	4200	3575	3500	2611	2976	1298	8944
MLT Debt Outstanding and Disbursed	36835	39601	45140	47222	54749	54803	62900	59998	63931	64223
Commercial Banks c/	28394	29425	33403	33188	37600	38261	38092	34590	35368	31751
Bilateral	1654	3290	3621	5132	5809	5585	10921	11302	12287	14173
Bonds d/	4208	4307	3922	3638	3528	2915	5907	5668	7772	8683
IBRD	534	503	700	1140	1802	2101	2196	2366	2790	3037
IDB	873	936	1205	1405	2185	2263	2667	2990	3170	3697
IMF	1173	1140	2289	2719	3825	3678	3117	3082	2544	2882
MLT Disbursements (Gross)	8593	14926	8843	7984	5027	4298	5198	4188	5675	4052
Commercial Banks	6106	12698	6584	5446	2202	2562	2391	1966	2350	0
Bilateral	704	1814	510	1238	571	477	1755	908	1122	400
Bonds	451	171	130	183	83	0	0	0	956	1200
IBRD	70	96	144	408	795	487	316	405	460	481
IDB	89	147	326	162	123	231	503	399	450	748
IMF purchases	1173	0	1149	547	1253	541	233	510	337	1223
MLT Amortiztions	4209	11504	4778	1612	2490	2463	1891	3375	2699	3964
Commercial Banks	3214	11057	3956	583	1226	943	0	1289	0	127
Bilateral	510	178	179	258	187	0	483	756	610	1065
Bonds	400	72	515	467	179	656	309	226	561	1433
IBRD	40	80	71	110	133	188	221	235	322	233
IDB	45	84	57	77	94	153	160	174	208	221
IMF repurchases	0	33	0	117	671	523	718	695	998	885
MLT Disbursements (Net)	4384	3422	4065	6372	2537	1835	3308	812	2976	88
Commercial Banks	2892	1641	2628	4863	976	1619	2391	677	2350	-127
Bilateral	194	1636	331	980	384	477	1272	152	512	-665
Bonds	51	99	-385	-284	-96	-656	-309	-226	395	-233
IBRD	30	16	73	298	662	299	96	169	138	248
IDB	44	63	269	85	29	78	343	225	242	527
IMF	1173	-33	1149	430	582	18	-485	-185	-661	338
Interest Payments	5423	5537	5132	4291	4362	5198	5194	5777	4935	2954
Commercial Banks	..	4427	3802	3098	2998	3452	3359	3230	2546	1103
Bilateral	..	189	297	122	482	513	645	1070	937	568
Bonds	..	437	449	320	490	323	232	598	588	436
IBRD	36	56	46	75	91	159	196	182	209	165
IDB	56	80	72	108	180	158	167	193	175	131
IMF charges	74	90	140	159	121	282	262	243	314	331
Short Term	..	258	326	409	0	311	333	261	166	220

a/ Disbursements and amortizations may not explain yearly changes in debt stock due to valuation changes.

b/ Figures adjusted by the changes in cross-rates between US dollar and other currencies.

c/ Commercial Bank debt includes arrears.

d/ Change in debt stock from 1988 to 1989 includes BONEX conversion.

Source: IBRD staff estimates based on data from the Central Bank of the Republic of Argentina, IMF and IDB.

Table 6.1: ARGENTINA - BALANCE OF PAYMENTS, 1970-1992 a/
(Millions of US dollars)

	1970	1971	1972	1973	1974	1975	1976	1977	1978	1979	1980	1981	1982	1983	1984	1985	1986	1987	1988	1989	1990	1991	1992 b/
Exports (FOB)	1773	1740	1941	3266	3930	2961	3918	5651	6401	7810	8021	9143	7624	7836	8107	8396	6853	6358	8942	9573	12354	12019	12218
Imports (CIF)	1694	1868	1905	2230	3635	3947	3033	4162	3834	6700	10541	9430	5337	4505	4584	3814	4724	5817	5322	4202	4079	8036	13909
	79	-128	36	1036	295	-986	885	1489	2567	1110	-2520	-287	2287	3331	3523	4582	2129	541	3620	5371	8275	3983	-1691
Non-Factor Services (net)	-12	-2	78	68	164	172	272	387	-100	-762	-739	-705	43	-341	-205	-231	-573	-285	-255	-265	-379	-1007	-938
Receipts	424	457	458	557	861	743	836	1117	1314	1791	2744	2402	1901	1676	1921	1846	1865	2112	2210	2381	2599	2736	2737
Payments	437	459	380	489	696	571	564	730	1414	2553	3483	3107	1858	2017	2125	2077	2438	2397	2465	2646	2978	3743	3675
Balance of Goods and NFS	67	-130	114	1104	459	-814	1157	1876	2467	348	-3259	-992	2330	2990	3318	4351	1556	256	3365	5106	7896	2976	-2629
Net Factor Service Income	-223	-256	-334	-394	-333	-475	-508	-618	-681	-920	-1531	-3700	-4719	-5408	-5712	-5304	-4416	-4485	-5127	-6422	-6203	-5740	-4632
Net Interest Payments			-273	-317	-298	-460	-465	-370	-405	-493	-947	-2965	-4403	-4983	-5273	-4879	-3934	-3927	-4467	-5759	-5724	-4828	-3679
Interest Receipts									769	907	1228	885	523	440	264	253	357	218	211	265	280	378	456
Interest Payments									1174	1400	2175	3850	4926	5423	5537	5132	4291	4145	4678	6024	6004	5206	4135
Direct Investment Income			-60	-78	-36	-16	-27	-208	-276	-427	-584	-735	-316	-425	-439	-425	-482	-558	-660	-664	-716	-912	-953
Other Factor Services						1	-16	-40													237		
Current Transfers (net)	-3	-3	-4	11	0	5	18	31	48	35	23	-22	32	16	3	0	2	-8	0	8	71	29	-49
Balance on Current Account	-159	-389	-223	721	126	-1284	667	1289	1834	-537	-4767	-4714	-2357	-2402	-2391	-953	-2858	-4237	-1762	-1308	1764	-2735	-7310
Direct Investment	11	11	10	10	10			145	273	265	788	944	257	183	268	919	574	-19	1147	1028	2008	2439	2441
Total M&LT Loans (net) c/	229	208	-1	-136	8	-12	1230	875	907	2648	3400	8557	7401	2610	-756	2786	5763	2653	446	1444	-969	1288	-250
Total Short-term Loans (net)	185	-240	-74	157	-62	226	-923	31	-1215	1635	-1780	-8093	-5446	-935	2340	-2384	-4186	-720	-1899	-956	365	0	7646
Net Use of IMF Resources d/			189		-131	219	237	-132	-423	370				1227		987	146	615	30	-478	-257	-590	338
Capital Transactions n.e.i. d/	-130.9	19.1	273.8	83.7	44.4	-6	-54	-491	503		-390	-131	-613	-1937	480	675	6	698	3784	-1630	164	1586	134
Changes in Gross Reserves (- = increase)	-135	390	-175	-835	4	857	-1157	-1717	-1879	-4381	2749	3437	758	1254	59	-2030	555	1010	-1746	1900	-3075	-1988	-2999.2

Source: Central Bank of the Republic of Argentina (BCRA); IBRD estimates.
a/ For 1970-1974, private sector transactions include "banking" sector.
b/ Preliminary.
c/ 1985-1992 data on public and private disbursements and amortizations are IBRD estimates,
   based on data provided by the Central Bank.
d/ Valuation adjustments, SDRs, changes in arrears and errors and omissions.

Table 6.2: Argentina - Nominal Official Exchange Rate, 1970-1992
(Annual Averages; Pesos/US$)

	Exchange Rate
1970	0.000000000038
1971	0.000000000045
1972	0.000000000050
1973	0.000000000050
1974	0.000000000050
1975	0.000000000235
1976	0.000000001400
1977	0.000000004080
1978	0.000000007960
1979	0.000000013170
1980	0.000000018560
1981	0.000000044170
1982	0.000000259000
1983	0.000001053000
1984	0.000006765000
1985	0.000060406000
1986	0.000094303000
1987	0.000214509083
1988	0.000877030000
1989	0.042333960833
1990	0.487589083333
1991	0.953554416667
1992	0.990633333333

Source: IMF, International Financial Statistics (IFS).

Table 7.1: ARGENTINA - GROSS DOMESTIC PRODUCT BY SECTORAL ORIGIN, 1970-1990
(1970 Pesos)

	1970	1971	1972	1973	1974	1975	1976	1977	1978	1979	1980	1981	1982	1983	1984	1985	1986	1987	1988	1989	1990
GDP AT MARKET PRICES	0.87746	0.91050	0.92940	0.96420	1.01630	1.01030	1.01020	1.07470	1.04000	1.11217	1.12919	1.05471	1.00259	1.03279	1.06015	1.01405	1.07210	1.09634	1.06658	1.01664	1.02296
NET INDIRECT TAXES	0.10004	0.10377	0.10610	0.10997	0.11594	0.11518	0.11518	0.12255	0.11856	0.12680	0.12873	0.12025	0.11430	0.11775	0.12087	0.11559	0.12222	0.12488	0.12159	0.11615	0.11663
GDP AT FACTOR COST	0.77742	0.80673	0.82330	0.85423	0.90036	0.89512	0.89502	0.95215	0.92144	0.98537	1.00046	0.93446	0.88829	0.91504	0.93928	0.89846	0.94988	0.97046	0.94499	0.90249	0.90633
Agriculture	0.10232	0.10393	0.10593	0.11728	0.12048	0.11717	0.12270	0.12570	0.12920	0.13289	0.12557	0.12799	0.13701	0.14026	0.14455	0.14213	0.13838	0.14243	0.14237	0.13826	0.15180
Mining	0.01777	0.01916	0.01972	0.01916	0.01962	0.01932	0.01979	0.02148	0.02189	0.02328	0.02462	0.02478	0.02491	0.02496	0.02481	0.02416	0.02323	0.02327	0.02550	0.02632	0.02591
Manufacturing	0.20986	0.22275	0.23170	0.24089	0.25504	0.24853	0.24099	0.25982	0.23248	0.25616	0.24640	0.20778	0.19725	0.21704	0.22569	0.20239	0.22878	0.22752	0.21236	0.19721	0.18762
Construction	0.05025	0.05342	0.05291	0.04671	0.05041	0.05272	0.06058	0.06797	0.06474	0.06444	0.06518	0.05671	0.04373	0.03801	0.03041	0.02838	0.03114	0.03571	0.03054	0.02090	0.01697
Electricity, Gas and Water	0.01810	0.01979	0.02174	0.02338	0.02477	0.02627	0.02724	0.02850	0.02945	0.03261	0.03514	0.03474	0.03581	0.03868	0.04119	0.04175	0.04486	0.04758	0.04989	0.04922	0.04894
Commerce, Restaurants and Hotels	0.11833	0.12210	0.12420	0.12730	0.13490	0.13420	0.12970	0.14010	0.13140	0.14780	0.16191	0.14644	0.12612	0.13150	0.13737	0.12603	0.13708	0.13896	0.13019	0.11966	0.11769
Transport and Communication	0.08811	0.08950	0.08930	0.09420	0.09670	0.09594	0.09530	0.10040	0.09820	0.10542	0.10614	0.10200	0.09932	0.10340	0.10907	0.10489	0.11013	0.11297	0.10984	0.10652	0.11034
Banking	0.05915	0.05982	0.05850	0.06112	0.06918	0.06338	0.06074	0.06915	0.07381	0.07969	0.08952	0.08474	0.07500	0.06978	0.07065	0.06979	0.07471	0.07689	0.07643	0.07455	0.07605
Public and Private Services a/	0.11353	0.11626	0.11930	0.12419	0.12926	0.13759	0.13798	0.13903	0.14027	0.14308	0.14598	0.14928	0.14914	0.15141	0.15554	0.15894	0.16157	0.16513	0.16787	0.16985	0.17081

Source: Central Bank of the Republic of Argentina (BCRA).
a/ 1970-1975 figures for public and private services are estimates.

July 1992

Table 7.2: ARGENTINA - GROSS DOMESTIC PRODUCT BY SECTORAL ORIGIN, 1970-1990
(Growth Rates)

	1970	1971	1972	1973	1974	1975	1976	1977	1978	1979	1980	1981	1982	1983	1984	1985	1986	1987	1988	1989	1990
GDP AT MARKET PRICES		3.8	2.1	3.7	5.4	-0.6	0.0	6.4	-3.2	6.9	1.5	-6.6	-4.9	3.0	2.6	-4.3	5.7	2.2	-2.6	-4.5	0.4
NET INDIRECT TAXES		3.7	2.2	3.6	5.4	-0.7	0.0	6.4	-3.3	7.0	1.5	-6.6	-4.9	3.0	2.6	-4.4	5.7	2.2	-2.6	-4.5	0.4
GDP AT FACTOR COST		3.8	2.1	3.8	5.4	-0.6	0.0	6.4	-3.2	6.9	1.5	-6.6	-4.9	3.0	2.6	-4.3	5.7	2.2	-2.6	-4.5	0.4
Agriculture		1.6	1.9	10.7	2.7	-2.7	4.7	2.4	2.8	2.9	-5.5	1.9	7.0	2.4	3.1	-1.7	-2.6	2.9	0.0	-2.9	9.8
Mining		7.8	2.9	-2.8	2.4	-1.5	2.4	8.5	1.9	6.3	5.8	0.6	0.5	0.2	-0.6	-2.6	-3.8	0.2	9.6	3.2	-1.6
Manufacturing		6.1	4.0	4.0	5.9	-2.6	-3.0	7.8	-10.5	10.2	-3.8	-15.7	-5.1	10.0	4.0	-10.3	13.0	-0.6	-6.7	-7.1	-4.8
Construction		6.3	-1.0	-11.7	7.9	4.6	14.9	12.2	-4.8	-0.5	1.1	-13.0	-22.9	-13.1	-20.0	-6.7	9.7	14.7	-14.5	-31.6	-18.8
Electricity, Gas and Water		9.3	9.9	7.5	5.9	6.1	3.7	4.6	3.3	10.7	7.8	-1.1	3.1	8.0	6.5	1.4	7.4	6.1	4.9	-1.3	-0.6
Commerce, Restaurants and Hotels		3.2	1.7	2.5	6.0	-0.5	-3.4	8.0	-6.2	12.5	9.5	-9.6	-13.9	4.3	4.5	-8.3	8.8	1.4	-6.3	-8.1	-1.6
Transport and Communication		1.6	-0.2	5.5	2.7	-0.8	-0.7	5.4	-2.2	7.4	0.7	-3.9	-2.6	4.1	5.5	-3.8	5.0	2.6	-2.8	-3.0	3.6
Banking		1.1	-2.2	4.5	13.2	-8.4	-4.2	13.8	6.7	8.0	12.3	-5.3	-11.5	-7.0	1.2	-1.2	7.0	2.9	42.9	39.4	48.0
Public and Private Services a/		2.4	2.6	4.1	4.1	6.4	0.3	0.8	0.9	2.0	2.0	2.3	-0.1	1.5	2.7	2.2	1.7	2.2	-53.7	-55.6	-55.2

Source: Table 7.1
a/ 1970-1975 figures for public and private services are estimates.

July 1992

Table 7.3: ARGENTINA - GROSS DOMESTIC PRODUCT BY SECTORAL ORIGIN, 1970-1990
(Percent of GDP at Factor Cost, 1970 Prices)

	1970	1971	1972	1973	1974	1975	1976	1977	1978	1979	1980	1981	1982	1983	1984	1985	1986	1987	1988	1989	1990
GDP AT MARKET PRICES	112.9	112.9	112.9	112.9	112.9	112.9	112.9	112.9	112.9	112.9	112.9	112.9	112.9	112.9	112.9	112.9	112.9	112.9	112.9	112.9	112.9
NET INDIRECT TAXES	12.9	12.9	12.9	12.9	12.9	12.9	12.9	12.9	12.9	12.9	12.9	12.9	12.9	12.9	12.9	12.9	12.9	12.9	12.9	12.9	12.9
GDP AT FACTOR COST	100.0	100.0	100.0	100.0	100.0	100.0	100.0	100.0	100.0	100.0	100.0	100.0	100.0	100.0	100.0	100.0	100.0	100.0	100.0	100.0	100.0
Agriculture	13.2	12.9	12.9	13.7	13.4	13.1	13.7	13.2	14.0	13.5	12.6	13.7	15.4	15.3	15.4	15.8	14.6	14.7	15.1	15.3	16.7
Mining	2.3	2.4	2.4	2.2	2.2	2.2	2.2	2.3	2.4	2.4	2.5	2.7	2.8	2.7	2.6	2.7	2.4	2.4	2.7	2.9	2.9
Manufacturing	27.0	27.6	28.1	28.2	28.3	27.8	26.9	27.3	25.2	26.0	24.6	22.2	22.2	23.7	24.0	22.5	24.1	23.4	22.5	21.9	20.7
Construction	6.5	6.6	6.4	5.5	5.6	5.9	6.8	7.1	7.0	6.5	6.5	6.1	4.9	4.2	3.2	3.2	3.3	3.7	3.2	2.3	1.9
Electricity, Gas and Water	2.3	2.5	2.6	2.7	2.8	2.9	3.0	3.0	3.2	3.3	3.5	3.7	4.0	4.2	4.4	4.6	4.7	4.9	5.3	5.5	5.4
Commerce, Restaurants and Hotels	15.2	15.1	15.1	14.9	15.0	15.0	14.5	14.7	14.3	15.0	16.2	15.7	14.2	14.4	14.6	14.0	14.4	14.3	13.8	13.3	13.0
Transport and Communication	11.3	11.1	10.8	11.0	10.7	10.7	10.6	10.5	10.7	10.7	10.6	10.9	11.2	11.3	11.6	11.7	11.6	11.6	11.6	11.8	12.2
Banking	7.6	7.4	7.1	7.2	7.7	7.1	6.8	7.3	8.0	8.1	8.9	9.1	8.4	7.6	7.5	7.8	7.9	7.9	11.6	11.8	12.2
Public and Private Services a/	14.6	14.4	14.5	14.5	14.4	15.4	15.4	14.6	15.2	14.5	14.8	16.0	16.8	16.5	16.6	17.7	17.0	17.0	8.1	8.3	8.4

Source: Table 7.1
a/ 1970-1975 figures for public and private services are estimates.

July 1992

Table 7.4: ARGENTINA - GROSS DOMESTIC PRODUCT BY SECTORAL ORIGIN, 1970-1990 a/
(Thousands of Pesos)

	1970	1971	1972	1973	1974	1975	1976	1977	1978	1979	1980	1981	1982	1983	1984	1985	1986	1987	1988	1989	1990
GROSS DOMESTIC PRODUCT	0.00088	0.00125	0.00207	0.00355	0.00486	0.0143	0.07587	0.20934	0.52342	1.4251	2.8336	5.4752	14.7613	68.2652	528.100	3,959.26	7,430.90	17,310.9	78,479.3	2,558,026	51,564,375
Agriculture	0.00011	0.00018	0.00031	0.00056	0.00066	0.00127	0.00833	0.02293	0.05307	0.1504	0.2436	0.4939	1.7383	8.6377	66.834	0,501.07	0,940.43	2,190.8	9,932.1	323,734	6,525,798
Mining	0.00002	0.00002	0.00004	0.00007	0.00010	0.00028	0.00148	0.00258	0.01012	0.0343	0.0669	0.1590	0.4514	2.6955	20.886	0,156.58	0,293.88	0,684.6	3,103.8	101,167	2,039,312
Manufacturing	0.00026	0.00038	0.00063	0.00101	0.00139	0.00464	0.02505	0.06501	0.15131	0.3951	0.7082	1.3147	4.1918	21.0154	162.599	1,219.04	2,287.94	5,330.0	24,163.4	787,604	15,876,420
Construction	0.00005	0.00007	0.00012	0.00018	0.00027	0.00112	0.00548	0.01476	0.03813	0.0991	0.2000	0.3306	0.7206	4.2344	32.721	0,245.32	0,460.42	1,072.6	4,862.6	158,495	3,194,922
Electricity	0.00002	0.00003	0.00004	0.00007	0.00010	0.00026	0.00191	0.00553	0.01449	0.0304	0.0718	0.1632	0.2513	1.7216	13.305	0,099.75	0,187.21	0,436.1	1,977.2	64,447	1,299,117
Commmerce	0.00015	0.00020	0.00035	0.00053	0.00074	0.00224	0.01320	0.03515	0.08840	0.2522	0.5106	0.9716	2.4499	11.2520	87.024	0,652.43	1,224.51	2,852.6	12,932.4	421,529	8,497,132
Transport	0.00008	0.00011	0.00017	0.00028	0.00038	0.00112	0.00600	0.01753	0.04431	0.1143	0.2171	0.4414	0.9244	3.8661	29.936	0,224.44	0,421.23	0,981.3	4,448.7	145,006	2,923,013
Banking	0.00007	0.00010	0.00016	0.00035	0.00045	0.00118	0.00585	0.02341	0.05615	0.1659	0.3885	0.7583	2.1383	4.3522	33.649	0,252.27	0,473.48	1,103.0	5,000.5	162,991	3,285,558
Government	0.00012	0.00016	0.00025	0.00049	0.00075	0.00220	0.00857	0.02244	0.06744	0.1835	0.4270	0.8426	1.8952	10.4903	81.145	0,608.36	1,141.79	2,659.9	12,058.7	393,052	7,923,104

Source: Central Bank of the Republic of Argentina (BCRA).
a/ GDP distribution by sector for 1984-1990 are estimates.

July 1992

Table 7.5: ARGENTINA - GROSS DOMESTIC PRODUCT BY SECTORAL ORIGIN, 1970-1990 a/

(Percent)

	1970	1971	1972	1973	1974	1975	1976	1977	1978	1979	1980	1981	1982	1983	1984	1985	1986	1987	1988	1989	1990
GROSS DOMESTIC PRODUCT	100.0	100.0	100.0	100.0	100.0	100.0	100.0	100.0	100.0	100.0	100.0	100.0	100.0	98.6	100.0	100.0	100.0	100.0	100.0	100.0	100.0
Agriculture	12.2	14.4	14.8	15.8	13.6	8.9	11.0	11.0	10.1	10.6	8.6	9.0	11.8	12.7	12.7	12.7	12.7	12.7	12.7	12.7	12.7
Mining	2.0	2.0	1.8	2.0	2.1	2.0	2.0	1.2	1.9	2.4	2.4	2.9	3.1	3.9	4.0	4.0	4.0	4.0	4.0	4.0	4.0
Manufacturing	30.1	30.2	30.7	28.5	28.6	32.4	33.0	31.1	28.9	27.7	25.0	24.0	28.4	30.8	30.8	30.8	30.8	30.8	30.8	30.8	30.8
Construction	5.8	6.0	5.7	5.1	5.6	7.8	7.2	7.0	7.3	7.0	7.1	6.0	4.9	6.2	6.2	6.2	6.2	6.2	6.2	6.2	6.2
Electricity	2.3	2.1	2.1	2.1	2.1	1.8	2.5	2.6	2.8	2.1	2.5	3.0	1.7	2.5	2.5	2.5	2.5	2.5	2.5	2.5	2.5
Commmerce	16.7	16.0	16.8	14.9	15.3	15.7	17.4	16.8	16.9	17.7	18.0	17.7	16.6	16.5	16.5	16.5	16.5	16.5	16.5	16.5	16.5
Transport	9.6	8.5	8.4	7.8	7.8	7.8	7.9	8.4	8.5	8.0	7.7	8.1	6.3	5.7	5.7	5.7	5.7	5.7	5.7	5.7	5.7
Banking	8.0	7.9	7.7	9.8	9.4	8.2	7.7	11.2	10.7	11.6	13.7	13.8	14.5	5.0	6.4	6.4	6.4	6.4	6.4	6.4	6.4
Government	13.3	13.0	12.1	13.9	15.4	15.4	11.3	10.7	12.9	12.9	15.1	15.4	12.8	15.4	15.4	15.4	15.4	15.4	15.4	15.4	15.4

Source: Table 7.4

a/ GDP distribution by sector for 1984-1990 are estimates

July 1992

Table 7.6. ARGENTINA - GROSS DOMESTIC PRODUCT BY EXPENDITURE, 1970-1990
(1970 Pesos)

	1970	1971	1972	1973	1974	1975	1976	1977	1978	1979	1980	1981	1982	1983	1984	1985	1986	1987	1988	1989	1990
Gross Domestic Product	0.8775	0.9105	0.9294	0.9642	1.0163	1.0103	1.0102	1.0747	1.0400	1.1122	1.1292	1.0547	1.0026	1.0328	1.0602	1.0141	1.0721	1.0953	1.0666	1.0186	1.0230
Terms of Trade Effect	0.0000	0.0107	0.0134	0.0302	0.0138	-0.0026	-0.0118	0.0002	-0.0084	0.0058	0.0258	0.0328	0.0033	0.0022	0.0145	-0.0010	-0.0134	-0.0471	-0.0465	-0.0552	-0.0710
Gross Domestic Income	0.8775	0.9212	0.9428	0.9944	1.0301	1.0077	0.9984	1.0749	1.0316	1.1180	1.1550	1.0875	1.0059	1.0350	1.0747	1.0131	1.0587	1.0482	1.0201	0.9635	0.9520
Imports of Goods and NFS a/	0.0789	0.0883	0.0840	0.0829	0.0874	0.0890	0.0703	0.0964	0.0914	0.1413	0.2068	0.1869	0.1077	0.1026	0.1089	0.0931	0.1094	0.1160	0.1027	0.0849	0.0850
Exports of Goods and NFS a/	0.0810	0.0729	0.0744	0.0848	0.0850	0.0771	0.1014	0.1291	0.1406	0.1361	0.1291	0.1362	0.1410	0.1519	0.1508	0.1697	0.1577	0.1539	0.1824	0.1964	0.2320
Exports Adjusted by Terms of Trade	0.0810	0.0836	0.0878	0.1150	0.0988	0.0745	0.0896	0.1293	0.1322	0.1419	0.1549	0.1690	0.1443	0.1541	0.1653	0.1687	0.1443	0.1067	0.1359	0.1412	0.1610
Resource Gap b/	-0.0021	0.0047	-0.0038	-0.0321	-0.0114	0.0145	-0.0193	-0.0329	-0.0408	-0.0006	0.0519	0.0179	-0.0366	-0.0515	-0.0564	-0.0756	-0.0349	0.0093	-0.0333	-0.0563	-0.0760
Total Expenditures	0.8754	0.9259	0.9390	0.9623	1.0187	1.0222	0.9791	1.0420	0.9908	1.1174	1.2069	1.1054	0.9693	0.9835	1.0183	0.9375	1.0239	1.0575	0.9868	0.9072	0.8760
	0.0000	0.0000	0.0000	0.0000	0.0000	0.0000	0.0000	0.0000	0.0000	0.0000	0.0000	0.0000	0.0000	0.0000	0.0000	0.0000	0.0000	0.0000	0.0000	0.0000	0.0000
Consumption	0.6694	0.7195	0.7305	0.7636	0.8179	0.8176	0.7605	0.7776	0.7685	0.8724	0.9395	0.9005	0.8049	0.8365	0.8875	0.8329	0.9010	0.9138	0.8587	0.8183	0.7928
Public	0.0908	0.0949	0.0932	0.0992	0.1069	0.1070	0.1119	0.1167	0.1204	0.1271	0.1288	0.1308	0.1215	0.1248	0.1274	0.1252	0.1318	0.1371	0.1288	0.1227	0.1189
Private	0.5986	0.6246	0.6373	0.6644	0.7110	0.7106	0.6486	0.6609	0.6481	0.7453	0.8107	0.7697	0.6834	0.7117	0.7601	0.7077	0.7692	0.7767	0.7299	0.6955	0.6739
Gross Domestic Investment	0.1860	0.2063	0.2085	0.1987	0.2009	0.2045	0.2186	0.2644	0.2223	0.2450	0.2675	0.2049	0.1645	0.1470	0.1307	0.1046	0.1228	0.1437	0.1282	0.0889	0.0832
Changes in Inventories	-0.0001	0.0051	0.0050	0.0100	0.0046	0.0078	0.0014	0.0018	-0.0067	0.0005	0.0099	-0.0073	0.0107	0.0012	-0.0020	-0.0126	-0.0048	-0.0018	0.0059	-0.0003	0.0061
Gross Domestic Fixed Investment	0.1861	0.2012	0.2035	0.1887	0.1963	0.1967	0.2172	0.2626	0.2290	0.2445	0.2576	0.2122	0.1538	0.1458	0.1326	0.1172	0.1276	0.1454	0.1223	0.0892	0.0771
Public	0.0708	0.0780	0.0795	0.0661	0.0684	0.0778	0.0989	0.1219	0.1068	0.1017	0.1010	0.0907	0.0712	0.0671	0.0491	0.0410	0.0519	0.0623	0.0649	0.0405	0.0308
Private	0.1153	0.1232	0.1240	0.1226	0.1279	0.1189	0.1183	0.1407	0.1222	0.1428	0.1566	0.1215	0.0826	0.0787	0.0835	0.0762	0.0757	0.0831	0.0574	0.0486	0.0462
Gross Domestic Savings c/	0.1882	0.2016	0.2123	0.2308	0.2123	0.1900	0.2379	0.2973	0.2631	0.2456	0.2156	0.1870	0.2011	0.1985	0.1871	0.1802	0.1577	0.1344	0.1614	0.1452	0.1592
Net Factor Income Payments	-0.0096	-0.0039	-0.0120	-0.0145	-0.0117	-0.0124	-0.0127	-0.0143	-0.0174	-0.0209	-0.0308	-0.0620	-0.0854	-0.0854	-0.0857	-0.0712	-0.0574	-0.0578	-0.0635	-0.0758	-0.0707
Net Transfers	-0.0001	-0.0001	-0.0001	0.0003	0.0000	0.0001	0.0004	0.0007	0.0010	0.0006	0.0004	-0.0003	0.0004	0.0002	0.0000	0.0000	0.0000	-0.0001	0.0000	0.0001	0.0008
Gross National Savings	0.1784	0.1976	0.2002	0.2166	0.2006	0.1778	0.2256	0.2836	0.2466	0.2253	0.1852	0.1247	0.1249	0.1133	0.1014	0.1090	0.1003	0.0765	0.0979	0.0695	0.0893
Gross National Product	0.8677	0.9065	0.9173	0.9500	1.0046	0.9980	0.9979	1.0611	1.0236	1.0919	1.0987	0.9924	0.9264	0.9476	0.9745	0.9429	1.0147	1.0374	1.0031	0.9429	0.9531
Gross National Income	0.8678	0.9172	0.9307	0.9802	1.0184	0.9954	0.9861	1.0613	1.0152	1.0977	1.1245	1.0252	0.9297	0.9498	0.9890	0.9419	1.0014	0.9903	0.9565	0.8877	0.8821

Source: Central Bank of the Republic of Argentina (BCRA) and IBRD staff estimates.
a/ Balance of Payments figures deflated by respective price indices and converted at 1970 exchange rate (3.8 pesos per US$)
b/ - (Exports adjusted by terms of trade - imports).
c/ Gross domestic investment - resource gap.

Jly 1992

Table 7.7: ARGENTINA - GROSS FIXED INVESTMENT, 1970-1990
(1970 Pesos)

	1970	1971	1972	1973	1974	1975	1976	1977	1978	1979	1980	1981	1982	1983	1984	1985	1986	1987	1988	1989	1990
Gross Fixed Investment, by sector	.1861	.2012	.2035	.1887	.1963	.1967	.2172	.2626	.2290	.2445	.2576	.2122	.1538	.1458	.1326	.1172	.1276	.1454	.1223	.0892	.0771
Public	.0708	.0780	.0795	.0661	.0684	.0778	.0989	.1214	.1068	.1017	.1010	.0907	.0712	.0671	.0491	.0410	.0519	.0623	.0649	.0405	.0308
Private	.1153	.1233	.1240	.1226	.1279	.1189	.1184	.1412	.1222	.1428	.1566	.1215	.0826	.0787	.0835	.0762	.0757	.0831	.0574	.0486	.0462
Gross Fixed Investment, by sector	.1861	.2012	.2035	.1887	.1963	.1967	.2172	.2626	.2290	.2445	.2576	.2122	.1538	.1458	.1326	.1172	.1276	.1454	.1223	.0892	.0771
Construction	.1161	.1244	.1221	.1089	.1172	.1226	.1393	.1531	.1452	.1449	.1457	.1279	.0999	.0885	.0737	.0670	.0718	.0817	.0700	.0492	.0412
Public	.0463	.0516	.0529	.0440	.0469	.0412	.0595	.0790	.0709	.0623	.0603	.0511	.0399	.0361	.0219	.0197	.0284	.0331	.0274	.0164	.0135
Private	.0698	.0729	.0692	.0649	.0703	.0814	.0798	.0741	.0743	.0826	.0854	.0768	.0599	.0524	.0518	.0472	.0435	.0486	.0426	.0328	.0277
Machinery and Equipment	.0700	.0768	.0814	.0798	.0791	.0741	.0779	.1096	.0838	.0996	.1119	.0843	.0540	.0573	.0569	.0502	.0558	.0637	.0523	.0400	.0359
Public	.0245	.0264	.0266	.0221	.0215	.0366	.0394	.0424	.0359	.0394	.0407	.0396	.0313	.0310	.0272	.0213	.0235	.0292	.0375	.0242	.0174
Private	.0455	.0504	.0548	.0577	.0576	.0375	.0385	.0672	.0479	.0602	.0712	.0447	.0227	.0263	.0317	.0289	.0323	.0345	.0148	.0159	.0185
of which:																					
Machinery, tools and furniture	.0482	.0527	.0541	.0519	.0543	.0521	.0573	.0795	.0594	.0680	.0803	.0634	.0411	.0417	.0425	.0363	.0392	.0452	.0369	.0271	.0250
Domestic	.0274	.0305	.0322	.0356	.0388	.0344	.0416	.0500	.0335	.0358	.0303	.0204	.0187	.0254	.0281	.0211	.0260	.0275	.0225	.0162	.0148
Imported	.0208	.0222	.0219	.0163	.0155	.0177	.0157	.0295	.0259	.0322	.0500	.0430	.0224	.0164	.0144	.0153	.0131	.0176	.0144	.0109	.0101
Transport Equipment	.0219	.0240	.0272	.0279	.0249	.0121	.0207	.0300	.0245	.0316	.0315	.0209	.0128	.0155	.0163	.0139	.0166	.0185	.0154	.0129	.0109
Domestic	.0215	.0230	.0257	.0269	.0240	.0109	.0196	.0244	.0209	.0250	.0252	.0147	.0115	.0138	.0144	.0128	.0164	.0181	.0152	.0122	.0098
Imported	.0004	.0010	.0015	.0010	.0009	.0012	.0011	.0056	.0036	.0067	.0063	.0062	.0014	.0018	.0019	.0011	.0002	.0004	.0003	.0007	.0012
Memo item:																					
Residential Construction	.0493	.0486	.0457	.0426	.0476	.0596	.0567	.0502	.0502	.0545	.0558	.0488	.0391	.0339	.0337	.0315	..	..	..	..	..
Non-residential Construction	.0668	.0758	.0764	.0663	.0696	.0630	.0826	.1029	.0950	.0904	.0899	.0791	.0608	.0546	.0400	.0355	..	..	..	..	..

Source: Central Bank of the Republic of Argentina (BCRA) and IBRD estimates.

July 1992

Table 7.8: ARGENTINA - GROSS FIXED INVESTMENT, 1970-1990
(Growth Rates)

	1971	1972	1973	1974	1975	1976	1977	1978	1979	1980	1981	1982	1983	1984	1985	1986	1987	1988	1989	1990
Gross Fixed Investment, by sector	8.1	1.1	-7.3	4.0	0.2	10.4	20.9	-12.8	6.8	5.4	-17.6	-27.5	-5.2	-9.0	-11.7	8.9	14.0	-15.9	-27.1	-13.6
Public	10.2	2.0	-16.9	3.5	13.8	27.0	22.8	-12.0	-4.7	-0.7	-10.2	-21.4	-5.8	-26.8	-16.5	26.5	20.1	4.1	-37.5	-24.0
Private	6.9	0.6	-1.1	4.3	-7.0	-0.4	19.3	-13.5	16.8	9.7	-22.4	-32.1	-4.7	6.2	-8.8	-0.6	9.7	-30.9	-15.3	-4.9
Gross Fixed Investment, by sector	8.1	1.1	-7.3	4.0	0.2	10.4	20.9	-12.8	6.8	5.3	-17.6	-27.5	-5.2	-9.1	-11.6	8.9	14.0	-15.9	-27.1	-13.6
Construction	7.2	-1.9	-10.8	7.6	4.6	13.6	9.9	-5.1	-0.2	0.6	-12.2	-21.9	-11.3	-16.7	-9.2	7.3	13.8	-14.3	-29.8	-16.2
Public	11.4	2.7	-16.9	6.6	-12.1	44.2	32.9	-10.3	-12.1	-3.2	-15.3	-21.8	-9.6	-39.3	-10.0	44.0	16.6	-17.3	-40.2	-17.8
Private	4.4	-5.1	-6.2	8.2	15.8	-1.9	-7.2	0.3	11.2	3.4	-10.1	-22.0	-12.5	-1.1	-8.9	-8.0	11.9	-12.3	-23.1	-15.4
Machinery and Equipment	9.7	6.0	-2.0	-0.9	-6.3	5.1	40.7	-23.5	18.9	12.3	-24.6	-36.0	6.1	2.8	-14.6	11.0	14.2	-17.9	-23.5	-10.3
Public	7.8	0.8	-16.9	-2.7	70.2	7.7	7.6	-15.3	9.9	3.2	-2.7	-21.0	-1.0	-12.3	-21.7	10.3	24.4	28.3	-35.8	-28.1
Private	10.8	8.7	5.3	-0.2	-34.9	2.7	74.5	-28.7	25.7	18.2	-37.2	-49.3	15.9	20.5	-8.6	11.6	6.7	-57.1	7.3	16.7
of which:																				
Machinery, tools and furniture	9.4	2.7	-4.1	4.6	-4.1	10.0	38.7	-25.3	14.5	18.1	-21.0	-35.2	1.5	1.9	-14.6	7.8	15.3	-18.4	-26.5	-7.8
Domestic	11.4	5.6	10.6	9.0	-11.3	20.9	20.2	-33.0	6.9	-15.4	-32.7	-5.2	35.6	10.7	-25.0	23.6	5.7	-18.3	-28.2	-8.1
Imported	6.7	-1.4	-25.6	-4.9	14.2	-11.3	87.9	-12.2	24.3	55.4	-14.0	-47.9	-27.0	-11.8	5.8	-14.0	34.3	-18.5	-23.9	-7.4
Transport Equipment	9.6	13.6	2.4	-10.7	-51.4	71.1	44.9	-18.3	29.1	-0.3	-33.8	-38.6	21.1	5.2	-14.9	19.5	11.6	-16.7	-18.2	-15.6
Domestic	7.0	12.0	4.5	-10.7	-54.6	79.8	24.5	-14.3	19.5	1.0	-41.8	-21.9	19.9	4.7	-11.0	27.7	10.6	-16.2	-19.4	-20.1
Imported	150.0	50.0	-33.3	-10.0	33.3	-8.3	409.1	-35.7	85.0	-5.4	-1.9	-78.2	31.9	8.4	-44.0	-77.8	79.2	-37.2	163.0	62.0
Memo item:																				
Residential Construction	-1.4	-6.0	-6.8	11.7	25.2	-4.9	-11.5	0.0	8.6	2.4	-12.5	-19.9	-13.3	-0.6	-6.5	..	..	..	..	..
Non-residential Construction	13.6	0.8	-13.2	4.9	-9.4	31.0	24.5	-7.7	-4.9	-0.5	-12.1	-23.2	-10.1	-26.7	-11.5	..	..	..	..	..

Source: Table 7.7

July 1992

Table 7.9: ARGENTINA - GROSS FIXED INVESTMENT, 1970-1990
(Percent of GDP, 1970 Prices)

	1970	1971	1972	1973	1974	1975	1976	1977	1978	1979	1980	1981	1982	1983	1984	1985	1986	1987	1988	1989	1990
Gross Fixed Investment, by sector	21.2	22.1	21.9	19.6	19.3	19.5	21.5	24.4	22.0	22.0	22.8	20.1	15.3	14.1	12.5	11.6	11.9	13.3	11.5	8.8	7.5
Public	8.1	8.6	8.6	6.9	6.7	7.7	9.8	11.3	10.3	9.1	8.9	8.6	7.1	6.5	4.6	4.0	4.8	5.7	6.1	4.0	3.0
Private	13.1	13.5	13.3	12.7	12.6	11.8	11.7	13.1	11.8	12.8	13.9	11.5	8.2	7.6	7.9	7.5	7.1	7.6	5.4	4.8	4.5
Gross Fixed Investment, by sector	21.2	22.1	21.9	19.6	19.3	19.5	21.5	24.4	22.0	22.0	22.8	20.1	15.3	14.1	12.5	11.6	11.9	13.3	11.5	8.8	7.5
Construction	13.2	13.7	13.1	11.3	11.5	12.1	13.8	14.2	14.0	13.0	12.9	12.1	10.0	8.6	7.0	6.6	6.7	7.5	6.6	4.8	4.0
Public	5.3	5.7	5.7	4.6	4.6	4.1	5.9	7.3	6.8	5.6	5.3	4.8	4.0	3.5	2.1	1.9	2.6	3.0	2.6	1.6	1.3
Private	8.0	8.0	7.4	6.7	6.9	8.1	7.9	6.9	7.1	7.4	7.6	7.3	6.0	5.1	4.9	4.7	4.1	4.4	4.0	3.2	2.7
Machinery and Equipment	8.0	8.4	8.8	8.3	7.8	7.3	7.7	10.2	8.1	9.0	9.9	8.0	5.4	5.5	5.6	5.0	5.2	5.8	4.9	3.9	3.5
Public	2.8	2.9	2.9	2.3	2.1	3.6	3.9	3.9	3.5	3.5	3.6	3.8	3.1	3.0	2.6	2.1	2.2	2.7	3.5	2.4	1.7
Private	5.2	5.5	5.9	6.0	5.7	3.7	3.8	6.3	4.6	5.4	6.3	4.2	2.3	2.5	3.0	2.9	3.0	3.1	1.4	1.6	1.8
of which:																					
Machinery, tools and furniture	5.5	5.8	5.8	5.4	5.3	5.2	5.7	7.4	5.7	6.1	7.1	6.0	4.1	4.0	4.0	3.6	3.7	4.1	3.5	2.7	2.4
Domestic	3.1	3.3	3.5	3.7	3.8	3.4	4.1	4.7	3.2	3.2	2.7	1.9	1.9	2.5	2.6	2.1	2.4	2.5	2.1	1.6	1.5
Imported	2.4	2.4	2.4	1.7	1.5	1.8	1.6	2.7	2.5	2.9	4.4	4.1	2.2	1.6	1.4	1.5	1.2	1.6	1.3	1.1	1.0
Transport Equipment	2.5	2.6	2.9	2.9	2.5	1.2	2.0	2.8	2.4	2.8	2.8	2.0	1.3	1.5	1.5	1.4	1.5	1.7	1.4	1.3	1.1
Domestic	2.4	2.5	2.8	2.8	2.4	1.1	1.9	2.3	2.0	2.2	2.2	1.4	1.1	1.3	1.4	1.3	1.5	1.7	1.4	1.2	1.0
Imported	0.0	0.1	0.2	0.1	0.1	0.1	0.1	0.5	0.3	0.6	0.6	0.6	0.1	0.2	0.2	0.1	0.0	0.0	0.0	0.1	0.1
Memo Item:																					
Residential Construction	5.6	5.3	4.9	4.4	4.7	5.9	5.6	4.7	4.8	4.9	4.9	4.6	3.9	3.3	3.2	3.1	..	..	..	..	..
Non-residential Construction	7.6	8.3	8.2	6.9	6.8	6.2	8.2	9.6	9.1	8.1	8.0	7.5	6.1	5.3	3.8	3.5	..	..	..	..	..

Source: Table 7.7

July 1992

Table 8.1: Argentina - Principal Price Indicators, Annual Percentage Change 1960-1991 a/

Year	WHOLESALE PRICE INDEX						CONSUMER PRICE INDEX	CONSTRUCTION COST INDEX
	General	Total Domestic	Agriculture	Non-agriculture				
				Total	Domestic	Imported		
1961	8.3	8.8	5.8	9.3	10.1	(3.2)	12.1	22.0
1962	30.6	30.2	37.0	27.7	27.5	33.0	27.0	30.1
1963	28.5	29.0	35.1	26.1	26.3	21.9	25.5	24.4
1964	26.1	26.7	28.2	25.3	25.9	13.8	22.0	20.8
1965	23.9	23.7	9.5	30.5	30.5	30.1	29.2	42.3
1966	20.0	20.0	21.3	19.5	19.5	19.6	32.3	28.9
1967	25.6	25.0	25.8	25.5	24.6	41.4	29.3	28.8
1968	9.6	9.7	9.9	9.5	9.6	8.0	15.7	7.6
1969	6.1	5.9	8.0	5.3	4.9	10.7	7.6	9.6
1970	14.1	14.0	15.8	13.4	13.2	16.6	13.6	11.9
1971	39.5	40.3	48.3	35.9	36.7	23.1	34.7	30.9
1972	77.0	76.0	94.8	69.1	67.2	100.6	58.7	54.3
1973	50.0	69.0	19.8	52.8	70.5	55.1	60.1	72.2
1974	20.0	5.4	30.8	25.7	11.4	43.7	29.9	38.8
1975	192.5	188.7	144.9	212.5	208.6	257.5	170.6	251.5
1976	499.0	485.2	529.6	489.0	469.2	690.4	444.1	360.6
1977	149.4	151.7	163.6	144.5	146.9	126.2	176.0	97.4
1978	146.0	152.1	141.6	147.6	156.6	75.9	175.5	137.0
1979	149.3	152.7	150.8	148.7	153.5	93.0	159.5	161.2
1980	75.4	75.5	63.0	80.1	80.4	74.5	100.8	109.0
1981	109.0	106.7	91.6	113.2	109.8	170.0	104.5	97.3
1982	257.3	250.4	298.1	247.6	238.5	355.3	164.8	172.5
1983	360.9	362.9	373.5	356.6	358.8	335.7	343.8	435.6
1984	573.6	575.4	552.8	586.9	588.6	568.9	626.7	647.7
1985	664.5	653.4	490.2	694.2	686.1	766.8	672.2	553.9
1986	63.9	64.2	111.5	58.1	57.9	60.2	90.1	69.6
1987	122.9	122.1	116.2	124.0	123.1	130.7	131.3	127.5
1988	412.5	409.7	378.4	417.8	415.2	438.8	343.0	372.6
1989	3,433.1	3,397.1	3,485.6	3,594.3	3,382.7	3,748.3	3,079.1	3,602.6
1990	1,606.7	1,669.9	1,492.0	1,701.1	1,699.7	1,098.4	2,314.1	1,615.5
1991	110.5	111.8	95.1	112.6	114.9	87.7	171.7	145.4
1992	6.0	6.6	18.2	4.5	4.8	0.4	24.9	21.3

Source: INDEC.
a/ change in annual average price indices

Table 9.1: Argentina - Private Sector Holdings of Financial Assets, Quarterly 1980-1991 a/
(December 1992 Million Pesos; stocks at the end of each quarter b/)

	Money (M1)				Quasi-Money			M2 c/
	Total	Currency	Demand Deposits		Total	Savings Accounts	Time Deposits	
1980 I	13,616	7,056	6,559		31,244	2,881	28,362	44,859
II	13,713	7,371	6,342		28,558	3,265	25,293	42,271
III	13,071	7,192	5,880		31,214	3,405	27,809	44,285
IV	15,296	9,182	6,114		29,541	3,510	26,031	44,836
1981 I	10,459	6,433	4,026		28,904	3,078	25,826	39,363
II	9,991	6,126	3,865		26,678	2,716	23,962	36,669
III	8,781	5,185	3,596		28,603	2,803	25,800	37,384
IV	11,146	7,304	3,842		27,490	2,892	24,598	38,636
1982 I	8,502	4,999	3,504		29,082	2,940	26,142	37,584
II	10,904	6,622	4,283		28,935	3,786	25,149	39,839
III	9,515	5,158	4,357		19,811	2,567	17,244	29,326
IV	11,605	6,820	4,784		18,314	2,324	15,990	29,919
1983 I	8,862	5,251	3,611		19,397	2,219	17,178	28,259
II	9,630	5,361	4,269		19,160	3,206	15,954	28,790
III	8,141	4,781	3,360		17,354	3,488	13,866	25,495
IV	10,233	6,779	3,454		18,087	4,512	13,575	28,320
1984 I	9,594	6,067	3,527		19,005	4,881	14,124	28,599
II	9,648	6,171	3,477		16,515	4,330	12,184	26,163
III	7,092	4,510	2,582		14,446	3,966	10,480	21,539
IV	8,072	5,818	2,254		14,085	4,460	9,625	22,157
1985 I	6,081	4,217	1,864		13,004	4,883	8,121	19,085
II	6,760	4,506	2,254		14,131	5,000	9,131	20,891
III	8,550	5,240	3,310		16,231	5,279	10,952	24,781
IV	11,528	7,734	3,794		17,631	5,647	11,984	29,159
1986 I	10,569	6,493	4,076		20,015	5,604	14,411	30,583
II	11,476	7,311	4,165		20,615	5,832	14,784	32,091
III	9,506	6,230	3,276		20,216	5,322	14,894	29,722
IV	11,747	8,388	3,359		22,373	5,387	16,986	34,120
1987 I	12,169	6,415	5,754		25,153	4,892	20,261	37,322
II	12,215	6,397	5,818		25,895	4,685	21,210	38,110
III	9,554	5,041	4,512		23,907	4,482	19,424	33,460
IV	10,696	5,878	4,818		23,299	4,149	19,150	33,995
1988 I	8,594	4,715	3,879		25,474	3,494	21,980	34,068
II	7,944	4,021	3,923		24,713	2,994	21,718	32,657
III	7,316	3,758	3,558		25,093	2,790	22,303	32,409
IV	9,002	5,320	3,682		28,661	3,157	25,504	37,662
1989 I	8,434	4,855	3,579		30,161	2,918	27,243	38,595
II	5,633	2,718	2,915		19,004	1,380	17,624	24,637
III	6,247	3,267	2,980		16,676	1,544	15,132	22,923
IV	9,066	4,476	4,590		12,699	1,352	11,347	21,766
1990 I	3,806	1,706	2,099		2,173	2,003	170	5,979
II	5,932	2,924	3,008		4,214	2,875	1,339	10,146
III	5,033	2,920	2,112		4,767	2,563	2,204	9,800
IV	6,194	3,906	2,288		5,922	2,921	3,001	12,116
1991 I	5,091	3,166	1,925		5,035	2,431	2,605	10,126
II	6,736	4,061	2,675		4,940	2,017	2,923	11,675
III	7,328	4,521	2,807		5,176	1,932	3,244	12,504
IV	9,239	5,553	3,686		5,662	2,086	3,576	14,901
1992 I	9,333	5,453	3,879		6,376	2,467	3,909	15,709
II	10,462	5,827	4,635		8,017	2,705	5,312	18,479
III	10,841	5,968	4,873		8,794	2,800	5,994	19,635
IV	11,667	6,757	4,910		8,903	2,683	6,220	20,570

Source: Central Bank of the Republic of Argentina (BCRA).
 a/ Does not include deposits issued by non-bank financial institutions.
 b/ deflated using the CPI, assuming an annual inflation of 12.2 % for 1992.
 c/ M1 plus quasi-money.

Table 9.2: Argentina - Evolution of Reserves and Monetary Base (US$ Million - end of period)

| | Central Bank Monetary Liabilities | Total Reserves | Gold | Liquid Reserves | | | ALADI (net) | Treasury Bonds Foreign Currency | Other | Coverage Ratios | |
				Total	Currency	Deposits				Liquid Reserves/ Liabilities	Total Reserves/ Liabilities
Mar-1991	4760	5482	1547	2464	28	2436	609	862	0	0.52	1.15
Jun-1991	5616	6406	1593	3281	18	3263	530	996	5	0.58	1.14
Sep-1991	6443	7270	1441	3947	7	3941	447	1141	294	0.61	1.13
Dec-1991	7565	9093	1433	6036	22	6013	97	1067	462	0.80	1.20
Jan-1992	7992	9129	1545	6040	17	6022	408	1077	60	0.76	1.14
Mar-1992	8028	9486	1485	6544	26	6518	0	1119	339	0.82	1.18
Apr-1992	8550	9895	1455	7096	15	7081	0	1126	219	0.83	1.16
May-1992	9352	10447	1459	7838	135	7703	24	1086	41	0.84	1.12
Jun-1992	9290	10290	1475	7885	39	7846	-91	972	48	0.85	1.11
Jul-1992	9918	10824	1545	8563	12	8551	-197	876	37	0.86	1.09
Aug-1992	9920	10749	1463	8722	21	8701	-298	828	34	0.88	1.08
Sep-1992	9459	11361	1511	8726	4	8722	-385	1475	34	0.92	1.20
Oct-1992	9714	11661	1472	9044	2	9042	-355	1466	33	0.93	1.20
Nov-1992 b/	9728	11151	1446	8641	100	8542	-421	1452	33	0.89	1.15
Dec-1992 c/	11010	12093	1437	9611	160	9451	-401	1288	158	0.87	1.10

Source: Central Bank of the Republic of Argentina, Macroeconómica and Carta Económica

a/ In Foreign Currency.
b/ Preliminary.
c/ December 23, 1992.

Table 10.1: ARGENTINA - POPULATION, 1960-1990

	Census Population a/ (Thousands)		Mid-year Population (Thousands)	Annual Growth Rate (%)	Five-year Growth Rate in Projection (%)
1960	20014	b/	20616	1.65	1.71
1965			22283	1.52	1.55
1970	23390	c/	23962	1.54	1.45
1975			26052	1.68	1.67
1980	27947		28237	1.61	1.61
1985			30564	1.55	1.58
1990			32293	1.19	1.11

Source: INDEC.and World Bank Atlas.
a/ 1980 census data.
b/ Census omissions are not included.
c/ Results obtained from sample.

June 1992

Distributors of World Bank Publications

ARGENTINA
Carlos Hirsch, SRL
Galeria Guemes
Florida 165, 4th Floor-Ofc. 453/465
1333 Buenos Aires

**AUSTRALIA, PAPUA NEW GUINEA,
FIJI, SOLOMON ISLANDS,
VANUATU, AND WESTERN SAMOA**
D.A. Information Services
648 Whitehorse Road
Mitcham 3132
Victoria

AUSTRIA
Gerold and Co.
Graben 31
A-1011 Wien

BANGLADESH
Micro Industries Development
    Assistance Society (MIDAS)
House 5, Road 16
Dhanmondi R/Area
Dhaka 1209

   Branch offices:
   Pine View, 1st Floor
   100 Agrabad Commercial Area
   Chittagong 4100

   76, K.D.A. Avenue
   Kulna 9100

BELGIUM
Jean De Lannoy
Av. du Roi 202
1060 Brussels

CANADA
Le Diffuseur
C.P. 85, 1501B rue Ampère
Boucherville, Québec
J4B 5E6

CHILE
Invertec IGT S.A.
Americo Vespucio Norte 1165
Santiago

CHINA
China Financial & Economic
    Publishing House
8, Da Fo Si Dong Jie
Beijing

COLOMBIA
Infoenlace Ltda.
Apartado Aereo 34270
Bogota D.E.

COTE D'IVOIRE
Centre d'Edition et de Diffusion
    Africaines (CEDA)
04 B.P. 541
Abidjan 04 Plateau

CYPRUS
Center of Applied Research
Cyprus College
6, Diogenes Street, Engomi
P.O. Box 2006
Nicosia

DENMARK
SamfundsLitteratur
Rosenoerns Allé 11
DK-1970 Frederiksberg C

DOMINICAN REPUBLIC
Editora Taller, C. por A.
Restauración e Isabel la Católica 309
Apartado de Correos 2190 Z-1
Santo Domingo

EGYPT, ARAB REPUBLIC OF
Al Ahram
Al Galaa Street
Cairo

The Middle East Observer
41, Sherif Street
Cairo

FINLAND
Akateeminen Kirjakauppa
P.O. Box 128
SF-00101 Helsinki 10

FRANCE
World Bank Publications
66, avenue d'Iéna
75116 Paris

GERMANY
UNO-Verlag
Poppelsdorfer Allee 55
D-5300 Bonn 1

HONG KONG, MACAO
Asia 2000 Ltd.
46-48 Wyndham Street
Winning Centre
2nd Floor
Central Hong Kong

INDIA
Allied Publishers Private Ltd.
751 Mount Road
Madras - 600 002

   Branch offices:
   15 J.N. Heredia Marg
   Ballard Estate
   Bombay - 400 038

   13/14 Asaf Ali Road
   New Delhi - 110 002

   17 Chittaranjan Avenue
   Calcutta - 700 072

   Jayadeva Hostel Building
   5th Main Road, Gandhinagar
   Bangalore - 560 009

   3-5-1129 Kachiguda
      Cross Road
   Hyderabad - 500 027

   Prarthana Flats, 2nd Floor
   Near Thakore Baug, Navrangpura
   Ahmedabad - 380 009

   Patiala House
   16-A Ashok Marg
   Lucknow - 226 001

   Central Bazaar Road
   60 Bajaj Nagar
   Nagpur 440 010

INDONESIA
Pt. Indira Limited
Jalan Borobudur 20
P.O. Box 181
Jakarta 10320

IRELAND
Government Supplies Agency
4-5 Harcourt Road
Dublin 2

ISRAEL
Yozmot Literature Ltd.
P.O. Box 56055
Tel Aviv 61560

ITALY
Licosa Commissionaria Sansoni SPA
Via Duca Di Calabria, 1/1
Casella Postale 552
50125 Firenze

JAPAN
Eastern Book Service
Hongo 3-Chome, Bunkyo-ku 113
Tokyo

KENYA
Africa Book Service (E.A.) Ltd.
Quaran House, Mfangano Street
P.O. Box 45245
Nairobi

KOREA, REPUBLIC OF
Pan Korea Book Corporation
P.O. Box 101, Kwangwhamun
Seoul

MALAYSIA
University of Malaya Cooperative
    Bookshop, Limited
P.O. Box 1127, Jalan Pantai Baru
59700 Kuala Lumpur

MEXICO
INFOTEC
Apartado Postal 22-860
14060 Tlalpan, Mexico D.F.

NETHERLANDS
De Lindeboom/InOr-Publikaties
P.O. Box 202
7480 AE Haaksbergen

NEW ZEALAND
EBSCO NZ Ltd.
Private Mail Bag 99914
New Market
Auckland

NIGERIA
University Press Limited
Three Crowns Building Jericho
Private Mail Bag 5095
Ibadan

NORWAY
Narvesen Information Center
Book Department
P.O. Box 6125 Etterstad
N-0602 Oslo 6

PAKISTAN
Mirza Book Agency
65, Shahrah-e-Quaid-e-Azam
P.O. Box No. 729
Lahore 54000

PERU
Editorial Desarrollo SA
Apartado 3824
Lima 1

PHILIPPINES
International Book Center
Suite 1703, Cityland 10
Condominium Tower 1
Ayala Avenue, H.V. dela
    Costa Extension
Makati, Metro Manila

POLAND
International Publishing Service
Ul. Piekna 31/37
00-677 Warzawa

For subscription orders:
IPS Journals
Ul. Okrezna 3
02-916 Warszawa

PORTUGAL
Livraria Portugal
Rua Do Carmo 70-74
1200 Lisbon

SAUDI ARABIA, QATAR
Jarir Book Store
P.O. Box 3196
Riyadh 11471

**SINGAPORE, TAIWAN,
MYANMAR,BRUNEI**
Information Publications
    Private, Ltd.
Golden Wheel Building
41, Kallang Pudding, #04-03
Singapore 1334

SOUTH AFRICA, BOTSWANA
For single titles:
Oxford University Press
    Southern Africa
P.O. Box 1141
Cape Town 8000

For subscription orders:
International Subscription Service
P.O. Box 41095
Craighall
Johannesburg 2024

SPAIN
Mundi-Prensa Libros, S.A.
Castello 37
28001 Madrid

Librería Internacional AEDOS
Consell de Cent, 391
08009 Barcelona

SRI LANKA AND THE MALDIVES
Lake House Bookshop
P.O. Box 244
100, Sir Chittampalam A.
    Gardiner Mawatha
Colombo 2

SWEDEN
For single titles:
Fritzes Fackboksforetaget
Regeringsgatan 12, Box 16356
S-103 27 Stockholm

For subscription orders:
Wennergren-Williams AB
P. O. Box 1305
S-171 25 Solna

SWITZERLAND
For single titles:
Librairie Payot
Case postale 3212
CH 1002 Lausanne

For subscription orders:
Librairie Payot
Service des Abonnements
Case postale 3312
CH 1002 Lausanne

THAILAND
Central Department Store
306 Silom Road
Bangkok

**TRINIDAD & TOBAGO, ANTIGUA
BARBUDA, BARBADOS,
DOMINICA, GRENADA, GUYANA,
JAMAICA, MONTSERRAT, ST.
KITTS & NEVIS, ST. LUCIA,
ST. VINCENT & GRENADINES**
Systematics Studies Unit
#9 Watts Street
Curepe
Trinidad, West Indies

TURKEY
Infotel
Narlabahçe Sok. No. 15
Cagaloglu
Istanbul

UNITED KINGDOM
Microinfo Ltd.
P.O. Box 3
Alton, Hampshire GU34 2PG
England

VENEZUELA
Libreria del Este
Aptdo. 60.337
Caracas 1060-A